noun	**n**		nom
nautical	**Naut**		nautisme
feminine noun	**nf**		nom féminin
masculine noun	**nm**		nom masculin
masculine and feminine noun	**nm,f**		nom masculin et féminin
masculine and feminine noun	**nmf**		nom masculin et féminin
proper noun	**npr**		nom propre
nuclear physics	**Nucl**		physique nucléaire
onomatopoeia	**onomat**		onomatopée
computing	**Ordinat**		informatique
pejorative	**pej, péj**		péjoratif
pharmacology	**Pharm**		pharmacie
philosophy	**Philos**		philosophie
phonetics, phonology	**Phon**		phonétique, phonologie
photography	**Phot**		photographie
physics	**Phys**		physique
physiology	**Physiol**		physiologie
plural	**pl**		pluriel
politics	**Pol**		politique
postal services	**Post**		postes
past participle	**pp**		participe passé
past participle adjective	**pp adj**		participe passé adjectif
present participle	**p prés**		participe présent
proper noun	**pr n**		nom propre
prepositional phrase	**prep phr**		locution prépositive
preposition	**prep, prép**		préposition
present participle adjective	**pres p adj**		participe présent adjectif
present	**pres, prés**		présent
preterit	**pret, prét**		prétérit
printing	**Print**		imprimerie
pronoun	**pron**		pronom
demonstrative pronoun	**pron dém**		pronom démonstratif
indefinite pronoun	**pron indéf**		pronom indéfini
interrogative pronoun	**pron inter**		pronom interrogatif
personal pronoun	**pron pers**		pronom personnel
pronominal phrase	**pron phr**		locution pronominale
possessive pronoun	**pron poss**		pronom possessif
relative pronoun	**pron rel**		pronom relatif
social security	**Prot Soc**		protection sociale
proverb	**Prov**		proverbe
psychology	**Psych**		psychologie
advertising	**Pub**		publicité
publishing	**Publg**		édition
something	**qch**		quelque chose
somebody	**qn**		quelqu'un
quantifier	**quantif**		quantificateur
religion	**Relig**		religion
somebody	**sb**		quelqu'un
school	**Sch**		école
sciences	**Sci**		sciences
school	**Scol**		école
Scottish	**Scot**		anglais d'Écosse
singular	**sg**		singulier
social security	**Soc Admin**		protection sociale
sociology	**Sociol**		sociologie
formal	**sout**		soutenu

specialist	**spec, spéc**		spécialiste
statistics	**Stat**		statistique
something	**sth**		quelque chose
technology	**Tech**		technologie
telecommunications	**Telecom, Télécom**		télécommunications
textiles	**Tex**		textile
theatre	**Theat, Théât**		théâtre
always	**tjrs**		toujours
transport	**Transp**		transport
horse racing	**Turf**		les courses
television	**TV**		télévision
European Union	**UE**		Union européenne
university	**Univ**		université
American	**US**		anglais américain
verb	**v**		verbe
impersonal verb	**v impers**		verbe impersonnel
reflexive verb	**v refl**		verbe pronominal
veterinary medicine	**Vet, Vét**		médecine vétérinaire
intransitive verb	**vi**		verbe intransitif
reflexive verb	**vpr**		verbe pronominal
transitive verb	**vtr**		verbe transitif
indirect transitive verb	**vtr ind**		verbe transitif indirect
zoology	**Zool**		zoologie
French headwords marked with an asterisk have an alternative spelling. Alternative spellings are given on pages xvi-xxi	*		Les entrées françaises suivies d'un astérisque ont une variante orthographique. La liste complète de ces variantes figure pp. xvi-xxi
More information will be found in the centre section	➡ 📖		Complément d'information dans les pages centrales
dated	†		vieilli
archaic	‡		archaïque
trademark*	®		marque déposée ou nom déposé*
informal	○		familier
very informal	◑		populaire
vulgar or taboo	●		vulgaire ou tabou
countable	C		dénombrable
uncountable	₡		non dénombrable
swung dash used as substitute for headword	~		tiret ondulé de substitution
British spelling only: US spelling varies	GB		graphie britannique: il existe une graphie nord-américaine
indicates an approximate translation equivalent	≈		pour signaler un équivalent approximatif
cross-reference	▶		renvoi

* **Proprietary terms** This dictionary includes some words which are, or are asserted to be, proprietary terms or trademarks. The presence or absence of such assertions should not be regarded as affecting the legal status of any proprietary name or trademark.

* **Les marques déposées** Les mots qui, à notre connaissance, sont considérés comme des marques ou des noms déposés sont signalés dans cet ouvrage par ®. La présence ou l'absence de cette mention ne peut pas être considérée comme ayant valeur juridique.

Contents / Table des matières

The Oxford–Hachette French Dictionary
Le Grand Dictionnaire Hachette–Oxford

Fourth Edition/ Quatrième Édition

Chief editors/ Direction éditoriale
Jean-Benoit Ormal-Grenon
Nicholas Rollin

Editors/Rédactrices
Joanna Rubery
Isabelle Stables-Lemoine
Mireille Snoeck
Valerie Grundy
Anne-Laure Jousse

The French spelling reform/Les rectifications de l'orthographe
Romain Muller

Proofreaders/ Correcteurs
Amanda Leigh
Alison Curr
Pat Bulhosen
Céline Cabrolier
Meic Haines
Beatriz Jarman

Third Edition/ Troisième Édition

Chief editors/ Direction éditoriale
Jean-Benoit Ormal-Grenon
Natalie Pomier

Editors/Rédactrices
Marianne Chalmers
Marie-Hélène Corréard

Cultural notes/ Notes culturelles
Martine Bouiller
Mary O'Neill
Annie Sussel

Guide to effective communication/ Communication mode d'emploi
Marianne Chalmers
Élodie Vialleton

Proofreaders/ Correctrices
Alison Curr
Sara Hawker
Isabelle Stables

Data-capture/ Saisie des données
Alison Curr

Design/Maquette
Information Design Unit, Newport Pagnell, UK
Maquette de couverture pour l'édition française
DDDP, Paris
Nous tenons également à remercier
Sabine Visbecq

Second Edition/ Deuxième Édition

Chief editor
Marie-Hélène Corréard

Editors
Marianne Chalmers
Françoise de Peretti

Associate Editor
Mary O'Neill

Translator/ Lexicographer
Susan Steinberg

An A–Z of Contemporary France
Richard Aplin

General advice on writing in French
Natalie Pomier

Proofreaders
Isabelle Lemoine
Genevieve Hawkins

Design
An A–Z of Contemporary France, General advice on writing in French:
Text Matters, Reading, UK

First Edition/ Première Édition

Chief editors/ Direction éditoriale
Marie-Hélène Corréard
Valerie Grundy

Editors/ Rédacteurs
Nicola Addyman
Jennifer Barnes
Marianne Chalmers
Glynnis Chantrell
Rosalind Combley
Gearóid Cronin
Laurence Delacroix
Françoise de Peretti
Janet Gough
Gérard G. Kahn
Pascal Lecler
Jacques Lesca
Mary O'Neill
Catherine Palmer
Martine Pierquin
Georges Pilard
Nicolas Rosec
Catherine Roux
Kathleen Shields
Susan Steinberg
Nicole Truchet

Lexicographical adviser/Conseiller en lexicographie
Beryl T. Atkins

Translator– lexicographers/ Traducteurs– lexicographes
Christopher Dawson
Robert Grundy
Hélène Haenen
Marie-Claude Harrison
Frances Illingworth
Thiên-Nga Lê
Natalie Pomier
Muriel Ranivoalison
Patrick Ros Gorasny
Tamsin Simmil
Thérèse Sepulchre
Jo Waite

Lexical usage notes and correspondence/ Notes d'usage lexicales et correspondance

Henri Béjoint
Richard Wakely

Assisted by/Assistés de
Ghislaine Ansieau
Lucy Atkins
Agnès Sauzet

Specialist terminology consultants/ Consultants en terminologie

Centre de Recherche en Traduction et Terminologie Université Lumière-Lyon II
Philippe Thoiron
Malcolm Harvey

University of Brighton
Tony Hartley

Malcolm Slater
Dimity Castellano

Consultants/Consultants

Martyn L. Bird
Rosalind Fergusson
Hélène M. A. Lewis
Janet Whitcut

North American English/Anglo-américain

Charles Lynn Clark

Georgie Boge
Amy Deanne Matthews

French outside France/Français d'ailleurs

Lilliam Hurst
Dominique Péladeau

Phonetics/Phonétique

Isabelle Vodoz
Jane Stuart-Smith

Administration/ Administration

Coordination/Coordination
Isabelle Lemoine

Marion Fox
Nadia Jamil

Data-capture/Saisie des données

Senior keyboarder/Responsable de la saisie
Philip Gerrish

Alison Curr
Annie Girardin
Alexander Ions
Fabienne Pearson
Muriel Ranivoalison
Tim Weekes

Proofreaders/ Correcteurs

Stephen Curtis
Genevieve Hawkins
Isabelle Lemoine

Design/Maquette

Text/texte: Fran Holdsworth
Diagrams/organigrammes:
Information Design Unit
Letters/correspondance: Raynor Design

Acknowledgements / Remerciements

The editors would like to extend their warmest thanks to a certain number of people and organizations not mentioned in the list of contributors, particularly Beth Levin of Northwestern University, who allowed us to make use of her work on English verb classification.

We are also indebted to all those who made it possible for us to build the corpus of contemporary French which, with the Oxford Corpus of Modern English, has been the cornerstone of this dictionary. In particular, our thanks go to Manuel Lucbert, Secrétaire Général of Le Monde, Jean-François Sailly, Gilbert Compagnon and his team, also from Le Monde, Christian Poulin from Libération, Joseph Laveille and Aimé Munoz from Le Progrès de Lyon.

Our thanks also go to Dora Carpenter, Colin Hope, Anne Judge, Helen Lawrence, Katherine Manville, Alain Pierrot, and Robin Sawers for their contribution at various stages of the project.

Finally we would like to thank all those people, too numerous to mention here, who have given us their support and the benefit of their knowledge in writing this dictionary.

Les auteurs tiennent à remercier un certain nombre de personnes et d'organismes qui n'ont pas été mentionnés dans la liste des collaborateurs du projet, en particulier Beth Levin, de Northwestern University, qui nous a permis d'utiliser son travail sur la classification des verbes anglais. Nous sommes également redevables à tous ceux qui nous ont aidés à constituer le corpus de français contemporain qui, avec le corpus d'anglais moderne d'Oxford, a été la pierre angulaire de ce dictionnaire. Nous remercions tout spécialement Manuel Lucbert, Secrétaire Général du journal Le Monde, ses collaborateurs Jean-François Sailly, Gilbert Compagnon et son équipe, Christian Poulin de Libération, Joseph Laveille et Aimé Munoz du Progrès de Lyon.

Nous remercions également Dora Carpenter, Colin Hope, Anne Judge, Helen Lawrence, Katherine Manville, Alain Pierrot, et Robin Sawers qui ont participé à diverses étapes du projet.

Nous adressons nos remerciements à tous ceux qui, trop nombreux pour être nommés ici, nous ont apporté leur soutien et fait bénéficier de leur savoir tout au long de notre entreprise.

Preface / Préface

Preface to the fourth edition

This new edition has been driven by two priorities. Firstly, the opportunity has been taken to update the dictionary's coverage in specialist and general vocabulary. This process has included adding many new words, additional senses of existing words, and the revision of existing entries. The opportunity has also been taken to enhance the dictionary's coverage of EU terminology.

Secondly, comprehensive information has been given on the French spelling reform, which is gradually gaining acceptance in France and the other francophone countries. New sections dealing with language problems and the practicalities of living in France and other French-speaking countries have also been added. They provide an enormous amount of valuable background information for students of French, and also for anyone who is contemplating working or living in France, or who uses French professionally.

Publishing Manager Vivian Marr
Development Editor Nicholas Rollin

Preface to the first edition

This dictionary is the fruit of six years' sustained cooperation between two of the world's foremost reference publishers. Being a completely original work, it is not constrained by previous editions or prior publications, and so is able to provide a truly fresh and contemporary description of the relationship between French and English.

The work was carried out by a team comprising equal numbers of French and English native-speakers, working together on the same site. Editors worked in bilingual pairs, each working only in his or her native language. Editors were able to consult constantly to establish accurate translations of every item in every entry. This team in turn drew on the resources of many freelance lexicographers, translators, consultants, and terminology specialists in the French- and English-speaking worlds.

This is the first French and English dictionary to have been written using electronic corpora: two huge databases of electronic texts, one of current French and the other of current English. Each database contained over 10 million words of language in use. Access to these databases has provided accounts of words and their translations which are always authentic and often revealing. Users of the dictionary can feel confident that translations presented derive from study of real language as it has actually been used in a wide range of contexts. The resulting text provides modern idiomatic coverage of general French and English, with many new words, extensive treatment of colloquial expressions, and thousands of example sentences showing real language in action. A wide range of literary vocabulary has been included, together with vocabulary from the specialized fields of science, business, technology, and medicine.

The aim of the Publishers has been to provide translators, students at all levels, teachers, and business people with a reference work that is without rival in authority, currency, and accuracy.

The Publishers
Oxford University Press
Project Director Timothy Benbow
Commissioning Editor Robert Scriven

Préface de la nouvelle édition

Deux priorités ont guidé nos travaux de mise à jour et d'enrichissement pour cette nouvelle édition.

Outil indispensable à la maîtrise de la langue, le dictionnaire reflète son évolution constante. De nombreux mots et sens nouveaux de la langue courante ou spécialisée ont été ajoutés à la nomenclature, avec une attention particulière portée aux mots issus de la terminologie de l'Union européenne.

Nous présentons également les rectifications de l'orthographe française, qui s'installent peu à peu dans les réalités langagières francophones et dans l'enseignement.

De nouvelles rubriques pratiques sur la langue anglaise et la vie au Royaume-Uni et aux États-Unis sont proposées. Elles fourniront une multitude de renseignements utiles à tous ceux et celles qui sont en relation avec des interlocuteurs anglo-saxons dans le cadre de leurs études ou de leur profession, ou qui partent s'installer dans l'un de ces pays.

Direction Carola Strang
Responsable d'édition Jean-Benoit Ormal-Grenon

Préface de la première édition

Ce dictionnaire est le fruit de six années d'étroite collaboration entre deux grands éditeurs d'ouvrages de référence. C'est une œuvre totalement nouvelle et originale qui offre une description actuelle et moderne des langues anglaise et française, et de leurs relations.

Des rédacteurs anglophones et francophones ont uni leurs compétences et ont constitué des équipes bilingues qui ont travaillé ensemble, en un même lieu. Tout au long de l'élaboration du dictionnaire, chaque rédacteur a travaillé dans sa langue maternelle et a pu vérifier, grâce à un échange constant avec les autres membres de l'équipe, la justesse et la pertinence des traductions. Les rédacteurs ont par ailleurs fait appel à de nombreux collaborateurs extérieurs : lexicographes, traducteurs, consultants et terminologues, tous spécialistes des mondes anglophone et francophone.

Les rédacteurs ont, pour la première fois dans l'histoire de la lexicographie bilingue, utilisé un corpus électronique composé de deux bases de données textuelles de français et d'anglais. Les bases de données française et anglaise comportent chacune plus de 10 millions de mots de la langue usuelle. L'utilisation de ces bases de données a permis un repérage des mots et des traductions, toujours authentique et pertinent. Les utilisateurs peuvent en toute confiance se servir des traductions proposées : elles sont issues de la langue réelle et employées en contexte. Le dictionnaire recense et traite de nombreux mots nouveaux, des expressions familières, des expressions idiomatiques et des tournures actuelles du français et de l'anglais. Il accorde également une large place à la langue littéraire, aux américanismes et au vocabulaire de domaines spécialisés : scientifique, commercial, technologique, médical . . .

Les éditeurs se sont fixé un seul but : allier recherche linguistique et effort éditorial afin d'offrir aux traducteurs, étudiants de tous niveaux, enseignants et au monde des affaires, un ouvrage de référence inégalé à ce jour en matière d'autorité, d'actualité et de fiabilité.

Les éditeurs
Hachette Dictionnaires
Direction Mireille Maurin   *Responsable d'édition* Héloïse Neefs

Introduction

Users of this dictionary will find it an effective tool for tackling practical linguistic tasks. In designing this dictionary we have ensured that every entry provides as much information as possible for each of the following users and tasks:
- the native English speaker trying to understand French,
- the native English speaker trying to write or speak French,
- the native French speaker trying to understand English,
- the native French speaker trying to write or speak English.

Users have different levels of skills and knowledge. For the advanced user, we provide thorough coverage of up-to-date language. We include a wide range of vocabulary in specialist but nonetheless highly topical areas such as business, politics, sport, information technology, marketing, social administration, and the environment. Advances in technology and the electronic information revolution are reflected in this new edition, as are new developments in popular culture and contemporary lifestyles.

For intermediate users, we have designed the dictionary to enable them to work with the foreign language, using it correctly and well. Particular care has been taken in the selection of the translations. Our electronic corpora give us a wealth of examples of words in use in real, everyday circumstances. When one good translation has been identified and checked in many contexts, it will often be given as the only general translation for one sense of the headword. It has been our policy throughout to give two or more translations only in those rare cases where they are consistently interchangeable, and to avoid adding less safe alternatives when one equivalent is adequate. Where appropriate, other equivalents, which have been found to work in more restricted contexts, will be shown in examples.

Where nuances of meaning within a sense of the headword are translated in different ways, these nuances are pinpointed by means of semantic indicators and/or typical collocates. For a step-by-step guide to using this type of information to arrive at the most suitable translation, see the section *Using this dictionary* on p. xxii.

Translations given in isolation are, however, not enough to enable someone to work in a foreign language: grammatical constructions are also needed if the translation is to be used correctly. For this reason, one of our principal concerns has been to include these constructions wherever they are required. This is a significant feature of our dictionary.

Headwords, compounds, and phrasal verbs stand out clearly on the page. English compounds are found in their proper place within the overall alphabetical order of headwords. Phrasal verbs are given a very full and explicit presentation which avoids ambiguous meta-language and, for the French user, shows clearly the positioning of the noun object.

The dictionary has a wide coverage of North American as well as British English, and exclusively British or North American usage is marked. Where appropriate, American variants are given in translations of French words and phrases. The existence of standard American spelling variants is indicated in translations in the French–English side of the dictionary.

The needs of users extend beyond the bounds of individual dictionary entries. To make this dictionary an effective aid for somebody working in a language not their own, we offer access to the language in several different ways. The user thumbing through this dictionary will find lexical usage notes, notes

Ce dictionnaire est conçu comme un outil pratique et efficace : il s'est donné comme objectif de répondre, par chacun de ses articles et le plus complètement possible, aux questions et besoins que peuvent rencontrer :
- le francophone qui veut comprendre l'anglais,
- le francophone qui veut s'exprimer en anglais,
- l'anglophone qui veut comprendre le français,
- l'anglophone qui veut s'exprimer en français.

Aux utilisateurs d'un niveau avancé, l'ouvrage présente un vaste panorama de la langue contemporaine, et notamment les domaines spécialisés que sont les affaires, la politique, les sports, l'informatique, l'environnement et la protection sociale. Les progrès technologiques et la révolution de l'information électronique ont leur place dans cette nouvelle édition, tout comme les nouvelles tendances culturelles et l'évolution des modes de vie.

Aux utilisateurs d'un niveau moins avancé, ce dictionnaire permet de travailler avec aisance et en toute confiance. Le choix des traductions a fait l'objet d'un soin particulier. En règle générale, à chaque acception d'un terme correspond une seule traduction. Cette traduction a été vérifiée dans les très nombreux exemples de langue réelle tirés de nos corpus électroniques. On ne trouvera deux ou plusieurs traductions équivalentes que dans les rares cas où elles sont vraiment interchangeables. Nous avons délibérément écarté les synonymes douteux et avons illustré par des exemples les traductions qui ne peuvent convenir que dans certains contextes.

Divers éléments (indicateurs de contexte et/ou indicateurs de collocations, décrits en détail dans *Comment se servir du dictionnaire ?*, p. xxvii) distinguent une acception et ses différentes nuances. On peut ainsi choisir la traduction la plus appropriée.

Mais une traduction n'est pleinement utilisable que si elle est accompagnée des structures grammaticales qu'elle requiert. L'un des atouts de ce dictionnaire est de fournir ces structures chaque fois qu'elles sont nécessaires.

Pour faciliter l'accès à l'information, les mots composés anglais et les mots composés français avec trait d'union figurent à leur place, dans l'ordre alphabétique.

La présentation des verbes à particule anglais met en évidence la position du complément.

La nomenclature anglaise accorde une large place à l'anglo-américain et les usages britanniques ou les américanismes sont spécifiés comme tels. La nomenclature française prend en compte le français des pays francophones autres que la France, qu'il s'agisse d'entrées à part entière ou d'acceptions. Dans la partie français-anglais, nous proposons des traductions en anglo-américain chaque fois qu'une variante graphique ou lexicale s'impose.

Les besoins de l'utilisateur vont souvent au-delà de ce qu'un article de dictionnaire peut offrir, aussi nous lui proposons, pour aborder la langue qu'il apprend, des notes d'usage sur le lexique et sur les mots grammaticaux, des notes culturelles, un guide complet pour communiquer efficacement, des tableaux de conjugaison, et des organigrammes.

on function words, cultural notes, a complete guide to communicating effectively, verb tables, and organizational diagrams.

The French spelling reform

A summary of the main changes is included in the introductory pages. This is followed by a list of the changes affecting individual headwords. All affected headwords in the dictionary have been marked with an asterisk immediately following the headword, or its variant, if it has one. A list of the new spellings is given on page xii of the introduction. As the old spellings remain valid, the reform has not been implemented wholesale throughout the dictionary. If they become the norm, the new spellings will in due course be presented as the preferred forms.

Lexical usage notes

These are boxed notes which appear within the dictionary text. They give the user facts about certain types of words that behave alike, for example, names of countries, languages, colour terms, and days of the week, and provide ways of discussing topics such as age, dates, time, and measurement. A full index to these notes is given on p. 1948.

The purpose of these notes is to make generalizations across lexical items, by summarizing syntactic facts that are common to most members of the set, thus supplementing the coverage of individual entries: in a one-volume dictionary it is not possible to give all the facts at each headword. Cross-references to the notes are given at all relevant entries, normally immediately after the pronunciation of the headword. The reference is to the page in the dictionary on which the usage note appears.

These notes are intended for specific users: people seeking to express themselves in a language not their own. Thus, the usage notes which appear in the English–French half of the dictionary are written in English and present facts about expression in French, and vice versa in the French–English half. Since they are designed to help translation into a foreign language, they do not represent a systematic analysis of linguistic facts, nor do they set out to give a comprehensive survey of all possible translations. Their purpose is to allow someone to say or write specific things accurately and naturally in the foreign language.

Many of the lexical usage notes represent a functional approach to language use, grouping the basic structures and expressions necessary in order to write or talk about a specific topic. Thus, as well as being readily usable reference aids for the individual user, they will also serve as valuable vocabulary-teaching material for teachers of French and English.

Notes on function words

The words of a language may be seen to be of two types: those with lexical meaning like *table* and *slowly* and *jump*, and those with function rather than meaning. The latter are the joints and sinews of the language, uniting the other elements into sentences which carry meaning. Examples of such function words are pronouns like *you* and *it*, verbs such as *be* and *have*, and determiners such as *this* and *that*.

The notes within or near function word entries are again intended for use by the person seeking to work in a foreign language. They provide basic information on grammatical words.

The function word notes are easily identifiable in the dictionary. In cases where the information can be presented fairly briefly, the note will be found at the top of the entry, immediately under the headword. In cases where the necessary information is more lengthy and complex, the notes are boxed and clearly visible, appearing as close as possible to the headword concerned.

Les rectifications de l'orthographe

Nous avons fait une place, au début de l'ouvrage, aux rectifications de l'orthographe approuvées par l'Académie française et parues au Journal officiel en 1990. Comme aucune des deux graphies, "l'ancienne" ou la "nouvelle", ne peut être tenue pour fautive, nous continuons de présenter dans la nomenclature les mots touchés par les rectifications dans leur "ancienne" graphie ; nous les avons cependant agrémentés d'un astérisque qui renvoie à la liste p. xiv des ajustements faits à ces mots.

Notes d'usage

On pourrait dire qu'il y a deux sortes de mots : les mots lexicaux qui ont un sens en eux-mêmes, comme *table*, *lentement*, *sauter*, et les mots grammaticaux dont la fonction l'emporte sur le sens, comme les prépositions *à*, *contre*, *pour* ou les conjonctions *quand*, *que*, *et*, *mais*. C'est pour ces deux sortes de mots que nous proposons, au fil du dictionnaire, des notes d'usage lexicales et grammaticales. L'utilisateur y trouvera les particularités d'expression de l'une et l'autre langue. Les notes d'usage sont rédigées en français dans la partie français-anglais et en anglais dans la partie anglais-français pour permettre à l'utilisateur de faire du thème.

• **Notes d'usage lexicales** Elles apparaissent en encadré dans le corps du dictionnaire. Elles renseignent le lecteur sur l'utilisation de certains termes. Leur objectif est de donner, sous une entrée générique (pays, langues, couleurs, jours de la semaine, âge, date, etc.), l'essentiel des exemples de construction qu'on ne peut, faute de place, faire figurer sous chacun des mots spécifiques qui constituent cet ensemble générique. Points de repère pratiques pour tout utilisateur, elles offrent aussi à l'enseignant un matériau pédagogique appréciable. La liste de ces notes lexicales se trouve p. 1948.

• **Notes d'usage grammaticales** Leur objectif est d'aider l'utilisateur qui apprend une langue étrangère. Elles mettent en évidence la façon dont les mots lexicaux s'articulent autour des mots grammaticaux pour donner un sens aux phrases. Elles rassemblent des éléments essentiels d'usage et de structure. Les notes courtes figurent au début de l'article, les plus longues apparaissent en encadré à proximité de celui-ci.

• **Notes culturelles** Le dictionnaire comprend un grand nombre de notes culturelles qui abordent des points spécifiques de la civilisation et des institutions de la France, du Royaume-Uni et des États-Unis. Elles apparaissent au fil du texte, dans l'ordre alphabétique, et apportent ainsi un complément d'information aux mots ou expressions qu'il est difficile de traduire ou dont la traduction seule ne suffit pas à véhiculer tout le sens du terme de départ. La liste complète de ces notes peut être consultée pp. 1946–1947.

Communication mode d'emploi

La partie centrale de l'ouvrage est destinée à l'acquisition des techniques et du vocabulaire nécessaires pour communiquer efficacement, tant à l'oral qu'à l'écrit.

• **L'anglais efficace** Les conventions utilisées dans les pays anglophones pour la rédaction de textes divers (compte rendus, dissertations, etc.) sont souvent différentes des nôtres. Ce guide vous donnera les notions essentielles et des conseils pour écrire et vous exprimer correctement en anglais.

• **Les difficultés de l'anglais** Parmi les difficultés qu'un francophone peut rencontrer quand il s'exprime en anglais, certaines sont dues au fait que les deux langues comportent un certain nombre de mots similaires dans leur forme mais qui peuvent avoir des sens différents. Nous nous attachons à présenter la diversité de ces "faux amis" et les mots du "franglais" avec leur sens réel en anglais.

Cultural notes

The dictionary incorporates a wide variety of cultural notes covering aspects of French, English and American society, institutions, and culture. These are conveniently located at the relevant alphabetical position in the wordlist to provide additional information on a term where a translation is impossible or cannot convey enough information on its own. A full list of these notes is also provided at the end of the book for reference.

Guide to communication

The central section of the dictionary is devoted to equipping the user with the techniques and vocabulary required for effective written and verbal communication in a variety of media.

• **Effective French** *Effective French* offers guidance on how to express yourself in French and highlights the cultural differences in approach to writing reports, essays, etc., which are often not obvious and not easily found.

• **Difficulties of French** *Difficulties of French* looks at some of the problems of using French faced by the English native-speaker. These are often the result of English and French using the same or similar words with different meanings. The phenomenon of *franglais* is discussed and examples of *franglais* terms and their real meanings in English are given.

• **Varieties of French** In this section the varieties of French in different French-speaking territories are discussed with examples.

• **Letters** A rich and comprehensive set of model letters and documents is to be found in a special section in the centre of the dictionary. Once again, these are designed for people seeking to write in a language not their own. Thus, the model letters for the English-speakers are written in French but introduced in English, and vice versa. French and English letters are grouped according to broad themes covering general correspondence, travel, business letters and employment. The letters in the two languages are shown on facing pages for ease of comparison but are not direct translations. Each pair of letters provides a typically idiomatic treatment of a similar theme in order to highlight the differences in letter-writing conventions between English and French. A selection of useful phrases provides a choice of possible openings and closures in different situations.

• **French Link words and expressions** This section offers a selection of helpful linking words and phrases to add structure to written work.

• **Living in France** *Living in France* summarizes important aspects of life in France. These cover such topics as immigration procedures for an extended stay, social security, health and tax matters, renting a house, operating a bank account, etc.

• **Email and the Internet** In order to reflect the prominence of electronic communications in contemporary society, the basic vocabulary of email and the Internet is presented and illustrated in sample email messages and web pages.

• **Using the telephone** This section offers practical advice on the language of calling procedures. The essentials of telephone manners are illustrated in a series of brief dialogues.

• **SMS (electronic text messaging)** Text messages have become an important element in modern communications. This section describes common conventions in texting in French.

• **Glossary of grammatical terms** In response to demand from some of our readers, a glossary of grammatical terms has been included in this edition. Each term is defined and an example is given to show its use in context.

• **Les variétés d'anglais** Cette rubrique offre un aperçu des différences dans le vocabulaire et l'orthographe de l'anglais selon les régions et les pays.

• **Correspondance** Dans la partie centrale du dictionnaire, l'utilisateur trouvera un vaste ensemble de lettres et de documents qui lui permettront, dans diverses situations, de s'exprimer correctement dans l'autre langue. Pour les anglophones, les modèles de correspondance française ont des titres anglais, et inversement. Les lettres en français et en anglais sont classées par grands thèmes qui couvrent la correspondance générale, la correspondance commerciale et l'emploi. Les lettres anglaises et les lettres françaises qui portent sur un même sujet sont placées sur des pages en vis-à-vis afin de pouvoir les comparer facilement, mais ce ne sont pas des traductions exactes.

Dans chaque couple de lettres, un même thème est abordé de façon idiomatique dans les deux langues afin de souligner les différences entre l'anglais et le français dans les formulations épistolaires.

Enfin, une sélection d'expressions utiles fournit des exemples de débuts de lettres et de formules de politesse à choisir en fonction du destinataire.

• **Les mots et expressions de liaison anglais** Cette section propose une sélection de mots et d'expressions de liaison qui permettent de structurer les productions écrites.

• **Vivre dans un pays anglophone** Cette rubrique propose des informations pratiques et utiles pour la vie quotidienne au Royaume-Uni et aux États-Unis : procédures d'immigration, systèmes de santé et de soins, impositions diverses, ouverture d'un compte, location ou achat d'un logement, etc.

• **Le courrier électronique et l'Internet** Pour faire écho à la prédominance des communications électroniques dans la société contemporaine, nous présentons le vocabulaire de base de l'e-mail et de l'Internet illustré d'exemples de messages électroniques et de pages web.

• **Le téléphone** Cette rubrique propose des conseils pratiques sur les formulations employées au cours des conversations téléphoniques. La plupart des expressions courantes sont mises en contexte dans une série de courts dialogues.

• **Les SMS (minimessages)** Les minimessages connaissent un essor grandissant parmi les outils de communication modernes. Cette section vous aidera à décoder ou à rédiger des SMS en anglais.

• **Glossaire de termes grammaticaux** Nous avons ajouté ce guide pour répondre au souhait de nombreux lecteurs. Les termes grammaticaux sont accompagnés d'une définition simple et d'un exemple pour une mise en contexte immédiate.

The French spelling reform

The following is a summary of the rules approved by the *Conseil supérieur de la langue française*, the *Académie française* and other French-language bodies. They have been published in the '*Journal Officiel* (*see* p. 472) and have been incorporated in school curriculums in Québec, Switzerland and Belgium. In France, the *Académie française* approved them and stated that "neither of the two written forms can be considered incorrect." Aspects of the reforms are now being widely used. However, full implementation of the reforms has been slower in France because of less public awareness of them than in the other countries mentioned above.

A summary of the changes is given below.

1.

Compound numbers are connected by hyphens.

Old spelling	New spelling
vingt et un	vingt-et-un
deux cents	deux-cents
trois millième	trois-millième

Notes
- Note the difference between *soixante et un tiers* (60 + ⅓) and *soixante-et-un tiers* (61⅓).

2.

In compound nouns (with a hyphen) such as *pèse-lettre* (verb + noun) or *sans-abri* (preposition + noun), the second element of the compound now takes a plural ending in the plural.

Old spelling	New spelling
un compte-gouttes, ➜ des compte-gouttes	un compte-goutte, ➜ des compte-gouttes
un après-midi, ➜ des après-midi	un après-midi, ➜ des après-midis

Notes
- Words such as *prie-Dieu* (because of the capital letter) or *trompe-la-mort* (because of the article) remain invariable.
- The form *des garde-pêches* should be used whether a person or an object.

3.

A grave accent (instead of an acute accent) is used in certain words (to standardize their spelling), in the future and conditional forms of verbs which conjugate like *céder*, and in forms such as *puissè-je*.

Old spelling	New spelling
événement	évènement
réglementaire	règlementaire
je céderai	je cèderai
ils régleraient	ils règleraient

Notes
- Before a silent syllable, è is to be used, except in the prefixes *dé-* or *pré-*, and initial *é* in *médecin* and *médecine*.
- The general rule is to follow the model of the source word: *évènement* is treated like *avènement*; *règlementaire* is written like *règlement*.

4.

The circumflex accent is no longer used with *i* and *u*. It is, however, used in verb endings in the simple past tense, in the subjunctive and to avoid possible ambiguity.

Old spelling	New spelling
coût	cout
entraîner, nous entraînons	entrainer, nous entrainons
paraître, il paraît	paraitre, il parait

Notes
- Words in which the circumflex is kept to maintain semantic differentiation are: the singular masculine adjectives *dû*, *mûr* and *sûr*, *jeûne(s)* and the forms of the verb *croitre* which, without an accent, could be confused with those of the verb *croire* (*je croîs*, *tu croîs*, etc.).

5.

Verbs ending in *-eler* or *-eter* are conjugated following the pattern of *peler* or *acheter*. Derivatives ending in *-ment* follow the verbs they are derived from. Exceptions to this rule are *appeler*, (and *rappeler*), *jeter* and its derivatives.

Old spelling	New spelling
j'amoncelle	j'amoncèle
amoncellement	amoncèlement
tu époussetteras	tu époussèteras

6.

Words borrowed from foreign languages form the plural in the same way as native French words and are accented according to the normal rules of French grammar.

Old spelling	New spelling
des matches	des matchs
des misses	des miss
revolver	révolver

7.

Elision affects spelling in a number of words, in particular:
- in compound words which begin with *contr(e)-* and *entr(e)-* :
- in onomatopoeic words and words of foreign origin.
- in compound words with specialist meanings.

Old spelling	New spelling
contre-appel, entre-temps	contrappel, entretemps
tic-tac, week-end	tictac, weekend
agro-alimentaire	agroalimentaire
porte-monnaie	portemonnaie

8.

Words formerly ending in *-olle* and verbs formerly ending in *-otter* are now to be written with only one consonant. Derivatives of *-otter* verbs are likewise written with one consonant. Exceptions to this rule are *colle*, *folle*, *molle* and words derived from nouns ending in *-otte* (such as *botter*, from *botte*).

Old spelling	New spelling
corolle	corole
frisotter, frisottis	frisoter, frisotis

Notes

• This rule ensures consistency of spelling in words like *corole* and *bestiole*; *mangeoter* and *neigeoter*.

9.

The dieresis is written over the letter u in the following cases - *güe-* and *-güi-* and is added in some words.

Old spelling	New spelling
aiguë, ambiguë	aigüe, ambigüe
ambiguïté	ambigüité
arguer	argüer

Notes

• The words in which a dieresis is added are: argüer (*j'argüe, nous argüons, etc.*), *gageüre, mangeüre, rongeüre, vergeüre*.

10.

The past participle of *laisser*, when followed by an infinitive, is invariable in the same way as the past participle of *faire* followed by an infinitive.

Old spelling	New spelling
elle s'est laissée maigrir	elle s'est laissé maigrir
je les ai laissés partir	je les ai laissé partir

11.

In order to avoid anomalies, the following written forms are to be used:

— absout, absoute (*past participle*) ;
— appâts (*plural masculine noun*) ;
— assoir, mes soir, ras soir, sur soir ;
— bizut ;
— bonhommie ;
— boursouflement, boursoufler, boursouflure ;
— cahutte ;
— chariot, chariotage, charioter ;
— chaussetrappe [*formerly* chausse-trape] ;
— combatif, combative, combativité ;
— cuisseau (*in all cases*) ;
— déciller [*formerly* dessiller] ;
— dentelier ;
— dissout, dissoute (*past participle*) ;
— douçâtre ;
— embattre ;
— exéma, exémateux, exémateuse ;
— guilde ;
— imbécilité ;
— innommé, innommée ;
— interpeler (j'interpelle, nous interpelons, *etc.*) ;
— levreau ;
— lunetier ;
— nénufar ;
— ognon, ognonade, ognonière ;
— pagaille ;
— persiflage, persifler, persifleur, persifleuse ;
— ponch (*the drink*) ;
— prudhommal, prudhommale, prudhommie ;
— prunelier ;
— relai ;
— saccarine (and its many derivatives) ;
— sconse ;
— sorgo ;
— sottie ;
— tocade, tocante, tocard, tocarde ;
— ventail.

• Some words where accents were omitted or whose pronunciation has changed, have been given accents: *asséner, papèterie, québécois*, etc.

• Words formerly ending in *-illier* now end with *-iller*, where the *i* following the consonant is silent: *joailler, serpillère*, etc. Exceptions are names of trees: *groseillier*.

Entrées concernées par les rectifications de l'orthographe / Entries affected by the French spelling reform

ancienne graphie existing spelling	nouvelle graphie new spelling
abaisse-langue *nm inv*	abaisse-langue *des abaisse-langues*
abat-jour *nm inv*	abat-jour *des abat-jours*
abat-son *nm inv*	abat-son *des abat-sons*
abat-vent *nm inv*	abat-vent *des abat-vents*
abîme	abime
abîmer	abimer
abrégement	abrègement
accroche-plat *nm inv*	accroche-plat *des accroche-plats*
accroître	accroitre
a contrario	à contrario
acupuncteur	acuponcteur
acupuncture	acuponcture
addenda *nm inv*	addenda *des addendas*
aéro-club	aéroclub
afféterie	affèterie
affût	affut
affûtage	affutage
affûter	affuter
affûteur	affuteur
agro-alimentaire	agroalimentaire
aide-mémoire *nm inv*	aide-mémoire *des aide-mémoires*
aigu, aiguë	aigu, aigüe
aîné	ainé
aînesse	ainesse
allégement	allègement
allégrement	allègrement
allegretto	allégretto
allegro	allégro
allô	allo
allume-cigare(s) *nm inv*	allume-cigare *des allume-cigares*
allume-feu *nm inv*	allume-feu *des allume-feux*
alpha *nm inv*	alpha *des alphas*
ambigu, ambiguë	ambigu, ambigüe
ambiguïté	ambigüité
amoncellement	amoncèlement
amuse-gueule *nm inv*	amuse-gueule *des amuse-gueules*
ana *nm inv*	ana *des anas*
anarcho-syndicalisme	anarchosyndicalisme
anarcho-syndicaliste	anarchosyndicaliste
angström	angstrœm
août	aout
aoûtat	aoutat
aoûtien	aoutien
à-pic *nm inv*	à-pic *des à-pics*
a posteriori	à postériori
apparaître	apparaitre
appas	appâts
appui-main *des appuis-main*	appuie-main *des appuie-mains*
appui-tête *des appuis-têtes*	appuie-tête *des appuie-têtes*
après-midi *nm inv*	après-midi *des après-midis*
après-ski *nm inv*	après-ski *des après-skis*
après-vente *adj inv*	après-vente *après-ventes*

ancienne graphie existing spelling	nouvelle graphie new spelling
a priori *loc adj inv, loc adv*	à priori
a priori *nm inv*	apriori *des aprioris*
arboretum	arborétum
arc-boutant	arcboutant
arc-bouter	arcbouter
arguer	argüer
arrache-pied (d')	arrachepied (d')
arrière-goût	arrière-gout
assener	asséner
assidûment	assidument
asseoir	assoir
attrape-mouches *nm inv*	attrape-mouche *des attrape-mouches*
auto-adhésif	autoadhésif
auto-allumage	autoallumage
auto-école	autoécole
auto-érotique	autoérotique
auto-érotisme	autoérotisme
auto-stop	autostop
auto-stoppeur	autostoppeur
avant-goût	avant-gout
avant-midi *nm inv*	avant-midi *des avant-midis*
baby-boom	babyboum
baby-foot *nm inv*	babyfoot *des babyfoots*
baby-sitter	babysitteur
baby-sitting	babysitting
bachi-bouzouk	bachibouzouk
ballottage	ballotage
ballottement	ballotement
ballotter	balloter
ball-trap	balltrap
barcarolle	barcarole
barman *des barmen*	barman *des barmans*
base-ball	baseball
basket-ball	basketball
basse-cour	bassecour
bat-flanc *nm inv*	bat-flanc *des bat-flancs*
benoît	benoit
benoîtement	benoitement
besicles	bésicles
best-seller	bestseller
bêta *nm inv*	bêta *des bêtas*
bien-aimé	bienaimé
bien-fondé	bienfondé
biodiesel	biodiésel
bizut(h)	bizut
black-out *nm inv*	blackout *des blackouts*
blue-jean	bluejean
body	body *des bodys*
bog(g)ie	bogie
boîte	boite
boîtier	boitier
bolchevik, bolchevique	bolchévik, bolchévique
bolchevisme	bolchévisme
bonhomie	bonhommie
bonneterie	bonnèterie
bookmaker	bookmakeur
boom	boum
bossa-nova	bossanova
bossellement	bossèlement
boui-boui	bouiboui

ancienne graphie existing spelling	nouvelle graphie new spelling
boulotter	bouloter
boursouflé	boursoufflé
boursouflage, boursouflement,	boursoufflage, boursoufflement
boursoufler	boursouffler
boursouflure	boursoufflure
boute-en-train *nm inv*	boutentrain *des boutentrains*
bouterolle	bouterole
boy-scout	boyscout
branle-bas	branlebas
brasero	braséro
briqueterie	briquèterie
brise-béton *nm inv*	brise-béton *des brise-bétons*
brise-bise *nm inv*	brise-bise *des brise-bises*
brise-fer *nm inv*	brise-fer *des brise-fers*
brise-glace *nm inv*	brise-glace *des brise-glaces*
brise-jet *nm inv*	brise-jet *des brise-jets*
brise-lames *nm inv*	brise-lame *des brise-lames*
brise-mottes *nm inv*	brise-motte *des brise-mottes*
brise-soleil *nm inv*	brise-soleil *des brise-soleils*
brise-tout *nm inv*	brisetout *des brisetouts*
brise-vent *nm inv*	brise-vent *des brise-vents*
broncho-pneumonie	bronchopneumonie
brûlage	brulage
brûlant	brulant
brûlé	brulé
brûle-gueule *nm inv*	brule-gueule *des brule-gueules*
brûle-parfum(s) *nm inv*	brule-parfum *des brule-parfums*
brûle-pourpoint (à)	brule-pourpoint (à)
brûler	bruler
brûlerie	brulerie
brûleur	bruleur
brûlis	brulis
brûlot	brulot
brûlure	brulure
bûche	buche
bûcher *(nom)*	bucher
bûcher *(verbe)*	bucher
bûcheron	bucheron
bûchette	buchette
bûcheur	bucheur
bulldozer	bulldozeur
businessman *des businessmen*	biznessman *des biznessmans*
cacahuète	cacahouète
cache-bagages *nm inv*	cache-bagage *des cache-bagages*
cache-cache *nm inv*	cachecache *des cachecaches*
cache-cœur *nm inv*	cache-cœur *des cache-cœurs*
cache-col *nm inv*	cache-col *des cache-cols*
cache-entrée *nm inv*	cache-entrée *des cache-entrées*
cache-misère *nm inv*	cache-misère *des cache-misères*

ancienne graphie existing spelling	nouvelle graphie new spelling	ancienne graphie existing spelling	nouvelle graphie new spelling	ancienne graphie existing spelling	nouvelle graphie new spelling
cache-plaque *nm inv*	cache-plaque *des cache-plaques*	check-up *nm inv*	checkup *des checkups*	contre-productif	contreproductif
cache-pot *nm inv*	cache-pot *des cache-pots*	chow-chow	chowchow	contre-programmation	contreprogrammation
cache-poussière *nm inv*	cache-poussière *des cache-poussières*	ciao	tchao	contre-projet	contreprojet
cache-prise *nm inv*	cache-prise *des cache-prises*	ci-gît	ci-git	contre-propagande	contrepropagande
		cigüe	cigüe	contre-proposition	contreproposition
cache-radiateur *nm inv*	cache-radiateur *des cache-radiateurs*	ciné-parc	cinéparc	contre-publicité	contrepublicité
		claire-voie	clairevoie	contre-rail	contrerail
cache-sexe *nm inv*	cache-sexe *des cache-sexes*	cloche-pied (à)	clochepied (à)	contre-réforme	contreréforme
		cloître	cloitre	contre-révolution	contrerévolution
cache-tampon *nm inv*	cache-tampon *des cache-tampons*	cloîtrer	cloitrer	contre-révolutionnaire	contrerévolutionnaire
		clopin-clopant	clopinclopant	contre-site	contresite
cachotterie	cachoterie	cocotter	cocoter	contre-sommet	contresommet
cachottier	cachotier	coin-coin	coincoin	contre-terrorisme	contreterrorisme
cahin-caha	cahincaha	combatif	combattif	contre-terroriste	contreterroriste
cahute	cahutte	combativité	combattivité	contre-torpilleur	contretorpilleur
call-girl	callgirl	come-back	comeback	contre-ut	contrut
cameraman *des cameramen*	caméraman *des caméramans*	comparaître	comparaitre	contre-valeur	contrevaleur
		complaître	complaire	contre-vérité	contrevérité
canada *nm inv*	canada *des canadas*	compte-fils *nm inv*	compte-fil *des compte-fils*	contre-visite	contrevisite
candela	candéla			contre-voie	contrevoie
cannelloni *nmpl*	cannelloni *des cannellonis*	compte-gouttes *nm inv*	compte-goutte *des compte-gouttes*	corollaire	corolaire
				corolle	corole
cañon	canyon	compte-tours *nm inv*	compte-tour *des compte-tours*	copra(h)	copra
cardio-pulmonaire	cardiopulmonaire			corollaire	corolaire
cardio-vasculaire	cardiovasculaire	connaître	connaitre	corolle	corole
car-ferry *des car-ferries*	carferry *des carferrys*	contigu, contiguë	contigu, contigüe	couci-couça	coucicouça
casse-cou *adj inv,* *nm inv, nmf inv*	casse-cou *(des) casse-cous*	contiguïté	contigüité	couguar	cougouar
		continûment	continument	coupe-carrelage *nm inv*	coupe-carrelage *des coupe-carrelages*
casse-couilles *nmf inv*	casse-couille *des casse-couilles*	contre-alizé	contralizé		
		contre-allée	contrallée	coupe-choux *nm inv*	coupe-chou *des coupe-choux*
casse-croûte *nm inv*	casse-croute *des casse-croutes*	contre-alliance	contralliance		
		contre-amiral	contramiral	coupe-circuit *nm inv*	coupe-circuit *des coupe-circuits*
casse-cul *adj inv, nmf inv*	casse-cul *(des) casse-culs*	contre-analyse	contranalyse		
		contre-argument	contrargument	coupe-coupe *nm inv*	coupe-coupe *des coupe-coupes*
casse-dalle *nm inv*	casse-dalle *des casse-dalles*	contre-attaque	contrattaque		
		contre-attaquer	contrattaquer	coupe-faim *nm inv*	coupe-faim *des coupe-faims*
casse-graine *nm inv*	casse-graine *des casse-graines*	contre-autopsie	contrautopsie		
		contre-braquer	contrebraquer	coupe-feu *nm inv*	coupe-feu *des coupe-feux*
casse-gueule *adj inv,* *nm inv*	casse-gueule *(des) casse-gueules*	contre-chant	contrechant	coupe-frites *nm inv*	coupe-frite *des coupe-frites*
		contre-courant	contrecourant		
casse-noisettes *nm inv*	casse-noisette *des casse-noisettes*	contre-culture	contreculture	coupe-gorge *nm inv*	coupe-gorge *des coupe-gorges*
		contre-écrou	contrécrou		
casse-pied *nm inv*	casse-pied *(des) casse-pieds*	contre-électromotrice	contrélectromotrice	coupe-jambon *nm inv*	coupe-jambon *des coupe-jambons*
		contre-emploi	contremploi		
casse-pipe *nm inv*	casse-pipe *des casse-pipes*	contre-enquête	contrenquête	coupe-jarret *nm inv*	coupe-jarret *des coupe-jarrets*
casse-tête *nm inv*	casse-tête *des casse-têtes*	contre-épreuve	contrépreuve		
céleri	cèleri	contre-espionnage	contrespionnage	coupe-légumes *nm inv*	coupe-légume *des coupe-légumes*
céphalo-rachidien	céphalorachidien	contre-essai	contressai	coupe-œuf *nm inv*	coupe-œuf *des coupe-œufs*
cérébro-spinal	cérébrospinal	contre-étiquette	contrétiquette		
cha-cha-cha	chachacha	contre-exemple	contrexemple	coupe-ongles *nm inv*	coupe-ongle *des coupe-ongles*
chaînage	chainage	contre-expertise	contrexpertise		
chaîne	chaine	contre-fenêtre	contrefenêtre	coupe-papier *nm inv*	coupe-papier *des coupe-papiers*
chaîner	chainer	contre-fer	contrefer		
chaînette	chainette	contre-feu	contrefeu	coupe-tomates *nm inv*	coupe-tomate *des coupe-tomates*
chaînon	chainon	contre-fil	contrefil		
chariot	charriot	contre-filet	contrefilet	coupe-vent *nm inv*	coupe-vent *des coupe-vents*
chasse-mouches *nm inv*	chasse-mouche *des chasse-mouches*	contre-indication	contrindication	coût	cout
		contre-indiqué	contrindiqué	coûtant	coutant
chasse-neige *nm inv*	chasse-neige *des chasse-neiges*	contre-insurrection	contrinsurrection	coûter	couter
		contre-interrogatoire	contrinterrogatoire	coûteusement	couteusement
chasse-pierres *nm inv*	chasse-pierre *des chasse-pierres*	contre-jour	contrejour	coûteux	couteux
		contremaître, contremaîtresse	contremaitre, contremaitresse	couvre-pieds *nm inv*	couvrepied *des couvrepieds*
chauffe-assiettes *nm inv*	chauffe-assiette *des chauffe-assiettes*	contre-manifestant	contremanifestant		
		contre-manifestation	contremanifestation	cover-girl	covergirl *des covergirls*
chauffe-biberon *nm inv*	chauffe-biberon *des chauffe-biberons*	contre-mesure	contremesure	cow-boy	cowboy *des cowboys*
		contre-offensive	controffensive	crécerelle	crècerelle
chauffe-eau *nm inv*	chauffe-eau *des chauffe-eaux*	contre-offre	controffre	credo	crédo
		contre-pente	contrepente	crémerie	crèmerie
chauffe-pieds *nm inv*	chauffe-pied *des chauffe-pieds*	contre-performance	contreperformance	crénelage	crènelage
		contre-pied	contrepied	crénelé	crènelé
chauffe-plat *nm inv*	chauffe-plat *des chauffe-plats*	contre-plongée	contreplongée	créneler	crèneler
		contre-porte	contreporte	crève-cœur *nm inv*	crève-cœur *des crève-cœurs*
chausse-pied	chaussepied				
chausse-trap(p)e	chaussetrappe	contre-pouvoir	contrepouvoir	croche-pied (à)	crochepied (à)
chauve-souris	chauvesouris				

ancienne graphie existing spelling	nouvelle graphie new spelling	ancienne graphie existing spelling	nouvelle graphie new spelling	ancienne graphie existing spelling	nouvelle graphie new spelling
croître	croitre	emboîtement	emboitement	fourre-tout *nm inv*	fourretout
croque-madame *nm inv*	croquemadame	emboîter	emboiter		*des fourretouts*
	des croquemadames	embûche	embuche	fraîche (*nom*)	fraiche
croque-mitaine	croquemitaine	emporte-pièce *nm inv*	emporte-pièce	fraîchement	fraichement
croque-monsieur *nm inv*	croquemonsieur		*des emporte-pièces*	fraîcheur	fraicheur
	des croquemonsieurs	en-cas	encas	fraîchir	fraichir
croque-mort	croquemort	enchaînement	enchainement	frais, fraîche	frais, fraiche
cross(-country)	crosscountry	enchaîner	enchainer	free-lance	freelance
croûte	croute	en-cours	encours	freezer	freezeur
croûter	crouter	encroûter	encrouter	freesia	frésia
croûton	crouton	en-tête	entête	fric-frac	fricfrac
crûment	crument	entraînant	entrainant	frisotter	frisoter
cui-cui	cuicui	entraînement	entrainement	fume-cigarette *nm inv*	fume-cigarette
cuissot	cuisseau	entraîner	entrainer		*des fume-cigarettes*
cure-dents *nm inv*	cure-dent	entraîneur	entraineur	fumerolle	fumerole
	des cure-dents	entre-rail	entrerail	fût (*nom*)	fut
cure-ongles *nm inv*	cure-ongle	entre-temps	entretemps	gageure	gageüre
	des cure-ongles	entre-tuer	entretuer	gagne-pain *nm inv*	gagne-pain
cure-pipes *nm inv*	cure-pipe *des cure-pipes*	envoûtant	envoutant		*des gagne-pains*
cuti-réaction	cutiréaction	envoûtement	envoutement	gagne-petit *adj inv,*	gagne-petit
cutter	cutteur	envoûter	envouter	*nm inv*	(*des*) gagne-petits
cyclo-cross	cyclocross	envoûteur	envouteur	gaiement	gaiment
cyclo-pousse	cyclopousse	épître	épitre	gaieté	gaité
dare-dare	daredare	epsilon *nm inv*	epsilon *des epsilons*	gamma *nm inv*	gamma *des gammas*
dealer (*nom*)	dealeur	errata *nm inv*	errata *des erratas*	gangreneux	grangréneux
déboîtement	déboitement	essuie-mains *nm inv*	essuie-main	garde-boue *nm inv*	garde-boue
déboîter	déboiter		*des essuie-mains*		*des garde-boues*
déchaîné	déchainé	essuie-phares *nm inv*	essuie-phare	garde-chiourme *nm inv*	garde-chiourme
déchaînement	déchainement		*des essuie-phares*		*des garde-chiourmes*
déchaîner	déchainer	essuie-pieds *nm inv*	essuie-pied	garde-feu *nm inv*	garde-feu *des garde-feux*
déchetterie	déchèterie		*des essuie-pieds*	garde-manger *nm inv*	garde-manger
decrescendo	décrescendo	essuie-verres *nm inv*	essuie-verre		*des garde-mangers*
décroître	décroitre		*des essuie-verres*	garde-meubles *nm inv*	garde-meuble
défraîchi	défraichi	essuie-vitres *nm inv*	essuie-vitre		*des garde-meubles*
défraîchir	défraichir		*des essuie-vitres*	garde-pêche *nm inv*	garde-pêche
dégot(t)er	dégoter	et cætera, et cetera	etcétéra		*des garde-pêches*
dégoût	dégout	étincellement	étincèlement	garotter	garoter
dégoûtant	dégoutant	étouffe-chrétien *adj inv,*	étouffe-chrétien	gastro-entérite	gastroentérite
dégoûtation	dégoutation	*nm inv*	(*des*) *étouffe-chrétiens*	gastro-entérologie	gastroentérologie
dégoûté	dégouté	événement	évènement	gastro-entérologue	gastroentérologue
dégoûter	dégouter	événementiel	évènementiel	gentleman	gentleman
deleatur *nm inv*	déléatur *des déléaturs*	exigu, exiguë	exigu, exigüe	*des gentlemen*	*des gentlemans*
delirium tremens *nm inv*	delirium trémens	exiguïté	exigüité	gentleman-farmer	gentleman-farmer
	des déliriums trémens	ex-libris	exlibris	*des gentlemen-farmers*	*des gentlemans-farmers*
delta *nm inv*	delta *des deltas*	extra *adj inv, nm inv*	extra (*des*) *extras*	girolle	girole
dentellier, dentellière	dentelier, dentelière	extra(-)fin	extrafin	gîte	gite
déplaîre	déplaire	extra-muros	extramuros	gîter	giter
déréglementation	dérèglementation	ex-voto *nm inv*	exvoto *des exvotos*	globe-trotter	globetrotteur
déréglementer	dérèglementer	fac-similé	facsimilé	golden *nf inv*	golden *des goldens*
désambiguïser	désambigüiser	faire-part *nm inv*	fairepart *des faireparts*	goulasch	goulach
desiderata *nmpl*	désidérata	fair-play	fairplay	goulûment	goulument
	des désidératas	faîtage	faitage	goût	gout
dessiller	déciller	faîte	faite	goûter	gouter
desperado	despérado	faîtière	faitière	goûteux	gouteux
dessaouler, dessoûler	dessouler	fast-food	fastfood	graffiti *nmpl*	graffiti *des graffitis*
diesel	diésel	favela	favéla	gratte-ciel *nm inv*	gratte-ciel
diktat	dictat	fayot(t)age	fayotage		*des gratte-ciels*
dîme	dime	fayot(t)er	fayoter	gratte-papier *nm inv*	gratte-papier
dînatoire	dinatoire	feed-back *nm inv*	feedback *des feedbacks*		*des gratte-papiers*
dîner (*verbe et nom*)	diner	féerie	féérie	grelottement	grelotement
dînette	dinette	féerique	féérique	grelotter	greloter
dîneur	dineur	ferry *des ferries*	ferry *des ferrys*	gri-gri	grigri
disparaître	disparaitre	ferry-boat	ferryboat	grille-pain *nm inv*	grille-pain
douceâtre	douçâtre	féverole	fèverole		*des grille-pains*
driver *nm*	driveur, driveuse	fjord	fiord	grolle	grole
dûment	dument	flash *des flashes*	flash *des flashs*	grommellement	grommèlement
duplicata *nm inv*	duplicata *des duplicatas*	flash-back	flashback	guibolle	guibole
dynamo-électrique	dynamoélectrique	flipper (*nom*)	flippeur	guérillero	guérilléro
eczéma	exéma	flûte	flute	guili-guili	guiliguili
eczémateux	exémateux	flûté	fluté	hache-légumes *nm inv*	hache-légume
edelweiss	édelweiss	flûtiau	flutiau		*des hache-légumes*
électro-aimant	électroaimant	flûtiste	flutiste	hache-paille *nm inv*	hache-paille
emboîtable	emboitable	fortissimo *nm inv*	fortissimo		*des hache-pailles*
emboîtage	emboitage		*des fortissimos*	hache-viande *nm inv*	hache-viande
					des hache-viandes
				hara-kiri	harakiri

xix •

Entries affected by the French spelling reform

ancienne graphie existing spelling	nouvelle graphie new spelling	ancienne graphie existing spelling	nouvelle graphie new spelling	ancienne graphie existing spelling	nouvelle graphie new spelling
hasch	hach	lave-linge *nm inv*	lave-linge *des lave-linges*	moût	mout
haschi(s)ch	hachich	lave-mains *nm inv*	lave-main *des lave-mains*	mû *(participe passé)*	mu
haute-contre	hautecontre			muezzin	muézine
haut-parleur	hautparleur	lave-vaisselle *nm inv*	lave-vaisselle *des lave-vaisselles*	mûre *(nom)*	mure
hébétement	hébètement			mûrement	murement
hi-fi *adj inv, nm inv*	hifi *(des) hifis*	lazzi *nmpl*	lazzi *des lazzis*	mûrier	murier
hi-han	hihan	leader	leadeur	mûrir	murir
hippy *des hippies*	hippy *des hippys*	leadership	leadeurship	mûrissage	murissage
hit-parade	hitparade	lèche-bottes *nmf inv*	lèche-botte *des lèche-bottes*	mûrissement	murissement
hors-bord *adj, nm inv*	hors-bord *(des) hors-bords*	lèche-cul *nmf inv*	lèche-cul *des lèche-culs*	mûrisserie	murisserie
				musellement	musèlement
hors-jeu *nm inv*	hors-jeu *des hors-jeux*	lèche-vitrines *nm inv*	lèche-vitrine *des lèche-vitrines*	nævus *des nævi*	névus *des névus*
hors-média *nm inv*	hors-média *des hors-médias*	lèse-majesté *nm inv*	lèse-majesté *des lèse-majestés*	naître	naitre
				negro(-)spiritual	négrospiritual
hors-piste *nm inv*	hors-piste *des hors-pistes*	levraut	levreau	nénuphar	nénufar
		lieu-dit	lieudit	new-look	newlook
hors-sol *nm inv*	hors-sol *des hors-sols*	lobby *des lobbies*	lobby *des lobbys*	nivellement	nivèlement
hors-texte *nm inv*	hors-texte *des hors-textes*	lock-out *nm inv*	lockout *des lockouts*	noroît	noroit *(vent)*
		lumbago	lombago	nova *des novæ*	nova *des novas*
huître	huitre	maelström	malstrom	nu *nm inv*	nu *des nus*
huîtrier	huitrier	maf(f)ia	mafia	numerus clausus	numérus clausus
huîtrière	huitrière	maf(f)ioso	mafioso	offshore *adj inv, nm inv*	offshore *(des) offshores*
igloo	iglou	mahara(d)jah	maharadja *des maharadjas*	oignon	ognon
île	ile			oligo-élément	oligoélément
îlien	ilien	mah-jong	majong	oméga *nm inv*	oméga *des omégas*
îlot	ilot	main-forte	mainforte	osso buco	ossobuco
îlotage	ilotage	maître	maitre	oto-rhino	otorhino
îlotier	ilotier	maîtresse	maitresse	oto-rhino- laryngologiste	otorhinolaryngologiste
imbécillité	imbécilité	maître-à-danser	maitre-à-danser		
imprimatur *nm inv*	imprimatur *des imprimaturs*	maître-assistant	maitre-assistant	oto-rhino-laryngologie	otorhinolaryngologie
		maître-autel	maitre-autel	ouvre-boîtes *nm inv*	ouvre-boite *des ouvre-boites*
impedimenta *nmpl*	impédimenta *des impédimentas*	maître-chanteur	maitre-chanteur		
		maître-chien	maitre-chien	ouvre-bouteilles *nm inv*	ouvre-bouteille *des ouvre-bouteilles*
imprimatur *nm inv*	imprimatur *des imprimaturs*	maître-cylindre	maitre-cylindre		
		maître-nageur	maitre-nageur	pacemaker	pacemakeur
indûment	indument	maîtrisable	maitrisable	paella	paélia
in extremis	in extrémis	maîtrise	maitrise	paître	paitre
in-folio *adj inv, nm inv*	infolio *(des) infolios*	maîtriser	maitriser	papeterie	papèterie
in-octavo *adj inv, nm inv*	inoctavo *(des) inoctavos*	mange-tout *nm inv*	mangetout *des mangetouts*	papy-boom	papyboum
in-quarto *adj inv, nm inv*	inquarto *(des) inquartos*			paraître	paraitre
interpeller	interpeler	maniaco-dépressif	maniacodépressif	pare-balles *adj inv*	pare-balle pare-balles
iota *nm inv*	iota *des iotas*	maraîchage	maraichage	pare-boue *nm inv*	pare-boue *des pare-boues*
jamboree	jamborée	maraîcher	maraicher	pare-brise *nm inv*	pare-brise *des pare-brises*
jazzman *des jazzmen*	jazzman *des jazzmans*	marguillier	marguiller	pare-chocs *nm inv*	pare-choc *des pare-chocs*
jean-foutre	jeanfoutre	mariol(le)	mariole	pare-éclats *nm inv*	pare-éclat *des pare-éclats*
jeûner	jeuner	marketing	markéting	pare-étincelles *nm inv*	pare-étincelle *des pare-étincelles*
jeûneur	jeuneur	marqueterie	marquèterie		
jiu-jitsu	jiujitsu	mass media *nmpl*	mass média *des mass médias*	pare-feu *nm inv*	pare-feu *des pare-feux*
joaillier	joailler			pare-soleil *nm inv*	pare-soleil *des pare-soleils*
juke-box *des juke-boxes*	jukebox *des jukebox*	méconnaître	méconnaitre		
khi *nm inv*	khi *des khis*	médico-légal	médicolégal	pare-vent *nm inv*	pare-vent *des pare-vents*
kibboutz *des kibboutzim*	kibboutz *des kibboutz*	médico-social	médicosocial	passe-crassane *nf inv*	passe-crassane *des passe-crassanes*
kif-kif	kifkif	médico-sportif	médicosportif		
kleptomane	cleptomane	méli-mélo	mélimélo	passe-partout *adj inv, nm inv*	passepartout *(des) passepartouts*
kleptomanie	cleptomanie	messeoir	messoir		
knock-out	knockout	micro-ampère	microampère	passe-passe *nm inv*	passepasse *des passepasses*
lance-flammes *nm inv*	lance-flamme *des lance-flammes*	mille-pattes *nm inv*	millepatte *des millepattes*		
				passe-temps	passetemps
lance-fusées *nm inv* *des lance-fusées*	lance-fusée	mini-boom	miniboum	passe-thé *nm inv*	passe-thé *des passe-thés*
		minichaîne	minichaine	pécheresse	pècheresse
lance-grenades *nm inv*	lance-grenade *des lance-grenades*	mini-jupe	minijupe	pedigree	pédigrée
		mire-œufs *nm inv*	mire-œuf *des mire-œufs*	pêle-mêle *nm inv*	pêlemêle *des pêlemêles*
lance-harpon *adj inv*	lance-harpon *lance-harpons*	miss *nf inv*	miss *des miss*	penalty	pénalty
		monte-charge *nm inv*	monte-charge *des monte-charges*	péquenaud	pèquenaud
lance-missiles *nm inv*	lance-missile *des lance-missiles*			péquenot	pèquenot
		monte-meubles *nm inv*	monte-meuble *des monte-meubles*	perce-neige *nm or f inv*	perce-neige *des perce-neiges*
lance-pierres *nm inv*	lance-pierre *des lance-pierres*				
		monte-plats *nm inv*	monte-plat *des monte-plats*	perestroïka	pérestroïka
lance-roquettes *nm inv*	lance-roquette *des lance-roquettes*			persiflage	persifflage
		morcellement	morcèlement	persifler	persiffler
lance-satellites *nm inv*	lance-satellite *des lance-satellites*	motocross *nm inv*	motocross *des motocross*	persifleur	persiffleur
				pèse-alcool *nm inv*	pèse-alcool *des pèse-alcools*
lance-torpilles *nm inv*	lance-torpille *des lance-torpilles*	moudjahidin *nmpl*	moudjahidine *des moudjahidines*		
				pèse-denrées *nm inv*	pèse-denrée *des pèse-denrées*
lasagnes *nfpl*	lasagne *des lasagnes*				

ancienne graphie existing spelling	nouvelle graphie new spelling	ancienne graphie existing spelling	nouvelle graphie new spelling	ancienne graphie existing spelling	nouvelle graphie new spelling
peseta	péséta	portefaix *nm inv*	portefaix *des portefaix*	quote-part	quotepart
pète-sec	pètesec	porte-fusible *nm inv*	porte-fusible *des porte-fusibles*	rabat-joie *adj inv, nm inv*	rabat-joie *des rabat-joies*
photo-finish	photofinish			radio-taxi	radiotaxi
physico-chimique	physicochimique	porte-greffes *nm inv*	porte-greffe *des porte-greffes*	rafraîchir	rafraichir
physico-mathématique	physicomathématique	porte-hélicoptères *nm inv*	porte-hélicoptère *des porte-hélicoptères*	rafraîchissant	rafraichissant
pi *nm inv*	pi *des pis*			rafraîchissement	rafraichissement
piccolo	picolo	porte-jarretelles *nm inv*	porte-jarretelle *des porte-jarretelles*	ragoût	ragout
pick-up *nm inv*	pickup *des pickups*			ragoûtant	ragoutant
pietà *nf inv*	piéta *des piétas*	porte-monnaie *nm inv*	portemonnaie *des portemonnaies*	ramasse-miettes *nm inv*	ramasse-miette *des ramasse-miettes*
pince-fesses *nm inv*	pince-fesse *des pince-fesses*	porte-musique *nm inv*	porte-musique *des porte-musiques*	ramasse-monnaie *nm inv*	ramasse-monnaie *des ramasse-monnaies*
pince-monseigneur *des pinces-monseigneur*	pince-monseigneur *des pince-monseigneurs*	porte-outil *nm inv*	porte-outil *des porte-outils*	ramasse-poussière *nm inv*	ramasse-poussière *des ramasse-poussières*
pince-oreilles *nm inv*	pince-oreille *des pince-oreilles*	porte-parapluie *nm inv*	porte-parapluie *des porte-parapluies*	rase-mottes *nm inv*	rase-motte *des rase-mottes*
ping-pong	pingpong	porte-parole *nm inv*	porte-parole *des porte-paroles*	rasseoir	rassoir
pin-up *nf inv*	pinup *des pinups*	porte-pipes *nm inv*	porte-pipe *des porte-pipes*	réapparaître	réapparaitre
pique-assiette *nmf inv*	pique-assiette *des pique-assiettes*			receler	recéler
pique-feu *nm inv*	pique-feu *des pique-feux*	porte-plume *nm inv*	porteplume *des porteplumes*	receleur	recéleur
pique-fleurs *nm inv*	pique-fleur *des pique-fleurs*	porte-savon *nm inv*	porte-savon *des porte-savons*	reconnaître	reconnaitre
pique-nique	piquenique	porte-serviettes *nm inv*	porte-serviette *des porte-serviettes*	recordman *des recordmen*	recordman *des recordmans*
pique-niquer	piqueniquer	porte-skis *nm inv*	porte-ski *des porte-skis*	recordwoman *des recordwomen*	recordwoman *des recordwomans*
pique-niqueur	piqueniqueur	porte-vélo *nm inv*	porte-vélo *des porte-vélos*	reflex	réflex
piqûre	piqure			refréner	réfréner
pisse-copie *nmf inv*	pisse-copie *des pisse-copies*	porte-verres *nm inv*	porte-verre *des porte-verres*	réglementaire	règlementaire
				réglementairement	règlementairement
pisse-froid *nm inv*	pisse-froid *des pisse-froids*	porte-voix *nm inv*	porte-voix *des porte-voix*	réglementation	règlementation
pisse-vinaigre *nm inv*	pisse-vinaigre *des pisse-vinaigres*	post-partum *nm inv*	post-partum *des post-partums*	réglementer	règlementer
		post-scriptum *nm inv*	post-scriptum *des post-scriptums*	relais	relai
pizzeria	pizzéria	pot-pourri	potpourri	remboîter	remboiter
placebo	placébo	pousse-café *nm inv*	pousse-café *des pousse-cafés*	remonte-fesses *nm inv*	remonte-fesse *des remonte-fesses*
plate-bande	platebande				
plate-forme *des plates-formes*	plateforme *des plateformes*	pousse-pousse *nm inv*	poussepousse *des poussepousses*	remue-ménage *nm inv*	remue-ménage *des remue-ménages*
playback *nm inv*	playback *des playbacks*	prêchi-prêcha	prêchiprêcha	remue-méninges *nm inv*	remue-méninge *des remue-méninges*
play-boy	playboy	premier-maître *(in compounds of premier)*	premier-maitre	renaître	renaitre
pogrom(e)	pogrome			renouvellement	renouvèlement
pop-corn	popcorn	presqu'île	presqu'ile	repaître	repaitre
porte-aéronefs *nm inv*	porte-aéronef *des porte-aéronefs*	presse-agrumes *nm inv*	presse-agrume *des presse-agrumes*	reparaître	reparaitre
porte-aiguilles *nm inv*	porte-aiguille *des porte-aiguilles*	presse-bouton *nm inv*	presse-bouton *des presse-boutons*	repartie	répartie
porte-autos *nm inv*	porte-auto *des porte-autos*	presse-citron *nm inv*	presse-citron *des presse-citrons*	repose-tête *nm inv*	repose-tête *des repose-têtes*
porte-avions *nm inv*	porte-avion *des porte-avions*	presse-étoupe *nm inv*	presse-étoupe *des presse-étoupes*	réveille-matin *nm inv*	réveille-matin *des réveille-matins*
porte-bagages *nm inv*	porte-bagage *des porte-bagages*	presse-papiers *nm inv*	presse-papier *des presse-papiers*	revolver	révolver
porte-bébé *nm inv*	porte-bébé *des porte-bébés*	presse-purée *nm inv*	presse-purée *des presse-purées*	rhô *nm inv*	rho *des rhos*
porte-billets *nm inv*	porte-billet *des porte-billets*	presse-raquette *nm inv*	presse-raquette *des presse-raquettes*	ric-rac	ricrac
porte-bonheur *nm inv*	porte-bonheur *des porte-bonheurs*	prima donna *nf inv*	primadonna *des primadonnas*	rince-bouteilles *nm inv*	rince-bouteille *des rince-bouteilles*
porte-bouteilles *nm inv*	porte-bouteille *des porte-bouteilles*	prorata *nm inv*	prorata *des proratas*	rince-doigts *nm inv*	rince-doigt *des rince-doigts*
porte-cartes *nm inv*	porte-carte *des porte-cartes*	protège-dents *nm inv*	protège-dent *des protège-dents*	risque-tout *nm inv*	risquetout *des risquetouts*
		prud'homal	prudhommal	rond-point	rondpoint
porte-chéquier *nm inv*	porte-chéquier *des porte-chéquiers*	prud'homme	prudhomme	roulotter	rouloter
		prunellier	prunelier	rousserolle	rousserole
porte-cigares *nm inv*	porte-cigare *des porte-cigares*	psi *nm inv*	psi *des psis*	rugbyman *des rugbymen*	rugbyman *des rugbymans*
porte-cigarettes *nm inv*	porte-cigarette *des porte-cigarettes*	pudding	pouding	ruissellement	ruissèlement
porte-clés *nm inv*	porteclé *des porteclés*	puîné	puiné	rush *des rushes*	rush *des rushs*
porte-conteneur *nm inv*	porte-conteneur *des porte-conteneurs*	punch *(boisson)*	ponch	saccharine	saccarine
		pull-over	pullover	saccharose	saccarose
porte-crayons *nm inv*	porte-crayon *des porte-crayons*	puîné	puiné	sacro-saint	sacrosaint
porte-documents *nm inv*	porte-document *des porte-documents*	putsch *nm inv*	putsch *des putschs*	sage-femme *des sages-femmes*	sagefemme *des sagefemmes*
		quanta *nmpl*	quanta *des quantas*	sans-abri *nmf inv*	sans-abri *des sans-abris*
porte-drapeau *nm inv*	porte-drapeau *des porte-drapeaux*	quantum *nm*	quantum *des quantums*	sans-cœur *nmf inv*	sans-cœur *des sans-cœurs*
porte-étendard *nm inv*	porte-étendard *des porte-étendards*	quartier-maître	quartier-maitre	sans-emploi *nmf inv*	sans-emploi *des sans-emplois*
		quincaillier	quincailler	sans-faute *nm inv*	sans-faute *des sans-fautes*

ancienne graphie existing spelling	nouvelle graphie new spelling
sans-fil *nm inv*	sans-fil *des sans-fils*
sans-gêne *adj inv, nmf inv*	sans-gêne *(des) sans-gênes*
sans-grade *nm inv*	sans-grade *des sans-grades*
sanskrit	sanscrit
sans-logis *nmf inv*	sans-logis *des sans-logis*
sans-papiers *nm inv*	sans-papier *des sans-papiers*
satisfecit *nm inv*	satisfécit *des satisfécits*
sauf-conduit	saufconduit *des saufconduits*
saute-mouton *nm inv*	saute-mouton *des saute-moutons*
saute-ruisseau *nm inv*	saute-ruisseau *des saute-ruisseaux*
scampi *nmpl*	scampi *des scampis*
scooter	scooteur
scotch *des scotches*	scotch *des scotchs*
sèche-cheveux *nm inv*	sèche-cheveu *des sèche-cheveux*
sèche-linge *nm inv*	sèche-linge *des sèche-linges*
sèche-mains *nm inv*	sèche-main *des sèche-mains*
sécheresse	sècheresse
séneçon	sèneçon
sénevé	sènevé
senior	sénior
serpillière	serpillère
serre-livres *nm inv*	serre-livre *des serre-livres*
shaker	shakeur
shampooing	shampoing
side-car	sidecar
sigma *nm inv*	sigma *des sigmas*
sirocco	siroco
sketch *des sketches*	sketch *des sketchs*
skiff	skif
skipper	skippeur
smash *des smashes*	smash *des smashs*
snack-bar	snackbar
sniff	snif
sniffer	snifer
socio-démocrate	sociodémocrate
socio-économique	socioéconomique
socio-éducatif	socioéducatif
sombrero	sombréro
sorgho	sorgo
souffre-douleur *nm inv*	souffre-douleur *des souffre-douleurs*
soûl	soul
soûlant	soulant
soûlard	soulard
soûler	souler
soûlerie	soulerie
soûlographe	soulographe
soûlographie	soulographie
sous-main *nm inv*	sous-main *des sous-mains*
sous-seing *nm inv*	sous-seing *des sous-seings*
sous-tasse	soutasse
sous-verre *nm inv*	sous-verre *des sous-verres*
spaghetti *nm inv*	spaghetti *des spaghettis*
spatio-temporel	spatiotemporel
sprinter	sprinteur
squatter (*nom*)	squatteur
statu quo *nm inv*	statuquo *des statuquos*
stimulus *des stimuli*	stimulus *des stimulus*
strato-cumulus	stratocumulus
strip-tease	striptease
strip-teaseur	stripteaseur
subaigu, subaiguë	subaigu, subaigüe
supernova *des supernovae*	supernova *des supernovas*
supporter (*nom*)	supporteur
suraigu, suraiguë	suraigu, suraigüe
surcoût	surcout
surcroît	surcroit
surdi-mutité	surdimutité
sûrement	surement
surentraînement	surentrainement
surentraîner	surentrainer
sûreté	sureté
suroît	suroit
surpiqûre	surpiqure
surseoir	sursoir
tagliatelles *nfpl*	taliatelle *des taliatelles*
taille-crayons *nm inv*	taille-crayon *des taille-crayons*
tam-tam	tamtam
tartignolle	tartignole
taste-vin *nm inv*	taste-vin *des taste-vins*
tchin(-tchin)	tchintchin
teck	tek
tee-shirt	teeshirt
télé-achat	téléachat
tennisman *des tennismen*	tennisman *des tennismans*
terre-plein	terreplein
tête-bêche	têtebêche
teuf-teuf	teufteuf
thêta *nm inv*	thêta *des thêtas*
thriller	thrilleur
tie-break	tiebreak
tire-bouchon	tirebouchon
tire-bouchonner	tirebouchonner
tire-fesse *nm inv*	tire-fesse *des tire-fesses*
tire-fond *nm inv*	tirefond *des tirefonds*
tire-laine *nm inv*	tire-laine *des tire-laines*
tire-lait *nm inv*	tire-lait *des tire-laits*
tohu-bohu	tohubohu
tomahawk	tomawak
tord-boyaux *nm inv*	tord-boyau *des tord-boyaux*
torero	toréro
trachéo-bronchite	trachéobronchite
tragi-comédie	tragicomédie
tragi-comique	tragicomique
traînailler	trainailler
traînant	trainant
traînard	trainard
traînasser	trainasser
traîne	traine
traîne-savates *nm inv*	traine-savate *des traine-savates*
traîneau	traineau
traînée	trainée
traîne-misère *nmf inv*	traine-misère *des traine-misères*
traîner	trainer
train(-)train	traintrain
traître, traîtresse	traitre, traitresse
traîtreusement	traitreusement
traîtrise	traitrise
transparaître	transparaitre
trouble-fête *nmf inv*	trouble-fête *des trouble-fêtes*
tsé-tsé *nf inv*	tsétsé *des tsétsés*
tsoin-tsoin	tsointsoin
vade-mecum *nm inv*	vadémécum *des vadémécums*
vantail	ventail
va-nu-pieds *nmf inv*	vanupied *des vanupieds*
va-tout *nm inv*	vatout *des vatouts*
vélo-cross	vélocross
vénerie	vènerie
veto	véto
vide-greniers *nm inv*	vide-grenier *des vide-greniers*
vide-ordures *nm inv*	vide-ordure *des vide-ordures*
vide-poches *nm inv*	vide-poche *des vide-poches*
vilenie	vilénie
volapük	volapuk
volley(-ball)	volleyball
volte-face *nf inv*	volte-face *des volte-faces*
voûte	voute
voûté	vouté
voûter	vouter
wallaby *des wallabies*	wallaby *des wallabys*
water-polo	waterpolo
waters *nmpl*	water *des waters*
week-end	weekend
whisky *des whiskies*	whisky *des whiskys*
yachtman *des yachtmen*	yachtman *des yachtmans*
ya(c)k	yak
yé-yé	yéyé
yiddish	yidiche
yoghourt	yogourt
yo-yo	yoyo
zakouski *nmpl*	zakouski *des zakouskis*
zêta *nm inv*	zêta *des zêtas*

Using this dictionary

Each entry in the dictionary is organized hierarchically, by grammatical category, then sense category. Grammatical categories are always in the same order. In the English-French part of the dictionary, the rule is that if the word has a use as an irregular inflected form, like the entry *left* for example, this will come first. Next will come the noun category, if there is one, then the adjective, then the adverb. Verbs, idioms, and phrasal verbs come last, in that order. The way the entry *kindly* is constructed is shown in the diagram below. To translate *he thought kindly of her*, you would go through the steps shown on the right. The section that follows gives other examples of how to get the best out of the dictionary for various kinds of translation task.

As a general rule, all meanings of a word are to be found in one single entry, provided they are pronounced in the same way, exclusive of stress shifts. English compounds have their own place in the alphabetical order of the dictionary, either as separate entries or, where several fall together in the alphabet, grouped together under the first element.

The French-English entries follow a similar sequence, but adjectives precede nouns and non-hyphenated compounds appear together in a separate category at the end of the entry. French hyphenated compounds are given separate-entry status. On both sides of the dictionary, the order of sense categories reflects frequency of use, the most commonly used coming first. Within sense categories, distinctions between alternative translations are shown by means of sense indicators in round brackets and/or collocates giving typical context, which appear in square brackets.

(1) kindly /'kaɪndlɪ/

A *adj* [*person, nature*] gentil/-ille; [*smile, interest*] bienveillant; [*voice*] plein de gentillesse; [*face*] sympathique; **she's a ~ soul** elle est très gentille

(2) B *adv* [1] (in a kind, nice way) [*speak, look, treat*] avec gentillesse; **to speak ~ of sb** avoir un mot gentil pour qn; **thank you ~†** tous mes remerciements; [2] (obligingly) gentiment; **she ~ agreed to do** elle a gentiment accepté de faire; **would you ~ do/refrain from doing** auriez-vous l'amabilité de faire/de ne pas faire; **'would visitors ~ do', 'visitors are ~ requested to do'** GB 'les visiteurs sont priés de faire'; **(3)(4)(5)** [3] **(favourably) to look ~ on** approuver [*activity*]; **to think ~ of** avoir une bonne opinion de [*person*]; **to take ~ to** apprécier [*idea, suggestion, person*]; **I don't think he'll take ~ to being kept waiting** je ne crois pas qu'il va apprécier qu'on le fasse attendre

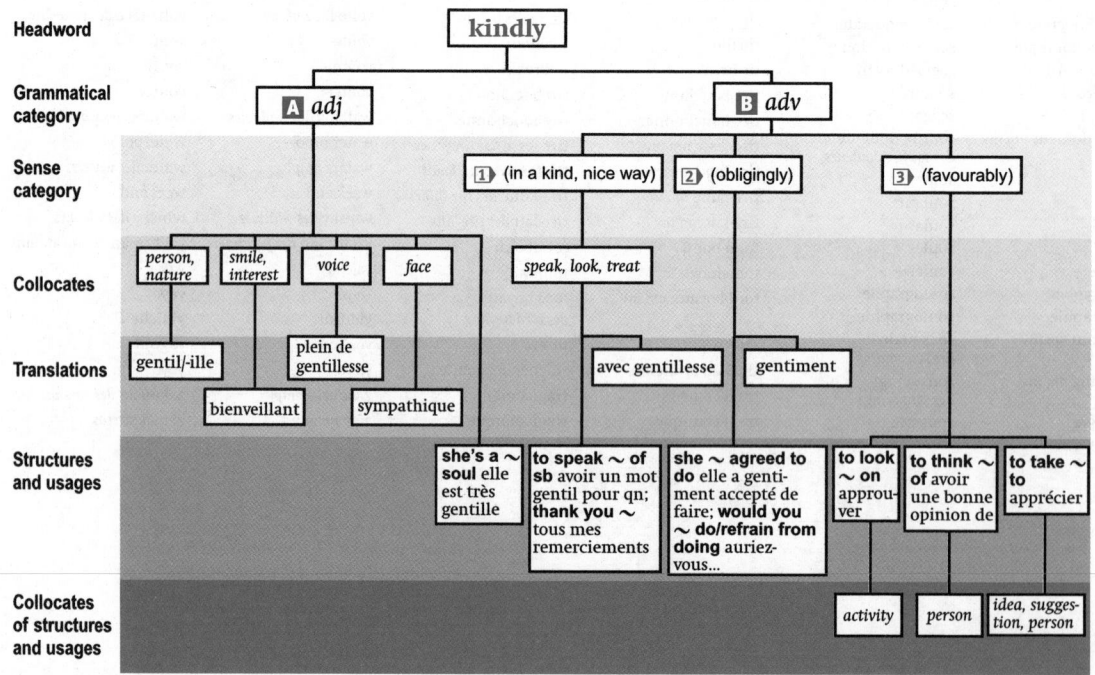

Goal 1	Translate	he treated her kindly

Process	**1** Identify the problem word or phrase. kindly	
	2 Look up *kindly* and choose the appropriate grammatical category. **B** *adv*	**kindly** /ˈkaɪndlɪ/ **A** *adj* [*person, nature*] gentil/-ille; [*smile, interest*] bienveillant; [*voice*] plein de gentillesse; [*face*] sympathique; **she's a ~ soul** elle est très gentille **B** *adv* **1** (in a kind, nice way) [*speak, look, treat*] avec gentillesse; **to speak ~ of sb** avoir un mot
	3 Choose the appropriate sense category. **1** (in a kind, nice way)	**B** *adv* **1** (in a kind, nice way) [*speak, look, treat*] avec gentillesse; **to speak ~ of sb** avoir un mot gentil pour qn; **thank you ~†** tous mes remerciements; **2** (obligingly) gentiment; **she ~ agreed to do** elle a gentiment accepté de faire; **would you ~ do/refrain from doing** auriez-vous l'amabilité de faire/de ne pas faire; **'would visitors ~ do', 'visitors are ~ requested to do'** GB 'les visiteurs sont priés de faire'; **3** (favourably) **to look ~ on** approuver [*activity*]; **to think ~ of** avoir une bonne
	4 Choose the most appropriate collocate or phrase included in the sense. treat	**B** *adv* **1** (in a kind, nice way) [*speak, look, **treat***] avec gentillesse; **to speak ~ of sb** avoir un mot gentil pour qn; **thank you ~†** tous mes remerciements; **2** (obligingly) gentiment; **she ~ agreed to do** elle a gentiment accepté de
	5 Note the translation. avec gentillesse	**B** *adv* **1** (in a kind, nice way) [*speak, look, treat*] **avec gentillesse**; **to speak ~ of sb** avoir un mot gentil pour qn; **thank you ~†** tous mes
	6 If necessary look up *treat* in the same way and *her* in the special grammatical note box, near the normal entry for *her*.	**ℹ her** When used as a direct object pronoun, *her* is translated by *la* (*l'* before a vowel). Note that the object pronoun normally comes before the verb in French and that, in compound tenses like perfect and past perfect, the past participle agrees with the pronoun: ***I know her*** = je la connais ***I've already seen her*** = je l'ai déjà vue In imperatives, the direct object pronoun is translated by *la* and comes after the verb: ***catch her!*** = attrape-la! (*note the hyphen*) When used as an indirect object pronoun, *her* is translated by *lui*: ***I've given her the book*** = je lui ai donné le livre ***I've given it to her*** = je le lui ai donné

Result	The translation	il l'a traitée avec gentillesse

| **Goal 2** | Translate *a sophisticated nightclub* in the phrase | they spent the rest of the evening in a sophisticated nightclub in Mayfair |

| **Process** | **1** Look up *nightclub*. English compounds appear in alphabetical order in the wordlist.

~club | **nightcap** /'naɪtkæp/ *n* ⬛1⟩ (hat) bonnet *m* de nuit; ⬛2⟩ (drink) **to have a** ~ boire quelque chose (avant d'aller se coucher)
night: ~**clothes** *npl* vêtements *mpl* pour la nuit; ~**club** *n* boîte *f* de nuit
nightclubbing *n* **to go** ~ aller en boîte○
night: ~**dress** *n* chemise *f* de nuit; ~ **editor** *n* Journ rédacteur/-trice *m/f* de nuit
nightfall /'naɪtfɔːl/ *n* tombée *f* de la nuit; **at** |

| | **2** Note the translation.

boîte *f* de nuit

Note the usage information in italics.
'*f*' indicates feminine gender. | **night**: ~**clothes** *npl* vêtements *mpl* pour la nuit; ~**club** *n* boîte *f* de nuit
nightclubbing *n* **to go** ~ aller en boîte○ |

| | **3** Look up *sophisticated* and select the most appropriate numbered sense category.

⬛1⟩ (smart) | **sophisticated** /sə'fɪstɪkeɪtɪd/ *adj* ⬛1⟩ (smart) [*person*] (worldly, cultured) raffiné, sophistiqué pej; (elegant) chic *inv*; [*clothes, fashion*] recherché; [*restaurant, resort*] chic *inv*; [*magazine*] sophistiqué; **she thinks it's** ~ **to smoke** elle pense que ça fait chic de fumer; **she was looking very** ~ **in black** elle était très chic en noir; ⬛2⟩ (discriminating) [*mind, taste*] raffiné; [*audience, public*] averti; **a book for the more** ~ **student** un livre pour les étudiants plus avancés; ⬛3⟩ (advanced) [*civilization*] évolué; ⬛4⟩ (elaborate, complex) [*equipment, machinery, technology*] |

| | **4** Look for the noun collocate, in square brackets, which is closest to your context.

restaurant | **sophisticated** /sə'fɪstɪkeɪtɪd/ *adj* ⬛1⟩ (smart) [*person*] (worldly, cultured) raffiné, sophistiqué pej; (elegant) chic *inv*; [*clothes, fashion*] recherché; [*restaurant, resort*] chic *inv*; [*magazine*] sophistiqué; **she thinks it's** ~ **to smoke** elle pense |

| | **5** Note the translation.

chic | [*person*] (worldly, cultured) raffiné, sophistiqué pej; (elegant) **chic** *inv*; [*clothes, fashion*] recherché; [*restaurant, resort*] chic *inv*; [*magazine*] sophistiqué; **she thinks it's** ~ **to smoke** elle pense |

| | **6** Note the usage information in italics.

inv

This means that the form of adjective *chic* does not change in the feminine or the plural. | [*person*] (worldly, cultured) raffiné, sophistiqué pej; (elegant) chic *inv*; [*clothes, fashion*] recherché; [*restaurant, resort*] chic **inv**; [*magazine*] sophistiqué; **she thinks it's** ~ **to smoke** elle pense |

| **Result** | The translation of the whole sentence | ils ont fini la soirée dans une boîte de nuit chic de Mayfair |

Goal 3	Translate	it's natural for her to want to stay

Process	**1** Look up *natural* and choose the appropriate grammatical category. **B** *adj*	**natural** /'nætʃrəl/ **A** *n* ① ○(person) **as an actress, she's a** ∼ c'est une actrice née; **he's a** ∼ **for the role of Hamlet** il est fait pour jouer Hamlet; ② Mus (sign) bécarre *m*; (note) note *f* naturelle; ③ ‡(simpleton) imbécile *mf* **B** *adj* ① (not artificial or man-made) [*phenomenon, force, disaster, harbour, light, resources, process, progression, beauty, material, food*] naturel/-elle; **the** ∼ **world** le monde naturel; **in its** ∼ **state**
	2 Choose the most appropriate numbered sense category. **②** (usual, normal)	**B** *adj* ① (not artificial or man-made) [*phenomenon, force, disaster, harbour, light, resources, process, progression, beauty, material, food*] naturel/-elle; **the** ∼ **world** le monde naturel; **in its** ∼ **state** à l'état naturel; **②** (usual, normal) naturel/-elle, normal; **it's** ∼ **to do/to be** c'est normal de faire/d'être; **it's** ∼ **for sb to do** c'est normal que qn fasse; **the** ∼ **thing to do would be to protest** la chose la plus normale serait de protester; **it's only** ∼ c'est tout à fait naturel; **it's not** ∼! ce n'est pas normal!; **to die of** ∼ **causes** mourir de mort naturelle *or* de sa belle mort; **death from** ∼ **causes** Jur mort naturelle; **for the rest of one's** ∼ **life** Jur à vie; **③** (innate) [*gift, talent, emotion, trait*] inné; [*artist, professional, storyteller*] né; [*affinity*] naturel/-elle; **a** ∼ **advantage** (of person, party, country) un atout; **④** (unaffected) [*person, manner*] simple, naturel/-elle; **try and look more** ∼
	3 Look for the basic structure you need. **it's** ∼ **for sb to do**	à l'état naturel; **②** (usual, normal) naturel/-elle, normal; **it's** ∼ **to do/to be** c'est normal de faire/d'être; **it's** ∼ **for sb to do** c'est normal que qn fasse; **the** ∼ **thing to do would be to**
	4 Note the translation. **c'est normal que qn fasse**	à l'état naturel; **②** (usual, normal) naturel/-elle, normal; **it's** ∼ **to do/to be** c'est normal de faire/d'être; **it's** ∼ **for sb to do** c'est normal que qn fasse; **the** ∼ **thing to do would be to**
	5 Use the translation of the basic structure to translate your sentence, noting that *fasse* is a subjunctive. If you are unsure about the conjugation of the irregular verb *vouloir*, look it up in the French verb tables at the back of the dictionary.	

Result	The translation	c'est normal qu'elle veuille rester

Goal 4	Translate	the police have sealed off the area

Process	1	*Seal off* is a phrasal verb, so go to the end of the entry *seal* where you will find the phrasal verbs listed in alphabetical order, each verb clearly signalled by a square bullet. ■ **seal off**	**E sealed** *pp adj* [*envelope*] cacheté; [*package*] scellé; [*bid, instructions, orders*] sous pli cacheté; [*jar*] fermé hermétiquement; [*door, vault*] scellé (Phrasal verbs) ■ **seal in** conserver [*flavour*] ■ **seal off**: ▶ ~ **[sth] off**, ~ **off [sth]** 1 (isolate) isoler [*corridor, wing*]; 2 (cordon off) boucler [*area, building*]; barrer [*street*] ■ **seal up**: ▶ ~ **[sth] up**, ~ **up [sth]** fermer [qch] hermétiquement [*jar*]; boucher [*gap*]
	2	Look for the appropriate phrasal verb pattern. ▶ ~ **[sth] off**, ~ **off [sth]**	■ **seal off**: ▶ ~ **[sth] off**, ~ **off [sth]** 1 (isolate) isoler [*corridor, wing*]; 2 (cordon off) boucler [*area, building*]; barrer [*street*]
	3	Select the appropriate sense category of the phrasal verb pattern. 2 **(cordon off)**	■ **seal off**: ▶ ~ **[sth] off**, ~ **off [sth]** 1 (isolate) isoler [*corridor, wing*]; 2 **(cordon off)** boucler [*area, building*]; barrer [*street*]
	4	Select the appropriate collocate showing context for the translation, in this case typical objects of the verb translations. *area*	■ **seal off**: ▶ ~ **[sth] off**, ~ **off [sth]** 1 (isolate) isoler [*corridor, wing*]; 2 (cordon off) boucler [**area**, *building*]; barrer [*street*]
	5	Identify the appropriate translation. boucler	■ **seal off**: ▶ ~ **[sth] off**, ~ **off [sth]** 1 (isolate) isoler [*corridor, wing*]; 2 (cordon off) **boucler** [*area, building*]; barrer [*street*]
	6	If necessary, look up *area* and select the appropriate translation. quartier *m*	**area** /'eərɪə/ **A** *n* 1 (region) (of land) région *f*; (of sky) zone *f*; (of city) zone *f*; (district) **quartier** *m*; **in the London/ Paris** ~ dans la région de Londres/de Paris; **residential/rural/slum** ~ zone *f* résidentielle/
	7	Now construct the translation of the sentence, putting the verb in the correct tense and person.	
Result		The translation	la police a bouclé le quartier

Comment se servir du dictionnaire?

Les articles du dictionnaire ont une structure hiérarchisée; ils sont subdivisés en catégories grammaticales (introduites par des majuscules sur fond noir et présentées dans un ordre fixe) qui sont elles-mêmes subdivisées en catégories sémantiques (introduites par des chiffres arabes). Les catégories sémantiques et les nuances de sens sont différenciées par des indicateurs sémantiques et/ou des indicateurs de collocations et apparaissent selon un ordre qui donne la priorité aux sens les plus fréquents. Pour traduire *tiède* dans la phrase *boire tiède* la démarche à suivre est indiquée par les numéros dans la figure ci-contre. La structure hiérarchisée est illustrée ci-dessous avec l'arborescence de l'entrée *tiède*.

En règle générale, les homographes homophones ont été regroupés sous la même entrée sans tenir compte de l'étymologie; dans les autres cas, l'entrée est répétée et on lui a attribué un numéro d'homographe. Locutions idiomatiques et proverbes sont regroupés en fin d'article.

Certaines caractéristiques liées à la structure de la langue sont particulières à un côté du dictionnaire. Ainsi dans la partie français-anglais, les mots composés sans trait d'union sont regroupés alphabétiquement en fin d'article.

Dans la partie anglais-français, les verbes à particule apparaissent toujours en fin d'article, dans l'ordre alphabétique. Les mots composés sont à leur place dans la nomenclature. On trouvera dans les pages suivantes quelques exemples d'utilisation du dictionnaire tant pour la compréhension que pour la traduction en anglais.

1 **tiède** /tjɛd/

A *adj* **1** lit (désagréablement) [*café, soupe*] lukewarm; [*bain*] tepid; (agréablement) [*eau, air, nuit*] warm; [*saison, température*] mild; ▸ **salade**; **2** fig (sans enthousiasme) [*sentiment, applaudissements, partisan*] lukewarm, half-hearted; [*accueil*] lukewarm

B *nmf* péj (membre d'un parti, groupe) lukewarm *ou* half-hearted supporter; (adepte) half-hearted believer

C *adv* **servez** ~ serve slightly warm; **dépêche-toi ou tu vas manger** ~ hurry up or your food will get cold; **il fait** ~ (dehors) it's mild; (dedans) it's nice and warm

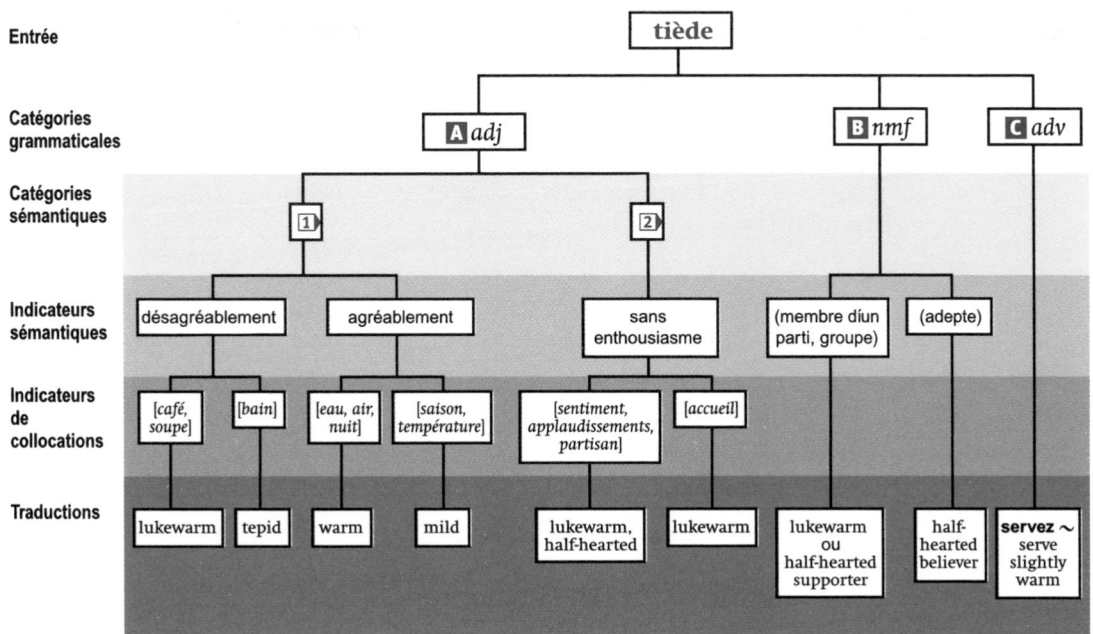

| **Objectif 3** | Traduire | il neigeait à notre départ de Moscou |

| **Méthode** | **1** | Rechercher l'entrée *neiger* dans la nomenclature. L'exemple est au présent et la phrase à traduire à l'imparfait, il suffit de changer le temps. | **neiger** /neʒe/ [13] *v impers* to snow; **il neige** it's snowing |

it was snowing

| | **2** | Rechercher l'entrée *départ* dans la nomenclature et choisir la catégorie sémantique adéquate. La première convient exactement. Une traduction générale est fournie. | **départ** /depaʀ/ *nm* ⓵ (d'un lieu) departure; **retarder son** ∼ to postpone one's departure; **heures de** ∼ departure times; ∼ **des gran-** |

departure

| | **3** | Mais un des exemples donnés plus bas a des points communs avec la phrase à traduire. | heures de ∼ departure times; ∼ **des gran-des lignes/des lignes de banlieue** Rail (platforms for) main line/suburban departures; **je l'ai vue avant mon** ∼ **pour Paris** I saw her before I left for Paris; **les** ∼**s en vacances** holiday GB *ou* vacation US departures; **avant mon** ∼ **en vacances** before I set off on holiday GB *ou* vacation US; **téléphone avant ton** ∼ phone before you leave; **c'est bientôt le** ∼, **le** ∼ **approche** it'll soon be time to leave; **se donner rendez-vous au** ∼ **du car** (au lieu) to arrange to meet at the coach GB *ou* bus US; **vols quotidiens au** ∼ **de Nice** daily flights from Nice; **le train a pris du retard au** ∼ **de Lyon** the train was late leaving Lyons; **être** |

je l'ai vue avant mon ∼ **pour Paris**
I saw her before I left for Paris

Le groupe nominal *mon départ* est traduit par la tournure verbale *I left*.

| | **4** | En cas de doute vérifier *left* dans la partie anglais-français. | **left** /left/ ▸ p. 1139
A *prét, pp* ▸ **leave**
B *n* ⓵ (side or direction) gauche *f*; **on the** ∼ sur la gauche; **on your** ∼ sur votre gauche; **to the** ∼ vers la gauche; **keep (to the)** ∼ Aut tenez la gauche; ⓶ Pol **the** ∼ la gauche; **on the** ∼ à gauche; **to the** ∼ **of sb** à gauche de qn; ⓷ Sport (poing *m*) gauche *m*
C *adj* [eye, hand, shoe] gauche
D *adv* [go, look, turn] à gauche |

| | **5** | Pour trouver la construction qui nous intéresse il faut consulter l'entrée *leave* toujours en employant la même méthode : rechercher dans la nomenclature, choisir la catégorie grammaticale qui convient et la parcourir en détail.

Un exemple peut servir utilement de modèle. Il ne reste plus qu'à trouver la traduction de *Moscou*. | **leave** /liːv/
A *n* ⓵ (also ∼ **of absence**) (time off) gen congé *m*; Mil permission *f*; **to take** ∼ prendre des congés; **to take three days'** ∼ prendre trois jours de congé; **I've taken all my** ∼ **for this year** j'ai pris tous mes congés pour cette année; **to be granted 24 hours'** ∼ Mil recevoir une permission de 24 heures; **to be on** ∼ gen être en congé; Mil être en permission; **to come home on** ∼ Mil rentrer en permission
B *vtr* (*prét, pp* **left**) ⓵ (depart from) gen partir de [house, station etc]; (more permanently) quitter [country, city etc]; (by going out) sortir de [room, building]; **he left home early** il est parti tôt de chez lui; **to** ∼ **school** (permanently) quitter l'école; **the plane/train** ∼**s Paris for Nice at 9.00** l'avion/le train pour Nice part de Paris à 9 heures; **to** ∼ **the road/table** quitter la route/table; **to** ∼ **France to live in Canada** quitter la France pour aller vivre au Canada; |

| **Résultat** | | La traduction n'est pas strictement parallèle au texte français mais elle est exacte et naturelle en anglais. | it was snowing when we left Moscow |

Objectif 4   Traduire *make out* dans la phrase   I couldn't make out what he was saying

---

Méthode   **1**   Rechercher l'entrée *make*.
Rechercher les verbes à particule
clairement signalés à la fin de l'article.

> (Phrasal verbs) ■ make after: ► ~ after [sb] poursuivre ■ make at: ► ~ at [sb] attaquer (with avec) ■ make away with = make off ■ make do: ► ~ do faire avec; to ~ do with se contenter de qch; ► ~ [sth] do se contenter de ■ make for: ► ~ for [sth] 1〉 (head for) se diriger vers [*door, town, home*]; 2〉 (help create) permettre, assurer [*easy life, happy marriage*]; ► ~ for [sb] 1〉 (attack) se jeter sur; 2〉 (approach) se diriger vers ■ make good: ► ~ good réussir; a poor

2   Rechercher *make out* dans les verbes
à particule présentés alphabétiquement.

3   Rechercher la structure qui se rapproche le
plus de celle à traduire c'est-à-dire la forme
transitive présentée de la façon suivante.

> ► ~ out [sth], ~ [sth] out

> ■ make out: ► ~ out 1〉 (manage) s'en tirer◦; how are you making out? comment ça marche◦?; 2〉 US (grope) se peloter◦; 3〉 (claim) affirmer (that que); he's not as stupid as he ~s out il n'est pas aussi bête qu'il (le) prétend; ► ~ out [sth], ~ [sth] out 1〉 (see, distinguish) distinguer [*shape, writing*]; 2〉 (claim) to ~ sth out to be prétendre que qch est; 3〉 (understand, work out) comprendre [*puzzle, mystery, character*]; to ~ out if *or* whether comprendre si; I can't ~ him out je n'arrive pas à le comprendre; 4〉 (write out) faire, rédiger [*cheque, will, list*]; to ~ out a cheque GB *ou* check US to sb faire un chèque à qn, signer un chèque à l'ordre de qn; it is made out to X il est à l'ordre de X; who shall I ~ the cheque out to? à quel ordre dois-je faire le chèque?; 5〉 (expound) to ~ out a case for sth argumenter en faveur de qch; ► ~ oneself out to be prétendre être [*rich, brilliant*]; faire semblant d'être [*stupid, incompetent*]

4   Examiner les traductions fournies.
Choisir celle qui convient au contexte.

> comprendre

> qu'il (le) prétend; ► ~ out [sth], ~ [sth] out 1〉 (see, distinguish) **distinguer** [*shape, writing*]; 2〉 (claim) to ~ sth out to be **prétendre que qch est**; 3〉 (understand, work out) comprendre [*puzzle, mystery, character*]; to ~ out if *or* whether comprendre si; I can't ~ him out je n'arrive pas à le comprendre; 4〉 (write out) faire, **rédiger** [*cheque, will, list*]; to ~ out a cheque GB *ou* check US to sb faire un chèque à qn, signer un chèque à l'ordre de qn; it is made out to X il est à l'ordre de X; who shall I ~ the cheque out to? à quel ordre dois-je faire le chèque?; 5〉 (expound) to ~ out a case for sth argumenter en faveur de qch; ► ~ oneself out to be prétendre être [*rich, brilliant*]; faire semblant d'être [*stupid, incompetent*]

Résultat   Traduction   je n'arrivais pas à comprendre ce qu'il disait

Structure du texte français–anglais

sigle/acronyme ● — **FIV** /fiv/
A *nf: abbr* ▸ **fécondation**
fivete /fivεt/ *nf* ZIFT, zygote intra-fallopian transfer

entrée ● — **flûtiste*** /flytist/ ▸ **p. 532** *nmf* flautist, flutist US — ● renvoi à une note d'usage lexicale

— ● renvoi à une entrée

foie /fwa/ *nm* ⬚1 Anat liver; **avoir mal au ∼** ≈ to have an upset stomach; **crise de ∼** indigestion; ⬚2 Culin liver

— ● tiret ondulé remplaçant l'entrée dans les exemples
— ● symbole indiquant un équivalent dans la langue cible

⬭Composés⬮ **∼ d'agneau** lamb's liver; **∼ de génisse** beef liver; **∼ gras** foie gras; **∼ de porc** pig's liver; **∼ de veau** calf's liver; **∼s de volaille** chicken livers

idiomes regroupés en fin d'article ● — ⬭Idiomes⬮ **se ronger les ∼s**○ to worry; **avoir les ∼s**○ to have the jitters○ — ● indicateurs de niveau de langue
 ○ familier
 ❶ populaire
 ● vulgaire ou tabou

mot composé avec trait d'union ● ayant valeur d'entrée à part entière — **foie-de-bœuf**, *pl* **foies-de-bœuf** /fwadbœf/ *nm* Bot beefsteak fungus

forme du féminin ● — **foliacé, ∼e** /foljase/ *adj* ⬚1 Bot foliaceous; ⬚2 Minér foliated — ● domaines

traduction avec sa variante ● nord-américaine — **formidablement** /fɔrmidabləmɑ̃/ *adj* awfully; **il a ∼ grossi** he's got GB *ou* gotten US awfully fat; **ça s'est ∼ amélioré** there's been

symbole marquant un mot archaïque ● — **fors**‡ /fɔr/ *prép liter* save, except

fournaise /furnεz/ *nf* ⬚1 (endroit chaud) blaze; **le bureau est une vraie ∼!** the office is like an oven!; **la ville est une ∼ en été** the town is baking hot in summer; ⬚2 Can (chaudière) boiler GB, furnace US — ● numéro de catégorie sémantique
— ● inclusion de mots ou sens d'autres pays francophones (ici canadianisme)

symbole marquant un mot vieilli ● — **freluquet**† /frəlykε/ *nm* little squirt○, whippersnapper†
frémir /fremir/ [3] *vi* ⬚1 (trembler) [*voile, feuille, aile, violon*] to quiver; [*lac*] to ripple; [*vitre*] to … — ● numéro de conjugaison

information sur l'existence d'une ● variante graphique nord-américaine (donnée sous l'entrée du côté anglais-français) — **vent faisait ∼ les eaux du port** the wind rippled the waters of the harbour^GB; ⬚2 (sous l'effet d'une émotion) [*lèvre, narine, main*] to tremble; [*personne*] (d'indignation, impatience, de colère, joie, plaisir) to quiver (**de** with); (de dégoût, d'horreur, effroi) to shudder (**de** with); **frémissant de rage/d'enthousiasme** quivering with rage/with enthusiasm; **je frémis à cette idée** I shudder at the thought; **tout mon être frémit** (d'horreur) my whole being shuddered; (de plaisir) my whole being thrilled; **ça fait ∼ de penser que…** it makes you shudder to think that…; **poésie/sensibilité frémissante** vibrant poetry/sensitivity; ⬚3 Culin [*liquide*] to start to — ● indicateur sémantique
— ● construction syntaxique
— ● exemple

indicateur de collocation ●
transcription phonétique ● — **frère** /frεr/ *nm* ⬚1 (dans la famille) brother; **c'est mon/grand/petit ∼** he's my big/little brother; **Dupont et ∼s** (enseigne) Dupont Brothers; **aimer qn comme un ∼** to love sb — ● partie du discours

mots composés sans trait d'union ● regroupés alphabétiquement — ⬭Composés⬮ **∼ d'armes** brother-in-arms; **∼ jumeau** twin brother; **∼ lai** lay brother; **∼ de lait** foster brother; **∼s maçons** brother Masons

fricandeau, *pl* **∼x** /frikɑ̃do/ *nm* braised veal ¢ — ● forme du pluriel

information grammaticale sur la ● langue cible (mot non dénombrable)
catégorie grammaticale ● — **frictionner** /friksjone/ [1]
A *vtr* to give a rub to [*personne*]; to rub [*pieds, tête*]
B **se frictionner** *vpr* to rub oneself down

nom déposé ● — **frigidaire®** /friʒidεr/ *nm* refrigerator

Structure du texte anglais–français

entrée •
matron /'meɪtrən/ n [1] GB (nurse) (in hospital) infirmière f en chef; (in school) infirmière f (*chargée également de l'intendance*); [2] (person in charge) (of orphanage, nursing home) directrice f; [3] US (warder) gardienne f; [4] (woman) péj matrone f pej
• glose explicative

numéro d'homographe •
mine² /maɪn/
A n [1] Mining mine f; to work in ou down the ∼s travailler dans les mines; to go down the ∼ (become a miner) descendre à la mine; [2] fig mine f; to be a ∼ of information être une mine de renseignements; to have a ∼ of experience to draw on pouvoir s'appuyer sur son expérience; [3] Mil (explosive) mine f; to lay a ∼ (on land) poser une mine; (in sea) mouiller une mine; to hit ou strike a ∼ heurter une mine
• traduction

tiret ondulé remplaçant l'entrée • dans les exemples

catégorie sémantique •

• genre des substantifs en français

catégorie grammaticale •
B vtr [1] Mining extraire [gems, mineral]; exploiter [area]; [2] Mil (lay mines in) miner [area]; (blow up) faire sauter [ship, tank]
• domaine

partie du discours •
C vi exploiter un gisement; to ∼ for extraire [gems, mineral]

verbe à particule •
(Phrasal verb) ■ **mine out**: ▶ ∼ **out** [sth], ∼ **[sth] out** extraire [mineral]; exploiter [area, pit]; the pit is completely ∼d out la mine est épuisée
• construction d'un verbe à particule

groupe de mots composés •
mine maɪn: ∼**sweeper** n dragueur m de mines; ∼**sweeping** n dragage m de mines; ∼**worker** ▶ p. 1683 n mineur m; ∼ **workings** npl chantier m de mine
• renvoi à une note d'usage lexicale

transcription phonétique de la • prononciation nord-américaine
minute² /maɪ'njuːt, US -'nuːt/ adj [particle, lettering] minuscule; [quantity] infime; [risk, rise, variation] minime; to describe sth in a ∼ detail décrire qch dans les moindres détails
• exemple

minutiae /maɪ'njuːʃɪː, US mɪ'nuːʃɪː/ npl menus détails mpl, minuties† fpl
• symbole marquant un mot vieilli

sigle/acronyme •
MIPS, **mips** /mɪps/ n (abrév = **millions of instructions per second**) millions d'instructions par seconde

transcription phonétique •
misbegotten /ˌmɪsbɪ'ɡɒtn/ adj [1] [plan] mal conçu; [person] qui ne vaut rien; [2] ‡(illegitimate) bâtard; ∼ **child** bâtard/-e m/f
• symbole marquant un mot archaïque

indicateurs de collocations •
miserable /'mɪzrəbl/ adj [1] (gloomy, unhappy) [person, expression] malheureux/-euse; [thoughts] noir; [event] malheureux/-euse; [weather] sale (before n); what a ∼ afternoon! quel après-midi maussade!; to look ∼ avoir l'air malheureux/-euse; to feel ∼ avoir le cafard; [2] ○(small, pathetic) [helping, quantity] misérable; [salary, wage] de misère; [attempt, failure, performance, result] lamentable; a ∼ 50 dollars 50 misérables dollars; [3] (poverty-stricken) [life] de misère; [dwelling] misérable; [4] (abject) a ∼ sinner un pécheur éhonté
• forme du féminin d'un adjectif

• indicateur de niveau de langue
○ familier
◑ populaire
● vulgaire ou tabou

indicateur sémantique •

mot composé ayant valeur d'entrée à • part entière
mother tongue n [1] (native tongue) langue f maternelle; [2] (from which another evolves) langue f mère

mouldy GB, **moldy** US /'məʊldɪ/ adj [bread, food] moisi; a ∼ smell une odeur de moisi; to go ∼ moisir
• variante graphique nord-américaine

mowing /'məʊɪŋ/ n (of lawn) tonte f; (of hay) fauchage m

renvoi à une entrée •
mown /məʊn/ pp ▶ **mow**

The pronunciation of French

The symbols used in this dictionary for the pronunciation of French are those of the IPA (International Phonetic Alphabet). Certain differences in pronunciation are shown in the phonetic transcription, although many speakers do not observe them—e.g. the long 'a' /ɑ/ in *pâte* and the short 'a' /a/ in *patte*, or the difference between the nasal vowels 'un' /œ̃/ as in *brun* and 'in' /ɛ̃/ as in *brin*.

Transcription

Each entry is followed by its phonetic transcription between slashes, with the following exceptions:
- written abbreviations (*bd, kW*, etc.)
- cross-references from an inflected to a base form (*yeux, fol*)
- cross-references from a variant spelling to the preferred form (*paraphe/parafe, peinard/pénard, plasticage/plastiquage*).

Alternative pronunciations

Where the speaker has a choice of pronunciations, these are shown in one of the following two ways:
- by the use of brackets e.g. *syllabe* /sil(l)ab/, *déficit* /defisi(t)/
- in full, separated by a comma e.g. *revenir* /ʀəvniʀ, ʀvəniʀ/, *patio* /pasjo, patjo/.

Morphological variations

The phonetic transcription of the plural and feminine forms of certain nouns and adjectives does not repeat the root, but shows only the change in ending. Therefore, in certain cases, the presentation of the entry does not correspond to that of the phonetic transcription e.g. *platonicien, -ienne* /platɔnisjɛ̃, ɛn/.

Phrases

Full phonetic transcription is given for adverbial or prepositional phrases which are shown in alphabetical order within the main headword e.g. *emblée, d'emblée* /dɑ̃ble/, *plain-pied, de plain-pied* /d(ə)plɛ̃pje/.

Consonants

Aspiration of 'h'
Where it is impossible to make a liaison this is indicated by /'/ immediately after the slash e.g. *haine* /'ɛn/.

Assimilation
A voiced consonant can become unvoiced when it is followed by an unvoiced consonant within a word e.g. *absorption* /apsɔʀpsjɔ̃/.

Vowels

Open 'e' and closed 'e'
A clear distinction is made at the end of a word between a closed 'e' and an open 'e' e.g. *pré* /pʀe/ and *près* /pʀɛ/, *complet* /kɔ̃plɛ/ and *combler* /kɔ̃ble/.

Within a word the following rules apply:
- 'e' is always open in a syllable followed by a syllable containing a mute 'e' e.g. *règle* /ʀɛɡl/, *réglementaire* /ʀɛɡləmɑ̃tɛʀ/
- in careful speech 'e' is pronounced as a closed 'e' when it is followed by a syllable containing a closed vowel (y, i, e) e.g. *pressé* /pʀese/
- 'e' is pronounced as an open 'e' when it is followed by a syllable containing an open vowel e.g. *pressant* /pʀesɑ̃/.

Mute 'e'
The pronunciation of mute 'e' varies considerably depending on the level of language used and on the region from which the speaker originates. As a general rule it is only pronounced at the end of a word in the South of France or in poetry and it is, therefore, not shown. In an isolated word the mute 'e' preceded by a single consonant is dropped e.g. *galetas* /ɡalta/, *parfaitement* /paʀfɛtmɑ̃/, but *agréablement* /aɡʀeabləmɑ̃/.

In many cases the pronunciation of the mute 'e' depends on the surrounding context. Thus one would say *une reconnaissance de dette* /ynʀəkɔnɛsɑ̃sdədɛt/, but, *ma reconnaissance est éternelle* /maʀkɔnɛsɑ̃setetɛʀnɛl/. The mute 'e' is shown in brackets in order to account for this phenomenon.

Open 'o' and closed 'o'
The difference between open 'o' and closed 'o' is not clear and speakers may hesitate, particularly in the pronunciation of compound words whose first element ends in 'o' e.g. *broncho-pneumonie, sociolinguistique, politologue* etc. It is not possible to opt for one or the other to apply to all cases. Where the word seems to function more like a single word the 'o' tends to be pronounced as an open 'o'. Where the two elements of the compound retain a degree of autonomy, as is often the case when they are hyphenated, the 'o' tends to be pronounced as a closed 'o' e.g. *psychosocial* /psikosɔsjal/, but, *psychologie* /psikɔlɔʒi/.

Stress
There is no real stress as such in French. In normal unemphasized speech a slight stress falls on the final syllable of a word or group of words, providing that it does not contain a mute 'e'. This is not shown in the phonetic transcription of individual entries. *I.V.*

Vowels

a	*as in*	patte	/pat/	œ	*as in*	leur	/lœʀ/
ɑ		pâte	/pɑt/	œ̃		brun	/bʀœ̃/
ɑ̃		clan	/klɑ̃/	ø		deux	/dø/
e		dé	/de/	u		fou	/fu/
ɛ		belle	/bɛl/	y		pur	/pyʀ/
ɛ̃		lin	/lɛ̃/				
ə		demain	/dəmɛ̃/		**Semi-vowels**		
i		gris	/ɡʀi/	j	*as in*	fille	/fij/
o		gros	/ɡʀo/	ɥ		huit	/ɥit/
ɔ		corps	/kɔʀ/	w		oui	/wi/
ɔ̃		long	/lɔ̃/				

Consonants

b	*as in*	bal	/bal/	ŋ	*as in*	dancing	/dɑ̃siŋ/
d		dent	/dɑ̃/	p		porte	/pɔʀt/
f		foire	/fwaʀ/	ʀ		rire	/ʀiʀ/
ɡ		gomme	/ɡɔm/	s		sang	/sɑ̃/
k		clé	/kle/	ʃ		chien	/ʃjɛ̃/
l		lien	/ljɛ̃/	t		train	/tʀɛ̃/
m		mer	/mɛʀ/	v		voile	/vwal/
n		nage	/naʒ/	z		zèbre	/zɛbʀ/
ɲ		gnon	/ɲɔ̃/	ʒ		jeune	/ʒœn/

Prononciation de l'anglais

Les sons et leur transcription

Alphabet phonétique

La prononciation de chaque entrée est donnée en notation phonétique entre des barres obliques / /. On trouvera le tableau des signes utilisés page suivante. A la différence de l'écriture orthographique de l'anglais dans laquelle la même lettre peut prendre des valeurs différentes, par exemple le *c* dans *cat* (/kæt/) et *city* (/'sɪtɪ/), dans l'alphabet phonétique, chaque signe représente un seul son.

Anglais britannique

La prononciation standard de l'anglais britannique suit immédiatement le mot-vedette. Cette prononciation correspond à la Received Pronunciation (RP) qui est la forme d'anglais britannique la plus répandue.

Prononciation du /r/

En anglais britannique, le *r* ou *re* à la fin d'un mot ne se prononce que si le mot qui suit commence par une voyelle. C'est pourquoi, dans la transcription phonétique, ces sons sont indiqués entre parenthèses, par exemple *hair* /heə(r)/, *hire* /haɪə(r)/.

L'accent

Accent d'intensité

Les mots anglais polysyllabiques comportent une syllabe plus fortement accentuée que les autres. L'accent d'intensité est indiqué au moyen du signe /'/ placé devant la syllabe qu'il affecte, par exemple *city* /'sɪtɪ/. Certains mots longs ont deux accents d'intensité, l'un plus fort, appelé accent primaire et également noté /'/, l'autre plus faible, appelé accent secondaire et noté /ˌ/ : *pronunciation* /prəˌnʌnsɪ'eɪʃn/.

Déplacement de l'accent d'intensité

En général on évite d'avoir à prononcer deux accents d'intensité dans des syllabes adjacentes. Ainsi dans la phrase *Lisa is thirteen*, on prononcera /ˌθɜː'tiːn/, mais dans *Lisa has thirteen bicycles*, on dira /ˌθɜːtiːn 'baɪsɪkls/. On notera que le déplacement de l'accent d'intensité est valable pour toutes les catégories de mots et que tout mot ayant un accent secondaire suivi d'un accent primaire peut perdre ce dernier lorsqu'il est suivi par un mot dont la première syllabe porte l'accent d'intensité primaire.

Variantes dans la prononciation

Variantes britanniques

Il arrive pour de nombreux mots que plusieurs prononciations soient acceptées. Dans ce cas les variantes sont données, la prononciation la plus courante étant placée en premier, par exemple *economic* /ˌiːkə'nɒmɪk, ˌekə'nɒmɪk/.

Formes fortes et formes faibles

Certains mots courants tels que *a, the, and, but, for, me, them, can, have*, etc. peuvent se prononcer de deux façons différentes (ou plus) : une forme forte et une forme faible. Des deux, la forme faible est la plus fréquente : c'est celle qui se rencontre dans la chaîne parlée.

La forme forte s'utilise pour un mot isolé, ou encore pour souligner le mot dans une phrase. On trouvera la prononciation des deux formes dans le dictionnaire, la forme forte étant donnée la première, par exemple *and* /ænd, ənd/.

Dans la chaîne parlée, les formes faibles de *be* et *have* suivent souvent un pronom personnel. On notera que pronom et verbe sont généralement combinés en une forme contractée qui est une forme faible, par exemple *you're* /jɔː(r)/, *I'm* /aɪm/.

Contractions

Dans la langue écrite, les contractions se font par omission d'une ou deux lettres auxquelles on substitue une apostrophe ('), par exemple *can't*. Dans la langue parlée, il y a contraction quand une syllabe disparaît et que la syllabe restante comporte une voyelle autre que /ə/. La contraction est très fréquente pour certains verbes auxiliaires suivis de *not*, par exemple *don't* /dəʊnt/. (Ces formes ne sont pas des formes faibles et peuvent être accentuées).

Mots étrangers

L'anglais possède un certain nombre de mots et expressions d'origine étrangère qui se sont intégrés à la langue et ont acquis une prononciation anglaise, par exemple *coffee* /'kɒfɪ:/, *bungalow* /'bʌŋgələʊ/.

D'autres, bien que d'emploi courant, continuent à être perçus comme étrangers, d'où de grandes variations dans la manière dont ils sont prononcés. Beaucoup de ces mots sont français et de ce fait contiennent des voyelles nasales qui n'existent pas en anglais, par exemple *salon, en route*. La prononciation de ces sons est complexe pour les locuteurs de l'anglais et l'on peut entendre des sons totalement transformés aussi bien qu'une prononciation française correcte. La prononciation adoptée dans ce dictionnaire est la forme anglicisée des mots étrangers et l'on trouvera /'sælɒn/, /ˌɒn 'ruːt/.

Prononciation de l'anglais d'Amérique du nord

Celle-ci est indiquée après la prononciation RP chaque fois qu'il y a une différence marquée entre les deux, ainsi pour le mot *graph* /grɑːf, US græf/.

La prononciation de l'anglais d'Amérique du nord donnée ici est celle du General American.

Bien que les symboles utilisés soient les mêmes que pour la RP, on notera que certains sons, en particulier les voyelles, ont une valeur différente. On notera également que /r/ se prononce toujours en anglais d'Amérique du nord, ce qui n'est pas le cas en anglais britannique : *car, start*. Dans la transcription phonétique, la prononciation donnée sera celle de l'anglais britannique /kɑː(r)/, /stɑːt/.

Dérivés et composés

Dérivés

Les dérivés apparaissant généralement comme des entrées à part entière dans le dictionnaire, leur prononciation sera indiquée systématiquement.

Mots composés

En anglais, les mots composés s'écrivent soit en un seul mot ('closed compounds'), soit en deux mots parfois reliés par un trait d'union. Pour économiser de la place, la prononciation n'est pas toujours donnée, mais il suffira de consulter la prononciation des deux éléments du mot.

Prononciation de l'anglais

Au cours de l'articulation d'un mot composé il se produit souvent des changements phonétiques. Sous l'influence du phonème qui le suit, un son peut changer de valeur, ou disparaître complètement, comme dans *windscreen* qui se prononce /ˈwɪnskriːn/. Ce phénomène d'assimilation, plus ou moins marqué selon la rapidité d'élocution, se rencontre constamment dans la chaîne parlée. Toutefois, c'est toujours la forme complète qui est donnée dans le dictionnaire.   J.S.-S.

Voyelles et diphtongues

iː	*de*	see	/siː/	ɜː	*de*	fur	/fɜː(r)/	
ɪ		sit	/sɪt/	ə		ago	/əˈɡəʊ/	
e		ten	/ten/	eɪ		page	/peɪdʒ/	
æ		hat	/hæt/	əʊ		home	/həʊm/	
ɑː		arm	/ɑːm/	aɪ		five	/faɪv/	
ɒ		got	/ɡɒt/	aʊ		now	/naʊ/	
ɔː		saw	/sɔː/	ɔɪ		join	/dʒɔɪn/	
ʊ		put	/pʊt/	ɪə		near	/nɪə(r)/	
uː		too	/tuː/	eə		hair	/heə(r)/	
ʌ		cup	/kʌp/	ʊə		pure	/pjʊə(r)/	

Consonnes

p	*de*	pen	/pen/	s	*de*	so	/səʊ/	
b		bad	/bæd/	z		zoo	/zuː/	
t		tea	/tiː/	ʃ		she	/ʃiː/	
d		did	/dɪd/	ʒ		vision	/ˈvɪʒn/	
k		cat	/kæt/	h		how	/haʊ/	
ɡ		got	/ɡɒt/	m		man	/mæn/	
tʃ		chin	/tʃɪn/	n		no	/nəʊ/	
dʒ		June	/dʒuːn/	ŋ		sing	/sɪŋ/	
f		fall	/fɔːl/	l		leg	/leg/	
v		voice	/vɔɪs/	r		red	/red/	
θ		thin	/θɪn/	j		yes	/jes/	
ð		then	/ðen/	w		wet	/wet/	

a, A

a, A /a, ɑ/
A nm inv (lettre) a, A; **vitamine A** vitamin A; **de A à Z** from A to Z; **le bricolage de A à Z** the A to Z of DIY; **démontrer/prouver qch par A plus B à qn** to demonstrate/prove sth conclusively to sb

B A nf Transp (abbr = **autoroute**) **prendre l'A5** take the (motorway GB or freeway US) A5

Composé ~ **commercial** at sign

à /a/ prép

> ⚠ La préposition à se traduit de multiples façons. Les expressions courantes du genre *machine à écrire, aller à la pêche, difficile à faire* etc sont traitées respectivement sous **machine, pêche, difficile** etc.
>
> Les emplois de à avec les verbes *avoir, être, aller, penser* etc sont traités sous les verbes.
>
> Pour trouver la traduction correcte de à on aura intérêt à se reporter aux mots qui précèdent la préposition ainsi qu'aux notes d'usage répertoriées ► p. 1948.
>
> On trouvera ci-dessous quelques exemples typiques de traductions de à.

[1] (avec un verbe de mouvement) **se rendre au travail/~ Paris/~ la campagne** to go to work/to Paris/to the country; **aller de Paris ~ Nevers** to go from Paris to Nevers
[2] (pour indiquer le lieu où l'on se trouve) **~ l'école/ la maison** at school/home; **~ Paris/la campagne** in Paris/the country
[3] (dans le temps) **~ l'aube/l'âge de 10 ans** at dawn/the age of 10; **au printemps** in (the) spring
[4] (dans une description) with; **le garçon aux cheveux bruns** the boy with dark hair; **la femme au manteau marron/chapeau noir** the woman with the brown coat/black hat
[5] (employé avec le verbe être) **la maison est ~ louer** the house is for rent ou to let GB; **'~ louer'** 'to let', 'for rent'; **la maison est ~ vendre** the house is for sale; **'~ vendre'** 'for sale'; **il est ~ plaindre** he's to be pitied; **je suis ~ vous tout de suite** I'll be with you in a minute; **maintenant je suis ~ vous** I'm all yours; **c'est ~ qui de jouer?** whose turn is it?; **c'est ~ Emma/~ toi** it's Emma's turn/ your turn; **~ moi (de jouer)** my turn (to play); **(c'est) ~ lui de décider** it's up to him to decide
[6] (marquant l'appartenance) **appartenir ~ qn** to belong to sb; **~ qui est cette montre?** whose is this watch?; **elle est ~ moi/lui/elle** it's mine/his/hers; **c'est ~ vous cette voiture?** is this your car?; **une amie ~ moi/eux** a friend of mine/theirs; **encore une idée ~ elle** another of her ideas; **un ami ~ mon père**° a friend of my father's
[7] (employé avec un nombre) **nous avons fait le travail ~ deux/trois/quatre** two/three/four of us did the work; **~ deux/dix on devrait y arriver** two/ten of us should be able to manage; **~ nous trois nous avons transporté la malle** the three of us carried the trunk; **~ nous tous on devrait y arriver** between all of us we should be able to manage; **~ trois on est déjà serrés mais ~ quatre c'est impossible** with three people

it's crowded but with four it's impossible; **mener 3 ~ 2** to lead 3 (to) 2; **mener par 3 jeux ~ 2** to lead by 3 games to 2; **rouler ~ 100 kilomètres-heure, rouler ~ 100 ~ l'heure**° to drive at 100 kilometres^GB per ou an hour; **au 74 de la rue Bossuet** at 74 rue Bossuet; **au 3° étage** on the third GB ou second US floor; **~ quatre kilomètres d'ici** four kilometres^GB from here; **des bananes ~ 2 euros le kilo** bananas at 2 euros a kilo; **un timbre ~ 46 centimes (d'euro)** a 46-cent stamp; **travailler (de) huit ~ dix heures par jour** to work between eight and ten hours a day, to work eight to ten hours a day; **(de) cinq ~ sept millions de personnes sont concernées** between five and seven million people are concerned, five to seven million people are concerned
[8] (marquant une hypothèse) **~ ce qu'il paraît, ~ ce que l'on prétend, ~ ce que l'on dit** apparently; **~ ce qu'il me semble** as far as I can see; **~ vous entendre, on croirait que** to hear you talk one would think that; **~ y bien réfléchir** when you really think about it; **~ trop vouloir se dépêcher/réclamer on risque de faire** if you hurry too much/ask for too much you run the risk of doing; **~ ne jamais écouter les autres voilà ce qui arrive** that's what happens when you don't listen to other people
[9] (dans phrases exclamatives) **~ nous/notre projet/tes vacances!** (en levant son verre) (here's) to us/our project/your vacation!; **~ ta santé, ~ la tienne!, ~ la vôtre!** cheers!; **~ tes souhaits** or **amours!** bless you!; **~ toi/vous l'honneur!** (de couper le gâteau) you do the honours!; (après vous) after you!; **~ nous la belle vie!** the good life starts here!; **~ nous (deux)!** (avant un règlement de compte) let's sort this out between us; (de commerçant à client) I'm all yours; **~ demain/ce soir/dans 15 jours** see you tomorrow/tonight/in two weeks; **~ lundi** see you on Monday!; **~ la prochaine** see you next time!
[10] (dans une dédicace) **'~ ma mère'** (dans un livre) 'to my mother'; (sur une tombe) 'in memory of my mother'; **'~ nos chers disparus'** 'in memory of our dear departed'

Aaron /aaʀɔ̃/ npr Aaron

abaissant, ~e /abɛsɑ̃, ɑ̃t/ adj degrading

abaisse /abɛs/ nf Culin rolled-out pastry **₵**

abaisse-langue* /abɛslɑ̃g/ nm inv spatula, tongue-depressor

abaissement /abɛsmɑ̃/ nm [1] (diminution) (de prix, taux) cut (**de** in); (de seuil, niveau) lowering; **l'~ de l'âge de la retraite à 60 ans** the lowering of the retirement age to 60; [2] (de manette) (en tirant) pulling down; (en poussant) pushing down; [3] (de mur, socle) lowering (**de** of); [4] (avilissement) (de soi-même) self-abasement; (d'autrui) debasement

abaisser /abese/ [1]
A vtr [1] (diminuer en valeur) to reduce [prix, taux] (**à** to; **de** by); to lower [niveau, seuil] (**à** to; **de** by); [2] (diminuer en hauteur) to lower [mur, socle] (**de** by); [3] (faire descendre) to pull down [manette, rideau de fer]; to lower [pont-levis, rideau de scène]; [4] Math to draw [perpendiculaire]; to bring down [chiffre de dividende]; [5] (avilir) liter [personne] to humiliate [adversaire, vaincu]; [douleur, vice] to degrade; [6] (rabattre) to

humble [prétentions, orgueil]; [7] Culin to roll out [pâte]

B s'abaisser vpr [1] (descendre) [rideau de scène] to fall; [2] (s'avilir) to demean oneself; **s'~ à faire qch** to stoop to doing sth; **ce n'est pas s'~ que de demander de l'aide** it is not demeaning to ask for help

abaisseur /abɛsœʀ/ nm [1] Anat (muscle) **~** depressor; [2] Électrotech step-down transformer

abajoue /abaʒu/ nf cheek pouch

abandon /abɑ̃dɔ̃/ nm [1] (état) state of neglect; **état d'~** neglected state; **à l'~** [maison, domaine] abandoned, deserted; [enfant] running wild; [jardin] neglected; **biens à l'~** Jur ownerless property; **laisser à l'~** to allow [sth] to fall into decay [maison]; to allow [sth] to become overgrown [jardin, terres]; [2] Jur (de véhicule) abandonment; (de personne) desertion; [3] (d'idée, de projet, méthode) abandonment; (de droit, privilège) relinquishment; (de bien) surrender; **faire ~ de** to relinquish [droit, bien]; **faire ~ de qch à qn** to make over ou surrender sth to sb; [4] (de cours, d'épreuve) Scol, Sport withdrawal (**de** from); (de fonctions) giving up (**de** of); **être contraint à l'~** to be forced to withdraw; **vainqueur par ~** winner by default; [5] (confiance) lack of restraint; **parler avec ~** to talk freely ou without restraint; [6] (attitude détendue) relaxed attitude; **pose pleine d'~** attitude of complete relaxation

Composés **~ de créance** composition between debtor and creditor; **~ du domicile conjugal** desertion of the marital home; **~ d'enfant** abandonment of a child; **~ d'épave** abandonment of a vehicle; **~ d'incapable** abandonment of a person in need of care; **~ de navire** notice of abandonment (of a vessel) ; **~ de poste** desertion (of one's post); **~ des poursuites** abandonment of action, nolle prosequi spéc

abandonné, ~e /abɑ̃dɔne/
A pp ► **abandonner**
B pp adj [1] (délaissé) [épouse, famille, ami, cause] deserted; [véhicule] abandoned; [domaine, maison] abandoned; [héros, nation, peuple] abandoned, forsaken sout; **chef ~ de tous** leader whose supporters have fled; **être ~ à soi-même** to be left to one's own devices; **être ~ par les médecins** to be considered past help by the doctors; [2] (désaffecté) [chemin, usine, mine] disused; [3] (qui n'a plus cours) [théorie, méthode] discarded; [modèle, format] discontinued; [4] (détendu) [pose, attitude] gén relaxed; (voluptueusement) abandoned

abandonner /abɑ̃dɔne/ [1]
A vtr [1] (renoncer à) to abandon, to give up [projet, théorie, activité, espoir]; to give up [habitude]; to give up, to forsake sout [confort, sécurité]; Scol to drop [matière]; **~ les recherches** to give up the search; **~ la cigarette/l'alcool** to give up smoking/ drinking; **les médecins l'ont abandonné** the doctors have given up on him; **je peignais, mais j'ai abandonné** I used to paint, but I gave it up; **c'est trop dur, j'abandonne** it's too hard, I give up; **la partie** or **lutte** to throw in the towel; [2] (céder) to give ou relinquish sout [bien] (**à qn** to sb); to hand [sth] over [gestion] (**à qn** to sb); **je vous abandonne le**

~ **à** to achieve [*célébrité, gloire*]; to acquire [*responsabilités*]; to obtain [*poste*]; to reach, to attain sout [*fonctions*]; ~ **à la propriété** to become a home-owner; ~ **au pouvoir** to come to power; ~ **au trône** to accede to the throne; ③ fml (satisfaire à) ~ **à** to grant, to accede to sout [*demande, prière, désir*]; ④ Ordinat ~ **à** to access

accélérateur, -trice /akseleratœr, tris/
Ⓐ*adj* accelerating
Ⓑ*nm* Aut accelerator; **câble d'~** accelerator cable; **appuyer sur l'~** to step on the accelerator; **coup d'~** touch on the accelerator; **donner un coup d'~** lit to step on the accelerator; **donner un coup d'~ à qch** fig to give sth a boost, to speed up sth; **jouer un rôle de ~** fig to act as a catalyst
(Composé) ~ **de particules** particle accelerator

accélération /akselerasjɔ̃/ *nf* (de vitesse) acceleration (**de** of); (de croissance, consommation, prix) sharp increase (**de** in); (de processus, travail, projet) speeding-up (**de** of); **l'~ de l'Histoire** the speeding-up of events

accéléré, ~e /akselere/
Ⓐ*pp* ▸ **accélérer**
Ⓑ*pp adj* accelerated; **à un rythme ~** at an increasingly fast rate; **stage de formation ~e** intensive learning course
Ⓒ*nm* Cin fast *ou* accelerated motion; **en ~** in fast *ou* accelerated motion

accélérer /akselere/ [14]
Ⓐ*vtr* (hâter) to speed up [*rythme, mouvement*]; to accelerate [*processus, réaction*]; **le pas** *or* **l'allure** to quicken one's step *ou* pace
Ⓑ*vi* ① Aut [*conducteur*] to accelerate, to speed up; **accélère!** speed up!; ② °fig (se dépêcher) to get a move on°
Ⓒ*s'accélérer vpr* ① (aller plus vite) [*pouls, mouvement*] to quicken; **les événements s'accélèrent** the pace of events is quickening; ② (s'intensifier) [*phénomène, tendance*] to accelerate

accent /aksɑ̃/ *nm* ① (façon de parler) accent; **avoir l'~ bordelais** to have a Bordeaux accent; **parler français sans ~/avec un léger ~ anglais** to speak French without an accent/with a slight English accent; ② (sur une lettre) accent; ~ **aigu/grave** acute/grave accent; ~ **circonflexe** circumflex (accent); **prendre un ~** [*mot, lettre*] to have an accent; **sourcils en ~ circonflexe** arched eyebrows; ③ Phon ~ **(d'intensité)** stress; ~ **fixe/libre** fixed/free stress; **l'~ porte sur la dernière syllabe** the stress is *ou* falls on the last syllable; **mettre l'~ sur qch** fig to put the emphasis on sth, to stress sth; ④ (nuance, note) **il n'y avait pas le moindre ~ de sincérité dans son discours** there wasn't the slightest hint of sincerity in his/her speech; **musique aux ~s mozartiens** music with Mozartian overtones; **un ~ de vérité** a ring of truth
(Composés) ~ **de hauteur** pitch; ~ **tonique** stress

accenteur /aksɑ̃tœr/ *nm* ~ **mouchet** hedge sparrow

accentuation /aksɑ̃tɥasjɔ̃/ *nf* ① (de crise, tension) escalation; (d'inégalités) heightening; (de phénomène) worsening; (de tendance) increase; ② Phon stress, (en poésie) accentuation; ③ (signes diacritiques) accents (*pl*)
(Composé) ~ **d'image** image enhancement

accentuel, -elle /aksɑ̃tɥɛl/ *adj* accentual, stress (*épith*); **groupe ~** stress group; **unité accentuelle** accentual unit

accentuer /aksɑ̃tɥe/ [1]
Ⓐ*vtr* ① (rendre plus évident) [*mesure, situation*] to accentuate [*inégalités, différences*]; to heighten [*tensions*]; to increase [*tendance*]; ② (tenter de faire ressortir) [*personne*] to highlight [*différences, trait de caractère, inégalités*]; to emphasize [*aspect*]; ③ Phon to stress, (en poésie) to accentuate [*syllabe*]; **syllabe accentuée/non accentuée** stressed/unstressed syllable, (en poésie) accented/unaccented syllable;

④ (écrire) to put an accent on [*lettre*]; **les lettres accentuées** letters with accents, accented letters
Ⓑ*s'accentuer vpr* [*déséquilibre, phénomène, tendance*] to become more marked, to become more pronounced; [*timidité*] to become worse

acceptabilité /aksɛptabilite/ *nf* acceptability

acceptable /aksɛptabl/ *adj* ① (tolérable) [*seuil, norme, condition, comportement*] acceptable; **rendre qch ~** to make sth acceptable (**à** to); ② (passable) [*travail, qualité*] passable; [*résultat*] satisfactory; **'comment est le nouveau professeur?'—'~'** 'what's the new teacher like?'—'he's/she's all right'

acceptation /aksɛptasjɔ̃/ *nf* acceptance; **sous réserve d'~** subject to acceptance (**de** of)

accepter /aksɛpte/ [1]
Ⓐ*vtr* ① (bien recevoir) to accept [*invitation, personne, proposition, cadeau*]; ~ **qch de qn** to accept sth from sb; ~ **de faire qch** to agree to do sth; ~ **que** to accept that; **s'il te plaît, accepte!** please say yes!; **je n'accepte pas qu'on m'interrompe!** I will not be interrupted!; ② (agréer) to agree to [*condition, contrat, devis*]; ③ (relever) to accept, to take up [*défi, pari*]; ④ (admettre) to accept [*excuse, théorie, personne*]; **elle a essayé de faire ~ son fiancé/projet** she tried to get her fiancé/plan accepted; **il aura du mal à se faire ~ par sa belle-famille** he'll have trouble getting himself accepted by his in-laws; ~ **l'idée de faire qch** to accept the idea of doing sth; ⑤ (se résigner à) to accept, to come to terms with [*situation, destin*]
Ⓑ*s'accepter vpr* ① (soi-même) **s'~ (tel qu'on est)** to accept oneself (for what one is); ② (l'un l'autre) **s'~ (mutuellement)** to accept one another

acception /aksɛpsjɔ̃/ *nf* ① (sens) sense; **dans toute l'~ du terme** *or* **mot** in every sense of the word; ② Jur (distinction) **sans ~ de** irrespective of

accès /aksɛ/ *nm inv* ① (moyen, possibilité d'atteindre) access; **moyens d'~** means of access; **être facile d'~** *or* **d'un ~ facile** to be easy to get to; **être difficile d'~** *or* **d'un ~ difficile** to be difficult to get to; **être facile d'~ avec une voiture** to be easily accessible *ou* easy to get to by car; **être d'un ~ facile/difficile** [*personne*] to be approachable/unapproachable; **l'~ au village** (possibilité d'atteindre) access to the village; (moyen d'atteindre) the way into the village, the road leading to the village; **l'~ au roi** access to the king; **cela donne ~ à** (mener) it leads to; **toutes les voies d'~ sont barrées** (portes) all entrances are sealed off; (routes) all approach roads are closed off; **'~ aux quais'** 'to the trains'; ② (moyen d'entrer) **l'~ à** access to; **les ~ du bâtiment** the entrances to the building; **les ~ de la ville** the approach roads *ou* approaches to the town; ③ (droit d'entrée) **ne pas avoir ~ à** not to be admitted to; **interdire l'~ aux enfants** not to admit children; **il s'est vu refuser l'~ de la maison** he was not allowed into the house; **'~ interdit'** 'no entry', 'no admittance'; **'~ interdit aux visiteurs'** 'visitors not admitted'; **'~ interdit aux chiens'** 'no dogs (allowed)'; **'~ réservé au personnel** *or* **au service'** 'staff only'; ④ (possibilité d'obtenir, d'utiliser) access; **avoir ~ à** to have access to [*documents, fonds, soins médicaux*]; **ne pas avoir libre ~ aux médias** not to have free access to the media; ⑤ (possibilité de participer à) **l'~ à** access to [*profession, cours*]; admission to [*club, grande école*]; **barrer l'~ d'une profession aux femmes** to keep women out of a profession; **ouvrir l'~ d'une profession aux femmes** to open up a profession to women; **faciliter l'~ à une profession** to open up a profession; ⑥ (possibilité de comprendre) **être d'un ~ facile** to be accessible; **être d'un ~ difficile** not to be very accessible; ⑦ (crise) ~ **de colère** fit of anger; ~ **de fièvre**

bout of fever; ~ **d'enthousiasme** burst of enthusiasm; **par ~** by fits and starts; ⑧ Ordinat access; ~ **aléatoire/séquentiel** random/sequential access; **voie d'~ à** access path to

accessibilité /aksesibilite/ *nf* ① (possibilité d'être atteint) accessibility (**de** of); (possibilité d'atteindre) access (**de** to); ② (droit) right; **l'~ de tous à l'emploi/au droit de vote** everyone's right to a job/to vote; ③ Ling, Psych accessibility

accessible /aksesibl/ *adj* ① [*lieu*] accessible; **un site ~ par les transports en commun** a site accessible by public transport; ② [*emploi*] ~ **à** open to; **la culture doit être ~ à tous** culture must be accessible to everyone; ③ [*ouvrage, théorie*] accessible; **un langage ~ à tous** a language which can be understood by everyone; ④ [*prix, tarif*] affordable (**à qn** to sb); ⑤ [*personne*] (qu'on peut approcher) approachable; (qu'on peut émouvoir) ~ **à** susceptible to [*compassion, pitié*]

accession /aksesjɔ̃/ *nf* ① (fait de parvenir) ~ **à** accession to [*pouvoir, trône*]; attainment of [*indépendance*]; ~ **à la propriété** home-buying; ② Jur accession

accessit /aksesit/ *nm* honourable^GB mention

accessoire /akseswar/
Ⓐ*adj* [*problème, détail, avantage*] incidental
Ⓑ*nm* ① (choses non essentielles) **distinguer l'~ de l'essentiel** to distinguish the non-essentials from the essentials; ② (équipement complémentaire) (d'auto, de moto, vêtement) accessory; (de perceuse, robot ménager, d'aspirateur) attachment; ③ Cin, Théât ~**s** props (*pl*)
(Composés) ~**s de salle de bains** bathroom accessories; ~**s de table** condiments and cutlery; ~**s de toilette** toilet requisites
(Idiome) **ranger qch au magasin des ~s** to shelve sth

accessoirement /akseswarmɑ̃/ *adv* (en plus) incidentally, as it happens; (le cas échéant) if desired; **'je peux amener Paul?'—'oui ~'** 'can I bring Paul along?'—'if you must'

accessoiriser /akseswarize/ [1] *vtr* to accessorize

accessoiriste /akseswarist/ ▸ p. 532 *nmf* Théât props man/woman

accident /aksidɑ̃/ *nm* ① (dommage) accident; ~ **grave** serious accident; **en cas d'~ prévenir...** in case of accident (please) notify...; **l'~ a fait deux morts et quinze blessés** two died and fifteen were injured as a result of the accident; **un ~ est si vite arrivé!** accidents can easily happen!; **il y a 10 000 morts par ~ chaque année** 10,000 people die in accidents every year; **il s'est tué par ~ en nettoyant son fusil** he accidentally killed himself while cleaning his gun; ② (problème) hitch; (événement inhabituel) one off°; hum accident; **une carrière qui évolue sans ~** a career which is progressing without a hitch; **une erreur qui n'est qu'un ~** an error which is just a one-off; **ils ont gagné! c'était un ~!** hum they won! that was an accident!; ~ **de parcours°** hitch; hum accident; **l'arrivée du (petit) dernier est un ~ (de parcours)** the birth of the last one was an accident; **les ~s de l'existence** the unforeseen events of life; **une découverte faite par ~** (par hasard) a chance discovery; ③ Méd accident; ~ **cérébral/vasculaire** cerebral/vascular accident; ~ **cardiaque** cardiac event; ~ **de santé** health problem; ④ (inégalité) ~ **de terrain** irregularity in the landscape, accident spéc; **maison cachée par un ~ de terrain** house obscured by an undulation in the land; **le satellite peut repérer le moindre ~ de terrain** the satellite can pick out every contour; ⑤ Mus accidental; ⑥ Philos accident
(Composés) ~ **d'avion** plane crash; ~ **de chasse** hunting accident; ~ **de la circulation** traffic accident; ~ **corporel**

a

accident involving injury; ～ **domestique** accident in the home; ～ **ferroviaire** rail accident; ～ **industriel** industrial accident; ～ **de montagne** climbing accident; ～ **nucléaire** nuclear accident; ～ **de la route** road accident; ～ **du travail** industrial accident; ～ **de voiture** car accident

accidenté, **～e** /aksidɑ̃te/
A *pp* ▸ accidenter
B *pp adj* ⓵ [*personne*] injured; [*véhicule*] involved in an accident (*après n*); ⓶ [*chemin, terrain, paysage*] uneven; ⓷ fig (plein d'événements) chequered GB *ou* checkered US; **après un parcours ～ il a pris la tête du parti** after a chequered GB *ou* checkered US career he has taken over leadership of the party
C *nm,f* casualty, accident victim; **les ～s de la route** road accident victims; **les ～s du travail** people injured at work

accidentel, -elle /aksidɑ̃tɛl/ *adj* accidental; **l'explosion n'avait rien d'～** there was nothing accidental about the explosion

accidentellement /aksidɑ̃tɛlmɑ̃/ *adv* ⓵ (dans un accident) [*mourir, tuer*] accidentally; **il s'est tué ～** he accidentally killed himself (**en faisant** while doing); ⓶ (par hasard) by accident; **le coup (de feu) est parti ～** the shot went off by accident

accidenter /aksidɑ̃te/ [1] *vtr* to bump [*véhicule*]; **sa camionnette a été accidentée plusieurs fois** he has bumped his van several times

acclamation /aklamasjɔ̃/ *nf* cheering ¢, acclamation; **sous les ～s de** to the cheering of; **vote par ～** vote by acclamation, voice vote US

acclamer /aklame/ [1] *vtr* to cheer, to acclaim [*personne, orateur, chef d'État*]

acclimatable /aklimatabl/ *adj* acclimatizable, acclimatable US

acclimatation /aklimatasjɔ̃/ *nf* acclimatization, acclimation US

acclimatement /aklimatmɑ̃/ *nm* acclimatization, acclimation US

acclimater /aklimate/ [1]
A *vtr* ⓵ Bot, Zool to acclimatize, to acclimate US [*plante, animal*]; ⓶ (introduire) to introduce [*mode, idée, procédé*]
B **s'acclimater** *vpr* ⓵ Bot, Zool to become acclimatized, to become acclimated US; ⓶ [*personne*] to adapt; [*idée*] to become accepted

accointances /akwɛ̃tɑ̃s/ *nfpl* contacts; **avoir des ～ avec qn** to have contacts with sb, to know sb; **il a des ～ en haut lieu** he's got friends in high places

accolade /akɔlad/ *nf* ⓵ (embrassade) embrace; **donner l'～ à qn** to embrace sb; ⓶ (cérémonie) accolade

accoler /akɔle/ [1] *vtr* ⓵ (mettre côte à côte) ～ **un bâtiment à qch** to build a building right next to sth; ～ **une étiquette/un nom à** to attach a label/a name to; ～ **une idée à** to associate an idea with; ⓶ Imprim to bracket (together) [*lignes, paragraphes*]

accommodant, **～e** /akɔmɔdɑ̃, ɑ̃t/ *adj* [*personne*] accommodating; [*politique*] flexible

accommodation /akɔmɔdasjɔ̃/ *nf* Physiol, Biol, Psych accommodation

accommodement /akɔmɔdmɑ̃/ *nm* ⓵ (transaction) arrangement; **parvenir à un ～ avec qn** to come to an arrangement with sb (**à propos de** about); ⓶ (expédient) hum agreement; **trouver des ～s avec sa conscience/avec le Ciel** to come to terms with one's conscience/with God

accommoder /akɔmɔde/ [1]
A *vtr* ⓵ Culin to prepare [*aliment, plat*]; **l'art d'～ les restes** the art of using up leftovers; ⓶ (adapter) to adapt; **il accommode ses propos aux circonstances** he adapts his remarks to suit the circumstances
B *vi* [*œil*] to focus
C **s'accommoder** *vpr* **s'～ de qch** (positif) to make the best of sth; (plus résigné) to put up

with sth; **s'～ à** to adapt to

accompagnateur, **-trice** /akɔ̃paɲatœʀ, tʀis/ *nm,f* ⓵ ▸ p. 532 Mus accompanist; ⓶ (d'enfants) accompanying adult; (de groupe touristique) courier; **vingt athlètes et ～s** twenty athletes and accompanying personnel

accompagnement /akɔ̃paɲmɑ̃/ *nm* ⓵ Mus accompaniment; **sans ～** unaccompanied; ⓶ Culin accompaniment; **en ～ à** as an accompaniment to; **avec ～ de** served with; ⓷ (de malade) caring (**de** for); (de touristes) accompanying; ⓸ (cortège) fig complement; (conséquence) result; **le chômage et son ～ de misères** unemployment and its attendant ills; ⓹ (soutien) support; **artillerie/aviation d'～** artillery/air support; **mesures/politiques d'～** attendant measures/policies
(Composés) ～ **musical** musical arrangement; ～ **social** social measures (*pl*); **crédits d'～ social** social funds

accompagner /akɔ̃paɲe/ [1]
A *vtr* ⓵ (se déplacer avec) (aller) to accompany, to go with; (venir) to accompany, to come with; (conduire) to take (**à** to); ～ **un convoi** to accompany a convoy; **accompagne-le au magasin** go with him to the shop GB *ou* store US; **tu m'accompagnes à la gare?** will you come to the station with me? **je vais vous (y) ～** (en voiture) I'll take you (there); (à pied) I'll come with you; ～ **un enfant à l'école** to take a child to school; **tous mes vœux vous accompagnent** all my good wishes go with you; **il s'est fait ～ par** *or* **d'un ami** he got a friend to go with *ou* accompany him; **être accompagné de** *or* **par** to be accompanied by; **20% de réduction à la personne qui vous accompagne** 20% reduction for any person travelling GB with you; **ces personnes vous accompagnent?** are these people with you?; **elle les accompagna du regard** her eyes followed them; **elle a accompagné son mari jusqu'à la fin** she stayed by her husband's side until the end; **accompagné/non accompagné** [*bagage, enfant*] accompanied/unaccompanied; ⓶ (aller de pair avec) to accompany, to go with; **les difficultés qui pourraient ～ la réforme** the difficulties which may accompany the reform; **fièvre accompagnée de maux de tête** fever accompanied by headaches; **une cassette accompagne le livre** there's a cassette with the book; **elle accompagna ces mots d'un sourire/clin d'œil** she smiled/winked as she said this; **CV accompagné de deux photos** CV *ou* resumé US together with two photographs; **l'inflation et les problèmes qui l'accompagnent** inflation and its attendant problems; ⓷ (soutenir) to back, to support; ～ **la réforme de garanties** to back up the reform with guarantees; ⓸ Mus to accompany (**à** on); ⓹ Culin [*sauce, vin, légumes*] (être servi avec) to be served with; (convenir à) to go with; **vin pour ～ un plat** wine to accompany a dish
B **s'accompagner** *vpr* ⓵ Mus to accompany oneself (**à** on); ⓶ (s'associer à) to be accompanied (**de** by); **la restructuration doit s'～ d'une modernisation** reorganization will have to be accompanied by modernization; **l'accord s'accompagne d'un contrat** the agreement comes with a contract; ⓷ Culin to be served with

accompli, **～e** /akɔ̃pli/
A *pp* ▸ accomplir
B *pp adj* (parfait) [*personne*] accomplished; (achevé) fulfilled, accomplished; **mission ～e!** mission accomplished!

accomplir /akɔ̃pliʀ/ [3]
A *vtr* ⓵ (s'acquitter de) to accomplish [*tâche, mission*]; to fulfil GB [*obligation*]; ～ **son devoir** to do one's duty; ⓶ (réaliser) to make [*progrès, effort*]; ～ **de grandes choses** to achieve great things; ⓷ Jur, Admin (faire) to do [*service militaire, peine de prison*]; ～ **des démarches/formalités** to go through procedures/formalities

B **s'accomplir** *vpr* ⓵ (se produire) [*événement*] to take place; ⓶ (se réaliser) [*vœu, souhait, prévisions*] to be fulfilled GB; ⓷ (s'épanouir) [*personne*] to find fulfilment GB (**dans** in)

accomplissement /akɔ̃plismɑ̃/ *nm* (d'activité, de mission) accomplishment, fulfilment GB; (réalisation) realization, achievement; (épanouissement) (self-)fulfilment GB

accord /akɔʀ/ *nm* ⓵ (consentement) consent (**à** to), agreement (**à** to); **donner son ～ à qch** to give one's consent to sth, to agree to sth; **d'un commun ～** by common consent *ou* mutual agreement; ⓶ (pacte) agreement (**portant sur** on); (non formel) understanding; ～ **de conciliation/cessez-le-feu** conciliation/ceasefire agreement; **conclure un ～** to enter into an agreement; ～**s de commerce** *or* **commerciaux** trade agreements; ～**s bilatéraux** bilateral agreements; ⓷ (avis partagé, entente) agreement (**sur** on); **décider qch en ～ avec qn** to decide sth in agreement with sb; **être d'～** to agree; **je suis/je ne suis pas d'～ avec toi là-dessus** I agree/I disagree with you on this; **je suis d'～ que** I agree (that); **Pierre est d'～ pour faire** Pierre has agreed to do; **je suis/je ne suis pas d'～ pour payer** I am/I am not willing to pay; **je ne suis pas d'～ pour que nous fassions** I am not in favour GB of our doing; **je demeure d'～ avec vous sur ce point** I am in agreement with you on this point; **se mettre** *or* **tomber d'～** to come to an agreement; **mettre tout le monde d'～** (du même avis) to bring everybody round GB to the same way of thinking; (mettre fin aux querelles) to put an end to the argument; **tu es d'～ pour la plage?** are you on for the beach?; **'on signe?'—'d'～!'** 'shall we sign?'—'OK!', 'all right', 'fine'; ⓸ (entre personnes, couleurs, styles) harmony; **vivre en ～** to live in harmony; **un ～ parfait règne entre eux** they have a very harmonious relationship; **être en ～ avec** (avec écrit, tradition, promesse) to be in keeping *ou* consistent with; **en ～ avec le reste du mobilier** in keeping with the rest of the furniture; **agir en ～ avec le règlement/ses principes** to act in accordance with the rules/one's principles; ⓹ Ling agreement; ～ **en genre/en nombre** gender/number agreement; **faire l'～** to make the agreement; ⓺ Mus (notes) chord; (réglage) tuning; **le piano tient l'～** the piano is in tune
(Composés) ～ **à l'amiable** informal agreement; ～ **d'association** UE association agreement; ～ **de contingentement** quota agreement; ～ **de gré à gré** mutual agreement; ～ **de paiement** Écon trade agreement; ～ **de principe** agreement in principle; ～ **salarial** Entr wage settlement; ～**s de crédit** Fin credit arrangements; **Accord général sur les tarifs douaniers et le commerce** Hist General Agreement on Tariffs and Trade, GATT

accordable /akɔʀdabl/ *adj* ⓵ (prêt) grantable, which may be granted; ⓶ Mus [*instrument*] tunable

accordage /akɔʀdaʒ/, **accordement** /akɔʀd(ə)mɑ̃/ *nm* Mus tuning

accord-cadre, *pl* **accords-cadres** /akɔʀkadʀ/ *nm* outline agreement

accordéon /akɔʀdeɔ̃/ ▸ p. 557
A *nm* accordion; **un air d'～** a tune on the accordion; **en ～** fig [*chaussettes, pantalon*] wrinkled; [*voiture accidentée*] concertinaed; **plier qch en ～** to fold sth into pleats; **être plié en ～** to be folded into a concertina
B **(-)accordéon** (in compounds) **cloison ～** sliding and folding partition; **porte ～** folding door
(Composés) ～ **chromatique** chromatic accordion; ～ **diatonique** diatonic accordion

accordéoniste /akɔʀdeɔnist/ ▸ p. 532, p. 557 *nmf* accordion-player

accorder /akɔʀde/ [1]
A *vtr* ⓵ (octroyer) ～ **qch à qn** to grant sth to sb,

d'un ridicule ∼/**d'une bêtise** ∼e to be utterly ridiculous/stupid; **être d'un comique** ∼/**d'une intelligence** ∼e [situation, œuvre] to be sheer comedy/intelligence; **il est d'une intelligence** ∼e he's extremely intelligent; **c'est un snob** ∼ he's a consummate snob; **c'est un idiot** ∼ he's a complete idiot

achèvement /aʃɛvmɑ̃/ nm (de travaux, projet, roman) completion; (de rencontre, discussions) conclusion; **en cours** or **voie d'**∼ nearing completion

achever /aʃve/ [16]
A vtr **1** (terminer) to finish [travail, repas, œuvre]; to conclude [discussions]; to complete [projet, visite, enquête, service militaire]; to end [vie]; ∼ **de faire** to finish doing; **il avait à peine achevé que tout le monde partait déjà** he had hardly finished speaking when everyone started to leave; **2** (réussir) **l'orage a achevé de décourager les spectateurs** the spectators were dispirited and the storm was the last straw; **il a achevé de me démoraliser avec ses mauvaises nouvelles** I was feeling downhearted and the bad news he gave me was the last straw; **ta démonstration a achevé de me convaincre** the proof you gave me finally convinced me; **3** (tuer) to destroy [animal]; to finish off [personne]; **4** ○(épuiser) [personne, effort] to wear [sb] out, to finish○; **5** ○(terrasser) [scandale, ruine] to finish [sb] off
B s'achever vpr to end (par with; sur on); **le jour s'achève** the day is drawing to a close; **s'**∼ **par un record** to end with a record; **s'**∼ **sur une victoire** to end on a victory

Achille /aʃil/ npr Achilles; **tendon d'**∼ Achilles tendon

Achkhabad /aʃkabad/ ▸ p. 894 npr Ashkhabad

achoppement /aʃɔpmɑ̃/ nm **pierre d'**∼ stumbling block

achopper /aʃɔpe/ [1] vi ∼ **sur** to stumble over; **les négociations ont achoppé sur ce point** the talks hit a snag over this issue

achromatique /akʁɔmatik/ adj achromatic

acide /asid/
A adj **1** (pas assez sucré) [goût] acid, sour; (agréablement) [goût] sharp; (comme propriété naturelle) [aliment] acidic; **2** [odeur] acrid; [couleur] acid; [remarque] acerbic; **3** Chimie acid, acidic
B nm **1** Chimie acid; ∼ **faible/fort** weak/strong acid; ∼ **gras** fatty acid; ∼ **chlorhydrique/sulfurique/urique** hydrochloric/sulphuric GB/uric acid; **2** ○(drogue) acid○
Composé ∼ **aminé** amino acid

acidifiant, ∼e /asidifjɑ̃, ɑ̃t/
A adj acidifying
B nm acidifying agent

acidification /asidifikasjɔ̃/ nf acidification

acidifier /asidifje/ [2]
A vtr to acidify
B s'acidifier vpr to acidify

acidité /asidite/ nf **1** (désagréable) gén acidity, sourness; (pas désagréable) tartness, sharpness; **2** (de personne, réflexion, discours) acerbity; **3** Chimie acidity

acidulé, ∼e /asidyle/ adj **1** lit slightly acid; **2** fig [parfum] tangy; [jaune, vert] acid

acier /asje/
A ▸ p. 202 adj inv **gris/bleu** ∼ steel(y) grey GB ou gray US/blue
B nm **1** (alliage) steel; **d'**∼ [cuve] steel (épith); [muscle] of steel; **d'**∼ [personne] to have nerves of steel; **avoir un moral d'**∼ to be made of stern stuff; **2** (industrie) steel industry
Composés ∼ **chirurgical** surgical steel; ∼ **inoxydable** stainless steel; ∼ **rapide** high-speed steel; ∼ **trempé** tempered steel

aciérie /asjeʁi/ nf steelworks (+ v sg ou pl)

aciériste /asjeʁist/ nm steel maker

acmé /akme/ nm **1** (apogée) liter acme littér; **2** Méd crisis

acné /akne/ nf Méd acne; ∼ **juvénile** teenage acne; ∼ **rosacée** acne rosacea

acnéique /akneik/ adj [peau] acned

acolyte /akɔlit/ nmf **1** (complice) péj henchman, acolyte; **2** Relig acolyte

acompte /akɔ̃t/ nm (premier versement) down payment; (arrhes) deposit; (versement échelonné) instalment GB; (versement partiel) part payment; ∼ **sur salaire** advance on salary; **verser un** ∼ **de** to make a deposit of; **1 000 euros d'**∼ or **en** ∼ a 1,000-euro deposit
Composé ∼ **provisionnel** Fisc first payment on account

aconit /akɔnit/ nm monkshood

a contrario* /akɔ̃tʁaʁjo/ loc adv on the contrary

acoquiner: s'acoquiner /akɔkine/ [1] vpr **s'**∼ **avec qn** to get thick○ with sb

Açores /asɔʁ/ ▸ p. 435 nprfpl **les** ∼ the Azores

à-côté, pl ∼s /akote/ nm **1** (problème) side issue; **2** (avantages) perk; (gains) **se faire de petits** ∼s to make a bit on the side○; **3** (dépenses) extra

à-coup, pl ∼s /aku/ nm (secousse) jolt; (de processus, négociations, travail, d'économie) hitch; **les** ∼s **du moteur** the coughs and splutters of the engine; **par** ∼s lit, fig by ou in fits and starts; **sans** ∼s lit, fig smoothly; **essayez d'éviter les** ∼s (dans le travail) try to keep things running smoothly; (dans la vie, les relations) try to keep things on an even keel

acouphène /akufɛn/ nm tinnitus

acousticien, **-ienne** /akustisjɛ̃, ɛn/ ▸ p. 532 nm,f acoustician

acoustique /akustik/
A adj acoustic
B nf **1** Phys acoustics (+ v sg); **2** (d'un lieu) acoustics (pl); **3** Mus acoustic quality

acquéreur /akeʁœʁ/ nm buyer, purchaser; **elle est** ∼ she's interested; **trouver un** ∼ **pour** to find a buyer for; **se porter** ∼ **de** to state one's intention to buy; **se rendre** ∼ **de** to purchase, to buy

acquérir /akeʁiʁ/ [35]
A vtr **1** (devenir propriétaire de) to acquire; (en achetant) to purchase; ∼ **qch par héritage** or **succession** to inherit sth; **2** (arriver à avoir) [personne] to acquire [habitude, connaissance, expérience, réputation]; ∼ **une formation** to undergo training; ∼ **la certitude que** to become convinced that; ∼ **la preuve de** to gain proof of; **cela vous a acquis le soutien de vos collègues** this has won you your colleagues' support; **3** (gagner) to acquire; ∼ **de la valeur** to gain in value; **cela a acquis de l'importance** it has become important; ∼ **de la vitesse** to gain speed; **4** (au passif) **il est acquis à notre cause** we have his support; **son bon vouloir nous est acquis** we can count on his good will; **il est acquis que** it is accepted that
B s'acquérir vpr **1** (s'obtenir) **s'**∼ **facilement** to be easy to acquire; **s'**∼ **par succession** or **héritage** to be inherited; **2** (s'apprendre) **c'est quelque chose qui s'acquiert** it's something you acquire ou pick up; **l'expérience s'acquiert avec l'âge** experience comes with age

acquêt /akɛ/ nm: property acquired in common by husband and wife

acquiescement /akjɛsmɑ̃/ fml nm acquiescence sout; **donner son** ∼ **à qch** to acquiesce to sth

acquiescer /akjese/ [12] vi to acquiesce; ∼ **d'un signe de tête** to nod in agreement; **et sa fille d'**∼ and the daughter agrees

acquis, ∼e /aki, iz/
A pp ▸ acquérir
B pp adj **1** Psych [comportement, idée] acquired; **2** (obtenu) [valeur, expérience, connaissance, conviction] acquired; **3** (reconnu) [principe, droit, fait] accepted, established; **les avantages** ∼ the gains; **tenir qch pour** ∼ to take sth for granted ou as read
C nm inv **1** (connaissances) knowledge; **vivre sur ses** ∼ to draw on one's knowledge; (réussite) achievement; **3** (avantage obtenu) ∼ **salariaux/syndicaux** wage/union gains; ∼ **sociaux** social benefits; **c'est un** ∼ that is one thing gained; **4** Psych, Philos **l'**∼ acquired knowledge; **l'inné et l'**∼ nature versus nurture; **5** ∼ **(communautaire)** UE acquis (communautaire)
Idiome **bien mal** ∼ **ne profite jamais** Prov ill-gotten gains never prosper

acquisition /akizisjɔ̃/ nf **1** (achat) purchase, acquisition; **prix d'**∼ purchase price; **faire l'**∼ **de** to purchase; **2** Ordinat data capture, data acquisition; **temps d'**∼ data capture time; **3** (de musée, bibliothèque) acquisition, accession spéc; **4** (processus) acquisition; **l'**∼ **du langage** language acquisition; **l'**∼ **automatique de la nationalité** the automatic acquisition of citizenship

acquit /aki/ nm Comm receipt; **pour** ∼ received
Idiome **par** ∼ **de conscience** to put one's mind at rest

acquit-à-caution, pl **acquits-à-caution** /akiakosjɔ̃/ nm (customs and excise) bond

acquittement /akitmɑ̃/ nm **1** Jur acquittal; **2** Fin settlement

acquitter /akite/ [1]
A vtr **1** Jur to acquit [personne]; **faire** ∼ **qn** to get sb acquitted; **2** (payer) to pay [impôt, loyer]; to settle, to pay [dette]; **3** (dégager) ∼ **qn d'une dette** to release sb from a debt
B s'acquitter vpr **bien s'**∼ **de son rôle** to fulfil GB a role; **s'**∼ **de son devoir** to discharge one's duty; **s'**∼ **d'une dette** lit to pay off a debt; fig to repay a debt of gratitude

acra /akʁa/ nm acra, akra

acre /akʁ/ ▸ p. 816 nf acre

âcre /ɑkʁ/ adj [goût, fruit] sharp; [fumée, odeur] acrid; [remarque] caustic

âcreté /ɑkʁəte/ nf (de fumée, d'odeur) acridity; (d'aliment, de goût) sharpness

acrimonie /akʁimɔni/ nf liter acrimony littér

acrimonieux, **-ieuse** /akʁimɔnjø, øz/ adj acrimonious

acrobate /akʁɔbat/ ▸ p. 532 nmf acrobat

acrobatie /akʁɔbasi/ nf **1** Sport (activité) **l'**∼ acrobatics (+ v sg); **faire de l'**∼ to do ou perform acrobatics; **un exercice d'**∼ an acrobatic exercise; **2** (mouvement) **une** ∼ Sport an acrobatic exercise; **faire des** ∼s Sport to do ou perform acrobatics; fig to jump through all sorts of hoops; **elle s'en tire toujours avec une** ∼ she always wriggles out of it
Composé ∼ **aérienne** aerobatics (+ v sg)

acrobatique /akʁɔbatik/ adj acrobatic

acronyme /akʁɔnim/ nm acronym

Acropole /akʁɔpɔl/ nprf **l'**∼ the Acropolis

acrostiche /akʁɔstiʃ/ nm acrostic

acrylique /akʁilik/
A adj acrylic
B nm acrylic; **un pull-over en** ∼ an acrylic jumper; **c'est de l'**∼ it's acrylic

actant /aktɑ̃/ nm Ling actor

acte /akt/
A nm **1** (action) act; ∼ **isolé/raciste** isolated/racist act; ∼ **de guerre/violence** act of war/violence; **l'**∼ **de chair** sexual congress; **un** ∼ **de foi** lit, fig an act of faith; **mes/tes** ∼s my/your actions; **être libre de ses** ∼s to do as one wishes; **faire** ∼ **d'allégeance/de bravoure/charité** to show allegiance/courage/charity; **faire** ∼ **d'autorité** to exercise one's authority; **faire** ∼ **de candidature** to put oneself forward as a candidate; **faire** ∼ **de citoyen** to perform one's duty as a citizen; **faire** ∼ **de présence** to put in an appearance; **2** Jur deed; **passer des** ∼s to execute

a

deeds; **demander/donner** ~ **de** to ask for/ make acknowledgement of; **prendre** ~ **de** gén to take note of; Jur to take cognizance of; **j'en prends** ~ I'll bear it in mind; **dont** ~ gén point noted; Jur which is hereby legally certified; ③ Théât act; **pièce en un** ~ one-act play; ④ Philos actual; **passer de la puissance à l'**~ to go from the potential to the actual; **en** ~ in actuality

B **actes** *nmpl* ① (de congrès, réunion) proceedings; ② Relig acts

〔Composés〕 ~ **d'accusation** bill of indictment; ~ **authentique** authenticated deed; ~ **de contrition** act of contrition; ~ **de décès** death certificate; ~ **de l'état civil** *birth, marriage or death certificate*; ~ **de foi** act of faith; ~ **gratuit** gratuitous act; ~ **manqué** parapraxis spéc, Freudian slip; ~ **de mariage** marriage certificate; ~ **médical** Méd medical treatment; ~ **de naissance** birth certificate; ~ **notarié** notarial deed; ~ **officiel** instrument; ~ **de parole** speech act; ~ **sexuel** sexual act; ~ **de vente** bill of sale; **l'Acte unique européen** Single European Act; **les Actes des apôtres** the Acts of the Apostles

acteur, -trice /aktœʀ, tʀis/ *nm,f* ① ▸ p. 532 Cin, Théât actor/actress; ~ **de cinéma/théâtre** film/stage actor; **les** ~**s du film/de la pièce** the actors in the film/play; ② (participant) ~**s de la scène politique** actors on the political stage; **tous les** ~**s de la vie économique** all the parties involved in economic life; **les** ~**s d'un drame** the protagonists of a tragedy; ③ (agent) agent (**de** of); ~**s du changement** agents for change

actif, -ive /aktif, iv/
A *adj* ① (occupé) [*personne, vie*] active; **les femmes actives** working women; **la vie active** working life; **service** ~ active service; **l'armée d'active** the regular army; ② (pas passif) [*association, participation*] active; [*propagande*] vigorous; **jouer/avoir un rôle** ~ **dans qch** to play/to have an active part in sth; **avoir/prendre une part active à qch** to play/to take an active part in sth; **militant** ~ activist; ③ (plein d'énergie) gén active; [*marché, secteur*] buoyant; ④ (agissant) [*substance, principe*] active; ⑤ Ling **voix active** active voice
B *nm,f* (qui travaille) working person; **les** ~**s** the working population
C *nm* Fin, Compta **l'**~ the assets (*pl*); **à l'**~ **du bilan** on the assets side; **à mettre à l'**~ **de qn** fig a point in sb's favour^{GB}
D **active** *nf* **l'armée d'active** the regular army

〔Composés〕 ~ **brut** gross assets (*pl*); ~ **disponible** liquid assets (*pl*); ~ **immobilisé** fixed assets (*pl*); ~ **net** net assets (*pl*)

actinium /aktinjɔm/ *nm* actinium

action /aksjɔ̃/ *nf* ① (fait d'agir) action; **il serait temps de passer à l'**~ gén it's time to act; (combattre) it's time for action; **entrer en** ~ Mil to go into action; **l'entrée en** ~ **de l'armée** the army's involvement in the conflict; **un homme/une femme d'**~ a man/a woman of action; **avoir toute liberté d'**~ to have complete freedom of action; **être en** ~ [*personne*] to be in action; **en** ~ [*machine, mécanisme*] in operation; **mettre qch en** ~ to put sth into operation [*mesure, plan*]; **un sportif en (pleine)** ~ a sportsman in action; **volonté d'**~ will to act; ② (façon d'agir) action; **programme** *or* **plan d'**~ plan of action; **moyens d'**~ courses of action; **avoir une unité d'**~ to have a common plan of action; **champ d'**~ field of action; ③ (effet) effect; **l'**~ **du temps** the effects of time; **avoir une** ~ **bénéfique/ néfaste/immunologique** to have a positive/a negative/an immunizing effect; **sous l'**~ **de qch** under the effect of sth; **l'**~ **de qch sur qch/qn** the effect of sth on sth/sb; **l'**~ **de qn sur qch/qn** sb's influence on sth/sb; ④ (acte) action, act; **une** ~ **irresponsable/stupide** an irresponsible/a stupid action; **des** ~**s criminelles/individuelles/racistes** criminal/ individual/racist acts; **une** ~ **d'éclat** a

remarkable feat; **faire une** ~ **d'éclat** to distinguish oneself; **une bonne/mauvaise** ~ a good/bad deed; **j'ai fait ma bonne** ~ **de la journée** I've done my good deed for the day; ⑤ (initiative) initiative; Mil, Jur action; **une** ~ **des Nations unies** a UN initiative; ~**s culturelles** culturel initiatives; **mener des** ~**s humanitaires** to carry out a programme^{GB} of humanitarian aid; **dégager des ressources pour des** ~**s sociales** to free money for social programmes^{GB}; **entreprendre une** ~ **militaire offensive** to take offensive action; **intenter une** ~ **en justice à qn** to take legal action against sb; **intenter une** ~ **en diffamation** to bring a libel action GB *ou* suit; ⑥ (histoire) action; **l'**~ **se situe à Venise** the action takes place in Venice; **un film d'**~ an action film; **un roman d'**~ an adventure novel; **j'aime quand il y a de l'**~ I like a bit of action; ⑦ Fin share; ~**s et obligations** securities; **une société par** ~**s** a joint stock company; ~ **A/B** A/B share; ~ **gratuite** free share; ~ **nominative** registered share; ~ **ordinaire** ordinary share GB, common share US; ~ **préférentielle** preference share GB, preferred share US

〔Composé〕 ~ **de grâce(s)** thanksgiving

actionnaire /aksjɔnɛʀ/ *nmf* shareholder, stockholder US; **être à 100%** to be the sole shareholder; **petit/gros** ~ minor/major shareholder; ~ **majoritaire/minoritaire** majority/minority shareholder

actionnariat /aksjɔnaʀja/ *nm* ① (fait d'être actionnaire) shareholding; ② (ensemble des actionnaires) shareholders (*pl*)

actionner /aksjɔne/ [1] *vtr* ① (mettre en marche) to activate, to turn on [*sirène, mécanisme*]; ② (faire fonctionner) to operate [*système, turbine*]; ③ Jur to sue

activation /aktivasjɔ̃/ *nf* activation

active ▸ **actif A, B, D**

activement /aktivmɑ̃/ *adv* actively; **participer** ~ **à** to take an active part in

activer /aktive/ [1]
A *vtr* ① (hâter) to speed up [*travail, débat, préparatifs*]; to stimulate [*digestion*]; ② (intensifier) [*vent*] to stir up [*flamme*]; [*personne*] to stoke [*feu*]; ③ Chimie to activate
B [○]*vi* to get a move on[○], to hurry up
C **s'activer** *vpr* ① (s'affairer) to be very busy (**pour faire** doing); **la cuisinière s'activait devant le fourneau** the cook was busy at the stove; ② [○](se dépêcher) to hurry up

activisme /aktivism/ *nm* activism

activiste /aktivist/ *adj, nmf* activist

activité /aktivite/ *nf* ① (occupation) activity; **leurs** ~**s de syndicalistes** their activities as trade unionists; ~ **professionnelle** occupation; **c'est une** ~ **manuelle** it's manual work; **exercer une** ~ **rémunérée** to be gainfully employed; **l'escroc qui exerçait son** ~ **sur la côte** the con-man who operated on the coast; **cesser ses** ~**s** [*entreprise, commerçant*] to stop trading; [*avocat, médecin*] to stop working; **reprendre ses** ~**s** [*entreprise, commerçant*] to start trading again; [*malade, vacancier*] to go back to work; **entrer en** ~ [*entreprise*] to start trading; **l'entrée en** ~ **de la société en 1993** the company's entry into the market in 1993; ② (fonctionnement) activity; ~ **économique** economic activity; **l'**~ **de la rue/ville** the bustle of the street/town; **l'**~ **du volcan** the active state of the volcano; **être en pleine** ~ [*atelier*] to be in full production; [*rue, ville, gare*] to be bustling with activity; **hum** [*personne*] to be very busy; **en** ~ [*volcan*] active; [*usine*] in operation; [*travailleur*] working; [*militaire*] in active service GB *ou* on active duty US; **ses années d'**~ his working years; ③ (énergie) (de personne) energy; **être d'une** ~ **débordante** to be brimming with energy

〔Composé〕 ~ **dirigée** Scol class work

actrice *nf* ▸ **acteur**

actuaire /aktɥɛʀ/ ▸ p. 532 *nmf* actuary

actualisation /aktɥalizasjɔ̃/ *nf* ① (mise à jour) (processus) updating **¢**; (résultat) update; ② Fin conversion to current value; ③ Philos actualization; ④ Ling realization

actualisé, ~**e** /aktɥalize/
A *pp* ▸ **actualiser**
B *pp adj* ① (mis à jour) updated; ② Fin converted to current value

actualiser /aktɥalize/ [1] *vtr* ① (mettre à jour) to update, to bring [sth] up to date [*ouvrage, fichier, méthode*]; ~ **ses connaissances** to brush up one's knowledge; ② Fin to convert [sth] to current value; ③ Philos to actualize; ④ Ling to realize

actualité /aktɥalite/
A *nf* ① (événements) current affairs (*pl*); **ne pas s'intéresser à l'**~ not to be interested in current affairs; **l'**~ **cinématographique** film news; **coller à l'**~ to be up to the minute with the news; **l'**~ **culturelle** cultural events (*pl*); **être sous les feux de l'**~ to be in the spotlight of the media; **être à la une de l'**~ to be in the headlines; ② (d'idées, de débat, livre) topicality; (de réflexion, de pensée) relevance; **sujets d'une brûlante** ~ burning issues; **d'**~ [*thème, question*] topical; **la démission du Premier ministre n'est plus d'**~ the Prime Minister's resignation is no longer at issue; **garder toute son** ~ [*texte, question*] to be still relevant today; ③ Philos actuality
B **actualités** *nfpl* news; (au cinéma) newsreel (*sg*); **les** ~**s télévisées** the television news

actuariel, -ielle /aktɥaʀjɛl/ *adj* Stat [*calcul*] actuarial (*épith*)

〔Composés〕 **taux (d'intérêt)** ~ **brut** Fin yield to maturity before tax; **taux (d'intérêt)** ~ **net** Fin yield to maturity after tax

actuel, -elle /aktɥɛl/ *adj* ① (présent) present, current; **la forme actuelle du traité** the present form of the treaty; **en l'état** ~ **de l'enquête** at the current stage of the enquiry^{GB}; **en l'état** ~ **des connaissances** in the present state of our knowledge; **en l'état** ~ **de la science** as far as science extends today; **à l'époque actuelle** in the present day; **dans le monde** ~ in today's world; **l'**~ **territoire de la Pologne** the territory of present-day Poland; **l'Italie actuelle** present-day Italy; ② (d'actualité) [*œuvre, débat, question*] topical; ③ Philos actual

actuellement /aktɥɛlmɑ̃/ *adv* (en ce moment précis) at the moment, at present; (à notre époque) currently

actus[○] /akty/ *nfpl* TV, Radio news

acuité /akɥite/ *nf* ① (d'intelligence, analyse, de perception) acuteness; **ressentir qch avec** ~ to feel sth keenly; ② (de son) shrillness; ③ (de douleur) intensity; ④ (de problème, crise) seriousness; **le problème se pose avec** ~ this is a burning issue

acupressing /akypʀesiŋ/ *nf* acupressure

acupuncteur, -trice* /akypɔ̃ktœʀ, tʀis/ ▸ p. 532 *nm,f* acupuncturist

acupuncture* /akypɔ̃ktyʀ/ *nf* acupuncture

acutangle /akytɑ̃gl/ *nm* acute-angled triangle

ADAC /adak/ *nm* (abrév = avion à décollage et atterrissage courts) STOL

adage /adaʒ/ *nm* saying, adage

adagio /ada(d)ʒjo/ *nm, adv* adagio

Adam /adɑ̃/ *npr* Adam; **être en tenue d'**~ fig to be in one's birthday suit; ▸ **Ève**

adamantin, ~**e** /adamɑ̃tɛ̃, in/ *adj* liter adamantine

adaptabilité /adaptabilite/ *nf* adaptability (**à** to)

adaptable /adaptabl/ *adj* ① (souple) [*personne, caractère, animal*] adaptable (**à** to); ② (réglable) [*hauteur, équipement*] adjustable; ~ **à toutes les circonstances** *or* **tous les besoins** all-purpose (*épith*)

adaptateur, -trice /adaptatœʀ, tʀis/
A ▸ p. 532 *nm,f* Cin, Théât adapter

a

B nm Tech adapter

adaptation /adaptasjɔ̃/ nf 1 gén, Biol (réajustement) adaptation; **processus/période d'~** process/period of adaptation; **faculté d'~** capacity for adaptation; **~ à** adjustment to; **accomplir un effort d'~** to try to adapt; **avoir des problèmes d'~** to have difficulty in adapting; 2 Cin, Mus, Théât adaptation; **~ au cinéma/à la télévision/au théâtre** film/TV/stage adaptation; **~ d'un roman** adaptation of a novel; **~ libre** loose adaptation

adapté, ~e /adapte/
A pp ▸ adapter
B pp adj 1 (approprié) [logement, emploi, produit, spectacle] suitable (à for); **~ aux circonstances** or **à la situation** suited to the circumstances; 2 (inséré) [personne] adjusted (à to); **un élève mal ~** a maladjusted pupil; **le personnel est maintenant ~ aux nouveaux horaires** the staff has now got GB ou gotten US used to the new timetable; 3 Cin, Théât adapted (à, pour for; de from); 4 Tech (modifié) [équipement, conception, version] adapted

adapter /adapte/ [1]
A vtr 1 Tech (poser) to fit [tuyau, pneu, moteur] (à to); 2 Tech (modifier) to adapt [équipement]; 3 (rendre conforme) to adapt [loi, formation] (à to); **~ l'offre à la demande** to adapt supply to demand; 4 (former) **~ le personnel aux nouvelles technologies** to get the staff to adapt to new technologies; 5 Cin, Théât [personne] to adapt [roman] (à, pour for)
B s'adapter vpr 1 Tech (s'insérer) [outil, pièce] to fit (dans into); 2 (s'habituer) [personne] to adapt (à to); 3 (être approprié) [discours, politique, méthode] to be suited (à to)

ADAV /adav/ nm (abbr = **avion à décollage et atterrissage verticaux**) VTOL

addenda* /adɛ̃da/ nm inv addendum; **des ~** addenda

Addis-Abeba /adisabeba/ ▸ p. 894 npr Addis Ababa

additif, -ive /aditif, iv/
A adj Math additive
B nm 1 Chimie, Ind (substance) additive; 2 Jur (article, clause) rider (à to)

addition /adisjɔ̃/ nf 1 Math addition ₵; **il sait déjà faire les ~s** he can already do addition; **faire une erreur d'~** to make a mistake in the addition; **vérifier des ~s** to check sums; **ton ~ est fausse** your sum is wrong; **l'~ des voix** the counting of the votes; 2 Chimie (ajout) addition; 3 (accumulation) accumulation; **l'~ des preuves** the accumulation of evidence; 4 (dans un restaurant) bill, check US; **une ~ de 100 euros** a bill for 100 euros; 5 (dépense) bill; **payer l'~** lit to foot the bill; fig to pay for it; **le projet a représenté une ~ de plusieurs milliards** the project has cost several billion

additionnel, -elle /adisjɔnɛl/ adj [taxe, clause] additional

additionner /adisjɔne/ [1]
A vtr 1 Math [personne, calculatrice] to add (up) [chiffres, quantités]; **~ qch à qch** to add sth to sth; 2 (ajouter) to add; **~ une sauce de cognac** to add cognac to a sauce; **vin additionné de sucre** wine with sugar added; 3 (accumuler) to accumulate [erreurs, échecs]; **elle additionne bêtise sur bêtise** she makes one stupid mistake after another
B s'additionner vpr 1 (s'accumuler) [problèmes, erreurs] to add up; 2 **les fractions s'additionnent** fractions can be added

additionneur /adisjɔnœr/ nm Ordinat adder; **~ complet/parallèle/série** full/parallel/serial adder

adducteur /adyktœr/ nm adductor

adduction /adyksjɔ̃/ nf Physiol adduction

(Composé) **~ d'eau** Gén Civ water conveyance; **travaux d'~ d'eau** work on the water supply system

Adélaïde /adelaid/ ▸ p. 894 npr Adelaide

Adélie /adeli/ npr Géog **terre ~** Adélie Land

Aden /adɛn/ ▸ p. 894 npr Aden

adénome /adenom/ nm adenoma

adénovirus /adenoviʀys/ nm inv adenovirus

adepte /adɛpt/ nmf (de secte) follower; (de doctrine) supporter; (de personne) disciple; (de sport, d'activité) enthusiast; **c'est une ~ de la bicyclette** she's a cycling enthusiast

adéquat, ~e /adekwa, at/ adj 1 (approprié) [réponse, environnement, choix] appropriate; [équipement, outil] suitable; 2 (suffisant) [niveau, formation, soins] adequate

adéquation /adekwasjɔ̃/ nf 1 (conformité) appropriateness (de of; à, avec to); **en ~ avec qch** in accord with sth; 2 Sci (de modèle) adequacy (à to)

adhérence /aderɑ̃s/ nf 1 Tech (de colle, papier) adhesion (à to); (de pneu, semelle) grip; 2 Méd adhesion

adhérent, ~e /aderɑ̃, ɑ̃t/
A adj [matière] which adheres (à to) (après n); [pneu] with a good grip (après n)
B nm,f (membre) member; **les ~s du parti/club** the party/club members

adhérer /adere/ [14] vtr ind 1 (coller) [colle, tissu] to stick (à to), to adhere (à to); **le pneu adhère à la route** the tyre GB ou tire US grips the road; 2 (s'inscrire) **~ à** to join [parti, syndicat]; to become a member of [organisme]; (être membre) to be a member of; 3 (se rallier) **~ à** to subscribe to [doctrine, thèse, politique]

adhésif, -ive /adezif, iv/
A adj adhesive
B nm (matière) adhesive; **~ thermocollant** iron-on adhesive

adhésion /adezjɔ̃/ nf 1 (appartenance) membership (à of GB, in US); 2 (inscription) **l'~ est gratuite** membership is free; **l'~ n'est pas obligatoire** you don't have to join; **l'~ d'un pays à la UE** the entry of a country into the EU; **le club a enregistré dix ~s** the club has enrolled ten members; 3 (soutien) support (à for); **~ à une cause** support for a cause; **mon ~ à votre point de vue est totale** I completely support your point of view

ad hoc /adɔk/ loc adj inv ad hoc

adieu, pl **~x** /adjø/ nm goodbye, farewell sout; **se dire ~** to say one's goodbyes, to say goodbye (to each other); **dire ~ à qn, faire ses ~x à qn** to say goodbye to sb, to bid sb farewell sout; **dire ~ à qch** to say goodbye to sth; **un discours/une lettre/un baiser d'~** a farewell speech/letter/kiss; **faire un geste/un sourire d'~** to wave/smile goodbye (à to); **donner** or **offrir un pot○/un dîner d'~** to give a farewell drink/dinner; **faire ses ~x à la scène** to take one's leave of the stage; **~ le ski** it's goodbye to skiing

adipeux, -euse /adipø, øz/ adj 1 Anat [tissu, cellule] fatty, adipose spéc; 2 gén [personne, visage] podgy; [ventre] fat

adiposité /adipozite/ nf 1 (caractère) adiposity spéc; 2 (amas graisseux) surplus fat ₵

adjacent, ~e /adʒasɑ̃, ɑ̃t/ adj adjacent (à to)

adjectif, -ive /adʒɛktif, iv/
A adj [forme, locution] adjectival
B nm adjective; **~ attribut/possessif/qualificatif** predicative/possessive/qualifying adjective; **~ déterminatif** determiner

adjectival, ~e, mpl **-aux** /adʒɛktival, o/ adj adjectival

adjoindre /adʒwɛ̃dr/ [56]
A vtr **on m'a adjoint un nouvel assistant** I've been assigned a new assistant; **~ de nouveaux collaborateurs à son personnel** to take on some extra staff; **~ une pièce au dossier** to attach a document to the file
B s'adjoindre vpr to take on [collaborateur, équipe]; **l'organisation vient de s'~ les services d'un juriste** the organization has just engaged the services of a lawyer

adjoint, ~e /adʒwɛ̃, ɛ̃t/
A nm,f Entr assistant; **l'~ du directeur** the manager's assistant
B nm Ling adjunct

(Composé) **~ au maire** Admin deputy mayor

adjonction /adʒɔ̃ksjɔ̃/ nf addition (à to)

adjudant /adʒydɑ̃/ ▸ p. 406 nm Mil (terre) ≈ warrant officer class II GB, ≈ warrant officer US; (air) intermediate rank between flight sergeant and warrant officer GB, ≈ warrant officer US; **oui, mon ~** lit yes, sir; fig yes, sergeant

adjudant-chef, pl **adjudants-chefs** /adʒydɑ̃ʃɛf/ ▸ p. 406 nm ≈ warrant officer class I GB, ≈ chief warrant officer US

adjudicataire /adʒydikatɛr/ nmf 1 (dans une vente) successful buyer; 2 (de contrat) contractor

adjudicateur, -trice /adʒydikatœr, tris/ nm,f 1 (possesseur) vendor; 2 (intermédiaire) auctioneer

adjudication /adʒydikasjɔ̃/ nf 1 (de biens) auction; **par ~** by auction; 2 (de contrat) tender; **~ ouverte** competitive tender; **par ~** by tender; 3 (d'emprunt) bid

(Composé) **~ judiciaire** Jur sale by order of the court

adjuger /adʒyʒe/ [13]
A vtr 1 (vendre aux enchères) to auction; **adjugé 1 000 euros** auctioned for 1,000 euros; **vase adjugé 400 euros à qn** vase sold to sb at auction for 400 euros; **une fois, deux fois adjugé! vendu!** going, going, gone!; 2 (attribuer) to award (à to); **prix littéraire adjugé à un jeune écrivain** literary prize awarded to a young writer; **se voir ~ un contrat** to win a contract; **~ une récompense à qn** to give sb a reward
B s'adjuger vpr [personne] to grant oneself [repas, part]; [sportif, équipe] to take [coupe, titre]; [action] to gain [plus-value]

adjuration /adʒyrasjɔ̃/ nf plea

adjurer /adʒyre/ [1] vtr to implore (de faire to do), to beg (de faire to do)

adjuvant /adʒyvɑ̃/ nm 1 Méd adjuvant; 2 Chimie additive

ad libitum /adlibitɔm/ loc adv [jouer, discuter] ad lib; [boire] as much as one likes

ADM /adeɛm/ nf (abbr = **arme de destruction massive**) WMD

admettre /admɛtr/ [60] vtr 1 (reconnaître) to accept, to admit [fait, hypothèse]; to admit [tort, échec, erreur]; **il faut (bien) ~ que la situation est difficile** it has to be admitted that the situation is difficult; **tout en admettant qu'ils ne l'aient pas fait exprès** whilst accepting that they didn't do it deliberately; **je dois ~ que j'ai eu tort/que tu avais raison** I have to admit I was wrong/you were right; 2 (accepter) to accept [principe, idée, droit]; to admit [personne] (dans to); **un club qui admet les enfants** a club which admits children; **avoir du mal à ~ qch** to have difficulty accepting sth; **la société admet mal ce genre de protestation** society does not readily accept this sort of protest; **tant qu'on ne voudra pas ~ cet état de fait** as long as there is a refusal to accept this state of affairs; **ils n'ont jamais bien admis leur nouveau chef** they've never really accepted their new boss; **le plus difficile à ~ pour eux** the most difficult thing for them to accept; **faire ~ qch à qn** to get sb to accept sth; **elle n'a pas réussi à se faire ~ comme déléguée/dans leur société/à ce poste** she didn't get accepted as a delegate/in their company/for this post; **je n'admets pas que l'on soit en retard** I won't tolerate people being late; **nous n'admettrons aucune exception** no exceptions will be made; **je n'admets pas qu'on me traite de cette façon/qu'on me parle sur ce ton** I won't be treated in this way/be spoken to in this way; 3 (supposer) **~ que** to suppose (that); **admettez qu'il vienne plus tôt que prévu** suppose he comes earlier than expected; **admettons que vous ayez raison/qu'il ne se soit rien passé** let's suppose (that) you're right/that nothing happened; **même en admettant que ce soit/que tu puisses** even supposing (that) it is/(that) you can; **'suppose que**

a

je gagne!'—'bon, admettons' 'suppose I win!'—'all right then, suppose you do'; **4** Scol, Univ (accepter) to admit (**en** to); **les professeurs n'ont pas voulu m'~ en classe supérieure sans examen** the teachers wouldn't let me move up unless I took an exam; **il n'a pas été admis à se présenter à l'examen** he wasn't allowed to take the exam; **les enfants admis à l'école** children admitted to school; **être admis à l'oral** to get through to the oral; **elle a été admise au concours** she passed the exam; **5** (recevoir) [*personne, local*] to admit (**à** to); **le roi l'admet à sa table** he's admitted to the king's table; **l'huissier m'a admis dans une salle d'attente** the usher showed me into a waiting room; **nos salles de classe ne peuvent ~ que 20 élèves** our classrooms can only hold 20 pupils; **le musée n'admet les visiteurs que par groupes de 20 personnes** visitors are only admitted to the museum in groups of 20; **être admis à la maternité/à l'hôpital** to be admitted to the maternity ward/to hospital; **6** (autoriser) fml **~ qn à faire** to allow sb to do; **7** Tech (laisser passer) to let [sth] through [*liquide, vapeur*]

administrateur, -trice /administʀatœʀ, tʀis/ ▸ p. 532 *nm,f* **1** Admin (d'organisme, de bibliothèque, théâtre) administrator; **~ général** general administrator; **2** Fin (membre du conseil d'administration) director; **~ délégué** executive director; **3** Jur (de fondation, succession) trustee; **4** (gestionnaire) administrator; **bon/mauvais ~** good/bad administrator; **avoir des qualités d'~** to have administrative skills

(Composés) **~ de biens** property manager; **~ civil** ≈ senior civil servant; **~ colonial** Hist colonial administrator; **~ judiciaire** (de faillite) receiver; (de succession) administrator; **~ légal** (des biens d'un mineur) guardian; (d'un patrimoine) trustee; **~ de site Internet** webmaster

administratif, -ive /administʀatif, iv/ **A** *adj* **1** (relatif à l'administration) [*bâtiment, retard, personnel, réforme*] administrative; **2** (émis par l'administration) official; **courrier/document/rapport ~** official mail/document/report **B** *nm,f* **être un ~** to work in administration; **les ~s** the administrative staff

administration /administʀasjɔ̃/ *nf* **1** Admin, Pol (appareil) administration; **~ centrale/civile/publique** central/civil/public administration; **~ américaine/française** American/French administration; **2** (fonction publique) civil service; **haute ~** senior civil service; **entrer dans l'~** to go into the civil service; **3** (contrôle) administration; **~ d'une ville** administration of a city; **sous ~ militaire** under military rule; **4** (gestion) management; **~ des entreprises** business management; **5** (octroi) (de médicament, sacrement) administration; (de preuve) furnishing

(Composés) **~ douanière** customs service; **~ fiscale** Fisc Inland Revenue GB, Internal Revenue US; **~ judiciaire** Jur receivership; **être placé sous ~ judiciaire** to go into receivership; **être sous ~ judiciaire** to be in receivership; **~ légale** Jur trusteeship; **~ militaire** military administration; **~ pénitentiaire** prison service; **~ territoriale** regional administration

administrativement /administʀativmɑ̃/ *adv* administratively

administré, ~e /administʀe/ **A** *pp* ▸ **administrer** **B** *pp adj* **bien/mal ~** well/badly run **C** *nm,f* constituent

administrer /administʀe/ [1] **A** *vtr* **1** (gérer) to administer [*projet, fonds*]; to run [*économie, pays, compagnie*]; **2** (donner) to administer [*médicament, sacrement*] (**à** to); to produce [*preuve*]; **3** (infliger) **~ une correction à qn** to give sb a good hiding; **~ des coups à qn** to deliver blows

B **s'administrer** *vpr* [*médicament*] to be administered

admirable /admiʀabl/ *adj* admirable; **être ~ de dévouement** to show admirable devotion; **des soldats ~s de courage** soldiers of exemplary courage; **se comporter de manière ~** to behave admirably; **s'exprimer dans une langue ~** to express oneself with admirable elegance

admirablement /admiʀabləmɑ̃/ *adv* [*s'exprimer, travailler, réussir, jouer*] admirably; [*ouvragé, brodé, vêtu, construit, cuisiné*] superbly

admirateur, -trice /admiʀatœʀ, tʀis/ *nm,f* admirer

admiratif, -ive /admiʀatif, iv/ *adj* [*personne, air, regard*] admiring (*épith*); **tous les spectateurs étaient ~s** all the spectators were full of admiration; **elle poussa un cri ~** she gave a cry of admiration

admiration /admiʀasjɔ̃/ *nf* admiration (**pour** for); **regarder qn/qch avec ~** to look at sb/sth in admiration; **être en ~ devant qn/qch** to be lost in admiration for sb/sth; **forcer l'~** to command admiration; **remplir qn d'~** to fill sb with admiration; **faire l'~ de qn** to be admired by sb; **avoir de l'~ pour qn** to admire sb; **être digne d'~** to be admirable

admirativement /admiʀativmɑ̃/ *adv* admiringly

admirer /admiʀe/ [1] *vtr* to admire; **c'est un homme très admiré** he's much admired; **~ qn de faire** to admire sb for doing

admis, ~e /admi, iz/ **A** *pp* ▸ **admettre** **B** *pp adj* (reconnu) [*opinion, pratique, théorie*] accepted, admitted; **selon une idée/thèse généralement ~e** according to a generally accepted idea/theory; **il est généralement ~ que** it is generally accepted *ou* admitted that; **être bien ~** [*principe, méthode, idée*] to be widely accepted **C** *nm,f* Scol, Univ successful candidate; **publier la liste des ~** to publish the list of successful candidates *ou* the pass list; **la liste des ~ au concours** the list of successful candidates in the exam

admissibilité /admisibilite/ *nf* **1** (d'étudiant) eligibility (*to take oral after written examination*); **2** (de preuve, témoignage) admissibility; **3** (d'hypothèse, argument) acceptability

admissible /admisibl/ *adj* **1** (tolérable) [*dose, seuil, comportement, écart*] acceptable; **2** Jur [*preuve, témoignage*] admissible; **3** Philos, Sci [*théorie, hypothèse, argument*] acceptable; **4** Univ [*étudiant*] eligible (*to take oral after written examination*)

admission /admisjɔ̃/ *nf* **1** (accueil) admission (**à, en** to); **~ d'un patient/élève/candidat** admission of a patient/pupil/candidate; **~ à la UE/au FMI** admission to the EU/to the IMF; **~ à l'hôpital/l'enseignement supérieur** admission to hospital/higher education; **~ en maison de retraite** admission to a retirement home; **~ sur examen** admission by entrance examination; **~ sur dossier** admission based on work experience and qualifications; **~ sur titres** admission based on certified qualifications; **demande** *or* **formulaire d'~** application form; **faire une demande d'~** to fill in an application form; **bureau** *or* **service des ~s** reception; **2** (droit) **~ à** eligibility for; **~ à l'aide sociale** eligibility for social security; **3** (reconnaissance) admission (**de la part de** by; **que** that); **4** Mécan intake; **régler l'~** to adjust the intake

(Composés) **~ à la cote** Fin listing; **~ temporaire** Fisc temporary importation

admonestation /admɔnɛstasjɔ̃/ *nf* admonition; **faire des ~s à qn** to admonish sb

admonester /admɔnɛste/ [1] *vtr* to admonish

admonition /admɔnisjɔ̃/ *nf* admonition

ADN /adeɛn/ *nm* (*abbr* = **acide désoxyribonucléique**) DNA

ado○ /ado/ *nmf* teenager

adolescence /adɔlesɑ̃s/ *nf* adolescence; **les premières années de l'~** early adolescence; **à l'~** during adolescence *ou* the teenage years

adolescent, ~e /adɔlesɑ̃, ɑ̃t/ **A** *adj* adolescent, teenage (*épith*) **B** *nm,f* teenager, adolescent

adonis /adɔnis/ *nm inv* fig Adonis

Adonis /adɔnis/ *npr* Mythol Adonis

adonner: s'adonner /adɔne/ [1] *vpr* **s'~ à** to devote oneself to [*travail, sport, art*]; **s'~ au plaisir** to live a debauched life; **il s'adonnait à la boisson** he used to drink too much

adopter /adɔpte/ [1] *vtr* **1** Jur to adopt [*enfant*]; **2** (prendre chez soi) to adopt, to take in [*animal, personne*]; **3** (accepter) to accept; **il a vite été adopté par le village** he was soon accepted by the village; **je me suis tout de suite senti adopté par mes nouveaux amis** I immediately felt at home with my new friends; **4** (choisir) to adopt [*méthode, style, attitude, mode*]; **5** (approuver) to take up [*projet*]; to adopt [*proposition, réforme*]; **~ une loi** to pass a law

adoptif, -ive /adɔptif, iv/ *adj* [*enfant*] adopted; [*parent, famille*] adoptive; [*village, pays*] adopted

adoption /adɔpsjɔ̃/ *nf* **1** Jur adoption; **2** (par choix) adoption; **pays/famille d'~** adopted country/family; **Anglais d'~** English by adoption; **3** (de loi) passing; (de proposition, politique, réforme, texte) adoption

adorable /adɔʀabl/ *adj* adorable

adorablement /adɔʀabləmɑ̃/ *adv* [*vêtu*] delightfully; [*naïf*] charmingly

adorateur, -trice /adɔʀatœʀ, tʀis/ *nm,f* **1** (d'un dieu) worshipperᴳᴮ; **2** (d'une personne) fervent admirer

adoration /adɔʀasjɔ̃/ *nf* **1** (action de rendre hommage) worship, adoration; **être en ~ devant qn/qch** to worship sb/sth; **2** (sentiment) adoration; **avoir de l'~ pour qn** to adore sb

adorer /adɔʀe/ [1] **A** *vtr* **1** (aimer) to love; (plus fort) to adore; **2** Relig to worship, to adore **B** **s'adorer** *vpr* **1** (l'un l'autre) to adore one another; **2** (soi-même) **elle s'adore** she thinks she's wonderful

(Idiome) **brûler ce qu'on a adoré** to turn against what one used to hold dear

adosser /adose/ [1] **A** *vtr* **1** (appuyer) to lean [sb/sth] (**à** on; **contre** against); **être adossé à qch** [*personne*] to be leaning against sth; **~ un meuble contre un mur** to stand a piece of furniture against a wall; (un peu incliné) to lean a piece of furniture against a wall; **2** (placer à côté) **~ une maison contre qch** to build a house backing on to sth **B** **s'adosser** *vpr* **1** (s'appuyer) [*personne*] **s'~ à/contre qch** to lean back on/against sth, to lean one's back on/against sth; **2** (être à côté de) [*maison, village*] **s'~ à qch** to back onto sth

adoubement /adubmɑ̃/ *nm* dubbing

adouber /adube/ [1] *vtr* **1** (aux échecs) to adjust; **2** Hist to dub

adoucir /adusiʀ/ [3] **A** *vtr* **1** (rendre plus doux) to soften [*peau, tissu, eau, éclairage, expression*]; to soothe [*gorge*]; to moderate [*son, voix*]; to tone down [*langage*]; to sweeten [*boisson, mets*]; **cette coiffure t'adoucit les traits** this hairstyle softens your features; **~ la réalité** to soften reality; **~ le métal** Tech to soften metal; **~ les angles** to soften the angles; **2** (rendre moins pénible) to alleviate [*misère, conditions*]; to ease [*sort, chagrin*]; to mitigate [*rigueur, régime*] **B** **s'adoucir** *vpr* **1** (devenir plus doux) [*température*] to become milder; [*lumière, voix*] to become softer; [*pente*] to become more gentle; ② (devenir moins pénible) [chagrin] to be soothed; [conditions] to be alleviated

(Idiome) **la musique adoucit les mœurs** music soothes the savage breast

adoucissant, ~e /adusisɑ̃, ɑ̃t/
A adj Cosmét [lotion, lait] soothing; **crème** ~e soothing skin cream
B nm Tex softener

adoucissement /adusismɑ̃/ nm (de température) improvement (**de** in); (de conditions) alleviation (**de** of); (de voix) softening (**de** of)

adoucisseur /adusisœʀ/ nm ~ **d'eau** water softener

ad patres /adpatʀɛs/ loc adv **envoyer qn** ~ to send sb to meet his/her maker

adragante /adʀagɑ̃t/ nf **gomme** ~ (gum) tragacanth

adrénaline /adʀenalin/ nf adrenalin

adressable /adʀesabl/ adj addressable; **mémoire** ~ addressable memory

adressage /adʀɛsaʒ/ nm addressing

(Composé) ~ **par domaines** Ordinat domain name system, DNS

adresse /adʀɛs/ nf ① (domicile) address; ~ **postale** postal GB ou mailing US address; **c'est une bonne** ~ [restaurant, magasin] it's a good place; **faire un changement d'**~ to notify one's change of address; **partir sans laisser d'**~ to leave without a forwarding address; **se tromper d'**~ fig (de personne) to pick the wrong person, to get the wrong number◦ US fig; (de lieu) to get the wrong address; **une remarque lancée à l'**~ **de qn** a remark directed at sb; **a-t-il dit à l'**~ **des participants** he said for the benefit of the participants; ② (habileté physique) dexterity; **jongler avec** ~ to juggle with dexterity; **exercer son** ~ **au tir** to practise[GB] one's shooting; ③ (habileté intellectuelle) skill; **avec** ~ skilfully[GB]; ④ (allocution) address; ~ **retransmise à la télévision** address broadcast on TV; ⑤ Ling (en lexicographie) headword; (en sociolinguistique) address; **forme** or **formule d'**~ form of address; ⑥ Ordinat address

(Composés) ~ **électronique** email address; ~ **e-mail** email address; ~ **réticulaire** universal resource locator, URL; ~ **universelle** universal resource locator, URL

adresser /adʀese/ [1]
A vtr ① (destiner) to direct [critique, menace, propos] (**à** at); to put [demande, question] (**à** to); to make [déclaration]; to deliver [ultimatum, message, mise en garde] (**à** to); to present [recommandation, pétition, témoignage] (**à** to); to put out [appel] (**à** to); to aim [coup] (**à** at); **cette remarque m'était adressée** that remark was directed at me; ~ **la parole à qn** to speak to sb; ~ **un sourire à qn** to smile at sb; ~ **un sourire complice à qn** to give sb a conspiratorial smile; ~ **un regard à qn** to look at sb; ~ **des éloges** or **louanges à qn** to praise sb; ~ **la parole à qn** to speak to sb; ② (expédier) to send [lettre, questionnaire]; **note adressée par télécopie** memorandum sent by fax; ③ (écrire l'adresse) to address [lettre, colis]; **lettre bien/mal adressée** correctly/incorrectly addressed letter; **adressé à mon nom** addressed to me personally; ④ (diriger) to refer [personne] (**à** to sb); ~ **un patient à un spécialiste** to refer a patient to a specialist
B s'adresser vpr ① (parler) **s'**~ **à qn** to speak to sb; **s'**~ **à la foule** to speak to ou to address the crowd; ② (contacter) **s'**~ **à** to contact; **s'**~ **au consulat** to contact the consulate; **s'**~ **à une firme japonaise** to go to a Japanese firm; **pour tous renseignements, s'**~ **à...** for all information, contact...; **adressez-vous au guichet 2** go to window 2; **adressez-vous au bureau d'information** go and ask at the information desk; **adresse-toi à ton père** ask your father; **pour les visas, adressez-vous au consulat** apply to the consulate for visas; ③ (être destiné) **s'**~ **à** [mesure, invention] to be aimed at; (toucher) **s'**~ **à** to appeal to [conscience, instinct]; ④ (échanger) to exchange [salut,

signe, reproche, lettres]; **s'**~ **la parole** to speak to each other

adret /adʀɛ/ nm sunny or south-facing side

adriatique /adʀijatik/ adj [côte] Adriatic

Adriatique /adʀijatik/ ▸ p. 579 npr f **la mer** ~, **l'**~ the Adriatic

adroit, ~e /adʀwa, at/ adj ① [jongleur, bricoleur, tireur, manœuvre] skilful[GB]; **d'un geste** ~ with a deft movement; **avoir des gestes** ~s to be nimble; **être** ~ **de ses mains** to be good with one's hands; ② [homme politique, diplomate] skilful[GB]; [réponse, discours] clever

adroitement /adʀwatmɑ̃/ adv skilfully[GB]

ADSL /adeɛsɛl/ nm (abbr = Asymmetric Digital Subscriber Line) ADSL; **une connexion** ~ a broadband connection

adulateur, **-trice** /adylatœʀ, tʀis/ nm,f liter adulator liter; pej flatterer

adulation /adylasjɔ̃/ nf adulation

aduler /adyle/ [1] vtr to worship, to adulate

adulte /adylt/
A adj [personne, comportement, relation] adult, grown-up; [démocratie, nation, électorat] mature; [animal, plante] full-grown; **l'âge** ~ adulthood
B nmf adult, grown-up

adultère /adyltɛʀ/
A adj adulterous
B nmf adulterer/adulteress
C nm adultery

adultérin, ~e /adylteʀɛ̃, in/ adj [enfant] born of adultery (après n)

advenir /advəniʀ/ [36] v impers fml ① (se produire) to happen; **quoi qu'il advienne** no matter what happens; **advienne que pourra** come what may; ② (devenir) ~ **de** to become of; **qu'adviendra-t-il de la démocratie?** what will become of democracy?

adventice /advɑ̃tis/ adj adventitious

adventiste /advɑ̃tist/ adj, nmf Adventist

adverbe /advɛʀb/ nm adverb; ~ **de temps/ de manière** adverb of time/manner

adverbial, ~e, pl **-iaux** /advɛʀbjal, o/ adj adverbial

adverbialement /advɛʀbjalmɑ̃/ adv adverbially

adversaire /advɛʀsɛʀ/ nmf gén opponent; Mil adversary

adversatif, **-ive** /advɛʀsatif, iv/ adj adversative

adverse /advɛʀs/ adj [équipe] opposing; [thèse] opposite; [attaque, manœuvre] from the opposite camp; **partie** ou **camp** ~ opposite camp

adversité /advɛʀsite/ nf adversity

ad vitam æternam◦ /advitametɛʀnam/ loc adv till kingdom come

AELE /aaɛla/ nf (abbr = Association européenne de libre échange) EFTA

aérage /aeʀaʒ/ nm Mines ventilation

aérateur /aeʀatœʀ/ nm ventilator

(Composé) ~ **transtympanique** Méd ventilating tube, grommet

aération /aeʀasjɔ̃/ nf (en ouvrant une fenêtre) airing; (avec un appareil) ventilation; **conduit d'**~ airduct

aéré, ~e /aeʀe/
A pp ▸ aérer
B pp adj ① lit (bien) ~ [pièce, chambre] airy, well-ventilated; [mine] well-ventilated; **mal** ~ [pièce, chambre] stuffy, badly-ventilated; [mine] badly-ventilated; ② (espacé) [document, texte] **bien** ~ nicely spaced out; **mal** ~ cramped

aérer /aeʀe/ [14]
A vtr ① (en ouvrant) to air [pièce, draps]; [appareil] to ventilate; ② (faire prendre l'air) **ça m'aère un peu** it gets me out into the fresh air; ③ (sur papier) to space out [devoir, document, lettre]; ④ Agric to aerate [terre, champ]
B s'aérer vpr [personne] to get some fresh air; **s'**~ **l'esprit** to think about something different for a change

aérien, **-ienne** /aeʀjɛ̃, ɛn/ adj ① Aviat [transport, désastre, base, attaque, carte] air (épith);

[photographie] aerial; **liaison aérienne** air link; ② Météo [courant, phénomène] air (épith); ③ (en l'air) [câble, circuit] overhead; [racine, plante] aerial; **métro** ~ elevated section of the underground GB ou subway US; ④ (léger) [démarche] floating; [grâce] exquisite; [musique] ethereal

aérobic /aeʀobik/ ▸ p. 469 nm aerobics (+ v sg)

aérobie /aeʀobi/
A adj aerobic
B nm aerobe

aérobiose /aeʀobjoz/ nf aerobiosis

aéro-club, pl ~**s*** /aeʀoklœb/ nm flying club

aérodrome /aeʀodʀom/ nm aerodrome GB, (small) airfield

(Composé) ~ **de dégagement** alternate aerodrome ou airfield

aérodynamique /aeʀodinamik/
A adj aerodynamic
B nf aerodynamics (+ v sg)

aérodynamisme /aeʀodinamism/ nm (de voiture, d'avion) aerodynamic properties

aérofrein /aeʀofʀɛ̃/ nm air brake

aérogare /aeʀogaʀ/ nf (air) terminal; ~ **2** terminal 2

aérogénérateur /aeʀoʒeneʀatœʀ/ nm wind generator

aéroglisseur /aeʀogliscœʀ/ nm hovercraft

aérogramme /aeʀogʀam/ nm aerogram, air letter

aérographe /aeʀogʀaf/ nm airbrush; **peinture à l'**~ airbrushing

aérolithe /aeʀolit/ nm aerolite

aéromaritime /aeʀomaʀitim/ adj [compagnie, filiale] air and sea

aéromodélisme /aeʀomodelism/ nm model aircraft making; **un club d'**~ a model aircraft club; **faire de l'**~ to make model aircraft

aéronaute /aeʀonot/ nmf aeronaut

aéronautique /aeʀonotik/
A adj [construction, industrie] aeronautics; [ingénieur] aeronautical
B nf aeronautics (+ v sg); **le marché de l'**~ the aeronautics market

aéronaval, ~e /aeʀonaval/
A adj [opération, forces, base] air and sea
B aéronavale nf Fleet Air Arm GB, Naval Aviation US

aéronef /aeʀonɛf/ nm aircraft

aérophagie /aeʀofaʒi/ ▸ p. 283 nf aerophagia spéc; **faire de l'**~ to suffer from aerophagia

aéroplane† /aeʀoplan/ nm aeroplane GB, airplane US

aéroport /aeʀopɔʀ/ nm airport

aéroporté, ~e /aeʀopɔʀte/ adj [troupes, opération] airborne; [missile, arme, matériel] transported by air

aéroportuaire /aeʀopɔʀtɥɛʀ/ adj [équipement, trafic, capacité] airport

aéropostal, ~e, mpl **-aux** /aeʀopɔstal, o/ adj [compagnie, service] airmail

aérosol /aeʀosɔl/ nm ① (suspension) aerosol; ② (bombe, système) aerosol; **un déodorant/ insecticide en** ~ an aerosol deodorant/ insecticide

aérospatial, ~e, mpl **-iaux** /aeʀospasjal, o/
A adj [industrie] aerospace (épith); [véhicule, lanceur] space
B aérospatiale nf (industrie) aerospace industry

aérostat /aeʀosta/ nm aerostat

aérostatique /aeʀostatik/
A adj Aviat [technique] aerostatic; **un vol** ~ a flight in an aerostat
B nf aerostatics (+ v sg)

aérostier /aeʀostje/ nm aerostat pilot

aéroterrestre /aeʁotɛʁɛstʁ/ adj [*division, opération*] air and land

aérotrain® /aeʁotʁɛ̃/ nm hovertrain

AFAT /afat, aɛfate/ nf (*abbr = auxiliaire féminin de l'armée de terre*) women's component of the French army

affabilité /afabilite/ nf courtesy, affability

affable /afabl/ adj [*personne, attitude, propos*] courteous, affable

affablement /afabləmɑ̃/ adv courteously

affabulateur, -trice /afabylatœʁ, tʁis/ nm,f storyteller

affabulation /afabylasjɔ̃/ nf ① (invention) fabrication ₵; **ce sont des ~s** that's pure fabrication; ② Littérat (de roman, récit) construction of the plot

affabuler /afabyle/ [1] vi to tell tall stories

affacturage /afaktyʁaʒ/ nm factoring

affadir /afadiʁ/ [3]
Ⓐ vtr ① lit to make [sth] tasteless ou insipid [*sauce, plat*]; ② fig [*auteur, corrections*] to make [sth] dull [*texte, personnage*]
Ⓑ **s'affadir** vpr ① lit [*plat*] to lose its flavour^GB; [*odeur*] to fade; ② fig [*intérêt*] to fade; [*argument*] to lose impact

affadissement /afadismɑ̃/ nm ① (de nourriture, goût) loss of flavour^GB; (de couleur, d'odeur) fading; ② (de style) weakening, loss of impact

affaiblir /afɛbliʁ/ [3]
Ⓐ vtr to weaken [*personne, démocratie, sens, monnaie*]; to reduce [*capacité, impact*]; to dull [*intelligence, sentiments*]; **~ les forces de qn** to sap sb's strength; **~ la portée d'un texte de loi** to reduce the scope of a law
Ⓑ **s'affaiblir** vpr [*autorité, gouvernement, économie, pont*] to be weakened; [*personne, voix, vue, détermination, volonté*] to get weaker; [*bruit*] to grow fainter; [*force, courage, capacité*] to diminish; [*santé, mémoire*] to deteriorate; **l'euro s'affaiblit (face au dollar)** the euro is weakening (against the dollar); **l'euro s'est affaibli face au dollar** the euro has fallen against the dollar; **le sens du mot s'est affaibli** the meaning of the word has weakened; **sortir affaibli d'une maladie** to be drained by an illness

affaiblissement /afɛblismɑ̃/ nm ① (de personne, pays, monnaie, sens) (processus) weakening; (état) weakened state; ② (de bruit, vue, santé) fading; ③ (de volonté, courage, détermination) diminishing; ④ (de style, d'œuvre) **les critiques ont remarqué l'~ de son style dans ses derniers écrits** critics have noted that his style lost its edge in his later writings; ⑤ (de volume, quantité) reduction (**de** in)

affaire /afɛʁ/
Ⓐ nf ① (ensemble de faits) gén affair; (à caractère politique, militaire) crisis, affair; (à caractère délictueux, scandaleux) (d'ordre général) scandal; (de cas unique) affair; (soumis à la justice) case; **une mystérieuse ~** a mysterious affair; **l'~ des otages** the hostage crisis ou affair; **l'~ de Suez** the Suez crisis; **une ~ politique/de corruption** a political/corruption scandal; **l'~ des fausses factures** the scandal of the bogus invoices; **~ civile/criminelle** civil/criminal case; **il a été condamné pour une ~ de drogue** he was convicted in a drug case; ② (histoire, aventure) affair; **une ~ délicate** a delicate matter ou affair; **une drôle d'~** an odd affair; **j'ignore tout de cette ~** I don't know anything about the matter; **pour une ~ de cœur** for an affair of the heart; **être mêlé à une sale ~** to be mixed up in some nasty business; **quelle ~!** what a business ou to-do!; **c'est une ~ d'argent/d'héritage** there's money/an inheritance involved; **et voilà toute l'~** and that's that; ③ (occupation, chose à faire) matter, business; **c'est une ~ qui m'a pris beaucoup de temps** it's a matter that has taken up a lot of my time; **il est parti pour une ~ urgente** he's gone off on some urgent business; **c'est toute une ~** it's quite a business; **c'est une**

(tout) autre ~ that's another matter (entirely); **ce n'est pas une petite** or **mince ~** it's no small ou simple matter; **c'est mon ~, pas la vôtre** that's my business, not yours; **c'est l'~ de tous** it's something which concerns everyone ou us all; **ça ne change rien à l'~** that doesn't change a thing; **l'~ se présente bien/mal** things are looking good/bad; **j'en fais mon ~** I'll deal with it
④ (spécialité) **il connaît bien son ~** he knows his business; **c'est une ~ d'hommes/de femmes** it's men's/women's business; **c'est une ~ de garçons/filles** it's boys'/girls' stuff péj; **la mécanique/soudure, c'est leur ~** mechanics/welding is their thing; **c'est une ~ de spécialistes** it's a case for the specialists
⑤ (transaction) deal; **une bonne/mauvaise ~** a good/bad deal; **conclure une ~** to make ou to strike a deal; **l'~ a été conclue** or **faite** the deal was settled; **faire ~ avec qn** to make a deal with sb; **la belle ~○!** big deal○!; ▸ **sac**
⑥ (achat avantageux) bargain; **à ce prix-là, c'est une ~** at that price, it's a bargain; **j'ai fait une ~** I got a bargain; **tu y feras des ~s** you'll find bargains there; **on ne fait plus beaucoup d'~s au marché aux puces** there aren't any bargains to be had at the flea market any more; **j'ai acheté cette robe en solde mais je n'ai pas fait une ~** I bought this dress in the sales but it wasn't a good buy
⑦ (entreprise) business, concern; **~ commerciale/d'import-export/de famille** commercial/import-export/family business ou concern; **de petites ~s** small businesses ou concerns; **~ industrielle** industrial concern; **leur fils a repris l'~** their son took over the business; **c'est elle qui fait marcher l'~** lit she runs the whole business; fig she runs the whole show; **une ~ en or** fig a gold mine
⑧ (question, problème) **c'est une ~ de temps/goût** it's a matter of time/taste; **c'est l'~ de quelques jours/d'un quart d'heure** it'll only take a few days/a quarter of an hour; **c'est ~ de politiciens** it's a matter for the politicians; **c'est l'~ des politiciens** it's the concern of politicians; **il en a fait une ~ personnelle** he took it personally; **en faire toute une ~○** to make a big deal○ of it ou a fuss○ about it; **on ne va pas en faire une ~ d'État○!** let's not make a big issue out of it!; **c'est une ~ de famille** fig it's a family affair
⑨ (difficulté, péril) **être hors** or **tiré d'~** [*malade*] to be in the clear; **s'il obtient le poste, il est tiré d'~** if he gets the job, his problems are over; **se tirer d'~** to get out of trouble; **tirer qn d'~** to get sb out of a spot; **on n'est pas encore sortis** or **tirés d'~** we're not out of the woods yet
⑩ (relation) **avoir ~ à** to be dealing with [*malfaiteur, fou, drogue, fausse monnaie*]; **nous avons ~ à un escroc/faux** we're dealing with a crook/fake; **je le connais mais je n'ai pas souvent ~ à lui** I know him but I don't have much to do with him; **j'ai eu ~ au directeur lui-même** I saw the manager himself; **tu auras ~ à moi!** you'll have me to contend with!
Ⓑ **affaires** nfpl ① (activités lucratives) gén business ₵; (d'une seule personne) business affairs; **être dans les ~s** to be in business; **faire des ~s avec** to do business with; **les ~s sont calmes/au plus bas** business is quiet/at its lowest ebb; **les ~s reprennent** or **marchent mieux** business is picking up; **il gère les ~s de son oncle** he runs his uncle's business affairs; **parler ~s** to talk business; **revenir aux ~s** to go back into business; **avoir le sens des ~s** to have business sense; **voir qn pour ~s** to see sb on business; **voyager pour ~s** to go on a business trip; **le monde des ~s** the business world; **quartier/milieu/lettre/rendez-vous d'~s** business district/circles/letter/appointment; **le français/chinois des ~s** business French/Chinese; **un**

homme dur en ~s a tough businessman
② (problèmes personnels) business ₵; **ça, c'est mes ~s○!** that's my business!; **occupe-toi de tes ~s!** mind your own business!; **se mêler** or **s'occuper des ~s des autres** to interfere ou meddle in other people's business ou affairs; **mettre de l'ordre dans ses ~s** to put one's affairs in order; **parler de ses ~s à tout le monde** to tell everybody one's business; **ça n'arrange pas mes ~s qu'elle vienne** her coming isn't very convenient for me
③ (effets personnels) things, belongings; **mets tes ~s dans le placard** put your things in the cupboard; **mes ~s de sport/de classe** my sports/school things
④ Admin, Pol affairs; **~s publiques/sociales/étrangères** public/social/foreign affairs; **les ~s intérieures d'un pays** a country's internal affairs; **les ~s de l'État** affairs of state

(Composé) **les ~s courantes** gén daily business (sg); Jur Pol day-to-day running of a country

(Idiomes) **être à son ~** to be in one's element; **il/ça fera l'~** he'll/that'll do; **il/ça ne peut pas faire l'~** he/that won't do; **ça a très bien fait l'~** it was just the job; **elle fait** or **fera notre ~** she's just the person we need; **ça fera leur ~** (convenir) that's just what they need; (être avantageux) it'll suit them; **faire** or **régler son ~ à qn○** (tuer) to bump sb off○; (sévir) to sort sb out

affairé, ~e /afeʁe/
Ⓐ pp ▸ **affairer**
Ⓑ pp adj [*personne, air, vie*] busy (**à qch** with sth; **à faire** doing); **avoir l'air ~** to look busy

affairement /afeʁmɑ̃/ nm bustling activity

affairer: s'affairer /afeʁe/ [1] vpr [*personne*] to bustle about; **s'~ auprès de** or **autour de qn** to fuss over sb; **s'~ à faire** to bustle about doing

affairisme /afeʁism/ nm pej wheeling and dealing○

affairiste /afeʁist/ nmf pej wheeler-dealer○

affaissé, ~e /afɛse/
Ⓐ pp ▸ **affaisser**
Ⓑ pp adj [*toiture, pont, joues, épaules, tête*] sagging

affaissement /afɛsmɑ̃/ nm ① (de sol, route) subsidence; (de toit, pont, joues) sagging; ② (de parti politique, valeurs morales) decline (**de** in)

affaisser: s'affaisser /afese/ [1] vpr ① [*route, terrain*] to subside, to sink; [*visage, épaules, chair, toit, pont*] to sag; **faire ~ le pont** to cause the bridge to sag; ② (s'effondrer) [*personne*] to collapse (**sur** on; **dans** into); [*tête*] to droop; ③ (se tasser) **un vieillard qui s'affaisse avec l'âge** an old man who is shrinking ou becoming hunched with age; ④ [*ventes, bénéfices*] to decline

affalé, ~e /afale/
Ⓐ pp ▸ **affaler**
Ⓑ pp adj slumped (**dans** in; **sur** on)

affaler /afale/ [1]
Ⓐ vtr Naut [*personne, marin*] to lower [*voile, cordage*]; **affalez!** lower away!
Ⓑ **s'affaler** vpr ① ○[*de fatigue*] to collapse; (par accident) to fall; ② Naut [*personne*] to slide; **s'~ par une échelle** to slide down a ladder

affamé, ~e /afame/
Ⓐ pp ▸ **affamer**
Ⓑ pp adj ① lit starving; ② fig **~ de** hungry for
Ⓒ nm,f lit, iron (adulte) starving man/woman; (enfant) starving child; **les ~s** the starving

(Idiome) **ventre ~ n'a pas d'oreilles** Prov ≈ a hungry man is an angry man

affamer /afame/ [1] vtr to starve [*personne, pays*]

affameur /afamœʁ/ nm ① lit person who exploits famine situations for financial gain; ② fig employer who pays starvation wages

affect /afɛkt/ nm Psych affect

a

affectation /afɛktasjɔ̃/ *nf* **1** (de bâtiment, matériel, d'argent) allocation (**à** to); **2** (nomination) aussi Mil (à un emploi, une fonction) appointment (**à** to); (dans un lieu, un pays) posting (**à** to); **recevoir une ~** to receive a posting; **lieu d'~** place of work; **3** (comportement) affectation; **sans ~** unaffectedly, without (any) affectation; **avec ~** in an affected way, affectedly; **4** Compta appropriation; **~s budgétaires** budget appropriations; **5** Math **l'~ d'un signe à un nombre** the modification of a number by a sign

affecté, ~e /afɛkte/
A *pp* ▸ **affecter**
B *pp adj* (non naturel) [*langage, manières, personne*] affected

affecter /afɛkte/ [1] *vtr* **1** (feindre) to feign, to affect [*pitié, gaieté, indifférence, tristesse*]; to affect [*genre, comportement*]; to take on, to assume [*forme*]; **~ la surprise** to feign surprise; **innocence/gaieté/pondération affectée** feigned innocence/cheerfulness/levelheadedness; **~ de faire** to pretend to do; **il affecte de ne pas être ému** he pretends not to be moved; **malgré sa tristesse il affecte la gaieté** despite his unhappiness he's putting on a show of cheerfulness; **~ de grands airs** to put on airs; **2** (allouer) to allocate, to assign [*matériel, lieu*] (**à** to); to allocate [*logement, argent*] (**à qn** to sb; **à qch** for sth); **3** (nommer) (à une activité, une fonction, un poste) to appoint (**à**, **en** to); (dans un lieu, un pays, une région) to post (**à**, **en** to); **4** (toucher, affliger) to affect [*pays, marché, cours, autorité, personne*]; **être affecté d'une légère surdité/myopie** to be slightly deaf/short-sighted; **5** Math to modify; **affecté de** modified by

affectif, -ive /afɛktif, iv/ *adj* gén emotional; Psych affective

affection /afɛksjɔ̃/ *nf* **1** (tendresse) affection; **avoir beaucoup d'~ pour** to have a lot of affection for; **prendre qn en ~, se prendre d'~ pour qn** to become fond of sb; **2** Méd complaint; **les ~ cardiaques** heart conditions

affectionné, ~e /afɛksjone/
A *pp* ▸ **affectionner**
B *pp adj* (dans une lettre) **votre neveu ~** your loving nephew; **votre ~** yours affectionately

affectionner /afɛksjone/ [1] *vtr* to be particularly fond of [*chose, activité*]; to be very fond of [*personne*]

affectivité /afɛktivite/ *nf* feelings (*pl*), affectivity spéc

affectueusement /afɛktɥøzmɑ̃/ *adv* affectionately, fondly

affectueux, -euse /afɛktɥø, øz/ *adj* [*personne, geste, lettre, animal*] affectionate; [*caresse, regard*] fond

afférent, ~e /aferɑ̃, ɑ̃t/ *adj* **1** Jur [*héritage*] accruing (**à** to); **2** Anat [*vaisseau, nerf*] afferent (**à** to); **3** [*renseignements, documents*] relative (**à** to), relating (**à** to)

affermage /afɛrmaʒ/ *nm* leasing

affermer /afɛrme/ [1] *vtr* [*propriétaire*] to lease (out) *ou* rent (out); [*locataire*] to rent *ou* lease [*terres, domaine*]

affermi, ~e /afɛrmi/
A *pp* ▸ **affermir**
B *pp adj* **1** [*pouvoir, autorité, paix*] consolidated; [*chairs*] firmed up; [*volonté, muscles, voix*] strengthened; [*santé*] better; **2** [*trait, style*] sharpened up, sharpened (up) US; [*écriture*] incisive

affermir /afɛrmir/ [3]
A *vtr* **1** (consolider) to strengthen [*autorité, conviction, volonté, voix*]; to consolidate [*pouvoir, position*]; to firm up [*muscle, chair*]; **2** (rendre plus défini) to sharpen up [*style, écriture*]
B **s'affermir** *vpr* **1** [*autorité, pouvoir, croissance*] to be consolidated; [*voix*] to become stronger; [*muscle, chair*] to firm up; [*terrain*] to become firmer; [*santé*] to become better; **2** [*style, écriture*] to become sharper

affermissement /afɛrmismɑ̃/ *nm* (de pouvoir, reprise) consolidation; (de volonté, muscles, voix) strengthening; (de santé, tendance, d'économie) improvement (**de** in)

affété, ~e /afete/ *adj* liter [*personne, style, manières*] affected

afféterie* /afetri/ *nf* liter (affectation, manières) affectation; **sans ~** without affectation

affichage /afiʃaʒ/ *nm* **1** (publicitaire, électoral) billsticking, billposting; **communiqué par voie d'~** [*résultat*] posted (up); **interdit à l'~** [*roman*] not for public display; **campagne d'~** poster campaign; **à ~ numérique** [*réveil*] with digital display; **2** Ordinat display; **3** (de connaissances, savoir) display

(Composés) **~ à cristaux liquides** liquid crystal display; **~ sauvage** flyposting GB, illegal *ou* unauthorized posting of bills

affiche /afiʃ/ *nf* (publicitaire, électorale) poster; (de cinéma, film, d'exposition) poster; (administrative, judiciaire) notice; **à l'~** Cin now showing; **plusieurs spectacles sont à l'~ du festival** several shows are on at the festival; **tenir le haut de l'~** to have top billing; **tenir l'~ pendant deux ans** [*pièce*] to run for two years; **la pièce/le film quitte l'~ cette semaine** the play/the film ends its run this week; **une belle ~** a fine cast; **mettre à l'~** to put [sth] on

(Composés) **~ lumineuse** neon sign; **~ publicitaire** advertisement, advertising poster; **~ de théâtre** playbill

affiché, ~e /afiʃe/
A *pp* ▸ **afficher**
B *pp adj* **1** [*photo, annonce*] put up; [*résultat, horaire, information*] posted (up); **2** Écon [*hausse, résultat*] published; [*bénéfice*] declared; **3** fig [*optimisme, volonté, dédain, objectif, opinion*] declared; **4** péj [*liaison*] flaunted; **5** Ordinat [*donnée, texte*] displayed

afficher /afiʃe/ [1]
A *vtr* **1** (coller) to put up [*affiche, photo*]; **'défense d'~'** 'no fly-posting', 'stick no bills'; **2** (faire connaître par voie d'affiche) to display [*prix*]; to post (up) [*décret, résultat*]; **3** Comm, Fin [*entreprise*] to show [*déficit, résultat*]; [*Bourse, marché*] to show [*hausse, baisse, excédent*]; **4** Cin, Théât [*cinéma*] to show [*film*]; [*théâtre*] to have [sth] on [*pièce, spectacle*]; **~ complet** Cin, Théât to be sold out; [*hôtel, voyage*] to be completely full, to be fully booked GB, to be booked up GB; [*parking*] to be full; **5** fig (montrer) to show [*admiration, confiance, détermination*]; to declare [*ambitions*]; to display [*mépris, autorité, opinions*]; to flaunt [*liaison, vie privée*]; **~ le sourire** lit to have a big smile; (feindre) to put on a big smile; **~ sa bonne santé/forme** to show how healthy/fit one is, to flaunt one's health/fitness péj; **6** Ordinat to display [*donnée, résultat*]
B **s'afficher** *vpr* **1** Tech [*résultat, texte, horaire*] to be displayed (**sur** on); **2** (avec ostentation) [*personne*] to flaunt oneself; **s'~ comme catholique** to declare oneself to be a Catholic; **un catholique qui s'affiche comme tel** an out-and-out Catholic; **3** [*sourire, joie*] to appear (**sur** on)

affichette /afiʃɛt/ *nf* (pour information) notice; (électorale) small poster

afficheur /afiʃœr/ *nm* **1** (entreprise) poster display firm; **2** (personne) manager of a poster display firm; **3** (écran) display

affichiste /afiʃist/ ▸ p. 532 *nmf* poster artist; **~ de cinéma** designer of cinema posters; **~ publicitaire** designer of advertising posters

affidé, ~e /afide/ *nm,f* littér, péj accomplice, conspirator

affilage /afilaʒ/ *nm* sharpening

affilé, ~e /afile/
A *pp* ▸ **affiler**
B *pp adj* **1** [*couteau, lame, outil*] sharpened; **2** fig [*intelligence*] keen; ▸ **langue**
C **d'affilée** *loc adv* in a row; **pendant deux semaines d'~e** for two weeks in a row;

parler trois heures d'~e [*amis*] to talk nonstop for three hours; [*politiciens, directeur*] to talk for three hours without a break; **boire trois verres d'~e** to have three drinks one after the other

affiler /afile/ [1] *vtr* to sharpen

affiliation /afiljasjɔ̃/ *nf* affiliation (**à** to)

affilié, ~e /afilje/ *nm,f* affiliated member (**à** of), affiliate; **les ~s à** the affiliated members of

affilier /afilje/ [2]
A *vtr* to affiliate (**à** to)
B **s'affilier** *vpr* to become affiliated (**à** to)

affiloir /afilwar/ *nm* **1** (instrument) gén sharpener; (à couteaux) steel; **2** (pierre) sharpening stone, whetstone

affinage /afinaʒ/ *nm* Tech (de métal) refining; (de verre) fining; (de fromage) maturing

affine /afin/ *adj* Math affine

affinement /afinmɑ̃/ *nm* refinement

affiner /afine/ [1]
A *vtr* **1** lit to refine [*métal*]; to fine [*verre*]; to mature [*fromage*]; **2** fig to refine [*stratégie, politique, idée, style, jugement*]; to sharpen [*ouïe*]; to slim down [*taille, silhouette*]
B **s'affiner** *vpr* [*jugement*] to become keener; [*politique, idée, style, goût*] to become (more) refined; [*personne, taille, silhouette*] to slim down; [*ligne, dessin*] to become (more) refined

affineur, -euse /afinœr, øz/ ▸ p. 532 *nm,f* (de métal) refiner; (de verre) finisher; (de fromage) *person in charge of the maturing process*

affinité /afinite/ *nf* affinity

affirmatif, -ive /afirmatif, iv/
A *adj* [*proposition, mot, réponse, signe*] affirmative; [*personne, ton*] assertive; **faire un signe de tête ~** to nod agreement
B *nm* Ling affirmative; **à l'~** in the affirmative
C *adv* affirmative
D **affirmative** *nf* affirmative; **répondre par l'affirmative** to reply in the affirmative; **dans l'affirmative** if so, if the answer is yes

affirmation /afirmasjɔ̃/ *nf* **1** (assertion) assertion; **2** (manifestation) (de sentiment, religion) affirmation; (de personnalité) assertion; **l'~ de soi** assertiveness; **3** Ling assertion

affirmative ▸ **affirmatif** A, D

affirmativement /afirmativmɑ̃/ *adv* affirmatively

affirmer /afirme/ [1]
A *vtr* **1** (soutenir) to maintain [*fait, vérité, contraire*]; **'je n'ai pas l'intention de démissionner', affirma-t-il** 'I have no intention of resigning,' he declared; **~ faire/avoir fait** to claim to do/to have done; **~ que** to maintain *ou* claim (that); **pouvez-vous l'~?** can you be sure about it?; **je vous l'affirme** I can assure you (of it); **2** (prouver) to assert [*talent, personnalité, autorité, originalité, indépendance*]; **3** (proclamer) to declare, to affirm [*volonté, désir*]
B **s'affirmer** *vpr* [*progrès, tendance*] to become apparent; [*majorité*] to be established; [*personnalité, style*] to assert itself; **s'~ comme** [*personne*] to establish oneself as; **s'~ comme une force nouvelle** to establish itself as a new force; **le festival s'affirme comme un événement majeur** the festival is becoming established as a major event

affixe /afiks/ *nm* Ling affix

affleurement /aflœrmɑ̃/ *nm* **1** lit (de roche, minerai) outcrop; (de récif) emergence; **2** fig (d'inconscient, de thème) appearance, surfacing; **3** Tech flushing

affleurer /aflœre/ [1]
A *vtr* **1** Tech to make [sth] flush [*planches, battants*]; **2** (arriver au même niveau) **la rivière affleure les quais** the river is almost level with the banks
B *vi* **1** lit [*roche, glace, récif*] to show on the surface; **~ au niveau du sol** [*eau, pétrole*] to come up to ground level; [*roche, minerai*] to come

a

through the soil, to outcrop spéc; 2▸ fig [thème, sentiment] to surface, to crop up

affliction /afliksjɔ̃/ nf fml affliction; **jeter** or **plonger qn dans l'~** to afflict sb deeply; **être dans l'~** to be in a state of distress

afflictive /afliktiv/ adj f peine ~ sentence that strips a person of their civil rights

affligé, **~e** /afliʒe/ nm,f les ~s the afflicted

affligeant, **~e** /afliʒɑ̃, ɑ̃t/ adj 1▸ (attristant) distressing; 2▸ (consternant) pathetic, depressing

affliger /afliʒe/ [13]
A vtr 1▸ (frapper) [destin, malheur, handicap] to afflict, to strike; ~ qn de qch to afflict sb with sth; être affligé de qch to be afflicted with sth; 2▸ (peiner) to distress
B s'affliger vpr to be distressed (de qch about sth)

affluence /aflɥɑ̃s/ nf (de personnes) crowd(s); (d'objets) abundance; l'~ des grands magasins the crowds in the department stores; les heures d'~ dans les magasins peak shopping periods

affluent /aflɥɑ̃/ nm Géog tributary

affluer /aflɥe/ [1] vi [foule, clients, passagers] to flock (à, vers to); [eau, air, sang] to rush (à, vers to); [argent, capitaux] to flow (à, vers to); [plaintes, lettres de protestation] to pour in

afflux /afly/ nm inv (de sang) rush; (de personnes) flood; (d'argent, de capitaux, produits) influx; Électron flow

affolant, **~e** /afɔlɑ̃, ɑ̃t/ adj (effrayant) [nouvelle, prix, situation] frightening, disturbing; il fume trois paquets par jour, c'est ~! he smokes three packets a day, it's awful!

affolé, **~e** /afɔle/
A pp ▸ affoler
B pp adj panic-stricken

affolement /afɔlmɑ̃/ nm panic; être en proie à l'~ to be in a state of panic; dans l'~ in the panic; pas d'~! don't panic!

affoler /afɔle/ [1]
A vtr to terrify, to throw [sb] into a panic [personne]
B s'affoler vpr 1▸ [personne, animal] to panic; [aiguille de boussole] to spin; ne t'affole pas don't get into a panic; 2▸ ○(se dépêcher) to get a move on○; (réagir) [élève] to stir oneself

affouiller /afuje/ [1] vtr Tech to undermine

affranchi, **~e** /afrɑ̃ʃi/ nm,f emancipated slave

affranchir /afrɑ̃ʃiʀ/ [3]
A vtr 1▸ Postes (en collant des timbres) to stamp, to put a stamp ou stamps on; (avec une machine) to frank; une lettre non affranchie an unstamped letter; tu n'as pas suffisamment affranchi le paquet you haven't put enough stamps on the parcel; une lettre insuffisamment affranchie a letter without enough stamps on it; 2▸ (libérer) lit, fig to free, to liberate [serf, population, pays] (de from); 3▸ ○(informer) to give [sb] the lowdown○; 4▸ Jeux (aux cartes) to clear
B s'affranchir vpr to free oneself (de from)

affranchissement /afrɑ̃sismɑ̃/ nm 1▸ Postes (action) (en collant des timbres) stamping; (avec une machine) franking; (coût) postage; l'~ va augmenter postage is going up; 2▸ (libération) (de peuple, pays) liberation; (de serf, d'esclave) freeing; (de groupe, minorité) emancipation

affres /afʀ/ nfpl littér agony; (de douleur) agony; (de faim) pangs; (de jalousie) throes; les ~ de la mort death throes

affrètement /afʀɛtmɑ̃/ nm (d'avion, de bateau, camion) chartering

affréter /afʀete/ [14] vtr Transp to charter [avion, bateau, camion]

affréteur /afʀetœʀ/ nm Comm, Naut charter company

affreusement /afʀøzmɑ̃/ adv 1▸ [se conduire, parler] abominably; [laid, blessé, défiguré, torturé] horribly; [malade] terribly, dreadfully;

2▸ ○(extrêmement) terribly; parler ~ mal to speak appallingly badly

affreux, **-euse** /afʀø, øz/ adj 1▸ (laid) [personne, visage, vêtement, couleur, style] ugly, hideous; [blessure, plaie, monstre] hideous; 2▸ (abject) [crime, attentat, tyrannie, personne] despicable, dreadful; 3▸ (désagréable) [temps, route, voyage, vacances] awful; c'est ~ ce qu'il est ennuyeux he really is terribly boring; c'est ~ le monde qu'il y a it really is terribly busy; c'est ~! it's awful ou dreadful!; 4▸ (extrême) [besoin, envie, soif] terrible; (cruel) [torture, douleur, accident, blessure] dreadful, terrible

affriander /afʀijɑ̃de/ [1] vtr to entice, to attract

affriolant, **~e** /afʀijɔlɑ̃, ɑ̃t/ adj [femme] alluring; [vêtement] titillating; [idée] tempting

affrioler /afʀijɔle/ [1] vtr to entice

affriqué, **~e** /afʀike/
A adj affricative; consonne ~e affricate
B affriquée nf affricate

affront /afʀɔ̃/ nm affront (à to); rougir sous l'~ to blush at the affront; faire à qn l'~ de faire to affront ou insult sb by doing; il m'a fait l'~ de refuser mon invitation he insulted me by refusing my invitation

affrontement /afʀɔ̃tmɑ̃/ nm confrontation, clash; au cours d'~s armés in armed clashes; tué dans des ~s avec l'armée killed in clashes with the army; des ~s ont eu lieu entre la police et les manifestants there were clashes between police and demonstrators

affronter /afʀɔ̃te/ [1]
A vtr to face, to confront [adversaire, mort, situation, troupe]; to brave [montagne, tempête, froid]
B s'affronter vpr [adversaires, armées, équipes] to confront one another; [idées, points de vue] to clash; [politiciens, théoriciens] to confront one another

affublement /afyblmɑ̃/ nm attire†

affubler /afyble/ [1]
A vtr péj ~ qn de to deck sb out in, to dress sb up in [vêtement, ornement]; to saddle sb with [prénom, surnom]; elle était affublée d'un chapeau de cow-boy she was wearing a stupid cowboy hat; il est affublé d'un prénom ridicule he's saddled with a ridiculous name
B s'affubler vpr s'~ de to deck oneself out in, to dress oneself up in [vêtement]; to deck oneself out in [ornement]; to take on, to assume [nom, surnom]

affût* /afy/ nm 1▸ Mil ~ (de canon) (gun) carriage; 2▸ Chasse hide GB, blind US; chasser à l'~ to hunt game from a hide GB ou blind US; se tenir or être à l'~ lit to lie in wait; fig to be on the lookout (de for)

affûtage* /afytaʒ/ nm gén sharpening; (avec une meule) grinding, sharpening

affûter* /afyte/ [1] vtr gén to sharpen; (avec une meule) to grind, to sharpen

affûteur* /afytœʀ/ nm 1▸ ▸ p. 532 (personne) grinder; 2▸ (outil) sharpener, grinder

afghan, **~e** /afgɑ̃, an/ ▸ p. 561, p. 483
A adj Afghan
B nm Ling Afghan

Afghan, **~e** /afgɑ̃, an/ ▸ p. 561 nm,f Afghan

Afghanistan /afganistɑ̃/ ▸ p. 333 nprm Afghanistan

afin /afɛ̃/
A afin de loc prép ~ de faire in order to do, so as to do; ~ de ne pas faire so as not to do
B afin que loc conj so that; faire cuire cinq minutes ~ que la sauce épaississe cook for five minutes so that the sauce thickens; prendre des mesures ~ que les jeunes trouvent du travail to take measures so that young people might find work; je lui écris régulièrement ~ qu'il ne se sente pas abandonné I write to him regularly so that he won't feel neglected

AFME /aɛfɛmə/ nf: abbr ▸ agence

AFNOR /afnɔʀ/ nf (abbr = Association française de normalisation) AFNOR (French standards authority)

afocal, **~e**, mpl **-aux** /afɔkal, o/ adj Phys afocal

a fortiori /afɔʀsjɔʀi/ loc adv all the more so, a fortiori sout

AFP /aɛfpe/ nf (abbr = Agence France-Presse) AFP (French news agency) ▸ presse

AFPA /afpa/ nf (abbr = Association pour la formation professionnelle des adultes) adult education and training organization

africain, **~e** /afʀikɛ̃, ɛn/ adj African

Africain, **~e** /afʀikɛ̃, ɛn/ nm,f African

africanisation /afʀikanizasjɔ̃/ nf Africanization

africaniser /afʀikanize/ [1] vtr to Africanize

africanisme /afʀikanism/ nm African-French expression

africaniste /afʀikanist/ nmf Africanist

afrikaans /afʀikans/ ▸ p. 483 nm Ling Afrikaans

afrikaner /afʀikanɛʀ/ adj Afrikaans

Afrikaner /afʀikanɛʀ/ nmf Afrikaner

Afrique /afʀik/ ▸ p. 333 nprf Africa; l'~ australe/du Nord/de l'Ouest/de l'Est Southern/North/West/East Africa; l'~ noire Black Africa; République d'~ du Sud Republic of South Africa

Afrique-Équatoriale /afʀikekwatɔʀjal/ nprf Hist ~ française French Equatorial Africa

Afrique-Occidentale /afʀikɔksidɑ̃tal/ nprf Hist ~ française French West Africa

afro /afʀo/
A adj inv coiffure ~ Afro haircut
B ○nmf African

afro- /afʀo/ préf ~-brésilien/-cubain Afro-Brazilian/-Cuban; **-jazz** African Jazz; **afrophobie** afrophobia; **afrocentrisme** afrocentrism

afro-américain, **~e**, mpl **~s** /afʀoameʀikɛ̃, ɛn/ adj Afro-American, African American

Afro-américain, **~e**, mpl **~s** /afʀoameʀikɛ̃, ɛn/ nm,f Afro-American, African American

afro-asiatique /afʀoazjatik/ adj Afro-Asian

Afro-asiatique /afʀoazjatik/ nmf Afro-Asian

afrocentrisme /afʀosɑ̃tʀism/ nm Afrocentrism

AG /aʒe/ nf: abbr ▸ assemblée

agaçant, **~e** /agasɑ̃, ɑ̃t/ adj annoying, irritating

agacement /agasmɑ̃/ nm 1▸ (ennui) irritation, annoyance; 2▸ (douleur) irritation

agacer /agase/ [12] vtr 1▸ (excéder) to annoy, to irritate; tu commences à m'~ you're starting to annoy me ou get on my nerves; tu commences à m'~ avec tes cris/pleurs your shouting/crying is starting to annoy me; que ça m'agace! this is really annoying!; ça m'agace qu'il ne comprenne pas it annoys me that he doesn't understand; tu m'agaces à ne jamais écouter ce que je te dis it annoys me that you never listen to what I say; tu m'agaces à te ronger les ongles it annoys me when you bite your nails; 2▸ (lanciner) to set [sth] on edge [dent]; to grate on [nerf]
(Idiome) ~ les nerfs de qn to set sb's nerves on edge

Agamemnon /agamɛmnɔ̃/ npr Agamemnon

agapes /agap/ nfpl feast (sg), banquet (sg)

agar-agar /agaʀagaʀ/ nm agar-agar

agate /agat/ nf 1▸ Minér agate; une coupe d'~ an agate cup; des yeux d'~ (couleur) agate-coloured GB eyes; 2▸ (bille) marble

(Composés) ∼ **de Dieu** Relig Lamb of God;
l'∼ pascal Relig the paschal lamb

(Idiome) **être doux comme un** ∼ to be as meek
as a lamb

agnelage /aɲəlaʒ/ nm lambing

agneler /aɲəle/ [19] vi to lamb

agnelet /aɲəlɛ/ nm baby lamb

agneline /aɲəlin/ nf virgin lamb's wool

agnelle /aɲɛl/ nf ewe lamb

agnosticisme /agnɔstisism/ nm agnosti-
cism

agnostique /agnɔstik/ adj, nmf agnostic

agonie /agɔni/ nf [1] (d'être vivant) death throes
(pl) littér (**de** of); **il est à l'∼** he's at death's
door, he's dying; **son ∼ a été longue/terrible**
he/she died a slow/terrible death; [2] (d'un
parti, régime) slow death (**de** of); **le régime politique est à l'∼** the political regime is dying
ou in its death throes

agonir /agɔniʀ/ [3] vtr ∼ **qn d'injures** to hurl
insults at sb; **se faire ∼ d'injures** to have
insults hurled at one; **en rentrant, il s'est fait
∼** when he got home he was told off
soundly

agonisant, ∼**e** /agɔnizɑ̃, ɑ̃t/
A adj dying
B nm,f dying person

agoniser /agɔnize/ [1] vi lit, fig to be dying

agora /agɔʀa/ nf agora

agoraphobe /agɔʀafɔb/ adj, nmf agoraphoᴏ-
bic

agoraphobie /agɔʀafɔbi/ nf agoraphobia

agrafage /agʀafaʒ/ nm [1] (de vêtement) fas-
tening; [2] (de papiers) stapling; [3] Méd fasten-
ing skin clips (pl)

agrafe /agʀaf/ nf [1] (pour vêtements) hook;
[2] (pour papiers) staple; [3] Méd skin clip; **on
m'a mis trois ∼s au front** they've put three
(skin) clips in my forehead

agrafer /agʀafe/ [1]
A vtr [1] (fermer) to fasten [vêtement]; [2] (attacher)
to staple (together) [papiers, tissu];
[3] ○(attraper) to nab○, to catch
B s'agrafer vpr [vêtement] to fasten

agrafeuse /agʀaføz/ nf stapler

agraire /agʀɛʀ/ adj [société] agrarian; [mesure,
réforme] land (épith)

agrammatical, ∼**e,** mpl **-aux** /agʀamati-
kal, o/ adj Ling ungrammatical

agrandir /agʀɑ̃diʀ/ [3]
A vtr [1] (en dimensions) to enlarge [ville, photo]; to
extend [pièce, maison, magasin]; to widen
[tunnel, marge, écart]; to make [sth] bigger, to
enlarge [trou]; **il me regardait, les yeux agran-
dis par la peur** he was looking at me, his eyes
wide with fear; **faire ∼ une maison** to have
an extension built; **faire ∼ une photo** to have
a photo enlarged; **la peinture blanche agran-
dit la pièce** white paint makes the room look
bigger ou larger; [2] (en importance) to extend
[famille]; to expand [entreprise, parti]
B s'agrandir vpr [1] (devenir plus grand) [trou] to
get bigger; [ville, famille, entreprise] to expand,
to grow; [marge, écart, yeux] to widen;
[2] ○(dans un logement) to have more room to
live in, to have more space; **déménager pour
s'∼** to move in order to have more space

agrandissement /agʀɑ̃dismɑ̃/ nm [1] Phot
enlargement; [2] (de maison, pièce) extension;
(d'ouverture) enlargement; (d'entreprise) expan-
sion; **faire des travaux d'∼** (dans une maison) to
build an extension; (dans un magasin) to extend
the floor space

agrandisseur /agʀɑ̃disœʀ/ nm enlarger

agraphie /agʀafi/ ▸ p. 283 nf agraphia

agrarien, -ienne /agʀaʀjɛ̃, ɛn/ adj, nm,f
Hist, Pol agrarian

agréable /agʀeabl/
A adj nice, pleasant; **avoir un physique ∼** to be
good-looking; **∼ à l'œil/au toucher/à l'oreille**
pleasing to the eye/to the touch/to the ear;
∼ à vivre [personne] pleasant ou nice to be
with; [ville] pleasant to live in; **être ∼ à qn**

[personne] to be nice to sb
B nm **l'∼ de qch** the agreeable aspect of sth;
▸ utile

agréablement /agʀeabləmɑ̃/ adv pleasant-
ly, agreeably

agréé, ∼**e** /agʀee/
A pp ▸ agréer
B pp adj [agence, concessionnaire] authorized (**par**
by); [médecin, ambulancier, nourrice] registered
(**par** with); [matériel, association, établissement]
approved (**par** by)

agréer /agʀee/ [11] vtr [1] (accepter) to agree to
[demande]; **faire ∼ qch par qn** to have sth
agreed by sb; **veuillez ∼, Messieurs, mes
salutations distinguées** (personne non nommée)
yours faithfully; (personne nommée) yours sin-
cerely; [2] (reconnaître officiellement) to recognize
[sb] officially [diplomate]; to authorize
[concessionnaire]; to register [taxi, nourrice,
médecin]; to approve [matériel, association,
établissement]

agrégat /agʀega/ nm [1] Biol, Constr, Écon
aggregate; [2] fig jumble (**de** of)

(Composé) ∼**s monétaires** Écon monetary
aggregates

agrégatif, -ive /agʀegatif, iv/ nm,f: candidate for the agrégation

agrégation /agʀegasjɔ̃/ nf [1] Univ examination for recruitment of teachers; [2] (de particules)
agregation

Agrégation

This qualification, awarded by competitive
examination or concours, entitles the
holder to teach at the highest level in secondary and tertiary education. In most
subjects, the number of candidates
exceeds the number of places available.
The successful agregé/-ée is then commit-
ted to five years of service in either a
state school or a university'.

---

agrégé, ∼**e** /agʀeʒe/ nm,f: holder of the
agrégation

agréger: s'agréger /agʀeʒe/ [15] vpr [1] (se
coller) [particules] to aggregate; [2] (se joindre)
s'∼ à [personne, groupe] to join

agrément /agʀemɑ̃/ nm [1] (validation officielle)
approval; **retirer son ∼ à une école de
langues** to withdraw a language school's
accreditation; [2] (accord) agreement; **recevoir
l'∼ de qn** to obtain sb's agreement;
[3] (charme) (d'activité, expérience) pleasure; (de personne, lieu, chose) charm; **un des ∼s de la vie à
l'étranger** one of the pleasures of living
abroad; **c'en est le principal ∼** that's its
main charm; **trouver de l'∼ à une ville** to
find a certain charm in a town; **plein d'∼**
[séjour] very pleasant; [lieu] full of charm
(après n); **sans ∼** [séjour, existence] dull; [visage,
maison] unattractive; [décor, pièce] cheerless;
voyage d'∼ pleasure trip

(Composés) ∼ **fiscal** tax relief; ∼ **mélo-
dique** ornament

agrémenter /agʀemɑ̃te/ [1]
A vtr to liven up [texte, histoire] (**de** with); to
cheer up [réunion] (**de** with); to brighten up
[jardin] (**de** with); to supplement [repas, plat]
(**de** with); **les petits plaisirs qui agrémentent
l'existence** the little things that brighten up
one's life; **un ensemble immobilier agrémenté de nombreux services** a property
development offering many facilities; **un
texte agrémenté d'illustrations** a text with
illustrations; **un chapeau agrémenté d'une
voilette** a hat trimmed with a veil; **une pièce
agrémentée de tableaux** a room decorated
with pictures
B s'agrémenter vpr **s'∼ de** [chapeau, vêtement]
to be trimmed with; [pièce] to be decorated
with; [conversation] to be laced with

agrès /agʀɛ/ nmpl [1] Sport apparatus ¢; **aux
∼** on the apparatus; [2] Naut tackle

agresser /agʀese/ [1] vtr [1] (physiquement)
[personne] to attack, to assault [personne]; (pour
voler) to mug [personne]; [pays, peuple] to attack

[pays, peuple]; **se faire ∼ dans la rue** to be
mugged in the street; [2] (moralement) [per-
sonne] to be aggressive with [personne]; **se
sentir agressé** to feel threatened (**par** by); **les
images télévisées nous agressent** we are
bombarded by pictures on television; [3] (être
trop fort) [shampooing, pluies acides, fumée] to
attack

agresseur /agʀesœʀ/ nm (individu) attacker;
(groupe, peuple) aggressor; **le pays ∼** the
aggressor

agressif, -ive /agʀesif, iv/ adj [1] (hostile)
[personne, animal] aggressive (**avec qn** with sb;
envers qn toward, towards GB sb); [tempéra-
ment, ton, air, environnement, publicité] aggressive; **d'un ton ∼** aggressively; [2] (trop fort)
[couleur] violent; [son] ear-splitting; [lumière,
shampooing] harsh; [images] threatening;
[3] (dynamique) [politique, campagne, jeu] aggressive; **mener une politique commerciale agres-
sive** to have an aggressive sales policy

agression /agʀesjɔ̃/ nf [1] (par une personne)
attack; (pour voler) mugging; (par un pays) act of
aggression; **une ∼ raciste** a racist attack;
être victime d'une ∼ gén to be attacked; (être
volé) to be mugged; **commettre une ∼ contre
qn** (pour attaquer) to attack sb; (pour voler) to mug sb; **∼ à
main armée** armed assault; [2] (par un fait) pro-
tégez votre visage contre les ∼s protect your
face from the wind and the cold; **les ∼s de
l'entourage/la vie urbaine** the stresses and
strains of one's surroundings/city life;
[3] Psych aggression

agressivement /agʀesivmɑ̃/ adv aggressively

agressivité /agʀesivite/ nf [1] gén aggres-
siveness; [2] Psych aggression

agreste /agʀɛst/ adj liter rustic

agricole /agʀikɔl/ adj [produit, ouvrier] farm;
[coopérative] farming; [méthode, problème] agri-
cultural; [syndicat] farm workers'

agriculteur, -trice /agʀikyltœʀ, tʀis/,
▸ p. 532 nm,f farmer; **une famille d'∼s** a farming family

agriculture /agʀikyltyʀ/ nf farming, agriculture spéc

(Composé) ∼ **biologique** organic farming;
∼ **raisonnée** integrated farming

agripper /agʀipe/ [1]
A vtr to grab [branche, personne]
B s'agripper vpr **s'∼ à** to cling to [paroi, bras];
il était agrippé à une branche he was cling-
ing to a branch

agro-alimentaire, pl ∼**s** /agʀoalimɑ̃tɛʀ/
A adj [industrie, filière, complexe] food processing;
la recherche ∼ food research
B nm food processing industry; **un géant de l'∼**
a food giant

agrochimie /agʀoʃimi/ nf agro-chemistry

agrochimique /agʀoʃimik/ adj agrochem-
ical

agro-industrie, pl ∼**s** /agʀoɛ̃dystʀi/ nf
agro-industry

agronome /agʀonɔm/ ▸ p. 532 nmf agronomist; **ingénieur ∼** agronomist

agronomie /agʀonɔmi/ nf agronomy

agronomique /agʀonɔmik/ adj agronomic

agrotechnologie /agʀotɛknɔlɔʒi/ nf
agrotechnology

agrume /agʀym/ nm citrus fruit; **les ∼s**
citrus fruits

aguerri, ∼**e** /ageʀi/
A pp ▸ aguerrir
B pp adj [1] Mil (accoutumé à la guerre) seasoned
(**par** by); [2] gén (endurci) hardened, inured sout
(**à, contre** to)

aguerrir /ageʀiʀ/ [3]
A vtr [expérience] to harden [personne] (**à qch** to
sth); ∼ **des troupes au combat** to toughen
soldiers for battle
B s'aguerrir vpr to become hardened ou
inured sout (**à, contre** to)

a

aguets: aux aguets /ozagɛ/ *loc adv* **être aux** ~ (à l'affût) to lie in wait; (se méfier) to be on one's guard; (surveiller de près) to be watching like a hawk

aguichant, ~**e** /agiʃɑ̃, ɑ̃t/ *adj* [*personne, pose, sourire*] alluring

aguicher /agiʃe/ [1] *vtr* (sexuellement) to lead [sb] on; (pour vendre) to attract [*client*]

aguicheur, **-euse** /agiʃœR, øz/
A *adj* [*personne, propos*] alluring
B **aguicheuse** *nf pej* tease *péj*

ah /ɑ/
A *nm inv* (d'étonnement, admiration) gasp; (de soulagement, satisfaction) sigh
B *excl* oh!; ~ **non alors!** certainly not!; ~, **tu vois!** see!; ~! **c'est dégoûtant!** ugh! it's revolting!; ~ **oui** *or* **bon?** really?; ~ ~, **il est parti en voyage d'affaires?** iron so, it's a business trip, is it? iron; ~ ~ ~! (rire) ha ha ha!

ahaner /aane/ [1] *vi* (grogner) to grunt with effort; (peiner) to strain, to heave

ahuri, ~**e** /ayRi/
A *pp* ▸ ahurir
B *pp adj* (hébété) dazed; (étonné) stunned
C *nf pej* halfwit *péj*

ahurir /ayRiR/ [3] *vtr* [*réponse, nouvelle*] to stun; **j'ai été ahuri d'apprendre que** I was stunned to hear that

ahurissant, ~**e** /ayRisɑ̃, ɑ̃t/ *adj* [*nouvelle, bruit*] incredible; [*personne, comportement, force*] incredible; [*chiffre*] staggering; **c'est** ~! it's absolutely incredible!

ahurissement /ayRismɑ̃/ *nm* amazement

aï /ai/ *nm* three-toed sloth

aidant, ~**e** /ɛdɑ̃, ɑ̃t/ *nm,f* carer

aide /ɛd/ ▸ p. 532
A *nmf* (dans un travail) assistant
B *nf* **[1]** (secours) (d'individu, de groupe) help, assistance; (d'État, organisme) assistance; **appeler à l'**~ to call for help; **à l'**~! help!; **avec/sans l'**~ **de qn** with/without sb's help; **à l'**~ **de** with the help *ou* aid of [*tournevis, dictionnaire, police*]; **proposer son** ~ **à qn** to offer to help sb; **apporter son** ~ **à qn** to help sb; **il m'a apporté une** ~ **considérable** he was a great help to me; **venir/aller à l'**~ **de qn** to come/to go to sb's aid *ou* assistance; **venir en** ~ **à qn** (financièrement) to help *ou* aid sb; **[2]** (en argent) (à un pays) aid; (aux démunis) aid ∉, allowance C; (à une industrie, un organisme) aid ∉, subsidy C; (pour un projet) aid ∉, grant C; **recevoir des** ~**s de** to receive financial backing *ou* aid from [*État, organisme*]; **les** ~**s à la famille** financial aid for families; **recevoir une** ~ **de 2 000 euros** to receive 2,000 euros in aid

(Composés) ~ **de camp** aide-de-camp; ~ **au développement** foreign aid; ~ **à domicile** home help GB, home helper US; ~ **familiale** mother's help GB, mother's helper US; ~ **française** international aid programme^GB; ~ **judiciaire** legal aid; ~ **légale** = ~ **judiciaire**; ~ **maternelle** = ~ **familiale**; ~ **médicale** health care; ~ **ménagère** = ~ **à domicile**; ~ **régionale** regional aid; ~ **au retour** *incentive for voluntary repatriation*; ~ **sociale** social security benefits GB, welfare benefits US

Aide française

This refers to the government programme of international aid, mainly directed to French-speaking countries in Africa.

Aide judiciaire

The legal aid available to those whose income is below a certain level. This includes awards for the costs of a case and also free initial legal consultations.

Aide au retour

A government measure to encourage the repatriation of foreign nationals who wish to return to their country of origin.

---

aide-anesthésiste, *pl* **aides-anesthésistes** /ɛdanɛstezist/ ▸ p. 532 *nmf* assistant anaesthetist^GB

aide-bibliothécaire, *pl* **aides-bibliothécaires** /ɛdbiblijotekɛR/ ▸ p. 532 *nmf* assistant librarian

aide-comptable, *pl* **aides-comptables** /ɛdkɔ̃tabl/ ▸ p. 532 *nmf* assistant accountant

aide-cuisinier, **-ière**, *pl* **aides-cuisiniers**, **aides-cuisinières** /ɛdkɥizinje, ɛR/ ▸ p. 532 *nm,f* assistant cook

aide-éducateur, **-trice**, *pl* **aides-éducateurs**, **aides-éducatrices** /ɛdedykatœR, tRis/ ▸ p. 532 *nm,f*: *classroom assistant*

aide-électricien, *pl* **aides-électriciens** /ɛdelɛktRisjɛ̃/ ▸ p. 532 *nm* electrician's mate GB, electrician's helper US

aide-mécanicien, *pl* **aides-mécaniciens** /ɛdmekanisjɛ̃/ ▸ p. 532 *nm* mechanic's mate GB, mechanic's helper US

aide-mémoire * /ɛdmemwaR/ *nm inv* aidemémoire *sout*; **c'est mon** ~ I use it to jog my memory

aider /ede/ [1]
A *vtr* **[1]** (prêter son concours à) to help; **il n'aide jamais** he never helps; ~ **qn à faire** to help sb to do; **en quoi puis-je vous** ~? how can I help you?; ~ **qn financièrement** to help sb financially; **(une fois)** to help sb out financially; **se faire** ~ **par qn** to get help from sb; ~ **qn de ses conseils** to give sb helpful advice; **il m'a aidé par sa présence** the fact he was there helped me; **le vin/la fatigue aidant** wine/tiredness playing its part; **le temps aidant** with time; **[2]** (subventionner) to aid [*industrie, déshérités*]; to give aid to [*pays pauvre*]
B **aider à** *vtr ind* to help toward(s) [*compréhension, insertion sociale, financement*]; ~ **à faire** to help in doing
C **s'aider** *vpr* **[1]** (soi-même) **s'**~ **de** to use [*dictionnaire, tableau, outil*]; **marcher en s'aidant d'une canne** to walk with the help of a stick; **[2]** (les uns les autres) to help each other

(Idiome) **aide-toi le Ciel t'aidera** *Prov* God helps those who help themselves *Prov*

aide-soignant, ~**e**, *pl* **aides-soignants**, **aides-soignantes** /ɛdswaɲɑ̃, ɑ̃t/ ▸ p. 532 *nm,f* nursing auxiliary GB, nurse's aide US

aïe /aj/ *excl* (de douleur) ouch!; (d'inquiétude) ~ (~ ~), **que se passe-t-il?** oh dear, what's going on?; (d'anticipation) ~ ~ ~!... oh no!...

aïeul, ~**e** /ajœl/ *nm,f* liter grandfather/grandmother

aïeux /ajø/ *nmpl* liter ancestors; **mes** ~**!** upon my word†!

aigle /ɛgl/
A *nm* **[1]** Zool eagle; ▸ petit; **[2]** (lutrin) lectern
B *nf* **[1]** Zool (female) eagle; **[2]** Hérald Hist Mil eagle; **les** ~**s romaines** the Roman eagles

(Composés) ~ **impérial** imperial eagle; ~ **royal** golden eagle

(Idiome) **ce n'est pas un** ~ he's not the brightest

aiglefin /ɛglǝfɛ̃/ *nm* haddock

aiglon /ɛglɔ̃/ *nm* eaglet

aigre /ɛgR/ *adj* **[1]** lit [*odeur, goût*] sour; [*vin, lait*] sour; [*fruit*] (acidulé) sharp; (pas mûr) sour; **[2]** fig [*paroles, ton*] sharp; [*caractère*] sour; **d'un ton** ~ sharply; **tourner** *or* **virer à l'**~ [*discussion, plaisanterie*] to turn sour

aigre-doux, **-douce**, *pl* **aigres-doux**, **aigres-douces** /ɛgRǝdu, dus/ *adj* **[1]** Culin [*fruit, goût*] bitter-sweet; [*cuisine, sauce*] sweet and sour; **[2]** fig [*propos, communiqué*] barbed

aigrefin /ɛgRǝfɛ̃/ *nm* swindler

aigrelet, **-ette** /ɛgRǝlɛ, ɛt/ *adj* **[1]** lit [*goût*] rather sour; [*fruit*] (acidulé) rather sharp; (pas mûr) rather sour; **un petit vin** ~ a sharpish wine; **[2]** fig [*voix*] shrill

aigrement /ɛgRǝmɑ̃/ *adv* fig sharply

aigrette /ɛgRɛt/ *nf* **[1]** Zool (oiseau) egret; (plumes) crest; **[2]** (ornement de coiffure) aigrette; **un casque à** ~ a plumed helmet; **[3]** Bot pappus

aigreur /ɛgRœR/ *nf* **[1]** gén (de lait) sourness; (de vin) sharpness; (de fruit) (acidulé) sharpness; (pas mûr) sourness; **[2]** Méd **des** ~**s d'estomac** heartburn ∉; **[3]** fig bitterness

aigri, ~**e** /ɛgRi/
A *pp* ▸ aigrir
B *pp adj* [*personne*] embittered

aigrir /ɛgRiR/ [3]
A *vtr* [*expérience*] to embitter [*personne*]
B **s'aigrir** *vpr* **[1]** [*personne*] to become embittered; **[2]** [*vin, aliment*] to turn sour

aigu, **-uë** * /egy/
A *adj* **[1]** (à l'oreille) [*son, voix, note*] high-pitched; **[2]** Méd, gén (violent) [*maladie, crise, douleur*] acute; [*symptôme, problème*] acute; [*phase*] critical; **[3]** (intense) [*perception, sens*] keen; **il a un sens** ~ **du devoir** he's got a keen sense of duty
B *nm* Mus (de chaîne stéréo) treble; (de voix) high notes (pl); **passer du grave à l'**~ to go from low notes to high notes

aigue-marine, *pl* **aigues-marines** /ɛgmaRin/ *nf* aquamarine

aiguière /ɛgjɛR/ *nf* ewer

aiguillage /egɥijaʒ/ *nm* **[1]** Rail (appareil) points (pl) GB, switch US; (manœuvre) switching to another line; **une erreur d'**~ a signalling^GB error; **poste d'**~ signal box; **[2]** fig (orientation) **il y a eu une erreur d'**~ (confusion) there's been a mix-up; **il y a eu une erreur d'**~ **dans leurs études** they were led to choose the wrong courses

aiguille /egɥij/ *nf* **[1]** (pour coudre) needle; ~ **à coudre/broder/repriser** sewing/embroidery/darning needle; ~ **à brider** poultry needle; ~ **à suture** suture needle; **travail à l'**~ needlework; **tirer l'**~† to ply one's needle†; **[2]** (de seringue) needle; (en acupuncture) needle; **[3]** (de montre, chronomètre) hand; (de jauge, d'altimètre) needle; (de balance) pointer; **l'**~ **des minutes/des heures** the minute/hour hand; **dans le sens des** ~**s d'une montre** clockwise; **dans le sens inverse des** ~**s d'une montre** anticlockwise; **[4]** Bot needle; **[5]** Géog peak; **[6]** Zool garfish

(Composés) ~ **aimantée** magnetic needle; ~ **de pin** pine needle; ~ **de radium** radium needle; ~ **à tricoter** knitting needle

(Idiomes) **autant chercher une** ~ **dans une botte** *or* **meule de foin** it's like looking for a needle in a haystack; **et de fil en** ~ and one thing leading to another

aiguillée /egɥije/ *nf* length of thread (*on a needle*)

aiguiller /egɥije/ [1] *vtr* **[1]** (vers un endroit) to direct [*personne*] (**vers** toward); to send [*courrier, dossier*] (**vers** to); (vers une profession, des études) to guide, to steer [*personne*] (**vers** toward, towards GB); (orienter) to steer [*conversation*] (**sur** toward, towards GB); **elle a été mal aiguillée dans ses études** she was badly advised about what to study; **c'est ce qui nous a aiguillés dans nos recherches** that's what put us on the right track in our research; **[2]** Rail ~ **un train** to switch a train to a new line; **[3]** Ordinat to route

aiguillette /egɥijɛt/ *nf* **[1]** Culin (de bœuf) tip of rump steak; (de volaille) breast fillet; (mince tranche de viande) fillet; **[2]** Hist Mil aiguillette

(Idiome) **nouer l'**~ **à qn** to render sb impotent by witchcraft

aiguilleur /egɥijœR/ ▸ p. 532 *nm* Rail pointsman GB, switchman US

(Composé) ~ **du ciel** air traffic controller

aiguillon /egɥijɔ̃/ *nm* **[1]** Zool sting; **[2]** (stimulant) incentive; **[3]** (bâton) goad; **[4]** Bot thorn

ajustement /aʒystəmɑ̃/ *nm* ⚊ Tech fit; ⚋ (adaptation) adjustment (**avec** with); **~ des prix** price adjustment; **plan d'~ structurel** structural adjustment programme^{GB}

ajuster /aʒyste/ [1] *vtr* ⚊ (régler) to adjust [*taux, prix, horaire*]; to alter [*robe, chemise*] (**à** to); to calibrate [*balance*]; to tighten [*rênes*]; **~ qch à** *or* **sur qch** lit to make sth fit sth; **~ un manche à une brosse** to adjust a handle to fit a brush; **~ la théorie à la pratique** to adapt the theory to the practice; ⚋ (arranger) to arrange [*coiffure*]; to adjust [*tenue*]; ⚌ (viser) to take aim at [*lapin*]; **~ son tir** *or* **coup** lit to adjust one's aim; fig to fix a more precise target

ajusteur /aʒystœʀ/ ▸ p. 532 *nm* fitter

akène /aken/ *nm* achene

Alabama /alabama/ ▸ p. 721 *nprm* Alabama

alacrité /alakʀite/ *nf* alacrity sout; **avec ~** with alacrity

Aladin /aladɛ̃/ *npr* Aladdin

alaise = **alèse**

alambic /alɑ̃bik/ *nm* Chimie still

alambiqué, **~e** /alɑ̃bike/ *adj* [*expression, style*] convoluted; [*explication*] tortuous

alangui, **~e** /alɑ̃gi/
A *pp* ▸ **alanguir**
B *pp adj* languid

alanguir /alɑ̃giʀ/ fml [3] *vtr* ⚊ (rendre langoureux) [*amour, musique*] to make [sb] languid; ⚋ (rendre languissant) [*maladie*] to sap [sb's] energy; [*chaleur*] to enervate, to make [sb] listless

alanguissement /alɑ̃gismɑ̃/ *nm* languor

alarmant, **~e** /alaʀmɑ̃, ɑ̃t/ *adj* alarming

alarme /alaʀm/ *nf* ⚊ (appareil) alarm; **sonner l'~** to sound the alarm; ⚋ (alerte) alarm, alert; **donner l'~** to raise the alarm; **c'est ce qui a donné l'~** that was what made us/them realize something was wrong; ⚌ (peur) alarm; **une population tenue en ~** a population kept perpetually on its guard; **en état d'~** in a state of perpetual alarm

alarmer /alaʀme/ [1]
A *vtr* to alarm [*personne, population*]
B *s'alarmer vpr* to become alarmed (**de qch** about sth); **vous n'avez aucune raison de vous ~** there's no cause for alarm

alarmisme /alaʀmism/ *nm* alarmism

alarmiste /alaʀmist/ *adj, nmf* alarmist

Alaska /alaska/ ▸ p. 721 *nprm* Alaska

albanais, **~e** /albanɛ, ɛz/
A ▸ p. 561 *adj* Albanian
B ▸ p. 483 *nm* Ling Albanian

Albanais, **~e** /albanɛ, ɛz/ ▸ p. 561 *nm,f* Albanian

Albanie /albani/ ▸ p. 333 *nprf* Albania

albanophone /albanɔfɔn/
A *adj* Albanian-speaking
B *nmf* Albanian speaker

albâtre /albɑtʀ/ *nm* alabaster; **un vase en ~** an alabaster vase; **une peau d'~** a skin as white as alabaster

(Idiome) **blanc comme l'~** as white as alabaster

albatros /albatʀos/ *nm inv* albatross

Alberta /albɛʀta/ ▸ p. 721 *nprm* Alberta

albigeois, **~e** /albiʒwa, az/ *adj* Albigensian

Albigeois /albiʒwa/ *nprmpl* **les ~** the Albigenses; **croisade contre les ~** crusade against the Albigenses

albinisme /albinism/ *nm* albinism

albinos /albinos/ *adj inv, nmf inv* albino

Albion /albjɔ̃/ *nprf* Albion; **la perfide ~** perfidious Albion

album /albɔm/ *nm* ⚊ (livre illustré) illustrated book; **~ de bandes dessinées** comic strip book; ⚋ (classeur, cahier) album; **~ de photographies/cartes postales/timbres** photograph/postcard/stamp album; ⚌ (disque) album; **double ~** double album

---

(Composés) **~ à colorier** colouring^{GB} book; **~ de famille** family album

albumen /albymɛn/ *nm* albumen

albumine /albymin/ *nf* albumin; **avoir de l'~**○ to suffer from albuminuria spéc

albumineux, **-euse** /albyminø, øz/ *adj* albuminous

albuminurie /albyminyʀi/ *nf* albuminuria

alcali /alkali/ *nm* ⚊ (ammoniaque) ammonia; **~ volatil** ammonia; ⚋ Chimie alkali

alcalin, **~e** /alkalɛ̃, in/ *adj* alkaline

alcalinité /alkalinite/ *nf* alkalinity

alcaloïde /alkalɔid/ *nm* alkaloid

Alceste /alsɛst/ *npr* Mythol Alcestis

alchimie /alʃimi/ *nf* alchemy

alchimique /alʃimik/ *adj* alchemic

alchimiste /alʃimist/ *nmf* alchemist

alcolo○ /alkolo/ *nmf* drunk

alcool /alkɔl/ *nm* ⚊ (boisson) alcohol; **boire de l'~** to drink alcohol; **vous prendrez bien un petit ~?** will you have a little drop of something?; **~ de poire** pear brandy; **sans ~** [*cocktail*] non-alcoholic; [*bière*] alcohol-free; **elle ne tient pas du tout l'~** she cannot take *ou* hold her drink at all; **l'~ m'est interdit** I'm not allowed to drink alcohol; ⚋ (alcoolisme) drink; **s'adonner à** *or* **sombrer dans l'~** to take to drink; **l'~ au volant** drinking and driving; ⚌ (substance) alcohol; **avoir une forte teneur en ~** to have a high alcohol content; ⚍ **un ~** a spirit; **il ne boit que des ~s forts** he only drinks spirits

(Composés) **~ absolu** absolute alcohol; **~ blanc** clear fruit brandy; **~ à brûler** methylated spirits, meths○ GB; **~ camphré** camphorated alcohol; **~ éthylique** ethyl alcohol; **~ à 90°** surgical spirit GB, rubbing alcohol US; **~ de menthe** mentholated alcohol

alcoolat /alkɔla/ *nm* alcohol-based medicine

alcoolémie /alkɔlemi/ *nf* presence of alcohol in the blood; **contrôle d'~** checking for alcohol in the blood; **taux d'~** level of alcohol in the blood

alcoolique /alkɔlik/ *adj, nmf* alcoholic

alcoolisation /alkɔlizasjɔ̃/ *nf* alcoholization

alcoolisé, **~e** /alkɔlize/
A *pp* ▸ **alcooliser**
B *pp adj* alcoholic; **une boisson peu/non ~e** a low-alcohol/non-alcoholic drink

alcooliser /alkɔlize/ [1]
A *vtr* to alcoholize
B *s'alcooliser*○ *vpr* hum to get drunk

alcoolisme /alkɔlism/ *nm* alcoholism

alcootest /alkɔtɛst/ *nm* ⚊ (appareil) Breathalyzer®; ⚋ (contrôle) breath test

> **Alcootest**
>
> A test carried out on drivers, sometimes randomly and always after a traffic accident, in order to measure the alcohol content in the bloodstream. The legal limit in France is 0.5g/l.

Alcotest® /alkɔtɛst/ *nm* Breathalyzer®

alcôve /alkov/ *nf* alcove; **d'~** [*histoires, secrets*] of the boudoir

alcyon /alsjɔ̃/ *nm* ⚊ Mythol halcyon; ⚋ Zool dead man's fingers (+ *v sg*)

aléa /alea/ *nm* (de temps, nature, marché) vagary; (économique, financier) hazard; **les ~s du métier** occupational hazards

aléatoire /aleatwaʀ/ *adj* ⚊ [*événements, succès, résultat*] unpredictable; [*profession*] insecure, risky; **le caractère ~ de** the unpredictability of [*résultat*]; the unstable nature of [*emploi*]; ⚋ Littérat, Mus aleatory; ⚌ Math, Stat random; ⚍ Jur [*acte, contrat*] aleatory

alémanique /alemanik/ ▸ p. 483 *adj, nm* Alemannic

ALÉNA /alɛna/ *nm* (abbr = **Accord de libre-échange nord-américain**) NAFTA

alêne /alɛn/ *nf* awl

alentour /alɑ̃tuʀ/
A *adv* surrounding; **visite de la ville et de la région ~** visit of the town and surrounding area; **les maisons d'~** the surrounding houses
B *alentours nmpl* (environs) surrounding area (*sg*); **les ~s de la ferme/ville** the area around the farm/town; **il n'y a personne aux** *or* **dans les ~s** there is no-one in the surrounding area
C **aux alentours de** *loc prép* ⚊ (de lieu) around; **aux ~s de la place/Nîmes** around the square/Nîmes; ⚋ (de chiffre, date) about, around; **aux ~s de l'an 2000** about the year 2000; **il y avait aux ~s de 1 000 personnes** there were about 1,000 people

aléoute /aleut/ ▸ p. 483
A *adj* Aleutian
B *nm* Ling Aleut

Aléoute /aleut/ *nmf* Aleut

Aléoutiennes /aleusjɛn/ ▸ p. 435 *adj fpl* **les îles ~** the Aleutian islands

alerte /alɛʀt/
A *adj* (vif) [*personne, esprit*] alert; [*démarche*] brisk; [*style, jeu, interprétation*] lively
B *nf* alert; **être en état d'~** lit to be in a state of alert; fig to be on the alert; **en cas d'~ grave...** in the event of a serious alert...; **donner l'~** to raise the alarm; **donner l'~ à qn** to alert sb; **fausse ~** false alarm; **~ générale** full alert

(Composés) **~ aérienne** air raid warning; **~ à la bombe** bomb scare

alerter /alɛʀte/ [1] *vtr* ⚊ (donner l'alerte) to alert [*police, autorités*]; ⚋ (informer) to alert [*opinion publique*] (**sur qch** to sth); to inform [*personne, service*]; **les pompiers alertés sont arrivés rapidement** the firemen arrived soon after being alerted

alésage /alezaʒ/ *nm* ⚊ (usinage) boring; ⚋ (partie alésée) bore; ⚌ Aut (diamètre des cylindres) cylinder bore

alèse /alɛz/ *nf* undersheet, mattress protector; (imperméable) waterproof undersheet, waterproof mattress protector

alésé, **~e** /aleze/ *adj* Hérald couped

aléser /aleze/ [14] *vtr* to bore

aléseur /alezœʀ/ *nm* ⚊ ▸ p. 532 boring-machine operator; ⚋ Mines reamer; **~ à rouleaux** rotary reamer

aléseuse /alezœz/ *nf* Mécan boring machine

aléseuse-fraiseuse, *pl* **aléseuses-fraiseuses** /alezœzfʀɛzœz/ *nf* boring and milling machine

alésoir /alezwaʀ/ *nm* Mécan reamer

alevin /alvɛ̃/ *nm* young fish

alevinage /alvinaʒ/ *nm* stocking with young fish

Alexandre /alɛksɑ̃dʀ/ *npr* Alexander; **~ le Grand** Alexander the Great

Alexandrie /alɛksɑ̃dʀi/ ▸ p. 894 *npr* ⚊ (en Égypte) Alexandria; ⚋ (en Italie) Alessandria

alexandrin /alɛksɑ̃dʀɛ̃/ *adj m, nm* alexandrine

alezan, **~e** /alzɑ̃, an/
A *adj* [*cheval*] chestnut
B *nm* chestnut (horse)

alfa /alfa/ *nm* ⚊ (herbe) esparto grass; ⚋ (fibre) esparto; ⚌ (papier) esparto paper, alfa paper

algarade /algaʀad/ *nf* quarrel; **avoir une ~ avec qn** to have a quarrel with sb

algèbre /alʒɛbʀ/ *nf* algebra

algébrique /alʒebʀik/ *adj* algebraic

algébriquement /alʒebʀikmɑ̃/ *adv* algebraically

algébriste /alʒebʀist/ ▸ p. 532 *nmf* algebraist

algéco® /alʒeko/ *nm* portakabin®

Alger /alʒe/ ▸ p. 894 *npr* Algiers

Algérie /alʒeʀi/ ▸ p. 333 nprf Algeria

algérien, -ienne /alʒeʀjɛ̃, ɛn/ ▸ p. 561 adj Algerian

Algérien, -ienne /alʒeʀjɛ̃, ɛn/ ▸ p. 561 nm,f Algerian

algérois, ∼e /alʒeʀwa, az/ ▸ p. 894 adj of Algiers

Algérois, ∼e /alʒeʀwa, az/ ▸ p. 894 nm,f (natif) native of Algiers; (habitant) inhabitant of Algiers

algicide /alʒisid/ nm algicide

algie /alʒi/ nf pain; ∼ **dentaire** toothache, odontalgia spéc

ALGOL /algɔl/ nm (abbr = algorithmic language) ALGOL

algonquin /algɔ̃kɛ̃/ ▸ p. 483 nm Ling [1] (famille de langues) Algonquian languages (pl); [2] (langue) Algonquin

algorithme /algɔʀitm/ nm algorithm

algorithmique /algɔʀitmik/ adj algorithmic

algue /alg/ nf [1] Bot (d'eau douce) alga; (marine) seaweed ℂ, alga spéc; **des ∼s (marines)** seaweed, algae spéc; [2] Culin seaweed ℂ

(Composés) **∼s brunes** brown algae; **∼s rouges** red algae; **∼s vertes** green algae

alias /aljas/
A nm Ordinat alias
B adv alias

Ali Baba /alibaba/ npr ∼ **et les quarante voleurs** Ali Baba and the forty thieves; **une vraie caverne d'∼** a real Aladdin's cave

alibi /alibi/ nm [1] Jur alibi; **fournir un ∼ très solide** to give a watertight alibi; [2] (prétexte) excuse; **il a invoqué l'∼ d'une importante réunion de travail** he gave an important business meeting as his excuse; **servir d'∼** to do as an excuse

alicament /alikamɑ̃/ nm nutraceutical, functional food

aliénabilité /aljenabilite/ nf Jur alienability

aliénable /aljenabl/ adj Jur alienable

aliénant, ∼e /aljenɑ̃, ɑ̃t/ adj alienating

aliénataire /aljenatɛʀ/ nm,f Jur alienee

aliénateur, -trice /aljenatœʀ, tʀis/ nm,f Jur alienator

aliénation /aljenasjɔ̃/ nf [1] (asservissement) alienation (de of); [2] Jur alienation; [3] †Méd ∼ **(mentale)** insanity, (mental) alienation†

aliéné, ∼e /aljene/ nm,f Méd insane person

aliéner /aljene/ [14]
A vtr [1] Jur (céder) to alienate [terre]; [2] (perdre) to lose [liberté]; (par renoncement) to give up; [3] (détourner) ∼ **qn à qn** to alienate sb from sb; **ces mesures lui ont aliéné une partie du vote socialiste** these measures have lost him a section of the socialist vote; [4] Philos, Sociol to alienate [personne]
B s'aliéner vpr [1] (détourner) to alienate [confrères, électorat, opinion publique]; **s'∼ qch** to lose sth; **tu t'es aliéné leur estime** you have lost their esteem; [2] Philos, Sociol to be alienated (**à** from); **s'∼ par le travail** to be alienated by work

aliéniste /aljenist/ nm,f alienist†, psychiatrist

aligné, ∼e /aliɲe/
A pp ▸ aligner
B pp adj Pol [pays] aligned; **non ∼** nonaligned

alignement /aliɲ(ə)mɑ̃/
A nm [1] (rang) row, line; **mettre qch à l'∼ de qch** to line sth up with sth, to align sth with sth; **se mettre à/sortir de l'∼** [soldat] to fall into/to step out of line; **∼!** Mil fall in!; [2] (mise côte à côte) alignment; [3] (pour la conformité) alignment; ∼ **de qch sur qch** [monnaie, salaires, parti, politique] alignment of sth with sth; **l'∼ de sa conduite sur celle de qn d'autre** bringing one's behaviour^GB into line with sb else's; [4] (de voie publique) alignment
B alignements nmpl Archéol alignments

aligner /aliɲe/ [1]
A vtr [1] (mettre côte à côte) to put [sth] in a line, to line [sth] up; (mettre en ligne droite) to line [sth] up, to align [objets, points]; **alignés contre le mur** lined up ou in a line against the wall; **des objets alignés** objects in a line; **stands alignés le long de la route** rows of stalls along the road; (rendre conforme à) ∼ **qch sur qch** to bring sth into line with sth; [3] (énumérer) to give a list of [statistiques, arguments, chiffres]; (accumuler) to line up [somme]; to notch up^○ [kilomètres, bons résultats]; [4] ^○(payer) **tu peux ∼ tes 100 balles**^○ you can fork out^○ your 100 francs; ∼ **les fautes/les excuses** to make one mistake/excuse after another ou the other; [5] (présenter) to line up [joueurs, équipe]
B s'aligner vpr [1] (être côte à côte) to be in a line; [2] (se mettre en file) to line up; (en formation militaire) to fall into line; [3] **s'∼ sur** to align oneself with [pays, parti, idées]; **s'∼ sur le règlement** to conform with the rules; [4] ^○(dans une compétition) **ils peuvent toujours s'∼!** they can try but they don't stand a chance!

aligot /aligo/ nm: creamed potato with cheese

aligoté /aligɔte/
A adj [cépage, vin] aligoté (épith)
B nm white wine

aliment /alimɑ̃/
A nm [1] (pour êtres humains) food; **un ∼ rare** a rare food; **certains ∼s** certain foods; **lavez/faites cuire vos ∼s** wash/cook your food; **∼s énergétiques/surgelés** high-energy/frozen foods; **dans quels ∼s trouve-t-on du fer?** which foods contain iron?; **un ∼ de base** a staple food; [2] (pour animaux) gén food; (pour animaux d'élevage) feed; **les ∼s pour chats/chiens** catfood/dogfood; **les ∼s pour volailles** poultry feed; [3] (pour plantes) nutrient; **les plantes puisent leurs ∼s dans le sol** plants take their nutrients from the soil; [4] fig **fournir** or **être un ∼ à qch** to feed sth
B aliments nmpl Jur alimony, maintenance

alimentaire /alimɑ̃tɛʀ/ adj [1] lit [besoins, comportement, habitudes] dietary; [ration, aide, industrie, pénurie] food; **prix ∼s** food prices; **produits** or **denrées ∼s** foodstuffs; **régime ∼** diet; **trouble du comportement ∼** eating disorder; [2] fig (pour survivre) **un travail purement ∼** a job done purely to make a living; **roman ∼** potboiler; **il fait de la traduction/peinture ∼** he churns out translations/paintings for money

alimentation /alimɑ̃tasjɔ̃/ nf [1] (manière de se nourrir) diet; **avoir une ∼ saine** to have a healthy diet; **surveiller son ∼** to watch one's diet; **une ∼ riche en** a diet rich in; **l'∼ de base** staple food; [2] (action de se nourrir) feeding; ∼ **artificielle** Méd artificial feeding; **être sous ∼ artificielle** to be artificially fed; [3] Comm (produits alimentaires) food; (industrie) food industry; (commerce) food retailing; **20% de leur budget est consacré à l'∼** 20% of their budget is devoted to food; **le rayon ∼** the food section; **magasin d'∼** food shop, grocery store; [4] (approvisionnement) (en papier, oxygène) feeding (de of); **l'∼ en électricité/eau/mazout de qch** the electricity/water/fuel supply of sth; **l'∼ d'une arme à feu** loading a firearm

alimenter /alimɑ̃te/ [1]
A vtr [1] to feed [personne, animal]; ∼ **au biberon** to bottle-feed; ∼ **qn artificiellement** to feed sb artificially; [2] (approvisionner) [torrent, eau] to feed [lac, rivière, barrage, turbine]; [tuyau, système] to feed [chaudière, poêle, moteur]; ∼ **qch en** to feed sth with [papier, grain, données]; ∼ **une chaudière en mazout** to feed ou supply a stove with oil; ∼ **un appareil en électricité** to power an appliance with electricity; **la centrale alimente toute la ville** the power station supplies the whole town with electricity; ∼ **un budget** to fund a budget; [3] fig to fuel [conversation, hostilité, feu]
B s'alimenter vpr [1] [personne] to eat; [animal] to feed; **il s'alimente bien/mal** he eats well/

badly; **s'∼ de** [personne] to live on; [animal] to feed on; [2] (en eau, gaz, électricité) [ville, bâtiment] **s'∼ en** to be supplied with; [3] [conversation, jalousie, haine] **s'∼ de** to thrive on

alinéa /alinea/ nm (rentré) indentation; (ligne rentrée) indented line; (paragraphe) paragraph; **l'article 49, ∼ 3 de la Constitution** article 49, paragraph 3 of the Constitution

alisier /alizje/ nm sorb

(Composé) ∼ **blanc** whitebeam mountain ash

alitement /alitmɑ̃/ nm bed rest

aliter: s'aliter /alite/ [1] vpr to take to one's bed; **être/rester alité** to be/to remain confined to bed

alizé /alize/
A adj m **vent ∼** trade wind
B nm trade wind; **les ∼s** trade winds

Allah /alla/ npr Allah

allaitement /alɛtmɑ̃/ nm (humain) feeding ℂ; (animal) suckling ℂ

(Composés) ∼ **artificiel** bottle-feeding; ∼ **maternel** breast-feeding; ∼ **mixte** mixed feeding

allaiter /alete/ [1] vtr [femme] to breast-feed; [animal] to suckle; ∼ **au biberon** to bottle-feed

allant, ∼e /alɑ̃, ɑ̃t/
A adj active, lively
B nm drive, bounce; **avoir de l'∼, être plein d'∼** to have plenty of drive, to be full of bounce; **perdre son ∼** to run out of steam

alléchant, ∼e /aleʃɑ̃, ɑ̃t/ adj tempting

allécher /aleʃe/ [14] vtr to tempt; ∼ **qn avec des promesses** to tempt sb with promises

allée /ale/
A nf [1] (chemin) (de jardin, bois, parc) path; (de château) drive; (rue) road; **une petite ∼** a little path; **une ∼ de peupliers** an avenue of poplars; **les ∼s du pouvoir** fig the corridors of power; [2] (entre des rangées de sièges) aisle; ∼ **(centrale)** aisle; ∼ **latérale** side aisle; [3] (escalier) staircase
B allées nfpl ∼s **et venues** comings and goings; **surveiller les ∼s et venues de qn** to watch sb's movements; **faire des ∼s et venues entre les bureaux** to go back and forth between offices

(Composés) ∼ **cavalière** bridleway, bridle path; ∼ **forestière** forest trail

allégation /alegasjɔ̃/ nf allegation; ∼s **mensongères** false allegations

allégé, ∼e /aleʒe/
A pp ▸ alléger
B pp adj [beurre, yaourt, menu, cuisine] low-fat; [sucre, confiture] diet

allégeance /aleʒɑ̃s/ nf allegiance; **faire acte d'∼** to pledge one's allegiance

allégement* /aleʒmɑ̃/ nm [1] (en poids) lightening; [2] (réduction) (de dette, charges) reduction; (de contrôles) relaxing; (de structures, procédures) simplification; ∼ **des effectifs** Scol reduction in numbers; ∼ **de la fiscalité** tax cuts (pl); ∼ **fiscal** tax relief; [3] Sport (en ski) unweighting; [4] (de conditions de détention) improvement, easing

alléger /aleʒe/ [15]
A vtr [1] (rendre moins lourd) to lighten [véhicule, fardeau, bagages]; [2] (rendre moins important) to reduce [dette, charges] (**de** by); to cut [impôt]; to simplify [structure, procédure]; to relax [contrôle]; ∼ **les horaires scolaires** to reduce the school day; ∼ **les programmes** Scol, Univ to cut the content of courses; [3] (rendre moins pénible) to improve [conditions de détention]; to alleviate [souffrances]
B s'alléger vpr [1] (devenir moins lourd) [fardeau, véhicule, bagages] to get lighter; [2] (devenir moins important) [dette, impôt, charges] to be reduced; [dispositif, structure, procédure] to be simplified; [embargo, contrôle] to be relaxed; [3] (devenir moins pénible) [conditions de détention] to be improved

allégorie /alegɔʀi/ nf allegory

allégorique /alegɔʀik/ *adj* allegorical

allégoriquement /alegɔʀikmɑ̃/ *adv* allegorically

allègre /alɛgʀ/ *adj* [*texte, style*] light; [*récit, ton*] light-hearted; [*pas, humeur*] buoyant

allégrement* /alegʀəmɑ̃/ *adv* **1** (avec allégresse) joyfully; **2** *iron* (sans souci) blithely; **elle est partie ~ au Népal** she blithely went off to Nepal; **promettre ~ un allégement des impôts** to promise tax cuts blithely, to make a blithe promise of tax cuts; **mettre ~ qn en prison** to throw sb in jail without a second thought

allégresse /alegʀɛs/ *nf* joy; **dans l'~** in joyful mood; **participer à l'~ générale** to share in the general rejoicing; **explosion d'~** joyous outburst

allegretto* /alegʀɛto/ *nm, adv* allegretto

allegro* /alegʀo/ *adv* allegro

alléguer /alege/ [14] *vtr* **1** (invoquer) to invoke [*exemple, précédent*]; **2** (prétexter) to allege, to claim

allèle /alɛl/ *nm* allele

alléluia /aleluja/ *nm* hallelujah

Allemagne /almaɲ/ ▸ p. 333 *nprf* Germany; **la République fédérale d'~** the Federal Republic of Germany; **les deux ~s** the two Germanies; **l'~ unie** unified Germany; **l'ancienne ~ de l'Est** the former East Germany

allemand, ~e /almɑ̃, ɑ̃d/
A ▸ p. 561 *adj* German
B ▸ p. 483 *nm* Ling German
C allemande *nf* Danse, Mus allemande.

Allemand, ~e /almɑ̃, ɑ̃d/ ▸ p. 561 *nm,f* German; **~ de l'Est/de l'Ouest** East/West German

aller¹ /ale/ [9]
A *v aux* **1** (marque le futur) **je vais partir** I'm leaving; **je vais rentrer chez moi/me coucher** I'm going home/to bed; **j'allais partir** I was just leaving; **j'allais partir quand il est arrivé** I was about to leave when he arrived; **l'homme qui allait inventer la bombe atomique** the man who was to invent the atomic bomb; **il allait le regretter** he was to regret it; **il va le regretter** he'll regret it; **elle va avoir un an** she'll soon be one; **il va faire nuit** it'll soon be dark; **ça va ~ mal**○ there'll be trouble; **tu vas me laisser tranquille?** will you please leave me alone!

2 (marque le futur programmé) **je vais leur dire ce que je pense** I'm going to tell them what I think; **elle va peindre sa cuisine en bleu** she's going to paint her kitchen blue; **j'allais te le dire** I was just going to tell you

3 (marque le mouvement) **~ rouler de l'autre côté de la rue** to go rolling across the street; **~ valser**○ **à l'autre bout de la pièce** to go flying across the room; **~ atterrir**○ **en plein champ/sur mon bureau** to end up in the middle of a field/on my desk

4 (marque l'inclination, l'initiative) **qu'est-ce que tu vas imaginer là?** what a ridiculous idea!; **va savoir!** who knows?; **va** *or* **allez (donc) savoir ce qui s'est passé** who knows what happened?; **qu'es-tu allé te mettre en tête?** where did you pick up that idea?; **qui irait le soupçonner?** who would suspect him?; **vous n'iriez pas leur dire ça?** you're not going to go and say that, are you?; **pourquoi es-tu allé faire ça?** why did you have to go and do that?; **n'allez pas croire une chose pareille!** (pour réfuter) don't you believe it!; (pour tempérer l'enthousiasme) don't get carried away!; **allez y comprendre quelque chose!** just try and work that out!

5 (marque l'évolution) **la situation va (en) se compliquant** the situation is getting more and more complicated; **~ (en) s'améliorant/s'aggravant** to be improving/getting worse; **la tristesse ira (en) s'atténuant** the grief will diminish

B *vi* **1** (se porter, se dérouler, fonctionner) **comment vas-tu, comment ça va?** how are you?; **ça va (bien)** I'm fine; **les enfants vont bien?** are the children all right?; **et ta femme/ton épaule, comment ça va?** how's your wife/your shoulder?; **comment va la santé?** how are you keeping?; **ça va la vie**○? how's life○?; **ça va les amours**○? how's the love life going?; **~ beaucoup mieux** to be much better; **bois ça, ça ira mieux** drink this, you'll feel better; **tout va bien pour toi?** is everything going all right?; **si tout va bien** if everything goes all right; **vous êtes sûr que ça va?** are you sure you're all right?; **les affaires vont bien/mal** business is good/bad; **ça va l'école?** how are things at school?; **ça ne va pas très fort** *or* **bien** (ma santé) I'm not feeling very well; (la vie) things aren't too good; (le moral) I'm feeling a bit low; **ça pourrait ~ mieux, ça va plus ou moins** (réponse) so-so; **ça va mal entre eux** things aren't too good between them; **qu'est-ce qui ne va pas?** what's the matter?; **la voiture a quelque chose qui ne va pas** there's something wrong with the car; **tout va pour le mieux** everything's fine; **tout est allé si vite!** it all happened so quickly!; **ne pas ~ sans peine** *or* **mal** not to be easy; **ne pas ~ sans hésitations** to take some thinking about; **ça va de soi** *or* **sans dire** it goes without saying; **ça devrait ~ de soi** it should be obvious; **ainsi vont les choses** that's the way it goes; **ainsi va le monde** that's the way of the world; **ainsi allait la France** this was the state of affairs in France; **l'amour ne va**

jamais de soi love is never straightforward; **ça va tout seul** (c'est facile) it's a doddle○ GB, it's as easy as pie; **ça ne va pas tout seul** it's not that easy, it's no picnic○; **les choses vont très vite** things are moving fast; **on fait ~**○ struggling on○; **ça peut ~**○, **ça ira**○ could be worse○; **ça va pas, non** *or* **la tête**○? are you mad○ GB *ou* crazy○?; **ça va pas, non, de crier** *or* **gesticuler comme ça**○? what's the matter with you, carrying on like that○?; ▸ **pis**

2 (se déplacer) to go; **tu vas trop vite** you're going too fast; **allez tout droit** go straight ahead; **~ et venir** (dans une pièce) to pace up and down; (d'un lieu à l'autre) to run in and out; **la liberté d'~ et venir** the freedom to come and go at will; **je préfère ~ à pied/en avion** I'd rather walk/fly; **les nouvelles vont vite** news travels fast; **~ d'un pas rapide** to walk quickly; **je sais ~ à bicyclette/cheval** I can ride a bike/horse; **où vas-tu?** where are you going?, where are you off○ to?; **je vais en Pologne** I'm going to Poland; **~ au marché/en ville** to go to the market/into town; **~ chez le médecin/dentiste** to go to the doctor's/dentist's; **va dans ta chambre** go to your room; **je suis allé de Bruxelles à Anvers** I went from Brussels to Antwerp; **je suis allé jusqu'en Chine/au marché** (et pas plus loin) I went as far as China/the market; (et c'était loin) I went all the way to China/the market; **je préfère ne pas y ~** I'd rather not go; **allons-y!** let's go!; **je l'ai rencontré en allant au marché** I met him on the way to the market; **~ vers le nord** to head north; **j'y vais** (je m'en occupe) I'll see to it; (je pars)○ I'm going, I'm off○; **où va-t-il encore?** where is he off to now○?; **~ sur** *or* **vers Paris** to head for Paris; **où va-t-on**○?, **où allons-nous**○? *fig* what are things coming to?, what's the world coming to?; **va donc, eh, abruti**○! get lost○, you idiot!; ▸ **cruche**

3 (pour se livrer à une activité, chercher un produit) **~ à l'école/au travail** to go to school/to work; **~ à la chasse/pêche** to go hunting/fishing; **allez-vous à la piscine?** do you go to the swimming pool?; **il est allé au golf/tennis** he's gone to play golf/tennis; **~ aux champignons/framboises** to go mushroom/raspberry-picking; **~ au pain** to go and get the bread; **dans quelle boulangerie allez-vous?** which bakery do you go to?; **~ aux courses** *or* **commissions**○ to go shopping; **~ au ravitaillement** to go and stock up; **~ aux nouvelles** *or* **informations** to go and see if there's any news

4 (s'étendre dans l'espace) **la route va au village** the road leads to the village; **la rue va de la gare à l'église** the street goes from the station to the church

5 (convenir) **ma robe/la traduction, ça va?** is my dress/the translation all right?; **ça va, ça ira**○, **ça peut aller**○ (en quantité) that'll do; (en qualité) it'll do; **ça va comme ça** it's all right as it is; **ça ne va pas du tout** that's no good at all; **ça ne va pas du tout, tu dois mettre une cravate** you can't go like that, you have to wear a tie; **la traduction n'allait pas** the translation was no good; **lundi ça (te) va?** would Monday suit you *ou* be okay○?; **une soupe, ça (te) va?** how about some soup?; **va pour une soupe**○ soup is okay○; **ça irait si on se voyait demain?** would it it be all right if we met tomorrow?; **si le contrat ne te va pas, ne le signe pas** don't sign the contract if you're not happy with it; **si ça va pour toi, ça va pour moi**○ *or* **ça me va**○ if it's okay by you, it's okay by me○; **ça n'irait pas du tout** (inacceptable) that would never do; **ma scie ne va pas pour le métal** my saw is no good for metal; **ça te va bien de faire la morale/parler comme ça**○ *iron* you're hardly the person to preach/make that sort of remark

6 (être de la bonne taille, de la bonne forme) **~ à qn** to fit sb; **tes chaussures sont trop grandes, elles ne me vont pas** your shoes are too big,

6 aller¹

they don't fit me; **cette vis/clé ne va pas** this screw/key doesn't fit
▸ **7** (flatter, mettre en valeur) ∼ **à qn** to suit sb; **le rouge ne me va pas** *or* **me va mal** red doesn't suit me; **sa robe lui allait (très) bien** her dress really suited her; **le rôle t'irait parfaitement** the part would suit you perfectly; **ta cravate ne va pas avec ta chemise** your tie doesn't go with your shirt; **les tapis vont bien ensemble** the rugs go together well; **les meubles vont bien ensemble** the furniture all matches; **je trouve que ta sœur et son petit ami vont très bien ensemble** I think your sister and her boyfriend are ideally suited
▸ **8** (se ranger) to go; **les assiettes vont dans le placard** the plates go in the cupboard; **la chaise pliante va derrière la porte** the folding chair goes behind the door
▸ **9** (faculté) **pouvoir** ∼ **dans l'eau** to be waterproof; **le plat ne va pas au four** the dish is not ovenproof
▸ **10** (dans une évaluation) **la voiture peut** ∼ **jusqu'à 200 km/h** the car can do up to 200 km/h; **certains modèles peuvent** ∼ **jusqu'à 1 000 euros** some models can cost up to 1,000 euros; **une peine allant jusqu'à cinq ans de prison** a sentence of up to five years in prison
▸ **11** (en arriver à) ∼ **jusqu'au président** to take it right up to the president; ∼ **jusqu'à mentir/tuer** to go as far as to lie/kill; **leur amour est allé jusqu'à la folie** their love bordered on madness
▸ **12** (dans le temps) ∼ **jusqu'en 1914** to go up to 1914; **pendant la période qui va du 8 février au 13 mars** between 8 February and 13 March; **la période qui va de 1918 à 1939** the period between 1918 and 1939; **l'offre va jusqu'à jeudi** the offer lasts until Thursday; **le contrat allait jusqu'en 2007** the contract ran until 2007; **va-t-on vers une nouvelle guerre?** are we heading for another war?; ∼ **sur ses 17 ans** to be going on 17
▸ **13** (agir, raisonner) **vas-y doucement** *or* **gentiment, le tissu est fragile** careful, the fabric is delicate; **ils n'y sont pas allés doucement avec les meubles**○ they were rather rough with the furniture; **tu vas trop vite** you're going too fast; **j'y vais**○ (je vais agir) here we go!; **si tu vas par là** *or* **dans ce sens, rien n'est entièrement vrai** if you take that line, nothing is entirely true
▸ **14** (pour inciter, encourager) **vas-y, demandeleur!**○ (incitation) go on, ask them!; **vas-y, disle!**○ (provocation) come on, out with it!; **allons!, allez!**○ (pour encourager, inciter) come on!; **allez Zidane!, vas-y Zidane!**○ come on Zidane; **allez les Bleus!**○ (Sport) come on France!; **allez-y!**○ (après vous) after you!
▸ **15** (contribuer) **y** ∼ **de sa petite larme** to shed a little tear; **y** ∼ **de sa petite chanson** to do one's party piece; **y** ∼ **de ses économies** to dip into one's savings; **y** ∼ **de sa personne** to pitch in; **y** ∼ **de 100 euros** Jeux to put in 100 euros
▸ **16** ○(se succéder) **ça y va la vodka avec lui** he certainly gets through the vodka; **ça y allait les coups** the fur was flying○
▸ **17** (servir) **où est allé l'argent?** where has the money gone?; **l'argent ira à la réparation de l'église** the money will go toward(s) repairing the church
▸ **18** (enfreindre) ∼ **contre la loi** [*personne*] to break the law; [*acte*] to be against the law; **je ne peux pas** ∼ **contre ce qu'il a décidé** I can't go against his decision

C s'en aller *vpr* ▸ **1** (partir, se rendre) **il faut que je m'en aille** I must go *ou* leave; **je m'en vais en Italie cet été** I'm going to Italy this summer; **je m'en vais du Japon l'année prochaine** I'll be leaving Japan next year; **va-t'en!** go away!; **s'en** ∼ **en vacances/au travail** to go off on vacation/to work; **ils s'en allaient chantant†** they went off singing
▸ **2** (disparaître) **les nuages vont s'en** ∼ the clouds will clear away; **la tache ne s'en va pas** the stain won't come out; **avec le temps,**

tout s'en va everything fades with time; **les années s'en vont** the years go by
▸ **3** fml (mourir) to pass away
▸ **4** (avoir l'intention de, essayer) **je m'en vais leur dire ce que je pense** I'm going to tell them what I think; **ne t'en va pas imaginer une chose pareille** (pour réfuter) don't you believe it!; (pour tempérer l'enthousiasme) don't get carried away!; **va-t'en savoir ce qu'il a voulu dire!** who knows what he meant?

D *v impers* ▸ **1** (être en jeu) **il y va de ma réputation** my reputation is at stake; **il y va de ta santé** your health is at stake
▸ **2** (se passer) **il en va souvent ainsi** that's often what happens; **tout le monde doit aider et il en va de même pour toi** everyone must help, and that goes for you too; **il en ira de même pour eux** the same goes for them; **il en va autrement en Corée** things are different in Korea; **il en ira de lui comme de ses prédécesseurs** he'll go the same way as his predecessors
▸ **3** Math **40 divisé par 12 il y a 3 fois et il reste 4** 12 into 40 goes 3 times with 4 left over

aller² /ale/ *nm* ▸ **1** (trajet) **j'ai fait une escale à l'**∼ I made a stopover on the way out; **j'ai pris le bus à l'**∼ (en allant là) I took the bus there; (en venant ici) I took the bus here; **l'**∼ **a pris trois heures** the journey there took three hours; **il n'arrête pas de faire des** ∼**s et retours entre chez lui et son bureau** he keeps running to and fro from his house to the office; **je suis pressé, je ne fais que l'**∼ **et le retour**○ I'm in a hurry, I've just popped in○; **billet** ∼ gén single ticket GB, one-way ticket US; (d'avion) one-way ticket; **billet** ∼ **(et) retour** return ticket GB, round trip (ticket) US; ▸ **2** (ticket) ∼ **(simple)** single (ticket); **deux** ∼**s (pour) Lille** two singles to Lille; ∼ **(et) retour** return ticket; ▸ **3** Sport (match) first leg; **à l'**∼ in the first leg; **match** *or* **rencontre** ∼ first leg

allergène /alɛʀʒɛn/ *nm* allergen

allergie /alɛʀʒi/ *nf* Méd allergy; **avoir une** ∼ **à qch** Méd to have an allergy to sth; fig to be allergic to sth; **une** ∼ **médicamenteuse** an allergy to a medicine; ∼ **professionnelle** work-related allergy

allergique /alɛʀʒik/ *adj* Méd, fig allergic (**à** to); **réaction** ∼ allergic reaction

allergisant, ∼**e** /alɛʀʒizɑ̃, ɑ̃t/ *adj* Méd [*produit*] allergenic; **sans effet** ∼ hypoallergenic; **un produit qui a une action** ∼**e** a product which causes allergic reactions

allergologie /alɛʀɡɔlɔʒi/ *nf* Méd study of allergies; **se spécialiser en** ∼ to specialize in (the study of) allergies

allergologue /alɛʀɡɔlɔɡ/ ▸ p. 532 *nmf* allergist

alliacé, ∼**e** /aljase/ *adj* [*odeur, plante*] alliaceous

alliage /aljaʒ/ *nm* ▸ **1** (produit) alloy; **en** ∼ alloy (épith); **en** ∼ **d'aluminium** in aluminium GB *ou* aluminum US alloy (après n); ▸ **2** (action) formation of an alloy (**de qch avec qch** of sth and sth); ▸ **3** fig (association) combination

alliance /aljɑ̃s/ *nf* ▸ **1** (bague) wedding ring; ▸ **2** (entente) (entre pays, personnes, groupes) alliance; **faire** ∼ **avec** to form an alliance with; **rompre une** ∼ to break off an alliance; ∼ **militaire** military alliance; ▸ **3** Relig Covenant; **l'ancienne/la nouvelle** ∼ the old/the new Covenant; ▸ **4** (mariage) fml union sout, marriage; **cousin par** ∼ cousin by marriage; ▸ **5** (combinaison) fml combination; **une** ∼ **d'autorité et de douceur** a combination of authority and gentleness

(Composés) **l'**∼ **atlantique** the Atlantic Alliance; ∼ **de mots** Ling oxymoron

allié, ∼**e** /alje/
A *pp* ▸ allier
B *pp adj* (uni) (par un mariage) related by marriage (**à qn** to sb); (par un traité) [*nation, peuple*] allied; **le débarquement** ∼ the Allied landings
C *nm,f* (proche) ally; (parent) relative; **il s'en est fait une** ∼**e** he made an ally of her; **parents et**

∼**s** immediate family and other relatives; **les** ∼**s** Mil Hist the Allies

allier /alje/ [2]
A *vtr* ▸ **1** Tech to alloy [*métaux*] (**à, avec** with); ▸ **2** (combiner) to combine (**et, à** with); **elle réussit à** ∼ **fantaisie et rigueur dans ses œuvres** she successfully combines imagination with precision in her works; ▸ **3** (par un mariage) to unite [sth] by marriage [*familles*]
B s'allier *vpr* ▸ **1** Pol, Mil (s'unir) to form an alliance (**avec, à** with); ▸ **2** (s'harmoniser) [*sons, couleurs*] to go (well) together

Allier /alje/ ▸ p. 372, p. 721 *nprm* (rivière, département) **l'**∼ the Allier

alligator /aligatɔʀ/ *nm* alligator

allitération /al(l)iteʀasjɔ̃/ *nf* alliteration **C**; **une** ∼ **en s/t** alliterative 's's/'t's

allô* /alo/ *excl* hello!, hallo!; ∼**? bonjour! ici Sarah, pourrais-je parler à Yves?** hello, Sarah here, could I speak to Yves?

allocataire /al(l)ɔkatɛʀ/ *nmf* person entitled to a state benefit

allocation /al(l)ɔkasjɔ̃/ *nf* ▸ **1** (action) allocation, granting; ▸ **2** (somme) benefit, benefits (pl) US; **verser une** ∼ to pay sb benefit *ou* benefits US; **toucher des** ∼**s** to get benefit *ou* benefits US; **toucher une** ∼ **de 10 000 euros par an** to get 10,000 euros in benefit *ou* benefits US a year; ▸ **3** Fin (de prêt) granting

(Composés) ∼ **chômage** unemployment benefit *ou* benefits US; ∼ **de devises** foreign currency allowance; ∼ **de fin de droits** income support (after the period of unemployment benefit has ended); ∼ **logement** housing benefit *ou* benefits US; ∼ **de maternité** maternity benefit *ou* benefits US; ∼ **de recherche** Univ research grant; ∼ **vieillesse** discretionary retirement pension; ∼**s familiales** family allowance (sg)

Allocations familiales

Known colloquially as *les allocs*, they cover both maternity benefits and child benefit generally. For a first child, a working mother is entitled to sixteen weeks of paid maternity leave financed by the state. After the birth of a second child, child benefit is payable monthly.

allocs○ /alɔk/ *nfpl* family allowance

allocutaire /al(l)ɔkytɛʀ/ *nmf* Ling addressee

allocution /al(l)ɔkysjɔ̃/ *nf* address; **une** ∼ **de bienvenue/clôture** a welcome/closing address; **prononcer une** ∼ **télévisée** to make a televised address

allogène /al(l)ɔʒɛn/
A *adj* [*population, peuple*] non-indigenous
B *nmf* non-indigenous person

allogreffe /alogʀɛf/ *nf* (de tissu) allograft; (d'organe) allotransplant

allomorphe /alomɔʀf/ *nm* allomorph

allonge /alɔ̃ʒ/ *nf* ▸ **1** (de table) leaf; ▸ **2** (électrique) extension cord, extension lead GB; ▸ **3** Sport (en boxe) reach; ▸ **4** (crochet de boucherie) meat-hook

allongé, ∼**e** /alɔ̃ʒe/
A *pp* ▸ allonger
B *pp adj* ▸ **1** (longiforme) elongated; **visage** ∼ elongated face; ▸ **2** Équit [*pas, trot, galop*] extended

allongement /alɔ̃ʒmɑ̃/ *nm* ▸ **1** (de liste, procédure, délais) lengthening; (de vacances) extension; ▸ **2** (de voyelle) lengthening; ▸ **3** Aviat aspect ratio; ▸ **4** Phys (de ressort) extension

allonger /alɔ̃ʒe/ [13]
A *vtr* ▸ **1** (coucher) to lay [sb] down; ▸ **2** (agrandir) to lengthen [*robe, rideau*] (**de** by); to extend [*itinéraire, liste, vacances*] (**de** by); to prolong [*espérance de vie*] (**de** by); ∼ **le visage de qn** to make sb's face look longer; ∼ **la silhouette de qn** to make sb look slimmer; ∼ **le pas** to quicken one's step; ▸ **3** (étirer) to stretch [sth] out [*bras, cou, jambes*]; **allonge tes jambes sur le canapé** stretch your legs out on the sofa;

elle avait les jambes allongées her legs were stretched out; ④ (diluer) to water [sth] down [café, vin]; **allongé d'eau** watered down; ⑤ ○(dans un combat) to floor° [adversaire, personne]; ⑥ ○(donner) ~ **200 euros** to give 200 euros; **200 euros, allez, allonge!** 200 euros, go on, hand them over!; ~ **un coup de poing à qn** to throw a punch at sb
B vi [jours] to lengthen
C s'allonger vpr ① (pour se reposer, dormir) to lie down; (s'étirer) to stretch out; **allongé sur son lit/le dos** lying on his bed/his back; ② (tomber)○ **s'~ sur le trottoir** to fall flat on the pavement GB ou sidewalk US; (s'agrandir) [liste, délais] to get longer; **ta silhouette s'allonge** you look slimmer; **leur pas s'allonge** they are quickening their step

allopathe /al(l)ɔpat/ nmf allopath

allopathie /al(l)ɔpati/ nf allopathy

allopathique /al(l)ɔpatik/ adj [méthode, traitement] allopathic

allophone /alɔfɔn/
A adj [personne] allophonic
B nmf allophone
C nm Ling allophone

allotir /alɔtiʀ/ [3] vtr to divide up

allotropie /al(l)ɔtʀɔpi/ nf allotropy

allotropique /al(l)ɔtʀɔpik/ adj [état, variétés] allotropic

allouer /alwe/ [1] vtr ① (donner) to allocate [somme, pension, prime, budget] (**à qn** to sb; **à qch** for sth); **la somme qui nous est allouée** the sum allocated to us; ② (accorder) to grant [prêt, indemnité, subvention] (**à qn** to sb; **à qch** for sth); to allot, to allow [temps] (**à qn** to sb; **à qch** for sth); **le temps qui nous est alloué** the time allotted to us

allumage /alymaʒ/ nm ① Aut ignition; **double ~** dual ignition; ② (de lampe, chauffage) switching on; **l'~ est automatique** it switches on automatically

allumé°, ~e /alyme/
A adj ① (fou) mad°; ② (ivre) tipsy°; **être bien ~** to be well oiled°
B nm,f (fou) **c'est un ~** he's mad°; **les ~s du sport** sport fanatics

allume-cigare(s)* /alymsigaʀ/ nm inv cigar lighter

allume-feu* /alymfø/ nm inv fire-lighter

allume-gaz /alymgaz/ nm inv gas lighter

allumer /alyme/ [1]
A vtr ① (par la flamme) to light [bougie, poêle, briquet, gaz]; to strike [allumette]; to start [incendie]; **le feu ne va pas rester allumé** the fire is not going to stay alight GB, lighted US; ② (électriquement) to switch [sth] on, to turn [sth] on [lumière, appareil, électricité]; ~ **la chambre** to switch on ou turn on the light in the bedroom; **le couloir est allumé** the light is (switched ou turned) on in the corridor; **laisser ses phares allumés** to leave one's headlights on; **laisser sa chambre allumée** to leave the lights in one's room on; **allume!** switch on ou turn on the light!; **c'est allumé chez elle** her lights are on; ③ (exciter) [imagination] to arouse [désir, jalousie, colère]; to turn [sb] on° [personne]
B **s'allumer** vpr ① (électriquement) [lampe, radio, chauffage] to switch on; **le chauffage s'allume automatiquement** the heating switches on automatically; **le couloir s'allume où?** where do you switch on the light in the corridor?; ② (s'exciter) [désir, colère] to be aroused; [regard] to light up

allumette /alymɛt/ nf match, matchstick
(Composés) ~ **au fromage** Culin cheese straw GB, cheese stick US; ~ **suédoise** or **de sûreté** safety match
(Idiome) **avoir des jambes commes des ~s** to have legs like matchsticks

allumeur, -euse /alymœʀ, øz/ ▸ p. 532
A nm,f ① ~ **de réverbères** lamplighter; ② ○(séducteur) tease
B nm Aut, Mécan distributor

allure /alyʀ/ nf ① (de marcheur) pace; (de véhicule) speed; **rouler à vive** or **grande/faible ~** to drive at high/low speed; **l'entreprise s'est développée à grande ~** the company expanded at a tremendous pace; **modérer** or **ralentir son ~** to slow down; **presser l'~** (à pied) to quicken one's pace; (en véhicule) to speed up; **à toute ~** (conduire, marcher) at top speed; (réciter, manger, noter) really fast; **partir à toute ~** to speed off; **à cette ~ nous allons être en retard** at this rate we're going to be late; ② (apparence) (de personne) appearance; (de vêtement) look; (d'événement) aspect; **avoir des ~s de** to look like; **il a une drôle d'~** he's a funny-looking chap; **tu as une ~** or **de l'~ avec ce chapeau!** you look really daft in that hat!; **ses vêtements lui donnent l'~ d'un bandit** his clothes make him look like a gangster; **prendre l'~** or **les ~s de** [changement, révolte] to begin to look like; [personne] to make oneself out to be; ③ (distinction) style; **elle a beaucoup d'~** she's got a lot of style; **avoir belle ~** to look very stylish; **une personne de belle ~** a distinguished-looking person; **le salon a de l'~** the sitting room is stylish; **avoir fière ~** to cut a fine figure; ④ Naut sailing trim; ⑤ (d'animal) gait

allusif, -ive /alyzif, iv/ adj ① (qui contient une allusion) [propos, phrase, réponse] allusive; ② (qui parle par allusions) [personne] indirect; **elle est restée très allusive** she spoke very indirectly; **répondre de façon allusive** to give an indirect reply, to reply indirectly

allusion /alyzjɔ̃/ nf (évocation, sous-entendu) allusion (**à** to); **faire ~ à** to allude to; **une ~ littéraire** a literary allusion; **une ~ perfide** an innuendo; **sans faire la moindre ~ au conflit** without alluding at all to the conflict; **l'~ n'était pas innocente** it was not an innocent allusion

allusivement /alyzivmɑ̃/ adv [s'exprimer, répondre] indirectly

alluvial, ~e, mpl -iaux /alyvjal, o/ adj alluvial

alluvion /alyvjɔ̃/ nf alluvium; **des ~s** alluvia

alluvionnement /alyvjɔnmɑ̃/ nm alluviation

alluvionner /alyvjɔne/ [1] vi to deposit alluvia

Alma-Ata /almaata/ ▸ p. 894 npr Alma-Ata

almanach /almana(k)/ nm almanac

almée /alme/ nf Hist, littér almah

aloès /alɔɛs/ nm inv aloe

aloi /alwɑ/ nm **un succès de bon/mauvais ~** a well-deserved/an undeserved success; **une plaisanterie de bon/mauvais ~** a joke in good taste/a tasteless joke; **une gaieté de bon ~** a simple cheerfulness

alopécie /alopesi/ nf hair loss, alopecia spéc

alors /alɔʀ/
A adv ① (à ce moment-là) (dans le passé ou dans le futur) then; **nous pourrons ~ réaliser nos projets** then we will be able to carry out our plans; **j'ai les mêmes amis qu'~** I've got the same friends as I had then; **il est aussi timide qu'~** he's as shy as he was then; **il avait ~ 18 ans** he was 18 at the time; ~ **seulement tu pourras faire** only then will you be able to do; ~ **enfin** il put sortir then at last he could go out; **l'usine, ~ en pleine activité** the factory, which was then at full production; **le président, ~ gravement malade** the president, who was seriously ill at the time; **le pays, ~ sorti de la crise, pourra** the country which by then will be out of recession, will be able to; **la mode/les habitudes d'~** the fashion/the custom in those days; **c'étaient les mœurs d'~** that was the custom in those days; **le propriétaire/patron/premier ministre d'~** the then owner/boss/prime minister; **le premier ministre britannique d'~** the British Prime Minister at the time; **les enfants d'~ craignaient le maître** in those days children were scared of their teachers; **mes amis**

d'~ **étaient surtout des peintres** my friends at the time were mainly painters; **mes toiles/romans d'~** my paintings/novels of the time; **jusqu'~** until then; **il n'avait cessé jusqu'~ de refuser** until then he had kept on refusing; **une organisation terroriste jusqu'~ inconnue** a terrorist organization which nobody had heard of before then; **c'est ~ qu'il prit la parole** it was then that he started to speak; **c'est ~ qu'il prendra une décision** then he'll come to a decision; **c'est seulement ~ que nous saurons s'il est sauvé** only then will we know whether he's been saved or not
② (dans ce cas-là) then; **s'il venait à mourir, ~ elle hériterait** if he should die, then she would inherit; ~ **je m'en vais** I'm going then; **(mais)** ~ **cela change tout!** but that changes everything!; **et (puis)** ~? so what?; ~ **quoi?** on est encore en retard? what's this? late again are we?; ~ **quoi? qu'est-ce que j'entends?** on n'est pas content? what's this I hear? complaining are we?; ~**? que faisons-nous?** so? what shall we do?; ~**? qu'en penses-tu?** so? what do you think?
③ (de ce fait) so; **il y avait grève du métro, ~ j'ai pris un taxi** there was a tube GB ou subway US strike, so I took a taxi
④ (pour résumer) then; **on se voit demain ~?** we'll see each other tomorrow then?; **tu n'as rien trouvé d'autre ~?** you couldn't find anything else then?
⑤ (ou bien) **ou ~** or else; **il a oublié le rendez-vous ou ~ il a eu un accident** he's forgotten the appointment, or else he's had an accident; **je serai dans la cuisine ou ~ dans le jardin** I'll be in the kitchen or in the garden
⑥ ○(dans un récit) so; ~ **il me dit..., ~ je lui dis...** so he said to me..., so I said to him...; ~ **le type s'en va** so the guy goes off
⑦ (pour renforcer une exclamation) **non mais ~!** honestly!; **ça ~!** (étonnement) good grief!; ~ **ça!** (indignation) that's not on!; **chic** or **chouette ~!** (hey) that's great!; **mince** or **zut ~!** (étonnement) wow°!; (colère) blast°! GB, darn°! US
B alors que loc conj ① (pendant que) while; **j'ai appris la nouvelle ~ que j'étais à Rome** I heard the news while I was in Rome; **il fait chaud ici ~ que dehors il gèle** it's hot in here while outside it's freezing; ② (tandis que) when; **vous jouez ~ qu'il faudrait travailler** you're playing when you should be working; **tu lui souris ~ que tu le détestes** you smile at him while (in fact) you hate him
C alors même que loc conj even though

alose /aloz/ nf shad

alouette /alwɛt/ nf lark
(Composé) ~ **des champs** skylark
(Idiome) **attendre que les ~s vous tombent toutes rôties dans le bec** Prov to expect everything just to drop into one's lap

alourdir /aluʀdiʀ/ [3]
A vtr ① (rendre plus lourd) [fardeau] to weigh [sb] down [personne]; [problème] to make [sth] tense [atmosphère]; **le subjonctif/l'adverbe alourdit la phrase** the subjunctive/the adverb weighs the sentence down; **la valise était alourdie par les livres** the suitcase was weighed down by the books; **un manteau alourdi par la pluie** a coat heavy with rain; ② (rendre plus important) to increase [impôt, charges, déficit]; **le dernier témoignage a alourdi les accusations** the statement by the last witness weighed heavily against the accused
B s'alourdir vpr ① (devenir plus lourd) [paupières] to grow heavy; [air, atmosphère] to get heavy; ② (devenir plus important) [dépenses, dette] to increase; **le bilan de victimes s'est alourdi** the death toll has risen

alourdissement /aluʀdismɑ̃/ nm ① (en poids) heaviness; ② Fin (de l'impôt, de prélèvement) increase (**de** in)

aloyau /alwajo/ nm (Culin) sirloin; **un bifteck dans l'~** a sirloin steak

a

alpaga /alpaga/ *nm* (animal, laine) alpaca

alpage /alpaʒ/ *nm* mountain pasture

alpaguer /alpage/ [1] *vtr* to collar [*personne*]; **se faire ~ par qn** to be collared by sb

alpe /alp/ *nf* alpine pasture

Alpes /alp/ ▸ p. 721 *nprfpl* **les ~s** the Alps

Alpes-de-Haute-Provence /alpdəotpRɔvɑ̃s/ ▸ p. 721 *nprfpl* (département) **les ~** the Alpes-de-Haute-Provence

Alpes-Maritimes /alpmaRitim/ ▸ p. 721 *nprfpl* (département) **les ~** the Alpes-Maritimes

alpestre /alpɛstR/ *adj* alpine

alpha* /alfa/ *nm inv* (lettre) alpha

(Idiome) **être l'~ et l'omega** to be the alpha and omega

alphabet /alfabɛ/ *nm* [1] (signes) alphabet; [2] (manuel) ABC (book)

(Composés) **~ morse** Morse alphabet; **~ phonétique international, API** International Phonetic Alphabet, IPA

alphabétique /alfabetik/ *adj* alphabetical; **dans l'ordre** *or* **par ordre ~** in alphabetical order

alphabétiquement /alfabetikmɑ̃/ *adv* alphabetically

alphabétisation /alfabetizasjɔ̃/ *nf* [1] (enseignement de l'écriture) literacy tuition; **une politique d'~** a policy of promoting literacy; **un cours d'~** a literacy class; [2] (mise en ordre alphabétique) alphabetizing

alphabétiser /alfabetize/ [1] *vtr* [1] (enseigner) to teach [sb] to read and write [*personne, groupe*]; to promote literacy in [*population, pays*]; [2] (mettre en ordre alphabétique) to put [sth] in alphabetical order, to alphabetize

alphafétoprotéine /alfafetopRɔtein/ *nf* alphafetoprotein

alpha-immunothérapie, *pl* **~s** /alfaimynoteRapi/ *nf* alpha ray therapy

alphanumérique /alfanymeRik/ *adj* alphanumeric

alpin, **~e** /alpɛ̃, in/ *adj* alpine

alpinisme /alpinism/ ▸ p. 469 *nm* mountaineering

alpiniste /alpinist/ *nmf* mountaineer

Al-Quaida /alkaida/ *nm* Al-Quaeda

Alsace /alzas/ ▸ p. 721 *nprf* **l'~** Alsace

alsacien, **-ienne** /alzasjɛ̃, ɛn/
A ▸ p. 721 *adj* [*personne*] from Alsace; [*cuisine, population, paysage*] of Alsace
B ▸ p. 483 *nm* Ling Alsatian

Alsacien, **-ienne** /alzasjɛ̃, ɛn/ *nm,f* Alsatian

altérable /alteRabl/ *adj* [*couleur*] unstable; [*revêtement*] easily damaged

altération /alteRasjɔ̃/ *nf* [1] (détérioration) (de facultés) impairment (**de** of); (de denrée) spoiling (**de** of); (d'environnement) deterioration (**de** in); (de sentiment, couleur) change (**de** in); **l'~ de sa santé** the deterioration in his health; [2] (falsification) (de texte, faits) distortion; (de monnaie) falsification; [3] Mus **~ (accidentelle)** accidental; **~ constitutive** key signature

altercation /altɛRkasjɔ̃/ *nf* altercation

alter ego /altɛRego/ *nm inv* alter ego

altérer /alteRe/ [14]
A *vtr* [1] (détériorer) to impair [*saveur, caractère, relation*]; to affect [*santé*]; to spoil [*denrée*]; to mar [*joie*]; to alter [*sentiment, composition*]; to change [*expression, visage*]; to fade [*couleur*]; **d'une voix altérée** in a faltering voice; [2] (falsifier) to distort [*fait, texte*]; to falsify [*monnaie*]; to adulterate [*substance*]; [3] *fml* (donner soif) to make [sb] feel parched; **être altéré de sang** to thirst for blood
B s'altérer *vpr* [*santé, faculté, relation, saveur*] to become impaired; [*denrée*] to spoil; [*voix*] to falter; [*sentiments, expression*] to change

altérité /alteRite/ *nf* otherness

altermondialisation /altɛRmɔ̃djalizasjɔ̃/ *nf* alterglobalization

altermondialiste /altɛRmɔ̃djalist/ *adj, nmf* alterglobalist

alternance /altɛRnɑ̃s/ *nf* [1] gén alternation; **~ d'ondées et d'éclaircies** showers with intermittent bright spells; **en ~ avec** alternately with; **en ~** alternately; **'l'Avare' se joue en ~** 'l'Avare' is on every other night; **formation en ~** work-based learning **⊄**; [2] Pol **choisir l'~** [*électorat, pays*] to opt for a change in power

alternant, **~e** /altɛRnɑ̃, ɑ̃t/ *adj* alternating

alternateur /altɛRnatœR/ *nm* Électrotech alternator

alternatif, **-ive** /altɛRnatif, iv/
A *adj* [1] gén alternate; [2] Électrotech alternating; [3] Sociol alternative
B alternative *nf* alternative

alternativement /altɛRnativmɑ̃/ *adv* alternately, in turn

alterne /altɛRn/ *adj* [1] Bot alternate; [2] Math [*angles*] alternate

alterné, **~e** /altɛRne/ *adj* alternating

alterner /altɛRne/ [1]
A *vtr* gén to alternate; **nous alternons cours pratique et cours théorique** we alternate between practical work and lessons in theory; **~ les cultures** to rotate crops
B *vi* [1] (se succéder) [*périodes, couleurs, objets*] to alternate (**avec** with); [2] (se relayer) [*personnes, groupe*] **~ avec qn pour faire qch** to take turns with sb (at) doing sth; **les deux partis ont alterné au pouvoir pendant 30 ans** the two parties have been alternately in and out of power for 30 years

altesse /altɛs/ *nf* [1] (titre) highness; **son Altesse royale** His/Her Royal Highness; [2] (personne) prince/princess

altier, **-ière** /altje, ɛR/ *adj* [*personne, attitude, démarche*] haughty; **avoir un port ~** to have a haughty bearing

altimètre /altimɛtR/ *nm* altimeter

altimétrie /altimetRi/ *nf* altimetry

altiport /altipɔR/ *nm* mountain airstrip

altiste /altist/ ▸ p. 557, p. 532 *nmf* viola player GB, violist US

altitude /altityd/ *nf* [1] (hauteur) altitude; **perdre/prendre de l'~** [*avion, ballon*] to lose/to gain altitude *or* height; **à basse/haute ~** [*neiger, voler*] at low/high altitude; **vol à basse/haute ~** low/high altitude flight; **à une ~ de 2 000 mètres** [*avion*] at an altitude of 2,000 metres^GB; [*montagne, plateau*] at a height of 2,000 metres^GB (above sea-level), at an altitude of 2,000 metres^GB; **quelle est l'~ du mont Blanc?** how high is Mont Blanc?, what is the altitude of Mont Blanc?; **des sommets de plus de 6 000 mètres d'~** peaks more than 6,000 metres^GB high; **avoir une faible ~** [*plateau, ville*] to be close to sea-level; [2] (haute montagne) **en ~** [*pousser, neiger*] high up (in the mountains), at altitude spéc; **station d'~** mountain resort

alto /alto/
A *adj* [*saxophone, clarinette*] alto
B *nm* [1] ▸ p. 557 (instrument) viola; [2] ▸ p. 532 (musicien) viola player GB, violin US; [3] ▸ p. 141 (voix) alto

altocumulus /altokymylys/ *nm inv* altocumulus

altostratus /altostRatys/ *nm inv* altostratus

altruisme /altRɥism/ *nm* altruism

altruiste /altRɥist/
A *adj* altruistic
B *nmf* altruist

alu /aly/ *nm* aluminium GB, aluminum US; **papier ~** kitchen foil

aluminate /alyminat/ *nm* aluminate

alumine /alymin/ *nf* alumina

aluminer /alymine/ [1] *vtr* to aluminize

aluminium /alyminjɔm/ *nm* aluminium GB, aluminum US; **d'~** [*resine, production*] aluminium GB, aluminum US; **en ~** [*casseroles, jantes*] aluminium (épith) GB, aluminum (épith) US

alun /alœ̃/ *nm* alum

alunir /alyniR/ [3] *vi* controv to land on the moon

alunissage /alynisaʒ/ *nm* controv moon landing

alvéolaire /alveolɛR/ *adj* [1] Anat [*arcade, point*] alveolar; [2] Ling [*consonne, articulation*] alveolar; [3] Géol [*structure*] alveolate

alvéole /alveol/ *nf* [1] (de ruche) alveolus; [2] Anat (de poumon) alveolus; (de dent) tooth socket, alveolus spéc; [3] Géol cavity

alvéolé, **~e** /alveole/ *adj* [*caoutchouc, carton, métal*] honeycombed

Alzheimer /alzajmœR/ ▸ p. 283 *npr* **la maladie d'~** Alzheimer's disease

amabilité /amabilite/
A *nf* [1] (gentillesse) kindness; **avec ~** kindly; **veuillez avoir l'~ de** please; **il est toujours plein d'~** he's always very pleasant; **quelle ~!** iron charming!; [2] (politesse) courtesy; **avec ~** politely, courteously
B amabilités *nfpl* (prévenances) **faire des ~s à qn** to be polite to sb; **se dire des ~s** lit to exchange pleasantries; iron to exchange insults; **après cet échange d'~s** lit after this exchange of pleasantries; iron after this exchange of insults

amadou /amadu/ *nm* tinder, touchwood

amadouer /amadwe/ [1]
A *vtr* to coax, to cajole [*personne, animal*]; **~ qn pour qu'il fasse qch** to cajole sb into doing sth; **elle cherche à nous ~ avec des promesses** she's trying to cajole us with promises; **se laisser ~** to let oneself be coaxed
B s'amadouer *vpr* [*personne*] to soften

amaigrir /amegRiR/ [3] *vtr* [*maladie, régime*] to make [sb] thinner [*personne*]; **je l'ai trouvée très amaigrie** I found her much thinner; **un visage amaigri par la maladie** a face made thin by illness

amaigrissant, **~e** /amegRisɑ̃, ɑ̃t/ *adj* [*régime, produit*] slimming

amaigrissement /amegRismɑ̃/ *nm* weight loss, loss of weight

amalgamation /amalgamasjɔ̃/ *nf* amalgamation

amalgame /amalgam/ *nm* [1] (de qualités, sentiments) mixture; (d'idées) pej hotchpotch GB, hodgepodge US; (d'objets, de personnes) mixture; **faire l'~ entre des problèmes/situations** pej to lump together various problems/situations; [2] Dent, Chimie amalgam

amalgamer /amalgame/ [1] *vtr* [1] (associer) pej to lump together [*idées, problèmes*]; to combine, to mix [*qualité, sentiments*]; to mix [*personnes, communautés*]; [2] (mélanger) to blend, to amalgamate [*ingrédients*]

amande /amɑ̃d/ *nf* Bot [1] (fruit) almond; **en ~** almond-shaped; **yeux en ~** almond(-shaped) eyes; **huile d'~ douce** almond oil; [2] (dans un noyau) kernel

amandier /amɑ̃dje/ *nm* almond tree

amandine /amɑ̃din/ *nf* almond tart

amanite /amanit/ *nf* amanita

(Composés) **~ phalloïde** death cap; **~ tue-mouche** fly agaric; **~ vireuse** destroying angel

amant /amɑ̃/ *nm* lover; **prendre un ~** to take a lover

amante‡ /amɑ̃t/ *nf* mistress†, lover

amarante /amaRɑ̃t/
A ▸ p. 202 *adj inv* amaranthine
B *nm* [1] (couleur) red; [2] (arbre) purple heart; **bois d'~** purple heart
C *nf* [1] (plante) amaranth; [2] (colorant) amaranth

amariner /amaRine/ [1] *vtr* [1] (habituer à la mer) to accustom [sb] to life at sea [*personne*];

analphabète /analfabɛt/ *adj, nmf* illiterate

analphabétisme /analfabetism/ *nm* illiteracy

analysable /analizabl/ *adj* analysable^{GB}

analyse /analiz/ *nf* ① gén (examen) analysis; ~ **politique/financière** political/financial analysis; **ton** ~ **de la situation est très juste** your analysis of the situation is very accurate; ~ **d'un produit/d'une substance** analysis of a product/of a substance; **faire l'~ de qch** to analyse^{GB} sth; **en dernière** ~ in the final analysis; **avoir l'esprit d'**~ to have an analytical mind; ② Méd test; **elle s'est fait faire des** ~**s** she's had tests done; ③ Math (discipline) calculus; ④ Psych psychoanalysis; **faire une** ~, **être en** ~ to be in analysis

(Composés) ~ **combinatoire** combinatorial analysis; ~ **coût-efficacité** cost-effectiveness analysis; ~ **coûts-avantages** cost-benefit analysis; ~ **économique** economic analysis; ~ **fonctionnelle** functional analysis; ~ **grammaticale** parsing; **faire l'~ grammaticale d'une phrase** to parse a sentence; ~ **harmonique** harmonic analysis; ~ **logique** clause analysis; ~ **numérique** numerical analysis; ~ **organique** organic analysis; ~ **de sang** blood test; ~ **spectrale** spectrum analysis; ~ **transactionnelle** transactional analysis; ~ **d'urine** urine test; ~ **de la valeur** value engineering; ~ **vectorielle** vector analysis

analyser /analize/ [1] *vtr* ① gén to analyse^{GB} [*problème, situation, produit, substance, texte*]; ② Méd to test [*sang, urine*]; ③ Psych to psychoanalyse^{GB}; **se faire** ~ to be in analysis

analyseur /analizœr/ *nm* ~ **différentiel** Ordinat differential analyser^{GB}; ~ **d'ondes** Phys wave analyser^{GB}; ~ **de spectre** Phys spectrum analyser^{GB}

analyste /analist/ ▸ p. 532 *nmf* ① gén, Ordinat analyst; ② Psych analyst

(Composé) ~ **financier** Fin financial analyst

analyste-programmeur, **-euse**, *mpl* **analystes-programmeurs** /analist-prɔgramœr, øz/ ▸ p. 532 *nm,f* analyst-programmer

analytique /analitik/ ① *adj* ① gén, Philos analytical; ② Psych analytic ② *nf* Philos analytics (+ *v sg*)

analytiquement /analitikmɑ̃/ *adv* analytically

anamorphose /anamɔrfoz/ *nf* anamorphosis

ananas /anana(s)/ *nm inv* pineapple

anapeste /anapɛst/ *nm* anapaest

anaphore /anafɔr/ *nf* anaphora

anaphylactique /anafilaktik/ *adj* anaphylactic; **choc** ~ anaphylactic shock, anaphylaxis

anar[○] /anar/ *adj inv, nmf* (*abbr* = **anarchiste**) anarchist

anarchie /anarʃi/ *nf* lit, fig anarchy

anarchique /anarʃik/ *adj* lit, fig anarchic

anarchiquement /anarʃikmɑ̃/ *adv* anarchically

anarchisant, ~**e** /anarʃizɑ̃, ɑ̃t/ *adj* anarchistic

anarchisme /anarʃism/ *nm* anarchism

anarchiste /anarʃist/ ① *adj* anarchistic ② *nmf* anarchist

anarcho-syndicalisme* /anarkosɛ̃dikalism/ *nm* anarcho-syndicalism

anarcho-syndicaliste, *pl* ~**s*** /anarko-sɛ̃dikalist/ *adj, nmf* anarcho-syndicalist

anastigmatique /anastigmatik/ *adj* anastigmatic

anastrophe /anastrɔf/ *nf* anastrophe

anathème /anatɛm/ *nm* anathema; **prononcer l'~ contre qn, frapper qn d'~** to excommunicate sb; **jeter l'~ sur qn/qch** fig to curse *ou* anathematize sout sb/sth

Anatolie /anatɔli/ ▸ p. 721 *nprf* Anatolia

anatolien, **-ienne** /anatɔljɛ̃, ɛn/ *adj* Anatolian

anatomie /anatɔmi/ *nf* ① Anat (science) anatomy; (structure) anatomy; ② ○(silhouette) figure; **elle a une belle** ~ she's got a good figure; ③ (analyse) analysis; **faire l'~ d'une crise économique** to analyse^{GB} an economic crisis

(Composé) ~ **artistique** (spécialité) life drawing; (œuvre) life study

anatomique /anatɔmik/ *adj* [*étude, planche, dessin*] anatomical; [*forme, objet*] anatomically designed

anatomiquement /anatɔmikmɑ̃/ *adv* anatomically

anatomiste /anatɔmist/ *nmf* anatomist

ancestral, ~**e**, *mpl* **-aux** /ɑ̃sestral, o/ *adj* ancestral

ancêtre /ɑ̃sɛtr/ *nmf* ① (aïeul) ancestor; **mes** ~**s** my ancestors, my forebears; **nos** ~**s les Gaulois** our ancestors the Gauls; ② ○(personne âgée) old man/woman; ③ (forme ancienne) ancestor; (précurseur) father, forerunner; **l'~ de l'homme/du catamaran** the ancestor of man/of the catamaran

anche /ɑ̃ʃ/ *nf* Mus reed

anchois /ɑ̃ʃwa/ *nm inv* anchovy

ancien, **-ienne** /ɑ̃sjɛ̃, ɛn/ ① *adj* ① (qui a été autrefois) [*champion, mari, président, coiffeur, toxicomane, capitale*] former; **mon ancienne école** my old school; ② (vieux) [*église, connaissance, modèle, famille*] old; **dans l'~ temps** in the olden days; ③ Antiq [*histoire, langue, civilisation*] ancient; **la Grèce ancienne** ancient Greece; **l'~ français** Old French; ④ Art, Comm [*style, monnaie, tableau*] old; [*voiture*] vintage; [*meuble*] antique; [*livre*] old, antiquarian; ⑤ (dans une profession, une fonction, un grade) senior ② *nm* ① (vétéran) (de congrégation, tribu) elder; (d'entreprise) senior member; **les** ~**s du village** the village elders; **les** ~**s** (les personnes âgées) the older people; ② (qui a été membre) (d'école, entreprise) old member; (de grande école) graduate; ③ (immobilier) **l'**~ older property; ④ Comm (vieilles choses) antiques (*pl*); **acheter de l'**~ to buy antiques; ⑤ (pour distinguer des générations) elder; **Caton l'**~ Cato the Elder ③ *anciens nmpl* Antiq ancients; **littérature des** ~**s** literature of the ancients ④ *ancienne nf* **à l'ancienne** [*confiture, meuble*] traditional; [*préparé, fabriqué*] in the traditional way

(Composés) ~ **combattant** veteran; ~ **élève** Scol old boy; Univ graduate; ~ **franc** old franc; **l'**~ **monde** the Old World; **l'Ancien Régime** the Ancien Régime; **l'Ancien Testament** the Old Testament

anciennement /ɑ̃sjɛnmɑ̃/ *adv* formerly

ancienneté /ɑ̃sjɛnte/ *nf* ① (de personne) seniority (dans in); **elle a plus d'**~ **que lui** she has more seniority than him; **avoir peu d'**~ to have little seniority; **promotion à l'**~ promotion based on seniority; **trois mois/ans d'**~ three months'/years' service; **jour d'**~ Entr, Ind service-related leave *ou* holiday GB; ~ **dans le chômage** average period of unemployment; ② (de tradition, relique) antiquity; ③ (âge) age; ④ (temps écoulé depuis) **l'**~ **de leur immigration** the time elapsed since they immigrated; **en raison de l'**~ **des faits** because the events happened a long time ago

ancillaire /ɑ̃silɛr/ *adj* **amours** ~**s** amorous liaisons with the servants

ancrage /ɑ̃kraʒ/ *nm* ① Naut (action d'ancrer) anchoring; (mouillage) anchorage; ② Constr (de mur) cramping

ancre /ɑ̃kr/ *nf* ① Naut anchor; **jeter l'**~ lit to cast anchor; fig to settle down; **lever l'**~ lit to weigh anchor; fig[○] to get a move on[○]; **être à l'**~ to be *ou* lie *ou* ride at anchor; ② Tech (dans le bâtiment) cramp-iron; (en horlogerie) anchor escapement

(Composé) ~ **de salut** *or* **miséricorde** sheet anchor

ancrer /ɑ̃kre/ [1] ① *vtr* ① Naut to anchor [*navire*]; **les navires ancrés dans la baie** the ships lying at anchor *ou* anchored in the bay; ② (fixer) ~ **une idée dans les esprits** to fix an idea in people's minds; ~ **un parti dans une région** to establish a party in an area; ~ **qch dans la réalité** to anchor sth to reality; ③ Constr to cramp [*bâtiment*] ② *s'ancrer vpr* ① Naut to anchor, to cast anchor; ② fig [*idée*] to become fixed (**dans** in); [*parti, coutume*] to become established (**dans** in); **tradition bien ancrée** well-established tradition; **société trop ancrée dans ses habitudes** society which is too set in its ways

andain /ɑ̃dɛ̃/ *nm* swathe

andalou, **-ouse** /ɑ̃dalu, uz/ *adj* Andalusian

Andalou, **-ouse** /ɑ̃dalu, uz/ *nm,f* Andalusian

Andalousie /ɑ̃daluzi/ ▸ p. 721 *nprf* Andalusia

andante /ɑ̃dɑ̃t(e)/ *nm, adv* andante

Andes /ɑ̃d/ *nprfpl* **les** ~ the Andes

andin, ~**e** /ɑ̃dɛ̃, in/ *adj* Andean

andorran, ~**e** /ɑ̃dɔrɑ̃, an/ ▸ p. 561 *adj* Andorran

Andorran, ~**e** /ɑ̃dɔrɑ̃, an/ ▸ p. 561 *nm,f* Andorran

Andorre /ɑ̃dɔr/ ▸ p. 333 *nprf* Andorra

andouille /ɑ̃duj/ *nf* ① Culin andouille; ② ○fool; **faire l'**~ to act the fool GB, to goof around US

andouiller /ɑ̃duje/ *nm* branch of an antler, tine spéc

andouillette /ɑ̃dujɛt/ *nf* andouillette (*small sausage made from chitterlings*)

androgène /ɑ̃drɔʒɛn/ ① *adj* androgenic ② *nm* androgen

androgenèse /ɑ̃drɔʒənɛz/ *nf* androgenesis

androgyne /ɑ̃drɔʒin/ ① *adj* androgynous ② *nm* androgyne

androïde /ɑ̃drɔid/ *nm* android

Andromaque /ɑ̃drɔmak/ *npr* Andromache

andropause /ɑ̃drɔpoz/ *nf* male menopause

androstérone /ɑ̃drosterɔn/ *nf* androsterone

âne /ɑn/ *nm* ① Zool donkey, ass; ② ○(personne stupide) dimwit[○]; Scol dunce

(Composé) ~ **bâté** stupid clot

(Idiomes) **faire l'~ pour avoir du son** to act dumb to find out more; **être comme l'~ de Buridan** to be chronically indecisive

anéantir /aneɑ̃tir/ [3] ① *vtr* ① (détruire) to ruin [*récoltes*]; to lay waste to [*ville, région*]; to wipe out [*peuple, armée*]; to shatter [*espoir, rêve, autorité*]; ② (abattre) [*nouvelle, chagrin*] to crush; [*effort, fatigue*] to exhaust; [*chaleur*] to overwhelm; **anéanti par la fatigue** utterly exhausted ② *s'anéantir vpr* [*espoir, rêve*] to be shattered

anéantissement /aneɑ̃tismɑ̃/ *nm* ① (de ville, pays) destruction; (de peuple, armée) annihilation; (de récolte) devastation; ② (d'espoir) shattering; (d'une personne) total collapse; **la nouvelle a provoqué l'~ de tous leurs espoirs** the news completely shattered all their hopes

anecdote /anɛkdɔt/ *nf* anecdote; **ton article tient plus de l'~ que de l'analyse** your article is more anecdotal than analytical; **un auteur qui se perd dans l'~** an author who digresses on trivial topics; **pour l'~** as a matter of interest

anecdotique /anɛgdɔtik, anɛkdɔtik/ *adj* anecdotal

anémie /anemi/ *nf* ① ▸ p. 283 Méd anaemia; ② fig weakness

(Composé) ~ **pernicieuse** pernicious anaemia

anémier /anemje/ [2]
A *vtr* ① Méd to make [sb] anaemic [*personne*]; ② fig to weaken
B **s'anémier** *vpr* ① Méd to become anaemic; ② fig to grow feeble

anémique /anemik/ *adj* ① Méd anaemic; ② fig weak, anaemic

anémomètre /anemomɛtR/ *nm* anemometer

anémone /anemɔn/ *nf* anemone

(Composé) ~ **de mer** Zool sea anemone

ânerie /anRi/ *nf* (parole) silly remark; (action) silly blunder; **dire des** ~**s** to talk rubbish○ *ou* nonsense; **faire des** ~**s** to do silly things

anéroïde /aneRɔid/ *adj* **baromètre** ~ aneroid barometer

ânesse /anɛs/ *nf* she-ass, female donkey; **lait d'**~ asses' milk

anesthésiant, ~**e** /anɛstezjã, ãt/ *adj* ① Méd anaesthetic; ② fig stupefying

anesthésie /anɛstezi/ *nf* ① Méd anaesthesia; **provoquer une** ~ to induce anaesthesia; **faire une** ~ **locale/générale** to give sb a local/ general anaesthetic; **sous** ~ **locale/générale** under local/general anaesthetic; **il ne supporterait pas l'**~ he would not tolerate the anaesthetic; ② fig (de l'opinion publique, de la population) anaesthetizing

anesthésier /anɛstezje/ [2] *vtr* ① Méd to anaesthetize; ② fig to anaesthetize [*opinion publique, population*]

anesthésique /anɛstezik/ *adj, nm* anaesthetic

anesthésiste /anɛstezist/ ▸ p. 532 *nmf* (spécialiste) anaesthetist GB, anesthesiologist US

aneth /anɛt/ *nm* dill

anévrisme /anevRism/ *nm* aneurysm

anfractuosité /ãfRaktɥozite/ *nf* crevice

ange /ãʒ/ *nm* ① Relig angel; **être le bon** ~ **de qn** fig to be sb's good angel; **être le mauvais** ~ **de qn** fig to be a bad influence on sb; **être un** ~ **de beauté** to be angelically beautiful; **être un** ~ **de patience** to be patience itself; ② (terme d'affection) angel, darling; **va me chercher mes cigarettes, tu seras un** ~! be an angel and get my cigarettes for me!

(Composés) ~ **déchu** fallen angel; ~ **exterminateur** avenging angel; ~ **gardien** guardian angel; ~ **de mer** angel shark; ~ **de la mort** Angel of Death; ~ **de la route** motorbike patrolman

(Idiomes) **être aux** ~**s** to be in seventh heaven, to be walking on air; **'un** ~ **passe!'** 'somebody's walked over my grave!'; **un** ~ **passa** there was a lull in the conversation; **sourire aux** ~**s** to smile serenely; **il est beau comme un** ~ he looks like a cherub; **être patient comme un** ~ to have the patience of a saint; **être doux comme un** ~ to be sweet-natured; **discuter sur le sexe des** ~**s** to count how many angels can dance on the head of a pin

angélique /ãʒelik/
A *adj* angelic
B *nf* Bot, Culin angelica

angéliquement /ãʒelikmã/ *adv* angelically

angélisme /ãʒelism/ *nm* angelism

angelot /ãʒlo/ *nm* cherub

angélus /ãʒelys/ *nm inv* Relig angelus

angevin, ~**e** /ãʒvɛ̃, in/ ▸ p. 894 *adj* Angevin (épith), of Anjou (après n)

Angevin, ~**e** /ãʒvɛ̃, in/ *nm,f* ① ▸ p. 894 (natif d'Angers); (habitant d'Angers) inhabitant of Angers; ② ▸ p. 721 (natif de l'Anjou); (habitant de l'Anjou) inhabitant of Anjou

angine /ãʒin/ ▸ p. 283 *nf* Méd throat infection

(Composés) ~ **diphtérique** angina diphtherica; ~ **de poitrine** angina pectoris; ~ **rouge** tonsillitis; ~ **de Vincent** Vincent's angina *ou* disease

angiocardiogramme /ãʒjokaRdjɔgram/ *nm* angiocardiogram

angiocardiographie /ãʒjokaRdjɔgrafi/ *nf* angiocardiography

angiogenèse /ãʒjoʒənɛz/ *nf* angiogenesis

angiogramme /ãʒjogram/ *nm* angiogram

angiographie /ãʒjografi/ *nf* angiography

angiologie /ãʒjolɔʒi/ *nf* angiology

angiologue /ãʒjolɔg/ ▸ p. 532 *nmf* angiologist

angiome /ãʒjom/ ▸ p. 283 *nm* angioma

angioplastie /ãʒjoplasti/ *nf* angioplasty

angiosperme /ãʒjospɛRm/ *nf* angiosperm

anglais, ~**e** ➡ 🔲 /ãglɛ, ɛz/
A *adj* English
B ▸ p. 483 *nm* Ling English; **parler l'**~ to speak English
C **anglaise** *nf* ① (écriture) slanted script; ② (boucle) ringlet

(Idiome) **filer à l'**~**e** to take French leave

Anglais, ~**e** /ãglɛ, ɛz/ *nm,f* Englishman/ Englishwoman; **les** ~ the English

angle /ãgl/ *nm* ① Math angle; ~ **de 90°** ninety-degree angle; ② (coin) corner; **être à** *ou* **faire l'**~ **de deux rues** to be at the corner of two streets; **le bâtiment qui fait l'**~ the building on the corner; **bibliothèque/cheminée d'**~ corner bookcase/fireplace; **faire un** ~ [*rue*] to bend; ③ (point de vue) angle; **prendre une photo sous le bon** ~ to take a photo from the right angle; **vu sous cet** ~ viewed from this angle

(Composés) ~ **aigu** Math acute angle; ~ **d'arrivée** Mil angle of incidence; ~ **d'attaque** Astronaut, Aviat angle of attack; Tech (d'un outil) angle of clearance; ~ **de braquage** Aut steering lock; ~ **de carrossage** Aut camber angle; ~ **de champ** Phot angle of field; ~ **de contingence** Math angle of contingence; ~ **de déphasage** Phys phase angle; ~ **droit** Math right angle; **faire un** ~ **droit avec qch** to make a right angle with sth; **se couper à** ~ **droit** to intersect at right angles; ~ **d'éclairage** Phot angle of reflection; ~ **de gîte** Naut angle of list; ~ **de hausse** (au tir) angle of elevation, elevation firing angle; ~ **horaire** Aviat, Phot angle of incidence; ~ **d'inclinaison** Math bank angle; Phot angle of tilt; ~ **de montée** Aviat angle of climb; ~ **mort** Aut, Aviat blind spot; Mil dead angle; ~ **obtus** Math obtuse angle; ~ **d'ouverture** Phot, Phys aperture angle; ~ **plat** Math straight angle; ~ **de prise de vue** viewing angle; ~ **de réflexion** Phot, Phys angle of reflection; ~ **de réfraction** Phys angle of refraction; ~ **rentrant** Math reentrant angle; ~ **de route** Aviat track angle; ~ **saillant** Math salient angle; ~ **solide** Math solid angle; ~ **de tir** Mil firing angle; ~ **visuel** Phot visual angle; ~**s adjacents** Math adjacent angles; ~**s alternes externes** Math alternate exterior angles; ~**s complémentaires** Math complementary angles; ~**s opposés par le sommet** Math opposite angles; ~**s supplémentaires** Math supplementary angles

Angleterre /ãglətɛR/ ▸ p. 721 *nprf* Géog England

anglican, ~**e** /ãglikã, an/ *adj, nm,f* Anglican

anglicanisme /ãglikanism/ *nm* Anglicanism

anglicisation /ãglisizasjɔ̃/ *nf* anglicization

angliciser /ãglisize/ [1]
A *vtr* to anglicize
B **s'angliciser** *vpr* to become anglicized

anglicisme /ãglisism/ *nm* Anglicism

angliciste /ãglisist/ *nmf* (spécialiste) Anglicist; (étudiant) student of English

anglo-américain, ~**e**, *mpl* ~**s** /ãgloameRikɛ̃, ɛn/
A *adj* gén Anglo-American; Ling American English (épith)
B ▸ p. 483 *nm* Ling American English

anglomanie /ãglomani/ *nf* Anglomania

anglo-normand, ~**e**, *mpl* ~**s** /ãglonɔRmã, ãd/
A *adj* Hist Anglo-Norman
B *nm* Ling Anglo-Norman

Anglo-Normande /ãglonɔRmãd/ ▸ p. 435 *adj f* **les îles** ~**s** the Channel Islands

anglophile /ãglofil/ *adj, nmf* Anglophile

anglophone /ãglofɔn/
A *adj* [*pays, province, groupe, personne*] English-speaking; **littérature** ~ Univ literature of the English-speaking countries; **civilisations** ~**s** Univ the English-speaking world
B *nmf* gén English speaker; (au Canada) Anglophone

anglo-saxon, **-onne**, *mpl* ~**s** /ãglosaksɔ̃, ɔn/
A *adj* ① Hist, Ling Anglo-Saxon; ② (de langue anglaise) [*littérature*] English language (épith)
B ▸ p. 483 *nm* Ling Anglo-Saxon

Anglo-Saxon, **-onne**, *mpl* ~**s** /ãglosaksɔ̃, ɔn/ *nm,f* Anglo-Saxon

angoissant, ~**e** /ãgwasã, ãt/ *adj* (alarmant) [*question, futur, réalité*] alarming; (effrayant) [*silence, film, pénombre*] frightening

angoisse /ãgwas/ *nf* ① gén, Psych anxiety (**devant, de** about); **vivre dans l'**~ **permanente** to live in a state of perpetual anxiety; **ce boulot c'est l'**~○! this work is torture!; **je suis arrivée tôt dans l'**~ **de rater mon avion** I arrived early for fear of missing my plane; ② (crise d'anxiété) anxiety; **tous les soirs elle a des** ~**s** she suffers from anxiety every night; ③ Philos anguish, angst

angoissé, ~**e** /ãgwase/
A *pp* ▸ **angoisser**
B *pp adj* [*voix, visage, personne*] anxious
C *nm,f* worrier

angoisser /ãgwase/ [1]
A *vtr* [*personne, situation, question*] to worry [*personne*]; **ma santé m'angoisse** my health is a source of worry *ou* anxiety to me
B ○*vi* to be anxious *ou* nervous; **j'ai angoissé toute la nuit avant l'examen** I was anxious all night before my exam
C **s'angoisser** *vpr* to get anxious (**de faire** doing)

Angola /ãgola/ ▸ p. 333 *nprm* Angola

angolais, ~**e** /ãgolɛ, ɛz/ ▸ p. 561 *adj* Angolan

Angolais, ~**e** /ãgolɛ, ɛz/ ▸ p. 561 *nm,f* Angolan

angora /ãgoRa/
A *adj* [*animal, laine*] angora (épith)
B *nm* Tex angora; **pull-over en** ~ angora sweater

angström* /ãgstRœm/ *nm* angstrom

anguille /ãgij/ *nf* Zool, Culin eel

(Composés) ~ **de mer** conger eel; ~ **des sables** sand eel

(Idiomes) **il y a** ~ **sous roche** there's something going on; **se faufiler comme une** ~ to slip in and out; **filer** *or* **glisser comme une** ~ to be as slippery as an eel

angulaire /ãgylɛR/ *adj* Math, Phys angular

anguleux, **-euse** /ãgylø, øz/ *adj* [*visage, traits, coude*] bony; [*aspect, contours*] jagged; [*personne, caractère, esprit*] prickly

angusture /ãgystyR/ *nf* angostura

anhydre /anidR/ *adj* anhydrous

anhydride /anidRid/ *nm* anhydride

anicroche /anikRɔʃ/ *nf* hitch; **sans** ~(s) without a hitch

ânier, **-ière** /anje, ɛR/ ▸ p. 532 *nm,f* donkey-driver

aniline /anilin/ *nf* aniline

➡ 🔲   *voir* Variétés d'anglais

B *nf* antepenultimate syllable

antéposé, ~e /ãtepoze/ *adj* Ling **en anglais l'adjectif est** ~ in English the adjective comes before the noun

antérieur, ~e /ãteʀjœʀ/ *adj* ① (précédent) [*salaire, situation, œuvre*] previous; **le texte est** ~ **à 1986** the text was written prior to 1986; **toutes les estimations sont** ~**es au lundi noir** all the estimates were made prior to Black Monday; **sa nomination est très** ~**e à la guerre** his nomination dates back to long before the war; ② (placé devant) [*partie, face*] front; [*membre, ligament*] anterior; ③ Phon [*voyelle*] front

antérieurement /ãteʀjœʀmã/ *adv* previously; ~ **à** prior to

antériorité /ãteʀjɔʀite/ *nf* anteriority; **l'**~ **de qch sur** the anteriority of sth in relation to

anthologie /ãtɔlɔʒi/ *nf* anthology

anthozoaire /ãtozɔɛʀ/ *nm* anthozoan; **les** ~**s** Anthozoa

anthracite /ãtʀasit/
A ▸ p. 202 *adj inv* (couleur) charcoal grey GB *ou* gray US
B *nm* anthracite

anthrax /ãtʀaks/ *nm inv* Méd carbuncle

anthropocentrisme /ãtʀopɔsãtʀism/ *nm* anthropocentrism

anthropoïde /ãtʀɔpoid/
A *adj* anthropoid
B *nm* (singe) anthropoid ape

anthropologie /ãtʀopɔlɔʒi/ *nf* anthropology

anthropologique /ãtʀopɔlɔʒik/ *adj* anthropological

anthropologiste /ãtʀopɔlɔʒist/, **anthropologue** /ãtʀopɔlɔg/ ▸ p. 532 *nmf* anthropologist

anthropométrie /ãtʀopɔmetʀi/ *nf* anthropometry

anthropométrique /ãtʀopɔmetʀik/ *adj* anthropometric; **service** ~ anthropometry department

anthropomorphe /ãtʀopɔmɔʀf/ *adj* anthropomorphic

anthropomorphique /ãtʀopɔmɔʀfik/ *adj* anthropomorphic

anthropomorphisme /ãtʀopɔmɔʀfism/ *nm* anthropomorphism

anthropophage /ãtʀopɔfaʒ/
A *adj* cannibalistic, anthropophagous spéc
B *nmf* cannibal, anthropophagite spéc

anthropophagie /ãtʀopɔfaʒi/ *nf* cannibalism, anthropophagy spéc

anthropopithèque /ãtʀopɔpitɛk/ *nm* Anthropopithecus

anti- /ãti/ *pref* anti(-); **anti-européen** anti-European

antiacarien, **-ienne** /ãtiakaʀjɛ̃, ɛn/ *adj* anti-dust mite (*épith*)

antiacide /ãtiasid/ *adj inv, nm* antacid

antiacnéique /ãtiakneik/ *adj* for the treatment of acne

antiadhésif, **-ive** /ãtiadezif, iv/ *adj* nonstick

antiaérien, **-ienne** /ãtiaeʀjɛ̃, ɛn/ *adj* [*défense, missile*] antiaircraft (*épith*)

antialcoolique /ãtialkɔlik/ *adj* **mesure/campagne** ~ anti-alcohol measure/campaign; **ligue** ~ temperance league; **centre de cure** ~ (alcohol) detoxification centre^GB

antiallergique /ãtialɛʀʒik/ *adj* anti-allergic

antianémique /ãtianemik/ *adj* haematinic

anti-apartheid /ãtiapaʀtɛd/ *adj* anti-apartheid

antiasthénique /ãtiastenik/ *adj* for the treatment of asthenia

antiatomique /ãtiatɔmik/ *adj* [*vêtement*] (anti-)radiation (*épith*); **abri** ~ nuclear fall-out shelter

antiaveuglant, ~e /ãtiavøglã, ãt/ *adj* Aut antiglare, antidazzle

antibactérien, **-ienne** /ãtibakteʀjɛ̃, ɛn/ *adj* antibacterial

antibalistique /ãtibalistik/ *adj* anti-ballistic

antibiothérapie /ãtibjoteʀapi/ *nf* antibiotic therapy

antibiotique /ãtibjotik/ *adj, nm* antibiotic; **traiter qn aux** ~**s** to treat sb with antibiotics; **être sous** ~**s** to be on antibiotics

antiblocage /ãtiblokaʒ/ *adj inv* **système** ~ **des roues** anti-lock braking system, ABS

antibrouillard /ãtibʀujaʀ/ Aut
A *adj inv* **phare** ~ fog lamp GB, fog light
B *nm* fog lamp GB, fog light

antibruit /ãtibʀɥi/ *adj inv* [*mur, revêtement*] soundproof

antibuée /ãtibye/ *adj inv* **dispositif** ~ demister

anticalcaire /ãtikalkɛʀ/ *adj* **agent** *or* **produit** ~ water softener

anticancéreux, **-euse** /ãtikãseʀø, øz/ *adj* [*traitement*] cancer (*épith*); [*médicament*] anti-cancer (*épith*); **centre** ~ (hôpital) cancer hospital; (laboratoire) cancer research centre^GB

anticerne /ãtisɛʀn/ *nm* concealer

antichambre /ãtiʃãbʀ/ *nf* lit, fig anteroom, antechamber; **faire** ~ to wait in the anteroom; **l'**~ **de la gloire** fig the way to stardom

antichar /ãtiʃaʀ/ *adj* antitank (*épith*)

antichoc /ãtiʃɔk/ *adj inv* ① (protecteur) **casque** ~ crash helmet; ② (incassable) [*montre*] shockproof

anticipation /ãtisipasjɔ̃/ *nf* ① (prévision) anticipation; **faire qch par** ~ to do sth in advance; ② Cin, Littérat **film/roman d'**~ science fiction film/novel

anticipé, ~e /ãtisipe/
A *pp* ▸ **anticiper**
B *pp adj* [*départ, élection, libération*] early; **il a demandé à partir en retraite** ~**e** he asked for early retirement; **avec mes remerciements** ~**s** thanking you in advance; **faire qch de façon** ~**e** to do sth in advance

anticiper /ãtisipe/ [1]
A *vtr* ① (prévoir) to anticipate [*réaction, coup, victoire, changement*]; to foresee [*invention*]; ~ **qch de plusieurs années/trois mois** to anticipate sth by several years/three months; **n'anticipons pas!** let's not get ahead of ourselves!; ② (effectuer à l'avance) to bring [sth] forward [*paiement, remboursement*]; **ils ont anticipé la construction du pont d'un an** they brought the building of the bridge forward by a year
B *anticiper sur* *vtr ind* to anticipate [*événements, évolution, mouvement*]; **vous anticipez sur le récit en révélant ce détail** by mentioning that detail you are anticipating the next part of the story
C *vi* Jeux, Sport (au tennis, aux échecs) to think ahead

anticlérical, ~e, *mpl* **-aux** /ãtikleʀikal, o/ *adj, nm,f* anticlerical

anticléricalisme /ãtikleʀikalism/ *nm* anticlericalism

anticlinal, ~e, *mpl* **-aux** /ãtiklinal, o/
A *adj* anticlinal
B *nm* anticline

anticoagulant, ~e /ãtikoagylã, ãt/
A *adj* anticoagulant
B *nm* anticoagulant

anticolonialisme /ãtikolɔnjalism/ *nm* anti-colonialism

anticolonialiste /ãtikolɔnjalist/ *adj, nmf* anti-colonialist

anticommunisme /ãtikɔmynism/ *nm* anti-communism

anticommuniste /ãtikɔmynist/ *adj, nmf* anti-communist

anticonceptionnel, **-elle** /ãtikɔ̃sɛpsjonɛl/ *adj* [*pilule, méthode*] contraceptive; [*propagande*] birth control (*épith*)

anticoncurrentiel, **-ielle** /ãtikɔ̃kyʀãsjɛl/ *adj* anticompetitive

anticonformisme /ãtikɔ̃fɔʀmism/ *nm* nonconformism

anticonformiste /ãtikɔ̃fɔʀmist/ *adj, nmf* nonconformist

anticonstitutionnel, **-elle** /ãtikɔ̃stitysjonɛl/ *adj* unconstitutional

anticonstitutionnellement /ãtikɔ̃stitysjonɛlmã/ *adv* unconstitutionally

anticorps /ãtikɔʀ/ *nm inv* antibody; **fabriquer des** ~ to produce antibodies

anticorrosion /ãtikɔʀozjɔ̃/ *adj inv* rust-proof

anti-crevaison /ãtikʀəvɛzɔ̃/ *adj inv* **bombe** ~ Aut puncture sealant spray

anticyclone /ãtisiklon/ *nm* anticyclone, high

anticyclonique /ãtisiklɔnik/ *adj* anticyclonic

antidater /ãtidate/ [1] *vtr* to antedate

antidéflagrant, ~e /ãtideflagʀã, ãt/ *adj* explosion-proof

antidémarrage /ãtidemaʀaʒ/ *nm* immobilizer; ~ **électronique** electronic immobilizer

antidémocratique /ãtidemokʀatik/ *adj* undemocratic

antidépresseur /ãtidepʀesœʀ/ *nm* antidepressant

antidérapant, ~e /ãtideʀapã, ãt/ *adj* [*pneu, chaussée*] nonskid; [*semelle*] nonslip

antidétonant, ~e /ãtidetɔnã, ãt/
A *adj* antiknock
B *nm* antiknock

antidiphtérique /ãtidifteʀik/ *adj* diphtheria (*épith*)

antidiscriminatoire /ãtidiskʀiminatwaʀ/ *adj* antidiscriminatory

antidopage /ãtidopaʒ/ *adj* [*contrôle, test*] dope; [*mesure, lutte*] against doping (*après n*); **subir un contrôle** ~ to be dope-tested

antidote /ãtidot/ *nm* lit, fig antidote (**contre** against; **à, de** for)

antidrogue /ãtidʀɔg/ *adj inv* antidrug

antiéconomique /ãtiekɔnɔmik/ *adj* uneconomical

antiémeute /ãtiemøt/ *adj inv* **police/véhicule** ~ riot police/vehicle

antienne /ãtjɛn/ *nf* ① (refrain) refrain; ② Relig antiphon

antiesclavagisme /ãtiɛsklavaʒism/ *nm* opposition to slavery; (aux États-Unis) abolitionism

antiesclavagiste /ãtiɛsklavaʒist/
A *adj* anti-slavery; (aux États-Unis) abolitionist
B *nmf* opponent of slavery; (aux États-Unis) abolitionist

antifasciste /ãtifaʃist/ *adj, nmf* antifascist

antifatigue /ãtifatig/ *adj inv* [*bas, collant*] support (*épith*)

antifongique /ãtifɔ̃ʒik/ *adj* antifungal

anti-g /ãtiʒe/ *adj inv* anti-g; **combinaison** ~ G suit

antigang /ãtigãg/ *adj inv* **brigade** ~ crime squad

antigel /ãtiʒɛl/ *adj inv, nm* antifreeze

antigène /ãtiʒɛn/ *nm* antigen

antigivre /ãtiʒivʀ/ *nm* antifreeze

antiglisse /ãtiglis/ *adj inv* non-slip

Antigone /ãtigɔn/ *npr* Antigone

antigouvernemental, ~e, *mpl* **-aux** /ãtiguvɛʀnmãtal, o/ *adj* anti-government

Antigue et Barbude /ãtigebaʀbyd/ ▸ p. 333, p. 435 *nprf* Antigua and Barbuda

Legal Identifiers

Technically, legal identifiers must be composed of only Unicode characters, numbers, currency symbols, and connecting characters (like underscores). The exam doesn't dive into the details of which ranges of the Unicode character set are considered to qualify as letters and digits. So, for example, you won't need to know that Tibetan digits range from `\u0420` to `\u0f29`. Here are the rules you *do* need to know:

- Identifiers must start with a letter, a currency character ($), or a connecting character such as the underscore (_). Identifiers cannot start with a number!
- After the first character, identifiers can contain any combination of letters, currency characters, connecting characters, or numbers.
- In practice, there is no limit to the number of characters an identifier can contain.
- You can't use a Java keyword as an identifier. Table 1-1 lists all of the Java keywords including one new one for 5.0, `enum`.
- Identifiers in Java are case-sensitive; `foo` and `FOO` are two different identifiers.

Examples of legal and illegal identifiers follow, first some legal identifiers:

```
int _a;
int $c;
int _____2_w;
int _$;
int this_is_a_very_detailed_name_for_an_identifier;
```

The following are illegal (it's your job to recognize why):

```
int :b;
int -d;
int e#;
int .f;
int 7g;
```

TABLE 1-1	Complete List of Java Keywords (`assert` added in 1.4, `enum` added in 1.5)				
abstract	boolean	break	byte	case	catch
char	class	const	continue	default	do
double	else	extends	final	finally	float
for	goto	if	implements	import	instanceof
int	interface	long	native	new	package
private	protected	public	return	short	static
strictfp	super	switch	synchronized	this	throw
throws	transient	try	void	volatile	while
assert	enum				

Sun's Java Code Conventions

Sun estimates that over the lifetime of a standard piece of code, 20 percent of the effort will go into the original creation and testing of the code, and 80 percent of the effort will go into the subsequent maintenance and enhancement of the code. Agreeing on, and coding to, a set of code standards helps to reduce the effort involved in testing, maintaining, and enhancing any piece of code. Sun has created a set of coding standards for Java, and published those standards in a document cleverly titled "Java Code Conventions," which you can find at java.sun.com. It's a great document, short and easy to read and we recommend it highly.

That said, you'll find that many of the questions in the exam don't follow the code conventions, because of the limitations in the test engine that is used to deliver the exam internationally. One of the great things about the Sun certifications is that the exams are administered uniformly throughout the world. In order to achieve that, the code listings that you'll see in the real exam are often quite cramped, and do not follow Sun's code standards. In order to toughen you up for the exam, we'll often present code listings that have a similarly cramped look and feel, often indenting our code only two spaces as opposed to the Sun standard of four.

We'll also jam our curly braces together unnaturally, and sometimes put several statements on the same line...ouch! For example:

```
1. class Wombat implements Runnable {
2.    private int i;
3.    public synchronized void run() {
4.      if (i%5 != 0) { i++; }
5.      for(int x=0; x<5; x++, i++)
```

```
 6.        { if (x > 1) Thread.yield(); }
 7.      System.out.print(i + " ");
 8.    }
 9.    public static void main(String[] args) {
10.      Wombat n = new Wombat();
11.      for(int x=100; x>0; --x) { new Thread(n).start(); }
12. } }
```

Consider yourself forewarned—you'll see lots of code listings, mock questions, and real exam questions that are this sick and twisted. Nobody wants you to write your code like this. Not your employer, not your coworkers, not us, not Sun, and not the exam creation team! Code like this was created only so that complex concepts could be tested within a universal testing tool. The one standard that *is* followed as much as possible in the real exam are the naming standards. Here are the naming standards that Sun recommends, and that we use in the exam and in most of the book:

- **Classes and interfaces**   The first letter should be capitalized, and if several words are linked together to form the name, the first letter of the inner words should be uppercase (a format that's sometimes called "camelCase"). For classes, the names should typically be nouns. For example:

```
Dog
Account
PrintWriter
```

   For interfaces, the names should typically be adjectives like

```
Runnable
Serializable
```

- **Methods**   The first letter should be lowercase, and then normal camelCase rules should be used. In addition, the names should typically be verb-noun pairs. For example:

```
getBalance
doCalculation
setCustomerName
```

- **Variables**   Like methods, the camelCase format should be used, starting with a lowercase letter. Sun recommends short, meaningful names, which sounds good to us. Some examples:

```
buttonWidth
accountBalance
myString
```

- **Constants**   Java constants are created by marking variables `static` and `final`. They should be named using uppercase letters with underscore characters as separators:

```
MIN_HEIGHT
```

JavaBeans Standards

The JavaBeans spec is intended to help Java developers create Java components that can be easily used by other Java developers in a visual Integrated Development Environment (IDE) tool (like Eclipse or NetBeans). As a Java programmer, you want to be able to use components from the Java API, but it would be great if you could also buy the Java component you want from "Beans 'R Us," that software company down the street. And once you've found the components, you'd like to be able to access them through a development tool in such a way that you don't have to write all your code from scratch. By using naming rules, the JavaBeans spec helps guarantee that tools can recognize and use components built by different developers. The JavaBeans API is quite involved, but you'll need to study only a few basics for the exam.

First, JavaBeans are Java classes that have *properties*. For our purposes, think of properties as `private` instance variables. Since they're `private`, the only way they can be accessed from outside of their class is through *methods* in the class. The methods that change a property's value are called *setter* methods, and the methods that retrieve a property's value are called *getter* methods. The JavaBean naming rules that you'll need to know for the exam are the following:

JavaBean Property Naming Rules

- If the property is not a boolean, the getter method's prefix must be *get*. For example, `getSize()` is a valid JavaBeans getter name for a property named "size." Keep in mind that you do not need to have a variable named *size* (although some IDEs expect it). The name of the property is *inferred* from the getters and setters, not through any variables in your class. What you return from `getSize()` is up to you.

■ If the property is a boolean, the getter method's prefix is either `get` or `is`. For example, `getStopped()` or `isStopped()` are both valid JavaBeans names for a boolean property.

■ The setter method's prefix must be *set*. For example, `setSize()` is the valid JavaBean name for a property named *size*.

■ To complete the name of a getter or setter method, change the first letter of the property name to uppercase, and then append it to the appropriate prefix (`get`, `is`, or `set`).

■ Setter method signatures must be marked `public`, with a `void` return type and an argument that represents the property type.

■ Getter method signatures must be marked `public`, take no arguments, and have a return type that matches the argument type of the setter method for that property.

Second, the JavaBean spec supports *events*, which allow components to notify each other when something happens. The event model is often used in GUI applications when an event like a mouse click is multicast to many other objects that may have things to do when the mouse click occurs. The objects that receive the information that an event occurred are called *listeners*. For the exam, you need to know that the methods that are used to add or remove listeners from an event must also follow JavaBean naming standards:

JavaBean Listener Naming Rules

■ Listener method names used to "register" a listener with an event source must use the prefix `add`, followed by the listener type. For example, `addActionListener()` is a valid name for a method that an event source will have to allow others to register for Action events.

■ Listener method names used to remove ("unregister") a listener must use the prefix `remove`, followed by the listener type (using the same rules as the registration add method).

■ The type of listener to be added or removed must be passed as the argument to the method.

bounce() and setBounceFactor() methods." Figure 1-1 illustrates the relationship between interfaces and classes.

```
interface Bounceable

void bounce( );
void setBounceFactor(int bf);
```

What you declare.

```
interface Bounceable

public abstract void bounce( );
public abstract void setBounceFactor(int bf);
```

What the compiler sees.

```
Class Tire implements Bounceable
public void bounce( ){...}
public void setBounceFactor(int bf){ }
```

What the implementing class must do.

(All interface methods must be implemented, and must be marked public.)

Think of an interface as a 100-percent abstract class. Like an abstract class, an interface defines abstract methods that take the following form:

```
abstract void bounce();   // Ends with a semicolon rather than
                          // curly braces
```

But while an abstract class can define both abstract and non-abstract methods, an interface can have only abstract methods. Another way interfaces differ from abstract classes is that interfaces have very little flexibility in how the methods and variables defined in the interface are declared. These rules are strict:

- ■ All interface methods are implicitly public and abstract. In other words, you do not need to actually type the public or abstract modifiers in the method declaration, but the method is still always public and abstract.
- ■ All variables defined in an interface must be public, static, and final—in other words, interfaces can declare only constants, not instance variables.

- Interface methods must not be `static`.
- Because interface methods are abstract, they cannot be marked `final`, `strictfp`, or `native`. (More on these modifiers later.)
- An interface can *extend* one or more other interfaces.
- An interface cannot extend anything but another interface.
- An interface cannot implement another interface or class.
- An interface must be declared with the keyword `interface`.
- Interface types can be used polymorphically (see Chapter 2 for more details).

The following is a legal interface declaration:

```
public abstract interface Rollable { }
```

Typing in the `abstract` modifier is considered redundant; interfaces are implicitly abstract whether you type `abstract` or not. You just need to know that both of these declarations are legal, and functionally identical:

```
public abstract interface Rollable { }
public interface Rollable { }
```

The `public` modifier is required if you want the interface to have public rather than default access.

We've looked at the interface declaration but now we'll look closely at the methods within an interface:

```
public interface Bounceable {
    public abstract void bounce();
    public abstract void setBounceFactor(int bf);
}
```

Typing in the `public` and `abstract` modifiers on the methods is redundant, though, since all interface methods are implicitly `public` and `abstract`. Given that rule, you can see that the following code is exactly equivalent to the preceding interface:

```
public interface Bounceable {
    void bounce();                    // No modifiers
    void setBounceFactor(int bf);    // No modifiers
}
```

You must remember that all interface methods are public and abstract regardless of what you see in the interface definition.

Look for interface methods declared with any combination of `public`, `abstract`, or no modifiers. For example, the following five method declarations, if declared within their own interfaces, are legal and identical!

```
void bounce();
public void bounce();
abstract void bounce();
public abstract void bounce();
abstract public void bounce();
```

The following interface method declarations won't compile:

```
final void bounce();      // final and abstract can never be used
                          // together, and abstract is implied
static void bounce();     // interfaces define instance methods
private void bounce();    // interface methods are always public
protected void bounce();    // (same as above)
```

Declaring Interface Constants

You're allowed to put constants in an interface. By doing so, you guarantee that any class implementing the interface will have access to the same constant.

By placing the constants right in the interface, any class that implements the interface has direct access to the constants, just as if the class had inherited them.

You need to remember one key rule for interface constants. They must always be

```
public static final
```

So that sounds simple, right? After all, interface constants are no different from any other publicly accessible constants, so they obviously must be declared `public`, `static`, and `final`. But before you breeze past the rest of this discussion, think about the implications: **Because interface constants are defined in an interface, they don't have to be *declared* as `public`, `static`, or `final`. They must be public, static, and final, but you don't have to actually declare them that way.** Just as interface methods are always public and abstract whether you say so in the code or not, any variable defined in an interface must be—and implicitly is—a public constant. See if you can spot the problem with the following code (assume two separate files):

```
interface Foo {
   int BAR = 42;
   void go();
}

class Zap implements Foo {
   public void go() {
      BAR = 27;
   }
}
```

You can't change the value of a constant! Once the value has been assigned, the value can never be modified. The assignment happens in the interface itself (where the constant is declared), so the implementing class can access it and use it, but as a read-only value. So the BAR = 27 assignment will not compile.

e **x** a m

w a t c h *Look for interface definitions that define constants, but without explicitly using the required modifiers. For example, the following are all identical:*

```
public int x = 1;          // Looks non-static and non-final,
                           // but isn't!
int x = 1;                 // Looks default, non-final,
                           // non-static, but isn't!
static int x = 1;          // Doesn't show final or public
final int x = 1;           // Doesn't show static or public
public static int x = 1;      // Doesn't show final
public final int x = 1;       // Doesn't show static
static final int x = 1        // Doesn't show public
public static final int x = 1;  // what you get implicitly
```

Any combination of the required (but implicit) modifiers is legal, as is using no modifiers at all! On the exam, you can expect to see questions you won't be able to answer correctly unless you know, for example, that an interface variable is final *and can never be given a value by the implementing (or any other) class.*

Whereas default access doesn't extend any special consideration to subclasses (you're either in the package or you're not), the protected modifier respects the parent-child relationship, even when the child class moves away (and joins a new package). So, when you think of *default* access, think *package* restriction. No exceptions. But when you think *protected*, think *package* + *kids*. A class with a protected member is marking that member as having package-level access for all classes, but with a special exception for subclasses outside the package.

But what does it mean for a subclass-outside-the-package to have access to a superclass (parent) member? It means the subclass inherits the member. It does not, however, mean the subclass-outside-the-package can access the member using a reference to an instance of the superclass. In other words, protected = inheritance. Protected does not mean that the subclass can treat the protected superclass member as though it were public. So if the subclass-outside-the-package gets a reference to the superclass (by, for example, creating an instance of the superclass somewhere in the subclass' code), the subclass cannot use the dot operator on the superclass reference to access the protected member. To a subclass-outside-the-package, a protected member might as well be default (or even private), when the subclass is using a reference to the superclass. **The subclass can see the** `protected` **member only through inheritance.**

Are you confused? So are we. Hang in there and it will all become clear with the next batch of code examples. (And don't worry; we're not actually confused. We're just trying to make you feel better if you are. You know, like it's OK for you to feel as though nothing makes sense, and that it isn't your fault. Or is it? <insert evil laugh>)

Protected Details

Let's take a look at a `protected` instance variable (remember, an instance variable is a member) of a superclass.

```
package certification;
public class Parent {
   protected int x = 9; // protected access
}
```

The preceding code declares the variable x as `protected`. This makes the variable *accessible* to all other classes *inside* the certification package, as well as *inheritable* by any subclasses *outside* the package. Now let's create a subclass in a different package, and attempt to use the variable x (that the subclass inherits):

```
package other; // Different package
import certification.Parent;
class Child extends Parent {
   public void testIt() {
      System.out.println("x is " + x); // No problem; Child
                                        // inherits x
   }
}
```

The preceding code compiles fine. Notice, though, that the Child class is accessing the `protected` variable through inheritance. Remember, any time we talk about a subclass having access to a superclass member, we could be talking about the subclass inheriting the member, not simply accessing the member through a reference to an instance of the superclass (the way any other nonsubclass would access it). Watch what happens if the subclass Child (outside the superclass' package) tries to access a `protected` variable using a Parent class reference.

```
package other;
import certification.Parent;
class Child extends Parent {
   public void testIt() {
      System.out.println("x is " + x); // No problem; Child
                                        // inherits x
      Parent p = new Parent(); // Can we access x using the
                               // p reference?
      System.out.println("X in parent is " + p.x); // Compiler
                                                    // error!
   }
}
```

The compiler is more than happy to show us the problem:

```
%javac -d . other/Child.java
other/Child.java:9: x has protected access in certification.Par
ent
System.out.println("X in parent is " + p.x);
                                         ^
1 error
```

So far we've established that a protected member has essentially package-level or default access to all classes except for subclasses. We've seen that subclasses outside the package can inherit a protected member. Finally, we've seen that subclasses outside the package can't use a superclass reference to access a protected member. *For a subclass outside the package, the protected member can be accessed only through inheritance.*

But there's still one more issue we haven't looked at...what does a `protected` member look like to other classes trying to use the subclass-outside-the-package to get to the subclass' inherited `protected` superclass member? For example, using our previous Parent/Child classes, what happens if some other class—Neighbor, say—in the same package as the Child (subclass), has a reference to a Child instance and wants to access the member variable x ? In other words, how does that `protected` member behave once the subclass has inherited it? Does it maintain its `protected` status, such that classes in the Child's package can see it?

No! Once the subclass-outside-the-package inherits the `protected` member, that member (as inherited by the subclass) becomes private to any code outside the subclass, with the exception of subclasses of the subclass. So if class Neighbor instantiates a Child object, then even if class Neighbor is in the same package as class Child, class Neighbor won't have access to the Child's inherited (but protected) variable x. The bottom line: when a subclass-outside-the-package inherits a `protected` member, the member is essentially private inside the subclass, such that only the subclass and its subclasses can access it. Figure 1-4 illustrates the effect of protected access on classes and subclasses in the same or different packages.

Whew! That wraps up `protected`, the most misunderstood modifier in Java. Again, it's used only in very special cases, but you can count on it showing up on the exam. Now that we've covered the `protected` modifier, we'll switch to default member access, a piece of cake compared to `protected`.

Default Details

Let's start with the default behavior of a member in a superclass. We'll modify the Parent's member x to make it default.

```
package certification;
public class Parent {
  int x = 9; // No access modifier, means default
             // (package) access
}
```

Notice we didn't place an access modifier in front of the variable x. Remember that if you don't type an access modifier before a class or member declaration, the access control is default, which means package level. We'll now attempt to access the default member from the Child class that we saw earlier.

FIGURE 1-4

Effects of protected access

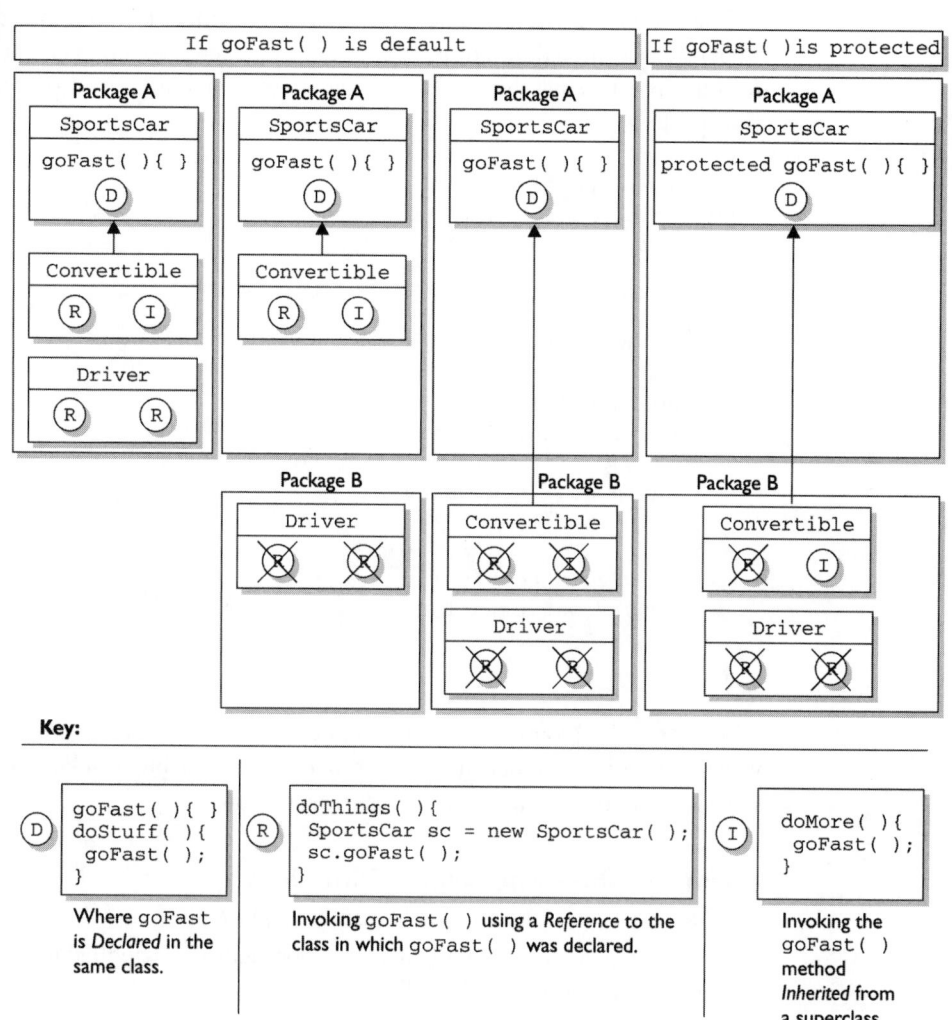

When we compile the child file, we get an error something like this:

```
Child.java:4: Undefined variable: x
     System.out.println("Variable x is " + x);
1 error
```

The compiler gives the same error as when a member is declared as `private`. The subclass Child (in a different package from the superclass Parent) can't see or use the default superclass member x ! Now, what about default access for two classes in the same package?

```
package certification;
public class Parent{
  int x = 9; // default access
}
```

And in the second class you have the following:

```
package certification;
class Child extends Parent{
  static public void main(String[] args) {
    Child sc = new Child();
    sc.testIt();
  }
  public void testIt() {
    System.out.println("Variable x is " + x); // No problem;
  }
}
```

The preceding source file compiles fine, and the class Child runs and displays the value of x. Just remember that default members are visible to subclasses only if those subclasses are in the same package as the superclass.

Local Variables and Access Modifiers

Can access modifiers be applied to local variables? NO!

There is never a case where an access modifier can be applied to a local variable, so watch out for code like the following:

```
class Foo {
  void doStuff() {
    private int x = 7;
    this.doMore(x);
  }
}
```

You can be certain that any local variable declared with an access modifier will not compile. In fact, there is only one modifier that can ever be applied to local variables—`final`.

That about does it for our discussion on member access modifiers. Table 1-2 shows all the combinations of access and visibility; you really should spend some time with it. Next, we're going to dig into the other (nonaccess) modifiers that you can apply to member declarations.

TABLE 1-2 Determining Access to Class Members

Visibility	Public	Protected	Default	Private
From the same class	Yes	Yes	Yes	Yes
From any class in the same package	Yes	Yes	Yes	No
From a subclass in the same package	Yes	Yes	Yes	No
From a subclass outside the same package	Yes	Yes, *through inheritance*	No	No
From any non-subclass class outside the package	Yes	No	No	No

Nonaccess Member Modifiers

We've discussed member access, which refers to whether code from one class can invoke a method (or access an instance variable) from another class. That still leaves a boatload of other modifiers you can use on member declarations. Two you're already familiar with—`final` and `abstract`—because we applied them to class declarations earlier in this chapter. But we still have to take a quick look at `transient`, `synchronized`, `native`, `strictfp`, and then a long look at the Big One—`static`.

We'll look first at modifiers applied to methods, followed by a look at modifiers applied to instance variables. We'll wrap up this section with a look at how `static` works when applied to variables and methods.

```
    private String manager;
    // other code goes here including access methods for private
    // fields
}
```

The preceding Employee class says that each employee instance will know its own name, title, and manager. In other words, each instance can have its own unique values for those three fields. If you see the term "field," "instance variable," "property," or "attribute," they mean virtually the same thing. (There actually are subtle but occasionally important distinctions between the terms, but those distinctions aren't used on the exam.)

For the exam, you need to know that instance variables

- Can use any of the four access *levels* (which means they can be marked with any of the three access *modifiers*)
- Can be marked `final`
- Can be marked `transient`
- Cannot be marked `abstract`
- Cannot be marked `synchronized`
- Cannot be marked `strictfp`
- Cannot be marked `native`
- Cannot be marked `static`, because then they'd become class variables.

We've already covered the effects of applying access control to instance variables (it works the same way as it does for member methods). A little later in this chapter we'll look at what it means to apply the `final` or `transient` modifier to an instance variable. First, though, we'll take a quick look at the difference between instance and local variables. Figure 1-7 compares the way in which modifiers can be applied to methods vs. variables.

We can also declare multidimensional arrays, which are in fact arrays of arrays. This can be done in the following manner:

```
String[][][] occupantName;
String[] ManagerName [];
```

The first example is a three-dimensional array (an array of arrays of arrays) and the second is a two-dimensional array. Notice in the second example we have one square bracket before the variable name and one after. This is perfectly legal to the compiler, proving once again that just because it's legal doesn't mean it's right.

In Chapter 3, we'll spend a lot of time discussing arrays, how to initialize and use them, and how to deal with multi-dimensional arrays...stay tuned!

Final Variables

Declaring a variable with the `final` keyword makes it impossible to reinitialize that variable once it has been initialized with an explicit value (notice we said explicit rather than default). For primitives, this means that once the variable is assigned a value, the value can't be altered. For example, if you assign 10 to the `int` variable x, then x is going to stay 10, forever. So that's straightforward for primitives, but what does it mean to have a `final` object reference variable? A reference variable marked `final` can't ever be reassigned to refer to a different object. The data within the object can be modified, but the reference variable cannot be changed. In other words, a `final` reference still allows you to modify the state of the object it refers to, but you can't modify the reference variable to make it refer to a different object. Burn this in: there are no `final` objects, only `final` references. We'll explain this in more detail in Chapter 3.

We've now covered how the `final` modifier can be applied to classes, methods, and variables. Figure 1-8 highlights the key points and differences of the various applications of `final`.

FIGURE 1-8   Effect of `final` on variables, methods, and classes

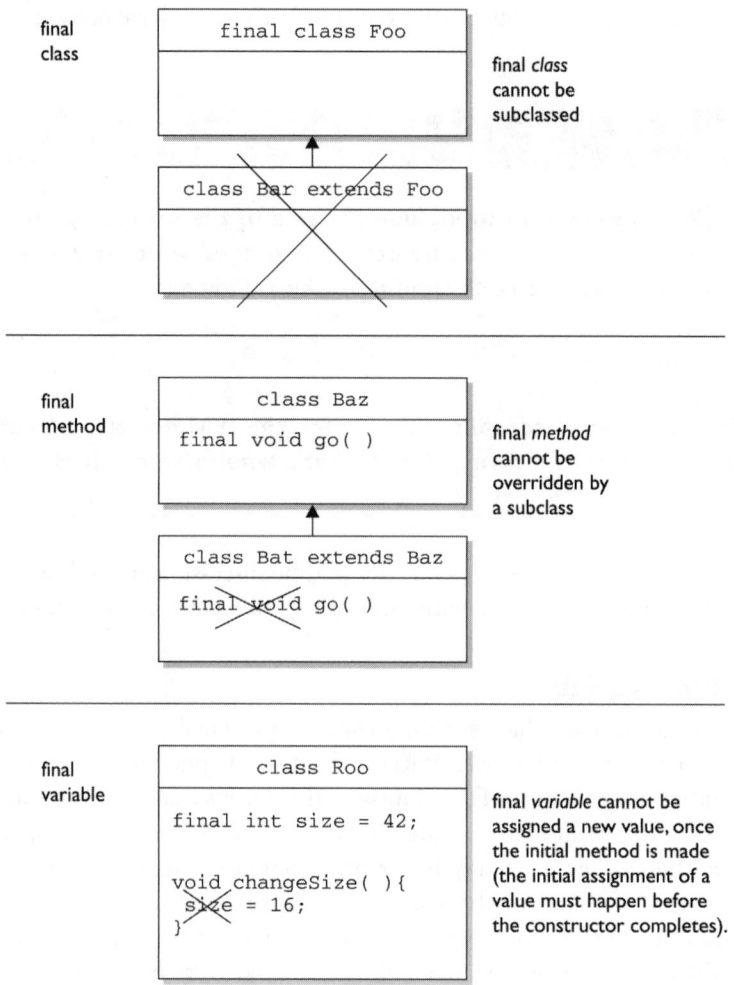

final
class

final *class*
cannot be
subclassed

final
method

final *method*
cannot be
overridden by
a subclass

final
variable

final *variable* cannot be
assigned a new value, once
the initial method is made
(the initial assignment of a
value must happen before
the constructor completes).

Transient Variables

If you mark an instance variable as `transient`, you're telling the JVM to skip (ignore) this variable when you attempt to serialize the object containing it. Serialization is one of the coolest features of Java; it lets you save (sometimes called "flatten") an object by writing its state (in other words, the value of its instance variables) to a special type of I/O stream. With serialization you can save an object to a file, or even ship it over a wire for reinflating (deserializing) at the other end, in another JVM. Serialization has been added to the exam as of Java 5, and we'll cover it in great detail in Chapter 6.

Volatile Variables

The `volatile` modifier tells the JVM that a thread accessing the variable must always reconcile its own private copy of the variable with the master copy in memory. Say what? Don't worry about it. For the exam, all you need to know about `volatile` is that, as with `transient`, it can be applied only to instance variables. Make no mistake, the idea of multiple threads accessing an instance variable is scary stuff, and very important for any Java programmer to understand. But as you'll see in Chapter 11, you'll probably use synchronization, rather than the `volatile` modifier, to make your data thread-safe.

The `volatile` *modifier may also be applied to project managers :)*

Static Variables and Methods

The `static` modifier is used to create variables and methods that will exist independently of any instances created for the class. In other words, `static` members exist before you ever make a new instance of a class, and there will be only one copy of the `static` member regardless of the number of instances of that class. In other words, all instances of a given class share the same value for any given `static` variable. We'll cover `static` members in great detail in the next chapter.

Things you can mark as `static`:

- Methods
- Variables
- A class nested within another class, but not within a method (more on this in Chapter 8).
- Initialization blocks

Things you can't mark as `static`:

- Constructors (makes no sense; a constructor is used only to create instances)
- Classes (unless they are nested)
- Interfaces
- Method local inner classes (we'll explore this in Chapter 8)
- Inner class methods and instance variables
- Local variables

Declaring Enums

As of 5.0, Java lets you restrict a variable to having one of only a few pre-defined values—in other words, one value from an enumerated list. (The items in the enumerated list are called, surprisingly, `enums`.)

Using enums can help reduce the bugs in your code. For instance, in your coffee shop application you might want to restrict your size selections to BIG, HUGE, and OVERWHELMING. If you let an order for a LARGE or a GRANDE slip in, it might cause an error. Enums to the rescue. With the following simple declaration, you can guarantee that the compiler will stop you from assigning anything to a `CoffeeSize` except BIG, HUGE, or OVERWHELMING:

```
enum CoffeeSize { BIG, HUGE, OVERWHELMING };
```

From then on, the only way to get a `CoffeeSize` will be with a statement something like this:

```
CoffeeSize cs = CoffeeSize.BIG;
```

It's not required that `enum` constants be in all caps, but borrowing from the Sun code convention that constants are named in caps, it's a good idea.

The basic components of an `enum` are its constants (i.e., BIG, HUGE, and OVERWHELMING), although in a minute you'll see that there can be a lot more to an enum. Enums can be declared as their own separate class, or as a class member, however they must not be declared within a method!

Declaring an enum *outside* a class:

```
enum CoffeeSize { BIG, HUGE, OVERWHELMING }  // this cannot be
                                             // private or protected

class Coffee {
   CoffeeSize size;
}

public class CoffeeTest1 {
   public static void main(String[] args) {
      Coffee drink = new Coffee();
      drink.size = CoffeeSize.BIG;        // enum outside class
   }
}
```

The preceding code can be part of a single file. (Remember, the file must be named CoffeeTest1.java because that's the name of the public class in the file.) The key point to remember is that the enum can be declared with only the public or default modifier, just like a non-inner class. Here's an example of declaring an enum *inside* a class:

```
class Coffee2 {
   enum CoffeeSize {BIG, HUGE, OVERWHELMING }

   CoffeeSize size;
}

public class CoffeeTest2 {
   public static void main(String[] args) {
      Coffee2 drink = new Coffee2();
      drink.size = Coffee2.CoffeeSize.BIG;   // enclosing class
                                             // name required
   }
}
```

The key points to take away from these examples are that enums can be declared as their own class, or enclosed in another class, and that the syntax for accessing an enum's members depends on where the enum was declared.

The following is NOT legal:

```
public class CoffeeTest1 {
  public static void main(String[] args) {
    enum CoffeeSize { BIG, HUGE, OVERWHELMING } // WRONG! Cannot
                                                 // declare enums
                                                 // in methods

    Coffee drink = new Coffee();
    drink.size = CoffeeSize.BIG;
  }
}
```

To make it more confusing for you, the Java language designers made it optional to put a semicolon at the end of the enum declaration:

```
public class CoffeeTest1 {

  enum CoffeeSize { BIG, HUGE, OVERWHELMING }; // <--semicolon
                                               // is optional here
  public static void main(String[] args) {
    Coffee drink = new Coffee();
    drink.size = CoffeeSize.BIG;
  }
}
```

So what gets created when you make an enum? The most important thing to remember is that enums are not Strings or ints! Each of the enumerated CoffeeSize types are actually instances of CoffeeSize. In other words, BIG is of type CoffeeSize. Think of an enum as a kind of class, that looks something (but not exactly) like this:

```
// conceptual example of how you can think
// about enums

class CoffeeSize {
    public static final CoffeeSize BIG =
                           new CoffeeSize("BIG", 0);
    public static final CoffeeSize HUGE =
                           new CoffeeSize("HUGE", 1);
    public static final CoffeeSize OVERWHELMING =
                           new CoffeeSize("OVERWHELMING", 2);
```

```
public CoffeeSize(String enumName, int index) {
      // stuff here
  }
  public static void main(String[] args) {
    System.out.println(CoffeeSize.BIG);
  }
}
```

Notice how each of the enumerated values, BIG, HUGE, and OVERWHELMING, are instances of type CoffeeSize. They're represented as `static` and `final`, which in the Java world, is thought of as a constant. Also notice that each enum value knows its index or position...in other words, the order in which enum values are declared matters. You can think of the CoffeeSize enums as existing in an array of type CoffeeSize, and as you'll see in a later chapter, you can iterate through the values of an enum by invoking the `values()` method on any enum type. (Don't worry about that in this chapter.)

Declaring Constructors, Methods, and Variables in an enum

Because an enum really is a special kind of class, you can do more than just list the enumerated constant values. You can add constructors, instance variables, methods, and something really strange known as a *constant specific class body*. To understand why you might need more in your enum, think about this scenario: imagine you want to know the actual size, in ounces, that map to each of the three CoffeeSize constants. For example, you want to know that BIG is 8 ounces, HUGE is 10 ounces, and OVERWHELMING is a whopping 16 ounces.

You could make some kind of a lookup table, using some other data structure, but that would be a poor design and hard to maintain. The simplest way is to treat your enum values (BIG, HUGE, and OVERWHELMING), as objects that can each have their own instance variables. Then you can assign those values at the time the enums are initialized, by passing a value to the enum constructor. This takes a little explaining, but first look at the following code:

```
enum CoffeeSize {

    BIG(8), HUGE(10), OVERWHELMING(16);
    // the arguments after the enum value are "passed"
    // as values to the constructor

    CoffeeSize(int ounces) {
```

```
            this.ounces = ounces;   // assign the value to
                                     // an instance variable
     }

     private int ounces;         // an instance variable each enum
                                 // value has
   public int getOunces() {
     return ounces;
   }
}

class Coffee {
   CoffeeSize size;       // each instance of Coffee has-a
                          // CoffeeSize enum

   public static void main(String[] args) {
     Coffee drink1 = new Coffee();
     drink1.size = CoffeeSize.BIG;

     Coffee drink2 = new Coffee();
     drink2.size = CoffeeSize.OVERWHELMING;

     System.out.println(drink1.size.getOunces()); // prints 8
     System.out.println(drink2.size.getOunces()); // prints 16
   }
}
```

The key points to remember about enum constructors are

■ You can NEVER invoke an enum constructor directly. The enum constructor is invoked automatically, with the arguments you define after the constant value. For example, BIG(8) invokes the CoffeeSize constructor that takes an int, passing the int literal 8 to the constructor. (Behind the scenes, of course, you can imagine that BIG is also passed to the constructor, but we don't have to know—or care—about the details.)

■ You can define more than one argument to the constructor, and you can overload the enum constructors, just as you can overload a normal class constructor. We discuss constructors in much more detail in Chapter 2. To initialize a CoffeeType with both the number of ounces and, say, a lid type, you'd pass two arguments to the constructor as BIG(8, "A"), which means you have a constructor in CoffeeSize that takes both an int and a String.

And finally, you can define something really strange in an enum that looks like an anonymous inner class (which we talk about in Chapter 8). It's known as a constant specific class body, and you use it when you need a particular constant to override a method defined in the enum.

Imagine this scenario: you want enums to have two methods—one for ounces and one for lid code (a String). Now imagine that most coffee sizes use the same lid code, "B", but the OVERWHELMING size uses type "A". You can define a getLidCode() method in the CoffeeSize enum that returns "B", but then you need a way to override it for OVERWHELMING. You don't want to do some hard-to-maintain if/then code in the getLidCode() method, so the best approach might be to somehow have the OVERWHELMING constant override the getLidCode() method.

This looks strange, but you need to understand the basic declaration rules:

```
enum CoffeeSize {
    BIG(8),
    HUGE(10),
    OVERWHELMING(16) {      // start a code block that defines
                            // the "body" for this constant

      public String getLidCode() {    // override the method
                                      // defined in CoffeeSize
        return "A";
      }
    };    // <-- the semicolon is REQUIRED when you have a body

    CoffeeSize(int ounces) {
      this.ounces = ounces;
    }

    private int ounces;

    public int getOunces() {
      return ounces;
    }
    public String getLidCode() {  // this method is overridden
                                  // by the OVERWHELMING constant

      return "B";    // the default value we want to return for
                     // CoffeeSize constants
    }
}
```

CERTIFICATION SUMMARY

After absorbing the material in this chapter, you should be familiar with some of the nuances of the Java language. You may also be experiencing confusion around why you ever wanted to take this exam in the first place. That's normal at this point. If you hear yourself saying, "What was I thinking?" just lie down until it passes. We would like to tell you that it gets easier...that this was the toughest chapter and it's all downhill from here...

Let's briefly review what you'll need to know for the exam.

There will be many questions dealing with keywords indirectly, so be sure you can identify which are keywords and which aren't.

Although naming conventions like the use of camelCase won't be on the exam directly, you will need to understand the basics of JavaBeans naming, which uses camelCase.

You need to understand the rules associated with creating legal identifiers, and the rules associated with source code declarations, including the use of `package` and `import` statements.

You now have a good understanding of access control as it relates to classes, methods, and variables. You've looked at how access modifiers (`public`, `protected`, and `private`) define the access control of a class or member.

You learned that `abstract` classes can contain both `abstract` and nonabstract methods, but that if even a single method is marked `abstract`, the class must be marked `abstract`. Don't forget that a concrete (nonabstract) subclass of an `abstract` class must provide implementations for all the `abstract` methods of the superclass, but that an `abstract` class does not have to implement the `abstract` methods from its superclass. An `abstract` subclass can "pass the buck" to the first concrete subclass.

We covered interface implementation. Remember that interfaces can extend another interface (even multiple interfaces), and that any class that implements an interface must implement all methods from all the interfaces in the inheritance tree of the interface the class is implementing.

You've also looked at the other modifiers including `static`, `final`, `abstract`, `synchronized`, and so on. You've learned how some modifiers can never be combined in a declaration, such as mixing `abstract` with either `final` or `private`.

Keep in mind that there are no `final` objects in Java. A reference variable marked `final` can never be changed, but the object it refers to can be modified.

You've seen that final applied to methods means a subclass can't override them, and when applied to a class, the final class can't be subclassed.

Remember that as of Java 5, methods can be declared with a var-arg parameter (which can take from zero to many arguments of the declared type), but that you can have only one var-arg per method, and it must be the method's last parameter.

Make sure you're familiar with the relative sizes of the numeric primitives. Remember that while the values of non-final variables can change, a reference variable's type can never change.

You also learned that arrays are objects that contain many variables of the same type. Arrays can also contain other arrays.

Remember what you've learned about static variables and methods, especially that static members are per-class as opposed to per-instance. Don't forget that a static method can't directly access an instance variable from the class it's in, because it doesn't have an explicit reference to any particular instance of the class.

Finally, we covered a feature new to Java 5, enums. An enum is a much safer and more flexible way to implement constants than was possible in earlier versions of Java. Because they are a special kind of class, enums can be declared very simply, or they can be quite complex—including such attributes as methods, variables, constructors, and a special type of inner class called a constant specific class body.

Before you hurl yourself at the practice test, spend some time with the following optimistically named "Two-Minute Drill." Come back to this particular drill often, as you work through this book and especially when you're doing that last-minute cramming. Because—and here's the advice you wished your mother had given you before you left for college—it's not what you know, it's when you know it.

For the exam, knowing what you can't do with the Java language is just as important as knowing what you can do. Give the sample questions a try! They're very similar to the difficulty and structure of the real exam questions, and should be an eye opener for how difficult the exam can be. Don't worry if you get a lot of them wrong. If you find a topic that you are weak in, spend more time reviewing and studying. Many programmers need two or three serious passes through a chapter (or an individual objective) before they can answer the questions confidently.

✓ TWO-MINUTE DRILL

Remember that in this chapter, when we talk about classes, we're referring to non-inner classes, or *top-level* classes. We'll devote all of Chapter 8 to inner classes.

Identifiers (Objective 1.3)

❏ Identifiers can begin with a letter, an underscore, or a currency character.

❏ After the first character, identifiers can also include digits.

❏ Identifiers can be of any length.

❏ JavaBeans methods must be named using camelCase, and depending on the method's purpose, must start with set, get, is, add, or remove.

Declaration Rules (Objective 1.1)

❏ A source code file can have only one public class.

❏ If the source file contains a public class, the filename must match the public class name.

❏ A file can have only one package statement, but multiple imports.

❏ The package statement (if any) must be the first (non-comment) line in a source file.

❏ The import statements (if any) must come after the package and before the class declaration.

❏ If there is no package statement, import statements must be the first (non-comment) statements in the source file.

❏ package and import statements apply to all classes in the file.

❏ A file can have more than one nonpublic class.

❏ Files with no public classes have no naming restrictions.

Class Access Modifiers (Objective 1.1)

❏ There are three access modifiers: public, protected, and private.

❏ There are four access levels: public, protected, default, and private.

❏ Classes can have only public or default access.

❏ A class with default access can be seen only by classes within the same package.

❏ A class with public access can be seen by all classes from all packages.

❑ Class visibility revolves around whether code in one class can

  ❑ Create an instance of another class

  ❑ Extend (or subclass), another class

  ❑ Access methods and variables of another class

Class Modifiers (Nonaccess) (Objective 1.2)

❑ Classes can also be modified with `final`, `abstract`, or `strictfp`.

❑ A class cannot be both `final` and `abstract`.

❑ A `final` class cannot be subclassed.

❑ An `abstract` class cannot be instantiated.

❑ A single `abstract` method in a class means the whole class must be abstract.

❑ An `abstract` class can have both `abstract` and nonabstract methods.

❑ The first concrete class to extend an `abstract` class must implement all of its `abstract` methods.

Interface Implementation (Objective 1.2)

❑ Interfaces are contracts for what a class can do, but they say nothing about the way in which the class must do it.

❑ Interfaces can be implemented by any class, from any inheritance tree.

❑ An interface is like a 100-percent `abstract` class, and is implicitly abstract whether you type the `abstract` modifier in the declaration or not.

❑ An interface can have only abstract methods, no concrete methods allowed.

❑ Interface methods are by default `public` and `abstract`—explicit declaration of these modifiers is optional.

❑ Interfaces can have constants, which are always implicitly `public`, `static`, and `final`.

❑ Interface constant declarations of `public`, `static`, and `final` are optional in any combination.

❑ A legal nonabstract implementing class has the following properties:

  ❑ It provides concrete implementations for the interface's methods.

  ❑ It must follow all legal override rules for the methods it implements.

  ❑ It must not declare any new checked exceptions for an implementation method.

- ❑ It must not declare any checked exceptions that are broader than the exceptions declared in the interface method.
- ❑ It may declare runtime exceptions on any interface method implementation regardless of the interface declaration.
- ❑ It must maintain the exact signature (allowing for covariant returns) and return type of the methods it implements (but does not have to declare the exceptions of the interface).
- ❑ A class implementing an interface can itself be `abstract`.
- ❑ An `abstract` implementing class does not have to implement the interface methods (but the first concrete subclass must).
- ❑ A class can extend only one class (no multiple inheritance), but it can implement many interfaces.
- ❑ Interfaces can extend one or more other interfaces.
- ❑ Interfaces cannot extend a class, or implement a class or interface.
- ❑ When taking the exam, verify that interface and class declarations are legal before verifying other code logic.

Member Access Modifiers (Objectives 1.3 and 1.4)

- ❑ Methods and instance (nonlocal) variables are known as "members."
- ❑ Members can use all four access levels: public, protected, default, private.
- ❑ Member access comes in two forms:
  - ❑ Code in one class can access a member of another class.
  - ❑ A subclass can inherit a member of its superclass.
- ❑ If a class cannot be accessed, its members cannot be accessed.
- ❑ Determine class visibility before determining member visibility.
- ❑ `public` members can be accessed by all other classes, even in other packages.
- ❑ If a superclass member is public, the subclass inherits it—regardless of package.
- ❑ Members accessed without the dot operator (.) must belong to the same class.
- ❑ `this.` always refers to the currently executing object.
- ❑ `this.aMethod()` is the same as just invoking `aMethod()`.
- ❑ `private` members can be accessed only by code in the same class.
- ❑ `private` members are not visible to subclasses, so private members cannot be inherited.

❑ Default and `protected` members differ only when subclasses are involved:

   ❑ Default members can be accessed only by classes in the same package.

   ❑ `protected` members can be accessed by other classes in the same package, plus subclasses regardless of package.

   ❑ `protected` = package plus kids (kids meaning subclasses).

   ❑ For subclasses outside the package, the `protected` member can be accessed only through inheritance; a subclass outside the package cannot access a `protected` member by using a reference to a superclass instance (in other words, inheritance is the only mechanism for a subclass outside the package to access a `protected` member of its superclass).

   ❑ A `protected` member inherited by a subclass from another package is not accessible to any other class in the subclass package, except for the subclass' own subclasses.

Local Variables (Objective 1.3)

❑ Local (method, automatic, or stack) variable declarations cannot have access modifiers.

❑ `final` is the only modifier available to local variables.

❑ Local variables don't get default values, so they must be initialized before use.

Other Modifiers—Members (Objective 1.3)

❑ `final` methods cannot be overridden in a subclass.

❑ `abstract` methods are declared, with a signature, a return type, and an optional throws clause, but are not implemented.

❑ `abstract` methods end in a semicolon—no curly braces.

❑ Three ways to spot a non-abstract method:

   ❑ The method is not marked `abstract`.

   ❑ The method has curly braces.

   ❑ The method has code between the curly braces.

❑ The first nonabstract (concrete) class to extend an `abstract` class must implement all of the `abstract` class' `abstract` methods.

❑ The `synchronized` modifier applies only to methods and code blocks.

❑ `synchronized` methods can have any access control and can also be marked `final`.

- ❑ `abstract` methods must be implemented by a subclass, so they must be inheritable. For that reason:
  - ❑ `abstract` methods cannot be `private`.
  - ❑ `abstract` methods cannot be `final`.
- ❑ The `native` modifier applies only to methods.
- ❑ The `strictfp` modifier applies only to classes and methods.

Methods with var-args (Objective 1.4)

- ❑ As of Java 5, methods can declare a parameter that accepts from zero to many arguments, a so-called var-arg method.
- ❑ A var-arg parameter is declared with the syntax `type... name`; for instance: `doStuff(int... x) { }`
- ❑ A var-arg method can have only one var-arg parameter.
- ❑ In methods with normal parameters and a var-arg, the var-arg must come last.

Variable Declarations (Objective 1.3)

- ❑ Instance variables can
  - ❑ Have any access control
  - ❑ Be marked `final` or `transient`
- ❑ Instance variables can't be `abstract`, `synchronized`, `native`, or `strictfp`.
- ❑ It is legal to declare a local variable with the same name as an instance variable; this is called "shadowing."
- ❑ `final` variables have the following properties:
  - ❑ `final` variables cannot be reinitialized once assigned a value.
  - ❑ `final` reference variables cannot refer to a different object once the object has been assigned to the `final` variable.
  - ❑ `final` reference variables must be initialized before the constructor completes.
- ❑ There is no such thing as a `final` object. An object reference marked `final` does not mean the object itself is immutable.
- ❑ The `transient` modifier applies only to instance variables.
- ❑ The `volatile` modifier applies only to instance variables.

Array Declarations (Objective 1.3)

❑ Arrays can hold primitives or objects, but the array itself is always an object.

❑ When you declare an array, the brackets can be to the left or right of the variable name.

❑ It is never legal to include the size of an array in the declaration.

❑ An array of objects can hold any object that passes the IS-A (or instanceof) test for the declared type of the array. For example, if Horse extends Animal, then a Horse object can go into an Animal array.

Static Variables and Methods (Objective 1.4)

❑ They are not tied to any particular instance of a class.

❑ No classes instances are needed in order to use `static` members of the class.

❑ There is only one copy of a `static` variable / class and all instances share it.

❑ `static` methods do not have direct access to non-static members.

Enums (Objective 1.3)

❑ An enum specifies a list of constant values that can be assigned to a particular type.

❑ An enum is NOT a String or an int; an enum constant's type is the enum type. For example, WINTER, SPRING, SUMMER, and FALL are of the enum type Season.

❑ An enum can be declared outside or inside a class, but NOT in a method.

❑ An enum declared outside a class must NOT be marked `static`, `final`, `abstract`, `protected`, or `private`.

❑ Enums can contain constructors, methods, variables, and constant class bodies.

❑ enum constants can send arguments to the enum constructor, using the syntax BIG(8), where the int literal 8 is passed to the `enum` constructor.

❑ enum constructors can have arguments, and can be overloaded.

❑ enum constructors can NEVER be invoked directly in code. They are always called automatically when an `enum` is initialized.

❑ The semicolon at the end of an enum declaration is optional. These are legal:

```
enum Foo { ONE, TWO, THREE}
enum Foo { ONE, TWO, THREE};
```

SELF TEST

The following questions will help you measure your understanding of the material presented in this chapter. Read all of the choices carefully, as there may be more than one correct answer. Choose all correct answers for each question. Stay focused.

If you have a rough time with these at first, don't beat yourself up. Be positive. Repeat nice affirmations to yourself like, "I am smart enough to understand enums" and "OK, so that other guy knows enums better than I do, but I bet he can't <insert something you *are* good at> like me."

1. Given the following,

```
1. interface Base {
2.   boolean m1 ();
3.   byte m2(short s);
4. }
```

Which code fragments will compile? (Choose all that apply.)

A. `interface Base2 implements Base { }`

B. `abstract class Class2 extends Base {`
`public boolean m1() { return true; } }`

C. `abstract class Class2 implements Base { }`

D. `abstract class Class2 implements Base {`
`public boolean m1() { return (true); } }`

E. `class Class2 implements Base {`
`boolean m1() { return false; }`
`byte m2(short s) { return 42; } }`

2. Which declare a compilable `abstract` class? (Choose all that apply.)

A. `public abstract class Canine { public Bark speak(); }`

B. `public abstract class Canine { public Bark speak() { } }`

C. `public class Canine { public abstract Bark speak(); }`

D. `public class Canine abstract { public abstract Bark speak(); }`

3. Which is true? (Choose all that apply.)

A. "X extends Y" is correct if and only if X is a class and Y is an interface.

B. "X extends Y" is correct if and only if X is an interface and Y is a class.

C. "X extends Y" is correct if X and Y are either both classes or both interfaces.

D. "X extends Y" is correct for all combinations of X and Y being classes and/or interfaces.

4. Which are valid declarations? (Choose all that apply.)

A. `int $x;`

B. `int 123;`

C. `int _123;`

D. `int #dim;`

E. `int %percent;`

F. `int *divide;`

G. `int central_sales_region_Summer_2005_gross_sales;`

5. Which method names follow the JavaBeans standard? (Choose all that apply.)

A. `addSize`

B. `getCust`

C. `deleteRep`

D. `isColorado`

E. `putDimensions`

6. Given:

```
1. class Voop {
2.    public static void main(String [] args) {
3.       doStuff(1);
4.       doStuff(1,2);
5.    }
6.    // insert code here
7. }
```

Which, inserted independently at line 6, will compile? (Choose all that apply.)

A. `static void doStuff(int... doArgs) { }`

B. `static void doStuff(int[] doArgs) { }`

C. `static void doStuff(int doArgs...) { }`

D. `static void doStuff(int... doArgs, int y) { }`

E. `static void doStuff(int x, int... doArgs) { }`

7. Which are legal declarations? (Choose all that apply.)

A. `short x [];`

B. `short [] y;`

C. `short[5] x2;`

D. `short z2 [5];`

E. `short [] z [] [];`

F. `short [] y2 = [5];`

8.   Given:

```
1. enum Animals {
2.    DOG("woof"), CAT("meow"), FISH("burble");
3.    String sound;
4.    Animals(String s) { sound = s; }
5. }
6. class TestEnum {
7.    static Animals a;
8.    public static void main(String[] args) {
9.      System.out.println(a.DOG.sound + " " + a.FISH.sound);
10.   }
11. }
```

What is the result?

A. `woof burble`

B. Multiple compilation errors

C. Compilation fails due to an error on line 2

D. Compilation fails due to an error on line 3

E. Compilation fails due to an error on line 4

F. Compilation fails due to an error on line 9

9.   Given:

```
1. enum A { A }
2. class E2 {
3.    enum B { B }
4.    void C() {
5.      enum D { D }
6.    }
7. }
```

Which statements are true? (Choose all that apply.)

A. The code compiles.

B. If only line 1 is removed the code compiles.

C. If only line 3 is removed the code compiles.

D. If only line 5 is removed the code compiles.

E. If lines 1 and 3 are removed the code compiles.

F. If lines 1, 3 and 5 are removed the code compiles.

SELF TEST ANSWERS

I. Given the following,

```
1. interface Base {
2.    boolean m1 ();
3.    byte m2(short s);
4. }
```

Which code fragments will compile? (Choose all that apply.)

A. `interface Base2 implements Base { }`

B. `abstract class Class2 extends Base {`
`public boolean m1() { return true; } }`

C. `abstract class Class2 implements Base { }`

D. `abstract class Class2 implements Base {`
`public boolean m1() { return (true); } }`

E. `class Class2 implements Base {`
`boolean m1() { return false; }`
`byte m2(short s) { return 42; } }`

Answer:

☑ **C** and **D** are correct. **C** is correct because an `abstract` class doesn't have to implement any or all of its interface's methods. **D** is correct because the method is correctly implemented.

☒ **A** is incorrect because interfaces don't implement anything. **B** is incorrect because classes don't extend interfaces. **E** is incorrect because interface methods are implicitly `public`, so the methods being implemented must be `public`. (Objective 1.1)

2. Which declare a compilable `abstract` class? (Choose all that apply.)

A. `public abstract class Canine { public Bark speak(); }`

B. `public abstract class Canine { public Bark speak() { } }`

C. `public class Canine { public abstract Bark speak(); }`

D. `public class Canine abstract { public abstract Bark speak(); }`

Answer:

☑ **B** is correct. `abstract` classes don't have to have any `abstract` methods.

☒ **A** is incorrect because `abstract` methods must be marked as such. **C** is incorrect because you can't have an `abstract` method unless the class is `abstract`. **D** is incorrect because the keyword `abstract` must come before the class name. (Objective 1.1)

3. Which is true? (Choose all that apply.)

A. "X extends Y" is correct if and only if X is a class and Y is an interface.

B. "X extends Y" is correct if and only if X is an interface and Y is a class.

C. "X extends Y" is correct if X and Y are either both classes or both interfaces.

D. "X extends Y" is correct for all combinations of X and Y being classes and/or interfaces.

Answer:

☑ **C** is correct.

☒ **A** is incorrect because classes implement interfaces, they don't extend them. **B** is incorrect because interfaces only "inherit from" other interfaces. **D** is incorrect based on the preceding rules. (Objective 1.2)

4. Which are valid declarations? (Choose all that apply.)

A. `int $x;`

B. `int 123;`

C. `int _123;`

D. `int #dim;`

E. `int %percent;`

F. `int *divide;`

G. `int central_sales_region_Summer_2005_gross_sales;`

Answer:

☑ **A, C,** and **G** are legal identifiers.

☒ **B** is incorrect because an identifier can't start with a digit. **D, E,** and **F** are incorrect because identifiers must start with $, _, or a letter. (Objective 1.3)

5. Which method names follow the JavaBeans standard? (Choose all that apply.)

A. `addSize`

B. `getCust`

C. `deleteRep`

D. `isColorado`

E. `putDimensions`

Answer:

☑ **B** and **D** use the valid prefixes `'get'` and `'is'`.

☒ **A, C,** and **E** are incorrect because `'add'`, `'delete'` and `'put'` are not standard JavaBeans name prefixes. (Objective 1.4)

6. Given:
```
1. class Voop {
2.   public static void main(String[] args) {
3.     doStuff(1);
4.     doStuff(1,2);
5.   }
6.   // insert code here
7. }
```
Which, inserted independently at line 6, will compile? (Choose all that apply.)

A. `static void doStuff(int... doArgs) { }`

B. `static void doStuff(int[] doArgs) { }`

C. `static void doStuff(int doArgs...) { }`

D. `static void doStuff(int... doArgs, int y) { }`

E. `static void doStuff(int x, int... doArgs) { }`

Answer:

☑ **A** and **E** use valid var-args syntax.

☒ **B** and **C** are invalid var-arg syntax, and **D** is invalid because the var-arg must be the last of a method's arguments. (Objective 1.4)

7. Which are legal declarations? (Choose all that apply.)

A. `short x [];`

B. `short [] y;`

C. `short[5] x2;`

D. `short z2 [5];`

E. `short [] z [] [];`

F. `short [] y2 = [5];`

Answer:

☑ **A, B,** and **E** are correct array declarations; E is a three dimensional array.

☒ **C, D,** and **F** are incorrect, you can't include the size of your array in a declaration unless you also instantiate the array object. F uses invalid instantiation syntax. (Objective 1.3)

8. Given:
```
1. enum Animals {
2.   DOG("woof"), CAT("meow"), FISH("burble");
3.   String sound;
4.   Animals(String s) { sound = s; }
5. }
6. class TestEnum {
```

```
 7.    static Animals a;
 8.    public static void main(String [] args) {
 9.      System.out.println(a.DOG.sound + " " + a.FISH.sound);
10.    }
11. }
```

What is the result?

A. `woof burble`

B. Multiple compilation errors

C. Compilation fails due to an error on line 2

D. Compilation fails due to an error on line 3

E. Compilation fails due to an error on line 4

F. Compilation fails due to an error on line 9

Answer:

☑ **A** is correct; enums can have constructors and variables.

☒ **B, C, D, E,** and **F** are incorrect; these lines all use correct syntax. (Objective 1.3)

9.   Given:

```
1. enum A { A }
2. class E2 {
3.    enum B { B }
4.    void C() {
5.      enum D { D }
6.    }
7. }
```

Which statements are true? (Choose all that apply.)

A. The code compiles.

B. If only line 1 is removed the code compiles.

C. If only line 3 is removed the code compiles.

D. If only line 5 is removed the code compiles.

E. If lines 1 and 3 are removed the code compiles.

F. If lines 1, 3 and 5 are removed the code compiles.

Answer:

☑ **D** and **F** are correct. Line 5 is the only line that will not compile, because enums cannot be local to a method.

☒ **A, B, C** and **E** are incorrect based on the above. (Objective 1.3)

2

Object Orientation

Being a 1.5 SCJP means you must be at one with the object-oriented aspects of Java. You must dream of inheritance hierarchies, the power of polymorphism must flow through you, cohesion and loose coupling must become second nature to you, and composition must be your bread and butter. This chapter will prepare you for all of the object-oriented objectives and questions you'll encounter on the exam. We have heard of many experienced Java programmers who haven't really become fluent with the object-oriented tools that Java provides, so we'll start at the beginning.

CERTIFICATION OBJECTIVE

Encapsulation (Exam Objective 5.1)

5.1   Develop code that implements tight encapsulation, loose coupling, and high cohesion in classes, and describe the benefits.

Imagine you wrote the code for a class, and another dozen programmers from your company all wrote programs that used your class. Now imagine that later on, you didn't like the way the class behaved, because some of its instance variables were being set (by the other programmers from within their code) to values you hadn't anticipated. *Their* code brought out errors in *your* code. (Relax, this is just hypothetical.) Well, it is a Java program, so you should be able just to ship out a newer version of the class, which they could replace in their programs without changing any of their own code.

This scenario highlights two of the promises/benefits of Object Orientation: flexibility and maintainability. But those benefits don't come automatically. You have to do something. You have to write your classes and code in a way that supports flexibility and maintainability. So what if Java supports OO? It can't design your code for you. For example, imagine if you made your class with `public` instance variables, and those other programmers were setting the instance variables directly, as the following code demonstrates:

```
public class BadOO {
    public int size;
```

```
      public int weight;
      ...
}
public class ExploitBadOO {
   public static void main (String [] args) {
      BadOO b = new BadOO();
      b.size = -5; // Legal but bad!!
   }
}
```

And now you're in trouble. How are you going to change the class in a way that lets you handle the issues that come up when somebody changes the size variable to a value that causes problems? Your only choice is to go back in and write method code for adjusting size (a setSize(int a) method, for example), and then protect the size variable with, say, a private access modifier. But as soon as you make that change to your code, you break everyone else's!

The ability to make changes in your implementation code without breaking the code of others who use your code is a key benefit of encapsulation. You want to hide implementation details behind a public programming interface. By interface, we mean the set of accessible methods your code makes available for other code to call—in other words, your code's API. By hiding implementation details, you can rework your method code (perhaps also altering the way variables are used by your class) without forcing a change in the code that calls your changed method.

If you want maintainability, flexibility, and extensibility (and of course, you do), your design must include encapsulation. How do you do that?

- Keep instance variables protected (with an access modifier, often private).
- Make public accessor methods, and force calling code to use those methods rather than directly accessing the instance variable.
- For the methods, use the JavaBeans naming convention of set<someProperty> and get<someProperty>.

Figure 2-1 illustrates the idea that encapsulation forces callers of our code to go through methods rather than accessing variables directly.

FIGURE 2-1

The nature of
encapsulation

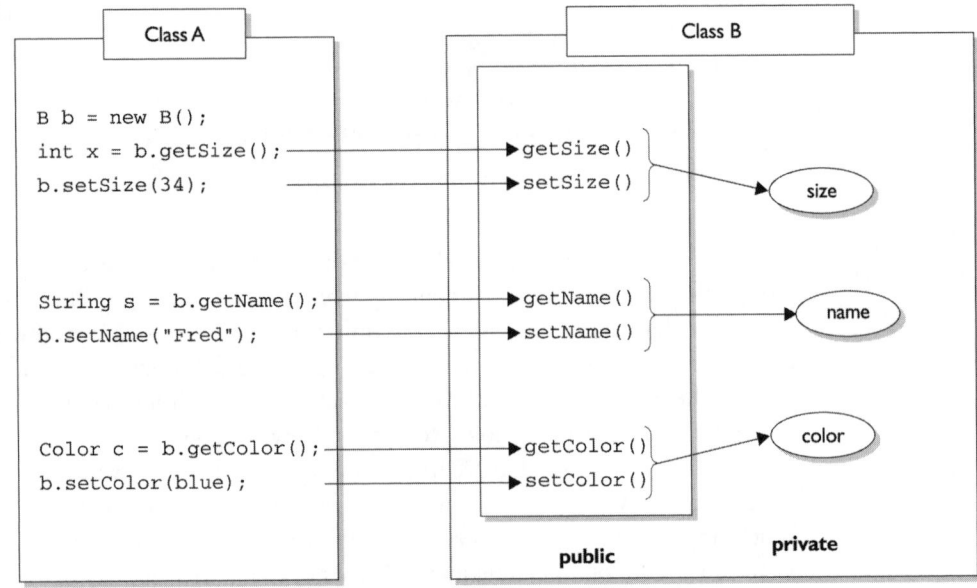

Class A cannot access Class B instance variable data
without going through getter and setter methods. Data is
marked private; only the accessor methods are public.

We call the access methods getters and setters although some prefer the fancier
terms accessors and mutators. (Personally, we don't like the word "mutate".)
Regardless of what you call them, they're methods that other programmers must go
through in order to access your instance variables. They look simple, and you've
probably been using them forever:

```
public class Box {
    // protect the instance variable; only an instance
    // of Box can access it " d " "dfdf"
    private int size;
    // Provide public getters and setters
    public int getSize() {
        return size;
```

```
    }
    public void setSize(int newSize) {
        size = newSize;
    }
}
```

Wait a minute...how useful is the previous code? It doesn't even do any validation or processing. What benefit can there be from having getters and setters that add no additional functionality? The point is, you can change your mind later, and add more code to your methods without breaking your API. Even if today you don't think you really need validation or processing of the data, good OO design dictates that you plan for the future. To be safe, force calling code to go through your methods rather than going directly to instance variables. *Always.* Then you're free to rework your method implementations later, without risking the wrath of those dozen programmers who know where you live.

exam

ᗯatch   *Look out for code that appears to be asking about the behavior of a method, when the problem is actually a lack of encapsulation. Look at the following example, and see if you can figure out what's going on:*

```
class Foo {
    public int left = 9;
    public int right = 3;
    public void setLeft(int leftNum) {
        left = leftNum;
        right = leftNum/3;
    }
    // lots of complex test code here
}
```

Now consider this question: Is the value of right always going to be one-third the value of left? It looks like it will, until you realize that users of the Foo *class don't need to use the* setLeft() *method! They can simply go straight to the instance variables and change them to any arbitrary* int *value.*

Inheritance, Is-A, Has-A (Exam Objective 5.5)

5.5 Develop code that implements "is-a" and/or "has-a" relationships.

Inheritance is everywhere in Java. It's safe to say that it's almost (almost?) impossible to write even the tiniest Java program without using inheritance. In order to explore this topic we're going to use the `instanceof` operator, which we'll discuss in more detail in Chapter 4. For now, just remember that `instanceof` returns `true` if the reference variable being tested is of the type being compared to. This code:

```
class Test {
  public static void main(String [] args) {
    Test t1 = new Test();
    Test t2 = new Test();
    if (!t1.equals(t2))
      System.out.println("they're not equal");
    if (t1 instanceof Object)
      System.out.println("t1's an Object");
  }
}
```

Produces the output:

```
they're not equal
t1's an Object
```

Where did that `equals` method come from? The reference variable `t1` is of type Test, and there's no `equals` method in the Test class. Or is there? The second `if` test asks whether `t1` is an instance of class Object, and because it *is* (more on that soon), the `if` test succeeds.

Hold on…how can `t1` be an instance of type Object, we just said it was of type Test? I'm sure you're way ahead of us here, but it turns out that every class in Java is a subclass of class Object, (except of course class Object itself). In other words, every class you'll ever use or ever write will inherit from class Object. You'll always have an `equals` method, a `clone` method, `notify`, `wait`, and others, available to use. Whenever you create a class, you automatically inherit all of class Object's methods.

Why? Let's look at that `equals` method for instance. Java's creators correctly assumed that it would be very common for Java programmers to want to compare instances of their classes to check for equality. If class Object didn't have an `equals` method, you'd have to write one yourself; you and every other Java programmer. That one `equals` method has been inherited billions of times. (To be fair, `equals` has also been *overridden* billions of times, but we're getting ahead of ourselves.)

For the exam you'll need to know that you can create inheritance relationships in Java by *extending* a class. It's also important to understand that the two most common reasons to use inheritance are

- To promote code reuse
- To use polymorphism

Let's start with reuse. A common design approach is to create a fairly generic version of a class with the intention of creating more specialized subclasses that inherit from it. For example:

```
class GameShape {
    public void displayShape() {
        System.out.println("displaying shape");
    }
    // more code
}

class PlayerPiece extends GameShape {
    public void movePiece() {
        System.out.println("moving game piece");
    }
    // more code
}


public class TestShapes {
    public static void main (String[] args) {
        PlayerPiece shape = new PlayerPiece();
        shape.displayShape();
        shape.movePiece();
    }
}
```

Outputs:

```
displaying shape
moving game piece
```

Notice that the PlayingPiece class inherits the generic display() method from the less-specialized class GameShape, and also adds its own method, movePiece(). Code reuse through inheritance means that methods with generic functionality (like display())—that could apply to a wide range of different kinds of shapes in a game—don't have to be reimplemented. That means all specialized subclasses of GameShape are guaranteed to have the capabilities of the more generic superclass. You don't want to have to rewrite the display() code in each of your specialized components of an online game.

But you knew that. You've experienced the pain of duplicate code when you make a change in one place and have to track down all the other places where that same (or very similar) code exists.

The second (and related) use of inheritance is to allow your classes to be accessed polymorphically—a capability provided by interfaces as well, but we'll get to that in a minute. Let's say that you have a GameLauncher class that wants to loop through a list of different kinds of GameShape objects, and invoke display() on each of them. At the time you write this class, you don't know every possible kind of GameShape subclass that anyone else will ever write. And you sure don't want to have to redo *your* code just because somebody decided to build a Dice shape six months later.

The beautiful thing about polymorphism ("many forms") is that you can treat any *subclass* of GameShape as a GameShape. In other words, you can write code in your GameLauncher class that says, "I don't care what kind of object you are as long as you inherit from (extend) GameShape. And as far as I'm concerned, if you extend GameShape then you've definitely got a display() method, so I know I can call it."

Imagine we now have two specialized subclasses that extend the more generic GameShape class, PlayerPiece and TilePiece:

```
class GameShape {
   public void displayShape() {
     System.out.println("displaying shape");
   }
   // more code
}
```

```
class PlayerPiece extends GameShape {
   public void movePiece() {
     System.out.println("moving game piece");
   }
   // more code
}

class TilePiece extends GameShape {
    public void getAdjacent() {
      System.out.println("getting adjacent tiles");
    }
    // more code
}
```

Now imagine a test class has a method with a declared argument type of GameShape, that means it can take any kind of GameShape. In other words, any subclass of GameShape can be passed to a method with an argument of type GameShape. This code

```
public class TestShapes {
   public static void main (String[] args) {
      PlayerPiece player = new PlayerPiece();
      TilePiece tile = new TilePiece();
      doShapes(player);
      doShapes(tile);
   }

   public static void doShapes(GameShape shape) {
     shape.displayShape();
   }
}
```

Outputs:

```
displaying shape
displaying shape
```

The key point is that the doShapes() method is declared with a GameShape argument but can be passed any subtype (in this example, a subclass) of GameShape. The method can then invoke any method of GameShape, without any concern for the actual runtime class type of the object passed to the method. There are implications, though. The `doShapes()` method knows only that the objects are a type of `GameShape`, since that's how the parameter is declared. And using a reference variable declared as type `GameShape`—regardless of whether the variable is a method parameter, local variable, or instance variable—means that *only* the methods of `GameShape` can be invoked on it. The methods you can call on a reference are totally dependent on the *declared* type of the variable, no matter what the actual object is, that the reference is referring to. That means you can't use a `GameShape` variable to call, say, the `getAdjacent()` method even if the object passed in *is* of type `TilePiece`. (We'll see this again when we look at interfaces.)

IS-A and HAS-A Relationships

For the exam you need to be able to look at code and determine whether the code demonstrates an IS-A or HAS-A relationship. The rules are simple, so this should be one of the few areas where answering the questions correctly is almost a no-brainer.

IS-A

In OO, the concept of IS-A is based on class inheritance or interface implementation. IS-A is a way of saying, "this thing is a type of that thing." For example, a Mustang is a type of horse, so in OO terms we can say, "Mustang IS-A Horse." Subaru IS-A Car. Broccoli IS-A Vegetable (not a very fun one, but it still counts). You express the IS-A relationship in Java through the keywords `extends` (for *class* inheritance) and `implements` (for *interface* implementation).

```
public class Car {
  // Cool Car code goes here
}

public class Subaru extends Car {
    // Important Subaru-specific stuff goes here
    // Don't forget Subaru inherits accessible Car members which
    // can include both methods and variables.
}
```

A Car is a type of Vehicle, so the inheritance tree might start from the Vehicle class as follows:

```
public class Vehicle { ... }
public class Car extends Vehicle { ... }
public class Subaru extends Car { ... }
```

In OO terms, you can say the following:

Vehicle is the superclass of Car.
Car is the subclass of Vehicle.
Car is the superclass of Subaru.
Subaru is the subclass of Vehicle.
Car inherits from Vehicle.
Subaru inherits from both Vehicle and Car.
Subaru is derived from Car.
Car is derived from Vehicle.
Subaru is derived from Vehicle.
Subaru is a subtype of both Vehicle and Car.

Returning to our IS-A relationship, the following statements are true:

"Car extends Vehicle" means "Car IS-A Vehicle."
"Subaru extends Car" means "Subaru IS-A Car."

And we can also say:

"Subaru IS-A Vehicle" because a class is said to be "a type of" anything further up in its inheritance tree. If the expression (`Foo instanceof Bar`) is `true`, then class `Foo` IS-A `Bar`, even if `Foo` doesn't directly extend `Bar`, but instead extends some other class that is a subclass of `Bar`. Figure 2-2 illustrates the inheritance tree for `Vehicle`, `Car`, and `Subaru`. The arrows move from the subclass to the superclass. In other words, a class' arrow points toward the class from which it extends.

FIGURE 2-2

Inheritance tree
for Vehicle, Car,
Subaru

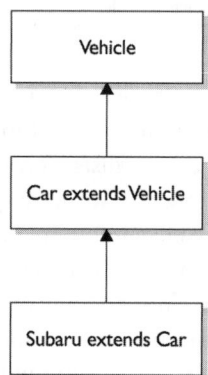

HAS-A

HAS-A relationships are based on usage, rather than inheritance. In other words, class A HAS-A B if code in class A has a reference to an instance of class B. For example, you can say the following,

A Horse IS-A Animal. A Horse HAS-A Halter.
The code might look like this:

```
public class Animal { }
public class Horse extends Animal {
    private Halter myHalter;
}
```

In the preceding code, the Horse class has an instance variable of type Halter, so you can say that "Horse HAS-A Halter." In other words, Horse has a reference to a Halter. Horse code can use that Halter reference to invoke methods on the Halter, and get Halter behavior without having Halter-related code (methods) in the Horse class itself. Figure 2-3 illustrates the HAS-A relationship between Horse and Halter.

FIGURE 2-3

HAS-A
relationship
between Horse
and Halter

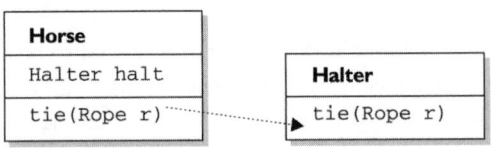

Horse class has a Halter, because Horse declares an instance variable of type Halter. When code invokes `tie()` on a Horse instance, the Horse invokes `tie()` on the Horse object's Halter instance variable.

HAS-A relationships allow you to design classes that follow good OO practices by not having monolithic classes that do a gazillion different things. Classes (and their resulting objects) should be specialists. As our friend Andrew says, "specialized classes can actually help reduce bugs." The more specialized the class, the more likely it is that you can reuse the class in other applications. If you put all the `Halter`-related code directly into the `Horse` class, you'll end up duplicating code in the `Cow` class, `UnpaidIntern` class, and any other class that might need `Halter` behavior. By keeping the `Halter` code in a separate, specialized `Halter` class, you have the chance to reuse the `Halter` class in multiple applications.

FROM THE CLASSROOM

Object-Oriented Design

IS-A and HAS-A relationships and encapsulation are just the tip of the iceberg when it comes to object-oriented design. Many books and graduate theses have been dedicated to this topic. The reason for the emphasis on proper design is simple: money. The cost to deliver a software application has been estimated to be as much as ten times more expensive for poorly designed programs. Having seen the ramifications of poor designs, I can assure you that this estimate is not far-fetched.

Even the best object-oriented designers make mistakes. It is difficult to visualize the relationships between hundreds, or even thousands, of classes. When mistakes are discovered during the implementation (code writing) phase of a project, the amount of code that has to be rewritten can sometimes cause programming teams to start over from scratch.

The software industry has evolved to aid the designer. Visual object modeling languages, like the Unified Modeling Language (UML), allow designers to design and easily modify classes without having to write code first,

because object-oriented components are represented graphically. This allows the designer to create a map of the class relationships and helps them recognize errors before coding begins. Another innovation in object-oriented design is design patterns. Designers noticed that many object-oriented designs apply consistently from project to project, and that it was useful to apply the same designs because it reduced the potential to introduce new design errors. Object-oriented designers then started to share these designs with each other. Now, there are many catalogs of these design patterns both on the Internet and in book form.

Although passing the Java certification exam does not require you to understand object-oriented design this thoroughly, hopefully this background information will help you better appreciate why the test writers chose to include encapsulation, and IS-A, and HAS-A relationships on the exam.

—Jonathan Meeks, Sun Certified Java Programmer

Users of the `Horse` class (that is, code that calls methods on a `Horse` instance), think that the `Horse` class has `Halter` behavior. The `Horse` class might have a `tie(LeadRope rope)` method, for example. Users of the `Horse` class should never have to know that when they invoke the `tie()` method, the `Horse` object turns around and delegates the call to its `Halter` class by invoking `myHalter.tie(rope)`. The scenario just described might look like this:

```
public class Horse extends Animal {
   private Halter myHalter;
   public void tie(LeadRope rope) {
      myHalter.tie(rope);  // Delegate tie behavior to the
                           // Halter object
   }
}
public class Halter {
   public void tie(LeadRope aRope) {
      // Do the actual tie work here
   }
}
```

In OO, we don't want callers to worry about which class or which object is actually doing the real work. To make that happen, the `Horse` class hides implementation details from `Horse` users. `Horse` users ask the `Horse` object to do things (in this case, tie itself up), and the `Horse` will either do it or, as in this example, ask something else to do it. To the caller, though, it always appears that the `Horse` object takes care of itself. Users of a `Horse` should not even need to know that there is such a thing as a `Halter` class.

CERTIFICATION OBJECTIVE

Polymorphism (Exam Objective 5.2)

5.2   Given a scenario, develop code that demonstrates the use of polymorphism. Further, determine when casting will be necessary and recognize compiler vs. runtime errors related to object reference casting.

Remember, any Java object that can pass more than one IS-A test can be considered polymorphic. Other than objects of type `Object`, *all* Java objects are polymorphic in that they pass the IS-A test for their own type and for class `Object`.

Remember that the only way to access an object is through a reference variable, and there are a few key things to remember about references:

■ A reference variable can be of only one type, and once declared, that type can never be changed (although the object it references can change).

■ A reference is a variable, so it can be reassigned to other objects, (unless the reference is declared `final`).

■ A reference variable's type determines the methods that can be invoked on the object the variable is referencing.

■ A reference variable can refer to any object of the same type as the declared reference, or—this is the big one—**it can refer to any** *subtype* **of the declared type!**

■ A reference variable can be declared as a class type or an interface type. If the variable is declared as an interface type, it can reference any object of any class that *implements* the interface.

Earlier we created a `GameShape` class that was extended by two other classes, `PlayerPiece` and `TilePiece`. Now imagine you want to animate some of the shapes on the game board. But not *all* shapes can be animatable, so what do you do with class inheritance?

Could we create a class with an `animate()` method, and have only *some* of the GameShape subclasses inherit from that class? If we can, then we could have PlayerPiece, for example, extend *both* the GameShape class and Animatable class, while the TilePiece would extend only GameShape. But no, this won't work! Java supports only single inheritance! That means a class can have only one immediate superclass. In other words, if PlayerPiece is a class, there is no way to say something like this:

```
class PlayerPiece extends GameShape, Animatable { // NO!
   // more code
}
```

A *class* cannot *extend* more than one class. That means one parent per class. A class *can* have multiple ancestors, however, since class B could extend class A, and class C could extend class B, and so on. So any given class might have multiple classes up its inheritance tree, but that's not the same as saying a class directly extends two classes.

on the job

Some languages (like C++) allow a class to extend more than one other class. This capability is known as "multiple inheritance." The reason that Java's creators chose not to allow multiple inheritance is that it can become quite messy. In a nutshell, the problem is that if a class extended two other classes, and both superclasses had, say, a doStuff() method, which version of doStuff() would the subclass inherit? This issue can lead to a scenario known as the "Deadly Diamond of Death," because of the shape of the class diagram that can be created in a multiple inheritance design. The diamond is formed when classes B and C both extend A, and both B and C inherit a method from A. If class D extends both B and C, and both B and C have overridden the method in A, class D has, in theory, inherited two different implementations of the same method. Drawn as a class diagram, the shape of the four classes looks like a diamond.

So if that doesn't work, what else could you do? You could simply put the `animate()` code in `GameShape`, and then disable the method in classes that can't be animated. But that's a bad design choice for many reasons, including it's more error-prone, it makes the `GameShape` class less cohesive (more on cohesion in a minute), and it means the `GameShape` API "advertises" that all shapes can be animated, when in fact that's not true since only some of the `GameShape` subclasses will be able to successfully run the `animate()` method.

So what *else* could you do? You already know the answer—create an `Animatable` *interface*, and have only the `GameShape` subclasses that can be animated implement that interface. Here's the interface:

```
public interface Animatable {
   public void animate();
}
```

And here's the modified `PlayerPiece` class that implements the interface:

```
class PlayerPiece extends GameShape implements Animatable {
    public void movePiece() {
        System.out.println("moving game piece");
    }
    public void animate() {
        System.out.println("animating...");
    }
    // more code
}
```

So now we have a `PlayerPiece` that passes the IS-A test for both the
`GameShape` class and the `Animatable` interface. That means a `PlayerPiece` can be
treated polymorphically as one of four things at any given time, depending on the
declared type of the reference variable:

- An `Object` (since any object inherits from `Object`)
- A `GameShape` (since `PlayerPiece` extends `GameShape`)
- A `PlayerPiece` (since that's what it really is)
- An `Animatable` (since `PlayerPiece` implements `Animatable`)

The following are all legal declarations. Look closely:

```
PlayerPiece player = new PlayerPiece();
      Object o = player;
      GameShape shape = player;
      Animatable mover = player;
```

There's only one object here—an instance of type `PlayerPiece`—but there
are four different types of reference variables, all referring to that one object on
the heap. Pop quiz: which of the preceding reference variables can invoke the
`display()` method? Hint: only two of the four declarations can be used to invoke
the `display()` method.

Remember that method invocations allowed by the compiler are based solely on
the declared type of the reference, regardless of the object type. So looking at the
four reference types again—`Object`, `GameShape`, `PlayerPiece`, and `Animatable`—
which of these four types know about the `display()` method?

You guessed it—both the `GameShape` class and the `PlayerPiece` class are known
(by the compiler) to have a `display()` method, so either of those reference types

can be used to invoke `display()`. Remember that to the compiler, a `PlayerPiece` IS-A `GameShape`, so the compiler says, "I see that the declared type is `PlayerPiece`, and since `PlayerPiece` extends `GameShape`, that means `PlayerPiece` inherited the `display()` method. Therefore, `PlayerPiece` can be used to invoke the `display()` method."

Which methods can be invoked when the `PlayerPiece` object is being referred to using a reference declared as type `Animatable`? Only the `animate()` method. Of course the cool thing here is that any class from any inheritance tree can also implement `Animatable`, so that means if you have a method with an argument declared as type `Animatable`, you can pass in `PlayerPiece` objects, `SpinningLogo` objects, and anything else that's an instance of a class that implements `Animatable`. And you can use that parameter (of type `Animatable`) to invoke the `animate()` method, but not the `display()` method (which it might not even have), or anything other than what is known to the compiler based on the reference type. The compiler always knows, though, that you can invoke the methods of class `Object` on any object, so those are safe to call regardless of the reference—class or interface—used to refer to the object.

We've left out one big part of all this, which is that even though the compiler only knows about the declared reference type, the JVM at runtime knows what the object really is. And that means that even if the `PlayerPiece` object's `display()` method is called using a `GameShape` reference variable, if the `PlayerPiece` overrides the `display()` method, the JVM will invoke the `PlayerPiece` version! The JVM looks at the real object at the other end of the reference, "sees" that it has overridden the method of the declared reference variable type, and invokes the method of the object's actual class. But one other thing to keep in mind:

Polymorphic method invocations apply only to *instance methods*. You can always refer to an object with a more general reference variable type (a superclass or interface), but at runtime, the ONLY things that are dynamically selected based on the actual *object* (rather than the *reference* type) are instance methods. Not *static* methods. Not *variables*. Only overridden instance methods are dynamically invoked based on the real object's type.

Since this definition depends on a clear understanding of overriding, and the distinction between static methods and instance methods, we'll cover those next.

CERTIFICATION OBJECTIVE

Overriding / Overloading (Exam Objectives 1.5 and 5.4)

1.5   Given a code example, determine if a method is correctly overriding or overloading another method, and identify legal return values (including covariant returns), for the method.

5.4   Given a scenario, develop code that declares and/or invokes overridden or overloaded methods and code that declares and/or invokes superclass, overridden, or overloaded constructors.

Overridden Methods

Any time you have a class that inherits a method from a superclass, you have the opportunity to override the method (unless, as you learned earlier, the method is marked `final`). The key benefit of overriding is the ability to define behavior that's specific to a particular subclass type. The following example demonstrates a Horse subclass of Animal overriding the Animal version of the eat() method:

```
public class Animal {
   public void eat() {
      System.out.println("Generic Animal Eating Generically");
   }
}
class Horse extends Animal {
   public void eat() {
      System.out.println("Horse eating hay, oats, "
                          + "and horse treats");
   }
}
```

For abstract methods you inherit from a superclass, you have no choice. You *must* implement the method in the subclass *unless the subclass is also abstract.* Abstract methods must be *implemented* by the concrete subclass, but this is a lot like saying that the concrete subclass *overrides* the abstract methods of the superclass. So you could think of abstract methods as methods you're forced to override.

The `Animal` class creator might have decided that for the purposes of polymorphism, all `Animal` subtypes should have an `eat()` method defined in a unique, specific way. Polymorphically, when someone has an `Animal` reference that refers not to an `Animal` instance, but to an `Animal` subclass instance, the caller should be able to invoke `eat()` on the `Animal` reference, but the actual runtime object (say, a `Horse` instance) will run its own specific `eat()` method. Marking the `eat()` method abstract is the Animal programmer's way of saying to all subclass developers, "It doesn't make any sense for your new subtype to use a generic `eat()` method, so you have to come up with your *own* eat() method implementation!" A (non-abstract), example of using polymorphism looks like this:

```
public class TestAnimals {
  public static void main (String [] args) {
    Animal a = new Animal();
    Animal b = new Horse();  //Animal ref, but a Horse object
    a.eat(); // Runs the Animal version of eat()
    b.eat(); // Runs the Horse version of eat()
  }
}
class Animal {
  public void eat() {
    System.out.println("Generic Animal Eating Generically");
  }
}
class Horse extends Animal {
  public void eat() {
    System.out.println("Horse eating hay, oats, "
                        + "and horse treats");
  }
  public void buck() { }
}
```

In the preceding code, the test class uses an Animal reference to invoke a method on a Horse object. Remember, the compiler will allow only methods in class Animal to be invoked when using a reference to an Animal. The following would not be legal given the preceding code:

```
Animal c = new Horse();
c.buck();  // Can't invoke buck();
           // Animal class doesn't have that method
```

To reiterate, the compiler looks only at the reference type, not the instance type. Polymorphism lets you use a more abstract supertype (including an interface) reference to refer to one of its subtypes (including interface implementers).

The overriding method cannot have a more restrictive access modifier than the method being overridden (for example, you can't override a method marked `public` and make it `protected`). Think about it: if the Animal class advertises a `public` eat() method and someone has an Animal reference (in other words, a reference declared as type Animal), that someone will assume it's safe to call eat() on the Animal reference regardless of the actual instance that the Animal reference is referring to. If a subclass were allowed to sneak in and change the access modifier on the overriding method, then suddenly at runtime—when the JVM invokes the true object's (Horse) version of the method rather than the reference type's (Animal) version—the program would die a horrible death. (Not to mention the emotional distress for the one who was betrayed by the rogue subclass.) Let's modify the polymorphic example we saw earlier in this section:

```
public class TestAnimals {
  public static void main (String [] args) {
    Animal a = new Animal();
    Animal b = new Horse();  //Animal ref, but a Horse object
    a.eat(); // Runs the Animal version of eat()
    b.eat(); // Runs the Horse version of eat()
  }
}
class Animal {
  public void eat() {
    System.out.println("Generic Animal Eating Generically");
  }
}
class Horse extends Animal {
  private void eat() {  // whoa! - it's private!
    System.out.println("Horse eating hay, oats, "
                    + "and horse treats");
  }
}
```

If this code compiled (which it doesn't), the following would fail at runtime:

```
Animal b = new Horse();  // Animal ref, but a Horse
                         // object , so far so good
b.eat();                 // Meltdown at runtime!
```

The variable b is of type `Animal`, which has a `public eat()` method. But remember that at runtime, Java uses virtual method invocation to dynamically select the actual version of the method that will run, based on the actual instance. An Animal reference can always refer to a Horse instance, because Horse IS-A(n) Animal. What makes that superclass reference to a subclass instance possible is that the subclass is guaranteed to be able to do everything the superclass can do. Whether the Horse instance overrides the inherited methods of Animal or simply inherits them, anyone with an Animal reference to a Horse instance is free to call all accessible Animal methods. For that reason, an overriding method must fulfill the contract of the superclass.

The rules for overriding a method are as follows:

- The argument list must exactly match that of the overridden method. If they don't match, you can end up with an overloaded method you didn't intend.
- The return type must be the same as, or a subtype of, the return type declared in the original overridden method in the superclass. (More on this in a few pages when we discuss covariant returns.)
- The access level can't be more restrictive than the overridden method's.
- The access level CAN be less restrictive than that of the overridden method.
- Instance methods can be overridden only if they are inherited by the subclass. A subclass within the same package as the instance's superclass can override any superclass method that is not marked `private` or `final`. A subclass in a different package can override only those non-`final` methods marked `public` or `protected` (since `protected` methods are inherited by the subclass).
- The overriding method CAN throw any unchecked (runtime) exception, regardless of whether the overridden method declares the exception. (More in Chapter 5.)
- The overriding method must NOT throw checked exceptions that are new or broader than those declared by the overridden method. For example, a method that declares a FileNotFoundException cannot be overridden by a method that declares a SQLException, Exception, or any other non-runtime exception unless it's a subclass of FileNotFoundException.
- The overriding method can throw narrower or fewer exceptions. Just because an overridden method "takes risks" doesn't mean that the overriding subclass' exception takes the same risks. Bottom line: an overriding method doesn't

have to declare any exceptions that it will never throw, regardless of what the overridden method declares.

- You cannot override a method marked `final`.

- You cannot override a method marked `static`. We'll look at an example in a few pages when we discuss `static` methods in more detail.

- If a method can't be inherited, you cannot override it. Remember that overriding implies that you're reimplementing a method you inherited! For example, the following code is not legal, and even if you added an `eat()` method to Horse, it wouldn't be an override of Animal's `eat()` method.

```
public class TestAnimals {
   public static void main (String [] args) {
      Horse h =  new Horse();
      h.eat(); // Not legal because Horse didn't inherit eat()
   }
}
class Animal {
   private void eat() {
      System.out.println("Generic Animal Eating Generically");
   }
}
class Horse extends Animal { }
```

Invoking a Superclass Version of an Overridden Method

Often, you'll want to take advantage of some of the code in the superclass version of a method, yet still override it to provide some additional specific behavior. It's like saying, "Run the superclass version of the method, then come back down here and finish with my subclass additional method code." (Note that there's no requirement that the superclass version run before the subclass code.) It's easy to do in code using the keyword `super` as follows:

```
public class Animal {
   public void eat() { }
   public void printYourself() {
      // Useful printing code goes here
   }
}
class Horse extends Animal {
   public void printYourself() {
      // Take advantage of Animal code, then add some more
```

```
        super.printYourself();   // Invoke the superclass
                                 // (Animal) code
                                 // Then do Horse-specific
                                 // print work here
    }
  }
```

Note: Using super to invoke an overridden method only applies to instance methods. (Remember, static methods can't be overridden.)

exam
ⓦatch
   If a method is overridden but you use a polymorphic (supertype) reference to refer to the subtype object with the overriding method, the compiler assumes you're calling the supertype version of the method. If the supertype version declares a checked exception, but the overriding subtype method does not, the compiler still thinks you are calling a method that declares an exception (more in Chapter 5). Let's take a look at an example:

```
    class Animal {
      public void eat() throws Exception {
        // throws an Exception
      }
    }
    class Dog2 extends Animal {
      public void eat() { // no Exceptions }
      public static void main(String [] args) {
        Animal a = new Dog2();
        Dog2 d = new Dog2();
        d.eat();              // ok
        a.eat();              // compiler error -
                              // unreported exception
      }
    }
```

   This code will not compile because of the Exception declared on the Animal eat() *method. This happens even though, at runtime, the* eat() *method used would be the Dog version, which does not declare the exception.*

Examples of Legal and Illegal Method Overrides

Let's take a look at overriding the eat() method of Animal:

```
public class Animal {
    public void eat() { }
}
```

Table 2-1 lists examples of illegal overrides of the Animal eat() method, given the preceding version of the Animal class.

TABLE 2-1   Examples of Illegal Overrides

Illegal Override Code	Problem with the Code
`private void eat() { }`	Access modifier is more restrictive
`public void eat() throws IOException { }`	Declares a checked exception not defined by superclass version
`public void eat(String food) { }`	A legal overload, not an override, because the argument list changed
`public String eat() { }`	Not an override because of the return type, not an overload either because there's no change in the argument list

Overloaded Methods

You're wondering what overloaded methods are doing in an OO chapter, but we've included them here since one of the things newer Java developers are most confused about are all of the subtle differences between over*loaded* and over*ridden* methods.

Over*loaded* methods let you reuse the same method name in a class, but with different arguments (and optionally, a different return type). Overloading a method often means you're being a little nicer to those who call your methods, because your code takes on the burden of coping with different argument types rather than forcing the caller to do conversions prior to invoking your method. The rules are simple:

- Overloaded methods MUST change the argument list.
- Overloaded methods CAN change the return type.
- Overloaded methods CAN change the access modifier.
- Overloaded methods CAN declare new or broader checked exceptions.

■ A method can be overloaded in the *same* class or in a *subclass*. In other words, if class A defines a `doStuff(int i)` method, the subclass B could define a `doStuff(String s)` method without overriding the superclass version that takes an int. So two methods with the same name but in different classes can still be considered overloaded, if the subclass inherits one version of the method and then declares another overloaded version in its class definition.

e x a m

ⓦ a t c h *Be careful to recognize when a method is overloaded rather than overridden. You might see a method that appears to be violating a rule for overriding, but that is actually a legal overload, as follows:*

```
public class Foo {
    public void doStuff(int y, String s) { }
    public void moreThings(int x) { }
}
class Bar extends Foo {
    public void doStuff(int y, long s) throws IOException { }
}
```

It's tempting to see the `IOException` *as the problem, because the overridden* `doStuff()` *method doesn't declare an exception, and* `IOException` *is checked by the compiler. But the* `doStuff()` *method is not overridden! Subclass* `Bar` *overloads the* `doStuff()` *method, by varying the argument list, so the* `IOException` *is fine.*

Legal Overloads

Let's look at a method we want to overload:

```
public void changeSize(int size, String name, float pattern) { }
```

The following methods are legal overloads of the changeSize() method:

```
public void changeSize(int size, String name) { }
public int changeSize(int size, float pattern) { }
public void changeSize(float pattern, String name)
                        throws IOException { }
```

Invoking Overloaded Methods

Note that there's a lot more to this discussion on how the compiler knows which method to invoke, but the rest is covered in Chapter 3 when we look at boxing and var-args—both of which have a huge impact on overloading. (You still have to pay attention to the part covered here, though.)

When a method is invoked, more than one method of the same name might exist for the object type you're invoking a method on. For example, the Horse class might have three methods with the same name but with different argument lists, which means the method is overloaded.

Deciding which of the matching methods to invoke is based on the arguments. If you invoke the method with a String argument, the overloaded version that takes a String is called. If you invoke a method of the same name but pass it a `float`, the overloaded version that takes a `float` will run. If you invoke the method of the same name but pass it a Foo object, and there isn't an overloaded version that takes a Foo, then the compiler will complain that it can't find a match. The following are examples of invoking overloaded methods:

```
class Adder {
  public int addThem(int x, int y) {
    return x + y;
  }

  // Overload the addThem method to add doubles instead of ints
  public double addThem(double x, double y) {
    return x + y;
  }
}
// From another class, invoke the addThem() method
public class TestAdder {
  public static void main (String [] args) {
    Adder a = new Adder();
    int b = 27;
    int c = 3;
    int result = a.addThem(b,c); // Which addThem is invoked?
    double doubleResult = a.addThem(22.5,9.3); // Which addThem?
  }
}
```

In the preceding TestAdder code, the first call to a.addThem(b,c) passes two ints to the method, so the first version of addThem()—the overloaded version that takes two int arguments—is called. The second call to a.addThem(22.5, 9.3) passes two doubles to the method, so the second version of addThem()—the overloaded version that takes two double arguments—is called.

Invoking overloaded methods that take object references rather than primitives is a little more interesting. Say you have an overloaded method such that one version takes an Animal and one takes a Horse (subclass of Animal). If you pass a Horse object in the method invocation, you'll invoke the overloaded version that takes a Horse. Or so it looks at first glance:

```
class Animal { }
class Horse extends Animal { }
class UseAnimals {
    public void doStuff(Animal a) {
        System.out.println("In the Animal version");
    }
    public void doStuff(Horse h) {
        System.out.println("In the Horse version");
    }
    public static void main (String [] args) {
        UseAnimals ua = new UseAnimals();
        Animal animalObj = new Animal();
        Horse horseObj = new Horse();
        ua.doStuff(animalObj);
        ua.doStuff(horseObj);
    }
}
```

The output is what you expect:

```
in the Animal version
in the Horse version
```

But what if you use an Animal reference to a Horse object?

```
Animal animalRefToHorse = new Horse();
 ua.doStuff(animalRefToHorse);
```

Which of the overloaded versions is invoked? You might want to say, "The one that takes a Horse, since it's a Horse object at runtime that's being passed to the method." But that's not how it works. The preceding code would actually print:

```
in the Animal version
```

Even though the actual object at runtime is a Horse and not an Animal, the choice of which overloaded method to call (in other words, the signature of the method) is NOT dynamically decided at runtime. Just remember, the *reference* type (not the object type) determines which overloaded method is invoked! To summarize, which over*ridden* version of the method to call (in other words, from which class in the inheritance tree) is decided at *runtime* based on *object* type, but which over*loaded* version of the method to call is based on the *reference* type of the argument passed at *compile* time. If you invoke a method passing it an Animal reference to a Horse object, the compiler knows only about the Animal, so it chooses the overloaded version of the method that takes an Animal. It does not matter that at runtime there's actually a Horse being passed.

Polymorphism in Overloaded and Overridden Methods

How does polymorphism work with overloaded methods? From what we just looked at, it doesn't appear that polymorphism matters when a method is overloaded. If you pass an Animal reference, the overloaded method that takes an Animal will be invoked, even if the actual object passed is a Horse. Once the Horse masquerading as Animal gets in to the method, however, the Horse object is still a Horse despite being passed into a method expecting an Animal. So it's true that polymorphism doesn't determine which overloaded version is called; polymorphism does come into play when the decision is about which overridden version of a method is called. But sometimes, a method is both overloaded and overridden. Imagine the Animal and Horse classes look like this:

```
public class Animal {
   public void eat() {
      System.out.println("Generic Animal Eating Generically");
   }
}
public class Horse extends Animal {
   public void eat() {
      System.out.println("Horse eating hay ");
   }
   public void eat(String s) {
      System.out.println("Horse eating " + s);
   }
}
```

Notice that the Horse class has both overloaded and overridden the eat() method. Table 2-2 shows which version of the three eat() methods will run depending on how they are invoked.

TABLE 2-2	Examples of Illegal Overrides

Method Invocation Code	Result
`Animal a = new Animal();` `a.eat();`	`Generic Animal Eating Generically`
`Horse h = new Horse();` `h.eat();`	`Horse eating hay`
`Animal ah = new Horse();` `ah.eat();`	`Horse eating hay` Polymorphism works—the actual object type (Horse), not the reference type (Animal), is used to determine which eat() is called.
`Horse he = new Horse();` `he.eat("Apples");`	`Horse eating Apples` The overloaded eat(String s) method is invoked.
`Animal a2 = new Animal();` `a2.eat("treats");`	Compiler error! Compiler sees that Animal class doesn't have an eat() method that takes a String.
`Animal ah2 = new Horse();` `ah2.eat("Carrots");`	Compiler error! Compiler *still* looks only at the reference, and sees that Animal doesn't have an eat() method that takes a String. Compiler doesn't care that the actual object might be a Horse at runtime.

exam

ⓦatch

Don't be fooled by a method that's overloaded but not overridden by a subclass. It's perfectly legal to do the following:

```
public class Foo {
    void doStuff() { }
}
class Bar extends Foo {
    void doStuff(String s) { }
}
```

The Bar class has two `doStuff()` *methods: the no-arg version it inherits from Foo (and does not override), and the overloaded* `doStuff(String s)` *defined in the Bar class. Code with a reference to a Foo can invoke only the no-arg version, but code with a reference to a Bar can invoke either of the overloaded versions.*

Table 2-3 summarizes the difference between overloaded and overridden methods.

TABLE 2-3	Differences Between Overloaded and Overridden Methods	
	Overloaded Method	**Overridden Method**
Argument(s)	Must change.	Must not change.
Return type	Can change.	Can't change except for covariant returns.
Exceptions	Can change.	Can reduce or eliminate. Must not throw new or broader checked exceptions.
Access	Can change.	Must not make more restrictive (can be less restrictive).
Invocation	*Reference* type determines which overloaded version (based on declared argument types) is selected. Happens at *compile* time. The actual *method* that's invoked is still a virtual method invocation that happens at runtime, but the compiler will already know the *signature* of the method to be invoked. So at runtime, the argument match will already have been nailed down, just not the *class* in which the method lives.	*Object* type (in other words, *the type of the actual instance on the heap*) determines which method is selected. Happens at *runtime*.

The current objective (5.4) covers both method and constructor overloading, but we'll cover constructor overloading in the next section, where we'll also cover the other constructor-related topics that are on the exam. Figure 2-4 illustrates the way overloaded and overridden methods appear in class relationships.

FIGURE 2-4

Overloaded and overridden methods in class relationships

Overriding

Tree
showLeaves()

Oak
showLeaves()

Overloading

Tree
setFeatures(String name)

Oak
setFeatures(String name, int leafSize) setFeatures(int leafSize)

CERTIFICATION OBJECTIVE

Reference Variable Casting (Objective 5.2)

5.2 Given a scenario, develop code that demonstrates the use of polymorphism. Further, determine when casting will be necessary and recognize compiler vs. runtime errors related to object reference casting.

We've seen how it's both possible and common to use generic reference variable types to refer to more specific object types. It's at the heart of polymorphism. For example, this line of code should be second nature by now:

```
Animal animal = new Dog();
```

But what happens when you want to use that `animal` reference variable to invoke a method that only class `Dog` has? You know it's referring to a `Dog`, and you want to do a `Dog`-specific thing? In the following code, we've got an array of `Animals`, and whenever we find a `Dog` in the array, we want to do a special `Dog` thing. Let's agree for now that all of this code is OK, except that we're not sure about the line of code that invokes the `playDead` method.

```
class Animal {
  void makeNoise() {System.out.println("generic noise"); }
}
class Dog extends Animal {
  void makeNoise() {System.out.println("bark"); }
  void playDead() { System.out.println("    roll over"); }
}

class CastTest2 {
  public static void main(String [] args) {
    Animal [] a = {new Animal(), new Dog(), new Animal() };
    for(Animal animal : a) {
      animal.makeNoise();
      if(animal instanceof Dog) {
        animal.playDead();        // try to do a Dog behavior ?
      }
    }
  }
}
```

When we try to compile this code, the compiler says something like this:

```
cannot find symbol
```

The compiler is saying, "Hey, class Animal doesn't have a `playDead()` method". Let's modify the `if` code block:

```
if(animal instanceof Dog) {
    Dog d = (Dog) animal;        // casting the ref. var.
    d.playDead();
}
```

The new and improved code block contains a cast, which in this case is sometimes called a *downcast*, because we're casting down the inheritance tree to a more specific class. Now, the compiler is happy. Before we try to invoke `playDead`, we cast the animal variable to type `Dog`. What we're saying to the compiler is, "We know it's really referring to a `Dog` object, so it's okay to make a new `Dog` reference variable to refer to that object." In this case we're safe because before we ever try the cast, we do an `instanceof` test to make sure.

It's important to know that the compiler is forced to trust us when we do a downcast, even when we screw up:

```
class Animal { }
class Dog extends Animal { }
class DogTest {
  public static void main(String [] args) {
    Animal animal = new Animal();
    Dog d = (Dog) animal;              // compiles but fails later
  }
}
```

It can be maddening! This code compiles! When we try to run it, we'll get an exception something like this:

```
java.lang.ClassCastException
```

Why can't we trust the compiler to help us out here? Can't it see that `animal` is of type `Animal`? All the compiler can do is verify that the two types are in the same inheritance tree, so that depending on whatever code might have come before the downcast, it's possible that `animal` is of type `Dog`. The compiler must allow things that might possibly work at runtime. However, if the compiler knows with certainty that the cast could not possibly work, compilation will fail. The following replacement code block will NOT compile:

```
Animal animal = new Animal();
Dog d = (Dog) animal;
String s = (String) animal;   // animal can't EVER be a String
```

In this case, you'll get an error something like this:

```
inconvertible types
```

Unlike downcasting, upcasting (casting *up* the inheritance tree to a more general type) works implicitly (i.e. you don't have to type in the cast) because when you upcast you're implicitly restricting the number of methods you can invoke, as opposed to *downcasting*, which implies that later on, you might want to invoke a more *specific* method. For instance:

```
class Animal { }
class Dog extends Animal { }

class DogTest {
  public static void main(String [] args) {
    Dog d = new Dog();
    Animal a1 = d;            // upcast ok with no explicit cast
    Animal a2 = (Animal) d;   // upcast ok with an explicit cast
  }
}
```

Both of the previous upcasts will compile and run without exception, because a Dog IS-A Animal, which means that anything an Animal can do, a Dog can do. A Dog can do more, of course, but the point is—anyone with an Animal reference can safely call Animal methods on a Dog instance. The Animal methods may have been overridden in the Dog class, but all we care about now is that a Dog can always do at least everything an Animal can do. The compiler and JVM know it too, so the implicit upcast is always legal for assigning an object of a subtype to a reference of one of its supertype classes (or interfaces). If Dog implements Pet, and Pet defines beFriendly(), then a Dog can be implicitly cast to a Pet, but the only Dog method you can invoke then is beFriendly(), which Dog was forced to implement because Dog implements the Pet interface.

One more thing…if `Dog implements Pet`, then if `Beagle extends Dog`, but Beagle does not *declare* that it implements Pet, Beagle is still a Pet! Beagle is a Pet simply because it extends Dog, and Dog's already taken care of the Pet parts of itself, and all its children. The Beagle class can always override any methods it inherits from Dog, including methods that Dog implemented to fulfill its interface contract.

And just one more thing…if Beagle does declare it implements Pet, just so that others looking at the Beagle class API can easily see that Beagle IS-A Pet, without having to look at Beagle's superclasses, Beagle still doesn't need to implement the beFriendly() method if the Dog class (Beagle's superclass) has already taken care of that. In other words, if Beagle IS-A Dog, and Dog IS-A Pet, then Beagle IS-A Pet, and has already met its Pet obligations for implementing the `beFriendly()` method since it inherits the `beFriendly()` method. The compiler is smart enough to say, "I know Beagle already IS a Dog, but it's OK to make it more obvious."

So don't be fooled by code that shows a concrete class that declares that it implements an interface, but doesn't implement the *methods* of the interface. Before you can tell whether the code is legal, you must know what the superclasses of this implementing class have declared. If any class in its inheritance tree has already provided concrete (i.e., non-abstract) method implementations, and has declared that it (the superclass) implements the interface, then the subclass is under no obligation to re-implement (override) those methods.

exam

ⓦatch   *The exam creators will tell you that they're forced to jam tons of code into little spaces "because of the exam engine." While that's partially true, they ALSO like to obfuscate. The following code:*

```
Animal a = new Dog();
Dog d = (Dog) a;
a.doDogStuff();
```

Can be replaced with this easy-to-read bit of fun:

```
Animal a = new Dog();
((Dog)a).doDogStuff();
```

In this case the compiler needs all of those parentheses, otherwise it thinks it's been handed an incomplete statement.

Implementing an Interface (Exam Objective 1.2)

1.2 Develop code that declares an interface…

When you implement an interface, you're agreeing to adhere to the contract defined in the interface. That means you're agreeing to provide legal implementations for every method defined in the interface, and that anyone who knows what the interface methods look like (not how they're implemented, but how they can be called and what they return) can rest assured that they can invoke those methods on an instance of your implementing class.

For example, if you create a class that implements the Runnable interface (so that your code can be executed by a specific thread), you must provide the `public void run()` method. Otherwise, the poor thread could be told to go execute your Runnable object's code and—surprise surprise—the thread then discovers the object has no `run()` method! (At which point, the thread would blow up and the JVM would crash in a spectacular yet horrible explosion.) Thankfully, Java prevents this meltdown from occurring by running a compiler check on any class that claims to implement an interface. If the class says it's implementing an interface, it darn well better have an implementation for each method in the interface (with a few exceptions we'll look at in a moment).

Assuming an interface, Bounceable, with two methods: `bounce()`, and `setBounceFactor()`, the following class will compile:

```
public class Ball implements Bounceable {   // Keyword
                                            // 'implements'
    public void bounce() { }
    public void setBounceFactor(int bf) { }
}
```

OK, we know what you're thinking: "This has got to be the worst implementation class in the history of implementation classes." It compiles, though. And runs. The interface contract guarantees that a class will have the method (in other words, others can call the method subject to access control), but it never guaranteed a good implementation—or even any actual implementation code in the body of the method. The compiler will never say to you, "Um, excuse me, but did you really mean to put nothing between those curly braces? HELLO. This is a method after all, so shouldn't it do something?"

Implementation classes must adhere to the same rules for method implementation as a class extending an `abstract` class. In order to be a legal implementation class, a nonabstract implementation class must do the following:

- Provide concrete (nonabstract) implementations for all methods from the declared interface.
- Follow all the rules for legal overrides.
- Declare no checked exceptions on implementation methods other than those declared by the interface method, or subclasses of those declared by the interface method.
- Maintain the signature of the interface method, and maintain the same return type (or a subtype). (But it does not have to declare the exceptions declared in the interface method declaration.)

But wait, there's more! An implementation class can itself be `abstract`! For example, the following is legal for a class Ball implementing Bounceable:

```
abstract class Ball implements Bounceable { }
```

Notice anything missing? We never provided the implementation methods. And that's OK. If the implementation class is `abstract`, it can simply pass the buck to its first concrete subclass. For example, if class BeachBall extends Ball, and BeachBall is not `abstract`, then BeachBall will have to provide all the methods from Bounceable:

```
class BeachBall extends Ball {
  // Even though we don't say it in the class declaration above,
  // BeachBall implements Bounceable, since BeachBall's abstract
  // superclass (Ball) implements Bounceable

  public void bounce() {
     // interesting BeachBall-specific bounce code
  }
  public void setBounceFactor(int bf) {
     // clever BeachBall-specific code for setting
     // a bounce factor
  }
```

```
        // if class Ball defined any abstract methods,
        // they'll have to be
        // implemented here as well.
    }
```

Look for classes that claim to implement an interface but don't provide the correct method implementations. Unless the implementing class is abstract, the implementing class must provide implementations for all methods defined in the interface.

Two more rules you need to know and then we can put this topic to sleep (or put you to sleep; we always get those two confused):

1. A class can implement more than one interface. It's perfectly legal to say, for example, the following:

```
public class Ball implements Bounceable, Serializable, Runnable
{ ... }
```

You can extend only one class, but implement many interfaces. But remember that subclassing defines who and what you are, whereas implementing defines a role you can play or a hat you can wear, despite how different you might be from some other class implementing the same interface (but from a different inheritance tree). For example, a Person extends HumanBeing (although for some, that's debatable). But a Person may also implement Programmer, Snowboarder, Employee, Parent, or PersonCrazyEnoughToTakeThisExam.

2. An interface can itself extend another interface, but never implement anything. The following code is perfectly legal:

```
public interface Bounceable extends Moveable { }    // ok!
```

What does that mean? The first concrete (nonabstract) implementation class of Bounceable must implement all the methods of Bounceable, plus all the methods of Moveable! The subinterface, as we call it, simply adds more requirements to the contract of the superinterface. You'll see this concept applied in many areas of Java, especially J2EE where you'll often have to build your own interface that extends one of the J2EE interfaces.

Hold on though, because here's where it gets strange. An interface can extend more than one interface! Think about that for a moment. You know that when we're talking about classes, the following is illegal:

```
public class Programmer extends Employee, Geek { } // Illegal!
```

As we mentioned earlier, a class is not allowed to extend multiple classes in Java. An interface, however, is free to extend multiple interfaces.

```
interface Bounceable extends Moveable, Spherical {    // ok!
   void bounce();
   void setBounceFactor(int bf);
}
interface Moveable {
   void moveIt();
}
interface Spherical {
   void doSphericalThing();
}
```

In the next example, Ball is required to implement Bounceable, plus all methods from the interfaces that Bounceable extends (including any interfaces those interfaces extend, and so on until you reach the top of the stack—or is it the bottom of the stack?). So Ball would need to look like the following:

```
class Ball implements Bounceable {

   public void bounce() { }    // Implement Bounceable's methods
   public void setBounceFactor(int bf) { }

   public void moveIt() { }     // Implement Moveable's method

   public void doSphericalThing() { }    // Implement Spherical
}
```

If class Ball fails to implement any of the methods from Bounceable, Moveable, or Spherical, the compiler will jump up and down wildly, red in the face, until it does. Unless, that is, class Ball is marked abstract. In that case, Ball could choose to implement any, all, or none of the methods from any of the interfaces, thus leaving the rest of the implementations to a concrete subclass of Ball, as follows:

```
abstract class Ball implements Bounceable {
   public void bounce() { ... }   // Define bounce behavior
   public void setBounceFactor(int bf) { ... }
   // Don't implement the rest; leave it for a subclass
}
class SoccerBall extends Ball {   // class SoccerBall must
            // implement the interface methods that Ball didn't
   public void moveIt() { ... }
   public void doSphericalThing() { ... }
   // SoccerBall can choose to override the Bounceable methods
   // implemented by Ball
   public void bounce() { ... }
}
```

Figure 2-5 compares concrete and abstract examples of extends and implements, for both classes and interfaces.

FIGURE 2-5   Comparing concrete and abstract examples of extends and implements

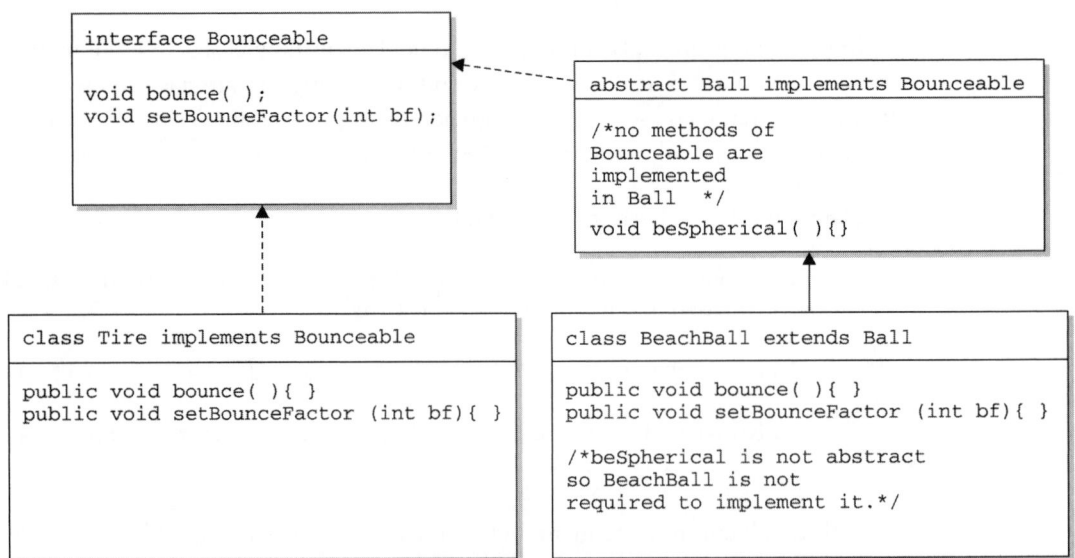

Because BeachBall is the first concrete class to implement Bounceable, it must provide implementations for all methods of Bounceable, except those defined in the abstract class Ball. Because Ball did not provide implementations of Bounceable methods, BeachBall was required to implement all of them.

exam
ⓦatch

Look for illegal uses of extends and implements. The following shows examples of legal and illegal class and interface declarations:

```
class Foo { }                          // OK
class Bar implements Foo  { }          // No! Can't implement a class
interface Baz { }                      // OK
interface Fi { }                       // OK
interface Fee implements Baz { }       // No! Interface can't
                                       // implement an interface
interface Zee implements Foo { }       // No! Interface can't
                                       // implement a class
interface Zoo extends Foo { }          // No! Interface can't
                                       // extend a class
interface Boo extends Fi { }           // OK. Interface can extend
                                       // an interface
class Toon extends Foo, Button { }     // No! Class can't extend
                                       // multiple classes
class Zoom implements Fi, Fee { }      // OK. class can implement
                                       // multiple interfaces
interface Vroom extends Fi, Fee { }    // OK. interface can extend
                                       // multiple interfaces
class Yow extends Foo implements Fi { } // OK. Class can do both
                                       // (extends must be 1st)
```

Burn these in, and watch for abuses in the questions you get on the exam. Regardless of what the question appears to be testing, the real problem might be the class or interface declaration. Before you get caught up in, say, tracing a complex threading flow, check to see if the code will even compile. (Just that tip alone may be worth your putting us in your will!) (You'll be impressed by the effort the exam developers put into distracting you from the real problem.) (How did people manage to write anything before parentheses were invented?)

Legal Return Types (Exam Objective 1.5)

1.5 Given a code example, determine if a method is correctly overriding or overloading another method, and identify legal return values (including covariant returns), for the method.

This objective covers two aspects of return types: what you can declare as a return type, and what you can actually return as a value. What you can and cannot declare is pretty straightforward, but it all depends on whether you're overriding an inherited method or simply declaring a new method (which includes overloaded methods). We'll take just a quick look at the difference between return type rules for overloaded and overriding methods, because we've already covered that in this chapter. We'll cover a small bit of new ground, though, when we look at polymorphic return types and the rules for what is and is not legal to actually return.

Return Type Declarations

This section looks at what you're allowed to declare as a return type, which depends primarily on whether you are overriding, overloading, or declaring a new method.

Return Types on Overloaded Methods

Remember that method overloading is not much more than name reuse. The overloaded method is a completely different method from any other method of the same name. So if you inherit a method but overload it in a subclass, you're not subject to the restrictions of overriding, which means you can declare any return type you like. What you can't do is change *only* the return type. To overload a method, remember, you must change the argument list. The following code shows an overloaded method:

```
public class Foo{
    void go() { }
}
public class Bar extends Foo {
    String go(int x) {
```

```
        return null;
    }
}
```

Notice that the Bar version of the method uses a different return type. That's perfectly fine. As long as you've changed the argument list, you're overloading the method, so the return type doesn't have to match that of the superclass version. What you're NOT allowed to do is this:

```
public class Foo{
    void go() { }
}
public class Bar extends Foo {
    String go() { // Not legal! Can't change only the return type
        return null;
    }
}
```

Overriding and Return Types, and Covariant Returns

When a subclass wants to change the method implementation of an inherited method (an override), the subclass must define a method that matches the inherited version exactly. Or, as of Java 5, you're allowed to change the return type in the overriding method as long as the new return type is a *subtype* of the declared return type of the overridden (superclass) method.

Let's look at a covariant return in action:

```
class Alpha {
  Alpha doStuff(char c) {
    return new Alpha();
  }
}

class Beta extends Alpha {
  Beta doStuff(char c) {      // legal override in Java 1.5
    return new Beta();
  }
}
```

As of Java 5, this code will compile. If you were to attempt to compile this code with a 1.4 compiler or with the source flag as follows:

```
javac -source 1.4 Beta.java
```

you would get a compiler error something like this:

```
attempting to use incompatible return type
```

(We'll talk more about compiler flags in Chapter 10.)

Other rules apply to overriding, including those for access modifiers and declared exceptions, but those rules aren't relevant to the return type discussion.

For the exam, be sure you know that overloaded methods can change the return type, but overriding methods can do so only within the bounds of covariant returns. Just that knowledge alone will help you through a wide range of exam questions.

Returning a Value

You have to remember only six rules for returning a value:

1. You can return `null` in a method with an object reference return type.

```java
public Button doStuff() {
  return null;
}
```

2. An array is a perfectly legal return type.

```java
public String[] go() {
  return new String[] {"Fred", "Barney", "Wilma"};
}
```

3. In a method with a primitive return type, you can return any value or variable that can be implicitly converted to the declared return type.

```java
public int foo() {
  char c = 'c';
  return c;  // char is compatible with int
}
```

4. In a method with a primitive return type, you can return any value or variable that can be explicitly cast to the declared return type.

```
public int foo () {
   float f = 32.5f;
   return (int) f;
}
```

5. You must *not* return anything from a method with a void return type.

```
public void bar() {
   return "this is it";   // Not legal!!
}
```

6. In a method with an object reference return type, you can return any object type that can be implicitly cast to the declared return type.

```
public Animal getAnimal() {
   return new Horse();   // Assume Horse extends Animal
}

public Object getObject() {
   int[] nums = {1,2,3};
   return nums;   // Return an int array,
                  // which is still an object
}

public interface Chewable { }
public class Gum implements Chewable { }

public class TestChewable {
    // Method with an interface return type
    public Chewable getChewable() {
      return new Gum();   // Return interface implementer
    }
}
```

e x a m

ⓦ a t c h

Watch for methods that declare an abstract class or interface return type, and know that any object that passes the IS-A test (in other words, would test true using the instanceof operator) can be returned from that method— for example:

```
public abstract class Animal { }
public class Bear extends Animal { }
public class Test {
   public Animal go() {
      return new Bear();   // OK, Bear "is-a" Animal
   }
}
```

This code will compile, the return value is a subtype.

CERTIFICATION OBJECTIVE

Constructors and Instantiation (Exam Objectives 1.6 and 5.4)

1.6 Given a set of classes and superclasses, develop constructors for one or more of the classes. Given a class declaration, determine if a default constructor will be created, and if so, determine the behavior of that constructor. Given a nested or non-nested class listing, write code to instantiate the class.

5.4 Given a scenario, develop code that declares and/or invokes overridden or overloaded methods and code that declares and/or invokes superclass, overridden, or overloaded constructors.

Objects are constructed. You can't make a new object without invoking a constructor. In fact, you can't make a new object without invoking not just the constructor of the object's actual class type, but also the constructor of each of its superclasses! Constructors are the code that runs whenever you use the keyword new. OK, to be a bit more accurate, there can also be initialization blocks that run when you say new, but we're going to cover them (init blocks), and their static initialization counterparts, in the next chapter. We've got plenty to talk about here—we'll look at how constructors are coded, who codes them, and how they work at runtime. So grab your hardhat and a hammer, and let's do some object building.

Constructor Basics

Every class, *including abstract classes*, MUST have a constructor. Burn that into your brain. But just because a class must have one, doesn't mean the programmer has to type it. A constructor looks like this:

```
class Foo {
    Foo() { } // The constructor for the Foo class
}
```

Notice what's missing? There's no return type! Two key points to remember about constructors are that they have no return type and their names must exactly match the class name. Typically, constructors are used to initialize instance variable state, as follows:

```
class Foo {
    int size;
    String name;
    Foo(String name, int size) {
        this.name = name;
        this.size = size;
    }
}
```

In the preceding code example, the Foo class does not have a no-arg constructor. That means the following will fail to compile:

```
Foo f = new Foo();  // Won't compile, no matching constructor
```

but the following will compile:

```
Foo f = new Foo("Fred", 43);   // No problem. Arguments match
                               // the Foo constructor.
```

So it's very common (and desirable) for a class to have a no-arg constructor, regardless of how many other overloaded constructors are in the class (yes, constructors can be overloaded). You can't always make that work for your classes; occasionally you have a class where it makes no sense to create an instance without supplying information to the constructor. A `java.awt.Color` object, for example, can't be created by calling a no-arg constructor, because that would be like saying to the JVM, "Make me a new Color object, and I really don't care what color it is...you pick." Do you seriously want the JVM making your style decisions?

Constructor Chaining

We know that constructors are invoked at runtime when you say new on some class type as follows:

```
Horse h = new Horse();
```

But what *really* happens when you say new `Horse()` ?
(Assume Horse extends Animal and Animal extends Object.)

1. Horse constructor is invoked. Every constructor invokes the constructor of its superclass with an (implicit) call to super(), unless the constructor invokes an overloaded constructor of the same class (more on that in a minute).

2. Animal constructor is invoked (Animal is the superclass of Horse).

3. Object constructor is invoked (Object is the ultimate superclass of all classes, so class Animal extends Object even though you don't actually type "extends Object" into the Animal class declaration. It's implicit.) At this point we're on the top of the stack.

4. Object instance variables are given their explicit values. By *explicit* values, we mean values that are assigned at the time the variables are declared, like "int x = 27", where "27" is the explicit value (as opposed to the default value) of the instance variable.

5. Object constructor completes.

6. Animal instance variables are given their explicit values (if any).

7. Animal constructor completes.

8. Horse instance variables are given their explicit values (if any).

9. Horse constructor completes.

Figure 2-6 shows how constructors work on the call stack.

| 4. `Object()` |
| 3. `Animal()` **calls** `super()` |
| 2. `Horse()` **calls** `super()` |
| 1. `main()` **calls** `new Horse()` |

Rules for Constructors

The following list summarizes the rules you'll need to know for the exam (and to
understand the rest of this section). You MUST remember these, so be sure to study
them more than once.

- Constructors can use any access modifier, including private. (A private
  constructor means only code within the class itself can instantiate an object
  of that type, so if the `private` constructor class wants to allow an instance
  of the class to be used, the class must provide a static method or variable that
  allows access to an instance created from within the class.)
- The constructor name must match the name of the class.
- Constructors must not have a return type.
- It's legal (but stupid) to have a method with the same name as the class,
  but that doesn't make it a constructor. If you see a return type, it's a method
  rather than a constructor. In fact, you could have both a method and a
  constructor with the same name—the name of the class—in the same class,
  and that's not a problem for Java. Be careful not to mistake a method for a
  constructor—be sure to look for a return type.
- If you don't type a constructor into your class code, a default constructor will
  be automatically generated by the compiler.
- The default constructor is ALWAYS a no-arg constructor.
- If you want a no-arg constructor and you've typed any other constructor(s)
  into your class code, the compiler won't provide the no-arg constructor (or

any other constructor) for you. In other words, if you've typed in a constructor with arguments, you won't have a no-arg constructor unless you type it in yourself!

■ Every constructor has, as its first statement, either a call to an overloaded constructor (this()) or a call to the superclass constructor (super()), although remember that this call can be inserted by the compiler.

■ If you do type in a constructor (as opposed to relying on the compiler-generated default constructor), and you do not type in the call to super() or a call to this(), the compiler will insert a no-arg call to super() for you, as the very first statement in the constructor.

■ A call to super() can be either a no-arg call or can include arguments passed to the super constructor.

■ A no-arg constructor is not necessarily the default (i.e., compiler-supplied) constructor, although the default constructor is always a no-arg constructor. The default constructor is the one the compiler provides! While the default constructor is always a no-arg constructor, you're free to put in your own no-arg constructor.

■ You cannot make a call to an instance method, or access an instance variable, until after the super constructor runs.

■ Only static variables and methods can be accessed as part of the call to super() or this(). (Example: super(Animal.NAME) is OK, because NAME is declared as a static variable.)

■ Abstract classes have constructors, and those constructors are always called when a concrete subclass is instantiated.

■ Interfaces do not have constructors. Interfaces are not part of an object's inheritance tree.

■ The only way a constructor can be invoked is from within another constructor. In other words, you can't write code that actually calls a constructor as follows:

```
 class Horse {
   Horse() { } // constructor
void doStuff() {
  Horse();  // calling the constructor - illegal!
 }
}
```

Determine Whether a Default Constructor Will Be Created

The following example shows a Horse class with two constructors:

```
class Horse {
   Horse() { }
   Horse(String name) { }
 }
```

Will the compiler put in a default constructor for the class above? No!
How about for the following variation of the class?

```
class Horse {
   Horse(String name) { }
}
```

Now will the compiler insert a default constructor? No!
What about this class?

```
class Horse { }
```

Now we're talking. The compiler will generate a default constructor for the
preceding class, because the class doesn't have any constructors defined.
OK, what about this class?

```
class Horse {
   void Horse() { }
}
```

It might look like the compiler won't create one, since there already is a constructor
in the Horse class. Or is there? Take another look at the preceding Horse class.
What's wrong with the Horse() constructor? It isn't a constructor at all! It's
simply a method that happens to have the same name as the class. Remember, the
return type is a dead giveaway that we're looking at a method, and not a constructor.

How do you know for sure whether a default constructor will be created?
Because you didn't write any constructors in your class.

How do you know what the default constructor will look like?

Because...

- The default constructor has the same access modifier as the class.
- The default constructor has no arguments.
- The default constructor includes a no-arg call to the super constructor (`super()`).

Table 2-4 shows what the compiler will (or won't) generate for your class.

What happens if the super constructor has arguments?

Constructors can have arguments just as methods can, and if you try to invoke a method that takes, say, an int, but you don't pass anything to the method, the compiler will complain as follows:

```
class Bar {
    void takeInt(int x) { }
}

class UseBar {
  public static void main (String [] args) {
    Bar b = new Bar();
    b.takeInt();  // Try to invoke a no-arg takeInt() method
  }
}
```

The compiler will complain that you can't invoke takeInt() without passing an int. Of course, the compiler enjoys the occasional riddle, so the message it spits out on some versions of the JVM (your mileage may vary) is less than obvious:

```
UseBar.java:7: takeInt(int) in Bar cannot be applied to ()
    b.takeInt();
      ^
```

But you get the idea. The bottom line is that there must be a match for the method. And by match, we mean that the argument types must be able to accept the values or variables you're passing, and in the order you're passing them. Which brings us back to constructors (and here you were thinking we'd never get there), which work exactly the same way.

| **TABLE 2-4** | Compiler-Generated Constructor Code |

Class Code (What You Type)	**Compiler Generated Constructor Code (in Bold)**

```class Foo { }```	```class Foo {```
	 ``` Foo() {```
	 ``` super();```
	 ``` }```
	 ```}```

```class Foo {```
 ``` Foo() { }```
 ```}```
	```class Foo {```
	 ``` Foo() {```
	 ``` super();```
	 ``` }```
	 ```}```

```public class Foo { }```	```class Foo {```
	 ``` public Foo() {```
	 ``` super();```
	 ``` }```
	 ```}```

```class Foo {```
 ``` Foo(String s) { }```
 ```}```
	```class Foo {```
	 ``` Foo(String s) {```
	 ``` super();```
	 ``` }```
	 ```}```

```class Foo {```
 ``` Foo(String s) {```
 ```   super();```
 ``` }```
 ```}```
	Nothing, compiler doesn't need to insert anything.

```class Foo {```
 ``` void Foo() { }```
 ```}```
	```class Foo {```
	 ``` void Foo() { }```
	 ``` Foo() {```
	 ``` super();```
	 ``` }```
	 ```}```
	 ```(void Foo()``` *is a method, not a constructor.)*

So if your super constructor (that is, the constructor of your immediate superclass/parent) has arguments, you must type in the call to super(), supplying the appropriate arguments. Crucial point: if your superclass does not have a no-arg constructor, you must type a constructor in your class (the subclass) because you need a place to put in the call to super with the appropriate arguments.

The following is an example of the problem:

```
class Animal {
   Animal(String name) { }
}

class Horse extends Animal {
   Horse() {
       super();   // Problem!
   }
}
```

And once again the compiler treats us with the stunningly lucid:

```
Horse.java:7: cannot resolve symbol
symbol  : constructor Animal  ()
location: class Animal
        super();  // Problem!
        ^
```

If you're lucky (and it's a full moon), *your* compiler might be a little more explicit. But again, the problem is that there just isn't a match for what we're trying to invoke with super()—an Animal constructor with no arguments.

Another way to put this is that if your superclass does *not* have a no-arg constructor, then in your subclass you will not be able to use the default constructor supplied by the compiler. It's that simple. Because the compiler can *only* put in a call to a no-arg super(), you won't even be able to compile something like this:

```
class Clothing {
   Clothing(String s) { }
}
class TShirt extends Clothing { }
```

Trying to compile this code gives us exactly the same error we got when we put a constructor in the subclass with a call to the no-arg version of super():

```
Clothing.java:4: cannot resolve symbol
symbol  : constructor Clothing  ()
location: class Clothing
```

```
class TShirt extends Clothing { }
      ^
```

In fact, the preceding Clothing and TShirt code is implicitly the same as the
following code, where we've supplied a constructor for TShirt that's identical to the
default constructor supplied by the compiler:

```
class Clothing {
    Clothing(String s) { }
}
class TShirt extends Clothing {
                  // Constructor identical to compiler-supplied
                  // default constructor
    TShirt() {
       super(); // Won't work!
    }             // Invokes a no-arg Clothing() constructor,
}                 // but there isn't one!
```

One last point on the whole default constructor thing (and it's probably
very obvious, but we have to say it or we'll feel guilty for years), *constructors
are never inherited.* They aren't methods. They can't be overridden (because
they aren't methods and only instance methods can be overridden). So the type
of constructor(s) your superclass has in no way determines the type of default
constructor you'll get. Some folks mistakenly believe that the default constructor
somehow matches the super constructor, either by the arguments the default
constructor will have (remember, the default constructor is always a no-arg), or by
the arguments used in the compiler-supplied call to super().

So, although constructors can't be overridden, you've already seen that they can
be overloaded, and typically are.

Overloaded Constructors

Overloading a constructor means typing in multiple versions of the constructor, each
having a different argument list, like the following examples:

```
class Foo {
    Foo() { }
    Foo(String s) { }
}
```

The preceding Foo class has two overloaded constructors, one that takes a string, and one with no arguments. Because there's no code in the no-arg version, it's actually identical to the default constructor the compiler supplies, but remember— since there's already a constructor in this class (the one that takes a string), the compiler won't supply a default constructor. If you want a no-arg constructor to overload the with-args version you already have, you're going to have to type it yourself, just as in the Foo example.

Overloading a constructor is typically used to provide alternate ways for clients to instantiate objects of your class. For example, if a client knows the animal name, they can pass that to an Animal constructor that takes a string. But if they don't know the name, the client can call the no-arg constructor and that constructor can supply a default name. Here's what it looks like:

```
1. public class Animal {
2.    String name;
3.    Animal(String name) {
4.       this.name = name;
5.    }
6.
7.    Animal() {
8.      this(makeRandomName());
9.    }
10.
11.   static String makeRandomName() {
12.      int x = (int) (Math.random() * 5);
13.      String name = new String[] {"Fluffy", "Fido",
                                     "Rover", "Spike",
                                     "Gigi"}[x];
14.      return name;
15.   }
16.
17.   public static void main (String [] args) {
18.     Animal a = new Animal();
19.     System.out.println(a.name);
20.     Animal b = new Animal("Zeus");
21.     System.out.println(b.name);
22.   }
23. }
```

Running the code four times produces this output:

```
% java Animal
Gigi
Zeus

% java Animal
Fluffy
Zeus

% java Animal
Rover
Zeus

% java Animal
Fluffy
Zeus
```

There's a lot going on in the preceding code. Figure 2-7 shows the call stack for constructor invocations when a constructor is overloaded. Take a look at the call stack, and then let's walk through the code straight from the top.

FIGURE 2-7

Overloaded constructors on the call stack

| 4. `Object()` |
| 3. `Animal(String s)` **calls** `super()` |
| 2. `Animal()` **calls** `this(randomlyChosenNameString)` |
| 1. `main()` **calls** `new Animal()` |

- **Line 2** Declare a String instance variable name.
- **Lines 3–5** Constructor that takes a String, and assigns it to instance variable name.
- **Line 7** Here's where it gets fun. Assume every animal needs a name, but the client (calling code) might not always know what the name should be, so you'll assign a random name. The no-arg constructor generates a name by invoking the makeRandomName() method.
- **Line 8** The no-arg constructor invokes its own overloaded constructor that takes a String, in effect calling it the same way it would be called if

client code were doing a `new` to instantiate an object, passing it a String for the name. The overloaded invocation uses the keyword `this`, but uses it as though it were a method name, `this()`. So line 8 is simply calling the constructor on line 3, passing it a randomly selected String rather than a client-code chosen name.

■ **Line 11** Notice that the `makeRandomName()` method is marked `static`! That's because you cannot invoke an instance (in other words, nonstatic) method (or access an instance variable) until after the super constructor has run. And since the super constructor will be invoked from the constructor on line 3, rather than from the one on line 7, line 8 can use only a static method to generate the name. If we wanted all animals not specifically named by the caller to have the same default name, say, "Fred," then line 8 could have read `this("Fred");` rather than calling a method that returns a string with the randomly chosen name.

■ **Line 12** This doesn't have anything to do with constructors, but since we're all here to learn...it generates a random integer between 0 and 4.

■ **Line 13** Weird syntax, we know. We're creating a new String object (just a single String instance), but we want the string to be selected randomly from a list. Except we don't have the list, so we need to make it. So in that one line of code we

1. Declare a String variable, name.

2. Create a String array (anonymously—we don't assign the array itself to anything).

3. Retrieve the string at index [x] (x being the random number generated on line 12) of the newly created String array.

4. Assign the string retrieved from the array to the declared instance variable name. We could have made it much easier to read if we'd just written

```
String[] nameList = {"Fluffy", "Fido", "Rover", "Spike",
                     "Gigi"};
String name = nameList[x];
```

But where's the fun in that? Throwing in unusual syntax (especially for code wholly unrelated to the real question) is in the spirit of the exam. Don't be startled! (OK, be startled, but then just say to yourself, "Whoa" and get on with it.)

- ■ **Line 18** We're invoking the no-arg version of the constructor (causing a random name from the list to be passed to the other constructor).
- ■ **Line 20** We're invoking the overloaded constructor that takes a string representing the name.

The key point to get from this code example is in line 8. Rather than calling super(), we're calling `this()`, and `this()` always means a call to another constructor in the same class. OK, fine, but what happens after the call to `this()`? Sooner or later the `super()` constructor gets called, right? Yes indeed. A call to `this()` just means you're delaying the inevitable. Some constructor, somewhere, must make the call to `super()`.

Key Rule: The first line in a constructor must be a call to super() or a call to this().

No exceptions. If you have neither of those calls in your constructor, the compiler will insert the no-arg call to `super()`. In other words, if constructor A() has a call to `this()`, the compiler knows that constructor A() will not be the one to invoke `super()`.

The preceding rule means a constructor can never have both a call to `super()` and a call to `this()`. Because each of those calls must be the first statement in a constructor, you can't legally use both in the same constructor. That also means the compiler will not put a call to `super()` in any constructor that has a call to `this()`.

Thought question: What do you think will happen if you try to compile the following code?

```
class A {
   A() {
     this("foo");
   }
   A(String s) {
      this();
   }
}
```

Your compiler may not actually catch the problem (it varies depending on your compiler, but most won't catch the problem). It assumes you know what you're doing. Can you spot the flaw? Given that a super constructor must always be called, where would the call to super() go? Remember, the compiler won't put in a default constructor if you've already got one or more constructors in your class. And when the compiler doesn't put in a default constructor, it still inserts a call to super() in any constructor that doesn't explicitly have a call to the super constructor—unless, that is, the constructor already has a call to this(). So in the preceding code, where can super() go? The only two constructors in the class both have calls to this(), and in fact you'll get exactly what you'd get if you typed the following method code:

```
public void go() {
    doStuff();
}

public void doStuff() {
    go();
}
```

Now can you see the problem? Of course you can. The stack explodes! It gets higher and higher and higher until it just bursts open and method code goes spilling out, oozing out of the JVM right onto the floor. Two overloaded constructors both calling this() are two constructors calling each other. Over and over and over, resulting in

```
% java A
Exception in thread "main" java.lang.StackOverflowError
```

The benefit of having overloaded constructors is that you offer flexible ways to instantiate objects from your class. The benefit of having one constructor invoke another overloaded constructor is to avoid code duplication. In the Animal example, there wasn't any code other than setting the name, but imagine if after line 4 there was still more work to be done in the constructor. By putting all the other constructor work in just one constructor, and then having the other constructors invoke it, you don't have to write and maintain multiple versions of that other important constructor code. Basically, each of the other not-the-real-one overloaded constructors will call another overloaded constructor, passing it whatever data it needs (data the client code didn't supply).

Constructors and instantiation become even more exciting (just when you thought it was safe), when you get to inner classes, but we know you can stand to have only so much fun in one chapter, so we're holding the rest of the discussion on instantiating inner classes until Chapter 8.

CERTIFICATION OBJECTIVE

Statics (Exam Objective 1.3)

1.3 Develop code that declares, initializes, and uses primitives, arrays, enums, and objects as static, instance, and local variables. Also, use legal identifiers for variable names.

Static Variables and Methods

The `static` modifier has such a profound impact on the behavior of a method or variable that we're treating it as a concept entirely separate from the other modifiers. To understand the way a `static` member works, we'll look first at a reason for using one. Imagine you've got a utility class with a method that always runs the same way; its sole function is to return, say, a random number. It wouldn't matter which instance of the class performed the method—it would always behave exactly the same way. In other words, the method's behavior has no dependency on the state (instance variable values) of an object. So why, then, do you need an object when the method will never be instance-specific? Why not just ask the class itself to run the method?

Let's imagine another scenario: Suppose you want to keep a running count of all instances instantiated from a particular class. Where do you actually keep that variable? It won't work to keep it as an instance variable within the class whose instances you're tracking, because the count will just be initialized back to a default value with each new instance. The answer to both the utility-method-always-runs-the-same scenario and the keep-a-running-total-of-instances scenario is to use the `static` modifier. Variables and methods marked `static` belong to the class, rather than to any particular instance. In fact, you can use a `static` method or variable without having any instances of that class at all. You need only have the class available to be able to invoke a `static` method or access a `static` variable. `static` variables, too, can be accessed without having an instance of a class. But if there are instances, a `static` variable of a class will be shared by all instances of that class; there is only one copy.

The following code declares and uses a `static` counter variable:

```
class Frog {
   static int frogCount = 0;   // Declare and initialize
                               // static variable
   public Frog() {
      frogCount += 1;  // Modify the value in the constructor
   }
   public static void main (String [] args) {
      new Frog();
      new Frog();
      new Frog();
      System.out.println("Frog count is now " + frogCount);
   }
}
```

In the preceding code, the static frogCount variable is set to zero when the Frog class is first loaded by the JVM, before any Frog instances are created! (By the way, you don't actually need to initialize a static variable to zero; static variables get the same default values instance variables get.) Whenever a Frog instance is created, the Frog constructor runs and increments the static `frogCount` variable. When this code executes, three Frog instances are created in `main()`, and the result is

```
Frog count is now 3
```

Now imagine what would happen if frogCount were an instance variable (in other words, nonstatic):

```
class Frog {
   int frogCount = 0;   // Declare and initialize
                        // instance variable
   public Frog() {
      frogCount += 1;   // Modify the value in the constructor
   }
   public static void main (String [] args) {
      new Frog();
      new Frog();
      new Frog();
      System.out.println("Frog count is now " + frogCount);
   }
}
```

When this code executes, it should still create three Frog instances in `main()`, but the result is...a compiler error! We can't get this code to compile, let alone run.

```
Frog.java:11: non-static variable frogCount cannot be referenced
from a static context
    System.out.println("Frog count is " + frogCount);
                                           ^

1 error
```

The JVM doesn't know which Frog object's frogCount you're trying to access. The problem is that `main()` is itself a `static` method, and thus isn't running against any particular instance of the class, rather just on the class itself. A `static` method can't access a nonstatic (instance) variable, because there is no instance! That's not to say there aren't instances of the class alive on the heap, but rather that even if there are, the `static` method doesn't know anything about them. The same applies to instance methods; a `static` method can't directly invoke a nonstatic method. Think static = class, nonstatic = instance. Making the method called by the JVM (`main()`) a `static` method means the JVM doesn't have to create an instance of your class just to start running code.

exam

🐶 **a t c h** *One of the mistakes most often made by new Java programmers is attempting to access an instance variable (which means nonstatic variable) from the static* `main()` *method (which doesn't know anything about any instances, so it can't access the variable). The following code is an example of illegal access of a nonstatic variable from a static method:*

```
class Foo {
    int x = 3;
    public static void main (String [] args) {
        System.out.println("x is " + x);
    }  }
```

Understand that this code will never compile, because you can't access a nonstatic (instance) variable from a static method. Just think of the compiler saying, "Hey, I have no idea which Foo object's x variable you're trying to print!" Remember, it's the class running the `main()` *method, not an instance of the class.*

e x a m

ⓦatch

(continued) Of course, the tricky part for the exam is that the question won't look as obvious as the preceding code. The problem you're being tested for— accessing a nonstatic variable from a static method—will be buried in code that might appear to be testing something else. For example, the preceding code would be more likely to appear as

```
class Foo {
    int x = 3;
    float y = 4.3f;
    public static void main (String [] args) {
        for (int z = x; z < ++x; z--, y = y + z) {
            // complicated looping and branching code
        }
    }
}
```

So while you're trying to follow the logic, the real issue is that x and y can't be used within `main()`, *because x and y are instance, not static, variables! The same applies for accessing nonstatic methods from a static method. The rule is, a static method of a class can't access a nonstatic (instance) method or variable of its own class.*

Accessing Static Methods and Variables

Since you don't need to have an instance in order to invoke a static method or access a static variable, then how do you invoke or use a static member? What's the syntax? We know that with a regular old instance method, you use the dot operator on a reference to an instance:

```
class Frog {
    int frogSize = 0;
    public int getFrogSize() {
        return frogSize;
    }
    public Frog(int s) {
        frogSize = s;
    }
    public static void main (String [] args) {
```

```
        Frog f = new Frog(25);
        System.out.println(f.getFrogSize()); // Access instance
                                             // method using f
    }
}
```

In the preceding code, we instantiate a Frog, assign it to the reference variable f, and then use that f reference to invoke a method on the Frog instance we just created. In other words, the getFrogSize() method is being invoked on a specific Frog object on the heap.

But this approach (using a reference to an object) isn't appropriate for accessing a static method, because there might not be any instances of the class at all! So, the way we access a static method (or static variable) is to use the dot operator on the class name, as opposed to using it on a reference to an instance, as follows:

```
class Frog {
    static int frogCount = 0;  // Declare and initialize
                               // static variable
    public Frog() {
        frogCount += 1;  // Modify the value in the constructor
    }
}

class TestFrog {
    public static void main (String [] args) {
        new Frog();
        new Frog();
        new Frog();
        System.out.print("frogCount:"+Frog.frogCount); //Access
                                                   // static variable
    }
}
```

But just to make it really confusing, the Java language also allows you to use an object reference variable to access a static member:

```
Frog f = new Frog();
int frogs = f.frogCount; // Access static variable
                         // FrogCount using f
```

In the preceding code, we instantiate a Frog, assign the new Frog object to the reference variable f, and then use the f reference to invoke a `static` method! But even though we are using a specific Frog instance to access the `static` method, the rules haven't changed. This is merely a syntax trick to let you use an object reference variable (but not the object it refers to) to get to a `static` method or variable, but the `static` member is still unaware of the particular instance used to invoke the `static` member. In the Frog example, the compiler knows that the reference variable f is of type Frog, and so the Frog class `static` method is run with no awareness or concern for the Frog instance at the other end of the f reference. In other words, the compiler cares only that reference variable f is declared as type Frog. Figure 2-8 illustrates the effects of the static modifier on methods and variables.

FIGURE 2-8

The effects of static on methods and variables

```
                class Foo

    int size = 42;
    static void doMore( ){
        int x = size;
    }
```

static method cannot access an instance (non-static) variable

```
                class Bar

    void go ( );
    static void doMore( ){
        go( );
    }
```

static method cannot access a non-static method

```
                class Baz

    static int count;
    static void woo( ){ }
    static void doMore( ){
        woo( );
        int x = count;
    }
```

static method *can* access a static method or variable

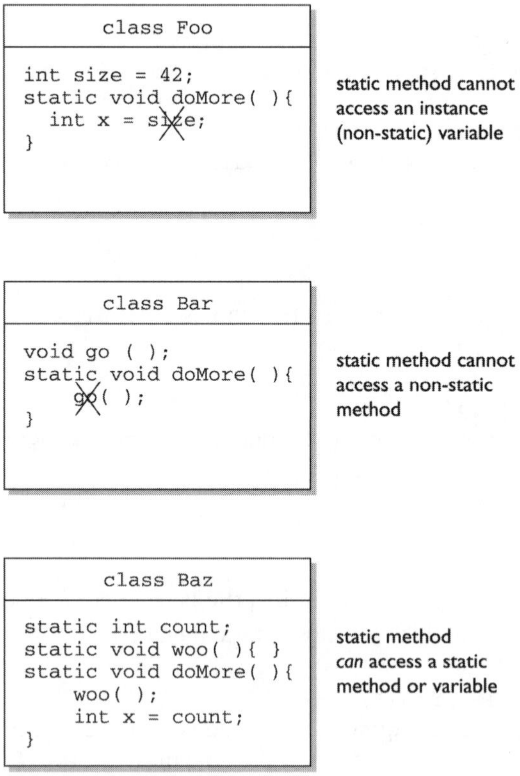

Finally, remember that *static methods can't be overridden*! This doesn't mean they can't be redefined in a subclass, but redefining and overriding aren't the same thing. Let's take a look at an example of a redefined (remember, not overridden), static method:

```
class Animal {
  static void doStuff() {
    System.out.print("a ");
  }
}
class Dog extends Animal {
  static void dostuff() {          // it's a redefinition,
                                   // not an override
    System.out.print("d ");
  }
  public static void main(String [] args) {
    Animal [] a = {new Animal(), new Dog(), new Animal()};
    for(int x = 0; x < a.length; x++)
      a[x].doStuff();             // invoke the static method
  }
}
```

Running this code produces the output:

```
a a a
```

Remember, the syntax `a[x].doStuff()` is just a shortcut (the syntax trick)...the compiler is going to substitute something like `Animal.doStuff()` instead. Notice that we didn't use the Java 1.5 *enhanced* `for` *loop* here (covered in Chapter 5), even though we could have. Expect to see a mix of both Java 1.4 and Java 5 coding styles and practices on the exam.

CERTIFICATION OBJECTIVE

Coupling and Cohesion (Exam Objective 5.1)

5.1   Develop code that implements tight encapsulation, loose coupling, and high cohesion in classes, and describe the benefits.

We're going to admit it up front. The Sun exam's definitions for cohesion and coupling are somewhat subjective, so what we discuss in this chapter is from the perspective of the exam, and by no means The One True Word on these two OO design principles. It may not be exactly the way that you've learned it, but it's what you need to understand to answer the questions. You'll have very few questions about coupling and cohesion on the real exam.

These two topics, coupling and cohesion, have to do with the quality of an OO design. In general, good OO design calls for *loose coupling* and shuns tight coupling, and good OO design calls for *high cohesion*, and shuns low cohesion. As with most OO design discussions, the goals for an application are

- Ease of creation
- Ease of maintenance
- Ease of enhancement

Coupling

Let's start by making an attempt at a definition of coupling. Coupling is the degree to which one class knows about another class. If the only knowledge that class A has about class B, is what class B has exposed through its interface, then class A and class B are said to be loosely coupled...that's a good thing. If, on the other hand, class A relies on parts of class B that are not part of class B's interface, then the coupling between the classes is tighter...*not* a good thing. In other words, if A knows more than it should about the way in which B was implemented, then A and B are tightly coupled.

Using this second scenario, imagine what happens when class B is enhanced. It's quite possible that the developer enhancing class B has no knowledge of class A, why would she? Class B's developer ought to feel that any enhancements that don't break the class's interface should be safe, so she might change some non-interface part of the class, which then causes class A to break.

At the far end of the coupling spectrum is the horrible situation in which class A knows non-API stuff about class B, and class B knows non-API stuff about class A... this is REALLY BAD. If either class is ever changed, there's a chance that the other class will break. Let's look at an obvious example of tight coupling, which has been enabled by poor encapsulation:

```
class DoTaxes {
  float rate;
```

```
  float doColorado() {
    SalesTaxRates str = new SalesTaxRates();
    rate = str.salesRate;        // ouch
                                 // this should be a method call:
                                 // rate = str.getSalesRate("CO");
    // do stuff with rate
  }
}

class SalesTaxRates {
  public float salesRate;              // should be private
  public float adjustedSalesRate;      // should be private

  public float getSalesRate(String region) {
    salesRate = new DoTaxes().doColorado();    // ouch again!
    // do region-based calculations
    return adjustedSalesRate;
  }
}
```

All non-trivial OO applications are a mix of many classes and interfaces working together. Ideally, all interactions between objects in an OO system should use the APIs, in other words, the contracts, of the objects' respective classes. Theoretically, if all of the classes in an application have well-designed APIs, then it should be possible for all interclass interactions to use those APIs exclusively. As we discussed earlier in this chapter, an aspect of good class and API design is that classes should be well encapsulated.

The bottom line is that coupling is a somewhat subjective concept. Because of this, the exam will test you on really obvious examples of tight coupling; you won't be asked to make subtle judgment calls.

Cohesion

While coupling has to do with how classes interact with each other, cohesion is all about how a single class is designed. The term *cohesion* is used to indicate the degree to which a class has a single, well-focused purpose. Keep in mind that cohesion is a subjective concept. The more focused a class is, the higher its cohesiveness—a good thing. The key benefit of high cohesion is that such classes are typically much easier to maintain (and less frequently changed) than classes with low cohesion. Another benefit of high cohesion is that classes with a well-focused purpose tend to be more reusable than other classes. Let's take a look at a pseudo-code example:

```
class BudgetReport {
  void connectToRDBMS(){ }
  void generateBudgetReport() { }
  void saveToFile() { }
  void print() { }
}
```

Now imagine your manager comes along and says, "Hey you know that accounting application we're working on? The clients just decided that they're also going to want to generate a revenue projection report, oh and they want to do some inventory reporting also. They do like our reporting features however, so make sure that all of these reports will let them choose a database, choose a printer, and save generated reports to data files..." Ouch!

Rather than putting all the printing code into one report class, we probably would have been better off with the following design right from the start:

```
class BudgetReport {
  Options getReportingOptions() { }
  void generateBudgetReport(Options o) { }
}

class ConnectToRDBMS {
  DBconnection getRDBMS() { }
}

class PrintStuff {
  PrintOptions getPrintOptions() { }
}

class FileSaver {
  SaveOptions getFileSaveOptions() { }
}
```

This design is much more cohesive. Instead of one class that does everything, we've broken the system into four main classes, each with a very specific, or *cohesive*, role. Because we've built these specialized, reusable classes, it'll be much easier to write a new report, since we've already got the database connection class, the printing class, and the file saver class, and that means they can be reused by other classes that might want to print a report.

CERTIFICATION SUMMARY

We started the chapter by discussing the importance of encapsulation in good OO design, and then we talked about how good encapsulation is implemented: with private instance variables and public getters and setters.

Next, we covered the importance of inheritance; so that you can grasp overriding, overloading, polymorphism, reference casting, return types, and constructors.

We covered IS-A and HAS-A. IS-A is implemented using inheritance, and HAS-A is implemented by using instance variables that refer to other objects.

Polymorphism was next. Although a reference variable's type can't be changed, it can be used to refer to an object whose type is a subtype of its own. We learned how to determine what methods are invocable for a given reference variable.

We looked at the difference between overridden and overloaded methods, learning that an overridden method occurs when a subclass inherits a method from a superclass, and then re-implements the method to add more specialized behavior. We learned that, at runtime, the JVM will invoke the subclass version on an instance of a subclass, and the superclass version on an instance of the superclass. Abstract methods must be "overridden" (technically, abstract methods must be implemented, as opposed to overridden, since there really isn't anything to override.

We saw that overriding methods must declare the same argument list and return type (or, as of Java 5, they can return a subtype of the declared return type of the superclass overidden method), and that the access modifier can't be more restrictive. The overriding method also can't throw any new or broader checked exceptions that weren't declared in the overridden method. You also learned that the overridden method can be invoked using the syntax `super.doSomething();`.

Overloaded methods let you reuse the same method name in a class, but with different arguments (and, optionally, a different return type). Whereas overriding methods must not change the argument list, overloaded methods must. But unlike overriding methods, overloaded methods are free to vary the return type, access modifier, and declared exceptions any way they like.

We learned the mechanics of casting (mostly downcasting), reference variables, when it's necessary, and how to use the `instanceof` operator.

Implementing interfaces came next. An interface describes a *contract* that the implementing class must follow. The rules for implementing an interface are similar to those for extending an abstract class. Also remember that a class can implement more than one interface, and that interfaces can extend another interface.

We also looked at method return types, and saw that you can declare any return type you like (assuming you have access to a class for an object reference return type), unless you're overriding a method. Barring a covariant return, an overriding method must have the same return type as the overridden method of the superclass. We saw that while overriding methods must not change the return type, overloaded methods can (as long as they also change the argument list).

Finally, you learned that it is legal to return any value or variable that can be implicitly converted to the declared return type. So, for example, a `short` can be returned when the return type is declared as an `int`. And (assuming Horse extends Animal), a Horse reference can be returned when the return type is declared an Animal.

We covered constructors in detail, learning that if you don't provide a constructor for your class, the compiler will insert one. The compiler-generated constructor is called the default constructor, and it is always a no-arg constructor with a no-arg call to super(). The default constructor will never be generated if there is even a single constructor in your class (regardless of the arguments of that constructor), so if you need more than one constructor in your class and you want a no-arg constructor, you'll have to write it yourself. We also saw that constructors are not inherited, and that you can be confused by a method that has the same name as the class (which is legal). The return type is the giveaway that a method is not a constructor, since constructors do not have return types.

We saw how all of the constructors in an object's inheritance tree will always be invoked when the object is instantiated using `new`. We also saw that constructors can be overloaded, which means defining constructors with different argument lists. A constructor can invoke another constructor of the same class using the keyword `this()`, as though the constructor were a method named `this()`. We saw that every constructor must have either `this()` or `super()` as the first statement (although the compiler can insert it for you).

We looked at `static` methods and variables. Static members are tied to the class, not an instance, so there is only one copy of any `static` member. A common mistake is to attempt to reference an instance variable from a `static` method. Use the class name with the dot operator to access `static` members.

We discussed the OO concepts of coupling and cohesion. Loose coupling is the desirable state of two or more classes that interact with each other only through their respective API's. Tight coupling is the undesirable state of two or more classes that know inside details about another class, details not revealed in the class's API. High cohesion is the desirable state of a single class whose purpose and responsibilities are limited and well-focused.

And once again, you learned that the exam includes tricky questions designed largely to test your ability to recognize just how tricky the questions can be.

✓ TWO-MINUTE DRILL

Here are some of the key points from each certification objective in this chapter.

Encapsulation, IS-A, HAS-A (Objective 5.1)

❑ Encapsulation helps hide implementation behind an interface (or API).

❑ Encapsulated code has two features:

    ❑ Instance variables are kept protected (usually with the private modifier).

    ❑ Getter and setter methods provide access to instance variables.

❑ IS-A refers to inheritance.

❑ IS-A is expressed with the keyword extends.

❑ IS-A, "inherits from," and "is a subtype of" are all equivalent expressions.

❑ HAS-A means an instance of one class "has a" reference to an instance of another class or another instance of the same class.

Inheritance (Objective 5.5)

❑ Inheritance allows a class to be a subclass of a superclass, and thereby inherit public and protected variables and methods of the superclass.

❑ Inheritance is a key concept that underlies IS-A, polymorphism, overriding, overloading, and casting.

❑ All classes (except class Object), are subclasses of type Object, and therefore they inherit Object's methods.

Polymorphism (Objective 5.2)

❑ Polymorphism means "many forms."

❑ A reference variable is always of a single, unchangeable type, but it can refer to a subtype object.

❑ A single object can be referred to by reference variables of many different types—as long as they are the same type or a supertype of the object.

❑ The reference variable's type (not the object's type), determines which methods can be called!

❑ Polymorphic method invocations apply only to overridden *instance* methods.

Overriding and Overloading (Objectives 1.5 and 5.4)

❑ Methods can be overridden or overloaded; constructors can be overloaded but not overridden.

❑ Abstract methods must be overridden by the first concrete (non-abstract) subclass.

❑ With respect to the method it overrides, the overriding method

   ❑ Must have the same argument list.

   ❑ Must have the same return type, except that as of Java 5, the return type can be a subclass—this is known as a covariant return.

   ❑ Must not have a more restrictive access modifier.

   ❑ May have a less restrictive access modifier.

   ❑ Must not throw new or broader checked exceptions.

   ❑ May throw fewer or narrower checked exceptions, or any unchecked exception.

❑ `final` methods cannot be overridden.

❑ Only inherited methods may be overridden, and remember that private methods are not inherited.

❑ A subclass uses `super.overriddenMethodName()` to call the superclass version of an overridden method.

❑ Overloading means reusing a method name, but with different arguments.

❑ Overloaded methods

   ❑ Must have different argument lists

   ❑ May have different return types, if argument lists are also different

   ❑ May have different access modifiers

   ❑ May throw different exceptions

❑ Methods from a superclass can be overloaded in a subclass.

❑ Polymorphism applies to overriding, not to overloading.

❑ Object type (not the reference variable's type), determines which overridden method is used at runtime.

❑ Reference type determines which overloaded method will be used at compile time.

Reference Variable Casting (Objective 5.2)

❑ There are two types of reference variable casting: downcasting and upcasting.

❑ Downcasting: If you have a reference variable that refers to a subtype object, you can assign it to a reference variable of the subtype. You must make an explicit cast to do this, and the result is that you can access the subtype's members with this new reference variable.

❑ Upcasting: You can assign a reference variable to a supertype reference variable explicitly or implicitly. This is an inherently safe operation because the assignment restricts the access capabilities of the new variable.

Implementing an Interface (Objective 1.2)

❑ When you implement an interface, you are fulfilling its contract.

❑ You implement an interface by properly and concretely overriding all of the methods defined by the interface.

❑ A single class can implement many interfaces.

Return Types (Objective 1.5)

❑ Overloaded methods can change return types; overridden methods cannot, except in the case of covariant returns.

❑ Object reference return types can accept `null` as a return value.

❑ An array is a legal return type, both to declare and return as a value.

❑ For methods with primitive return types, any value that can be implicitly converted to the return type can be returned.

❑ Nothing can be returned from a `void`, but you can return nothing. You're allowed to simply say `return`, in any method with a `void` return type, to bust out of a method early. But you can't return nothing from a method with a non-void return type.

❑ Methods with an object reference return type, can return a subtype.

❑ Methods with an interface return type, can return any implementer.

Constructors and Instantiation (Objectives 1.6 and 5.4)

❑ A constructor is always invoked when a new object is created.

- ❑ Each superclass in an object's inheritance tree will have a constructor called.
- ❑ Every class, even an abstract class, has at least one constructor.
- ❑ Constructors must have the same name as the class.
- ❑ Constructors don't have a return type. If you see code with a return type, it's a method with the same name as the class, it's not a constructor.
- ❑ Typical constructor execution occurs as follows:
  - ❑ The constructor calls its superclass constructor, which calls its superclass constructor, and so on all the way up to the Object constructor.
  - ❑ The Object constructor executes and then returns to the calling constructor, which runs to completion and then returns to its calling constructor, and so on back down to the completion of the constructor of the actual instance being created.
- ❑ Constructors can use any access modifier (even `private`!).
- ❑ The compiler will create a default constructor if you don't create any constructors in your class.
- ❑ The default constructor is a no-arg constructor with a no-arg call to `super()`.
- ❑ The first statement of every constructor must be a call to either `this()` (an overloaded constructor) or `super()`.
- ❑ The compiler will add a call to `super()` unless you have already put in a call to `this()` or `super()`.
- ❑ Instance members are accessible only after the super constructor runs.
- ❑ Abstract classes have constructors that are called when a concrete subclass is instantiated.
- ❑ Interfaces do not have constructors.
- ❑ If your superclass does not have a no-arg constructor, you must create a constructor and insert a call to `super()` with arguments matching those of the superclass constructor.
- ❑ Constructors are never inherited, thus they cannot be overridden.
- ❑ A constructor can be directly invoked only by another constructor (using a call to `super()` or `this()`).
- ❑ Issues with calls to `this()`
  - ❑ May appear only as the first statement in a constructor.
  - ❑ The argument list determines which overloaded constructor is called.

❑ Constructors can call constructors can call constructors, and so on, but sooner or later one of them better call `super()` or the stack will explode.

❑ Calls to `this()` and `super()` cannot be in the same constructor. You can have one or the other, but never both.

Statics (Objective 1.3)

❑ Use `static` methods to implement behaviors that are not affected by the state of any instances.

❑ Use `static` variables to hold data that is class specific as opposed to instance specific—there will be only one copy of a `static` variable.

❑ All `static` members belong to the class, not to any instance.

❑ A `static` method can't access an instance variable directly.

❑ Use the dot operator to access `static` members, but remember that using a reference variable with the dot operator is really a syntax trick, and the compiler will substitute the class name for the reference variable, for instance:

```
d.doStuff();
```

becomes:

```
Dog.doStuff();
```

❑ `static` methods can't be overridden, but they can be redefined.

Coupling and Cohesion (Objective 5.1)

❑ Coupling refers to the degree to which one class knows about or uses members of another class.

❑ Loose coupling is the desirable state of having classes that are well encapsulated, minimize references to each other, and limit the breadth of API usage.

❑ Tight coupling is the undesirable state of having classes that break the rules of loose coupling.

❑ Cohesion refers to the degree in which a class has a single, well-defined role or responsibility.

❑ High cohesion is the desirable state of a class whose members support a single, well-focused role or responsibility.

❑ Low cohesion is the undesirable state of a class whose members support multiple, unfocused roles or responsibilities.

SELF TEST

1. Which statement(s) are true? (Choose all that apply.)

A. Has-a relationships always rely on inheritance.

B. Has-a relationships always rely on instance variables.

C. Has-a relationships always require at least two class types.

D. Has-a relationships always rely on polymorphism.

E. Has-a relationships are always tightly coupled.

2. Given:

```
class Clidders {
  public final void flipper() { System.out.println("Clidder"); }
}
public class Clidlets extends Clidders {
  public void flipper() {
    System.out.println("Flip a Clidlet");
    super.flipper();
  }
  public static void main(String [] args) {
    new Clidlets().flipper();
  }
}
```

What is the result?

A. `Flip a Clidlet`

B. `Flip a Clidder`

C. `Flip a Clidder`
   `Flip a Clidlet`

D. `Flip a Clidlet`
   `Flip a Clidder`

E. Compilation fails.

3. Given:

```
public abstract interface Frobnicate { public void twiddle(String s); }
```

Which is a correct class? (Choose all that apply.)

A. ```
   public abstract class Frob implements Frobnicate {
       public abstract void twiddle(String s) { }
   }
   ```
   ```

B. `public abstract class Frob implements Frobnicate { }`

C.
```
public class Frob extends Frobnicate {
        public void twiddle(Integer i) { }
    }
```

D.
```
public class Frob implements Frobnicate {
        public void twiddle(Integer i) { }
    }
```

E.
```
public class Frob implements Frobnicate {
        public void twiddle(String i) { }
        public void twiddle(Integer s) { }
    }
```

4. Given:
```
class Top {
  public Top(String s) { System.out.print("B"); }
}
public class Bottom2 extends Top {
  public Bottom2(String s) { System.out.print("D"); }
  public static void main(String [] args) {
    new Bottom2("C");
    System.out.println(" ");
  }
}
```

What is the result?

A. BD

B. DB

C. BDC

D. DBC

E. Compilation fails.

5. Select the two statements that best indicate a situation with low coupling. (Choose two.)

A. The attributes of the class are all `private`.

B. The class refers to a small number of other objects.

C. The object contains only a small number of variables.

D. The object is referred to using an anonymous variable, not directly.

E. The reference variable is declared for an interface type, not a class. The interface provides a small number of methods.

F. It is unlikely that changes made to one class will require any changes in another.

6.   Given:

```
class Clidder {
  private final void flipper() { System.out.println("Clidder"); }
}

public class Clidlet extends Clidder {
  public final void flipper() { System.out.println("Clidlet");  }
  public static void main(String [] args) {
    new Clidlet().flipper();
  }
}
```

What is the result?

A. `Clidlet`

B. `Clidder`

C. `Clidder`
    `Clidlet`

D. `Clidlet`
    `Clidder`

E. Compilation fails.

7.   Using the **fragments** below, complete the following **code** so it compiles.
Note, you may not have to fill all of the slots.

Code:

```
class AgedP {

    _____  _____  _____  _____  _____

    public AgedP(int x) {

        _____  _____  _____  _____  _____

    }
}
public class Kinder extends AgedP {

    _____  _____  _____  _____  _____  _____

    public Kinder(int x) {

        _____  _____  _____  _____  _____ ();

    }
}
```

Fragments: Use the following fragments zero or more times:

AgedP	super	this	
(	)	{	}
;			

8. Given:

```
1. class Plant {
2.    String getName() { return "plant"; }
3.    Plant getType() { return this; }
4. }
5. class Flower extends Plant {
6.  // insert code here
7. }
8. class Tulip extends Flower { }
```

Which statement(s), inserted at line 6, will compile? (Choose all that apply.)

A. `Flower getType() { return this; }`

B. `String getType() { return "this"; }`

C. `Plant getType() { return this; }`

D. `Tulip getType() { return new Tulip(); }`

9. Given:

```
1. class Zing {
2.    protected Hmpf h;
3. }
4. class Woop extends Zing { }
5. class Hmpf { }
```

Which is true? (Choose all that apply.)

A. `Woop` is-a `Hmpf` and has-a `Zing`.

B. `Zing` is-a `Woop` and has-a `Hmpf`.

C. `Hmpf` has-a `Woop` and `Woop` is-a `Zing`.

D. `Woop` has-a `Hmpf` and `Woop` is-a `Zing`.

E. `Zing` has-a `Hmpf` and `Zing` is-a `Woop`.

10. Given:

```
1. class Programmer {
2.    Programmer debug() { return this; }
3. }
4. class SCJP extends Programmer {
5.    // insert code here
6. }
```

Which, inserted at line 5, will compile? (Choose all that apply.)

A. `Programmer debug() { return this; }`

B. `SCJP debug() { return this; }`

C. `Object debug() { return this; }`

D. `int debug() { return 1; }`

E. `int debug(int x) { return 1; }`

F. `Object debug(int x) { return this; }`

11. Given:

```
class Uber {
  static int y = 2;
  Uber(int x) { this(); y = y * 2; }
  Uber() { y++; }
}
class Minor extends Uber {
  Minor() { super(y);   y = y + 3; }
  public static void main(String [] args) {
    new Minor();
    System.out.println(y);
} }
```

What is the result?

A. 6

B. 7

C. 8

D. 9

E. Compilation fails.

F. An exception is thrown.

12. Which statement(s) are true? (Choose all that apply.)

A. Cohesion is the OO principle most closely associated with hiding implementation details.

B. Cohesion is the OO principle most closely associated with making sure that classes know about other classes only through their APIs.

C. Cohesion is the OO principle most closely associated with making sure that a class is designed with a single, well-focused purpose.

D. Cohesion is the OO principle most closely associated with allowing a single object to be seen as having many types.

13. Given:

```
1. class Dog { }
2. class Beagle extends Dog { }
3.
4. class Kennel {
5.   public static void main(String [] arfs) {
6.     Beagle b1 = new Beagle();
7.     Dog dog1 = new Dog();
8.     Dog dog2 = b1;
9.     // insert code here
10. } }
```

Which, inserted at line 9, will compile? (Choose all that apply.)

A. `Beagle b2 = (Beagle) dog1;`

B. `Beagle b3 = (Beagle) dog2;`

C. `Beagle b4 = dog2;`

D. None of the above statements will compile.

14. Given the following,

```
1. class X { void do1() { } }
2. class Y extends X { void do2() { } }
3.
4. class Chrome {
5.   public static void main(String [] args) {
6.     X x1 = new X();
7.     X x2 = new Y();
8.     Y y1 = new Y();
9.     // insert code here
10. } }
```

Which, inserted at line 9, will compile? (Choose all that apply.)

A. `x2.do2();`

B. `(Y)x2.do2();`

C. `((Y)x2).do2();`

D. None of the above statements will compile.

SELF TEST ANSWERS

1. Which statement(s) are true? (Choose all that apply.)

   A. Has-a relationships always rely on inheritance.

   B. Has-a relationships always rely on instance variables.

   C. Has-a relationships always require at least two class types.

   D. Has-a relationships always rely on polymorphism.

   E. Has-a relationships are always tightly coupled.

   Answer:

   ☑ **B** is correct.

   ☒ **A** and **D** describe other OO topics. **C** is incorrect because a class can have an instance of itself. **E** is incorrect because while has-a relationships can lead to tight coupling, it is by no means *always* the case.
   (Objective 5.5)

2. Given:

   ```
   class Clidders {
     public final void flipper() { System.out.println("Clidder"); }
   }

   public class Clidlets extends Clidders {
     public void flipper() {
       System.out.println("Flip a Clidlet");
       super.flipper();
     }
     public static void main(String [] args) {
       new Clidlets().flipper();
     }
   }
   ```

   What is the result?

   A. `Flip a Clidlet`

   B. `Flip a Clidder`

   C. `Flip a Clidder`
      `Flip a Clidlet`

   D. `Flip a Clidlet`
      `Flip a Clidder`

   E. Compilation fails.

Answer:

☑ **E** is correct. `final` methods cannot be overridden.

☒ **A, B, C,** and **D** are incorrect based on the above.
(Objective 5.3)

3. Given:

```
public abstract interface Frobnicate { public void twiddle(String s); }
```

Which is a correct class? (Choose all that apply.)

A. ```
public abstract class Frob implements Frobnicate {
        public abstract void twiddle(String s) { }
    }
```
B. ```
public abstract class Frob implements Frobnicate { }
```
C. ```
public class Frob extends Frobnicate {
        public void twiddle(Integer i) { }
    }
```
D. ```
public class Frob implements Frobnicate {
        public void twiddle(Integer i) { }
    }
```
E. ```
public class Frob implements Frobnicate {
        public void twiddle(String i) { }
        public void twiddle(Integer s) { }
    }
```

Answer:

☑ **B** is correct, an `abstract` class need not implement any or all of an interface's methods. **E** is correct, the class implements the interface method and additionally overloads the `twiddle()` method.

☒ **A** is incorrect because `abstract` methods have no body. **C** is incorrect because classes implement interfaces they don't extend them. **D** is incorrect because overloading a method is not implementing it.
(Objective 5.4)

4. Given:

```
class Top {
  public Top(String s) { System.out.print("B"); }
}
public class Bottom2 extends Top {
  public Bottom2(String s) { System.out.print("D"); }
  public static void main(String [] args) {
```
```

```
    new Bottom2("C");
    System.out.println(" ");
} }
```

What is the result?

A. BD

B. DB

C. BDC

D. DBC

E. Compilation fails.

Answer:

☑ **E** is correct. The implied `super()` call in Bottom2's constructor cannot be satisfied because there isn't a no-arg constructor in Top. A default, no-arg constructor is generated by the compiler only if the class has no constructor defined explicitly.

☒ **A, B, C,** and **D** are incorrect based on the above.
(Objective 1.6)

5.   Select the two statements that best indicate a situation with low coupling. (Choose two.)

A.   The attributes of the class are all `private`.

B.   The class refers to a small number of other objects.

C.   The object contains only a small number of variables.

D.   The object is referred to using an anonymous variable, not directly.

E.   The reference variable is declared for an interface type, not a class. The interface provides a small number of methods.

F.   It is unlikely that changes made to one class will require any changes in another.

Answer:

☑ **E** and **F** are correct. Only having access to a small number of methods implies limited coupling. If the access is via a reference of interface type, it may be argued that there is even less opportunity for coupling as the class type itself is not visible. Stating that changes in one part of a program are unlikely to cause consequences in another part is really the essence of low coupling. There is no such thing as an anonymous variable. Referring to only a small number of other objects might imply low coupling, but if each object has many methods, and all are used, then coupling is high. Variables (attributes) in a class should usually be private, but this describes encapsulation, rather than low coupling. Of course, good encapsulation tends to reduce coupling as a consequence.

☒ **A, B, C** and **D** are incorrect based on the preceding treatise.
(Objective 5.1)

6. Given:

```
class Clidder {
  private final void flipper() { System.out.println("Clidder"); }
}

public class Clidlet extends Clidder {
  public final void flipper() { System.out.println("Clidlet");  }
  public static void main(String [] args) {
    new Clidlet().flipper();
} }
```

What is the result?

A. `Clidlet`

B. `Clidder`

C. `Clidder`
`Clidlet`

D. `Clidlet`
`Clidder`

E. Compilation fails.

Answer:

☑ **A** is correct. Although a final method cannot be overridden, in this case, the method is private, and therefore hidden. The effect is that a new, accessible, method flipper is created. Therefore, no polymorphism occurs in this example, the method invoked is simply that of the child class, and no error occurs.

☒ **B, C, D,** and **E** are incorrect based on the preceding.
(Objective 5.3)

7. Using the **fragments** below, complete the following **code** so it compiles. Note, you may not have to fill all of the slots.

Code:

```
class AgedP {

  _____  _____  _____  _____  _____

  public AgedP(int x) {

    _____  _____  _____  _____  _____

  }
}
public class Kinder extends AgedP {

  _____  _____  _____  _____  _____
```

```
    public Kinder(int x) {
       _____  _____  _____  _____  _____  ();
    }
}
```

Fragments: Use the following fragments zero or more times:

AgedP	super	this	
(	)	{	}
;			

Answer:

```
class AgedP {
   AgedP() {}
   public AgedP(int x) {
   }
}
public class Kinder extends AgedP {
   public Kinder(int x) {
      super();
   }
}
```

As there is no droppable tile for the variable x and the parentheses (in the Kinder constructor), are already in place and empty, there is no way to construct a call to the superclass constructor that takes an argument. Therefore, the only remaining possibility is to create a call to the no-argument superclass constructor. This is done as: super();. The line cannot be left blank, as the parentheses are already in place. Further, since the superclass constructor called is the no-argument version, this constructor must be created. It will not be created by the compiler because there is another constructor already present.
(Objective 5.4)

8. Given:

```
1. class Plant {
2.    String getName() { return "plant"; }
3.    Plant getType() { return this; }
4. }
5. class Flower extends Plant {
6.   // insert code here
7. }
8. class Tulip extends Flower { }
```

Which statement(s), inserted at line 6, will compile? (Choose all that apply.)

A. `Flower getType() { return this; }`

B. `String getType() { return "this"; }`

C. `Plant getType() { return this; }`

D. `Tulip getType() { return new Tulip(); }`

Answer:

☑ **A, C,** and **D** are correct. **A** and **D** are examples of co-variant returns, i.e., `Flower` and `Tulip` are both subtypes of `Plant`.

☒ **B** is incorrect, `String` is not a subtype of `Plant`.
(Objective 1.5)

9. Given:

```
1. class Zing {
2.    protected Hmpf h;
3. }
4. class Woop extends Zing { }
5. class Hmpf { }
```

Which is true? (Choose all that apply.)

A. `Woop is-a Hmpf` and `has-a Zing`.

B. `Zing is-a Woop` and `has-a Hmpf`.

C. `Hmpf has-a Woop` and `Woop is-a Zing`.

D. `Woop has-a Hmpf` and `Woop is-a Zing`.

E. `Zing has-a Hmpf` and `Zing is-a Woop`.

Answer:

☑ **D** is correct, `Woop` inherits a `Hmpf` from `Zing`.

☒ **A, B, C,** and **E** are incorrect based on the preceding.
(Objective 5.5)

10. Given:

```
1. class Programmer {
2.    Programmer debug() { return this; }
3. }
4. class SCJP extends Programmer {
5.    // insert code here
6. }
```

Which, inserted at line 5, will compile? (Choose all that apply.)

A. `Programmer debug() { return this; }`

B. `SCJP debug() { return this; }`

C. `Object debug() { return this; }`

D. `int debug() { return 1; }`

E. `int debug(int x) { return 1; }`

F. `Object debug(int x) { return this; }`

Answer:

☑ **A, B, E,** and **F** are correct. **A** and **B** are examples of overriding, specifically, **B** is an example of overriding using a covariant return. **E** and **F** are examples of overloading.

☒ **C** and **D** are incorrect. They are illegal overrides because their return types are incompatible. They are illegal overloads because their arguments did not change. (Objective 5.4)

11. Given:

```
class Uber {
  static int y = 2;
  Uber(int x) { this(); y = y * 2; }
  Uber() { y++; }
}
class Minor extends Uber {
  Minor() { super(y);   y = y + 3; }
  public static void main(String [] args) {
    new Minor();
    System.out.println(y);
} }
```

What is the result?

A. 6

B. 7

C. 8

D. 9

E. Compilation fails.

F. An exception is thrown.

Answer:

☑ **D** is correct. Minor's constructor makes an explicit call to Uber's 1-arg constructor, which makes an explicit (`this`) call to Uber's no-arg constructor, which increments y, then returns to the 1-arg constructor, which multiples y * 2, and then returns to Minor's constructor, which adds 3 to y.

☒ **A, B, C, E,** and **F** are incorrect based on the preceding.
(Objective 1.6)

12. Which statement(s) are true? (Choose all that apply.)

   A. Cohesion is the OO principle most closely associated with hiding implementation details.

   B. Cohesion is the OO principle most closely associated with making sure that classes know about other classes only through their APIs.

   C. Cohesion is the OO principle most closely associated with making sure that a class is designed with a single, well-focused purpose.

   D. Cohesion is the OO principle most closely associated with allowing a single object to be seen as having many types.

Answer:

☑ Answer **C** is correct.

☒ **A** refers to encapsulation, **B** refers to coupling, and **D** refers to polymorphism.
(Objective 5.1)

13. Given:

```
1. class Dog { }
2. class Beagle extends Dog { }
3.
4. class Kennel {
5.   public static void main(String [] arfs) {
6.      Beagle b1 = new Beagle();
7.      Dog dog1 = new Dog();
8.      Dog dog2 = b1;
9.      // insert code here
10.  }
11. }
```

Which, inserted at line 9, will compile? (Choose all that apply.)

A. `Beagle b2 = (Beagle) dog1;`

B. `Beagle b3 = (Beagle) dog2;`

C. `Beagle b4 = dog2;`

D. None of the above statements will compile

Answer:

☑ **A** and **B** are correct. However, at runtime, **A** will throw a `ClassCastException` because `dog1` refers to a Dog object, which can't necessarily do Beagle stuff.

☒ **C** and **D** are incorrect based on the preceding.
(Objective 5.2).

14. Given the following,

```
1. class X { void do1() { } }
2. class Y extends X { void do2() { } }
3.
4. class Chrome {
5.   public static void main(String [] args) {
6.     X x1 = new X();
7.     X x2 = new Y();
8.     Y y1 = new Y();
9.     // insert code here
10.  }
11. }
```

Which, inserted at line 9, will compile? (Choose all that apply.)

A. `x2.do2();`

B. `(Y)x2.do2();`

C. `((Y)x2).do2();`

D. None of the above statements will compile.

Answer:

☑ **C** is correct. Before you can invoke Y's do2 method you have to cast x2 to be of type Y. Statement **B** looks like a proper cast but without the second set of parentheses, the compiler thinks it's an incomplete statement.

☒ **A, B** and **D** are incorrect based on the preceding.
(Objective 5.2)

3

Assignments

- Use Class Members

- Develop Wrapper Code & Autoboxing Code

- Determine the Effects of Passing Variables into Methods

- Recognize when Objects Become Eligible for Garbage Collection

✓ Two-Minute Drill

Q&A Self Test

Stack and Heap—Quick Review

For most people, understanding the basics of the stack and the heap makes it far easier to understand topics like argument passing, polymorphism, threads, exceptions, and garbage collection. In this section, we'll stick to an overview, but we'll expand these topics several more times throughout the book.

For the most part, the various pieces (methods, variables, and objects) of Java programs live in one of two places in memory: the stack or the heap. For now, we're going to worry about only three types of things: instance variables, local variables, and objects:

- Instance variables and objects live on the heap.

- Local variables live on the stack.

Let's take a look at a Java program, and how its various pieces are created and map into the stack and the heap:

```
1. class Collar { }
2.
3. class Dog {
4.    Collar c;          // instance variable
5.    String name;       // instance variable
6.
7.    public static void main(String [] args) {
8.
9.      Dog d;                              // local variable: d
10.     d = new Dog();
11.     d.go(d);
12.    }
13.    void go(Dog dog) {                    // local variable: dog
14.      c = new Collar();
15.      dog.setName("Fido");
16.    }
17.    void setName(String dogName) {    // local var: dogName
18.      name = dogName;
19.      // do more stuff
20.    }
21. }
```

Figure 3-1 shows the state of the stack and the heap once the program reaches line 19. Following are some key points:

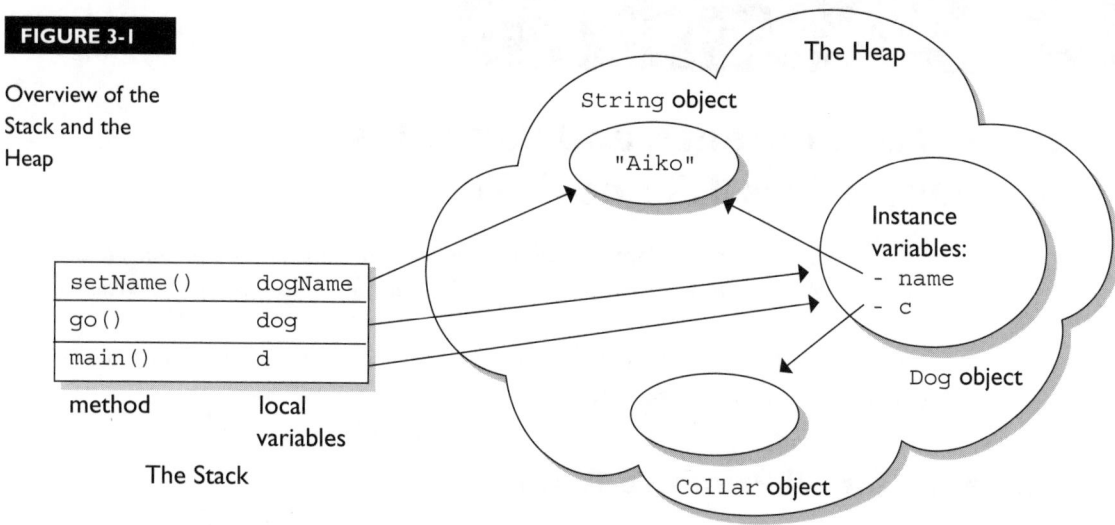

FIGURE 3-1

Overview of the Stack and the Heap

- Line 7—main() is placed on the stack.
- Line 9—reference variable d is created on the stack, but there's no Dog object yet.
- Line 10—a new Dog object is created and is assigned to the d reference variable.
- Line 11—a copy of the reference variable d is passed to the go() method.
- Line 13—the go() method is placed on the stack, with the dog parameter as a local variable.
- Line 14—a new Collar object is created on the heap, and assigned to Dog's instance variable.
- Line 17—setName() is added to the stack, with the dogName parameter as its local variable.
- Line 18—the name instance variable now also refers to the String object.
- Notice that two *different* local variables refer to the same Dog object.
- Notice that one local variable and one instance variable both refer to the same String Aiko.
- After Line 19 completes, setName() completes and is removed from the stack. At this point the local variable dogName disappears too, although the String object it referred to is still on the heap.

CERTIFICATION OBJECTIVE

Literals, Assignments, and Variables (Exam Objectives 1.3 and 7.6)

1.3   Develop code that declares, initializes, and uses primitives, arrays, enums, and objects as static, instance, and local variables. Also, use legal identifiers for variable names.

7.6   Write code that correctly applies the appropriate operators including assignment operators (limited to: =, +=, -=)...

Literal Values for All Primitive Types

A primitive literal is merely a source code representation of the primitive data types—in other words, an integer, floating-point number, boolean, or character that you type in while writing code. The following are examples of primitive literals:

```
'b'          // char literal
42           // int literal
false        // boolean literal
2546789.343  // double literal
```

Integer Literals

There are three ways to represent integer numbers in the Java language: decimal (base 10), octal (base 8), and hexadecimal (base 16). Most exam questions with integer literals use decimal representations, but the few that use octal or hexadecimal are worth studying for. Even though the odds that you'll ever actually use octal in the real world are astronomically tiny, they were included in the exam just for fun.

Decimal Literals   Decimal integers need no explanation; you've been using them since grade one or earlier. Chances are you don't keep your checkbook in hex. (If you do, there's a Geeks Anonymous (GA) group ready to help.) In the Java language, they are represented as is, with no prefix of any kind, as follows:

```
int length = 343;
```

Octal Literals Octal integers use only the digits 0 to 7. In Java, you represent an integer in octal form by placing a zero in front of the number, as follows:

```
class Octal {
  public static void main(String [] args) {
    int six = 06;       // Equal to decimal 6
    int seven = 07;     // Equal to decimal 7
    int eight = 010;    // Equal to decimal 8
    int nine = 011;     // Equal to decimal 9
    System.out.println("Octal 010 = " + eight);
  }
}
```

Notice that when we get past seven and are out of digits to use (we are allowed only the digits 0 through 7 for octal numbers), we revert back to zero, and one is added to the beginning of the number. You can have up to 21 digits in an octal number, not including the leading zero. If we run the preceding program, it displays the following:

```
Octal 010 = 8
```

Hexadecimal Literals Hexadecimal (hex for short) numbers are constructed using 16 distinct symbols. Because we never invented single digit symbols for the numbers 10 through 15, we use alphabetic characters to represent these digits. Counting from 0 through 15 in hex looks like this:

```
0 1 2 3 4 5 6 7 8 9 a b c d e f
```

Java will accept capital or lowercase letters for the extra digits (one of the few places Java is not case-sensitive!). You are allowed up to 16 digits in a hexadecimal number, not including the prefix 0x or the optional suffix extension L, which will be explained later. All of the following hexadecimal assignments are legal:

```
class HexTest {
  public static void main (String [] args) {
    int x = 0X0001;
    int y = 0x7fffffff;
    int z = 0xDeadCafe;
    System.out.println("x = " + x + " y = " + y + " z = " + z);
  }
}
```

Running HexTest produces the following output:

```
x = 1 y = 2147483647 z = -559035650
```

Don't be misled by changes in case for a hexadecimal digit or the 'x' preceding it. 0XCAFE and 0xcafe are both legal *and have the same value*.

All three integer literals (octal, decimal, and hexadecimal) are defined as int by default, but they may also be specified as long by placing a suffix of L or l after the number:

```
long jo = 110599L;
long so = 0xFFFFl;  // Note the lowercase 'l'
```

Floating-Point Literals

Floating-point numbers are defined as a number, a decimal symbol, and more numbers representing the fraction.

```
double d = 11301874.9881024;
```

In the preceding example, the number 11301874.9881024 is the literal value. Floating-point literals are defined as double (64 bits) by default, so if you want to assign a floating-point literal to a variable of type float (32 bits), you must attach the suffix F or f to the number. If you don't, the compiler will complain about a possible loss of precision, because you're trying to fit a number into a (potentially) less precise "container." The F suffix gives you a way to tell the compiler, "Hey, I know what I'm doing, and I'll take the risk, thank you very much."

```
float f = 23.467890;       // Compiler error, possible loss
                           // of precision
float g = 49837849.029847F;  // OK; has the suffix "F"
```

You may also optionally attach a D or d to double literals, but it is not necessary because this is the default behavior.

```
double d = 110599.995011D; // Optional, not required
double  g = 987.897;       // No 'D' suffix, but OK because the
                           // literal is a double by default
```

Look for numeric literals that include a comma, for example,

```
int x = 25,343;  // Won't compile because of the comma
```

Boolean Literals

Boolean literals are the source code representation for boolean values. A boolean value can only be defined as `true` or `false`. Although in C (and some other languages) it is common to use numbers to represent `true` or `false`, this will not work in Java. Again, repeat after me, "Java is not C++."

```
boolean t = true;  // Legal
boolean  f = 0;    // Compiler error!
```

Be on the lookout for questions that use numbers where booleans are required. You might see an `if` test that uses a number, as in the following:

```
int x = 1;  if (x) {  } // Compiler error!
```

Character Literals

A char literal is represented by a single character in single quotes.

```
char a = 'a';
char b = '@';
```

You can also type in the Unicode value of the character, using the Unicode notation of prefixing the value with \u as follows:

```
char letterN = '\u004E'; // The letter 'N'
```

Remember, characters are just 16-bit unsigned integers under the hood. That means you can assign a number literal, assuming it will fit into the unsigned 16-bit range (65535 or less). For example, the following are all legal:

```
char a = 0x892;        // hexadecimal literal
char b = 982;          // int literal
char c = (char)70000;  // The cast is required; 70000 is
                       // out of char range
```

```
char d = (char) -98;    // Ridiculous, but legal
```

And the following are not legal and produce compiler errors:

```
char e = -29;    // Possible loss of precision; needs a cast
char f = 70000   // Possible loss of precision; needs a cast
```

You can also use an escape code if you want to represent a character that can't be typed in as a literal, including the characters for linefeed, newline, horizontal tab, backspace, and single quotes.

```
char c = '\"';    // A double quote
char d = '\n';    // A newline
```

Literal Values for Strings

A string literal is a source code representation of a value of a String object. For example, the following is an example of two ways to represent a string literal:

```
String s = "Bill Joy";
System.out.println("Bill" + " Joy");
```

Although strings are not primitives, they're included in this section because they can be represented as literals—in other words, typed directly into code. The only other nonprimitive type that has a literal representation is an array, which we'll look at later in the chapter.

```
Thread t = ???   // what literal value could possibly go here?
```

Assignment Operators

Assigning a value to a variable seems straightforward enough; you simply assign the stuff on the right side of the = to the variable on the left. Well, sure, but don't expect to be tested on something like this:

```
x = 6;
```

No, you won't be tested on the no-brainer (technical term) assignments. You will, however, be tested on the trickier assignments involving complex expressions and casting. We'll look at both primitive and reference variable assignments. But before we begin, let's back up and peek inside a variable. What is a variable? How are the variable and its value related?

Variables are just bit holders, with a designated type. You can have an `int` holder, a `double` holder, a Button holder, and even a String[] holder. Within that holder is a bunch of bits representing the value. For primitives, the bits represent a numeric value (although we don't know what that bit pattern looks like for `boolean`, luckily, we don't care). A `byte` with a value of 6, for example, means that the bit pattern in the variable (the `byte` holder) is 00000110, representing the 8 bits.

So the value of a primitive variable is clear, but what's inside an object holder? If you say,

```
Button b = new Button();
```

what's inside the Button holder `b`? Is it the Button object? No! A variable referring to an object is just that—a *reference* variable. A reference variable bit holder contains bits representing a *way to get to the object*. We don't know what the format is. The way in which object references are stored is virtual-machine specific (it's a pointer to something, we just don't know what that something really is). All we can say for sure is that the variable's value is *not* the object, but rather a value representing a specific object on the heap. Or `null`. If the reference variable has not been assigned a value, or has been explicitly assigned a value of `null`, the variable holds bits representing—you guessed it—null. You can read

```
Button b = null;
```

as "The Button variable b is not referring to any object."

So now that we know a variable is just a little box o' bits, we can get on with the work of changing those bits. We'll look first at assigning values to primitives, and finish with assignments to reference variables.

Primitive Assignments

The equal (=) sign is used for assigning a value to a variable, and it's cleverly named the assignment operator. There are actually 12 assignment operators, but only the five most commonly used are on the exam, and they are covered in Chapter 4.

You can assign a primitive variable using a literal or the result of an expression.

Take a look at the following:

```
int x = 7;     // literal assignment
int y = x + 2; // assignment with an expression
               // (including a literal)
int z = x * y; // assignment with an expression
```

The most important point to remember is that a literal integer (such as 7) is always implicitly an int. Thinking back to Chapter 1, you'll recall that an int is a 32-bit value. No big deal if you're assigning a value to an int or a long variable, but what if you're assigning to a byte variable? After all, a byte-sized holder can't hold as many bits as an int-sized holder. Here's where it gets weird. The following is legal,

```
byte b = 27;
```

but only because the compiler automatically narrows the literal value to a byte. In other words, the compiler puts in the *cast*. The preceding code is identical to the following:

```
byte b = (byte) 27; // Explicitly cast the int literal to a byte
```

It looks as though the compiler gives you a break, and lets you take a shortcut with assignments to integer variables smaller than an int. (Everything we're saying about byte applies equally to char and short, both of which are smaller than an int.) We're not actually at the weird part yet, by the way.

We know that a literal integer is always an int, but more importantly, the result of an expression involving anything int-sized or smaller is always an int. In other words, add two bytes together and you'll get an int—even if those two bytes are tiny. Multiply an int and a short and you'll get an int. Divide a short by a byte and you'll get...an int. OK, now we're at the weird part. Check this out:

```
byte b = 3;     // No problem, 3 fits in a byte
byte c = 8;     // No problem, 8 fits in a byte
byte d = b + c; // Should be no problem, sum of the two bytes
                // fits in a byte
```

The last line won't compile! You'll get an error something like this:

```
TestBytes.java:5: possible loss of precision
found    : int
required: byte
    byte c = a + b;
                ^
```

We tried to assign the sum of two bytes to a `byte` variable, the result of which (11) was definitely small enough to fit into a `byte`, but the compiler didn't care. It knew the rule about `int`-or-smaller expressions always resulting in an `int`. It would have compiled if we'd done the *explicit* cast:

```
byte c = (byte) (a + b);
```

Primitive Casting

Casting lets you convert primitive values from one type to another. We mentioned primitive casting in the previous section, but now we're going to take a deeper look. (Object casting was covered in Chapter 2.)

Casts can be implicit or explicit. An implicit cast means you don't have to write code for the cast; the conversion happens automatically. Typically, an implicit cast happens when you're doing a widening conversion. In other words, putting a smaller thing (say, a `byte`) into a bigger container (like an `int`). Remember those `"possible loss of precision"` compiler errors we saw in the assignments section? Those happened when we tried to put a larger thing (say, a `long`) into a smaller container (like a `short`). The large-value-into-small-container conversion is referred to as *narrowing* and requires an explicit cast, where you tell the compiler that you're aware of the danger and accept full responsibility. First we'll look at an implicit cast:

```
int a = 100;
long b = a; // Implicit cast, an int value always fits in a long
```

An explicit casts looks like this:

```
float a = 100.001f;
int b = (int)a; // Explicit cast, the float could lose info
```

Integer values may be assigned to a `double` variable without explicit casting, because any integer value can fit in a 64-bit `double`. The following line demonstrates this:

```
double d = 100L; // Implicit cast
```

In the preceding statement, a `double` is initialized with a `long` value (as denoted by the `L` after the numeric value). No cast is needed in this case because a `double` can hold every piece of information that a `long` can store. If, however, we want to assign a `double` value to an integer type, we're attempting a narrowing conversion and the compiler knows it:

```
class Casting {
  public static void main(String [] args) {
    int x = 3957.229; // illegal
  }
}
```

If we try to compile the preceding code, we get an error something like:

```
%javac Casting.java
Casting.java:3: Incompatible type for declaration. Explicit cast
needed to convert double to int.
      int x = 3957.229; // illegal
1 error
```

In the preceding code, a floating-point value is being assigned to an integer variable. Because an integer is not capable of storing decimal places, an error occurs. To make this work, we'll cast the floating-point number into an `int`:

```
class Casting {
  public static void main(String [] args) {
    int x = (int)3957.229; // legal cast
    System.out.println("int x = " + x);
  }
}
```

When you cast a floating-point number to an integer type, the value loses all the digits after the decimal. The preceding code will produce the following output:

```
int x = 3957
```

We can also cast a larger number type, such as a `long`, into a smaller number type, such as a `byte`. Look at the following:

```
class Casting {
  public static void main(String [] args) {
    long l = 56L;
    byte b = (byte)l;
    System.out.println("The byte is " + b);
  }
}
```

The preceding code will compile and run fine. But what happens if the `long` value is larger than 127 (the largest number a `byte` can store)? Let's modify the code:

```
class Casting {
  public static void main(String [] args) {
    long l = 130L;
    byte b = (byte)l;
    System.out.println("The byte is " + b);
  }
}
```

The code compiles fine, and when we run it we get the following:

```
%java Casting
The byte is -126
```

You don't get a runtime error, even when the value being narrowed is too large for the type. The bits to the left of the lower 8 just...go away. If the leftmost bit (the sign bit) in the `byte` (or any integer primitive) now happens to be a 1, the primitive will have a negative value.

EXERCISE 3-1

Casting Primitives

Create a `float` number type of any value, and assign it to a `short` using casting.

1. Declare a `float` variable: `float f = 234.56F;`
2. Assign the `float` to a short: `short s = (short)f;`

Assigning Floating-Point Numbers   Floating-point numbers have slightly different assignment behavior than integer types. First, you must know that every floating-point literal is implicitly a `double` (64 bits), not a `float`. So the literal `32.3`, for example, is considered a `double`. If you try to assign a `double` to a `float`, the compiler knows you don't have enough room in a 32-bit `float` container to hold the precision of a 64-bit `double`, and it lets you know. The following code looks good, but won't compile:

```
float f = 32.3;
```

You can see that `32.3` should fit just fine into a float-sized variable, but the compiler won't allow it. In order to assign a floating-point literal to a `float` variable, you must either cast the value or append an `f` to the end of the literal. The following assignments will compile:

```
float f = (float) 32.3;
float g = 32.3f;
float h = 32.3F;
```

Assigning a Literal That Is Too Large for the Variable   We'll also get a compiler error if we try to assign a literal value that the compiler knows is too big to fit into the variable.

```
byte a = 128; // byte can only hold up to 127
```

The preceding code gives us an error something like

```
TestBytes.java:5: possible loss of precision
found    : int
required: byte
byte a = 128;
```

We can fix it with a cast:

```
byte a = (byte) 128;
```

But then what's the result? When you narrow a primitive, Java simply truncates the higher-order bits that won't fit. In other words, it loses all the bits to the left of the bits you're narrowing to.

Let's take a look at what happens in the preceding code. There, 128 is the bit pattern 10000000. It takes a full 8 bits to represent 128. But because the literal 128 is an int, we actually get 32 bits, with the 128 living in the right-most (lower-order) 8 bits. So a literal 128 is actually

00000000000000000000000010000000

Take our word for it; there are 32 bits there.

To narrow the 32 bits representing 128, Java simply lops off the leftmost (higher-order) 24 bits. We're left with just the 10000000. But remember that a byte is signed, with the leftmost bit representing the sign (and not part of the value of the variable). So we end up with a negative number (the 1 that used to represent 128 now represents the negative sign bit). Remember, to find out the value of a negative number using two's complement notation, you flip all of the bits and then add 1. Flipping the 8 bits gives us 01111111, and adding 1 to that gives us 10000000, or back to 128! And when we apply the sign bit, we end up with –128.

You must use an explicit cast to assign 128 to a byte, and the assignment leaves you with the value –128. A cast is nothing more than your way of saying to the compiler, "Trust me. I'm a professional. I take full responsibility for anything weird that happens when those top bits are chopped off."

That brings us to the compound assignment operators. The following will compile,

```
byte b = 3;
b += 7;         // No problem - adds 7 to b (result is 10)
```

and is equivalent to

```
byte b = 3;
b = (byte) (b + 7);  // Won't compile without the
                     // cast, since b + 7 results in an int
```

The compound assignment operator += lets you add to the value of b, without putting in an explicit cast. In fact, +=, -=, *=, and /= will all put in an implicit cast.

Assigning One Primitive Variable to Another Primitive Variable

When you assign one primitive variable to another, the contents of the right-hand variable are copied. For example,

```
int a = 6;
int b = a;
```

This code can be read as, "Assign the bit pattern for the number 6 to the int variable a. Then copy the bit pattern in a, and place the copy into variable b."

So, both variables now hold a bit pattern for 6, but the two variables have no other relationship. We used the variable a *only* to copy its contents. At this point, a and b have identical contents (in other words, identical values), but if we change the contents of *either* a or b, the other variable won't be affected.

Take a look at the following example:

```
class ValueTest {
    public static void main (String [] args) {
        int a = 10;  // Assign a value to a
        System.out.println("a = " + a);
        int b = a;
        b = 30;
        System.out.println("a = " + a + " after change to b");
    }
}
```

The output from this program is

```
%java ValueTest
a = 10
a = 10 after change to b
```

Notice the value of a stayed at 10. The key point to remember is that even after you assign a to b, a and b are not referring to the same place in memory. The a and b variables do not share a single value; they have identical copies.

Reference Variable Assignments

You can assign a newly created object to an object reference variable as follows:

```
Button b = new Button();
```

The preceding line does three key things:

- Makes a reference variable named b, of type Button
- Creates a new Button object on the heap
- Assigns the newly created Button object to the reference variable b

You can also assign null to an object reference variable, which simply means the variable is not referring to any object:

```
Button c = null;
```

The preceding line creates space for the Button reference variable (the bit holder for a reference value), but doesn't create an actual Button object.

As we discussed in the last chapter, you can also use a reference variable to refer to any object that is a subclass of the declared reference variable type, as follows:

```
public class Foo {
   public void doFooStuff() { }
}
public class Bar extends Foo {
   public void doBarStuff() { }
}
class Test {
   public static void main (String [] args) {
      Foo reallyABar = new Bar();  // Legal because Bar is a
                                   // subclass of Foo
      Bar reallyAFoo = new Foo();  // Illegal! Foo is not a
                                   // subclass of Bar

   }
}
```

The rule is that you can assign a subclass of the declared type, but not a superclass of the declared type. Remember, a Bar object is guaranteed to be able to do anything a Foo can do, so anyone with a Foo reference can invoke Foo methods even though the object is actually a Bar.

In the preceding code, we see that Foo has a method doFooStuff() that someone with a Foo reference might try to invoke. If the object referenced by the Foo variable is really a Foo, no problem. But it's also no problem if the object is a Bar, since Bar inherited the doFooStuff() method. You can't make it work in reverse, however. If somebody has a Bar reference, they're going to invoke `doBarStuff()`, but if the object is a Foo, it won't know how to respond.

Variable Scope

Once you've declared and initialized a variable, a natural question is "How long will this variable be around?" This is a question regarding the scope of variables. And not only is scope an important thing to understand in general, it also plays a big part in the exam. Let's start by looking at a class file:

```
class Layout {                          // class

  static int s = 343;                   // static variable

  int x;                                // instance variable

  { x = 7; int x2 = 5; }                // initialization block

  Layout() { x += 8; int x3 = 6;}       // constructor

  void doStuff() {                      // method

    int y = 0;                          // local variable

    for(int z = 0; z < 4; z++) {        // 'for' code block
      y += z + x;
    }
  }
}
```

As with variables in all Java programs, the variables in this program (s, x, x2, x3, y, and z) all have a scope:

- s is a static variable.
- x is an instance variable.
- y is a local variable (sometimes called a "method local" variable).
- z is a block variable.
- x2 is an init block variable, a flavor of local variable.
- x3 is a constructor variable, a flavor of local variable.

For the purposes of discussing the scope of variables, we can say that there are four basic scopes:

- Static variables have the longest scope; they are created when the class is loaded, and they survive as long as the class stays loaded in the JVM.
- Instance variables are the next most long-lived; they are created when a new instance is created, and they live until the instance is removed.
- Local variables are next; they live as long as their method remains on the stack. As we'll soon see, however, local variables can be alive, and still be "out of scope".
- Block variables live only as long as the code block is executing.

Scoping errors come in many sizes and shapes. One common mistake happens when a variable is *shadowed* and two scopes overlap. We'll take a detailed look at shadowing in a few pages. The most common reason for scoping errors is when you attempt to access a variable that is not in scope. Let's look at three common examples of this type of error:

- Attempting to access an instance variable from a static context (typically from `main()`).

```
class ScopeErrors {
  int x = 5;
  public static void main(String[] args) {
    x++;   // won't compile, x is an 'instance' variable
  }
}
```

- Attempting to access a local variable from a nested method.

  When a method, say `go()`, invokes another method, say `go2()`, `go2()` won't have access to `go()`'s local variables. While `go2()` is executing, `go()`'s local variables are still *alive*, but they are *out of scope*. When `go2()` completes, it is removed from the stack, and `go()` resumes execution. At this point, all of `go()`'s previously declared variables are back in scope. For example:

```
class ScopeErrors {
  public static void main(String [] args) {
    ScopeErrors s = new ScopeErrors();
    s.go();
  }
  void go() {
    int y = 5;
```

```
      go2();
      y++;            // once go2() completes, y is back in scope
    }
    void go2() {
      y++;            // won't compile, y is local to go()
    }
  }
```

- Attempting to use a block variable after the code block has completed.

  It's very common to declare and use a variable within a code block, but be careful not to try to use the variable once the block has completed:

```
void go3() {
  for(int z = 0; z < 5; z++) {
    boolean test = false;
    if(z == 3) {
      test = true;
      break;
    }
  }
  System.out.print(test);   // 'test' is an ex-variable,
                            // it has ceased to be...
}
```

In the last two examples, the compiler will say something like this:

```
cannot find symbol
```

This is the compiler's way of saying, "That variable you just tried to use? Well, it might have been valid in the distant past (like one line of code ago), but this is Internet time baby, I have no memory of such a variable."

Using a Variable or Array Element That Is Uninitialized and Unassigned

Java gives us the option of initializing a declared variable or leaving it uninitialized. When we attempt to use the uninitialized variable, we can get different behavior depending on what type of variable or array we are dealing with (primitives or objects). The behavior also depends on the level (scope) at which we are declaring our variable. An instance variable is declared within the class but outside any method or constructor, whereas a local variable is declared within a method (or in the argument list of the method).

Local variables are sometimes called stack, temporary, automatic, or method variables, but the rules for these variables are the same regardless of what you call them. Although you can leave a local variable uninitialized, the compiler complains if you try to use a local variable before initializing it with a value, as we shall see.

Primitive and Object Type Instance Variables

Instance variables (also called *member* variables) are variables defined at the class level. That means the variable declaration is not made within a method, constructor, or any other initializer block. Instance variables are initialized to a default value each time a new instance is created, although they may be given an explicit value after the object's super-constructors have completed. Table 3-1 lists the default values for primitive and object types.

TABLE 3-1   Default Values for Primitives and Reference Types

Variable Type	Default Value
Object reference	`null` (not referencing any object)
`byte, short, int, long`	`0`
`float, double`	`0.0`
`boolean`	`false`
`char`	`'\u0000'`

Primitive Instance Variables

In the following example, the integer `year` is defined as a class member because it is within the initial curly braces of the class and not within a method's curly braces:

```
public class BirthDate {
  int year;                                  // Instance variable
  public static void main(String [] args) {
    BirthDate bd = new BirthDate();
    bd.showYear();
  }
  public void showYear() {
    System.out.println("The year is " + year);
  }
}
```

When the program is started, it gives the variable `year` a value of zero, the default value for primitive number instance variables.

on the
Öo b

It's a good idea to initialize all your variables, even if you're assigning them with the default value. Your code will be easier to read; programmers who have to maintain your code (after you win the lottery and move to Tahiti) will be grateful.

Object Reference Instance Variables

When compared with uninitialized primitive variables, object references that aren't initialized are a completely different story. Let's look at the following code:

```
public class Book {
  private String title;                 // instance reference variable
  public String getTitle() {
    return title;
  }
  public static void main(String [] args) {
    Book b = new Book();
    System.out.println("The title is " + b.getTitle());
  }
}
```

This code will compile fine. When we run it, the output is

```
The title is null
```

The title variable has not been explicitly initialized with a String assignment, so the instance variable value is null. Remember that null is not the same as an empty String (""). A null value means the reference variable is not referring to any object on the heap. The following modification to the Book code runs into trouble:

```
public class Book {
  private String title;            // instance reference variable
  public String getTitle() {
    return title;
  }
  public static void main(String [] args) {
    Book b = new Book();
    String s = b.getTitle();      // Compiles and runs
    String t = s.toLowerCase();   // Runtime Exception!
  }
}
```

When we try to run the Book class, the JVM will produce something like this:

```
Exception in thread "main" java.lang.NullPointerException
      at Book.main(Book.java:9)
```

We get this error because the reference variable title does not point (refer) to an object. We can check to see whether an object has been instantiated by using the keyword null, as the following revised code shows:

```
public class Book {
  private String title;               // instance reference variable
  public String getTitle() {
    return title;
  }
  public static void main(String [] args) {
    Book b = new Book();
    String s = b.getTitle(); // Compiles and runs
    if (s != null) {
      String t = s.toLowerCase();
    }
```

```
    }
  }
```

The preceding code checks to make sure the object referenced by the variable s is not null before trying to use it. Watch out for scenarios on the exam where you might have to trace back through the code to find out whether an object reference will have a value of null. In the preceding code, for example, you look at the instance variable declaration for title, see that there's no explicit initialization, recognize that the title variable will be given the default value of null, and then realize that the variable s will also have a value of null. Remember, the value of s is a copy of the value of title (as returned by the getTitle() method), so if title is a null reference, s will be too.

Array Instance Variables

Later in this chapter we'll be taking a very detailed look at declaring, constructing, and initializing arrays and multidimensional arrays. For now, we're just going to look at the rule for an array element's default values.

An array is an object; thus, an array instance variable that's declared but not explicitly initialized will have a value of null, just as any other object reference instance variable. But…if the array is initialized, what happens to the elements contained *in* the array? All array elements are given their default values—the same default values that elements of that type get when they're instance variables. *The bottom line: Array elements are always, always, always given default values, regardless of where the array itself is declared or instantiated.*

If we initialize an array, object reference elements will equal null if they are not initialized individually with values. If primitives are contained in an array, they will be given their respective default values. For example, in the following code, the array year will contain 100 integers that all equal zero by default:

```java
public class BirthDays {
  static int [] year = new int[100];
  public static void main(String [] args) {
    for(int i=0;i<100;i++)
      System.out.println("year[" + i + "] = " + year[i]);
  }
}
```

When the preceding code runs, the output indicates that all 100 integers in the array equal zero.

Local (Stack, Automatic) Primitives and Objects

Local variables are defined within a method, and they include a method's parameters.

"Automatic" is just another term for "local variable." It does not mean the automatic variable is automatically assigned a value! The opposite is true. An automatic variable must be assigned a value in the code, or the compiler will complain.

Local Primitives

In the following time travel simulator, the integer year is defined as an automatic variable because it is within the curly braces of a method.

```
public class TimeTravel {
  public static void main(String [] args) {
    int year = 2050;
    System.out.println("The year is " + year);
  }
}
```

Local variables, including primitives, always, always, always must be initialized *before* you attempt to use them (though not necessarily on the same line of code). Java does not give local variables a default value; you must explicitly initialize them with a value, as in the preceding example. If you try to use an uninitialized primitive in your code, you'll get a compiler error:

```
public class TimeTravel {
  public static void main(String [] args) {
    int year; // Local variable (declared but not initialized)
    System.out.println("The year is " + year); // Compiler error
  }
}
```

Compiling produces output something like this:

```
%javac TimeTravel.java
TimeTravel.java:4: Variable year may not have been initialized.
          System.out.println("The year is " + year);
1 error
```

To correct our code, we must give the integer year a value. In this updated example, we declare it on a separate line, which is perfectly valid:

```
public class TimeTravel {
  public static void main(String [] args) {
    int year;       // Declared but not initialized
    int day;        // Declared but not initialized
    System.out.println("You step into the portal.");
    year = 2050;    // Initialize (assign an explicit value)
    System.out.println("Welcome to the year " + year);
  }
}
```

Notice in the preceding example we declared an integer called day that never gets initialized, yet the code compiles and runs fine. Legally, you can declare a local variable without initializing it as long as you don't use the variable, but let's face it, if you declared it, you probably had a reason (although we have heard of programmers declaring random local variables just for sport, to see if they can figure out how and why they're being used).

on the
Job

The compiler can't always tell whether a local variable has been initialized before use. For example, if you initialize within a logically conditional block (in other words, a code block that may not run, such as an if *block or* for *loop without a literal value of* true *or* false *in the test), the compiler knows that the initialization might not happen, and can produce an error. The following code upsets the compiler:*

```
public class TestLocal {
  public static void main(String [] args) {
    int x;
    if (args[0] != null) { // assume you know this will
                           // always be true
```

```
      x = 7;                      // compiler can't tell that this
                                  // statement will run
    }
    int y = x;                    // the compiler will choke here
  }
}
```

The compiler will produce an error something like this:

```
TestLocal.java:9: variable x might not have been initialized
```

Because of the compiler-can't-tell-for-certain problem, you will sometimes need to initialize your variable outside the conditional block, just to make the compiler happy. You know why that's important if you've seen the bumper sticker, "When the compiler's not happy, ain't nobody happy."

Local Object References

Objects references, too, behave differently when declared within a method rather than as instance variables. With instance variable object references, you can get away with leaving an object reference uninitialized, as long as the code checks to make sure the reference isn't `null` before using it. Remember, to the compiler, `null` is a value. You can't use the dot operator on a `null` reference, because *there is no object at the other end of it*, but a `null` reference is not the same as an *uninitialized* reference. Locally declared references can't get away with checking for `null` before use, unless you explicitly initialize the local variable to `null`. The compiler will complain about the following code:

```
import java.util.Date;
public class TimeTravel {
  public static void main(String [] args) {
    Date date;
    if (date == null)
      System.out.println("date is null");
  }
}
```

Compiling the code results in an error similar to the following:

```
%javac TimeTravel.java
TimeTravel.java:5: Variable date may not have been initialized.
          if (date == null)
1 error
```

Instance variable references are always given a default value of null, until explicitly initialized to something else. But local references are not given a default value; in other words, *they aren't null*. If you don't initialize a local reference variable, then by default, its value is…well that's the whole point—it doesn't have any value at all! So we'll make this simple: Just set the darn thing to `null` explicitly, until you're ready to initialize it to something else. The following local variable will compile properly:

```
Date date = null; // Explicitly set the local reference
                  // variable to null
```

Local Arrays

Just like any other object reference, array references declared within a method must be assigned a value before use. That just means you must declare and construct the array. You do not, however, need to explicitly initialize the elements of an array. We've said it before, but it's important enough to repeat: array elements are given their default values (0, `false`, `null`, `'\u0000'`, etc.) regardless of whether the array is declared as an instance or local variable. The array object itself, however, will not be initialized if it's declared locally. In other words, you must explicitly initialize an array reference if it's declared and used within a method, but at the moment you construct an array object, all of its elements are assigned their default values.

Assigning One Reference Variable to Another

With primitive variables, an assignment of one variable to another means the contents (bit pattern) of one variable are *copied* into another. Object reference variables work exactly the same way. The contents of a reference variable are a bit pattern, so if you assign reference variable a to reference variable b, the bit pattern in a is *copied* and the new *copy* is placed into b. (Some people have created a game around counting how many times we use the word *copy* in this chapter…this copy concept is a biggie!) If we assign an existing instance of an object to a new reference variable, then two reference variables will hold the same bit pattern—a bit pattern referring to a specific object on the heap. Look at the following code:

```
import java.awt.Dimension;
class ReferenceTest {
  public static void main (String [] args) {
    Dimension a = new Dimension(5,10);
    System.out.println("a.height = " + a.height);
    Dimension b = a;
    b.height = 30;
    System.out.println("a.height = " + a.height +
                      " after change to b");
  }
}
```

In the preceding example, a Dimension object a is declared and initialized with a width of 5 and a height of 10. Next, Dimension b is declared, and assigned the value of a. At this point, both variables (a and b) hold identical values, because the contents of a were copied into b. There is still only one Dimension object—the one that both a and b refer to. Finally, the height property is changed using the b reference. Now think for a minute: is this going to change the height property of a as well? Let's see what the output will be:

```
%java ReferenceTest
a.height = 10
a.height = 30 after change to b
```

From this output, we can conclude that both variables refer to the same instance of the Dimension object. When we made a change to b, the height property was also changed for a.

One exception to the way object references are assigned is String. In Java, String objects are given special treatment. For one thing, String objects are immutable; you can't change the value of a String object (lots more on this concept in Chapter 6). But it sure looks as though you can. Examine the following code:

```
class StringTest {
  public static void main(String [] args) {
    String x = "Java";  // Assign a value to x
    String y = x;       // Now y and x refer to the same
                        // String object

    System.out.println("y string = " + y);
    x = x + " Bean";    // Now modify the object using
                        // the x reference
```

```
        System.out.println("y string = " + y);
   }
}
```

You might think String y will contain the characters Java Bean after the variable x is changed, because Strings are objects. Let's see what the output is:

```
%java StringTest
y string = Java
y string = Java
```

As you can see, even though y is a reference variable to the same object that x refers to, when we change x, it doesn't change y! For any other object type, where two references refer to the same object, if either reference is used to modify the object, both references will see the change because there is still only a single object. *But any time we make any changes at all to a String, the VM will update the reference variable to refer to a different object.* The different object might be a new object, or it might not, but it will definitely be a different object. The reason we can't say for sure whether a new object is created is because of the String constant pool, which we'll cover in Chapter 6.

You need to understand what happens when you use a String reference variable to modify a string:

- A new string is created (or a matching String is found in the String pool), leaving the original String object untouched.
- The reference used to modify the String (or rather, make a new String by modifying a copy of the original) is then assigned the brand new String object.

So when you say

```
1. String s = "Fred";
2. String t = s;        // Now t and s refer to the same
                        // String object
3. t.toUpperCase();     // Invoke a String method that changes
                        // the String
```

you haven't changed the original String object created on line 1. When line 2 completes, both t and s reference the same String object. But when line 3 runs, rather than modifying the object referred to by t (which is the one and only String object up to this point), a brand new String object is created. And then abandoned. Because the new String isn't assigned to a String variable, the newly created String (which holds the string "FRED") is toast. So while two String objects were created in the preceding code, only one is actually referenced, and both t and s refer to it. The behavior of Strings is extremely important in the exam, so we'll cover it in much more detail in Chapter 6.

CERTIFICATION OBJECTIVE

Passing Variables into Methods (Objective 7.3)

7.3 Determine the effect upon object references and primitive values when they are passed into methods that perform assignments or other modifying operations on the parameters.

Methods can be declared to take primitives and/or object references. You need to know how (or if) the caller's variable can be affected by the called method. The difference between object reference and primitive variables, when passed into methods, is huge and important. To understand this section, you'll need to be comfortable with the assignments section covered in the first part of this chapter.

Passing Object Reference Variables

When you pass an object variable into a method, you must keep in mind that you're passing the object *reference*, and not the actual object itself. Remember that a reference variable holds bits that represent (to the underlying VM) a way to get to a specific object in memory (on the heap). More importantly, you must remember that you aren't even passing the actual reference variable, but rather a *copy* of the reference variable. A copy of a variable means you get a copy of the bits in that variable, so when you pass a reference variable, you're passing a copy of the bits representing how to get to a specific object. In other words, both the caller and the called method will now have identical copies of the reference, and thus both will refer to the same exact (*not* a copy) object on the heap.

For this example, we'll use the Dimension class from the java.awt package:

```
1. import java.awt.Dimension;
2. class ReferenceTest {
```

```
3.    public static void main (String [] args) {
4.       Dimension d = new Dimension(5,10);
5.       ReferenceTest rt = new ReferenceTest();
6.       System.out.println("Before modify() d.height = "
                                    + d.height);
7.       rt.modify(d);
8.       System.out.println("After modify() d.height = "
                                    + d.height);
9.    }
10.   void modify(Dimension dim) {
11.      dim.height = dim.height + 1;
12.      System.out.println("dim = " + dim.height);
13.   }
14. }
```

When we run this class, we can see that the modify() method was indeed able to modify the original (and only) Dimension object created on line 4.

```
C:\Java Projects\Reference>java ReferenceTest
Before modify() d.height = 10
dim = 11
After modify() d.height = 11
```

Notice when the Dimension object on line 4 is passed to the modify() method, any changes to the object that occur inside the method are being made to the object whose reference was passed. In the preceding example, reference variables d and dim both point to the same object.

Does Java Use Pass-By-Value Semantics?

If Java passes objects by passing the reference variable instead, does that mean Java uses pass-by-reference for objects? Not exactly, although you'll often hear and read that it does. Java is actually pass-by-value for all variables running within a single VM. Pass-by-value means pass-by-variable-value. And that means, pass-by-copy-of-the-variable! (There's that word *copy* again!)

It makes no difference if you're passing primitive or reference variables, you are always passing a copy of the bits in the variable. So for a primitive variable, you're passing a copy of the bits representing the value. For example, if you pass an int variable with the value of 3, you're passing a copy of the bits representing 3. The called method then gets its own copy of the value, to do with it what it likes.

And if you're passing an object reference variable, you're passing a copy of the bits representing the reference to an object. The called method then gets its own copy of the reference variable, to do with it what it likes. But because two identical reference variables refer to the exact same object, if the called method modifies the object (by invoking setter methods, for example), the caller will see that the object the caller's original variable refers to has also been changed. In the next section, we'll look at how the picture changes when we're talking about primitives.

The bottom line on pass-by-value: the called method can't change the caller's variable, although for object reference variables, the called method can change the object the variable referred to. What's the difference between changing the variable and changing the object? For object references, it means the called method can't reassign the caller's original reference variable and make it refer to a different object, or null. For example, in the following code fragment,

```java
void bar() {
    Foo f = new Foo();
    doStuff(f);
}
void doStuff(Foo g) {
    g.setName("Boo");
    g = new Foo();
}
```

reassigning g does not reassign f! At the end of the bar() method, two Foo objects have been created, one referenced by the local variable f and one referenced by the local (argument) variable g. Because the doStuff() method has a copy of the reference variable, it has a way to get to the original Foo object, for instance to call the setName() method. But, the doStuff() method does *not* have a way to get to the f reference variable. So doStuff() can change values within the object f refers to, but doStuff() can't change the actual contents (bit pattern) of f. In other words, doStuff() can change the state of the object that f refers to, but it can't make f refer to a different object!

Passing Primitive Variables

Let's look at what happens when a primitive variable is passed to a method:

```java
class ReferenceTest {
  public static void main (String [] args) {
```

```
        int a = 1;
        ReferenceTest rt = new ReferenceTest();
        System.out.println("Before modify() a = " + a);
        rt.modify(a);
        System.out.println("After modify() a = " + a);
    }
    void modify(int number) {
        number = number + 1;
        System.out.println("number = " + number);
    }
}
```

In this simple program, the variable a is passed to a method called modify(), which increments the variable by 1. The resulting output looks like this:

```
Before modify() a = 1
number = 2
After modify() a = 1
```

Notice that a did not change after it was passed to the method. Remember, it was a copy of a that was passed to the method. When a primitive variable is passed to a method, it is passed by value, which means pass-by-copy-of-the-bits-in-the-variable.

FROM THE CLASSROOM

The Shadowy World of Variables

Just when you think you've got it all figured out, you see a piece of code with variables not behaving the way you think they should. You might have stumbled into code with a shadowed variable. You can shadow a variable in several ways. We'll look at the one most likely to trip you up: hiding an instance variable by shadowing it with a local variable. Shadowing involves redeclaring a variable that's already been declared somewhere else.

The effect of shadowing is to hide the previously declared variable in such a way that it may look as though you're using the hidden variable, but you're actually using the shadowing variable. You might find reasons to shadow a variable intentionally, but typically it happens by accident and causes hard-to-find bugs. On the exam, you can expect to see questions where shadowing plays a role.

FROM THE CLASSROOM

You can shadow an instance variable by declaring a local variable of the same name, either directly or as part of an argument:

```
class Foo {
  static int size = 7;
  static void changeIt(int size) {
    size = size + 200;
    System.out.println("size in changeIt is " + size);
  }
  public static void main (String [] args) {
    Foo f = new Foo();
    System.out.println("size = " + size);
    changeIt(size);
    System.out.println("size after changeIt is " + size);
  }
}
```

The preceding code appears to change the size instance variable in the changeIt() method, but because changeIt() has a parameter named size, the local size variable is modified while the instance variable size is untouched. Running class Foo prints

```
%java Foo
size = 7
size in changeIt is 207
size after changeIt is 7
```

Things become more interesting when the shadowed variable is an object reference, rather than a primitive:

```
class Bar {
  int barNum = 28;
}
```

FROM THE CLASSROOM

```
class Foo {
  Bar myBar = new Bar();
  void changeIt(Bar myBar) {
    myBar.barNum = 99;
    System.out.println("myBar.barNum in changeIt is " + myBar.barNum);
    myBar = new Bar();
    myBar.barNum = 420;
    System.out.println("myBar.barNum in changeIt is now " + myBar.barNum);
  }
  public static void main (String [] args) {
    Foo f = new Foo();
    System.out.println("f.myBar.barNum is " + f.myBar.barNum);
    f.changeIt(f.myBar);
    System.out.println("f.myBar.barNum after changeIt is "
                       + f.myBar.barNum);
  }
}
```

The preceding code prints out this:

```
f.myBar.barNum is 28
myBar.barNum in changeIt is 99
myBar.barNum in changeIt is now 420
f.myBar.barNum after changeIt is 99
```

You can see that the shadowing variable (the local parameter myBar in changeIt()) can still affect the myBar instance variable, because the myBar parameter receives a reference to the same Bar object. But when the local myBar is reassigned a new Bar object, which we then modify by changing its barNum value, Foo's original myBar instance variable is untouched.

Declaring an Array (Exam Objective 1.3) **209**

CERTIFICATION OBJECTIVE

Array Declaration, Construction, and Initialization (Exam Objective 1.3)

1.3 Develop code that declares, initializes, and uses primitives, arrays, enums, and objects as static, instance, and local variables. Also, use legal identifiers for variable names.

Arrays are objects in Java that store multiple variables of the same type. Arrays can hold either primitives or object references, but the array itself will always be an object on the heap, even if the array is declared to hold primitive elements. In other words, there is no such thing as a primitive array, but you can make an array of primitives. For this objective, you need to know three things:

- How to make an array reference variable (declare)
- How to make an array object (construct)
- How to populate the array with elements (initialize)

There are several different ways to do each of those, and you need to know about all of them for the exam.

Arrays are efficient, but most of the time you'll want to use one of the Collection types from java.util (including HashMap, ArrayList, TreeSet). Collection classes offer more flexible ways to access an object (for insertion, deletion, and so on) and unlike arrays, can expand or contract dynamically as you add or remove elements (they're really managed arrays, since they use arrays behind the scenes). There's a Collection type for a wide range of needs. Do you need a fast sort? A group of objects with no duplicates? A way to access a name/value pair? A linked list? Chapter 7 covers them in more detail.

on the **Job**

Declaring an Array

Arrays are declared by stating the type of element the array will hold, which can be an object or a primitive, followed by square brackets to the left or right of the identifier.

Declaring an array of primitives:

```
int[] key;   // brackets before name (recommended)
int key [];  // brackets after name (legal but less readable)
             // spaces between the name and [] legal, but bad
```

Declaring an array of object references:

```
Thread[] threads;    // Recommended
Thread threads[];    // Legal but less readable
```

When declaring an array reference, you should always put the array brackets immediately after the declared type, rather than after the identifier (variable name). That way, anyone reading the code can easily tell that, for example, key is a reference to an int array object, and not an int primitive.

We can also declare multidimensional arrays, which are in fact arrays of arrays. This can be done in the following manner:

```
String[][][] occupantName;   // recommended
String[] ManagerName [];     // yucky, but legal
```

The first example is a three-dimensional array (an array of arrays of arrays) and the second is a two-dimensional array. Notice in the second example we have one square bracket before the variable name and one after. This is perfectly legal to the compiler, proving once again that just because it's legal doesn't mean it's right.

It is never legal to include the size of the array in your declaration. Yes, we know you can do that in some other languages, which is why you might see a question or two that include code similar to the following:

```
int[5] scores;
```

The preceding code won't make it past the compiler. Remember, the JVM doesn't allocate space until you actually instantiate the array object. That's when size matters.

Constructing an Array

Constructing an array means creating the array object on the *heap* (where all objects live)—i.e., doing a new on the array type. To create an array object, Java must know how much space to allocate on the heap, so you must specify the size of the array at creation time. The size of the array is the number of elements the array will hold.

Constructing One-Dimensional Arrays

The most straightforward way to construct an array is to use the keyword new followed by the array type, with a bracket specifying how many elements of that type the array will hold. The following is an example of constructing an array of type int:

```
int[] testScores;          // Declares the array of ints
testScores = new int[4]; // constructs an array and assigns it
                           // the testScores variable
```

The preceding code puts one new object on the heap—an array object holding four elements—with each element containing an int with a default value of 0. Think of this code as saying to the compiler, "Create an array object that will hold four ints, and assign it to the reference variable named testScores. Also, go ahead and set each int element to zero. Thanks." (The compiler appreciates good manners.) Figure 3-2 shows the testScores array on the heap, after construction.

FIGURE 3-2	

A one-dimensional array on the Heap

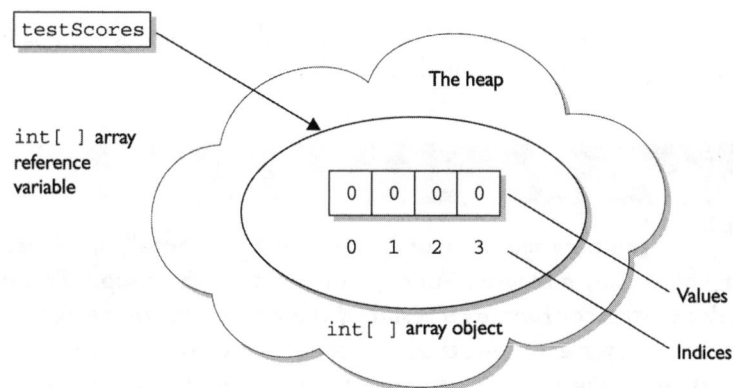

You can also declare and construct an array in one statement as follows:

```
int[] testScores = new int[4];
```

This single statement produces the same result as the two previous statements. Arrays of object types can be constructed in the same way:

```
Thread[] threads = new Thread[5];
```

Remember that—despite how the code appears—the Thread constructor is not being invoked. We're not creating a Thread instance, but rather a single Thread array object. After the preceding statement, there are still no actual Thread objects!

Think carefully about how many objects are on the heap after a code statement or block executes. The exam will expect you to know, for example, that the preceding code produces just one object (the array assigned to the reference variable named threads). The single object referenced by threads holds five Thread reference variables, but no Thread objects have been created or assigned to those references.

Remember, arrays must always be given a size at the time they are constructed. The JVM needs the size to allocate the appropriate space on the heap for the new array object. It is never legal, for example, to do the following:

```
int[] carList = new int[]; // Will not compile; needs a size
```

So don't do it, and if you see it on the test, run screaming toward the nearest answer marked "Compilation fails."

You may see the words "construct", "create", and "instantiate" used interchangeably. They all mean, "An object is built on the heap." This also implies that the object's constructor runs, as a result of the construct/create/instantiate code. You can say with certainty, for example, that any code that uses the keyword new, will (if it runs successfully) cause the class constructor and all superclass constructors to run.

In addition to being constructed with new, arrays can also be created using a kind of syntax shorthand that creates the array while simultaneously initializing the array elements to values supplied in code (as opposed to default values). We'll look at that in the next section. For now, understand that because of these syntax shortcuts, objects can still be created even without you ever using or seeing the keyword new.

Constructing Multidimensional Arrays

Multidimensional arrays, remember, are simply arrays of arrays. So a two-dimensional array of type int is really an object of type int array (int []), with each element in that array holding a reference to another int array. The second dimension holds the actual int primitives. The following code declares and constructs a two-dimensional array of type int:

```
int[][] myArray = new int[3][];
```

Notice that only the first brackets are given a size. That's acceptable in Java, since the JVM needs to know only the size of the object assigned to the variable myArray. Figure 3-3 shows how a two-dimensional int array works on the heap.

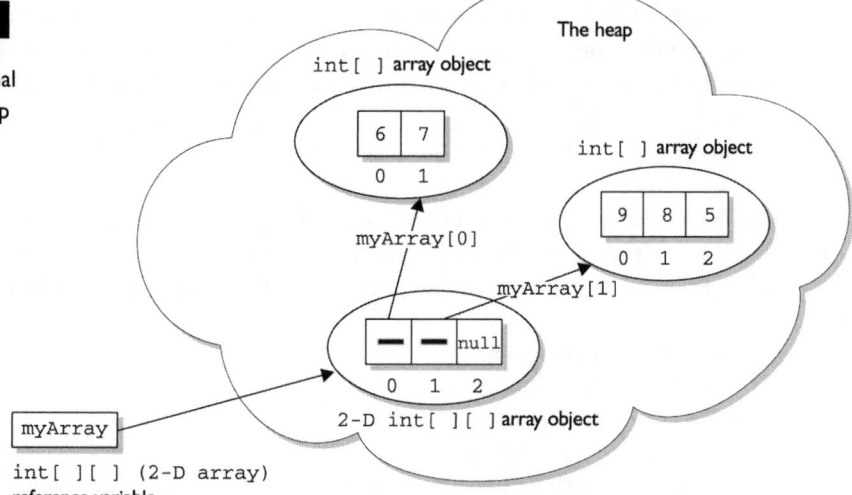

FIGURE 3-3

A two-dimensional array on the Heap

Picture demonstrates the result of the following code:

```
int[][] myArray = new int[3][];
myArray[0] = new int[2];
myArray[0][0] = 6;
myArray[0][1] = 7;
myArray[1] = new int[3];
myArray[1][0] = 9;
myArray[1][1] = 8;
myArray[1][2] = 5;
```

Initializing an Array

Initializing an array means putting things into it. The "things" in the array are the array's elements, and they're either primitive values (2, x, `false`, and so on), or objects referred to by the reference variables in the array. If you have an array of objects (as opposed to primitives), the array doesn't actually hold the objects, just as any other nonprimitive variable never actually holds the object, but instead holds a *reference* to the object. But we talk about arrays as, for example, "an array of five strings," even though what we really mean is, "an array of five references to String objects." Then the big question becomes whether or not those references are actually pointing (oops, this is Java, we mean referring) to real String objects, or are simply `null`. Remember, a reference that has not had an object assigned to it is a `null` reference. And if you try to actually use that `null` reference by, say, applying the dot operator to invoke a method on it, you'll get the infamous NullPointerException.

The individual elements in the array can be accessed with an index number. The index number always begins with zero, so for an array of ten objects the index numbers will run from 0 through 9. Suppose we create an array of three Animals as follows:

```
Animal [] pets = new Animal[3];
```

We have one array object on the heap, with three `null` references of type Animal, but we don't have any Animal objects. The next step is to create some Animal objects and assign them to index positions in the array referenced by `pets`:

```
pets[0] = new Animal();
pets[1] = new Animal();
pets[2] = new Animal();
```

This code puts three new Animal objects on the heap and assigns them to the three index positions (elements) in the `pets` array.

exam

ⓦatch
Look for code that tries to access an out-of-range array index. For example, if an array has three elements, trying to access the [3] element will raise an `ArrayIndexOutOfBoundsException`, because in an array of three elements, the legal index values are 0, 1, and 2. You also might see an attempt to use a negative number as an array index. The following are examples of legal and illegal array access attempts. Be sure to recognize that these cause runtime exceptions and not compiler errors!

Nearly all of the exam questions list both runtime exception and compiler error as possible answers.

```
int[] x = new int[5];
x[4] = 2; // OK, the last element is at index 4
x[5] = 3; // Runtime exception. There is no element at index
5!

int[] z = new int[2];
int y = -3;
z[y] = 4; // Runtime exception.; y is a negative number
```

These can be hard to spot in a complex loop, but that's where you're most likely to see array index problems in exam questions.

A two-dimensional array (an array of arrays) can be initialized as follows:

```
int[][] scores = new int[3][];
// Declare and create an array holding three references
// to int arrays

scores[0] = new int[4];
// the first element in the scores array is an int array
// of four int elements

scores[1] = new int[6];
// the second element in the scores array is an int array
// of six int elements

scores[2] = new int[1];
// the third element in the scores array is an int array
// of one int element
```

Initializing Elements in a Loop

Array objects have a single public variable, `length` that gives you the number of elements in the array. The last index value, then, is always one less than the `length`. For example, if the `length` of an array is 4, the index values are from 0 through 3. Often, you'll see array elements initialized in a loop as follows:

```
Dog[] myDogs = new Dog[6]; // creates an array of 6
                           // Dog references
for(int x = 0; x < myDogs.length; x++) {
    myDogs[x] = new Dog(); // assign a new Dog to the
                           // index position x
}
```

The `length` variable tells us how many elements the array holds, but it does not tell us whether those elements have been initialized. As we'll cover in Chapter 5, as of Java 5, we could have written the `for` loop without using the `length` variable:

```
for(Dog d : myDogs)
  d = new Dog();
```

Declaring, Constructing, and Initializing on One Line

You can use two different array-specific syntax shortcuts to both initialize (put explicit values into an array's elements) and construct (instantiate the array object itself) in a single statement. The first is used to declare, create, and initialize in one statement as follows:

```
1.  int x = 9;
2.  int[] dots = {6,x,8};
```

Line 2 in the preceding code does four things:

- Declares an `int` array reference variable named `dots`.
- Creates an `int` array with a length of three (three elements).
- Populates the array's elements with the values 6, 9, and 8.
- Assigns the new array object to the reference variable `dots`.

The size (length of the array) is determined by the number of comma-separated items between the curly braces. The code is functionally equivalent to the following longer code:

```
int[] dots;
dots = new int[3];
int x = 9;
dots[0] = 6;
dots[1] = x;
dots[2] = 8;
```

This begs the question, "Why would anyone use the longer way?" One reason come to mind. You might not know—at the time you create the array—the values that will be assigned to the array's elements. This array shortcut alone (combined with the stimulating prose) is worth the price of this book.

With object references rather than primitives, it works exactly the same way:

```
Dog puppy = new Dog("Frodo");
Dog[] myDogs = {puppy, new Dog("Clover"), new Dog("Aiko")};
```

The preceding code creates one Dog array, referenced by the variable myDogs, with a length of three elements. It assigns a previously created Dog object (assigned to the reference variable puppy) to the first element in the array. It also creates two new Dog objects (Clover and Aiko), and adds them to the last two Dog reference variable elements in the myDogs array. Figure 3-4 shows the result.

FIGURE 3-4

Declaring, constructing, and initializing an array of objects

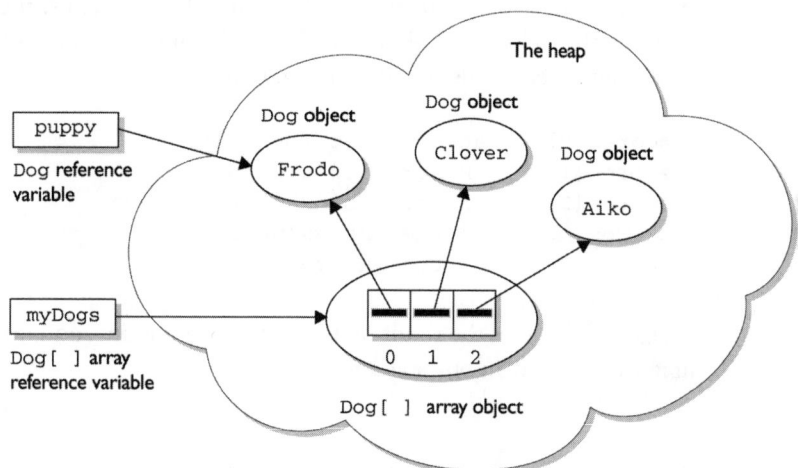

Picture demonstrates the result of the following code:

```
Dog puppy = new Dog("Frodo");
Dog[] myDogs = {puppy, new Dog("Clover"), new Dog("Aiko")};
```

Four objects are created:
1 Dog object referenced by puppy and by myDogs(0)
1 Dog[ ] array referenced by myDogs
2 Dog objects referenced by myDogs[1] and myDogs[2]

You can also use the shortcut syntax with multidimensional arrays, as follows:

```
int[][] scores = {{5,2,4,7}, {9,2}, {3,4}};
```

The preceding code creates a total of four objects on the heap. First, an array of int arrays is constructed (the object that will be assigned to the scores reference variable). The scores array has a length of three, derived from the number of items (comma-separated) between the outer curly braces. Each of the three elements in the scores array is a reference variable to an int array, so the three int arrays are constructed and assigned to the three elements in the scores array.

The size of each of the three int arrays is derived from the number of items within the corresponding inner curly braces. For example, the first array has a length of four, the second array has a length of two, and the third array has a length of two. So far, we have four objects: one array of int arrays (each element is a reference to an int array), and three int arrays (each element in the three int arrays is an int value). Finally, the three int arrays are initialized with the actual int values within the inner curly braces. Thus, the first int array contains the values 5, 2, 4, and 7. The following code shows the values of some of the elements in this two-dimensional array:

```
scores[0]     // an array of four ints
scores[1]     // an array of 2 ints
scores[2]     // an array of 2 ints
scores[0][1]  // the int value 2
scores[2][1]  // the int value 4
```

Figure 3-5 shows the result of declaring, constructing, and initializing a two-dimensional array in one statement.

Constructing and Initializing an Anonymous Array

The second shortcut is called "anonymous array creation" and can be used to construct and initialize an array, and then assign the array to a previously declared array reference variable:

```
int[] testScores;
testScores = new int[] {4,7,2};
```

Declaring, constructing, and initializing a two-dimensional array

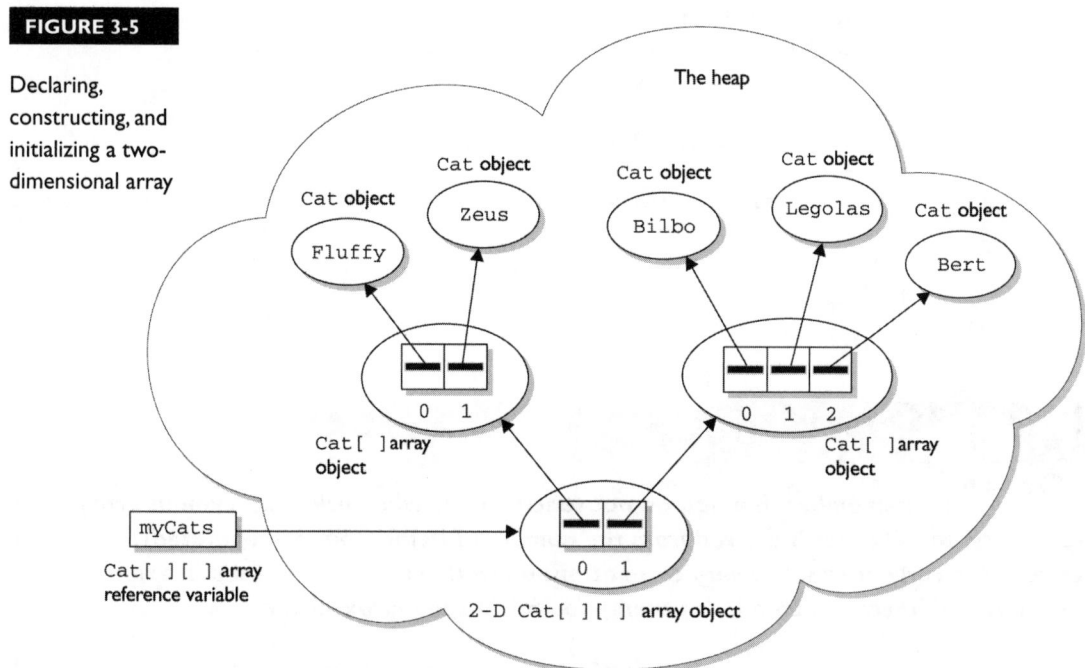

Picture demonstrates the result of the following code:

```
Cat[ ][ ] myCats = {{new Cat("Fluffy"), new Cat("Zeus")},
{new Cat("Bilbo"), new Cat("Legolas"), new Cat("Bert")}}
```

Eight objects are created:
1 2-D `Cat[ ][ ]` array object
2 `Cat[ ]` array objects
5 `Cat` objects

The preceding code creates a new `int` array with three elements, initializes the three elements with the values 4, 7, and 2, and then assigns the new array to the previously declared `int` array reference variable `testScores`. We call this anonymous array creation because with this syntax you don't even need to assign the new array to anything. Maybe you're wondering, "What good is an array if you don't assign it to a reference variable?" You can use it to create a just-in-time array to use, for example, as an argument to a method that takes an array parameter. The following code demonstrates a just-in-time array argument:

```
public class Foof {
  void takesAnArray(int []  someArray) {
    // use the array parameter
  }
  public static void main (String [] args) {
    Foof f = new Foof();
    f.takesAnArray(new int[] {7,7,8,2,5}); // we need an array
                                           // argument
  }
}
```

exam
watch

Remember that you do not specify a size when using anonymous array creation syntax. The size is derived from the number of items (comma-separated) between the curly braces. Pay very close attention to the array syntax used in exam questions (and there will be a lot of them). You might see syntax such as

```
new Object[3] {null, new Object(), new Object()};
// not legal;size must not be specified
```

Legal Array Element Assignments

What can you put in a particular array? For the exam, you need to know that arrays can have only one declared type (int [], Dog[], String [], and so on), but that doesn't necessarily mean that only objects or primitives of the declared type can be assigned to the array elements. And what about the array reference itself? What kind of array object can be assigned to a particular array reference? For the exam, you'll need to know the answers to all of these questions. And, as if by magic, we're actually covering those very same topics in the following sections. Pay attention.

Arrays of Primitives

Primitive arrays can accept any value that can be promoted implicitly to the declared type of the array. For example, an int array can hold any value that can fit into a 32-bit int variable. Thus, the following code is legal:

```
int[] weightList = new int[5];
byte b = 4;
char c = 'c';
short s = 7;
weightList[0] = b;   // OK, byte is smaller than int
weightlist[1] = c;   // OK, char is smaller than int
weightList[2] = s;   // OK, short is smaller than int
```

Arrays of Object References

If the declared array type is a class, you can put objects of any subclass of the declared type into the array. For example, if Subaru is a subclass of Car, you can put both Subaru objects and Car objects into an array of type Car as follows:

```
class Car {}
class Subaru extends Car {}
class Ferrari extends Car {}
...
Car [] myCars = {new Subaru(), new Car(), new Ferrari()};
```

It helps to remember that the elements in a Car array are nothing more than Car reference variables. So anything that can be assigned to a Car reference variable can be legally assigned to a Car array element.

If the array is declared as an interface type, the array elements can refer to any instance of any class that implements the declared interface. The following code demonstrates the use of an interface as an array type:

```
interface Sporty {
  void beSporty();
}

class Ferrari extends Car implements Sporty {
  public void beSporty() {
    // implement cool sporty method in a Ferrari-specific way
  }
}
class RacingFlats extends AthleticShoe implements Sporty {
  public void beSporty() {
    // implement cool sporty method in a RacingShoe-specific way
  }
```

```
    }
    class GolfClub { }
    class TestSportyThings {
      public static void main (String [] args) {
        Sporty[] sportyThings = new Sporty [3];
        sportyThings[0] = new Ferrari();        // OK, Ferrari
                                                // implements Sporty

        sportyThings[1] = new RacingFlats();    // OK, RacingFlats
                                                // implements Sporty

        sportyThings[2] = new GolfClub();

            // Not OK; GolfClub does not implement Sporty
            // I don't care what anyone says

      }
    }
```

The bottom line is this: any object that passes the "IS-A" test for the declared array type can be assigned to an element of that array.

Array Reference Assignments for One-Dimensional Arrays

For the exam, you need to recognize legal and illegal assignments for array reference variables. We're not talking about references in the array (in other words, array elements), but rather references to the array object. For example, if you declare an int array, the reference variable you declared can be reassigned to any int array (of any size), but cannot be reassigned to anything that is not an int array, including an int value. Remember, all arrays are objects, so an int array reference cannot refer to an int primitive. The following code demonstrates legal and illegal assignments for primitive arrays:

```
int[] splats;
int[] dats = new int[4];
char[] letters = new char[5];
splats = dats; // OK, dats refers to an int array
splats = letters; // NOT OK, letters refers to a char array
```

It's tempting to assume that because a variable of type byte, short, or char can be explicitly promoted and assigned to an int, an array of any of those types could be assigned to an int array. You can't do that in Java, but it would be just like those cruel, heartless (but otherwise attractive) exam developers to put tricky array assignment questions in the exam.

Arrays that hold object references, as opposed to primitives, aren't as restrictive. Just as you can put a Honda object in a Car array (because Honda extends Car), you can assign an array of type Honda to a Car array reference variable as follows:

```
Car[] cars;
Honda[] cuteCars = new Honda[5];
cars = cuteCars; // OK because Honda is a type of Car
Beer[] beers = new Beer [99];
cars = beers; // NOT OK, Beer is not a type of Car
```

Apply the IS-A test to help sort the legal from the illegal. Honda IS-A Car, so a Honda array can be assigned to a Car array. Beer IS-A Car is not true; Beer does not extend Car (plus it doesn't make sense, unless you've already had too much of it).

exam

ⓦatch
You cannot reverse the legal assignments. A Car array cannot be assigned to a Honda array. A Car is not necessarily a Honda, so if you've declared a Honda array, it might blow up if you assigned a Car array to the Honda reference variable. Think about it: a Car array could hold a reference to a Ferrari, so someone who thinks they have an array of Hondas could suddenly find themselves with a Ferrari. Remember that the IS-A test can be checked in code using the `instanceof` *operator.*

The rules for array assignment apply to interfaces as well as classes. An array declared as an interface type can reference an array of any type that implements the interface. Remember, any object from a class implementing a particular interface will pass the IS-A (`instanceof`) test for that interface. For example, if Box implements Foldable, the following is legal:

```
Foldable[] foldingThings;
Box[] boxThings = new Box[3];
foldingThings = boxThings;
// OK, Box implements Foldable, so Box IS-A Foldable
```

Array Reference Assignments for Multidimensional Arrays

When you assign an array to a previously declared array reference, the array you're assigning must be the same dimension as the reference you're assigning it to. For example, a two-dimensional array of int arrays cannot be assigned to a regular int array reference, as follows:

```
int[] blots;
int[][] squeegees = new int[3][];
blots = squeegees;          // NOT OK, squeegees is a
                            // two-d array of int arrays
int[] blocks = new int[6];
blots = blocks;             // OK, blocks is an int array
```

Pay particular attention to array assignments using different dimensions. You might, for example, be asked if it's legal to assign an int array to the first element in an array of int arrays, as follows:

```
int[][]  books = new int[3][];
int[] numbers = new int[6];
int aNumber = 7;
books[0] = aNumber;       // NO, expecting an int array not an int
books[0] = numbers;       // OK, numbers is an int array
```

Figure 3-6 shows an example of legal and illegal assignments for references to an array.

Initialization Blocks

We've talked about two places in a class where you can put code that performs operations: methods and constructors. Initialization blocks are the third place in a Java program where operations can be performed. Initialization blocks run when the class is first loaded (a static initialization block) or when an instance is created (an instance initialization block). Let's look at an example:

```
class SmallInit {
  static int x;
  int y;

  static { x = 7 ; }        // static init block
  { y = 8; }                // instance init block
}
```

FIGURE 3-6   Legal and illegal array assignments

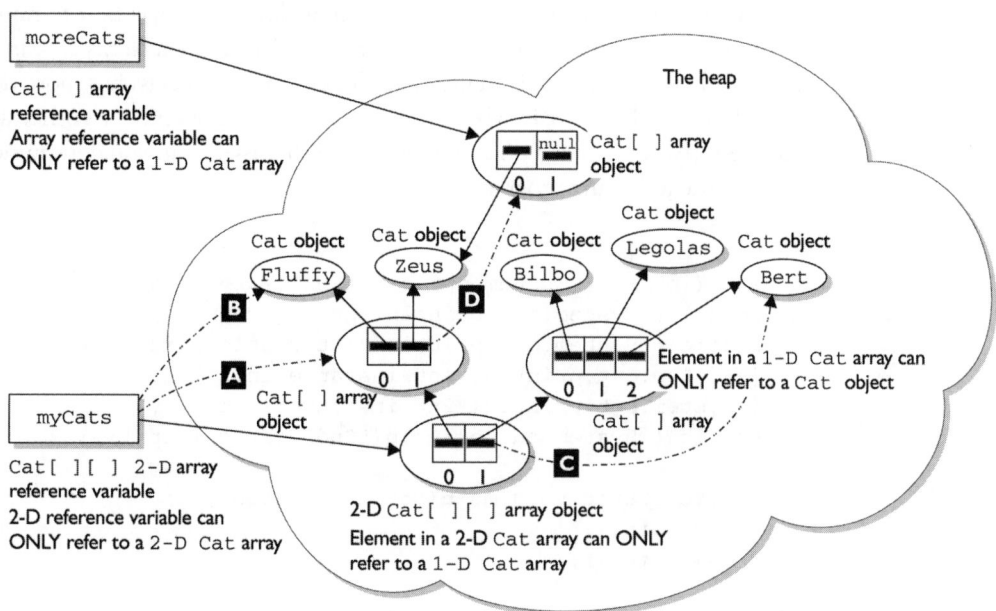

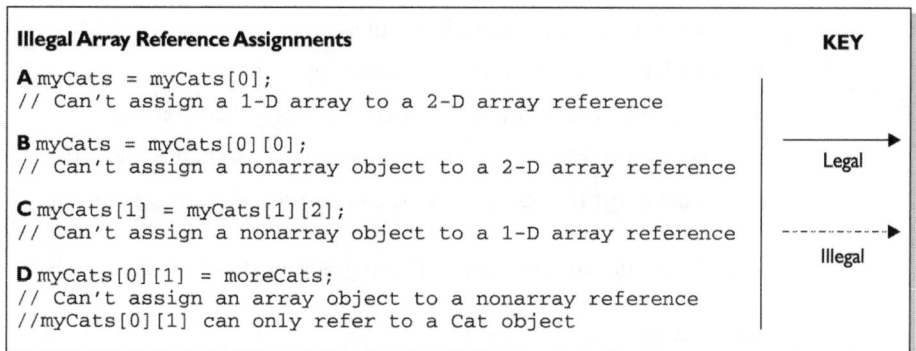

Illegal Array Reference Assignments   **KEY**

A myCats = myCats[0];
// Can't assign a 1-D array to a 2-D array reference

B myCats = myCats[0][0];   Legal
// Can't assign a nonarray object to a 2-D array reference

C myCats[1] = myCats[1][2];
// Can't assign a nonarray object to a 1-D array reference   Illegal

D myCats[0][1] = moreCats;
// Can't assign an array object to a nonarray reference
//myCats[0][1] can only refer to a Cat object

As you can see, the syntax for initialization blocks is pretty terse. They don't have names, they can't take arguments, and they don't return anything. A *static* initialization block runs *once*, when the class is first loaded. An *instance* initialization block runs once *every time a new instance is created*. Remember when we talked about the order in which constructor code executed? Instance init block code runs right after the call to super() in a constructor, in other words, after all super-constructors have run.

You can have many initialization blocks in a class. It is important to note that unlike methods or constructors, *the order in which initialization blocks appear in a class matters*. When it's time for initialization blocks to run, if a class has more than one, they will run in the order in which they appear in the class file...in other words, from the top down. Based on the rules we just discussed, can you determine the output of the following program?

```
class Init {
  Init(int x) { System.out.println("1-arg const"); }
  Init() { System.out.println("no-arg const"); }
  static { System.out.println("1st static init"); }
  { System.out.println("1st instance init"); }
  { System.out.println("2nd instance init"); }
  static { System.out.println("2nd static init"); }

  public static void main(String [] args) {
    new Init();
    new Init(7);
  }
}
```

To figure this out, remember these rules:

- Init blocks execute in the order they appear.
- Static init blocks run once, when the class is first loaded.
- Instance init blocks run every time a class instance is created.
- Instance init blocks run after the constructor's call to super().

With those rules in mind, the following output should make sense:

```
1st static init
2nd static init
1st instance init
2nd instance init
no-arg const
1st instance init
2nd instance init
1-arg const
```

As you can see, the instance init blocks each ran twice. Instance init blocks are often used as a place to put code that all the constructors in a class should share. That way, the code doesn't have to be duplicated across constructors.

Finally, if you make a mistake in your static init block, the JVM can throw an `ExceptionInIninitalizationError`. Let's look at an example,

```
class InitError {
  static int [] x = new int[4];
  static { x[4] = 5; }            // bad array index!
  public static void main(String [] args) { }
}
```

which produces something like:

```
Exception in thread "main" java.lang.ExceptionInInitializerError
Caused by: java.lang.ArrayIndexOutOfBoundsException: 4
        at InitError.<clinit>(InitError.java:3)
```

exam
watch

By convention, init blocks usually appear near the top of the class file, somewhere around the constructors. However, this is the SCJP exam we're talking about. Don't be surprised if you find an init block tucked in between a couple of methods, looking for all the world like a compiler error waiting to happen!

CERTIFICATION OBJECTIVE

Using Wrapper Classes and Boxing (Exam Objective 3.1)

3.1   Develop code that uses the primitive wrapper classes (such as Boolean, Character, Double, Integer, etc.), and/or autoboxing & unboxing. Discuss the differences between the String, StringBuilder, and StringBuffer classes.

The wrapper classes in the Java API serve two primary purposes:

- ■ To provide a mechanism to "wrap" primitive values in an object so that the primitives can be included in activities reserved for objects, like being added to Collections, or returned from a method with an object return value. Note: With Java 5's addition of autoboxing (and unboxing), which we'll get to in a few pages, many of the wrapping operations that programmers used to do manually are now handled automatically.

- ■ To provide an assortment of utility functions for primitives. Most of these functions are related to various conversions: converting primitives to and from String objects, and converting primitives and String objects to and from different bases (or radix), such as binary, octal, and hexadecimal.

An Overview of the Wrapper Classes

There is a wrapper class for every primitive in Java. For instance, the wrapper class for int is Integer, the class for float is Float, and so on. Remember that the primitive name is simply the lowercase name of the wrapper except for char, which maps to Character, and int, which maps to Integer. Table 3-2 lists the wrapper classes in the Java API.

TABLE 3-2	Wrapper Classes and Their Constructor Arguments	
Primitive	**Wrapper Class**	**Constructor Arguments**
boolean	Boolean	boolean or String
byte	Byte	byte or String
char	Character	char
double	Double	double or String
float	Float	float, double, or String
int	Integer	int or String
long	Long	long or String
short	Short	short or String

Creating Wrapper Objects

For the exam you need to understand the three most common approaches for creating wrapper objects. Some approaches take a String representation of a primitive as an argument. Those that take a String throw NumberFormatException if the String provided cannot be parsed into the appropriate primitive. For example "two" can't be parsed into "2". *Wrapper objects are immutable.* Once they have been given a value, that value cannot be changed. We'll talk more about wrapper immutability when we discuss boxing in a few pages.

The Wrapper Constructors

All of the wrapper classes except Character provide two constructors: one that takes a primitive of the type being constructed, and one that takes a String representation of the type being constructed—for example,

```
Integer i1 = new Integer(42);
Integer i2 = new Integer("42");
```

or

```
Float f1 = new Float(3.14f);
Float f2 = new Float("3.14f");
```

The Character class provides only one constructor, which takes a char as an argument—for example,

```
Character c1 = new Character('c');
```

The constructors for the Boolean wrapper take either a `boolean` value `true` or `false`, or a case-insensitive String with the value "true" or "false". Until Java 5, a Boolean object couldn't be used as an expression in a boolean test—for instance,

```
Boolean b = new Boolean("false");
if (b)      // won't compile, using Java 1.4 or earlier
```

As of Java 5, a Boolean object *can* be used in a boolean test, because the compiler will automatically "un-box" the Boolean to a `boolean`. We'll be focusing on Java 5's autoboxing capabilities in the very next section—so stay tuned!

The valueOf() Methods

The two (well, usually two) static `valueOf()` methods provided in most of the wrapper classes give you another approach to creating wrapper objects. Both methods take a String representation of the appropriate type of primitive as their first argument, the second method (when provided) takes an additional argument, `int radix`, which indicates in what base (for example binary, octal, or hexadecimal) the first argument is represented—for example,

```
Integer i2 = Integer.valueOf("101011", 2);   // converts 101011
                                              // to 43 and
                                              // assigns the value
                                              // 43 to the
                                              // Integer object i2
```

or

```
Float f2 = Float.valueOf("3.14f");    // assigns 3.14 to the
                                      // Float object f2
```

Using Wrapper Conversion Utilities

As we said earlier, a wrapper's second big function is converting stuff. The following methods are the most commonly used, and are the ones you're most likely to see on the test.

xxxValue()

When you need to convert the value of a wrapped numeric to a primitive, use one of the many `xxxValue()` methods. All of the methods in this family are no-arg methods. As you can see by referring to Table 3-3, there are 36 `xxxValue()` methods. Each of the six numeric wrapper classes has six methods, so that any numeric wrapper can be converted to any primitive numeric type—for example,

```
Integer i2 = new Integer(42);    //  make a new wrapper object
byte b = i2.byteValue();         //  convert i2's value to a byte
                                 //  primitive
short s = i2.shortValue();       //  another of Integer's xxxValue
                                 //  methods
double d = i2.doubleValue();     //  yet another of Integer's
                                 //  xxxValue methods
```

or

```
Float f2 = new Float(3.14f);    // make a new wrapper object
short s = f2.shortValue();      // convert f2's value to a short
                                // primitive
System.out.println(s);          // result is 3  (truncated, not
                                // rounded)
```

parseXxx() and valueOf()

The six `parseXxx()` methods (one for each numeric wrapper type) are closely related to the `valueOf()` method that exists in all of the numeric wrapper classes. Both `parseXxx()` and `valueOf()` take a String as an argument, throw a NumberFormatException (a.k.a. NFE) if the String argument is not properly formed, and can convert String objects from different bases (radix), when the underlying primitive type is any of the four integer types. (See Table 3-3.) The difference between the two methods is

- `parseXxx()` returns the named primitive.
- `valueOf()` returns a newly created wrapped object of the type that invoked the method.

Here are some examples of these methods in action:

```
double d4 = Double.parseDouble("3.14");   // convert a String
                                          // to a primitive
System.out.println("d4 = " + d4);         // result is d4 = 3.14

Double d5 = Double.valueOf("3.14");       // create a Double obj
System.out.println(d5 instanceof Double); // result is "true"
```

The next examples involve using the radix argument (in this case binary):

```
long L2 = Long.parseLong("101010", 2);    // binary String to a
                                          // primitive
System.out.println("L2 = " + L2);         // result is: L2 = 42

Long L3 = Long.valueOf("101010", 2);      // binary String to
                                          // Long object
System.out.println("L3 value = " + L3);   // result is:
                                          // L3 value = 42
```

toString()

Class Object, the alpha class, has a `toString()` method. Since we know that all other Java classes inherit from class Object, we also know that all other Java classes have a `toString()` method. The idea of the `toString()` method is to allow you to get some meaningful representation of a given object. For instance, if you have a Collection of various types of objects, you can loop through the Collection and print out some sort of meaningful representation of each object using the `toString()` method, which is guaranteed to be in every class. We'll talk more about `toString()` in the Collections chapter, but for now let's focus on how `toString()` relates to the wrapper classes which, as we know, are marked `final`. All of the wrapper classes have a no-arg, nonstatic, instance version of `toString()`. This method returns a String with the value of the primitive wrapped in the object—for instance,

```
Double d = new Double("3.14");
System.out.println("d = "+ d.toString() ); // result is d = 3.14
```

All of the numeric wrapper classes provide an overloaded, `static toString()` method that takes a primitive numeric of the appropriate type (`Double.toString()` takes a `double`, `Long.toString()` takes a `long`, and so on) and, of course, returns a String:

```
String d = Double.toString(3.14);      // d = "3.14"
```

Finally, Integer and Long provide a third toString() method. It's static, its first argument is the primitive, and its second argument is a radix. The radix tells the method to take the first argument, which is radix 10 (base 10) by default, and convert it to the radix provided, then return the result as a String—for instance,

```
String s = "hex = "+ Long.toString(254,16); // s = "hex = fe"
```

toXxxString() (Binary, Hexadecimal, Octal)

The Integer and Long wrapper classes let you convert numbers in base 10 to other bases. These conversion methods, `toXxxString()`, take an `int` or `long`, and return a String representation of the converted number, for example,

```
String s3 = Integer.toHexString(254);  // convert 254 to hex
System.out.println("254 is " + s3);    // result: "254 is fe"

String s4 = Long.toOctalString(254); // convert 254 to octal
System.out.print("254(oct) ="+ s4);  // result: "254(oct) =376"
```

Studying Table 3-3 is the single best way to prepare for this section of the test. If you can keep the differences between `xxxValue()`, `parseXxx()`, and `valueOf()` straight, you should do well on this part of the exam.

| **TABLE 3-3** | Common Wrapper Conversion Methods |

Method s = static n = NFE exception	**Boolean**	**Byte**	**Character**	**Double**	**Float**	**Integer**	**Long**	**Short**
byteValue		x		x	x	x	x	x
doubleValue		x		x	x	x	x	x
floatValue		x		x	x	x	x	x
intValue		x		x	x	x	x	x
longValue		x		x	x	x	x	x
shortValue		x		x	x	x	x	x
parseXxx s,n		x		x	x	x	x	x
parseXxx s,n (with radix)		x				x	x	x
valueOf s,n	x	x		x	x	x	x	x
valueOf s,n (with radix)		x				x	x	x
toString	x	x	x	x	x	x	x	x
toString s (primitive)	x	x	x	x	x	x	x	x
toString s (primitive, radix)						x	x	

In summary, the essential method signatures for Wrapper conversion methods are

    primitive xxxValue()   – to convert a Wrapper to a primitive

    primitive parseXxx(String)   – to convert a String to a primitive

    Wrapper valueOf(String)   – to convert a String to a Wrapper

Autoboxing

New to Java 5 is a feature known variously as: autoboxing, auto-unboxing, boxing, and unboxing. We'll stick with the terms boxing and unboxing. Boxing and unboxing make using wrapper classes more convenient. In the old, pre–Java 5 days, if you wanted to make a wrapper, unwrap it, use it, and then rewrap it, you might do something like this:

```
Integer y = new Integer(567);    // make it
int x = y.intValue();            // unwrap it
x++;                             // use it
y = new Integer(x);              // re-wrap it
System.out.println("y = " + i);  // print it
```

Now, with new and improved Java 5 you can say

```
Integer y = new Integer(567);    // make it
y++;                             // unwrap it, increment it,
                                 // rewrap it
System.out.println("y = " + i);  // print it
```

Both examples produce the output:

```
y = 568
```

And yes, you read that correctly. The code appears to be using the post-increment operator on an object reference variable! But it's simply a convenience. Behind the scenes, the compiler does the unboxing and reassignment for you. Earlier we mentioned that wrapper objects are immutable... this example appears to contradict that statement. It sure looks like y's value changed from 567 to 568. What actually happened, is that a second wrapper object was created and its value was set to 568. If only we could access that first wrapper object, we could prove it...

Let's try this:

```
Integer y = 567;                 // make a wrapper
Integer x = y;                   // assign a second ref
                                 // var to THE wrapper

System.out.println(y==x);        // verify that they refer
                                 // to the same object
```

```
y++;                                // unwrap, use, "rewrap"
System.out.println(x + " " + y);    // print values

System.out.println(y==x);           // verify that they refer
                                    // to different objects
```

Which produces the output:

```
true
567 568
false
```

So, under the covers, when the compiler got to the line i++; it had to substitute something like this:

```
int x2 = y.intValue();              // unwrap it
x2++;                               // use it
y = new Integer(x2);                // re-wrap it
```

Just as we suspected, there's gotta be a call to new in there somewhere.

Boxing, ==, and equals()

We just used == to do a little exploration of wrappers. Let's take a more thorough look at how wrappers work with ==, !=, and equals(). We'll talk a lot more about the equals() method in later chapters. For now all we have to know is that the intention of the equals() method is to determine whether two instances of a given class are "meaningfully equivalent." This definition is intentionally subjective; it's up to the creator of the class to determine what "equivalent" means for objects of the class in question. The API developers decided that for all the wrapper classes, two objects are equal if they are of the same type and have the same value. It shouldn't be surprising that

```
Integer i1 = 1000;
Integer i2 = 1000;
if(i1 != i2) System.out.println("different objects");
if(i1.equals(i2)) System.out.println("meaningfully equal");
```

Produces the output:

```
different objects
meaningfully equal
```

It's just two wrapper objects that happen to have the same value. Because they have the same `int` value, the `equals()` method considers them to be "meaningfully equivalent", and therefore returns `true`. How about this one:

```
Integer i3 = 10;
Integer i4 = 10;
if(i3 == i4) System.out.println("same object");
if(i3.equals(i4)) System.out.println("meaningfully equal");
```

This example produces the output:

```
same object
meaningfully equal
```

Yikes! The `equals()` method seems to be working, but what happened with `==` and `!=` ? Why is `!=` telling us that `i1` and `i2` are different objects, when `==` is saying that `i3` and `i4` are the same object? In order to save memory, two instances of the following wrapper objects will always be `==` when their primitive values are the same:

- ■ `Boolean`
- ■ `Byte`
- ■ `Character` from `\u0000` to `\u007f`   (7f is 127 in decimal)
- ■ `Short` and `Integer` from -128 to 127

Where Boxing Can Be Used

As we discussed earlier, it's very common to use wrappers in conjunction with collections. Any time you want your collection to hold objects and primitives, you'll want to use wrappers to make those primitives collection-compatible. The general rule is that boxing and unboxing work wherever you can normally use a primitive or a wrapped object. The following code demonstrates some legal ways to use boxing:

```
class UseBoxing {
  public static void main(String [] args) {
    UseBoxing u = new UseBoxing();
    u.go(5);
  }

  boolean go(Integer i) {      // boxes the int it was passed
    Boolean ifSo = true;       // boxes the literal
    Short s = 300;             // boxes the primitive
```

```
        if(ifSo) {                      // unboxing
          System.out.println(++s);      // unboxes, increments, reboxes
        }
        return !ifSo;                   // unboxes, returns the inverse
      }
    }
```

exam
watch

Remember, wrapper reference variables can be null. That means that you have to watch out for code that appears to be doing safe primitive operations, but that could throw a `NullPointerException`:

```
class Boxing2 {
  static Integer x;
  public static void main(String [] args) {
    doStuff(x);
  }
  static void doStuff(int z) {
    int z2 = 5;
    System.out.println(z2 + z);
  } }
```

This code compiles fine, but the JVM throws a `NullPointerException` when it attempts to invoke `doStuff(x)`, because `x` doesn't refer to an `Integer` object, so there's no value to unbox.

CERTIFICATION OBJECTIVE

Overloading (Exam Objectives 1.5 and 5.4)

1.5   Given a code example, determine if a method is correctly overriding or overloading another method, and identify legal return values (including covariant returns), for the method.

5.4   Given a scenario, develop code that declares and/or invokes overridden or overloaded methods...

Overloading Made Hard—Method Matching

Although we covered some rules for overloading methods in Chapter 2, in this chapter we've added some new tools to our Java toolkit. In this section we're going to take a look at three factors that can make overloading a little tricky:

- Widening
- Autoboxing
- Var-args

When a class has overloaded methods, one of the compiler's jobs is to determine which method to use whenever it finds an invocation for the overloaded method. Let's look at an example that doesn't use any new Java 5 features:

```
class EasyOver {
  static void go(int x) { System.out.print("int "); }
  static void go(long x) { System.out.print("long "); }
  static void go(double x) { System.out.print("double "); }

  public static void main(String [] args) {
    byte b = 5;
    short s = 5;
    long l = 5;
    float f = 5.0f;

    go(b);
    go(s);
    go(l);
    go(f);
  }
}
```

Which produces the output:

```
int int long double
```

This probably isn't much of a surprise; the calls that use `byte` and the `short` arguments are implicitly widened to match the version of the `go()` method that takes an `int`. Of course, the call with the `long` uses the long version of `go()`, and finally, the call that uses a `float` is matched to the method that takes a `double`.

In every case, when an exact match isn't found, the JVM uses the method with the smallest argument that is wider than the parameter.

You can verify for yourself that if there is only one version of the go() method, and it takes a double, it will be used to match all four invocations of go().

Overloading with Boxing and Var-args

Now let's take our last example, and add *boxing* into the mix:

```
class AddBoxing {
  static void go(Integer x) { System.out.println("Integer"); }
  static void go(long x) { System.out.println("long"); }

  public static void main(String [] args) {
    int i = 5;
    go(i);             // which go() will be invoked?
  }
}
```

As we've seen earlier, if the only version of the go() method was one that took an Integer, then Java 5's boxing capability would allow the invocation of go() to succeed. Likewise, if only the long version existed, the compiler would use it to handle the go() invocation. The question is, given that both methods exist, which one will be used? In other words, does the compiler think that widening a primitive parameter is more desirable than performing an autoboxing operation? The answer is that the compiler will choose widening over boxing, so the output will be

```
long
```

Java 5's designers decided that the most important rule should be that pre-existing code should function the way it used to, so since widening capability already existed, a method that is invoked via widening shouldn't lose out to a newly created method that relies on boxing. Based on that rule, try to predict the output of the following:

```
class AddVarargs {
  static void go(int x, int y) { System.out.println("int,int");}
  static void go(byte... x) { System.out.println("byte... "); }
  public static void main(String[] args) {
    byte b = 5;
    go(b,b);           // which go() will be invoked?
  }
}
```

As you probably guessed, the output is

```
int,int
```

Because, once again, even though each invocation will require some sort of conversion, the compiler will choose the older style before it chooses the newer style, keeping existing code more robust. So far we've seen that

- Widening beats boxing
- Widening beats var-args

At this point, inquiring minds want to know, does boxing beat var-args?

```
class BoxOrVararg {
  static void go(Byte x, Byte y)
                 { System.out.println("Byte, Byte"); }
  static void go(byte... x) { System.out.println("byte... "); }

  public static void main(String [] args) {
    byte b = 5;
    go(b,b);            // which go() will be invoked?
  }
}
```

As it turns out, the output is

```
Byte, Byte
```

A good way to remember this rule is to notice that the var-args method is "looser" than the other method, in that it could handle invocations with any number of `int` parameters. A var-args method is more like a catch-all method, in terms of what invocations it can handle, and as we'll see in Chapter 5, it makes most sense for catch-all capabilities to be used as a *last resort*.

Widening Reference Variables

We've seen that it's legal to widen a primitive. Can you widen a reference variable, and if so, what would it mean? Let's think back to our favorite polymorphic assignment:

```
Animal a = new Dog();
```

Along the same lines, an invocation might be:

```
class Animal {static void eat() { } }

class Dog3 extends Animal {
  public static void main(String[] args) {
    Dog3 d = new Dog3();
    d.go(d);                    // is this legal ?
  }
  void go(Animal a) { }
}
```

No problem! The `go()` method needs an Animal, and `Dog3` IS-A Animal. (Remember, the `go()` method thinks it's getting an Animal object, so it will only ask it to do Animal things, which of course anything that inherits from Animal can do.) So, in this case, the compiler widens the `Dog3` reference to an Animal, and the invocation succeeds. The key point here is that reference widening depends on inheritance, in other words the IS-A test. Because of this, it's not legal to widen from one wrapper class to another, because the wrapper classes are peers to one another. For instance, it's NOT valid to say that Short IS-A Integer.

Overloading When Combining Widening and Boxing

We've looked at the rules that apply when the compiler can match an invocation to a method by performing a single conversion. Now let's take a look at what happens when more than one conversion is required. In this case the compiler will have to widen and then autobox the parameter for a match to be made:

```
class WidenAndBox {
  static void go(Long x) { System.out.println("Long"); }

  public static void main(String [] args) {
    byte b = 5;
    go(b);                // must widen then box - illegal
  }
}
```

This is just too much for the compiler:

```
WidenAndBox.java:6: go(java.lang.Long) in WidenAndBox cannot be
applied to (byte)
```

Strangely enough, it IS possible for the compiler to perform a boxing operation followed by a widening operation in order to match an invocation to a method. This one might blow your mind:

```
class BoxAndWiden {
  static void go(Object o) {
    Byte b2 = (Byte) o;      // ok - it's a Byte object
    System.out.println(b2);
  }

  public static void main(String [] args) {
    byte b = 5;
    go(b);         // can this byte turn into an Object ?
  }
}
```

This compiles (!), and produces the output:

5

Wow! Here's what happened under the covers when the compiler, then the JVM, got to the line that invokes the `go()` method:

1. The `byte b` was boxed to a Byte.

2. The Byte reference was widened to an Object (since Byte extends Object).

3. The `go()` method got an Object reference that actually refers to a Byte object.

4. The `go()` method cast the Object reference back to a Byte reference (re member, there was never an object of type Object in this scenario, only an object of type Byte!).

5. The `go()` method printed the Byte's value.

Why didn't the compiler try to use the box-then-widen logic when it tried to deal with the WidenAndBox class? Think about it...if it tried to box first, the byte would have been converted to a Byte. Now we're back to trying to widen a Byte to a Long, and of course, the IS-A test fails.

Overloading in Combination with Var-args

What happens when we attempt to combine var-args with either widening or boxing in a method-matching scenario? Let's take a look:

```
class Vararg {
  static void wide_vararg(long... x)
                { System.out.println("long..."); }
  static void box_vararg(Integer... x)
                { System.out.println("Integer..."); }
  public static void main(String [] args) {
    int i = 5;
    wide_vararg(5,5);    // needs to widen and use var-args
    box_vararg(5,5);     // needs to box and use var-args
  }
}
```

This compiles and produces:

```
long...
Integer...
```

As we can see, you can successfully combine var-args with either widening or boxing. Here's a review of the rules for overloading methods using widening, boxing, and var-args:

- Primitive widening uses the "smallest" method argument possible.
- Used individually, boxing and var-args are compatible with overloading.
- You CANNOT widen from one wrapper type to another. (IS-A fails.)
- You CANNOT widen and then box. (An int can't become a Long.)
- You can box and then widen. (An int can become an Object, via Integer.)
- You can combine var-args with either widening or boxing.

There are more tricky aspects to overloading, but other than a few rules concerning generics (which we'll cover in Chapter 7), this is all you'll need to know for the exam. Phew!

CERTIFICATION OBJECTIVE

Garbage Collection (Exam Objective 7.4)

7.4 Given a code example, recognize the point at which an object becomes eligible for garbage collection, and determine what is and is not guaranteed by the garbage collection system. Recognize the behaviors of System.gc and finalization.

Overview of Memory Management and Garbage Collection

This is the section you've been waiting for! It's finally time to dig into the wonderful world of memory management and garbage collection.

Memory management is a crucial element in many types of applications. Consider a program that reads in large amounts of data, say from somewhere else on a network, and then writes that data into a database on a hard drive. A typical design would be to read the data into some sort of collection in memory, perform some operations on the data, and then write the data into the database. After the data is written into the database, the collection that stored the data temporarily must be emptied of old data or deleted and re-created before processing the next batch. This operation might be performed thousands of times, and in languages like C or C++ that do not offer automatic garbage collection, a small flaw in the logic that manually empties or deletes the collection data structures can allow small amounts of memory to be improperly reclaimed or lost. Forever. These small losses are called memory leaks, and over many thousands of iterations they can make enough memory inaccessible that programs will eventually crash. Creating code that performs manual memory management cleanly and thoroughly is a nontrivial and complex task, and while estimates vary, it is arguable that manual memory management can double the development effort for a complex program.

Java's garbage collector provides an automatic solution to memory management. In most cases it frees you from having to add any memory management logic to your application. The downside to automatic garbage collection is that you can't completely control when it runs and when it doesn't.

Overview of Java's Garbage Collector

Let's look at what we mean when we talk about garbage collection in the land of Java. From the 30,000 ft. level, garbage collection is the phrase used to describe automatic memory management in Java. Whenever a software program executes (in Java, C, C++, Lisp, Ruby, and so on), it uses memory in several different ways. We're not going to get into Computer Science 101 here, but it's typical for memory to be used to create a stack, a heap, in Java's case constant pools, and method areas. The heap is that part of memory where Java objects live, and it's the one and only part of memory that is in any way involved in the garbage collection process.

> *A heap is a heap is a heap. For the exam it's important to know that you can call it the heap, you can call it the garbage collectible heap, or you can call it Johnson, but there is one and only one heap.*

So, all of garbage collection revolves around making sure that the heap has as much free space as possible. For the purpose of the exam, what this boils down to is deleting any objects that are no longer reachable by the Java program running. We'll talk more about what reachable means, but let's drill this point in. When the garbage collector runs, its purpose is to find and delete objects that cannot be reached. If you think of a Java program as being in a constant cycle of creating the objects it needs (which occupy space on the heap), and then discarding them when they're no longer needed, creating new objects, discarding them, and so on, the missing piece of the puzzle is the garbage collector. When it runs, it looks for those discarded objects and deletes them from memory so that the cycle of using memory and releasing it can continue. Ah, the great circle of life.

When Does the Garbage Collector Run?

The garbage collector is under the control of the JVM. The JVM decides when to run the garbage collector. From within your Java program you can ask the JVM to run the garbage collector, but there are no guarantees, under any circumstances, that the JVM will comply. Left to its own devices, the JVM will typically run the garbage collector when it senses that memory is running low. Experience indicates that when your Java program makes a request for garbage collection, the JVM will usually grant your request in short order, but there are no guarantees. Just when you think you can count on it, the JVM will decide to ignore your request.

How Does the Garbage Collector Work?

You just can't be sure. You might hear that the garbage collector uses a mark and sweep algorithm, and for any given Java implementation that might be true, but the Java specification doesn't guarantee any particular implementation. You might hear that the garbage collector uses reference counting; once again maybe yes maybe no. The important concept to understand for the exam is when does an object become eligible for garbage collection? To answer this question fully, we have to jump ahead a little bit and talk about threads. (See Chapter 9 for the real scoop on threads.) In a nutshell, every Java program has from one to many threads. Each thread has its own little execution stack. Normally, you (the programmer) cause at least one thread to run in a Java program, the one with the `main()` method at the bottom of the stack. However, as you'll learn in excruciating detail in Chapter 9, there are many really cool reasons to launch additional threads from your initial thread. In addition to having its own little execution stack, each thread has its own lifecycle. For now, all we need to know is that threads can be alive or dead. With this background information, we can now say with stunning clarity and resolve that *an object is eligible for garbage collection when no live thread can access it.* (Note: Due to the vagaries of the String constant pool, the exam focuses its garbage collection questions on non-String objects, and so our garbage collection discussions apply to only non-String objects too.)

Based on that definition, the garbage collector does some magical, unknown operations, and when it discovers an object that can't be reached by any live thread, it will consider that object as eligible for deletion, and it might even delete it at some point. (You guessed it; it also might not ever delete it.) When we talk about reaching an object, we're really talking about having a reachable reference variable that refers to the object in question. If our Java program has a reference variable that refers to an object, and that reference variable is available to a live thread, then that object is considered reachable. We'll talk more about how objects can become unreachable in the following section.

Can a Java application run out of memory? Yes. The garbage collection system attempts to remove objects from memory when they are not used. However, if you maintain too many live objects (objects referenced from other live objects), the system can run out of memory. Garbage collection cannot ensure that there is enough memory, only that the memory that is available will be managed as efficiently as possible.

Writing Code That Explicitly Makes Objects Eligible for Collection

In the preceding section, we learned the theories behind Java garbage collection. In this section, we show how to make objects eligible for garbage collection using actual code. We also discuss how to attempt to force garbage collection if it is necessary, and how you can perform additional cleanup on objects before they are removed from memory.

Nulling a Reference

As we discussed earlier, an object becomes eligible for garbage collection when there are no more reachable references to it. Obviously, if there are no reachable references, it doesn't matter what happens to the object. For our purposes it is just floating in space, unused, inaccessible, and no longer needed.

The first way to remove a reference to an object is to set the reference variable that refers to the object to `null`. Examine the following code:

```
1. public class GarbageTruck {
2.   public static void main(String [] args) {
3.     StringBuffer sb = new StringBuffer("hello");
4.     System.out.println(sb);
5.     // The StringBuffer object is not eligible for collection
6.     sb = null;
7.     // Now the StringBuffer object is eligible for collection
8.   }
9. }
```

The StringBuffer object with the value `hello` is assigned to the reference variable sb in the third line. To make the object eligible (for GC), we set the reference variable sb to `null`, which removes the single reference that existed to the

StringBuffer object. Once line 6 has run, our happy little `hello` StringBuffer object is doomed, eligible for garbage collection.

Reassigning a Reference Variable

We can also decouple a reference variable from an object by setting the reference variable to refer to another object. Examine the following code:

```
class GarbageTruck {
   public static void main(String [] args) {
      StringBuffer s1 = new StringBuffer("hello");
      StringBuffer s2 = new StringBuffer("goodbye");
      System.out.println(s1);
      // At this point the StringBuffer "hello" is not eligible
      s1 = s2; // Redirects s1 to refer to the "goodbye" object
      // Now the StringBuffer "hello" is eligible for collection
   }
}
```

Objects that are created in a method also need to be considered. When a method is invoked, any local variables created exist only for the duration of the method. Once the method has returned, the objects created in the method are eligible for garbage collection. There is an obvious exception, however. If an object is returned from the method, its reference might be assigned to a reference variable in the method that called it; hence, it will not be eligible for collection. Examine the following code:

```
import java.util.Date;
public class GarbageFactory {
   public static void main(String [] args) {
      Date d = getDate();
      doComplicatedStuff();
      System.out.println("d = " + d);
   }

   public static Date getDate() {
      Date d2 = new Date();
      StringBuffer now = new StringBuffer(d2.toString());
      System.out.println(now);
      return d2;
   }
}
```

In the preceding example, we created a method called `getDate()` that returns a Date object. This method creates two objects: a Date and a StringBuffer containing the date information. Since the method returns the Date object, it will not be eligible for collection even after the method has completed. The StringBuffer object, though, will be eligible, even though we didn't explicitly set the `now` variable to `null`.

Isolating a Reference

There is another way in which objects can become eligible for garbage collection, even if they still have valid references! We call this scenario "islands of isolation."

A simple example is a class that has an instance variable that is a reference variable to another instance of the same class. Now imagine that two such instances exist and that they refer to each other. If all other references to these two objects are removed, then even though each object still has a valid reference, there will be no way for any live thread to access either object. When the garbage collector runs, it can *usually* discover any such islands of objects and remove them. As you can imagine, such islands can become quite large, theoretically containing hundreds of objects. Examine the following code:

```
public class Island {
  Island i;
  public static void main(String [] args) {

    Island i2 = new Island();
    Island i3 = new Island();
    Island i4 = new Island();

    i2.i = i3;   // i2 refers to i3
    i3.i = i4;   // i3 refers to i4
    i4.i = i2;   // i4 refers to i2

    i2 = null;
    i3 = null;
    i4 = null;

    // do complicated, memory intensive stuff
  }
}
```

When the code reaches `// do complicated`, the three Island objects (previously known as `i2`, `i3`, and `i4`) have instance variables so that they refer to each other, but their links to the outside world (i2, i3, and i4) have been nulled. These three objects are eligible for garbage collection.

This covers everything you will need to know about making objects eligible for garbage collection. Study Figure 3-7 to reinforce the concepts of objects without references and islands of isolation.

Forcing Garbage Collection

The first thing that should be mentioned here is that, contrary to this section's title, garbage collection cannot be forced. However, Java provides some methods that allow you to request that the JVM perform garbage collection. For example, if you are about to perform some time-sensitive operations, you probably want to minimize the chances of a delay caused by garbage collection. But you must remember that the methods that Java provides are requests, and not demands; the virtual machine will do its best to do what you ask, but there is no guarantee that it will comply.

| FIGURE 3-7 | "Island" objects eligible for garbage collection |

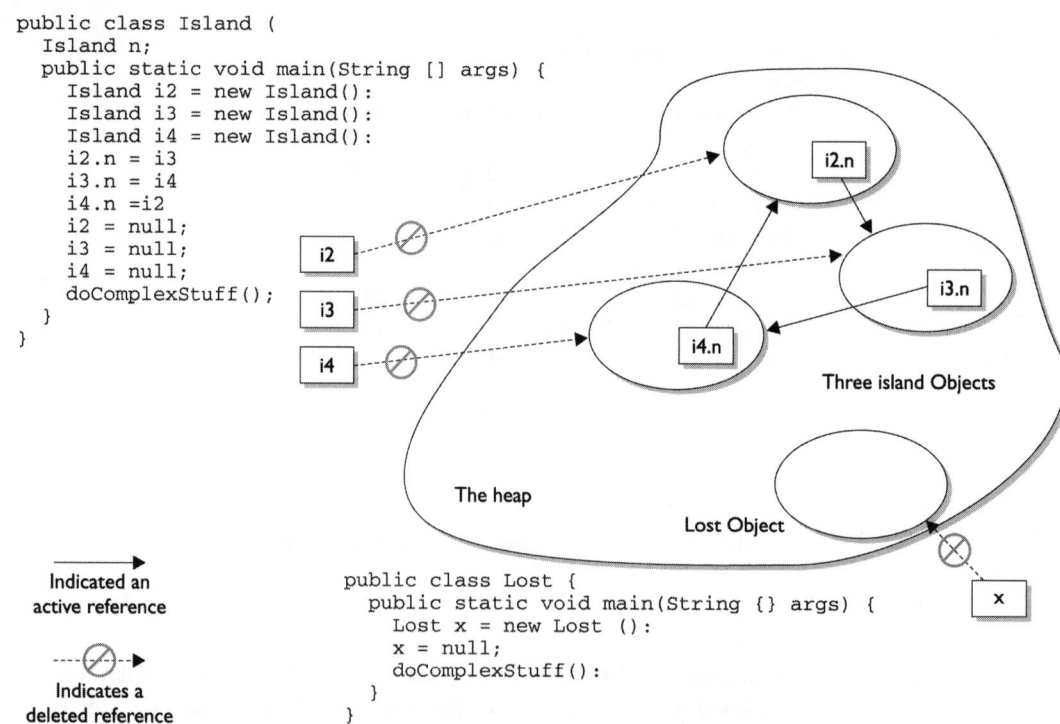

```
public class Island {
  Island n;
  public static void main(String [] args) {
    Island i2 = new Island():
    Island i3 = new Island():
    Island i4 = new Island():
    i2.n = i3
    i3.n = i4
    i4.n =i2
    i2 = null;
    i3 = null;
    i4 = null;
    doComplexStuff();
  }
}
```

Three island Objects

The heap

Lost Object

Indicated an
active reference

Indicates a
deleted reference

```
public class Lost {
  public static void main(String {} args) {
    Lost x = new Lost ():
    x = null;
    doComplexStuff():
  }
}
```

In reality, it is possible only to suggest to the JVM that it perform garbage collection. However, there are no guarantees the JVM will actually remove all of the unused objects from memory (even if garbage collection is run). It is essential that you understand this concept for the exam.

The garbage collection routines that Java provides are members of the Runtime class. The Runtime class is a special class that has a single object (a Singleton) for each main program. The Runtime object provides a mechanism for communicating directly with the virtual machine. To get the Runtime instance, you can use the method Runtime.getRuntime(), which returns the Singleton. Once you have the Singleton you can invoke the garbage collector using the gc() method. Alternatively, you can call the same method on the System class, which has static methods that can do the work of obtaining the Singleton for you. The simplest way to ask for garbage collection (remember—just a request) is

```
System.gc();
```

Theoretically, after calling `System.gc()`, you will have as much free memory as possible. We say theoretically because this routine does not always work that way. First, your JVM may not have implemented this routine; the language specification allows this routine to do nothing at all. Second, another thread (again, see the Chapter 9) might grab lots of memory right after you run the garbage collector.

This is not to say that `System.gc()` is a useless method—it's much better than nothing. You just can't rely on `System.gc()` to free up enough memory so that you don't have to worry about running out of memory. The Certification Exam is interested in guaranteed behavior, not probable behavior.

Now that we are somewhat familiar with how this works, let's do a little experiment to see if we can see the effects of garbage collection. The following program lets us know how much total memory the JVM has available to it and how much free memory it has. It then creates 10,000 Date objects. After this, it tells us how much memory is left and then calls the garbage collector (which, if it decides to run, should halt the program until all unused objects are removed). The final free memory result should indicate whether it has run. Let's look at the program:

```
1.   import java.util.Date;
2.   public class CheckGC {
3.      public static void main(String [] args) {
4.         Runtime rt = Runtime.getRuntime();
5.         System.out.println("Total JVM memory: "
                              + rt.totalMemory());
```

```
6.          System.out.println("Before Memory = "
                            + rt.freeMemory());
7.          Date d = null;
8.          for(int i = 0;i<10000;i++) {
9.              d = new Date();
10.             d = null;
11.         }
12.         System.out.println("After Memory = "
                            + rt.freeMemory());
13.         rt.gc();    // an alternate to System.gc()
14.         System.out.println("After GC Memory = "
                            + rt.freeMemory());
15.     }
16.  }
```

Now, let's run the program and check the results:

```
Total JVM memory: 1048568
Before Memory = 703008
After Memory = 458048
After GC Memory = 818272
```

As we can see, the JVM actually did decide to garbage collect (i.e., delete) the eligible objects. In the preceding example, we suggested to the JVM to perform garbage collection with 458,048 bytes of memory remaining, and it honored our request. This program has only one user thread running, so there was nothing else going on when we called rt.gc(). Keep in mind that the behavior when gc() is called may be different for different JVMs, so there is no guarantee that the unused objects will be removed from memory. About the only thing you can guarantee is that if you are running very low on memory, the garbage collector will run before it throws an OutOfMemoryException.

EXERCISE 3-2

Try changing the CheckGC program by putting lines 13 and 14 inside a loop. You might see that not all memory is released on any given run of the GC.

Cleaning Up Before Garbage Collection—the finalize() Method

Java provides you a mechanism to run some code just before your object is deleted by the garbage collector. This code is located in a method named `finalize()` that all classes inherit from class Object. On the surface this sounds like a great idea; maybe your object opened up some resources, and you'd like to close them before your object is deleted. The problem is that, as you may have gathered by now, you can't count on the garbage collector to ever delete an object. So, any code that you put into your class's overridden `finalize()` method is not guaranteed to run. The `finalize()` method for any given object might run, but you can't count on it, so don't put any essential code into your `finalize()` method. In fact, we recommend that in general you don't override `finalize()` at all.

Tricky Little finalize() Gotcha's

There are a couple of concepts concerning `finalize()` that you need to remember.

- For any given object, `finalize()` will be called only once (at most) by the garbage collector.
- Calling `finalize()` can actually result in saving an object from deletion.

Let's look into these statements a little further. First of all, remember that any code that you can put into a normal method you can put into `finalize()`. For example, in the `finalize()` method you could write code that passes a reference to the object in question back to another object, effectively *uneligiblizing* the object for garbage collection. If at some point later on this same object becomes eligible for garbage collection again, the garbage collector can still process this object and delete it. The garbage collector, however, will remember that, for this object, `finalize()` already ran, and it will not run `finalize()` again.

CERTIFICATION SUMMARY

This was a monster chapter! Don't worry if you find that you have to review some of these topics as you get into later chapters. This chapter has a lot of foundation stuff that will come into play later.

We started the chapter by reviewing the stack and the heap; remember local variables live on the stack, and instance variables live with their objects on the heap.

We reviewed legal literals for primitives and Strings, then we discussed the basics of assigning values to primitives and reference variables, and the rules for casting primitives.

Next we discussed the concept of scope, or "How long will this variable live?" Remember the four basic scopes, in order of lessening life span: static, instance, local, block.

We covered the implications of using uninitialized variables, and the importance of the fact that local variables MUST be assigned a value explicitly. We talked about some of the tricky aspects of assigning one reference variable to another, and some of the finer points of passing variables into methods, including a discussion of "shadowing."

The next topic was creating arrays, where we talked about declaring, constructing, and initializing one-, and multi-dimensional arrays. We talked about anonymous arrays, and arrays of references.

Next we reviewed static and instance initialization blocks, what they look like, and when they are called.

Phew!

We continued the chapter with a discussion of the wrapper classes; used to create immutable objects that hold a primitive, and also used to provide conversion capabilities for primitives: remember valueOf(), xxxValue(), and parseXxx().

Closely related to wrappers, we talked about a big new feature in Java 5, autoboxing. Boxing is a way to automate the use of wrappers, and we covered some of its trickier aspects such as how wrappers work with == and the equals() method.

Having added boxing to our toolbox, it was time to take a closer look at method overloading and how boxing and var-args, in conjunction with widening conversions, make overloading more complicated.

Finally, we dove into garbage collection, Java's automatic memory management feature. We learned that the heap is where objects live and where all the cool garbage collection activity takes place. We learned that in the end, the JVM will perform garbage collection whenever it wants to. You (the programmer) can request a garbage collection run, but you can't force it. We talked about garbage collection only applying to objects that are eligible, and that eligible means "inaccessible from any live thread." Finally, we discussed the rarely useful finalize() method, and what you'll have to know about it for the exam. All in all, one fascinating chapter.

✓ TWO-MINUTE DRILL

Here are some of the key points from this chapter.

Stack and Heap

- ❑ Local variables (method variables) live on the stack.
- ❑ Objects and their instance variables live on the heap.

Literals and Primitive Casting (Objective 1.3)

- ❑ Integer literals can be decimal, octal (e.g. 013), or hexadecimal (e.g. 0x3d).
- ❑ Literals for longs end in L or l.
- ❑ Float literals end in F or f, double literals end in a digit or D or d.
- ❑ The boolean literals are true and false.
- ❑ Literals for chars are a single character inside single quotes: 'd'.

Scope (Objectives 1.3 and 7.6)

- ❑ Scope refers to the lifetime of a variable.
- ❑ There are four basic scopes:
  - ❑ Static variables live basically as long as their class lives.
  - ❑ Instance variables live as long as their object lives.
  - ❑ Local variables live as long as their method is on the stack; however, if their method invokes another method, they are temporarily unavailable.
  - ❑ Block variables (e.g., in a for or an if) live until the block completes.

Basic Assignments (Objectives 1.3 and 7.6)

- ❑ Literal integers are implicitly ints.
- ❑ Integer expressions always result in an int-sized result, never smaller.
- ❑ Floating-point numbers are implicitly doubles (64 bits).
- ❑ Narrowing a primitive truncates the *high order* bits.
- ❑ Compound assignments (e.g. +=), perform an automatic cast.
- ❑ A reference variable holds the bits that are used to refer to an object.
- ❑ Reference variables can refer to subclasses of the declared type but not to superclasses.

❑ When creating a new object, e.g., `Button b = new Button();`, three things happen:
   ❑ Make a reference variable named b, of type Button
   ❑ Create a new Button object
   ❑ Assign the Button object to the reference variable b

Using a Variable or Array Element That Is Uninitialized and Unassigned (Objectives 1.3 and 7.6)

❑ When an array of objects is instantiated, objects within the array are not instantiated automatically, but all the references get the default value of null.

❑ When an array of primitives is instantiated, elements get default values.

❑ Instance variables are always initialized with a default value.

❑ Local/automatic/method variables are never given a default value. If you attempt to use one before initializing it, you'll get a compiler error.

Passing Variables into Methods (Objective 7.3)

❑ Methods can take primitives and/or object references as arguments.

❑ Method arguments are always copies.

❑ Method arguments are never actual objects (they can be references to objects).

❑ A primitive argument is an unattached copy of the original primitive.

❑ A reference argument is another copy of a reference to the original object.

❑ Shadowing occurs when two variables with different scopes share the same name. This leads to hard-to-find bugs, and hard-to-answer exam questions.

Array Declaration, Construction, and Initialization (Obj. 1.3)

❑ Arrays can hold primitives or objects, but the array itself is always an object.

❑ When you declare an array, the brackets can be left or right of the name.

❑ It is never legal to include the size of an array in the declaration.

❑ You must include the size of an array when you construct it (using new) unless you are creating an anonymous array.

❑ Elements in an array of objects are not automatically created, although primitive array elements are given default values.

❑ You'll get a NullPointerException if you try to use an array element in an object array, if that element does not refer to a real object.

- ❑ Arrays are indexed beginning with zero.
- ❑ An ArrayIndexOutOfBoundsException occurs if you use a bad index value.
- ❑ Arrays have a `length` variable whose value is the number of array elements.
- ❑ The last index you can access is always one less than the length of the array.
- ❑ Multidimensional arrays are just arrays of arrays.
- ❑ The dimensions in a multidimensional array can have different lengths.
- ❑ An array of primitives can accept any value that can be promoted implicitly to the array's declared type;. e.g., a `byte` variable can go in an `int` array.
- ❑ An array of objects can hold any object that passes the IS-A (or instanceof) test for the declared type of the array. For example, if Horse extends Animal, then a Horse object can go into an Animal array.
- ❑ If you assign an array to a previously declared array reference, the array you're assigning must be the same dimension as the reference you're assigning it to.
- ❑ You can assign an array of one type to a previously declared array reference of one of its supertypes. For example, a Honda array can be assigned to an array declared as type Car (assuming Honda extends Car).

Initialization Blocks (Objectives 1.3 and 7.6)

- ❑ Static initialization blocks run once, when the class is first loaded.
- ❑ Instance initialization blocks run every time a new instance is created. They run after all super-constructors and before the constructor's code has run.
- ❑ If multiple init blocks exist in a class, they follow the rules stated above, AND they run in the order in which they appear in the source file.

Using Wrappers (Objective 3.1)

- ❑ The wrapper classes correlate to the primitive types.
- ❑ Wrappers have two main functions:
  - ❑ To wrap primitives so that they can be handled like objects
  - ❑ To provide utility methods for primitives (usually conversions)
- ❑ The three most important method families are
  - ❑ `xxxValue()` Takes no arguments, returns a primitive
  - ❑ `parseXxx()` Takes a String, returns a primitive, throws NFE
  - ❑ `valueOf()` Takes a String, returns a wrapped object, throws NFE

❑ Wrapper constructors can take a String or a primitive, except for Character, which can only take a `char`.

❑ Radix refers to bases (typically) other than 10; octal is radix = 8, hex = 16.

Boxing (Objective 3.1)

❑ As of Java 5, boxing allows you to convert primitives to wrappers or to convert wrappers to primitives automatically.

❑ Using == with wrappers is tricky; wrappers with the same small values (typically lower than 127), will be ==, larger values will not be ==.

Advanced Overloading (Objectives 1.5 and 5.4)

❑ Primitive widening uses the "smallest" method argument possible.

❑ Used individually, boxing and var-args are compatible with overloading.

❑ You CANNOT widen from one wrapper type to another. (IS-A fails.)

❑ You CANNOT widen and then box. (An `int` can't become a Long.)

❑ You can box and then widen. (An `int` can become an Object, via an Integer.)

❑ You can combine var-args with either widening or boxing.

Garbage Collection (Objective 7.4)

❑ In Java, garbage collection (GC) provides automated memory management.

❑ The purpose of GC is to delete objects that can't be reached.

❑ Only the JVM decides when to run the GC, you can only suggest it.

❑ You can't know the GC algorithm for sure.

❑ Objects must be considered eligible before they can be garbage collected.

❑ An object is eligible when no live thread can reach it.

❑ To reach an object, you must have a live, reachable reference to that object.

❑ Java applications can run out of memory.

❑ Islands of objects can be GCed, even though they refer to each other.

❑ Request garbage collection with `System.gc();` (recommended).

❑ Class Object has a `finalize()` method.

❑ The `finalize()` method is guaranteed to run once and only once before the garbage collector deletes an object.

❑ The garbage collector makes no guarantees, `finalize()` may never run.

❑ You can uneligibilize an object for GC from within `finalize()`.

SELF TEST

I. Given:

```
class Scoop {
    static int thrower() throws Exception { return 42; }
    public static void main(String [] args) {
        try {
            int x = thrower();
        } catch (Exception e) {
            x++;
        } finally {
            System.out.println("x = " + ++x);
        }
    } } }
```

What is the result?

A. x = 42

B. x = 43

C. x = 44

D. Compilation fails.

E. The code runs with no output.

2. Given:

```
class CardBoard {
    Short story = 5;
    CardBoard go(CardBoard cb) {
        cb = null;
        return cb;
    }
    public static void main(String[] args) {
        CardBoard c1 = new CardBoard();
        CardBoard c2 = new CardBoard();
        CardBoard c3 = c1.go(c2);
        c1 = null;
        // do Stuff
    } }
```

When // doStuff is reached, how many objects are eligible for GC?

A. 0

B. 1

C. 2

D. Compilation fails.

E. It is not possible to know.

F. An exception is thrown at runtime.

3. Given:

```
class Alien {
  String invade(short ships) { return "a few"; }
  String invade(short... ships) { return "many"; }
}
class Defender {
  public static void main(String [] args) {
    System.out.println(new Alien().invade(7));
  }
}
```

What is the result?

A. many

B. a few

C. Compilation fails.

D. The output is not predictable.

E. An exception is thrown at runtime.

4. Given:

```
1. class Dims {
2.   public static void main(String[] args) {
3.     int[][] a = {{1,2,}, {3,4}};
4.     int[] b = (int[]) a[1];
5.     Object o1 = a;
6.     int[][] a2 = (int[][]) o1;
7.     int[] b2 = (int[]) o1;
8.     System.out.println(b[1]);
9. } }
```

What is the result?

A. 2

B. 4

C. An exception is thrown at runtime.

D. Compilation fails due to an error on line 4.

E. Compilation fails due to an error on line 5.

F. Compilation fails due to an error on line 6.

G. Compilation fails due to an error on line 7.

5. Given:

```
class Eggs {
  int doX(Long x, Long y) { return 1; }
  int doX(long... x) { return 2; }
  int doX(Integer x, Integer y) { return 3; }
  int doX(Number n, Number m) { return 4; }
  public static void main(String[] args) {
    new Eggs().go();
  }
  void go() {
    short s = 7;
    System.out.print(doX(s,s) + " ");
    System.out.println(doX(7,7));
  } }
```

What is the result?

- **A.** 1 1
- **B.** 2 1
- **C.** 3 1
- **D.** 4 1
- **E.** 2 3
- **F.** 3 3
- **G.** 4 3

6. Given:

```
class Mixer {
  Mixer() { }
  Mixer(Mixer m) { m1 = m; }
  Mixer m1;
  public static void main(String[] args) {
    Mixer m2 = new Mixer();
    Mixer m3 = new Mixer(m2);   m3.go();
    Mixer m4 = m3.m1;           m4.go();
    Mixer m5 = m2.m1;           m5.go();
  }
  void go() { System.out.print("hi "); }
}
```

What is the result?

- **A.** hi
- **B.** hi hi
- **C.** hi hi hi
- **D.** Compilation fails
- **E.** hi, followed by an exception
- **F.** hi hi, followed by an exception

7. Given:

```
1. class Zippy {
2.    String[] x;
3.    int[] a [] = {{1,2}, {1}};
4.    Object c = new long[4];
5.    Object[] d = x;
6. }
```

What is the result?

A. Compilation succeeds.

B. Compilation fails due only to an error on line 3.

C. Compilation fails due only to an error on line 4.

D. Compilation fails due only to an error on line 5.

E. Compilation fails due to errors on lines 3 and 5.

F. Compilation fails due to errors on lines 3, 4, and 5.

8. Given:

```
class Fizz {
   int x = 5;
   public static void main(String[] args) {
      final Fizz f1 = new Fizz();
      Fizz f2 = new Fizz();
      Fizz f3 = FizzSwitch(f1,f2);
      System.out.println((f1 == f3) + " " + (f1.x == f3.x));
   }
   static Fizz FizzSwitch(Fizz x, Fizz y) {
      final Fizz z = x;
      z.x = 6;
      return z;
   }
} }
```

What is the result?

A. `true true`

B. `false true`

C. `true false`

D. `false false`

E. Compilation fails.

F. An exception is thrown at runtime.

9. Given:

```
class Knowing {
   static final long tooth = 343L;
   static long doIt(long tooth) {
      System.out.print(++tooth + " ");
```

```
      return ++tooth;
    }
    public static void main(String[] args) {
      System.out.print(tooth + " ");
      final long tooth = 340L;
      new Knowing().doIt(tooth);
      System.out.println(tooth);
    }
  }
```

What is the result?

A. 343 340 340

B. 343 340 342

C. 343 341 342

D. 343 341 340

E. 343 341 343

F. Compilation fails.

G. An exception is thrown at runtime.

10. Which is true? (Choose all that apply.)

A. The invocation of an object's `finalize()` method is always the last thing that happens before an object is garbage collected (GCed).

B. When a stack variable goes out of scope it is eligible for GC.

C. Some reference variables live on the stack, and some live on the heap.

D. Only objects that have no reference variables referring to them can be eligible for GC.

E. It's possible to request the GC via methods in either `java.lang.Runtime` or `java.lang.System` classes.

11. Given:

```
1. class Convert {
2.   public static void main(String[] args) {
3.     Long xL = new Long(456L);
4.     long x1 = Long.valueOf("123");
5.     Long x2 = Long.valueOf("123");
6.     long x3 = xL.longValue();
7.     Long x4 = xL.longValue();
8.     Long x5 = Long.parseLong("456");
9.     long x6 = Long.parseLong("123");
10.   }
11. }
```

Which will compile using Java 5, but will NOT compile using Java 1.4? (Choose all that apply.)

A. Line 4

B. Line 5

C. Line 6

D. Line 7

E. Line 8

F. Line 9

12. Given:

```
1. class Eco {
2.   public static void main(String[] args) {
3.     Eco e1 = new Eco();
4.     Eco e2 = new Eco();
5.     Eco e3 = new Eco();
6.     e3.e = e2;
7.     e1.e = e3;
8.     e2 = null;
9.     e3 = null;
10.    e2.e = e1;
11.    e1 = null;
12.  }
13.  Eco e;
14. }
```

At what point is only a single object eligible for GC?

A. After line 8 runs.

B. After line 9 runs.

C. After line 10 runs.

D. After line 11 runs.

E. Compilation fails.

F. Never in this program.

G. An exception is thrown at runtime.

13. Given:

```
1. class Bigger {
2.   public static void main(String[] args) {
3.     // insert code here
4.   }
5. }
6. class Better {
7.   enum Faster {Higher, Longer};
8. }
```

Which, inserted independently at line 3, will compile? (Choose all that apply.)

A. `Faster f = Faster.Higher;`

B. `Faster f = Better.Faster.Higher;`

C. `Better.Faster f = Better.Faster.Higher;`

D. `Bigger.Faster f = Bigger.Faster.Higher;`

E. `Better.Faster f2;   f2 = Better.Faster.Longer;`

F. `Better b;   b.Faster = f3;   f3 = Better.Faster.Longer;`

14. Given:
```
class Bird {
  { System.out.print("b1 "); }
  public Bird() { System.out.print("b2 "); }
}
class Raptor extends Bird {
  static { System.out.print("r1 "); }
  public Raptor() { System.out.print("r2 "); }
  { System.out.print("r3 "); }
  static { System.out.print("r4 "); }
}
class Hawk extends Raptor {
  public static void main(String[] args) {
    System.out.print("pre ");
    new Hawk();
    System.out.println("hawk ");
  }
}
```

What is the result?

A. `pre b1 b2 r3 r2 hawk`

B. `pre b2 b1 r2 r3 hawk`

C. `pre b2 b1 r2 r3 hawk r1 r4`

D. `r1 r4 pre b1 b2 r3 r2 hawk`

E. `r1 r4 pre b2 b1 r2 r3 hawk`

F. `pre r1 r4 b1 b2 r3 r2 hawk`

G. `pre r1 r4 b2 b1 r2 r3 hawk`

H. The order of output cannot be predicted.

I. Compilation fails.

SELF TEST ANSWERS

1. Given:

```
class Scoop {
  static int thrower() throws Exception { return 42; }
  public static void main(String [] args) {
    try {
      int x = thrower();
    } catch (Exception e) {
      x++;
    } finally {
      System.out.println("x = " + ++x);
    } } }
```

What is the result?

A. x = 42

B. x = 43

C. x = 44

D. Compilation fails.

E. The code runs with no output.

Answer:

☑ **D** is correct, the variable x is only in scope within the try code block, it's not in scope in the catch or finally blocks. (For the exam, get used to those horrible closing } } } .)

☒ **A, B, C,** and **E** are incorrect based on the above. (Objective 1.3)

2. Given:

```
class CardBoard {
  Short story = 5;
  CardBoard go(CardBoard cb) {
    cb = null;
    return cb;
  }
  public static void main(String[] args) {
    CardBoard c1 = new CardBoard();
    CardBoard c2 = new CardBoard();
    CardBoard c3 = c1.go(c2);
    c1 = null;
    // do Stuff
  } }
```

When // doStuff is reached, how many objects are eligible for GC?

A. 0

B. 1

C. 2

D. Compilation fails.

E. It is not possible to know.

F. An exception is thrown at runtime.

Answer:

☑ **C** is correct. Only one `CardBoard object (c1)` is eligible, but it has an associated Short wrapper object that is also eligible.

☒ **A, B, D, E,** and **F** are incorrect based on the above. (Objective 7.4)

3. Given:

```
class Alien {
  String invade(short ships) { return "a few"; }
  String invade(short... ships) { return "many"; }
}
class Defender {
  public static void main(String [] args) {
    System.out.println(new Alien().invade(7));
} }
```

What is the result?

A. `many`

B. `a few`

C. Compilation fails.

D. The output is not predictable.

E. An exception is thrown at runtime.

Answer:

☑ **C** is correct, compilation fails. The var-args declaration is fine, but `invade` takes a `short`, so the argument 7 needs to be cast to a `short`. With the cast, the answer is **B**, 'a few'.

☒ **A, B, D,** and **E** are incorrect based on the above. (Objective 1.3)

4. Given:

```
1. class Dims {
2.   public static void main(String[] args) {
3.     int[][] a = {{1,2,}, {3,4}};
4.     int[] b = (int[]) a[1];
5.     Object o1 = a;
6.     int[][] a2 = (int[][]) o1;
7.     int[] b2 = (int[]) o1;
8.     System.out.println(b[1]);
9. } }
```

What is the result?

A. 2

B. 4

C. An exception is thrown at runtime

D. Compilation fails due to an error on line 4.

E. Compilation fails due to an error on line 5.

F. Compilation fails due to an error on line 6.

G. Compilation fails due to an error on line 7.

Answer:

☑ **C** is correct. A `ClassCastException` is thrown at line 7 because o1 refers to an int [] [] not an int []. If line 7 was removed, the output would be 4.

☒ **A, B, D, E, F,** and **G** are incorrect based on the above. (Objective 1.3)

5. Given:

```
class Eggs {
  int doX(Long x, Long y) { return 1; }
  int doX(long... x) { return 2; }
  int doX(Integer x, Integer y) { return 3; }
  int doX(Number n, Number m) { return 4; }
  public static void main(String[] args) {
    new Eggs().go();
  }
  void go() {
    short s = 7;
    System.out.print(doX(s,s) + " ");
    System.out.println(doX(7,7));
  } }
```

What is the result?

A. 1 1

B. 2 1

C. 3 1

D. 4 1

E. 2 3

F. 3 3

G. 4 3

Answer:

☑ **G** is correct. Two rules apply to the first invocation of doX(). You can't widen and then box in one step, and var-args are always chosen last. Therefore you can't widen shorts to either ints or longs, and then box them to Integers or Longs. But you can box shorts to Shorts and then widen them to Numbers, and this takes priority over using a var-args method. The second invocation uses a simple box from int to Integer.

☒ **A, B, C, D, E,** and **F** are incorrect based on the above. (Objective 3.1)

6. Given:

```
class Mixer {
  Mixer() { }
  Mixer(Mixer m) { m1 = m; }
  Mixer m1;
  public static void main(String[] args) {
    Mixer m2 = new Mixer();
    Mixer m3 = new Mixer(m2);  m3.go();
    Mixer m4 = m3.m1;          m4.go();
    Mixer m5 = m2.m1;          m5.go();
  }
  void go() { System.out.print("hi "); }
}
```

What is the result?

A. hi

B. hi hi

C. hi hi hi

D. Compilation fails

E. hi, followed by an exception

F. hi hi, followed by an exception

Answer:

☑ **F** is correct. The m2 object's m1 instance variable is never initialized, so when m5 tries to use it a NullPointerException is thrown.

☒ **A, B, C, D,** and **E** are incorrect based on the above. (Objective 7.3)

7. Given:

```
1. class Zippy {
2.   String[] x;
3.   int[] a [] = {{1,2}, {1}};
4.   Object c = new long[4];
5.   Object[] d = x;
6. }
```

What is the result?

A. Compilation succeeds.

B. Compilation fails due only to an error on line 3.

C. Compilation fails due only to an error on line 4.

D. Compilation fails due only to an error on line 5.

E. Compilation fails due to errors on lines 3 and 5.

F. Compilation fails due to errors on lines 3, 4, and 5.

Answer:

☑ **A** is correct, all of these array declarations are legal. Lines 4 and 5 demonstrate that arrays can be cast.

☒ **B, C, D, E,** and **F** are incorrect because this code compiles. (Objective 1.3)

8. Given:

```
class Fizz {
  int x = 5;
  public static void main(String[] args) {
    final Fizz f1 = new Fizz();
    Fizz f2 = new Fizz();
    Fizz f3 = FizzSwitch(f1,f2);
    System.out.println((f1 == f3) + " " + (f1.x == f3.x));
  }
  static Fizz FizzSwitch(Fizz x, Fizz y) {
    final Fizz z = x;
    z.x = 6;
    return z;
  } }
```

What is the result?

A. true true

B. false true

C. true false

D. false false

E. Compilation fails.

F. An exception is thrown at runtime.

Answer:

☑ **A** is correct. The references f1, z, and f3 all refer to the same instance of Fizz. The final modifier assures that a reference variable cannot be referred to a different object, but final doesn't keep the object's state from changing.

☒ **B, C, D, E,** and **F** are incorrect based on the above. (Objective 7.3)

9. Given:

```
class Knowing {
  static final long tooth = 343L;
  static long doIt(long tooth) {
    System.out.print(++tooth + " ");
```

```
        return ++tooth;
    }
    public static void main(String[] args) {
        System.out.print(tooth + " ");
        final long tooth = 340L;
        new Knowing().doIt(tooth);
        System.out.println(tooth);
    } }
```

What is the result?

- **A.** 343 340 340
- **B.** 343 340 342
- **C.** 343 341 342
- **D.** 343 341 340
- **E.** 343 341 343
- **F.** Compilation fails.
- **G.** An exception is thrown at runtime.

Answer:

☑ **D** is correct. There are three different `long` variables named tooth. Remember that you can apply the `final` modifier to local variables, but in this case the 2 versions of `tooth` marked `final` are not changed. The only `tooth` whose value changes is the one not marked `final`. This program demonstrates a bad practice known as shadowing.

☒ **A, B, C, E, F,** and **G** are incorrect based on the above. (Objective 7.3)

10. Which is true? (Choose all that apply.)

- **A.** The invocation of an object's `finalize()` method is always the last thing that happens before an object is garbage collected (GCed).
- **B.** When a stack variable goes out of scope it is eligible for GC.
- **C.** Some reference variables live on the stack, and some live on the `heap`.
- **D.** Only objects that have no reference variables referring to them can be eligible for GC.
- **E.** It's possible to request the GC via methods in either `java.lang.Runtime` or `java.lang.System` classes.

Answer:

☑ **C** and **E** are correct. When an object has a reference variable, the reference variable lives inside the object, on the heap.

☒ **A** is incorrect, because if, the first time an object's `finalize()` method runs, the object is saved from the GC, then the second time that object is about to be GCed, `finalize()` will not run. **B** is incorrect—stack variables are not dealt with by the GC. **D** is incorrect because objects can live in "islands of isolation" and be GC eligible. (Objective 7.4)

11. Given:

```
1. class Convert {
2.   public static void main(String[] args) {
3.     Long xL = new Long(456L);
4.     long x1 = Long.valueOf("123");
5.     Long x2 = Long.valueOf("123");
6.     long x3 = xL.longValue();
7.     Long x4 = xL.longValue();
8.     Long x5 = Long.parseLong("456");
9.     long x6 = Long.parseLong("123");
10.   }
11. }
```

Which will compile using Java 5, but will NOT compile using Java 1.4? (Choose all that apply.)

A. Line 4.

B. Line 5.

C. Line 6.

D. Line 7.

E. Line 8.

F. Line 9.

Answer:

☑ **A, D,** and **E** are correct. Because of the methods' return types, these method calls required autoboxing to compile.

☒ **B, C,** and **F** are incorrect based on the above. (Objective 3.1)

12. Given:

```
1. class Eco {
2.   public static void main(String[] args) {
3.     Eco e1 = new Eco();
4.     Eco e2 = new Eco();
5.     Eco e3 = new Eco();
6.     e3.e = e2;
7.     e1.e = e3;
8.     e2 = null;
9.     e3 = null;
10.    e2.e = e1;
11.    e1 = null;
12.  }
13.  Eco e;
14. }
```

At what point is only a single object eligible for GC?

A. After line 8 runs.

B. After line 9 runs.

C. After line 10 runs.

D. After line 11 runs.

E. Compilation fails.

F. Never in this program.

G. An exception is thrown at runtime.

Answer:

☑ **G** is correct. An error at line 10 causes a `NullPointerException` to be thrown because e2 was set to `null` in line 8. If line 10 was moved between lines 7 and 8, then **F** would be correct, because until the last reference is nulled none of the objects is eligible, and once the last reference is nulled, all three are eligible.

☒ **A, B, C, D, E,** and **F** are incorrect based on the above. (Objective 7.4)

13. Given:

```
1. class Bigger {
2.   public static void main(String[] args) {
3.     // insert code here
4.   }
5. }
6. class Better {
7.   enum Faster {Higher, Longer};
8. }
```

Which, inserted independently at line 3, will compile? (Choose all that apply.)

A. `Faster f = Faster.Higher;`

B. `Faster f = Better.Faster.Higher;`

C. `Better.Faster f = Better.Faster.Higher;`

D. `Bigger.Faster f = Bigger.Faster.Higher;`

E. `Better.Faster f2;  f2 = Better.Faster.Longer;`

F. `Better b;  b.Faster = f3;  f3 = Better.Faster.Longer;`

Answer:

☑ **C** and **E** are correct syntax for accessing an enum from another class.

☒ **A, B, D,** and **F** are incorrect syntax. (Objective 1.3)

14. Given:

```
class Bird {
  { System.out.print("b1 "); }
  public Bird() { System.out.print("b2 "); }
}
class Raptor extends Bird {
  static { System.out.print("r1 "); }
  public Raptor() { System.out.print("r2 "); }
  { System.out.print("r3 "); }
  static { System.out.print("r4 "); }
}
class Hawk extends Raptor {
  public static void main(String[] args) {
    System.out.print("pre ");
    new Hawk();
    System.out.println("hawk ");
  }
}
```

What is the result?

A. pre b1 b2 r3 r2 hawk

B. pre b2 b1 r2 r3 hawk

C. pre b2 b1 r2 r3 hawk r1 r4

D. r1 r4 pre b1 b2 r3 r2 hawk

E. r1 r4 pre b2 b1 r2 r3 hawk

F. pre r1 r4 b1 b2 r3 r2 hawk

G. pre r1 r4 b2 b1 r2 r3 hawk

H. The order of output cannot be predicted.

I. Compilation fails.

Answer:

☑ **D** is correct. Static init blocks are executed at class loading time, instance init blocks run right after the call to super() in a constructor. When multiple init blocks of a single type occur in a class, they run in order, from the top down.

☒ **A, B, C, E, F, G, H,** and **I** are incorrect based on the above. Note: you'll probably never see this many choices on the real exam! (Objective 1.3)

4

Operators

CERTIFICATION OBJECTIVES

- Using Operators
- ✓ Two-Minute Drill
- Q&A Self Test

I f you've got variables, you're going to modify them. You'll increment them, add them together, and compare one to another (in about a dozen different ways). In this chapter, you'll learn how to do all that in Java. For an added bonus, you'll learn how to do things that you'll probably never use in the real world, but that will almost certainly be on the exam.

CERTIFICATION OBJECTIVE

Java Operators (Exam Objective 7.6)

7.6   Write code that correctly applies the appropriate operators including assignment operators (limited to: =, +=, -=), arithmetic operators (limited to: +, -, *, /, %, ++, --), relational operators (limited to: <, <=, >, >=, ==, !=), the instanceof operator, logical operators (limited to: &, |, ^, !, &&, ||), and the conditional operator (? :), to produce a desired result. Write code that determines the equality of two objects or two primitives.

Java operators produce new values from one or more operands (just so we're all clear, remember the operands are the things on the right or left side of the operator). The result of most operations is either a `boolean` or numeric value. Because you know by now that Java is not C++, you won't be surprised that Java operators aren't typically overloaded. There are, however, a few exceptional operators that come overloaded:

- The + operator can be used to add two numeric primitives together, or to perform a concatenation operation if either operand is a String.

- The &, |, and ^ operators can all be used in two different ways, although as of this version of the exam, their bit-twiddling capabilities won't be tested.

Stay awake. Operators are often the section of the exam where candidates see their lowest scores. Additionally, operators and assignments are a part of many questions in other topics…it would be a shame to nail a really tricky threads question, only to blow it on a pre-increment statement.

Assignment Operators

We covered most of the functionality of the assignment operator, "=", in Chapter 3. To summarize:

- When assigning a value to a primitive, *size* matters. Be sure you know when implicit casting will occur, when explicit casting is necessary, and when truncation might occur.

- Remember that a reference variable isn't an object; it's a way to *get* to an object. (We know all you C++ programmers are just dying for us to say "it's a pointer", but we're not going to.)

- When assigning a value to a reference variable, *type* matters. Remember the rules for supertypes, subtypes, and arrays.

Next we'll cover a few more details about the assignment operators that are on the exam, and when we get to Chapter 7, we'll take a look at how the assignment operator "=" works with Strings (which are immutable).

e x a m

ⓦ a t c h

Don't spend time preparing for topics that are no longer on the exam! In a nutshell, the Java 5 exam differs from the 1.4 exam by moving away from bits, and towards the API. Many 1.4 topics related to operators have been removed from the exam, so in this chapter you WON'T see

- bit shifting operators
- bitwise operators
- two's complement
- divide by zero stuff

It's not that these aren't important topics, it's just that they're not on the exam anymore, and we're really focused on the exam.

Compound Assignment Operators

There are actually 11 or so compound assignment operators, but only the four most commonly used (+=, -=, *=, and /=), are on the exam (despite what the objectives say). The compound assignment operators let lazy typists shave a few keystrokes off their workload. Here are several example assignments, first without using a compound operator,

```
y = y - 6;
x = x + 2 * 5;
```

Now, with compound operators:

```
y -= 6;
x += 2 * 5;
```

The last two assignments give the same result as the first two.

e x a m

ⓦ a t c h   *Earlier versions of the exam put big emphasis on operator precedence (like: What's the result of:* `x = y++ + ++x/z;`*). Other than a very basic knowledge of precedence (such as: * and / are higher precedence than + and -), you won't need to study operator precedence, except that when using a compound operator, the expression on the right side of the = will always be evaluated first. For example, you might expect*

```
x *= 2 + 5;
```

to be evaluated like this:

```
x = (x * 2) + 5;   // incorrect precedence
```

since multiplication has higher precedence than addition. But instead, the expression on the right is always placed inside parentheses. it is evaluated like this:

```
x = x * (2 + 5);
```

Relational Operators

The exam covers six relational operators (<, <=, >, >=, ==, and !=). Relational operators always result in a boolean (`true` or `false`) value. This `boolean` value is most often used in an `if` test, as follows,

```
int x = 8;
if (x < 9) {
  // do something
}
```

but the resulting value can also be assigned directly to a `boolean` primitive:

```
class CompareTest {
  public static void main(String [] args) {
    boolean b = 100 > 99;
    System.out.println("The value of b is " + b);
  }
}
```

Java has four relational operators that can be used to compare any combination of integers, floating-point numbers, or characters:

- `>` greater than
- `>=` greater than or equal to
- `<` less than
- `<=` less than or equal to

Let's look at some legal comparisons:

```
class GuessAnimal {
  public static void main(String[] args) {
    String animal = "unknown";
    int weight = 700;
    char sex = 'm';
    double colorWaveLength = 1.630;
    if (weight >= 500) { animal = "elephant"; }
    if (colorWaveLength > 1.621) { animal = "gray " + animal; }
    if (sex <= 'f') { animal = "female " + animal; }
    System.out.println("The animal is a " + animal);
  }
}
```

In the preceding code, we are using a comparison between characters. It's also legal to compare a character primitive with any number (though it isn't great programming style). Running the preceding class will output the following:

```
The animal is a gray elephant
```

We mentioned that characters can be used in comparison operators. When comparing a character with a character, or a character with a number, Java will use the Unicode value of the character as the numerical value, for comparison.

"Equality" Operators

Java also has two relational operators (sometimes called "equality operators") that compare two similar "things" and return a `boolean` the represents what's true about the two "things" being equal. These operators are

■ == equals (also known as "equal to")

■ != not equals (also known as "not equal to")

Each individual comparison can involve two numbers (including `char`), two `boolean` values, or two object reference variables. You can't compare incompatible types, however. What would it mean to ask if a `boolean` is equal to a `char`? Or if a `Button` is equal to a `String` array? (Exactly, nonsense, which is why you can't do it.) There are four different types of things that can be tested:

■ numbers

■ characters

■ boolean primitives

■ Object reference variables

So what does == look at? The value in the variable—in other words, the bit pattern.

Equality for Primitives

Most programmers are familiar with comparing primitive values. The following code shows some equality tests on primitive variables:

```
class ComparePrimitives {
  public static void main(String[] args) {
    System.out.println("char 'a' == 'a'? " + ('a' == 'a'));
    System.out.println("char 'a' == 'b'? " + ('a' == 'b'));
    System.out.println("5 != 6? " + (5 != 6));
    System.out.println("5.0 == 5L? " + (5.0 == 5L));
    System.out.println("true == false? " + (true == false));
  }
}
```

This program produces the following output:

```
character 'a' == 'a'? true
character 'a' == 'b'? false
5 != 6? true
5.0 == 5L? true
true == false? false
```

As we can see, usually if a floating-point number is compared with an integer and the values are the same, the == operator returns `true` as expected.

Equality for Reference Variables

As we saw earlier, two reference variables can refer to the same object, as the following code snippet demonstrates:

```
JButton a = new JButton("Exit");
JButton b = a;
```

After running this code, both variable a and variable b will refer to the same object (a `JButton` with the label `Exit`). Reference variables can be tested to see if they refer to the same object by using the == operator. Remember, the == operator is looking at the bits in the variable, so for reference variables this means that if the

*Don't mistake **= for == in a boolean expression. The following is legal:***

```
11. boolean b = false;
12. if (b = true) { System.out.println("b is true");
13. } else { System.out.println("b is false");  }
```

Look carefully! You might be tempted to think the output is b is false *but look at the boolean test in line 12. The boolean variable* b *is not being compared to* true*, it's being set to* true*, so the* println *executes and we get* b is true *. The result of any assignment expression is the value of the variable following the assignment. This substitution of = for == works only with boolean variables, since the* if *test can be done only on boolean expressions. Thus, this does not compile:*

```
7. int x = 1;
8. if (x = 0) { }
```

Because x *is an integer (and not a* boolean*), the result of* (x = 0) *is 0 (the result of the assignment). Primitive* ints *cannot be used where a boolean value is expected, so the code in line 8 won't work unless changed from an assignment (=) to an equality test (==) as follows:*

```
8. if (x == 0) { }
```

bits in both reference variables are identical, then both refer to the same object. Look at the following code:

```
import javax.swing.JButton;
class CompareReference {
  public static void main(String[] args) {
    JButton a = new JButton("Exit");
    JButton b = new JButton("Exit");
    JButton c = a;
    System.out.println("Is reference a == b? " + (a == b));
    System.out.println("Is reference a == c? " + (a == c));
  }
}
```

This code creates three reference variables. The first two, a and b, are separate JButton objects that happen to have the same label. The third reference variable, c, is initialized to refer to the same object that a refers to. When this program runs, the following output is produced:

```
Is reference a == b? false
Is reference a == c? true
```

This shows us that a and c reference the same instance of a JButton. The == operator will not test whether two objects are "meaningfully equivalent," a concept we'll cover in much more detail in Chapter 7, when we look at the equals() *method* (as opposed to the equals *operator* we're looking at here).

Equality for Enums

Once you've declared an enum, it's not expandable. At runtime, there's no way to make additional enum constants. Of course, you can have as many variables as you'd like refer to a given enum constant, so it's important to be able to compare two enum reference variables to see if they're "equal," i.e. do they refer to the same enum constant. You can use either the == operator or the equals() method to determine if two variables are referring to the same enum constant:

```
class EnumEqual {
  enum Color {RED, BLUE}                        // ; is optional
  public static void main(String[] args) {
    Color c1 = Color.RED;  Color c2 = Color.RED;
    if(c1 == c2) { System.out.println("=="); }
    if(c1.equals(c2)) { System.out.println("dot equals"); }
} }
```

(We know } } is ugly, we're prepping you). This produces the output:

```
==
dot equals
```

instanceof Comparison

The `instanceof` operator is used for object reference variables only, and you can use it to check whether an object is of a particular type. By type, we mean class or interface type—in other words, if the object referred to by the variable on the left side of the operator passes the IS-A test for the class or interface type on the right side (Chapter 2 covered IS-A relationships in detail). The following simple example

```
public static void main(String[] args) {
  String s = new String("foo");
  if (s instanceof String) {
    System.out.print("s is a String");
  }
}
```

prints this: `s is a String`

Even if the object being tested is not an actual instantiation of the class type on the right side of the operator, `instanceof` will still return `true` if the object being compared is *assignment compatible* with the type on the right.

The following example demonstrates a common use for `instanceof`: testing an object to see if it's an instance of one of its subtypes, before attempting a "downcast":

```
class A { }
class B extends A {
  public static void main (String [] args) {
    A myA = new B();
    m2(myA);
  }
  public static void m2(A a) {
    if (a instanceof B)
      ((B)a).doBstuff();       // downcasting an A reference
                               // to a B reference
  }
  public static void doBstuff() {
    System.out.println("'a' refers to a B");
  }
}
```

The preceding code compiles and produces the output:

```
'a' refers to a B
```

In examples like this, the use of the `instanceof` operator protects the program from attempting an illegal downcast.

You can test an object reference against its own class type, or any of its superclasses. This means that *any* object reference will evaluate to `true` if you use the `instanceof` operator against type `Object`, as follows,

```
B b = new B();
if (b instanceof Object) {
    System.out.print("b is definitely an Object");
}
```

which prints this: `b is definitely an Object`

---

exam
watch

Look for instanceof questions that test whether an object is an instance of an interface, when the object's class implements the interface indirectly. An indirect implementation occurs when one of an object's superclasses implements an interface, but the actual class of the instance does not—for example,

```
interface Foo { }
class A implements Foo { }
class B extends A { }
...
A a = new A();
B b = new B();
```

the following are true:

```
a instanceof Foo
b instanceof A
b instanceof Foo  // implemented indirectly
```

An object is said to be of a particular interface type (meaning it will pass the `instanceof` *test) if any of the object's superclasses implement the interface.*

In addition, it is legal to test whether the `null` reference is an instance of a class. This will always result in `false`, of course. For example:

```
class InstanceTest {
   public static void main(String [] args) {
      String a = null;
      boolean b = null instanceof String;
      boolean c = a instanceof String;
      System.out.println(b + " " + c);
   }
}
```

prints this: `false false`

instanceof Compiler Error

You can't use the `instanceof` operator to test across two different class hierarchies. For instance, the following will NOT compile:

```
class Cat { }
class Dog {
  public static void main(String [] args) {
    Dog d = new Dog();
    System.out.println(d instanceof Cat);
  }
}
```

Compilation fails—there's no way d could ever refer to a `Cat` or a subtype of `Cat`.

Remember that arrays are objects, even if the array is an array of primitives. Watch for questions that look something like this:

```
int [] nums = new int[3];
if (nums instanceof Object) { } // result is true
```

An array is always an instance of Object. Any array.

Table 4-1 summarizes the use of the `instanceof` operator given the following:

```
interface Face { }
class Bar implements Face{ }
class Foo extends Bar { }
```

TABLE 4-1   Operands and Results Using *instanceof* Operator.

First Operand (Reference Being Tested)	instanceof Operand (Type We're Comparing the Reference Against)	Result
null	Any class or interface type	false
Foo instance	Foo, Bar, Face, Object	true
Bar instance	Bar, Face, Object	true
Bar instance	Foo	false
Foo [ ]	Foo, Bar, Face	false
Foo [ ]	Object	true
Foo [1]	Foo, Bar, Face, Object	true

Arithmetic Operators

We're sure you're familiar with the basic arithmetic operators.

- ■ + addition
- ■ – subtraction
- ■ * multiplication
- ■ / division

These can be used in the standard way:

```
int x = 5 * 3;
int y = x - 4;
System.out.println("x - 4 is " +  y);  // Prints 11
```

The Remainder (%) Operator

One operator you might not be as familiar with is the remainder operator, %. The remainder operator divides the left operand by the right operand, and the result is the remainder, as the following code demonstrates:

```
class MathTest {
  public static void main (String [] args) {
    int x = 15;
    int y = x % 4;
    System.out.println("The result of 15 % 4 is the "
      + "remainder of 15 divided by 4. The remainder is " + y);
  }
}
```

Running class MathTest prints the following:

```
The result of 15 % 4 is the remainder of 15 divided by 4. The
remainder is 3
```

(Remember: Expressions are evaluated from left to right by default. You can change this sequence, or *precedence*, by adding parentheses. Also remember that the * , / , and % operators have a higher precedence than the + and - operators.)

String Concatenation Operator

The plus sign can also be used to concatenate two strings together, as we saw earlier (and as we'll definitely see again):

```
String animal = "Grey " + "elephant";
```

String concatenation gets interesting when you combine numbers with Strings. Check out the following:

```
String a = "String";
int b = 3;
int c = 7;
System.out.println(a + b + c);
```

Will the + operator act as a plus sign when adding the int variables b + c? Or will the + operator treat 3 and 7 as characters, and concatenate them individually? Will the result be String10 or String37? OK, you've had long enough to think about it. The int values were simply treated as characters and glued on to the right side of the String, giving the result:

```
String37
```

So we could read the previous code as

> "Start with `String a`, `String`, and add the character `3` (the value of `b`) to it, to produce a new string `String3`, and then add the character `7` (the value of `c`) to that, to produce a new string `String37`, then print it out."

However, if you put parentheses around the two `int` variables, as follows,

```
System.out.println(a + (b + c));
```

you'll get this: `String10`

Using parentheses causes the `(b + c)` to evaluate first, so the rightmost `+` operator functions as the addition operator, given that both operands are `int` values. The key point here is that within the parentheses, the left-hand operand is not a `String`. If it were, then the `+` operator would perform `String` concatenation. The previous code can be read as

> "Add the values of `b + c` together, then take the sum and convert it to a `String` and concatenate it with the `String` from variable a."

The rule to remember is this:

> *If either operand is a* String, *the + operator becomes a* String *concatenation operator. If both operands are numbers, the + operator is the addition operator.*

You'll find that sometimes you might have trouble deciding whether, say, the left-hand operator is a `String` or not. On the exam, don't expect it to always be obvious. (Actually, now that we think about it, don't expect it ever to be obvious.) Look at the following code:

```
System.out.println(x.foo() + 7);
```

You can't know how the `+` operator is being used until you find out what the `foo()` method returns! If `foo()` returns a `String`, then `7` is concatenated to the returned

String. But if foo() returns a number, then the + operator is used to add 7 to the return value of foo().

Finally, you need to know that it's legal to mush together the compound additive operator (+=) and Strings, like so:

```
String s = "123";
s += "45";
s += 67;
System.out.println(s);
```

Since both times the += operator was used and the left operand was a String, both operations were concatenations, resulting in

```
1234567
```

exam

ⓦatch

If you don't understand how String concatenation works, especially within a print *statement, you could actually fail the exam even if you know the rest of the answer to the questions! Because so many questions ask, "What is the result?", you need to know not only the result of the code running, but also how that result is printed. Although there will be at least a few questions directly testing your String knowledge, String concatenation shows up in other questions on virtually every objective. Experiment! For example, you might see a line such as*

```
int b = 2;
System.out.println("" + b + 3);
```

which prints 23

but if the print statement changes to

```
System.out.println(b + 3);
```

then the result becomes 5

Increment and Decrement Operators

Java has two operators that will increment or decrement a variable by exactly one. These operators are composed of either two plus signs (++) or two minus signs (--):

- ■   ++   increment (prefix and postfix)
- ■   --   decrement (prefix and postfix)

The operator is placed either before (prefix) or after (postfix) a variable to change its value. Whether the operator comes before or after the operand can change the outcome of an expression. Examine the following:

```
1. class MathTest {
2.    static int players = 0;
3.      public static void main (String [] args) {
4.        System.out.println("players online: " + players++);
5.        System.out.println("The value of players is "
                                  + players);
6.        System.out.println("The value of players is now "
                                  + ++players);
7.    }
8. }
```

Notice that in the fourth line of the program the increment operator is *after* the variable `players`. That means we're using the postfix increment operator, which causes `players` to be incremented by one but only *after* the value of `players` is used in the expression. When we run this program, it outputs the following:

```
%java MathTest
players online: 0
The value of players is 1
The value of players is now 2
```

Notice that when the variable is written to the screen, at first it says the value is 0. Because we used the postfix increment operator, the increment doesn't happen until after the `players` variable is used in the `print` statement. Get it? The "post" in postfix means *after*. Line 5 doesn't increment `players`; it just outputs its value to the screen, so the newly incremented value displayed is 1. Line 6 applies the prefix increment operator to `players`, which means the increment happens *before* the value of the variable is used, so the output is 2.

Expect to see questions mixing the increment and decrement operators with other operators, as in the following example:

```
int x = 2;   int y = 3;
if ((y == x++) | (x < ++y)) {
  System.out.println("x = " + x + " y = " + y);
  }
```

The preceding code prints: x = 3 y = 4

You can read the code as follows: "If 3 is equal to 2 OR 3 < 4"

The first expression compares x and y, and the result is `false`, because the
increment on x doesn't happen until *after* the == test is made. Next, we increment
x, so now x is 3. Then we check to see if x is less than y, but we increment y *before*
comparing it with x! So the second logical test is (3 < 4). The result is `true`, so the
`print` statement runs.

As with String concatenation, the increment and decrement operators are used
throughout the exam, even on questions that aren't trying to test your knowledge
of how those operators work. You might see them in questions on `for` loops,
exceptions, even threads. Be ready.

e x a m

ⓦatch **Look out for questions that use the increment or decrement operators on**
a final variable. Because final variables can't be changed, the increment and decrement
operators can't be used with them, and any attempt to do so will result in a compiler
error. The following code won't compile:

```
final int x = 5;
int y = x++;
```

and produces the error:

```
Test.java:4: cannot assign a value to final variable x
int y = x++;
        ^
```

You can expect a violation like this to be buried deep in a complex piece
of code. If you spot it, you know the code won't compile and you can move on without
working through the rest of the code.
This question might seem to be testing you on some complex arithmetic
operator trivia, when in fact it's testing you on your knowledge of the final **modifier.**

Conditional Operator

The conditional operator is a *ternary* operator (it has *three* operands) and is used to evaluate `boolean` expressions, much like an `if` statement except instead of executing a block of code if the test is `true`, a conditional operator will assign a value to a variable. In other words, the goal of the conditional operator is to decide which of two values to assign to a variable. This operator is constructed using a ? (question mark) and a : (colon). The parentheses are optional. Its structure is:

```
x = (boolean expression) ? value to assign if true : value to assign if false
```

Let's take a look at a conditional operator in code:

```
class Salary {
  public static void main(String [] args) {
    int numOfPets = 3;
    String status = (numOfPets<4) ? "Pet limit not exceeded"
                       : "too many pets";
    System.out.println("This pet status is " + status);
  }
}
```

You can read the preceding code as

Set `numOfPets` equal to 3. Next we're going to assign a `String` to the status variable. If `numOfPets` is less than 4, assign `"Pet limit not exceeded"` to the status variable; otherwise, assign `"too many pets"` to the status variable.

A conditional operator starts with a `boolean` operation, followed by two possible values for the variable to the left of the assignment (=) operator. The first value (the one to the left of the colon) is assigned if the conditional (`boolean`) test is `true`, and the second value is assigned if the conditional test is `false`. You can even nest conditional operators into one statement:

```
class AssignmentOps {
  public static void main(String [] args) {
    int sizeOfYard = 10;
    int numOfPets = 3;
    String status = (numOfPets<4)?"Pet count OK"
        :(sizeOfYard > 8)? "Pet limit on the edge"
          :"too many pets";
    System.out.println("Pet status is " + status);
```

```
    }
}
```

Don't expect many questions using conditional operators, but remember that conditional operators are sometimes confused with assertion statements, so be certain you can tell the difference. Chapter 5 covers assertions in detail.

Logical Operators

The exam objectives specify six "logical" operators (&, |, ^, !, &&, and | |). Some Sun documentation uses other terminology for these operators, but for our purposes the "logical operators" are the six listed above, and in the exam objectives.

Bitwise Operators (Not on the Exam!)

Okay, this is going to be confusing. Of the six logical operators listed above, three of them (&, |, and ^) can also be used as "bitwise" operators. Bitwise operators were included in previous versions of the exam, but they're not on the Java 5 exam. Here are several legal statements that use bitwise operators:

```
byte b1 = 6 & 8;
byte b2 = 7 | 9;
byte b3 = 5 ^ 4;
System.out.println(b1 + " " + b2 + " " + b3);
```

Bitwise operators compare two variables bit by bit, and return a variable whose bits have been set based on whether the two variables being compared had respective bits that were either both "on" (&), one or the other "on" (|), or exactly one "on" (^). By the way, when we run the preceding code, we get

```
0 15 1
```

Having said all this about bitwise operators, the key thing to remember is this:

BITWISE OPERATORS ARE NOT ON THE EXAM!

So why did we bring them up? If you get hold of an old exam preparation book, or if you find some mock exams that haven't been properly updated, you're bound to find questions that perform bitwise operations. Unless you're a glutton for punishment, you can skip this kind of mock question.

Short-Circuit Logical Operators

There are five logical operators on the exam that are used to evaluate statements that contain more than one `boolean` expression. The most commonly used of the five are the two *short-circuit* logical operators. They are

- ▪ `&&` short-circuit AND
- ▪ `||` short-circuit OR

They are used to link little `boolean` expressions together to form bigger `boolean` expressions. The && and || operators evaluate only `boolean` values. For an AND (&&) expression to be `true`, both operands must be `true`—for example,

```
if ((2 < 3) && (3 < 4)) { }
```

The preceding expression evaluates to `true` because *both* operand one (2 < 3) and operand two (3 < 4) evaluate to `true`.

The short-circuit feature of the && operator is so named because it doesn't waste its time on pointless evaluations. A short-circuit && evaluates the left side of the operation first (operand one), and if it resolves to `false`, the && operator doesn't bother looking at the right side of the expression (operand two) since the && operator already *knows* that the complete expression can't possibly be `true`.

```
class Logical {
  public static void main(String [] args) {
    boolean b = true && false;
    System.out.println("boolean b = " + b);
  }
}
```

When we run the preceding code, we get

```
%java Logical
boolean b = false
```

The || operator is similar to the && operator, except that it evaluates to `true` if EITHER of the operands is true. If the first operand in an OR operation is `true`, the result will be `true`, so the short-circuit || doesn't waste time looking at the right side of the equation. If the first operand is `false`, however, the short-circuit || has to evaluate the second operand to see if the result of the OR operation will be true or `false`. Pay close attention to the following example; you'll see quite a few questions like this on the exam:

```
1. class TestOR {
2.   public static void main(String[] args) {
3.     if ((isItSmall(3)) || (isItSmall(7))) {
4.       System.out.println("Result is true");
5.     }
6.     if ((isItSmall(6)) || (isItSmall(9))) {
7.       System.out.println("Result is true");
8.     }
9.   }
10.
11.   public static boolean isItSmall(int i) {
12.     if (i < 5) {
13.       System.out.println("i < 5");
14.       return true;
15.     } else {
16.       System.out.println("i >= 5");
17.       return false;
18.     }
19.   }
20. }
```

What is the result?

```
% java TestOR
i < 5
Result is true
i >= 5
i >= 5
```

Here's what happened when the `main()` method ran:

1. When we hit line 3, the first operand in the `||` expression (in other words, the *left* side of the `||` operation) is evaluated.

2. The `isItSmall(3)` method is invoked, prints `"i < 5"`, and returns `true`.

3. Because the *first* operand in the `||` expression on line 3 is `true`, the `||` operator doesn't bother evaluating the second operand. So we never see the `"i >= 5"` that would have printed had the *second* operand been evaluated (which would have invoked `isItSmall(7)`).

4. Line 6 is evaluated, beginning with the *first* operand in the || expression.

5. The isItSmall(6) method is called, prints "i >= 5", and returns false.

6. Because the *first* operand in the || expression on line 6 is false, the || operator can't skip the *second* operand; there's still a chance the expression can be true, if the *second* operand evaluates to true.

7. The isItSmall(9) method is invoked and prints "i >= 5".

8. The isItSmall(9) method returns false, so the expression on line 6 is false, and thus line 7 never executes.

e x a m

ⓦatch

The || and && operators work only with boolean operands. The exam may try to fool you by using integers with these operators:

```
if (5 && 6) { }
```

It looks as though we're trying to do a bitwise AND on the bits representing the integers 5 and 6, but the code won't even compile.

Logical Operators (Not Short-Circuit)

There are two *non-short-circuit* logical operators.

- **&** non-short-circuit AND
- **|** non-short-circuit OR

These operators are used in logical expressions just like the && and || operators are used, but because they aren't the short-circuit operators, they evaluate both sides of the expression, always! They're inefficient. For example, even if the *first* operand (left side) in an & expression is false, the *second* operand will still be evaluated—even though it's now impossible for the result to be true! And the | is just as inefficient: if the *first* operand is true, the JVM still plows ahead and evaluates the *second* operand even when it knows the expression will be true regardless.

You'll find a lot of questions on the exam that use both the short-circuit and non-short-circuit logical operators. You'll have to know exactly which operands are evaluated and which are not, since the result will vary depending on whether the second operand in the expression is evaluated:

```
int z = 5;
if(++z > 5 || ++z > 6) z++;    // z = 7 after this code
```

versus:

```
int z = 5;
if(++z > 5 | ++z > 6) z++;    // z = 8 after this code
```

Logical Operators ^ and !

The last two logical operators on the exam are

- ^   exclusive-OR (XOR)
- !   boolean invert

The ^ (exclusive-OR) operator evaluates only `boolean` values. The ^ operator is related to the non-short-circuit operators we just reviewed, in that it always evaluates *both* the left and right operands in an expression. For an exclusive-OR (^) expression to be `true`, EXACTLY one operand must be `true`—for example,

```
System.out.println("xor " + ((2<3) ^ (4>3)));
```

produces the output: `xor false`

The preceding expression evaluates to **false** because BOTH operand one (2 < 3) and operand two (4 > 3) evaluate to `true`.

The ! (boolean invert) operator returns the opposite of a boolean's current value:

```
if(!(7 == 5)) { System.out.println("not equal"); }
```

can be read "if it's not true that 7 == 5," and the statement produces this output:

```
not equal
```

Here's another example using booleans:

```
boolean t = true;
boolean f = false;
System.out.println("! " + (t & !f) + " " + f);
```

produces the output:

```
! true false
```

In the preceding example, notice that the & test succeeded (printing `true`), and that the value of the `boolean` variable `f` did not change, so it printed `false`.

CERTIFICATION SUMMARY

If you've studied this chapter diligently, you should have a firm grasp on Java operators, and you should understand what equality means when tested with the == operator. Let's review the highlights of what you've learned in this chapter.

The logical operators (&& , | |, &, |, and ^) can be used only to evaluate two `boolean` expressions. The difference between && and & is that the && operator won't bother testing the right operand if the left evaluates to `false`, because the result of the && expression can never be `true`. The difference between | | and | is that the | | operator won't bother testing the right operand if the left evaluates to `true`, because the result is already known to be `true` at that point.

The == operator can be used to compare values of primitives, but it can also be used to determine whether two reference variables refer to the same object.

The `instanceof` operator is used to determine if the object referred to by a reference variable passes the IS-A test for a specified type.

The + operator is overloaded to perform `String` concatenation tasks, and can also concatenate `Strings` and primitives, but be careful—concatenation can be tricky.

The conditional operator (a.k.a. the "ternary operator") has an unusual, three-operand syntax—don't mistake it for a complex assert statement.

The ++ and -- operators will be used throughout the exam, and you must pay attention to whether they are prefixed or postfixed to the variable being updated.

Be prepared for a lot of exam questions involving the topics from this chapter. Even within questions testing your knowledge of another objective, the code will frequently use operators, assignments, object and primitive passing, and so on.

✓ TWO-MINUTE DRILL

Here are some of the key points from each section in this chapter.

Relational Operators (Objective 7.6)

❑ Relational operators always result in a `boolean` value (`true` or `false`).

❑ There are six relational operators: >, >=, <, <=, ==, and !=. The last two (== and !=) are sometimes referred to as *equality operators*.

❑ When comparing characters, Java uses the Unicode value of the character as the numerical value.

❑ Equality operators

    ❑ There are two equality operators: == and !=.

    ❑ Four types of things can be tested: numbers, characters, booleans, and reference variables.

❑ When comparing reference variables, == returns `true` only if both references refer to the same object.

instanceof Operator (Objective 7.6)

❑ `instanceof` is for reference variables only, and checks for whether the object is of a particular type.

❑ The `instanceof` operator can be used only to test objects (or `null`) against class types that are in the same class hierarchy.

❑ For interfaces, an object passes the `instanceof` test if any of its superclasses implement the interface on the right side of the `instanceof` operator.

Arithmetic Operators (Objective 7.6)

❑ There are four primary math operators: add, subtract, multiply, and divide.

❑ The remainder operator (%), returns the remainder of a division.

❑ Expressions are evaluated from left to right, unless you add parentheses, or unless some operators in the expression have higher precedence than others.

❑ The *, /, and % operators have higher precedence than + and -.

String Concatenation Operator (Objective 7.6)

❑ If either operand is a `String`, the + operator concatenates the operands.

❑ If both operands are numeric, the + operator adds the operands.

Increment/Decrement Operators (Objective 7.6)

❑ Prefix operators (++ and --) run before the value is used in the expression.

❑ Postfix operators (++ and --) run after the value is used in the expression.

❑ In any expression, both operands are fully evaluated *before* the operator is applied.

❑ Variables marked `final` cannot be incremented or decremented.

Ternary (Conditional Operator) (Objective 7.6)

❑ Returns one of two values based on whether a `boolean` expression is `true` or `false`.

   ❑ Returns the value after the ? if the expression is `true`.

   ❑ Returns the value after the : if the expression is `false`.

Logical Operators (Objective 7.6)

❑ The exam covers six "logical" operators: &, |, ^, !, &&, and ||.

❑ Logical operators work with two expressions (except for !) that must resolve to `boolean` values.

❑ The && and & operators return `true` only if both operands are `true`.

❑ The || and | operators return `true` if either or both operands are `true`.

❑ The && and || operators are known as short-circuit operators.

❑ The && operator does not evaluate the right operand if the left operand is `false`.

❑ The || does not evaluate the right operand if the left operand is `true`.

❑ The & and | operators always evaluate both operands.

❑ The ^ operator (called the "logical XOR"), returns `true` if exactly one operand is `true`.

❑ The ! operator (called the "inversion" operator), returns the opposite value of the `boolean` operand it precedes.

SELF TEST

1. Given:

```
class Hexy {
   public static void main(String[] args) {
      Integer i = 42;
      String s = (i<40)?"life":(i>50)?"universe":"everything";
      System.out.println(s);
   }
}
```

What is the result?

A. null

B. life

C. universe

D. everything

E. Compilation fails.

F. An exception is thrown at runtime.

2. Given:

```
1. class Example {
2.    public static void main(String[] args) {
3.       Short s = 15;
4.       Boolean b;
5.       // insert code here
6.    }
7. }
```

Which, inserted independently at line 5, will compile? (Choose all that apply.)

A. `b = (Number instanceof s);`

B. `b = (s instanceof Short);`

C. `b = s.instanceof(Short);`

D. `b = (s instanceof Number);`

E. `b = s.instanceof(Object);`

F. `b = (s instanceof String);`

3. Given:

```
1. class Comp2 {
2.    public static void main(String[] args) {
3.       float f1 = 2.3f;
4.       float[][] f2 = {{42.0f}, {1.7f, 2.3f}, {2.6f, 2.7f}};
5.       float[] f3 = {2.7f};
6.       Long x = 42L;
7.       // insert code here
8.          System.out.println("true");
9.    }
10. }
```

And the following five code fragments:

```
F1.   if(f1 == f2)
F2.   if(f1 == f2[2][1])
F3.   if(x == f2[0][0])
F4.   if(f1 == f2[1,1])
F5.   if(f3 == f2[2])
```

What is true?

A. One of them will compile, only one will be true.

B. Two of them will compile, only one will be true.

C. Two of them will compile, two will be true.

D. Three of them will compile, only one will be true.

E. Three of them will compile, exactly two will be true.

F. Three of them will compile, exactly three will be true.

4. Given:

```
class Fork {
  public static void main(String[] args) {
    if(args.length == 1 | args[1].equals("test")) {
      System.out.println("test case");
    } else {
      System.out.println("production " + args[0]);
    }
  }
}
```

And the command-line invocation:

```
java Fork live2
```

What is the result?

A. test case

B. production

C. test case live2

D. Compilation fails.

E. An exception is thrown at runtime.

5. Given:

```
class Foozit {
  public static void main(String[] args) {
    Integer x = 0;
    Integer y = 0;
    for(Short z = 0; z < 5; z++)
      if((++x > 2) || (++y > 2))
        x++;
    System.out.println(x + " " + y);
  }
}
```

What is the result?

A. 5 1

B. 5 2

C. 5 3

D. 8 1

E. 8 2

F. 8 3

G. 10 2

H. 10 3

6. Given:

```
class Titanic {
  public static void main(String[] args) {
    Boolean b1 = true;
    boolean b2 = false;
    boolean b3 = true;
    if((b1 & b2) | (b2 & b3) & b3)
      System.out.print("alpha ");
    if((b1 = false) | (b1 & b3) | (b1 | b2))
      System.out.print("beta ");
  }
}
```

What is the result?

A. beta

B. alpha

C. alpha beta

D. Compilation fails.

E. No output is produced.

F. An exception is thrown at runtime.

7. Given:

```
class Feline {
  public static void main(String[] args) {
    Long x = 42L;
    Long y = 44L;
    System.out.print(" " + 7 + 2 + " ");
    System.out.print(foo() + x + 5 + " ");
    System.out.println(x + y + foo());
  }
  static String foo() { return "foo"; }
}
```

What is the result?

A. 9 foo47 86foo

B. 9 foo47 4244foo

C. 9 foo425 86foo

D. `9 foo425 4244foo`

E. `72 foo47 86foo`

F. `72 foo47 4244foo`

G. `72 foo425 86foo`

H. `72 foo425 4244foo`

I. Compilation fails.

8. Place the fragments into the code to produce the output 33. Note, you must use each fragment exactly once.

CODE:
```
class Incr {
  public static void main(String[] args) {
    Integer x = 7;
    int y = 2;

    x    ___ ___;
    ___ ___ ___;
    ___ ___ ___;
    ___ ___ ___;

    System.out.println(x);
  }
}
```

FRAGMENTS:

y	y	y	y
y	x	x	
-=	*=	*=	*=

9. Given:

```
1. class Maybe {
2.   public static void main(String[] args) {
3.     boolean b1 = true;
4.     boolean b2 = false;
5.     System.out.print(!false ^ false);
6.     System.out.print(" " + (!b1 & (b2 = true)));
7.     System.out.println(" " + (b2 ^ b1));
8.   }
9. }
```

Which are true?

A. Line 5 produces true.

B. Line 5 produces false.

C. Line 6 produces true.

D. Line 6 produces false.

E. Line 7 produces true.

F. Line 7 produces false.

10. Given:

```
class Sixties {
  public static void main(String[] args) {
    int x = 5;  int y = 7;
    System.out.print(((y * 2) % x));
    System.out.print(" " + (y % x));
  }
}
```

What is the result?

A. 1 1

B. 1 2

C. 2 1

D. 2 2

E. 4 1

F. 4 2

G. Compilation fails.

H. An exception is thrown at runtime.

SELF TEST ANSWERS

1. Given:

```
class Hexy {
  public static void main(String[] args) {
    Integer i = 42;
    String s = (i<40)?"life":(i>50)?"universe":"everything";
    System.out.println(s);
  }
}
```

What is the result?

A. `null`

B. `life`

C. `universe`

D. `everything`

E. Compilation fails.

F. An exception is thrown at runtime.

Answer:

☑ **D** is correct. This is a ternary nested in a ternary with a little unboxing thrown in. Both of the ternary expressions are `false`.

☒ **A, B, C, E,** and **F** are incorrect based on the above.
(Objective 7.6)

2. Given:

```
1. class Example {
2.   public static void main(String[] args) {
3.     Short s = 15;
4.     Boolean b;
5.     // insert code here
6.   }
7. }
```

Which, inserted independently at line 5, will compile? (Choose all that apply.)

A. `b = (Number instanceof s);`

B. `b = (s instanceof Short);`

C. `b = s.instanceof(Short);`

D. `b = (s instanceof Number);`

E. `b = s.instanceof(Object);`

F. `b = (s instanceof String);`

Answer:

☑ **B** and **D** correctly use boxing and `instanceof` together.

☒ **A** is incorrect because the operands are reversed. **C** and **E** use incorrect `instanceof` syntax. **F** is wrong because `Short` isn't in the same inheritance tree as `String`. (Objective 7.6)

3. Given:

```
1. class Comp2 {
2.   public static void main(String[] args) {
3.     float f1 = 2.3f;
4.     float[][] f2 = {{42.0f}, {1.7f, 2.3f}, {2.6f, 2.7f}};
5.     float[] f3 = {2.7f};
6.     Long x = 42L;
7.     // insert code here
8.       System.out.println("true");
9.   }
10. }
```

And the following five code fragments:

```
F1.   if(f1 == f2)
F2.   if(f1 == f2[2][1])
F3.   if(x == f2[0][0])
F4.   if(f1 == f2[1,1])
F5.   if(f3 == f2[2])
```

What is true?

A. One of them will compile, only one will be `true`.

B. Two of them will compile, only one will be `true`.

C. Two of them will compile, two will be `true`.

D. Three of them will compile, only one will be `true`.

E. Three of them will compile, exactly two will be `true`.

F. Three of them will compile, exactly three will be `true`.

Answer:

- ☑ **D** is correct. Fragments `F2`, `F3`, and `F5` will compile, and only `F3` is `true`.
- ☒ **A, B, C, E,** and **F** are incorrect. `F1` is incorrect because you can't compare a primitive to an array. `F4` is incorrect syntax to access an element of a two-dimensional array. (Objective 7.6)

4. Given:

```
class Fork {
  public static void main(String[] args) {
    if(args.length == 1 | args[1].equals("test")) {
      System.out.println("test case");
    } else {
      System.out.println("production " + args[0]);
    }
  }
}
```

And the command-line invocation:

```
java Fork live2
```

What is the result?

A. `test case`

B. `production`

C. `test case live2`

D. Compilation fails.

E. An exception is thrown at runtime.

Answer:

- ☑ **E** is correct. Because the short circuit (`||`) is not used, both operands are evaluated. Since `args[1]` is past the args array bounds, an `ArrayIndexOutOfBoundsException` is thrown.
- ☒ **A, B, C,** and **D** are incorrect based on the above. (Objective 7.6)

5. Given:

```
class Foozit {
  public static void main(String[] args) {
    Integer x = 0;
    Integer y = 0;
    for(Short z = 0; z < 5; z++)
      if((++x > 2) || (++y > 2))
        x++;
    System.out.println(x + " " + y);
  }
}
```

What is the result?

A. 5 1

B. 5 2

C. 5 3

D. 8 1

E. 8 2

F. 8 3

G. 10 2

H. 10 3

Answer:

☑ **E** is correct. The first two times the `if` test runs, both `x` and `y` are incremented once (the `x++` is not reached until the third iteration). Starting with the third iteration of the loop, `y` is never touched again, because of the short-circuit operator.

☒ **A, B, C, D, F, G,** and **H** are incorrect based on the above.
(Objective 7.6)

6. Given:

```
class Titanic {
  public static void main(String[] args) {
    Boolean b1 = true;
    boolean b2 = false;
    boolean b3 = true;
    if((b1 & b2) | (b2 & b3) & b3)
      System.out.print("alpha ");
    if((b1 = false) | (b1 & b3) | (b1 | b2))
      System.out.print("beta ");
  }
}
```

What is the result?

A. beta

B. alpha

C. alpha beta

D. Compilation fails.

E. No output is produced.

F. An exception is thrown at runtime.

Answer:

☑ **E** is correct. In the second `if` test, the leftmost expression is an assignment, not a comparison. Once `b1` has been set to `false`, the remaining tests are all `false`.

☒ **A, B, C, D,** and **F** are incorrect based on the above. (Objective 7.6)

7. Given:

```
class Feline {
  public static void main(String[] args) {
    Long x = 42L;
    Long y = 44L;
    System.out.print(" " + 7 + 2 + " ");
    System.out.print(foo() + x + 5 + " ");
    System.out.println(x + y + foo());
  }
  static String foo() { return "foo"; }
}
```

What is the result?

A. 9 foo47 86foo

B. 9 foo47 4244foo

C. 9 foo425 86foo

D. 9 foo425 4244foo

E. 72 foo47 86foo

F. 72 foo47 4244foo

G. 72 foo425 86foo

H. 72 foo425 4244foo

I. Compilation fails.

Answer:

☑ **G** is correct. Concatenation runs from left to right, and if either operand is a `String`, the operands are concatenated. If both operands are numbers they are added together. Unboxing works in conjunction with concatenation.

☒ **A, B, C, D, E, F, H,** and **I** are incorrect based on the above. (Objective 7.6)

8. Place the fragments into the code to produce the output 33. Note, you must use each fragment exactly once.

CODE:

```
class Incr {
  public static void main(String[] args) {
    Integer x = 7;
    int y = 2;

    x    ___ ___;
    ___  ___ ___;
    ___  ___ ___;
    ___  ___ ___;

    System.out.println(x);
  }
}
```

FRAGMENTS:

y	y	y	y
y	x	x	
-=	*=	*=	*=

Answer:

```
class Incr {
  public static void main(String[] args) {
    Integer x = 7;
    int y = 2;
```

```
        x *= x;
        y *= y;
        y *= y;
        x -= y;

      System.out.println(x);
    }
  }
```

Yeah, we know it's kind of puzzle-y, but you might encounter something like it on the real exam. (Objective 7.6)

9. Given:

```
1. class Maybe {
2.   public static void main(String[] args) {
3.     boolean b1 = true;
4.     boolean b2 = false;
5.     System.out.print(!false ^ false);
6.     System.out.print(" " + (!b1 & (b2 = true)));
7.     System.out.println(" " + (b2 ^ b1));
8.   }
9. }
```

Which are true?

A. Line 5 produces `true`.

B. Line 5 produces `false`.

C. Line 6 produces `true`.

D. Line 6 produces `false`.

E. Line 7 produces `true`.

F. Line 7 produces `false`.

Answer:

☑ **A, D,** and **F** are correct. The `^` (`xor`) returns true if exactly one operand is `true`. The `!` inverts the operand's `boolean` value. On line 6 `b2 = true` is an assignment not a comparison, and it's evaluated because `&` does not short-circuit it.

☒ **B, C,** and **E** are incorrect based on the above.
(Objective 7.6)

10. Given:

```
class Sixties {
  public static void main(String[] args) {
    int x = 5;
    int y = 7;
    System.out.print(((y * 2) % x));
    System.out.print(" " + (y % x));
  }
}
```

What is the result?

A. 1 1

B. 1 2

C. 2 1

D. 2 2

E. 4 1

F. 4 2

G. Compilation fails.

H. An exception is thrown at runtime.

Answer:

☑ **F** is correct. The % (remainder a.k.a. modulus) operator returns the remainder of a division operation.

☒ **A, B, C, D, E, G,** and **H** are incorrect based on the above. (Objective 7.6)

5

Flow Control, Exceptions, and Assertions

C an you imagine trying to write code using a language that didn't give you a way to execute statements conditionally? Flow control is a key part of most any useful programming language, and Java offers several ways to do it. Some, like `if` statements and `for` loops, are common to most languages. But Java also throws in a couple of flow control features you might not have used before—exceptions and assertions.

The `if` statement and the `switch` statement are types of conditional/decision controls that allow your program to behave differently at a "fork in the road," depending on the result of a logical test. Java also provides three different looping constructs—`for`, `while`, and `do`—so you can execute the same code over and over again depending on some condition being true. Exceptions give you a clean, simple way to organize code that deals with problems that might crop up at runtime. Finally, the assertion mechanism, added to the language with version 1.4, gives you a way to do testing and debugging checks on conditions you expect to smoke out while developing, when you don't necessarily need or want the runtime overhead associated with exception handling.

With these tools, you can build a robust program that can handle any logical situation with grace. Expect to see a wide range of questions on the exam that include flow control as part of the question code, even on questions that aren't testing your knowledge of flow control.

CERTIFICATION OBJECTIVE

if and switch Statements (Exam Objective 2.1)

2.1 Develop code that implements an if or switch statement; and identify legal argument types for these statements.

The `if` and `switch` statements are commonly referred to as decision statements. When you use decision statements in your program, you're asking the program to evaluate a given expression to determine which course of action to take. We'll look at the `if` statement first.

if-else Branching

The basic format of an `if` statement is as follows:

```
if (booleanExpression) {
  System.out.println("Inside if statement");
}
```

The expression in parentheses must evaluate to (a boolean) `true` or `false`. Typically you're testing something to see if it's true, and then running a code block (one or more statements) if it is true, and (optionally) another block of code if it isn't. The following code demonstrates a legal `if-else` statement:

```
if (x > 3) {
  System.out.println("x is greater than 3");
} else {
  System.out.println("x is not greater than 3");
}
```

The `else` block is optional, so you can also use the following:

```
if (x > 3) {
  y = 2;
}
z += 8;
a = y + x;
```

The preceding code will assign 2 to y if the test succeeds (meaning x really is greater than 3), but the other two lines will execute regardless. Even the curly braces are optional if you have only one statement to execute within the body of the conditional block. The following code example is legal (although not recommended for readability):

```
if (x > 3)     // bad practice, but seen on the exam
  y = 2;
z += 8;
a = y + x;
```

Sun considers it good practice to enclose blocks within curly braces, even if there's only one statement in the block. Be careful with code like the above, because you might think it should read as,

"If x is greater than 3, then set y to 2, z to z + 8, and a to y + x."

But the last two lines are going to execute no matter what! They aren't part of the conditional flow. You might find it even more misleading if the code were indented as follows:

```
if (x > 3)
   y = 2;
   z += 8;
   a = y + x;
```

You might have a need to nest `if-else` statements (although, again, it's not recommended for readability, so nested `if` tests should be kept to a minimum). You can set up an `if-else` statement to test for multiple conditions. The following example uses two conditions so that if the first test fails, we want to perform a second test before deciding what to do:

```
if (price < 300) {
  buyProduct();
} else {
  if (price < 400) {
    getApproval();
  }
  else {
    dontBuyProduct();
  }
}
```

This brings up the other if-else construct, the `if, else if, else`. The preceding code could (and should) be rewritten:

```
if (price < 300) {
  buyProduct();
} else if (price < 400) {
    getApproval();
} else {
    dontBuyProduct();
}
```

There are a couple of rules for using `else` and `else if`:

- You can have zero or one `else` for a given `if`, and it must come after any `else if`s.
- You can have zero to many `else if`s for a given `if` and they must come before the (optional) `else`.
- Once an `else if` succeeds, none of the remaining `else if`s or `else`s will be tested.

The following example shows code that is horribly formatted for the real world. As you've probably guessed, it's fairly likely that you'll encounter formatting like this on the exam. In any case, the code demonstrates the use of multiple `else if`s:

```
int x = 1;
if ( x == 3 ) { }
else if (x < 4) {System.out.println("<4"); }
else if (x < 2) {System.out.println("<2"); }
else { System.out.println("else"); }
```

It produces the output:

```
<4
```

(Notice that even though the second `else if` is true, it is never reached.) Sometimes you can have a problem figuring out which `if` your `else` should pair with, as follows:

```
if (exam.done())
if (exam.getScore() < 0.61)
System.out.println("Try again.");
// Which if does this belong to?
else System.out.println("Java master!");
```

We intentionally left out the indenting in this piece of code so it doesn't give clues as to which `if` statement the `else` belongs to. Did you figure it out? Java law decrees that an `else` clause belongs to the innermost `if` statement to which it might possibly belong (in other words, the closest preceding `if` that doesn't have an `else`). In the case of the preceding example, the `else` belongs to the second `if` statement in the listing. With proper indenting, it would look like this:

```
if (exam.done())
  if (exam.getScore() < 0.61)
    System.out.println("Try again.");
  // Which if does this belong to?
  else
    System.out.println("Java master!");
```

Following our coding conventions by using curly braces, it would be even easier to read:

```
if (exam.done()) {
  if (exam.getScore() < 0.61) {
    System.out.println("Try again.");
  // Which if does this belong to?
  } else {
    System.out.println("Java master!");
  }
}
```

Don't get your hopes up about the exam questions being all nice and indented properly. Some exam takers even have a slogan for the way questions are presented on the exam: anything that can be made more confusing, will be.

Be prepared for questions that not only fail to indent nicely, but intentionally indent in a misleading way: Pay close attention for misdirection like the following:

```
if (exam.done())
  if (exam.getScore() < 0.61)
    System.out.println("Try again.");
else
  System.out.println("Java master!"); // Hmmmmm... now where does
                                       // it belong?
```

Of course, the preceding code is exactly the same as the previous two examples, except for the way it looks.

Legal Expressions for if Statements

The expression in an `if` statement must be a `boolean` expression. Any expression that resolves to a `boolean` is fine, and some of the expressions can be complex. Assume `doStuff()` returns `true`,

```
int y = 5;
int x = 2;
```

```
if (((x > 3) && (y < 2)) | doStuff()) {
    System.out.println("true");
}
```

which prints

```
true
```

You can read the preceding code as, "If both (x > 3) and (y < 2) are true, or if the result of doStuff() is true, then print true." So basically, if just doStuff() alone is true, we'll still get true. If doStuff() is false, though, then both (x > 3) and (y < 2) will have to be true in order to print true. The preceding code is even more complex if you leave off one set of parentheses as follows,

```
int y = 5;
int x = 2;
if ((x > 3) && (y < 2) | doStuff()) {
    System.out.println("true");
}
```

which now prints...nothing! Because the preceding code (with one less set of parentheses) evaluates as though you were saying, "If (x > 3) is true, and either (y < 2) or the result of doStuff() is true, then print true." So if (x > 3) is not true, no point in looking at the rest of the expression." Because of the short-circuit &&, the expression is evaluated as though there were parentheses around (y < 2) | doStuff(). In other words, it is evaluated as a single expression before the && and a single expression after the &&.

Remember that the only legal expression in an if test is a boolean. In some languages, 0 == false, and 1 == true. Not so in Java! The following code shows if statements that might look tempting, but are illegal, followed by legal substitutions:

```
int trueInt = 1;
int falseInt = 0;
if (trueInt)              // illegal
if (trueInt == true)      // illegal
if (1)                    // illegal
if (falseInt == false)    // illegal
if (trueInt == 1)         // legal
if (falseInt == 0)        // legal
```

e x a m

watch *One common mistake programmers make (and that can be difficult to spot), is assigning a boolean variable when you meant to test a boolean variable. Look out for code like the following:*

```
boolean boo = false;
if (boo = true) { }
```

You might think one of three things:
1. The code compiles and runs fine, and the `if` *test fails because* **boo** *is* `false`.
2. The code won't compile because you're using an assignment (=) rather than an equality test (==).
3. The code compiles and runs fine and the `if` *test succeeds because* **boo** *is SET to* `true` *(rather than TESTED for* `true`*) in the* `if` *argument!*

Well, number 3 is correct. Pointless, but correct. Given that the result of any assignment is the value of the variable after the assignment, the expression (`boo = true`*) has a result of* `true`*. Hence, the* `if` *test succeeds. But the only variable that can be assigned (rather than tested against something else) is a* `boolean`*; all other assignments will result in something non-boolean, so they're not legal, as in the following:*

```
int x = 3;
if (x = 5) { }  // Won't compile because x is not a boolean!
```

Because `if` *tests require boolean expressions, you need to be really solid on both logical operators and* `if` *test syntax and semantics.*

switch Statements

A way to simulate the use of multiple `if` statements is with the `switch` statement. Take a look at the following `if-else` code, and notice how confusing it can be to have nested `if` tests, even just a few levels deep:

```
int x = 3;
if(x == 1) {
```

```
    System.out.println("x equals 1");
}
else if(x == 2) {
    System.out.println("x equals 2");
  }
  else if(x == 3) {
      System.out.println("x equals 3");
    }
    else {
      System.out.println("No idea what x is");
    }
```

Now let's see the same functionality represented in a `switch` construct:

```
int x = 3;
switch (x) {
   case 1:
      System.out.println("x is equal to 1");
      break;
   case 2:
      System.out.println("x is equal to 2");
      break;
   case 3:
      System.out.println("x is equal to 3");
      break;
   default:
      System.out.println("Still no idea what x is");
}
```

Note: The reason this `switch` statement emulates the nested `if`s listed earlier is because of the `break` statements that were placed inside of the `switch`. In general, `break` statements are optional, and as we will see in a few pages, their inclusion or exclusion causes huge changes in how a `switch` statement will execute.

Legal Expressions for switch and case

The general form of the `switch` statement is:

```
switch (expression) {
  case constant1: code block
  case constant2: code block
  default: code block
}
```

A `switch`'s expression must evaluate to a `char`, `byte`, `short`, `int`, or, as of Java 5, an enum. That means if you're not using an `enum`, only variables and values that can be automatically promoted (in other words, implicitly cast) to an `int` are acceptable. You won't be able to compile if you use anything else, including the remaining numeric types of `long`, `float`, and `double`.

A `case` constant must evaluate to the same type as the `switch` expression can use, with one additional—and big—constraint: the `case` constant must be a compile time constant! Since the `case` argument has to be resolved at compile time, that means you can use only a constant or `final` variable that is assigned a literal value. It is not enough to be `final`, it must be a compile time *constant*. For example:

```
final int a = 1;
final int b;
b = 2;
int x = 0;
switch (x) {
  case a:      // ok
  case b:      // compiler error
```

Also, the `switch` can only check for equality. This means that the other relational operators such as greater than are rendered unusable in a `case`. The following is an example of a valid expression using a method invocation in a `switch` statement. Note that for this code to be legal, the method being invoked on the object reference must return a value compatible with an `int`.

```
String s = "xyz";
switch (s.length()) {
  case 1:
    System.out.println("length is one");
    break;
  case 2:
    System.out.println("length is two");
    break;
  case 3:
    System.out.println("length is three");
    break;
  default:
    System.out.println("no match");
}
```

One other rule you might not expect involves the question, "What happens if I switch on a variable smaller than an `int`?" Look at the following `switch`:

```
byte g = 2;
switch(g) {
  case 23:
  case 128:
}
```

This code won't compile. Although the `switch` argument is legal—a byte is implicitly cast to an `int`—the second `case` argument (128) is too large for a `byte`, and the compiler knows it! Attempting to compile the preceding example gives you an error something like

```
Test.java:6: possible loss of precision
found   : int
required: byte
    case 128:
        ^
```

It's also illegal to have more than one `case` label using the same value. For example, the following block of code won't compile because it uses two cases with the same value of 80:

```
int temp = 90;
switch(temp) {
  case 80 :  System.out.println("80");
  case 80 :  System.out.println("80");   // won't compile!
  case 90 :  System.out.println("90");
  default :  System.out.println("default");
}
```

It *is* legal to leverage the power of boxing in a `switch` expression. For instance, the following is legal:

```
switch(new Integer(4)) {
  case 4: System.out.println("boxing is OK");
}
```

Look for any violation of the rules for `switch` *and* `case` *arguments.*
For example, you might find illegal examples like the following snippets:

```
switch(x) {
  case 0 {
     y = 7;
  }
}

switch(x) {
  0: { }
  1: { }
}
```

In the first example, the `case` *uses a curly brace and omits the colon.*
The second example omits the keyword `case`.

Break and Fall-Through in switch Blocks

We're finally ready to discuss the `break` statement, and more details about flow control within a `switch` statement. The most important thing to remember about the flow of execution through a `switch` statement is this:

> `case` **constants are evaluated from the top down, and the first** `case` **constant that matches the** `switch`**'s expression is the execution** *entry point.*

In other words, once a `case` constant is matched, the JVM will execute the associated code block, and ALL subsequent code blocks (barring a `break` statement) too! The following example uses an enum in a `case` statement.

```
enum Color {red, green, blue}
class SwitchEnum {
  public static void main(String [] args) {
    Color c = Color.green;
    switch(c) {
```

```
        case red: System.out.print("red ");
        case green: System.out.print("green ");
        case blue: System.out.print("blue ");
        default: System.out.println("done");
      }
    }
  }
```

In this example `case green:` matched, so the JVM executed that code block and all subsequent code blocks to produce the output:

```
green blue done
```

Again, when the program encounters the keyword `break` during the execution of a `switch` statement, execution will immediately move out of the `switch` block to the next statement after the `switch`. If `break` is omitted, the program just keeps executing the remaining `case` blocks until either a `break` is found or the `switch` statement ends. Examine the following code:

```
int x = 1;
switch(x) {
  case 1:  System.out.println("x is one");
  case 2:  System.out.println("x is two");
  case 3:  System.out.println("x is three");
}
System.out.println("out of the switch");
```

The code will print the following:

```
x is one
x is two
x is three
out of the switch
```

This combination occurs because the code didn't hit a `break` statement; execution just kept dropping down through each `case` until the end. This dropping down is actually called "fall-through," because of the way execution falls from one `case` to the next. Remember, the matching `case` is simply your entry point into the `switch` block! In other words, you must *not* think of it as, "Find the matching `case`, execute just that code, and get out." That's *not* how it works. If you do want that "just the matching code" behavior, you'll insert a `break` into each `case` as follows:

```
int x = 1;
switch(x) {
  case 1:  {
    System.out.println("x is one");  break;
  }
  case 2:  {
    System.out.println("x is two");  break;
  }
  case 3:  {
    System.out.println("x is two");  break;
  }
}
System.out.println("out of the switch");
```

Running the preceding code, now that we've added the `break` statements, will print

```
x is one
out of the switch
```

and that's it. We entered into the `switch` block at `case 1`. Because it matched the `switch()` argument, we got the `println` statement, then hit the `break` and jumped to the end of the `switch`.

An interesting example of this fall-through logic is shown in the following code:

```
int x = someNumberBetweenOneAndTen;

switch (x) {
  case 2:
  case 4:
  case 6:
  case 8:
  case 10: {
    System.out.println("x is an even number");  break;
  }
}
```

This `switch` statement will print `x is an even number` or nothing, depending on whether the number is between one and ten and is odd or even. For example, if x is 4, execution will begin at `case 4`, but then fall down through 6, 8, and 10, where it prints and then breaks. The `break` at `case 10`, by the way, is not needed; we're already at the end of the `switch` anyway.

Note: Because fall-through is less than intuitive, Sun recommends that you add a comment like: `// fall through` when you use fall-through logic.

The Default Case

What if, using the preceding code, you wanted to print "x is an odd number" if none of the cases (the even numbers) matched? You couldn't put it after the switch statement, or even as the last case in the switch, because in both of those situations it would always print x is an odd number. To get this behavior, you'll use the default keyword. (By the way, if you've wondered why there is a default keyword even though we don't use a modifier for default access control, now you'll see that the default keyword is used for a completely different purpose.) The only change we need to make is to add the default case to the preceding code:

```java
int x = someNumberBetweenOneAndTen;

switch (x) {
  case 2:
  case 4:
  case 6:
  case 8:
  case 10: {
    System.out.println("x is an even number");
    break;
  }
  default: System.out.println("x is an odd number");
}
```

exam
watch

*The default **case doesn't have to come at the end of the** switch. Look for it in strange places such as the following:*

```java
int x = 2;
switch (x) {
  case 2:  System.out.println("2");
  default: System.out.println("default");
  case 3:  System.out.println("3");
  case 4:  System.out.println("4");
}
```

Running the preceding code prints

```
2
default
3
4
```

And if we modify it so that the only match is the default case:

```
int x = 7;
switch (x) {
  case 2:  System.out.println("2");
  default: System.out.println("default");
  case 3: System.out.println("3");
  case 4: System.out.println("4");
}
```

Running the preceding code prints

```
default
3
4
```

The rule to remember is that default *works just like any other* case *for fall-through!*

EXERCISE 5-1

Creating a switch-case Statement

Try creating a switch statement using a char value as the case. Include a default behavior if none of the char values match.

■ Make sure a char variable is declared before the switch statement.

■ Each case statement should be followed by a break.

■ The default case can be located at the end, middle, or top.

Loops and Iterators (Exam Objective 2.2)

2.2   Develop code that implements all forms of loops and iterators, including the use of for, the enhanced for loop (for-each), do, while, labels, break, and continue; and explain the values taken by loop counter variables during and after loop execution.

Java loops come in three flavors: while, do, and for (and as of Java 5, the for loop has two variations). All three let you repeat a block of code as long as some condition is true, or for a specific number of iterations. You're probably familiar with loops from other languages, so even if you're somewhat new to Java, these won't be a problem to learn.

Using while Loops

The while loop is good for scenarios where you don't know how many times a block or statement should repeat, but you want to continue looping as long as some condition is true. A while statement looks like this:

```
while (expression) {
  // do stuff
}
    or


int x = 2;
while(x == 2) {
  System.out.println(x);
  ++x;
}
```

In this case, as in all loops, the expression (test) must evaluate to a boolean result. The body of the while loop will only execute if the expression (sometimes called the "condition") results in a value of true. Once inside the loop, the loop body will repeat until the condition is no longer met because it evaluates to false. In the previous example, program control will enter the loop body because x is equal to 2. However, x is incremented in the loop, so when the condition is checked again it will evaluate to false and exit the loop.

Any variables used in the expression of a `while` loop must be declared before the expression is evaluated. In other words, you can't say

```
while (int x = 2) { }   // not legal
```

Then again, why would you? Instead of testing the variable, you'd be declaring and initializing it, so it would always have the exact same value. Not much of a test condition!

The key point to remember about a `while` loop is that it might not ever run. If the test expression is `false` the first time the `while` expression is checked, the loop body will be skipped and the program will begin executing at the first statement *after* the `while` loop. Look at the following example:

```
int x = 8;
while (x > 8) {
  System.out.println("in the loop");
  x = 10;
}
System.out.println("past the loop");
```

Running this code produces

```
past the loop
```

Because the expression `(x > 8)` evaluates to `false`, none of the code within the `while` loop ever executes.

Using do Loops

The `do` loop is similar to the `while` loop, except that the expression is not evaluated until after the `do` loop's code is executed. Therefore the code in a `do` loop is guaranteed to execute at least once. The following shows a `do` loop in action:

```
do {
   System.out.println("Inside loop");
} while(false);
```

The `System.out.println()` statement will print once, even though the expression evaluates to `false`. Remember, the `do` loop will always run the code in the loop body at least once. Be sure to note the use of the semicolon at the end of the `while` expression.

As with if *tests, look for* while *loops (and the* while *test in a* do *loop) with an expression that does not resolve to a* boolean. *Take a look at the following examples of legal and illegal* while *expressions:*

```
int x = 1;
while (x) { }          // Won't compile; x is not a boolean
while (x = 5) { }      // Won't compile; resolves to 5
                       //(as the result of assignment)
while (x == 5) { }     // Legal, equality test
while (true) { }       // Legal
```

Using for Loops

As of Java 5, the `for` loop took on a second structure. We'll call the old style of `for` loop the "basic `for` loop", and we'll call the new style of `for` loop the "enhanced `for` loop" (even though the Sun objective 2.2 refers to it as the `for-each`). Depending on what documentation you use (Sun's included), you'll see both terms, along with `for-in`. The terms `for-in`, `for-each`, and "enhanced `for`" all refer to the same Java construct.

The basic `for` loop is more flexible than the enhanced `for` loop, but the enhanced `for` loop was designed to make iterating through arrays and collections easier to code.

The Basic for Loop

The `for` loop is especially useful for flow control when you already know how many times you need to execute the statements in the loop's block. The `for` loop declaration has three main parts, besides the body of the loop:

- Declaration and initialization of variables
- The `boolean` expression (conditional test)
- The iteration expression

The three `for` declaration parts are separated by semicolons. The following two examples demonstrate the `for` loop. The first example shows the parts of a `for` loop in a pseudocode form, and the second shows a typical example of a `for` loop.

```
for (/*Initialization*/ ; /*Condition*/ ;  /* Iteration */) {
  /* loop body */
}

for (int i = 0; i<10; i++) {
  System.out.println("i is " + i);
}
```

The Basic for Loop: Declaration and Initialization

The first part of the `for` statement lets you declare and initialize zero, one, or multiple variables of the same type inside the parentheses after the `for` keyword. If you declare more than one variable of the same type, then you'll need to separate them with commas as follows:

```
for (int x = 10, y = 3; y > 3; y++) { }
```

The declaration and initialization happens before anything else in a `for` loop. And whereas the other two parts—the boolean test and the iteration expression—will run with each iteration of the loop, the declaration and initialization happens just once, at the very beginning. You also must know that the scope of variables declared in the `for` loop ends with the `for` loop! The following demonstrates this:

```
for (int x = 1; x < 2; x++) {
  System.out.println(x);   // Legal
}
System.out.println(x);   // Not Legal! x is now out of scope
                         // and can't be accessed.
```

If you try to compile this, you'll get something like this:

```
Test.java:19: cannot resolve symbol
symbol  : variable x
location: class Test
  System.out.println(x);
                     ^
```

Basic for Loop: Conditional (boolean) Expression

The next section that executes is the conditional expression, which (like all other conditional tests) must evaluate to a `boolean` value. You can have only one logical expression, but it can be very complex. Look out for code that uses logical expressions like this:

```
for (int x = 0; ((((x < 10) && (y-- > 2)) | x == 3)); x++) { }
```

The preceding code is legal, but the following is not:

```
for (int x = 0; (x > 5), (y < 2); x++) { } // too many
                                          //expressions
```

The compiler will let you know the problem:

```
TestLong.java:20: ';' expected
for (int x = 0; (x > 5), (y < 2); x++) { }
                       ^
```

The rule to remember is this: *You can have only one test expression.*

In other words, you can't use multiple tests separated by commas, even though the other two parts of a for statement can have multiple parts.

Basic for Loop: Iteration Expression

After each execution of the body of the for loop, the iteration expression is executed. This is where you get to say what you want to happen with each iteration of the loop. Remember that it always happens after the loop body runs! Look at the following:

```
for (int x = 0; x < 1; x++) {
  // body code that doesn't change the value of x
}
```

The preceding loop executes just once. The first time into the loop x is set to 0, then x is tested to see if it's less than 1 (which it is), and then the body of the loop executes. After the body of the loop runs, the iteration expression runs, incrementing x by 1. Next, the conditional test is checked, and since the result is now false, execution jumps to below the for loop and continues on.

Keep in mind that barring a forced exit, evaluating the iteration expression and then evaluating the conditional expression are always the last two things that happen in a for loop!

Examples of forced exits include a `break`, a return, a `System.exit()`, or an exception, which will all cause a loop to terminate abruptly, without running the iteration expression. Look at the following code:

```
static boolean doStuff() {
  for (int x = 0; x < 3; x++) {
    System.out.println("in for loop");
    return true;
  }
  return true;
}
```

Running this code produces

```
in for loop
```

The statement only prints once, because a return causes execution to leave not just the current iteration of a loop, but the entire method. So the iteration expression never runs in that case. Table 5-1 lists the causes and results of abrupt loop termination.

| TABLE 5-I | Causes of Early Loop Termination |

Code in Loop	What Happens
`break`	Execution jumps immediately to the 1st statement after the `for` loop.
`return`	Execution jumps immediately back to the calling method.
`System.exit()`	All program execution stops; the VM shuts down.

Basic for Loop: for Loop Issues

None of the three sections of the `for` declaration are required! The following example is perfectly legal (although not necessarily good practice):

```
for( ; ; ) {
  System.out.println("Inside an endless loop");
}
```

In the preceding example, all the declaration parts are left out so the `for` loop will act like an endless loop. For the exam, it's important to know that with the absence of the initialization and increment sections, the loop will act like a `while` loop. The following example demonstrates how this is accomplished:

```
int i = 0;

for (;i<10;) {
  i++;
  //do some other work
}
```

The next example demonstrates a `for` loop with multiple variables in play. A comma separates the variables, and they must be of the same type. Remember that the variables declared in the `for` statement are all local to the `for` loop, and can't be used outside the scope of the loop.

```
for (int i = 0,j = 0; (i<10) && (j<10); i++, j++) {
  System.out.println("i is " + i + " j is " +j);
}
```

exam
ⓦatch

Variable scope plays a large role in the exam. You need to know that a variable declared in the `for` loop can't be used beyond the `for` loop. But a variable only initialized in the `for` statement (but declared earlier) can be used beyond the loop. For example, the following is legal,

```
int x = 3;
for (x = 12; x < 20; x++) { }
System.out.println(x);
```

while this is not

```
for (int x = 3; x < 20; x++) { } System.out.println(x);
```

The last thing to note is that all three sections of the `for` loop are independent of each other. The three expressions in the `for` statement don't need to operate on the same variables, although they typically do. But even the iterator expression, which many mistakenly call the "increment expression," doesn't need to increment or set anything; you can put in virtually any arbitrary code statements that you want to happen with each iteration of the loop. Look at the following:

```
int b = 3;
for (int a = 1;  b != 1; System.out.println("iterate")) {
  b = b - a;
}
```

The preceding code prints

```
iterate
iterate
```

The Enhanced for Loop (for Arrays)

The enhanced `for` loop, new to Java 5, is a specialized `for` loop that simplifies looping through an array or a collection. In this chapter we're going to focus on using the enhanced `for` to loop through arrays. In Chapter 7 we'll revisit the enhanced `for` as we discuss collections—where the enhanced `for` really comes into its own.

Instead of having *three* components, the enhanced `for` has *two*. Let's loop through an array the basic (old) way, and then using the enhanced `for`:

```
int [] a = {1,2,3,4};
for(int x = 0; x < a.length; x++)    // basic for loop
  System.out.print(a[x]);
for(int n : a)                       // enhanced for loop
  System.out.print(n);
```

Which produces this output:

```
12341234
```

More formally, let's describe the enhanced for as follows:

```
for(declaration : expression)
```

The two pieces of the for statement are

- **declaration**   The *newly declared* block variable, of a type compatible with the elements of the array you are accessing. This variable will be available within the for block, and its value will be the same as the current array element.
- **expression**   This must evaluate to the array you want to loop through. This could be an array variable or a method call that returns an array. The array can be any type: primitives, objects, even arrays of arrays.

Using the above definitions, let's look at some legal and illegal enhanced for declarations:

```
int x;
long x2;
Long [] La = {4L, 5L, 6L};
long [] la = {7L, 8L, 9L};
int [] [] twoDee = {{1,2,3}, {4,5,6}, {7,8,9}};
String [] sNums = {"one", "two", "three"};
Animal [] animals = {new Dog(), new Cat()};

// legal 'for' declarations
for(long y : la ) ;          // loop thru an array of longs
for(long lp : La) ;          // autoboxing the Long objects
                             // into longs
for(int[] n : twoDee) ;      // loop thru the array of arrays
for(int n2 : twoDee[2]) ;    // loop thru the 3rd sub-array
for(String s : sNums) ;      // loop thru the array of Strings
for(Object o : sNums) ;      // set an Object reference to
                             // each String
for(Animal a : animals) ;    // set an Animal reference to each
                             // element
```

```
// ILLEGAL 'for' declarations
for(x2 : la) ;            // x2 is already declared
for(int x2 : twoDee) ;    // can't stuff an array into an int
for(int x3 : la) ;        // can't stuff a long into an int
for(Dog d : animals) ;    // you might get a Cat!
```

The enhanced `for` loop assumes that, barring an early exit from the loop, you'll always loop through every element of the array. The following discussions of `break` and `continue` apply to both the basic and enhanced `for` loops.

Using break and continue

The `break` and `continue` keywords are used to stop either the entire loop (`break`) or just the current iteration (`continue`). Typically if you're using `break` or `continue`, you'll do an `if` test within the loop, and if some condition becomes `true` (or `false` depending on the program), you want to get out immediately. The difference between them is whether or not you continue with a new iteration or jump to the first statement below the loop and continue from there.

Remember, `continue` *statements must be inside a loop; otherwise, you'll get a compiler error.* `break` *statements must be used inside either a loop or* `switch` *statement. (Note: this does not apply to labeled* `break` *statements.).*

The `break` statement causes the program to stop execution of the innermost loop and start processing the next line of code after the block.

The `continue` statement causes only the current iteration of the innermost loop to cease and the next iteration of the same loop to start if the condition of the loop is met. When using a `continue` statement with a `for` loop, you need to consider the effects that `continue` has on the loop iteration. Examine the following code:

```
for (int i = 0; i < 10; i++) {
  System.out.println("Inside loop");
  continue;
}
```

The question is, is this an endless loop? The answer is no. When the `continue` statement is hit, the iteration expression still runs! It runs just as though the current iteration ended "in the natural way." So in the preceding example, `i` will still increment before the condition (`i < 10`) is checked again. Most of the time, a `continue` is used within an `if` test as follows:

```
for (int i = 0; i < 10; i++) {
  System.out.println("Inside loop");
  if (foo.doStuff() == 5) {
    continue;
  }
  // more loop code, that won't be reached when the above if
  // test is true
}
```

Unlabeled Statements

Both the `break` statement and the `continue` statement can be unlabeled or labeled. Although it's far more common to use `break` and `continue` unlabeled, the exam expects you to know how labeled `break` and `continue` statements work. As stated before, a `break` statement (unlabeled) will exit out of the innermost looping construct and proceed with the next line of code beyond the loop block. The following example demonstrates a `break` statement:

```
boolean problem = true;
while (true) {
  if (problem) {
    System.out.println("There was a problem");
    break;
  }
}
// next line of code
```

In the previous example, the `break` statement is unlabeled. The following is an example of an unlabeled `continue` statement:

```
while (!EOF) {
  //read a field from a file
  if (wrongField) {
    continue;    // move to the next field in the file
  }
  // otherwise do other stuff with the field
}
```

In this example, a file is being read one field at a time. When an error is encountered, the program moves to the next field in the file and uses the `continue` statement to go back into the loop (if it is not at the end of the file) and keeps reading the various fields. If the `break` command were used instead, the code would stop reading the file once the error occurred and move on to the next line of code after the loop. The `continue` statement gives you a way to say, "This particular iteration of the loop needs to stop, but not the whole loop itself. I just don't want the rest of the code in this iteration to finish, so do the iteration expression and then start over with the test, and don't worry about what was below the `continue` statement."

Labeled Statements

Although many statements in a Java program can be labeled, it's most common to use labels with loop statements like `for` or `while`, in conjunction with `break` and `continue` statements. A label statement must be placed just before the statement being labeled, and it consists of a valid identifier that ends with a colon (:).

You need to understand the difference between labeled and unlabeled `break` and `continue`. The labeled varieties are needed only in situations where you have a nested loop, and need to indicate which of the nested loops you want to break from, or from which of the nested loops you want to continue with the next iteration. A `break` statement will exit out of the labeled loop, as opposed to the innermost loop, if the `break` keyword is combined with a label. An example of what a label looks like is in the following code:

```
foo:
  for (int x = 3; x < 20; x++) {
    while(y > 7) {
      y--;
    }
  }
```

The label must adhere to the rules for a valid variable name and should adhere to the Java naming convention. The syntax for the use of a label name in conjunction with a `break` statement is the `break` keyword, then the label name, followed by a semicolon. A more complete example of the use of a labeled `break` statement is as follows:

```
boolean isTrue = true;
outer:
  for(int i=0; i<5; i++) {
    while (isTrue) {
```

```
      System.out.println("Hello");
      break outer;
   } // end of inner while loop
   System.out.println("Outer loop."); // Won't print
 } // end of outer for loop
System.out.println("Good-Bye");
```

Running this code produces

```
Hello
Good-Bye
```

In this example the word Hello will be printed one time. Then, the labeled break statement will be executed, and the flow will exit out of the loop labeled outer. The next line of code will then print out Good-Bye. Let's see what will happen if the continue statement is used instead of the break statement. The following code example is similar to the preceding one, with the exception of substituting continue for break:

```
outer:
   for (int i=0; i<5; i++) {
     for (int j=0; j<5; j++) {
       System.out.println("Hello");
       continue outer;
     } // end of inner loop
     System.out.println("outer"); // Never prints
   }
System.out.println("Good-Bye");
```

Running this code produces

```
Hello
Hello
Hello
Hello
Hello
Good-Bye
```

In this example, Hello will be printed five times. After the continue statement is executed, the flow continues with the next iteration of the loop identified with the label. Finally, when the condition in the outer loop evaluates to false, this loop will finish and Good-Bye will be printed.

EXERCISE 5-2

Creating a Labeled while Loop

Try creating a labeled `while` loop. Make the label `outer` and provide a condition to check whether a variable `age` is less than or equal to 21. Within the loop, increment `age` by one. Every time the program goes through the loop, check whether `age` is 16. If it is, print the message "get your driver's license" and continue to the outer loop. If not, print "Another year."

- The `outer` label should appear just before the `while` loop begins.
- Make sure `age` is declared outside of the `while` loop.

Labeled `continue` *and* `break` *statements must be inside the loop that has the same label name; otherwise, the code will not compile.*

CERTIFICATION OBJECTIVE

Handling Exceptions (Exam Objectives 2.4 and 2.5)

2.4 Develop code that makes use of exceptions and exception handling clauses (try, catch, finally), and declares methods and overriding methods that throw exceptions.

2.5 Recognize the effect of an exception arising at a specific point in a code fragment. Note that the exception may be a runtime exception, a checked exception, or an error.

An old maxim in software development says that 80 percent of the work is used 20 percent of the time. The 80 percent refers to the effort required to check and handle errors. In many languages, writing program code that checks for and deals with errors is tedious and bloats the application source into confusing spaghetti.

Still, error detection and handling may be the most important ingredient of any robust application. Java arms developers with an elegant mechanism for handling errors that produces efficient and organized error-handling code: exception handling.

Exception handling allows developers to detect errors easily without writing special code to test return values. Even better, it lets us keep exception-*handling* code cleanly separated from the exception-*generating* code. It also lets us use the same exception-handling code to deal with a range of possible exceptions.

The exam has three objectives covering exception handling. We'll cover the first two in this section, and in the next section we'll cover those aspects of exception handling that are new to the exam as of Java 5.

Catching an Exception Using try and catch

Before we begin, let's introduce some terminology. The term "exception" means "exceptional condition" and is an occurrence that alters the normal program flow. A bunch of things can lead to exceptions, including hardware failures, resource exhaustion, and good old bugs. When an exceptional event occurs in Java, an exception is said to be "thrown." The code that's responsible for doing something about the exception is called an "exception handler," and it "catches" the thrown exception.

Exception handling works by transferring the execution of a program to an appropriate exception handler when an exception occurs. For example, if you call a method that opens a file but the file cannot be opened, execution of that method will stop, and code that you wrote to deal with this situation will be run. Therefore, we need a way to tell the JVM what code to execute when a certain exception happens. To do this, we use the `try` and `catch` keywords. The `try` is used to define a block of code in which exceptions may occur. This block of code is called a guarded region (which really means "risky code goes here"). One or more `catch` clauses match a specific exception (or group of exceptions—more on that later) to a block of code that handles it. Here's how it looks in pseudocode:

```
1. try {
2.    // This is the first line of the "guarded region"
3.    // that is governed by the try keyword.
4.    // Put code here that might cause some kind of exception.
5.    // We may have many code lines here or just one.
6. }
7. catch(MyFirstException) {
8.    // Put code here that handles this exception.
```

```
9.    // This is the next line of the exception handler.
10.   // This is the last line of the exception handler.
11. }
12. catch(MySecondException) {
13.   // Put code here that handles this exception
14. }
15.
16. // Some other unguarded (normal, non-risky) code begins here
```

In this pseudocode example, lines 2 through 5 constitute the guarded region that is governed by the `try` clause. Line 7 is an exception handler for an exception of type MyFirstException. Line 12 is an exception handler for an exception of type MySecondException. Notice that the `catch` blocks immediately follow the `try` block. This is a requirement; if you have one or more `catch` blocks, they must immediately follow the `try` block. Additionally, the `catch` blocks must all follow each other, without any other statements or blocks in between. Also, the order in which the `catch` blocks appear matters, as we'll see a little later.

Execution of the guarded region starts at line 2. If the program executes all the way past line 5 with no exceptions being thrown, execution will transfer to line 15 and continue downward. However, if at any time in lines 2 through 5 (the `try` block) an exception is thrown of type MyFirstException, execution will immediately transfer to line 7. Lines 8 through 10 will then be executed so that the entire `catch` block runs, and then execution will transfer to line 15 and continue.

Note that if an exception occurred on, say, line 3 of the `try` block, the rest of the lines in the `try` block (4 and 5) would never be executed. Once control jumps to the `catch` block, it never returns to complete the balance of the `try` block. This is exactly what you want, though. Imagine your code looks something like this pseudocode:

```
try {
  getTheFileFromOverNetwork
  readFromTheFileAndPopulateTable
}
catch(CantGetFileFromNetwork) {
  displayNetworkErrorMessage
}
```

The preceding pseudocode demonstrates how you typically work with exceptions. Code that's dependent on a risky operation (as populating a table with file data is dependent on getting the file from the network) is grouped into a `try` block in such a way that if, say, the first operation fails, you won't continue trying to run other code that's also guaranteed to fail. In the pseudocode example, you won't be able to read from the file if you can't get the file off the network in the first place.

One of the benefits of using exception handling is that code to handle any particular exception that may occur in the governed region needs to be written only once. Returning to our earlier code example, there may be three different places in our `try` block that can generate a MyFirstException, but wherever it occurs it will be handled by the same `catch` block (on line 7). We'll discuss more benefits of exception handling near the end of this chapter.

Using finally

Although `try` and `catch` provide a terrific mechanism for trapping and handling exceptions, we are left with the problem of how to clean up after ourselves if an exception occurs. Because execution transfers out of the `try` block as soon as an exception is thrown, we can't put our cleanup code at the bottom of the `try` block and expect it to be executed if an exception occurs. Almost as bad an idea would be placing our cleanup code in each of the `catch` blocks—let's see why.

Exception handlers are a poor place to clean up after the code in the `try` block because each handler then requires its own copy of the cleanup code. If, for example, you allocated a network socket or opened a file somewhere in the guarded region, each exception handler would have to close the file or release the socket. That would make it too easy to forget to do cleanup, and also lead to a lot of redundant code. To address this problem, Java offers the `finally` block.

A `finally` block encloses code that is always executed at some point after the `try` block, whether an exception was thrown or not. Even if there is a `return` statement in the `try` block, the `finally` block executes right after the `return` statement is encountered, and before the `return` executes!

This is the right place to close your files, release your network sockets, and perform any other cleanup your code requires. If the `try` block executes with no exceptions, the `finally` block is executed immediately after the `try` block completes. If there was an exception thrown, the `finally` block executes immediately after the proper `catch` block completes. Let's look at another pseudocode example:

```
1: try {
2:    // This is the first line of the "guarded region".
3: }
4: catch(MyFirstException) {
```

```
 5:    // Put code here that handles this exception
 6: }
 7: catch(MySecondException) {
 8:    // Put code here that handles this exception
 9: }
10: finally {
11:    // Put code here to release any resource we
12:    // allocated in the try clause.
13: }
14:
15: // More code here
```

As before, execution starts at the first line of the `try` block, line 2. If there are no exceptions thrown in the `try` block, execution transfers to line 11, the first line of the `finally` block. On the other hand, if a `MySecondException` is thrown while the code in the `try` block is executing, execution transfers to the first line of that exception handler, line 8 in the `catch` clause. After all the code in the `catch` clause is executed, the program moves to line 11, the first line of the `finally` clause. Repeat after me: `finally` always runs! OK, we'll have to refine that a little, but for now, start burning in the idea that `finally` always runs. If an exception is thrown, `finally` runs. If an exception is not thrown, `finally` runs. If the exception is caught, `finally` runs. If the exception is not caught, `finally` runs. Later we'll look at the few scenarios in which `finally` might not run or complete.

Remember, `finally` clauses are not required. If you don't write one, your code will compile and run just fine. In fact, if you have no resources to clean up after your `try` block completes, you probably don't need a `finally` clause. Also, because the compiler doesn't even require `catch` clauses, sometimes you'll run across code that has a `try` block immediately followed by a `finally` block. Such code is useful when the exception is going to be passed back to the calling method, as explained in the next section. Using a `finally` block allows the cleanup code to execute even when there isn't a `catch` clause.

The following legal code demonstrates a `try` with a `finally` but no `catch`:

```
try {
  // do stuff
} finally {
  //clean up
}
```

The following legal code demonstrates a `try`, `catch`, and `finally`:

```
try {
  // do stuff
} catch (SomeException ex) {
  // do exception handling
} finally {
  // clean up
}
```

The following ILLEGAL code demonstrates a `try` without a `catch` or `finally`:

```
try {
  // do stuff
}
// need a catch or finally here
System.out.println("out of try block");
```

The following ILLEGAL code demonstrates a misplaced `catch` block:

```
try {
  // do stuff
}
// can't have code between try/catch
System.out.println("out of try block");
catch(Exception ex) { }
```

*It is illegal to use a `try` **clause without either a** `catch` **clause or a** `finally` **clause. A** `try` **clause by itself will result in a compiler error. Any** `catch` **clauses must immediately follow the** `try` **block. Any** `finally` **clause must immediately follow the last** `catch` **clause (or it must immediately follow the** `try` **block if there is no** `catch`**). It is legal to omit either the** `catch` **clause or the** `finally` **clause, but not both.***

You can't sneak any code in between the try, catch, **or** finally **blocks. The following won't compile:**

```
try {
  // do stuff
}
System.out.print("below the try");  //Illegal!
catch(Exception ex) { }
```

Propagating Uncaught Exceptions

Why aren't catch clauses required? What happens to an exception that's thrown in a try block when there is no catch clause waiting for it? Actually, there's no requirement that you code a catch clause for every possible exception that could be thrown from the corresponding try block. In fact, it's doubtful that you could accomplish such a feat! If a method doesn't provide a catch clause for a particular exception, that method is said to be "ducking" the exception (or "passing the buck").

So what happens to a ducked exception? Before we discuss that, we need to briefly review the concept of the call stack. Most languages have the concept of a method stack or a call stack. Simply put, the call stack is the chain of methods that your program executes to get to the current method. If your program starts in method main() and main() calls method a(), which calls method b(), which in turn calls method c(), the call stack consists of the following:

```
c
b
a
main
```

We will represent the stack as growing upward (although it can also be visualized as growing downward). As you can see, the last method called is at the top of the stack, while the first calling method is at the bottom. The method at the very top of the stack trace would be the method you were currently executing. If we move back down the call stack, we're moving from the current method to the previously called method. Figure 5-1 illustrates a way to think about how the call stack in Java works.

FIGURE 5-1

The Java method
call stack

1) The call stack while method3() is running.

4	method3()	method2 invokes method3
3	method2()	method1 invokes method2
2	method1()	main invokes method1
1	main()	main begins

The order in which methods are put on the call stack

2) The call stack after method3() completes
Execution returns to method2()

1	method2()	method2() will complete
2	method1()	method1() will complete
3	main()	main() will complete and the JVM will exit

The order in which methods complete

Now let's examine what happens to ducked exceptions. Imagine a building, say, five stories high, and at each floor there is a deck or balcony. Now imagine that on each deck, one person is standing holding a baseball mitt. Exceptions are like balls dropped from person to person, starting from the roof. An exception is first thrown from the top of the stack (in other words, the person on the roof), and if it isn't caught by the same person who threw it (the person on the roof), it drops down the call stack to the previous method, which is the person standing on the deck one floor down. If not caught there, by the person one floor down, the exception/ball again drops down to the previous method (person on the next floor down), and so on until it is caught or until it reaches the very bottom of the call stack. This is called exception propagation.

If an exception reaches the bottom of the call stack, it's like reaching the bottom of a very long drop; the ball explodes, and so does your program. An exception that's never caught will cause your application to stop running. A description (if one is available) of the exception will be displayed, and the call stack will be "dumped." This helps you debug your application by telling you what exception was thrown, from what method it was thrown, and what the stack looked like at the time.

exam
watch

You can keep throwing an exception down through the methods on the stack. But what about when you get to the `main()` *method at the bottom? You can throw the exception out of* `main()` *as well. This results in the Java Virtual Machine (JVM) halting, and the stack trace will be printed to the output.*

The following code throws an exception,

```
class TestEx {
  public static void main (String [] args) {
    doStuff();
  }
  static void doStuff() {
    doMoreStuff();
  }
  static void doMoreStuff() {
    int x = 5/0;   // Can't divide by zero!
                   // ArithmeticException is thrown here
  }
}
```

which prints out a stack trace something like,

```
%java TestEx
Exception in thread "main" java.lang.ArithmeticException: /
by zero
at TestEx.doMoreStuff(TestEx.java:10)
at TestEx.doStuff(TestEx.java:7)
at TestEx.main(TestEx.java:3)
```

EXERCISE 5-3

Propagating and Catching an Exception

In this exercise you're going to create two methods that deal with exceptions. One of the methods is the `main()` method, which will call another method. If an exception is thrown in the other method, `main()` must deal with it. A `finally` statement will be included to indicate that the program has completed. The method that `main()`

will call will be named `reverse`, and it will reverse the order of the characters in a String. If the String contains no characters, `reverse` will propagate an exception up to the `main()` method.

- Create a class called `Propagate` and a `main()` method, which will remain empty for now.
- Create a method called `reverse`. It takes an argument of a `String` and returns a `String`.
- In `reverse`, check if the `String` has a length of 0 by using the `String.length()` method. If the length is 0, the `reverse` method will throw an exception.
- Now include the code to reverse the order of the `String`. Because this isn't the main topic of this chapter, the reversal code has been provided, but feel free to try it on your own.

```
String reverseStr = "";
for(int i=s.length()-1;i>=0;--i) {
  reverseStr += s.charAt(i);
}
return reverseStr;
```

- Now in the `main()` method you will attempt to call this method and deal with any potential exceptions. Additionally, you will include a `finally` statement that displays when `main()` has finished.

Defining Exceptions

We have been discussing exceptions as a concept. We know that they are thrown when a problem of some type happens, and we know what effect they have on the flow of our program. In this section we will develop the concepts further and use exceptions in functional Java code. Earlier we said that an exception is an occurrence that alters the normal program flow. But because this is Java, anything that's not a primitive must be…an object. Exceptions are no, well, exception to this rule. Every exception is an instance of a class that has class `Exception` in its inheritance hierarchy. In other words, exceptions are always some subclass of `java.lang.Exception`.

When an exception is thrown, an object of a particular `Exception` subtype is instantiated and handed to the exception handler as an argument to the `catch` clause. An actual `catch` clause looks like this:

```
try {
    // some code here
}
catch (ArrayIndexOutOfBoundsException e) {
    e.printStackTrace();
}
```

In this example, `e` is an instance of the `ArrayIndexOutOfBoundsException` class. As with any other object, you can call its methods.

Exception Hierarchy

All exception classes are subtypes of class `Exception`. This class derives from the class `Throwable` (which derives from the class `Object`). Figure 5-2 shows the hierarchy for the exception classes.

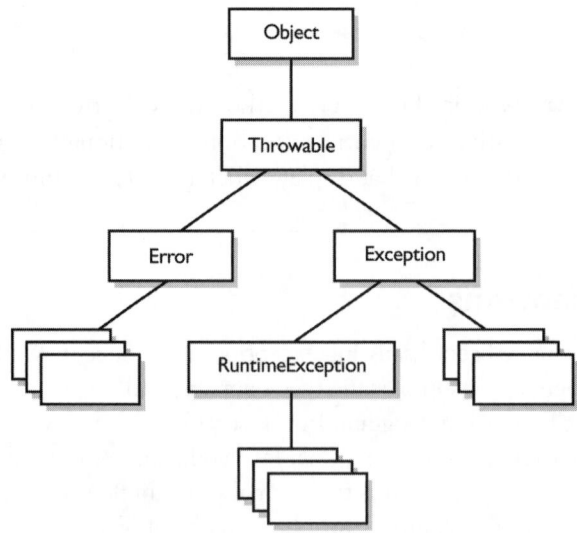

As you can see, there are two subclasses that derive from `Throwable`: `Exception` and `Error`. Classes that derive from `Error` represent unusual situations that are not caused by program errors, and indicate things that would not normally happen during program execution, such as the JVM running out of memory. Generally, your application won't be able to recover from an `Error`, so you're not required to handle them. If your code does not handle them (and it usually won't), it will still compile with no trouble. Although often thought of as exceptional conditions, Errors are technically not exceptions because they do not derive from class `Exception`.

In general, an exception represents something that happens not as a result of a programming error, but rather because some resource is not available or some other condition required for correct execution is not present. For example, if your application is supposed to communicate with another application or computer that is not answering, this is an exception that is not caused by a bug. Figure 5-2 also shows a subtype of `Exception` called `RuntimeException`. These exceptions are a special case because they sometimes do indicate program errors. They can also represent rare, difficult-to-handle exceptional conditions. Runtime exceptions are discussed in greater detail later in this chapter.

Java provides many exception classes, most of which have quite descriptive names. There are two ways to get information about an exception. The first is from the type of the exception itself. The next is from information that you can get from the exception object. Class `Throwable` (at the top of the inheritance tree for exceptions) provides its descendants with some methods that are useful in exception handlers. One of these is `printStackTrace()`. As expected, if you call an exception object's `printStackTrace()` method, as in the earlier example, a stack trace from where the exception occurred will be printed.

We discussed that a call stack builds upward with the most recently called method at the top. You will notice that the `printStackTrace()` method prints the most recently entered method first and continues down, printing the name of each method as it works its way down the call stack (this is called unwinding the stack) from the top.

---

e x a m

ⓦatch   *For the exam, it is not necessary to know any of the methods contained in the `Throwable` classes, including `Exception` and `Error`. You are expected to know that `Exception`, `Error`, `RuntimeException`, and `Throwable` types can all be thrown using the `throw` keyword, and can all be caught (although you rarely will catch anything other than `Exception` subtypes).*

Handling an Entire Class Hierarchy of Exceptions

We've discussed that the `catch` keyword allows you to specify a particular type of exception to catch. You can actually catch more than one type of exception in a single `catch` clause. If the exception class that you specify in the `catch` clause has no subclasses, then only the specified class of exception will be caught. However, if the class specified in the `catch` clause does have subclasses, any exception object that subclasses the specified class will be caught as well.

For example, class `IndexOutOfBoundsException` has two subclasses, `ArrayIndexOutOfBoundsException` and `StringIndexOutOfBoundsException`. You may want to write one exception handler that deals with exceptions produced by either type of boundary error, but you might not be concerned with which exception you actually have. In this case, you could write a `catch` clause like the following:

```
try {
  // Some code here that can throw a boundary exception
}
catch (IndexOutOfBoundsException e) {
  e.printStackTrace();
}
```

If any code in the `try` block throws `ArrayIndexOutOfBoundsException` or `StringIndexOutOfBoundsException`, the exception will be caught and handled. This can be convenient, but it should be used sparingly. By specifying an exception class's superclass in your `catch` clause, you're discarding valuable information about the exception. You can, of course, find out exactly what exception class you have, but if you're going to do that, you're better off writing a separate `catch` clause for each exception type of interest.

on the **job**

Resist the temptation to write a single catchall exception handler such as the following:

```
try {
  // some code
}
catch (Exception e) {
  e.printStackTrace();
}
```

This code will catch every exception generated. Of course, no single exception handler can properly handle every exception, and programming in this way defeats the design objective. Exception handlers that trap many errors at once will probably reduce the reliability of your program because it's likely that an exception will be caught that the handler does not know how to handle.

Exception Matching

If you have an exception hierarchy composed of a superclass exception and a number of subtypes, and you're interested in handling one of the subtypes in a special way but want to handle all the rest together, you need write only two catch clauses.

When an exception is thrown, Java will try to find (by looking at the available catch clauses from the top down) a catch clause for the exception type. If it doesn't find one, it will search for a handler for a supertype of the exception. If it does not find a catch clause that matches a supertype for the exception, then the exception is propagated down the call stack. This process is called exception matching. Let's look at an example:

```
 1: import java.io.*;
 2: public class ReadData {
 3:    public static void main(String args[]) {
 4:      try {
 5:        RandomAccessFile raf =
 6:          new RandomAccessFile("myfile.txt", "r");
 7:        byte b[] = new byte[1000];
 8:        raf.readFully(b, 0, 1000);
 9:      }
10:      catch(FileNotFoundException e) {
11:        System.err.println("File not found");
12:        System.err.println(e.getMessage());
13:        e.printStackTrace();
14:      }
15:      catch(IOException e) {
16:        System.err.println("IO Error");
17:        System.err.println(e.toString());
18:        e.printStackTrace();
19:      }
20:    }
21: }
```

This short program attempts to open a file and to read some data from it. Opening and reading files can generate many exceptions, most of which are some type of IOException. Imagine that in this program we're interested in knowing only whether the exact exception is a FileNotFoundException. Otherwise, we don't care exactly what the problem is.

FileNotFoundException is a subclass of IOException. Therefore, we could handle it in the catch clause that catches all subtypes of IOException, but then we would have to test the exception to determine whether it was a FileNotFoundException. Instead, we coded a special exception handler for the FileNotFoundException and a separate exception handler for all other IOException subtypes.

If this code generates a FileNotFoundException, it will be handled by the catch clause that begins at line 10. If it generates another IOException—perhaps EOFException, which is a subclass of IOException—it will be handled by the catch clause that begins at line 15. If some other exception is generated, such as a runtime exception of some type, neither catch clause will be executed and the exception will be propagated down the call stack.

Notice that the catch clause for the FileNotFoundException was placed above the handler for the IOException. This is really important! If we do it the opposite way, the program will not compile. The handlers for the most specific exceptions must always be placed above those for more general exceptions. The following will not compile:

```
try {
  // do risky IO things
} catch (IOException e) {
  // handle general IOExceptions
} catch (FileNotFoundException ex) {
  // handle just FileNotFoundException
}
```

You'll get a compiler error something like this:

```
TestEx.java:15: exception java.io.FileNotFoundException has
 already been caught
} catch (FileNotFoundException ex) {
  ^
```

If you think back to the people with baseball mitts (in the section "Propagating Uncaught Exceptions"), imagine that the most general mitts are the largest, and can thus catch many different kinds of balls. An IOException mitt is large enough and flexible enough to catch any type of IOException. So if the person on the fifth floor (say, Fred) has a big 'ol IOException mitt, he can't help but catch a FileNotFoundException ball with it. And if the guy (say, Jimmy) on the second floor is holding a FileNotFoundException mitt, that FileNotFoundException ball will never get to him, since it will always be stopped by Fred on the fifth floor, standing there with his big-enough-for-any-IOException mitt.

So what do you do with exceptions that are siblings in the class hierarchy? If one Exception class is not a subtype or supertype of the other, then the order in which the catch clauses are placed doesn't matter.

Exception Declaration and the Public Interface

So, how do we know that some method throws an exception that we have to catch? Just as a method must specify what type and how many arguments it accepts and what is returned, the exceptions that a method can throw must be *declared* (unless the exceptions are subclasses of RuntimeException). The list of thrown exceptions is part of a method's public interface. The throws keyword is used as follows to list the exceptions that a method can throw:

```
void myFunction() throws MyException1, MyException2 {
  // code for the method here
}
```

This method has a void return type, accepts no arguments, and declares that it can throw one of two types of exceptions: either type MyException1 or type MyException2. (Just because the method declares that it throws an exception doesn't mean it always will. It just tells the world that it might.)

Suppose your method doesn't directly throw an exception, but calls a method that does. You can choose not to handle the exception yourself and instead just declare it, as though it were your method that actually throws the exception. If you do declare the exception that your method might get from another method, and you don't provide a try/catch for it, then the method will propagate back to the method that called your method, and either be caught there or continue on to be handled by a method further down the stack.

Any method that might throw an exception (unless it's a subclass of RuntimeException) must declare the exception. That includes methods that aren't actually throwing it directly, but are "ducking" and letting the exception pass down to the next method in the stack. If you "duck" an exception, it is just as if you were the one actually throwing the exception. RuntimeException subclasses are exempt, so the compiler won't check to see if you've declared them. But all non-RuntimeExceptions are considered "checked" exceptions, because the compiler checks to be certain you've acknowledged that "bad things could happen here." Remember this:

Each method must either handle all checked exceptions by supplying a catch *clause or list each unhandled checked exception as a thrown exception.*

This rule is referred to as Java's "handle or declare" requirement. (Sometimes called "catch or declare.")

exam ⓦatch

Look for code that invokes a method declaring an exception, where the calling method doesn't handle or declare the checked exception. The following code (which uses the throw **keyword to throw an exception manually—more on this next) has two big problems that the compiler will prevent:**

```
void doStuff() {
  doMore();
}
void doMore() {
  throw new IOException();
}
```

First, the doMore() **method throws a checked exception, but does not declare it! But suppose we fix the** doMore() **method as follows:**

```
void doMore() throws IOException { … }
```

The doStuff() **method is still in trouble because it, too, must declare the** IOException, **unless it handles it by providing a** try/catch, **with a** catch **clause that can take an** IOException.

Again, some exceptions are exempt from this rule. An object of type RuntimeException may be thrown from any method without being specified as part of the method's public interface (and a handler need not be present). And even if a method does declare a RuntimeException, the calling method is under no obligation to handle or declare it. RuntimeException, Error, and all of their subtypes are unchecked exceptions and unchecked exceptions do not have to be specified or handled. Here is an example:

```
import java.io.*;
class Test {
  public int myMethod1() throws EOFException {
    return myMethod2();
  }
  public int myMethod2() throws EOFException {
    // code that actually could throw the exception goes here
    return 1;
  }
}
```

Let's look at myMethod1(). Because EOFException subclasses IOException and IOException subclasses Exception, it is a checked exception and must be declared as an exception that may be thrown by this method. But where will the exception actually come from? The public interface for method myMethod2() called here declares that an exception of this type can be thrown. Whether that method actually throws the exception itself or calls another method that throws it is unimportant to us; we simply know that we have to either catch the exception or declare that we throw it. The method myMethod1() does not catch the exception, so it declares that it throws it. Now let's look at another legal example, myMethod3().

```
public void myMethod3() {
  // code that could throw a NullPointerException goes here
}
```

According to the comment, this method can throw a NullPointerException. Because RuntimeException is the superclass of NullPointerException, it is an unchecked exception and need not be declared. We can see that myMethod3() does not declare any exceptions.

Runtime exceptions are referred to as *unchecked* exceptions. All other exceptions are *checked* exceptions, and they don't derive from java.lang.RuntimeException. A checked exception must be caught somewhere in your code. If you invoke a method that throws a checked exception but you don't catch the checked exception somewhere, your code will not compile. That's why they're called checked exceptions; the compiler checks to make sure that they're handled or declared. A number of the methods in the Java 2 Standard Edition libraries throw checked exceptions, so you will often write exception handlers to cope with exceptions generated by methods you didn't write.

You can also throw an exception yourself, and that exception can be either an existing exception from the Java API or one of your own. To create your own exception, you simply subclass `Exception` (or one of its subclasses) as follows:

```
class MyException extends Exception { }
```

And if you throw the exception, the compiler will guarantee that you declare it as follows:

```
class TestEx {
  void doStuff() {
    throw new MyException();  // Throw a checked exception
  }
}
```

The preceding code upsets the compiler:

```
TestEx.java:6: unreported exception MyException; must be caught
or
declared to be thrown
  throw new MyException();
  ^
```

w a t c h

When an object of a subtype of `Exception` *is thrown, it must be handled or declared. These objects are called checked exceptions, and include all exceptions except those that are subtypes of* `RuntimeException`, *which are unchecked exceptions. Be ready to spot methods that don't follow the "handle or declare" rule, such as*

```
class MyException extends Exception {
  void someMethod () {
    doStuff();
  }
```

```
            void doStuff() throws MyException {
              try {
                throw new MyException();
              }
              catch(MyException me) {
                throw me;
              }
            }
          }
```

You need to recognize that this code won't compile. If you try, you'll get

```
MyException.java:3: unreported exception MyException; must
be caught or declared to be thrown
doStuff();
        ^
```

Notice that someMethod() ***fails to either handle or declare the exception that* can *be thrown by* doStuff().

You need to know how an Error compares with checked and unchecked exceptions. Objects of type Error are not Exception objects, although they do represent exceptional conditions. Both Exception and Error share a common superclass, Throwable, thus both can be thrown using the throw keyword. When an Error or a subclass of Error is thrown, it's unchecked. You are not required to catch Error objects or Error subtypes. You can also throw an Error yourself (although other than AssertionError you probably won't ever want to), and you can catch one, but again, you probably won't. What, for example, would you actually do if you got an OutOfMemoryError? It's not like you can tell the garbage collector to run; you can bet the JVM fought desperately to save itself (and reclaimed all the memory it could) by the time you got the error. In other words, don't expect the JVM at that point to say, "Run the garbage collector? Oh, thanks so much for telling me. That just never occurred to me. Sure, I'll get right on it." Even better, what would you do if a VirtualMachineError arose? Your program is toast by the time you'd catch the Error, so there's really no point in trying to catch one of these babies. Just remember, though, that you can! The following compiles just fine:

```
class TestEx {
  public static void main (String [] args) {
    badMethod();
  }
  static void badMethod() {  // No need to declare an Error
    doStuff()
  }
  static void doStuff() {  //No need to declare an Error
    try {
      throw new Error();
    }
    catch(Error me) {
      throw me; // We catch it, but then rethrow it
    }
  }
}
```

If we were throwing a checked exception rather than `Error`, then the `doStuff()` method would need to declare the exception. But remember, since `Error` is not a subtype of `Exception`, it doesn't need to be declared. You're free to declare it if you like, but the compiler just doesn't care one way or another when or how the `Error` is thrown, or by whom.

on the Job

Because Java has checked exceptions, it's commonly said that Java forces developers to handle exceptions. Yes, Java forces us to write exception handlers for each exception that can occur during normal operation, but it's up to us to make the exception handlers actually do something useful. We know software managers who melt down when they see a programmer write:

```
try {
  callBadMethod();
} catch (Exception ex) { }
```

Notice anything missing? Don't "eat" the exception by catching it without actually handling it. You won't even be able to tell that the exception occurred, because you'll never see the stack trace.

Rethrowing the Same Exception

Just as you can throw a new exception from a `catch` clause, you can also throw the same exception you just caught. Here's a `catch` clause that does this:

```
catch(IOException e) {
  // Do things, then if you decide you can't handle it...
  throw e;
}
```

All other `catch` clauses associated with the same `try` are ignored, if a `finally` block exists, it runs, and the exception is thrown back to the calling method (the next method down the call stack). If you throw a checked exception from a `catch` clause, you must also declare that exception! In other words, you must handle *and* declare, as opposed to handle *or* declare. The following example is illegal:

```
public void doStuff() {
  try {
    // risky IO things
  } catch(IOException ex) {
    // can't handle it
      throw ex;  // Can't throw it unless you declare it
  }
}
```

In the preceding code, the `doStuff()` method is clearly able to throw a checked exception—in this case an `IOException`—so the compiler says, "Well, that's just peachy that you have a `try/catch` in there, but it's not good enough. If you might rethrow the `IOException` you catch, then you must declare it!"

EXERCISE 5-4

Creating an Exception

In this exercise we attempt to create a custom exception. We won't put in any new methods (it will have only those inherited from `Exception`), and because it extends `Exception`, the compiler considers it a checked exception. The goal of the program is to determine whether a command-line argument, representing a particular food (as a string), is considered bad or OK.

■ Let's first create our exception. We will call it `BadFoodException`. This exception will be thrown when a bad food is encountered.

■ Create an enclosing class called `MyException` and a `main()` method, which will remain empty for now.

- Create a method called `checkFood()`. It takes a `String` argument and throws our exception if it doesn't like the food it was given. Otherwise, it tells us it likes the food. You can add any foods you aren't particularly fond of to the list.

- Now in the `main()` method, you'll get the command-line argument out of the `String` array, and then pass that `String` on to the `checkFood()` method. Because it's a checked exception, the `checkFood()` method must declare it, and the `main()` method must handle it (using a `try/catch`). Do not have `main()` declare the exception, because if `main()` ducks the exception, who else is back there to catch it?

- As nifty as exception handling is, it's still up to the developer to make proper use of it. Exception handling makes organizing our code and signaling problems easy, but the exception handlers still have to be written. You'll find that even the most complex situations can be handled, and your code will be reusable, readable, and maintainable.

CERTIFICATION OBJECTIVE

Common Exceptions and Errors (Exam Objective 2.6)

2.6 Recognize situations that will result in any of the following being thrown: ArrayIndexOutOfBoundsException, ClassCastException, IllegalArgumentException, IllegalStateException, NullPointerException, NumberFormatException, AssertionError, ExceptionInInitializerError, StackOverflowError, or NoClassDefFoundError. Understand which of these are thrown by the virtual machine and recognize situations in which others should be thrown programmatically.

Exception handling is another area that the exam creation team decided to expand for the SCJP 5 exam. This section discusses the aspects of exceptions that were added for this new version. The intention of Objective 2.6 is to make sure that you are familiar with some of the most common exceptions and errors you'll encounter as a Java programmer.

e **x** a m

ⓦatch

The questions from this section are likely to be along the lines of, "Here's some code that just did something bad, which exception will be thrown?"

Throughout the exam, questions will present some code and ask you to determine whether the code will run, or whether an exception will be thrown. Since these questions are so common, understanding the causes for these exceptions is critical to your success.

This is another one of those objectives that will turn up all through the real exam (does "An exception is thrown at runtime" ring a bell?), so make sure this section gets a lot of your attention.

Where Exceptions Come From

Jump back a page and take a look at the last sentence of Objective 2.6. It's important to understand what causes exceptions and errors, and where they come from. For the purposes of exam preparation, let's define two broad categories of exceptions and errors:

- **JVM exceptions** Those exceptions or errors that are either exclusively or most logically thrown by the JVM.
- **Programmatic exceptions** Those exceptions that are thrown explicitly by application and/or API programmers.

JVM Thrown Exceptions

Let's start with a very common exception, the `NullPointerException`. As we saw in Chapter 3, this exception occurs when you attempt to access an object using a reference variable with a current value of `null`. There's no way that the compiler can hope to find these problems before runtime. Let's look at the following:

```
class NPE {
  static String s;
  public static void main(String [] args) {
    System.out.println(s.length());
  }
}
```

Surely, the compiler can find the problem with that tiny little program! Nope, you're on your own. The code will compile just fine, and the JVM will throw a `NullPointerException` when it tries to invoke the `length()` method.

Earlier in this chapter we discussed the call stack. As you recall, we used the convention that `main()` would be at the bottom of the call stack, and that as `main()` invokes another method, and that method invokes another, and so on, the stack grows upward. Of course the stack resides in memory, and even if your OS gives you a gigabyte of RAM for your program, it's still a finite amount. It's possible to grow the stack so large that the OS runs out of space to store the call stack. When this happens you get (wait for it...), a `StackOverflowError`. The most common way for this to occur is to create a recursive method. A recursive method is one that invokes itself in the method body. While that may sound weird, it's a very common and useful technique for such things as searching and sorting algorithms. Take a look at this code:

```
void go() {    // recursion gone bad
  go();
}
```

As you can see, if you ever make the mistake of invoking the `go()` method, your program will fall into a black hole; `go()` invoking `go()` invoking `go()`, until, no matter how much memory you have, you'll get a `StackOverflowError`. Again, only the JVM knows when this moment occurs, and the JVM will be the source of this error.

Programmatically Thrown Exceptions

Now let's look at programmatically thrown exceptions. Remember we defined "programmatically" as meaning something like this:

Created by an application and/or API developer.

For instance, many classes in the Java API have methods that take `String` arguments, and convert these `Strings` into numeric primitives. A good example of these classes are the so-called "wrapper classes" that we studied in Chapter 3.

At some point long ago, some programmer wrote the `java.lang.Integer` class, and created methods like `parseInt()` and `valueOf()`. That programmer wisely decided that if one of these methods was passed a `String` that could not be converted into a number, the method should throw a `NumberFormatException`. The partially implemented code might look something like this:

```
int parseInt(String s) throws NumberFormatException {
  boolean parseSuccess = false;
  int result = 0;
  // do complicated parsing
  if (!parseSuccess)   // if the parsing failed
    throw new NumberFormatException();
  return result;
}
```

Other examples of programmatic exceptions include an `AssertionError` (okay, it's not an exception, but it IS thrown programmatically), and throwing an `IllegalArgumentException`. In fact, our mythical API developer could have used `IllegalArgumentException` for her `parseInt()` method. But it turns out that `NumberFormatException` extends `IllegalArgumentException`, and is a little more precise, so in this case, using `NumberFormatException` supports the notion we discussed earlier: that when you have an exception hierarchy, you should use the most precise exception that you can.

Of course, as we discussed earlier, you can also make up your very own special, custom exceptions, and throw them whenever you want to. These homemade exceptions also fall into the category of "programmatically thrown exceptions."

A Summary of the Exam's Exceptions and Errors

Objective 2.6 lists ten specific exceptions and errors. In this section we discussed the `StackOverflowError`. The other nine exceptions and errors listed in the objective are covered elsewhere in this book. Table 5-2 summarizes this list and provides chapter references to the exceptions and errors we did not discuss here.

TABLE 5-2	Descriptions and Sources of Common Exceptions.	
Exception (Chapter Location)	**Description**	**Typically Thrown**
ArrayIndexOutOfBoundsException (Chapter 3, "Assignments")	Thrown when attempting to access an array with an invalid index value (either negative or beyond the length of the array).	By the JVM
ClassCastException (Chapter 2, "Object Orientation")	Thrown when attempting to cast a reference variable to a type that fails the IS-A test.	By the JVM
IllegalArgumentException (Chapter 3, "Assignments")	Thrown when a method receives an argument formatted differently than the method expects.	Programmatically
IllegalStateException (Chapter 6, "Formatting")	Thrown when the state of the environment doesn't match the operation being attempted, e.g., using a Scanner that's been closed.	Programmatically
NullPointerException (Chapter 3, "Assignments")	Thrown when attempting to access an object with a reference variable whose current value is `null`.	By the JVM
NumberFormatException (Chapter 6, "Formatting")	Thrown when a method that converts a String to a number receives a String that it cannot convert.	Programmatically
AssertionError (This chapter)	Thrown when a statement's boolean test returns `false`.	Programmatically
ExceptionInInitializerError (Chapter 3, "Assignments")	Thrown when attempting to initialize a static variable or an initialization block.	By the JVM
StackOverflowError (This chapter)	Typically thrown when a method recurses too deeply. (Each invocation is added to the stack.)	By the JVM
NoClassDefFoundError (Chapter 10, "Development")	Thrown when the JVM can't find a class it needs, because of a command-line error, a classpath issue, or a missing `.class` file.	By the JVM

Working with the Assertion Mechanism (Exam Objective 2.3)

2.3   Develop code that makes use of assertions, and distinguish appropriate from inappropriate uses of assertions.

You know you're not supposed to make assumptions, but you can't help it when you're writing code. You put them in comments:

```
if (x > 2 && y) {
  // do something
} else if (x < 2 || y) {
  // do something
} else {
  // x must be 2
  // do something else
}
```

You write print statements with them:

```
while (true) {
  if (x > 2) {
    break;
  }
  System.out.print("If we got here " +
                   "something went horribly wrong");
}
```

Added to the Java language beginning with version 1.4, assertions let you test your assumptions during development, without the expense (in both your time and program overhead) of writing exception handlers for exceptions that you assume will never happen once the program is out of development and fully deployed.

Starting with exam 310-035 (version 1.4 of the Sun Certified Java Programmer exam) and continuing with the current exam 310-055 (version 5), you're expected to know the basics of how assertions work, including how to enable them, how to use them, and how *not* to use them.

Assertions Overview

Suppose you assume that a number passed into a method (say, `methodA()`) will never be negative. While testing and debugging, you want to validate your assumption, but you don't want to have to strip out `print` statements, runtime exception handlers, or `if/else` tests when you're done with development. But leaving any of those in is, at the least, a performance hit. Assertions to the rescue! Check out the following code:

```
private void methodA(int num) {
  if (num >= 0) {
    useNum(num + x);
  } else {   // num must be < 0
             // This code should never be reached!
    System.out.println("Yikes! num is a negative number! "
                       + num);
  }
}
```

Because you're so certain of your assumption, you don't want to take the time (or program performance hit) to write exception-handling code. And at runtime, you don't want the `if/else` either because if you do reach the `else` condition, it means your earlier logic (whatever was running prior to this method being called) is flawed.

Assertions let you test your assumptions during development, but the assertion code basically evaporates when the program is deployed, leaving behind no overhead or debugging code to track down and remove. Let's rewrite `methodA()` to validate that the argument was not negative:

```
private void methodA(int num) {
  assert (num>=0);   // throws an AssertionError
                     // if this test isn't true
  useNum(num + x);
}
```

Not only do assertions let your code stay cleaner and tighter, but because assertions are inactive unless specifically "turned on" (enabled), the code will run as though it were written like this:

```
private void methodA(int num) {
  useNum(num + x); // we've tested this;
                   // we now know we're good here
}
```

Assertions work quite simply. You always assert that something is `true`. If it is, no problem. Code keeps running. But if your assertion turns out to be wrong (`false`), then a stop-the-world `AssertionError` is thrown (that you should never, ever handle!) right then and there, so you can fix whatever logic flaw led to the problem.

Assertions come in two flavors: *really simple* and *simple*, as follows:

Really simple:

```
private void doStuff() {
  assert (y > x);
  // more code assuming y is greater than x
}
```

Simple:

```
private void doStuff() {
  assert (y > x): "y is " + y + " x is " + x;
  // more code assuming y is greater than x
}
```

The difference between the two is that the simple version adds a second expression, separated from the first (boolean expression) by a colon, this expression's string value is added to the stack trace. Both versions throw an immediate `AssertionError`, but the simple version gives you a little more debugging help while the really simple version simply tells you only that your assumption was false.

Assertions are typically enabled when an application is being tested and debugged, but disabled when the application is deployed. The assertions are still in the code, although ignored by the JVM, so if you do have a deployed application that starts misbehaving, you can always choose to enable assertions in the field for additional testing.

Assertion Expression Rules

Assertions can have either one or two expressions, depending on whether you're using the "simple" or the "really simple." The first expression must always result in a `boolean` value! Follow the same rules you use for `if` and `while` tests. The whole point is to assert `aTest`, which means you're asserting that `aTest` is `true`. If it is `true`, no problem. If it's not `true`, however, then your assumption was wrong and you get an `AssertionError`.

The second expression, used only with the simple version of an `assert` statement, can be anything that results in a value. Remember, the second expression is used to generate a `String` message that displays in the stack trace to give you a little more debugging information. It works much like `System.out.println()` in that you can pass it a primitive or an object, and it will convert it into a `String` representation. It must resolve to a value!

The following code lists legal and illegal expressions for both parts of an `assert` statement. Remember, expression2 is used only with the simple `assert` statement, where the second expression exists solely to give you a little more debugging detail:

```
void noReturn() { }
int aReturn() { return 1; }
void go() {
  int x = 1;
  boolean b = true;

  // the following six are legal assert statements
  assert(x == 1);
  assert(b);
  assert true;
  assert(x == 1) : x;
  assert(x == 1) : aReturn();
  assert(x == 1) : new ValidAssert();

  // the following six are ILLEGAL assert statements
  assert(x = 1);  // none of these are booleans
  assert(x);
  assert 0;
  assert(x == 1) : ;             // none of these return a value
  assert(x == 1) : noReturn();
  assert(x == 1) : ValidAssert va;
}
```

e x a m
ⓦ a t c h

If you see the word "expression" in a question about assertions, and the question doesn't specify whether it means expression1 (the boolean test) or expression2 (the value to print in the stack trace), then always assume the word "expression" refers to expression1, the boolean test. For example, consider the following question:

Enabling Assertions

If you want to use assertions, you have to think first about how to compile with assertions in your code, and then about how to run with assertions enabled. Both require version 1.4 or greater, and that brings us to the first issue: how to compile with assertions in your code.

Identifier vs. Keyword

Prior to version 1.4, you might very well have written code like this:

```
int assert = getInitialValue();
if (assert == getActualResult()) {
  // do something
}
```

Notice that in the preceding code, `assert` is used as an identifier. That's not a problem prior to 1.4. But you cannot use a keyword/reserved word as an identifier, and beginning with version 1.4, `assert` is a keyword. The bottom line is this:

You can use `assert` as a keyword or as an identifier, but not both.

on the
job

If for some reason you're using a Java 1.4 compiler, and if you're using `assert` *as a keyword (in other words, you're actually trying to* `assert` *something in your code), then you must explicitly enable assertion-awareness at compile time, as follows:*

```
javac -source 1.4 com/geeksanonymous/TestClass.java
```

You can read that as "compile the class TestClass, in the directory com/geeksanonymous, *and do it in the 1.4 way, where* assert *is a keyword."*

Use Version 5 of java and javac

As far as the exam is concerned, you'll ALWAYS be using version 5 of the Java compiler (javac), and version 5 of the Java application launcher (java). You might see questions about older versions of source code, but those questions will always be in the context of compiling and launching old code with the current versions of javac and java.

Compiling Assertion-Aware Code

The Java 5 compiler will use the assert keyword by default. Unless you tell it otherwise, the compiler will generate an error message if it finds the word assert used as an identifier. However, you can tell the compiler that you're giving it an old piece of code to compile, and that it should pretend to be an old compiler! (More about compiler commands in Chapter 10.) Let's say you've got to make a quick fix to an old piece of 1.3 code that uses assert as an identifier. At the command line you can type

```
javac -source 1.3 OldCode.java
```

The compiler will issue warnings when it discovers the word assert used as an identifier, but the code will compile and execute. Suppose you tell the compiler that your code is version 1.4 or later, for instance:

```
javac -source 1.4 NotQuiteSoOldCode.java
```

In this case, the compiler will issue errors when it discovers the word assert used as an identifier.

If you want to tell the compiler to use Java 5 rules you can do one of three things: omit the -source option, which is the default, or add one of two source options:

-source 1.5 or -source 5. (See how clear Sun is about 1.5 vs. 5?)

If you want to use assert as an identifier in your code, you MUST compile using the -source 1.3 option. Table 5-3 summarizes how the Java 5 compiler will react to assert as either an identifier or a keyword.

TABLE 5-3   Using Java 5 to Compile Code That Uses assert as an Identifier or a Keyword

Command Line	If assert Is an Identifier	If assert Is a Keyword
`javac -source 1.3 TestAsserts.java`	Code compiles with warnings.	Compilation fails.
`javac -source 1.4 TestAsserts.java`	Compilation fails.	Code compiles.
`javac -source 1.5 TestAsserts.java`	Compilation fails.	Code compiles.
`javac -source 5 TestAsserts.java`	Compilation fails.	Code compiles.
`javac TestAsserts.java`	Compilation fails.	Code compiles.

Running with Assertions

Here's where it gets cool. Once you've written your assertion-aware code (in other words, code that uses assert as a keyword, to actually perform assertions at runtime), you can choose to enable or disable your assertions at runtime! Remember, assertions are disabled by default.

Enabling Assertions at Runtime

You enable assertions at runtime with

```
java -ea com.geeksanonymous.TestClass
```

or

```
java -enableassertions com.geeksanonymous.TestClass
```

The preceding command-line switches tell the JVM to run with assertions enabled.

Disabling Assertions at Runtime

You must also know the command-line switches for disabling assertions,

```
java -da com.geeksanonymous.TestClass
```

or

```
java -disableassertions com.geeksanonymous.TestClass
```

Because assertions are disabled by default, using the disable switches might seem unnecessary. Indeed, using the switches the way we do in the preceding example just gives you the default behavior (in other words, you get the same result regardless of whether you use the disabling switches). But…you can also selectively enable and disable assertions in such a way that they're enabled for some classes and/or packages, and disabled for others, while a particular program is running.

Selective Enabling and Disabling

The command-line switches for assertions can be used in various ways:

- **With no arguments (as in the preceding examples)**   Enables or disables assertions in all classes, except for the system classes.
- **With a package name**   Enables or disables assertions in the package specified, and any packages below this package in the same directory hierarchy (more on that in a moment).
- **With a class name**   Enables or disables assertions in the class specified.

You can combine switches to, say, disable assertions in a single class, but keep them enabled for all others, as follows:

```
java -ea  -da:com.geeksanonymous.Foo
```

The preceding command line tells the JVM to enable assertions in general, but disable them in the class com.geeksanonymous.Foo. You can do the same selectivity for a package as follows:

```
java -ea -da:com.geeksanonymous...
```

The preceding command line tells the JVM to enable assertions in general, but disable them in the package com.geeksanonymous, and all of its subpackages! You may not be familiar with the term subpackages, since there wasn't much use of that term prior to assertions. A subpackage is any package in a subdirectory of the named package. For example, look at the following directory tree:

```
com
    |_geeksanonymous
                    |_Foo
                    |_twelvesteps
                                |_StepOne
                                |_StepTwo
```

This tree lists three directories,

```
com
geeksanonymous
twelvesteps
and three classes:
com.geeksanonymous.Foo
com.geeksanonymous.twelvesteps.StepOne
com.geeksanonymous.twelvesteps.StepTwo
```

The subpackage of com.geeksanonymous is the twelvesteps package. Remember that in Java, the com.geeksanonymous.twelvesteps package is treated as a completely distinct package that has no relationship with the packages above it (in this example, the com.geeksanonymous package), except they just happen to share a couple of directories. Table 5-4 lists examples of command-line switches for enabling and disabling assertions.

TABLE 5-4   Assertion Command-Line Switches

Command-Line Example	What It Means
`java -ea` `java -enableassertions`	Enable assertions.
`java -da` `java -disableassertions`	Disable assertions (the default behavior of 1.5).
`java -ea:com.foo.Bar`	Enable assertions in class com.foo.Bar.
`java -ea:com.foo...`	Enable assertions in package com.foo and any of its subpackages.
`java -ea -dsa`	Enable assertions in general, but disable assertions in system classes.
`java -ea -da:com.foo...`	Enable assertions in general, but disable assertions in package com.foo and any of its subpackages.

Using Assertions Appropriately

Not all legal uses of assertions are considered appropriate. As with so much of Java, you can abuse the intended use of assertions, despite the best efforts of Sun's Java engineers to discourage you from doing so. For example, you're never supposed to handle an assertion failure. That means you shouldn't catch it with a `catch` clause and attempt to recover. Legally, however, `AssertionError` is a subclass of `Throwable`, so it can be caught. But just don't do it! If you're going to try to recover from something, it should be an exception. To discourage you from trying to substitute an assertion for an exception, the `AssertionError` doesn't provide access to the object that generated it. All you get is the `String` message.

So who gets to decide what's appropriate? Sun. The exam uses Sun's "official" assertion documentation to define appropriate and inappropriate uses.

Don't Use Assertions to Validate Arguments to a Public Method

The following is an inappropriate use of assertions:

```java
public void doStuff(int x) {
    assert (x > 0);                 // inappropriate !
    // do things with x
}
```

If you see the word "appropriate" on the exam, do not mistake that for "legal." "Appropriate" always refers to the way in which something is supposed to be used, according to either the developers of the mechanism or best practices officially embraced by Sun. If you see the word "correct" in the context of assertions, as in, "Line 3 is a correct use of assertions," you should also assume that correct is referring to how assertions SHOULD be used rather than how they legally COULD be used.

A `public` method might be called from code that you don't control (or from code you have never seen). Because `public` methods are part of your interface to the outside world, you're supposed to guarantee that any constraints on the arguments will be enforced by the method itself. But since assertions aren't guaranteed to actually run (they're typically disabled in a deployed application), the enforcement won't happen if assertions aren't enabled. You don't want publicly accessible code that works only conditionally, depending on whether assertions are enabled.

If you need to validate `public` method arguments, you'll probably use exceptions to throw, say, an `IllegalArgumentException` if the values passed to the `public` method are invalid.

Do Use Assertions to Validate Arguments to a Private Method

If you write a `private` method, you almost certainly wrote (or control) any code that calls it. When you assume that the logic in code calling your `private` method is correct, you can test that assumption with an assertion as follows:

```
private void doMore(int x) {
  assert (x > 0);
  // do things with x
}
```

The only difference that matters between the preceding example and the one before it is the access modifier. So, do enforce constraints on `private` methods' arguments, but do not enforce constraints on `public` methods. You're certainly free to compile assertion code with an inappropriate validation of `public` arguments, but for the exam (and real life) you need to know that you shouldn't do it.

Don't Use Assertions to Validate Command-Line Arguments

This is really just a special case of the "Do not use assertions to validate arguments to a public method" rule. If your program requires command-line arguments, you'll probably use the exception mechanism to enforce them.

Do Use Assertions, Even in Public Methods, to Check for Cases that You Know Are Never, Ever Supposed to Happen

This can include code blocks that should never be reached, including the default of a `switch` statement as follows:

```
switch(x) {
  case 1: y = 3;
  case 2: y = 9;
  case 3: y = 27;
  default: assert false; // We're never supposed to get here!
}
```

If you assume that a particular code block won't be reached, as in the preceding example where you assert that x must be either 2, 3, or 4, then you can use `assert false` to cause an `AssertionError` to be thrown immediately if you ever do reach that code. So in the `switch` example, we're not performing a boolean test—we've already asserted that we should never be there, so just getting to that point is an automatic failure of our assertion/assumption.

Don't Use Assert Expressions that Can Cause Side Effects!

The following would be a very bad idea:

```
public void doStuff() {
  assert (modifyThings());
  // continues on
}
public boolean modifyThings() {
  y = x++;
  return true;
}
```

The rule is, an `assert` expression should leave the program in the same state it was in before the expression! Think about it. `assert` expressions aren't guaranteed to always run, so you don't want your code to behave differently depending on whether assertions are enabled. Assertions must not cause any side effects. If assertions are enabled, the only change to the way your program runs is that an `AssertionError` can be thrown if one of your assertions (think: *assumptions*) turns out to be false.

on the
Job

Using assertions that cause side effects can cause some of the most maddening and hard-to-find bugs known to man! When a hot tempered Q.A. analyst is screaming at you that your code doesn't work, trotting out the old "well it works on MY machine" excuse won't get you very far.

CERTIFICATION SUMMARY

This chapter covered a lot of ground, all of which involves ways of controlling your program flow, based on a conditional test. First you learned about `if` and `switch` statements. The `if` statement evaluates one or more expressions to a `boolean` result. If the result is `true`, the program will execute the code in the block that is encompassed by the `if`. If an `else` statement is used and the `if` expression evaluates to `false`, then the code following the `else` will be performed. If no `else` block is defined, then none of the code associated with the `if` statement will execute.

You also learned that the `switch` statement can be used to replace multiple `if-else` statements. The `switch` statement can evaluate integer primitive types that can be implicitly cast to an `int` (those types are `byte`, `short`, `int`, and `char`), or it can evaluate enums.

At runtime, the JVM will try to find a match between the expression in the switch statement and a constant in a corresponding case statement. If a match is found, execution will begin at the matching case, and continue on from there, executing code in all the remaining case statements until a break statement is found or the end of the switch statement occurs. If there is no match, then the default case will execute, if there is one.

You've learned about the three looping constructs available in the Java language. These constructs are the for loop (including the basic for and the enhanced for which is new to Java 5), the while loop, and the do loop. In general, the for loop is used when you know how many times you need to go through the loop. The while loop is used when you do not know how many times you want to go through, whereas the do loop is used when you need to go through at least once. In the for loop and the while loop, the expression will have to evaluate to true to get inside the block and will check after every iteration of the loop. The do loop does not check the condition until after it has gone through the loop once. The major benefit of the for loop is the ability to initialize one or more variables and increment or decrement those variables in the for loop definition.

The break and continue statements can be used in either a labeled or unlabeled fashion. When unlabeled, the break statement will force the program to stop processing the innermost looping construct and start with the line of code following the loop. Using an unlabeled continue command will cause the program to stop execution of the current iteration of the innermost loop and proceed with the next iteration. When a break or a continue statement is used in a labeled manner, it will perform in the same way, with one exception: the statement will not apply to the innermost loop; instead, it will apply to the loop with the label. The break statement is used most often in conjunction with the switch statement. When there is a match between the switch expression and the case constant, the code following the case constant will be performed. To stop execution, a break is needed.

You've seen how Java provides an elegant mechanism in exception handling. Exception handling allows you to isolate your error-correction code into separate blocks so that the main code doesn't become cluttered by error-checking code. Another elegant feature allows you to handle similar errors with a single error-handling block, without code duplication. Also, the error handling can be deferred to methods further back on the call stack.

You learned that Java's try keyword is used to specify a guarded region—a block of code in which problems might be detected. An exception handler is the code that is executed when an exception occurs. The handler is defined by using Java's catch keyword. All catch clauses must immediately follow the related try block. Java also provides the finally keyword. This is used to define a block of code that is always executed, either immediately after a catch clause completes or immediately after the associated `try` block in the case that no exception was thrown (or there was a `try` but no `catch`). Use `finally` blocks to release system resources and to perform any cleanup required by the code in the `try` block. A `finally` block is not required, but if there is one it must immediately follow the last `catch`. (If there is no `catch` block, the `finally` block must immediately follow the `try` block.) It's guaranteed to be called except when the `try` or `catch` issues a `System.exit()`.

An exception object is an instance of class `Exception` or one of its subclasses. The `catch` clause takes, as a parameter, an instance of an object of a type derived from the `Exception` class. Java requires that each method either catches any checked exception it can throw or else declares that it throws the exception. The exception declaration is part of the method's public interface. To declare that an exception may be thrown, the `throws` keyword is used in a method definition, along with a list of all checked exceptions that might be thrown.

Runtime exceptions are of type `RuntimeException` (or one of its subclasses). These exceptions are a special case because they do not need to be handled or declared, and thus are known as "unchecked" exceptions. Errors are of type `java.lang.Error` or its subclasses, and like runtime exceptions, they do not need to be handled or declared. Checked exceptions include any exception types that are not of type `RuntimeException` or Error. If your code fails to either handle a checked exception or declare that it is thrown, your code won't compile. But with unchecked exceptions or objects of type `Error`, it doesn't matter to the compiler whether you declare them or handle them, do nothing about them, or do some combination of declaring and handling. In other words, you're free to declare them and handle them, but the compiler won't care one way or the other. It's not good practice to handle an `Error`, though, because you can rarely recover from one.

Exceptions can be generated by the JVM, or by a programmer.

Assertions, added to the language in version 1.4, are a useful debugging tool. You learned how you can use them for testing, by enabling them, but keep them disabled when the application is deployed. If you have older Java code that uses the word `assert` as an identifier, then you won't be able to use assertions, and you must recompile your older code using the `-source 1.3` flag. Remember that as of Java 5, assertions are compiled as a keyword by default, but must be enabled explicitly at runtime.

You learned how assert statements always include a boolean expression, and if the expression is `true` the code continues on, but if the expression is `false`, an `AssertionError` is thrown. If you use the two-expression `assert` statement, then the second expression is evaluated, converted to a `String` representation and inserted into the stack trace to give you a little more debugging info. Finally, you saw why assertions should not be used to enforce arguments to `public` methods, and why assert expressions must not contain side effects!

✓ TWO-MINUTE DRILL

Here are some of the key points from each certification objective in this chapter. You might want to loop through them several times.

Writing Code Using if and switch Statements (Obj. 2.1)

❑ The only legal expression in an `if` statement is a `boolean` expression, in other words an expression that resolves to a `boolean` or a `Boolean` variable.

❑ Watch out for `boolean` assignments (=) that can be mistaken for `boolean` equality (==) tests:

```
boolean x = false;
if (x = true) { } // an assignment, so x will always be true!
```

❑ Curly braces are optional for `if` blocks that have only one conditional statement. But watch out for misleading indentations.

❑ `switch` statements can evaluate only to `enums` or the `byte`, `short`, `int`, and `char` data types. You can't say,

```
long s = 30;
switch(s) { }
```

❑ The `case` constant must be a literal or `final` variable, or a constant expression, including an `enum`. You cannot have a case that includes a non-final variable, or a range of values.

❑ If the condition in a `switch` statement matches a `case` constant, execution will run through all code in the `switch` following the matching `case` statement until a `break` statement or the end of the `switch` statement is encountered. In other words, the matching `case` is just the entry point into the `case` block, but unless there's a `break` statement, the matching `case` is not the only `case` code that runs.

❑ The `default` keyword should be used in a `switch` statement if you want to run some code when none of the `case` values match the conditional value.

❑ The `default` block can be located anywhere in the `switch` block, so if no `case` matches, the `default` block will be entered, and if the `default` does not contain a `break`, then code will continue to execute (fall-through) to the end of the `switch` or until the `break` statement is encountered.

Writing Code Using Loops (Objective 2.2)

❑ A basic `for` statement has three parts: declaration and/or initialization, boolean evaluation, and the iteration expression.

❑ If a variable is incremented or evaluated within a basic `for` loop, it must be declared before the loop, or within the `for` loop declaration.

❑ A variable declared (not just initialized) within the basic `for` loop declaration cannot be accessed outside the `for` loop (in other words, code below the `for` loop won't be able to use the variable).

❑ You can initialize more than one variable of the same type in the first part of the basic `for` loop declaration; each initialization must be separated by a comma.

❑ An enhanced `for` statement (new as of Java 5), has two parts, the *declaration* and the *expression*. It is used only to loop through arrays or collections.

❑ With an enhanced `for`, the *expression* is the array or collection through which you want to loop.

❑ With an enhanced `for`, the *declaration* is the block variable, whose type is compatible with the elements of the array or collection, and that variable contains the value of the element for the given iteration.

❑ You cannot use a number (old C-style language construct) or anything that does not evaluate to a `boolean` value as a condition for an `if` statement or looping construct. You can't, for example, say `if(x)`, unless x is a `boolean` variable.

❑ The `do` loop will enter the body of the loop at least once, even if the test condition is not met.

Using break and continue (Objective 2.2)

❑ An unlabeled `break` statement will cause the current iteration of the innermost looping construct to stop and the line of code following the loop to run.

❑ An unlabeled `continue` statement will cause: the current iteration of the innermost loop to stop, the condition of that loop to be checked, and if the condition is met, the loop to run again.

❑ If the `break` statement or the `continue` statement is labeled, it will cause similar action to occur on the labeled loop, not the innermost loop.

Handling Exceptions (Objectives 2.4, 2.5, and 2.6)

❑ Exceptions come in two flavors: checked and unchecked.

❑ Checked exceptions include all subtypes of `Exception`, excluding classes that extend `RuntimeException`.

❑ Checked exceptions are subject to the handle or declare rule; any method that might throw a checked exception (including methods that invoke methods that can throw a checked exception) must either declare the exception using `throws`, or handle the exception with an appropriate try/catch.

❑ Subtypes of `Error` or `RuntimeException` are unchecked, so the compiler doesn't enforce the handle or declare rule. You're free to handle them, or to declare them, but the compiler doesn't care one way or the other.

❑ If you use an optional `finally` block, it will always be invoked, regardless of whether an exception in the corresponding `try` is thrown or not, and regardless of whether a thrown exception is caught or not.

❑ The only exception to the `finally`-will-always-be-called rule is that a `finally` will not be invoked if the JVM shuts down. That could happen if code from the `try` or `catch` blocks calls `System.exit()`.

❑ Just because `finally` is invoked does not mean it will complete. Code in the `finally` block could itself raise an exception or issue a `System.exit()`.

❑ Uncaught exceptions propagate back through the call stack, starting from the method where the exception is thrown and ending with either the first method that has a corresponding catch for that exception type or a JVM shutdown (which happens if the exception gets to `main()`, and `main()` is "ducking" the exception by declaring it).

❑ You can create your own exceptions, normally by extending `Exception` or one of its subtypes. Your exception will then be considered a checked exception, and the compiler will enforce the handle or declare rule for that exception.

❑ All `catch` blocks must be ordered from most specific to most general. If you have a `catch` clause for both `IOException` and `Exception`, you must put the `catch` for `IOException` first in your code. Otherwise, the `IOException` would be caught by `catch(Exception e)`, because a `catch` argument can catch the specified exception or any of its subtypes! The compiler will stop you from defining `catch` clauses that can never be reached.

❑ Some exceptions are created by programmers, some by the JVM.

Working with the Assertion Mechanism (Objective 2.3)

❑ Assertions give you a way to test your assumptions during development and debugging.

❑ Assertions are typically enabled during testing but disabled during deployment.

❑ You can use `assert` as a keyword (as of version 1.4) or an identifier, but not both together. To compile older code that uses `assert` as an identifier (for example, a method name), use the `-source 1.3` command-line flag to `javac`.

❑ Assertions are disabled at runtime by default. To enable them, use a command-line flag `-ea` or `-enableassertions`.

❑ Selectively disable assertions by using the `-da` or `-disableassertions` flag.

❑ If you enable or disable assertions using the flag without any arguments, you're enabling or disabling assertions in general. You can combine enabling and disabling switches to have assertions enabled for some classes and/or packages, but not others.

❑ You can enable and disable assertions on a class-by-class basis, using the following syntax:

```
java -ea  -da:MyClass  TestClass
```

❑ You can enable and disable assertions on a package-by-package basis, and any package you specify also includes any subpackages (packages further down the directory hierarchy).

❑ Do not use assertions to validate arguments to `public` methods.

❑ Do not use `assert` expressions that cause side effects. Assertions aren't guaranteed to always run, and you don't want behavior that changes depending on whether assertions are enabled.

❑ Do use assertions—even in `public` methods—to validate that a particular code block will never be reached. You can use `assert false;` for code that should never be reached, so that an assertion error is thrown immediately if the `assert` statement is executed.

SELF TEST

1. Given the following code:

```java
public class OrtegorumFunction {
  public int computeDiscontinuous(int x) {
    int r = 1;
    r += x;
    if ((x > 4) && (x < 10)) {
      r += 2 * x;
    } else (x <= 4) {
      r += 3 * x;
    } else {
      r += 4 * x;
    }
    r += 5 * x;
    return r;
  }

  public static void main(String [] args) {
    OrtegorumFunction o = new OrtegorumFunction();
    System.out.println("OF(11) is: " + o.computeDiscontinuous(11));
  }
}
```

What is the result?

A. OF(11) is: 45

B. OF(11) is: 56

C. OF(11) is: 89

D. OF(11) is: 111

E. Compilation fails.

F. An exception is thrown at runtime.

2. Given two files:

```java
1. class One {
2.   public static void main(String[] args) {
3.     int assert = 0;
4.   }
5. }
```

```java
1. class Two {
2.   public static void main(String[] args) {
```

```
3.      assert(false);
4.    }
5. }
```

And the four command-line invocations:

```
javac -source 1.3 One.java
javac -source 1.4 One.java
javac -source 1.3 Two.java
javac -source 1.4 Two.java
```

What is the result? (Choose all that apply.)

A. Only one compilation will succeed.

B. Exactly two compilations will succeed.

C. Exactly three compilations will succeed.

D. All four compilations will succeed.

E. No compiler warnings will be produced.

F. At least one compiler warning will be produced.

3. Given:

```
import java.io.*;
class Master {
  String doFileStuff() throws FileNotFoundException { return "a"; }
}
class Slave extends Master {
  public static void main(String[] args) {
    String s = null;
    try { s = new Slave().doFileStuff();
    } catch ( Exception x) {
      s = "b"; }
    System.out.println(s);
  }
  // insert code here
}
```

Which, inserted independently at `// insert code here`, will compile, and produce the output b? (Choose all that apply.)

A. `String doFileStuff() { return "b"; }`

B. `String doFileStuff() throws IOException { return "b"; }`

C. `String doFileStuff(int x) throws IOException { return "b"; }`

D. `String doFileStuff() throws FileNotFoundException { return "b"; }`

E. `String doFileStuff() throws NumberFormatException { return "b"; }`

F. `String doFileStuff() throws NumberFormatException,`

                                     `FileNotFoundException { return "b"; }`

4. Given:

```
class Input {
  public static void main(String[] args) {
    String s = "-";
    try {
      doMath(args[0]);
      s += "t ";          // line 6
    }
    finally { System.out.println(s += "f "); }
  }
  public static void doMath(String a) {
    int y = 7 / Integer.parseInt(a);
} }
```

And the command-line invocations:

```
java Input
java Input 0
```

Which are true? (Choose all that apply.)

A. Line 6 is executed exactly 0 times.

B. Line 6 is executed exactly 1 time.

C. Line 6 is executed exactly 2 times.

D. The `finally` block is executed exactly 0 times.

E. The `finally` block is executed exactly 1 time.

F. The `finally` block is executed exactly 2 times.

G. Both invocations produce the same exceptions.

H. Each invocation produces a different exception.

5. Given:

```
1. class Crivitch {
2.   public static void main(String [] args) {
3.     int x = 0;
4.     // insert code here
5.     do { } while (x++ < y);
6.     System.out.println(x);
7.   }
8. }
```

Which, inserted at line 4, produces the output 12?

A. `int y = x;`

B. `int y = 10;`

C. `int y = 11;`

D. `int y = 12;`

E. `int y = 13;`

F. None of the above will allow compilation to succeed.

6. Given:

```
class Plane {
  static String s = "-";
  public static void main(String[] args) {
    new Plane().s1();
    System.out.println(s);
  }
  void s1() {
    try { s2(); }
    catch (Exception e) { s += "c"; }
  }
  void s2() throws Exception  {
    s3();   s += "2";
    s3();   s += "2b";
  }
  void s3() throws Exception {
    throw new Exception();
  }
}
```

What is the result?

A. `-`

B. `-c`

C. `-c2`

D. `-2c`

E. `-c22b`

F. `-2c2b`

G. `-2c2bc`

H. Compilation fails.

7. Given:

```
try { int x = Integer.parseInt("two"); }
```

Which could be used to create an appropriate `catch` block? (Choose all that apply.)

A. `ClassCastException`

B. `IllegalStateException`

C. `NumberFormatException`

D. `IllegalArgumentException`

E. `ExceptionInInitializerError`

F. `ArrayIndexOutOfBoundsException`

8. Given:

```
1. class Ping extends Utils {
2.    public static void main(String [] args) {
3.      Utils u = new Ping();
4.      System.out.print(u.getInt(args[0]));
5.    }
6.    int getInt(String arg) {
7.      return Integer.parseInt(arg);
8.    }
9. }
10. class Utils {
11.    int getInt(String x) throws Exception { return 7; }
12. }
```

And the following three possible changes:

C1. Declare that `main()` throws an `Exception`.

C2. Declare that `Ping.getInt()` throws an `Exception`.

C3. Wrap the invocation of `getInt()` in a `try / catch` block.

Which change(s) allow the code to compile? (Choose all that apply.)

A. Just C1 is sufficient.

B. Just C2 is sufficient.

C. Just C3 is sufficient.

D. Both C1 and C2 are required.

E. Both C1 and C3 are required.

F. Both C2 and C3 are required.

G. All three changes are required.

9. Given:

```
class Swill {
  public static void main(String[] args) {
    String s = "-";
    switch(TimeZone.CST) {
      case EST: s += "e";
      case CST: s += "c";
      case MST: s += "m";
      default:  s += "X";
      case PST: s += "p";
    }
    System.out.println(s);
  }
}
enum TimeZone {EST, CST, MST, PST }
```

What is the result?

A. -c

B. -X

C. -cm

D. -cmp

E. -cmXp

F. Compilation fails.

G. An exception is thrown at runtime.

10. Given:

```
class Circus {
  public static void main(String[] args) {
    int x = 9;
    int y = 6;
    for(int z = 0; z < 6; z++, y--) {
      if(x > 2)  x--;
      label:
        if(x > 5) {
          System.out.print(x + " ");
          --x;
          continue label;
```

```
              }
          x--;
        }
      }
    }
```

What is the result?

A. 8

B. 8 7

C. 8 7 6

D. Compilation fails.

E. An exception is thrown at runtime.

11. Which are true? (Choose all that apply.)

A. It is appropriate to use assertions to validate arguments to methods marked `public`.

B. It is appropriate to catch and handle assertion errors.

C. It is NOT appropriate to use assertions to validate command-line arguments.

D. It is appropriate to use assertions to generate alerts when you reach code that should not be reachable.

E. It is NOT appropriate for assertions to change a program's state.

12. Given:

```
1. class Loopy {
2.   public static void main(String[] args) {
3.     int[] x = {7,6,5,4,3,2,1};
4.     // insert code here
5.       System.out.print(y + " ");
6.     }
7.   }
8. }
```

Which, inserted independently at line 4, compiles? (Choose all that apply.)

A. `for(int y : x) {`

B. `for(x : int y) {`

C. `int y = 0; for(y : x) {`

D. `for(int y=0, z=0; z<x.length; z++) { y = x[z];`

E. `for(int y=0, int z=0; z<x.length; z++) { y = x[z];`

F. `int y = 0; for(int z=0; z<x.length; z++) { y = x[z];`

13. Given:

```
1. class Ring {
2.    final static int x2 = 7;
3.    final static Integer x4 = 8;
4.    public static void main(String[] args) {
5.       Integer x1 = 5;
6.       String s = "a";
7.       if(x1 < 9) s += "b";
8.       switch(x1) {
9.         case 5:  s += "c";
10.        case x2: s += "d";
11.        case x4: s += "e";
12.       }
13.       System.out.println(s);
14.    }
15. }
```

What is the result?

A. abc

B. abcde

C. Compilation fails due only to an error on line 7.

D. Compilation fails due only to an error on line 8.

E. Compilation fails due only to an error on line 10.

F. Compilation fails due only to an error on line 11.

G. Compilation fails due to errors on multiple lines.

14. Given:

```
class Emu {
  static String s = "-";
  public static void main(String[] args) {
    try {
      throw new Exception();
    } catch (Exception e) {
      try {
        try { throw new Exception();
        } catch (Exception ex) { s += "ic "; }
        throw new Exception(); }
      catch (Exception x) { s += "mc "; }
      finally { s += "mf "; }
    } finally { s += "of "; }
    System.out.println(s);
  } }
```

What is the result?

A. -ic of

B. -mf of

C. -mc mf

D. -ic mf of

E. -ic mc mf of

F. -ic mc of mf

G. Compilation fails.

15. Given:

```
class Mineral { }
class Gem extends Mineral { }
class Miner {
  static int x = 7;
  static String s = null;
  public static void getWeight(Mineral m) {
    int y = 0 / x;
    System.out.print(s + " ");
  }
  public static void main(String[] args) {
    Mineral[] ma = {new Mineral(), new Gem()};
```

```
      for(Object o : ma)
        getWeight((Mineral) o);
    }
  }
```

And the command-line invocation:

```
    java Miner.java
```

What is the result?

- A. `null`
- B. `null null`
- C. A `ClassCastException` is thrown.
- D. A `NullPointerException` is thrown.
- E. A `NoClassDefFoundError` is thrown.
- F. An `ArithmeticException` is thrown.
- G. An `IllegalArgumentException` is thrown.
- H. An `ArrayIndexOutOfBoundsException` is thrown.

16. Which are most typically thrown by an API developer or an application developer as opposed to being thrown by the JVM? (Choose all that apply.)
    - A. `ClassCastException`
    - B. `IllegalStateException`
    - C. `NumberFormatException`
    - D. `IllegalArgumentException`
    - E. `ExceptionInInitializerError`

SELF TEST ANSWERS

1. Given the following code:

```
public class OrtegorumFunction {
  public int computeDiscontinuous(int x) {
    int r = 1;
    r += x;
    if ((x > 4) && (x < 10)) {
      r += 2 * x;
    } else (x <= 4) {
      r += 3 * x;
    } else {
      r += 4 * x;
    }
    r += 5 * x;
    return r;
  }

  public static void main(String [] args) {
    OrtegorumFunction o = new OrtegorumFunction();
    System.out.println("OF(11) is: " + o.computeDiscontinuous(11));
  } }
```

What is the result?

A. `OF(11) is: 45`

B. `OF(11) is: 56`

C. `OF(11) is: 89`

D. `OF(11) is: 111`

E. Compilation fails.

F. An exception is thrown at runtime.

Answer:

☑ **E** is correct. The `if` statement is illegal. The `if-else-else` must be changed to `if-else if-else`, which would result in `OF(11) is: 111`.

☒ **A, B, C, D,** and **F** are incorrect based on the above. (Objective 2.1)

2. Given two files:

```
1. class One {
2.   public static void main(String[] args) {
3.     int assert = 0;
4.   }
5. }
```

```
1. class Two {
2.   public static void main(String[] args) {
3.     assert(false);
4.   }
5. }
```

And the four command-line invocations:

```
javac -source 1.3 One.java
javac -source 1.4 One.java
javac -source 1.3 Two.java
javac -source 1.4 Two.java
```

What is the result? (Choose all that apply.)

A. Only one compilation will succeed.

B. Exactly two compilations will succeed.

C. Exactly three compilations will succeed.

D. All four compilations will succeed.

E. No compiler warnings will be produced.

F. At least one compiler warning will be produced.

Answer:

☑ **B** and **F** are correct. Class One will compile (and issue a warning) using the `1.3` flag, and class Two will compile using the `1.4` flag.

☒ **A, C, D,** and **E** are incorrect based on the above. (Objective 2.3)

3. Given:

```
import java.io.*;
class Master {
  String doFileStuff() throws FileNotFoundException { return "a"; }
}
class Slave extends Master {
  public static void main(String[] args) {
    String s = null;
    try { s = new Slave().doFileStuff();
    } catch ( Exception x) {
      s = "b"; }
    System.out.println(s);
  }
  // insert code here
}
```

Which, inserted independently at `// insert code here`, will compile, and produce the output b? (Choose all that apply.)

A. `String doFileStuff() { return "b"; }`

B. `String doFileStuff() throws IOException { return "b"; }`

C. `String doFileStuff(int x) throws IOException { return "b"; }`

D. `String doFileStuff() throws FileNotFoundException { return "b"; }`

E. `String doFileStuff() throws NumberFormatException { return "b"; }`

F. `String doFileStuff() throws NumberFormatException,`
`                                    FileNotFoundException { return "b"; }`

Answer:

☑ **A, D, E,** and **F** are correct. It's okay for an overriding method to throw the same exceptions, narrower exceptions, or no exceptions. And it's okay for the overriding method to throw any runtime exceptions.

☒ **B** is incorrect, because the overriding method is trying to throw a broader exception. **C** is incorrect. This method doesn't override, so the output is a. (Objective 2.4)

4. Given:

```
class Input {
  public static void main(String[] args) {
    String s = "-";
    try {
      doMath(args[0]);
      s += "t ";          // line 6
    }
    finally { System.out.println(s += "f "); }
  }
  public static void doMath(String a) {
    int y = 7 / Integer.parseInt(a);
  }
}
```

And the command-line invocations:

```
java Input
java Input 0
```

Which are true? (Choose all that apply.)

A. Line 6 is executed exactly 0 times.

B. Line 6 is executed exactly 1 time.

C. Line 6 is executed exactly 2 times.

D. The `finally` block is executed exactly 0 times.

E. The `finally` block is executed exactly 1 time.

F. The `finally` block is executed exactly 2 times.

G. Both invocations produce the same exceptions.

H. Each invocation produces a different exception.

Answer:

☑ **A, F,** and **H** are correct. Since both invocations throw exceptions, line 6 is never reached. Since both exceptions occurred within a `try` block, the `finally` block will always execute. The first invocation throws an `ArrayIndexOutOfBoundsException`, and the second invocation throws an `ArithmeticException` for the attempt to divide by zero.

☒ **B, C, D, E,** and **G** are incorrect based on the above. (Objective 2.5)

5. Given:

```
1. class Crivitch {
2.    public static void main(String [] args) {
3.       int x = 0;
4.       // insert code here
5.       do { } while (x++ < y);
6.       System.out.println(x);
7.    }
8. }
```

Which, inserted at line 4, produces the output 12?

A. `int y = x;`

B. `int y = 10;`

C. `int y = 11;`

D. `int y = 12;`

E. `int y = 13;`

F. None of the above will allow compilation to succeed.

Answer:

☑ **C** is correct. x reaches the value of `11`, at which point the `while` test fails. x is then incremented (after the comparison test!), and the `println()` method runs.

☒ **A, B, D, E,** and **F** are incorrect based on the above. (Objective 2.2)

6. Given:

```
class Plane {
  static String s = "-";
  public static void main(String[] args) {
    new Plane().s1();
    System.out.println(s);
  }
  void s1() {
    try { s2(); }
    catch (Exception e) { s += "c"; }
  }
  void s2() throws Exception {
    s3();  s += "2";
    s3();  s += "2b";
  }
  void s3() throws Exception {
    throw new Exception();
} }
```

What is the result?

A. -

B. -c

C. -c2

D. -2c

E. -c22b

F. -2c2b

G. -2c2bc

H. Compilation fails.

Answer:

☑ **B** is correct. Once `s3()` throws the exception to `s2()`, `s2()` throws it to `s1()`, and no more of `s2()`'s code will be executed.

☒ **A, C, D, E, F, G,** and **H** are incorrect based on the above. (Objective 2.5)

7. Given:

```
try { int x = Integer.parseInt("two"); }
```

Which could be used to create an appropriate `catch` block? (Choose all that apply.)

A. `ClassCastException`

B. `IllegalStateException`

C. `NumberFormatException`

D. `IllegalArgumentException`

E. `ExceptionInInitializerError`

F. `ArrayIndexOutOfBoundsException`

Answer:

☑ **C and D** are correct. `Integer.parseInt` can throw a `NumberFormatException`, and `IllegalArgumentException` is its superclass (i.e., a broader exception).

☒ **A, B, E,** and **F** are not in `NumberFormatException`'s class hierarchy. (Objective 2.6)

8. Given:

```
1. class Ping extends Utils {
2.    public static void main(String [] args) {
3.       Utils u = new Ping();
4.       System.out.print(u.getInt(args[0]));
5.    }
6.    int getInt(String arg) {
7.       return Integer.parseInt(arg);
8.    }
9. }
10. class Utils {
11.    int getInt(String x) throws Exception { return 7; }
12. }
```

And the following three possible changes:

C1. Declare that `main()` throws an `Exception`.

C2. Declare that `Ping.getInt()` throws an `Exception`.

C3. Wrap the invocation of `getInt()` in a `try / catch` block.

Which change(s) allow the code to compile? (Choose all that apply.)

A. Just C1 is sufficient.

B. Just C2 is sufficient.

C. Just C3 is sufficient.

D. Both C1 and C2 are required.

E. Both C1 and C3 are required.

F. Both C2 and C3 are required.

G. All three changes are required.

Answer:

☑ **A** and **C** are correct. Remember that line 4 is making a polymorphic call so the compiler knows that an exception might be thrown. If C1 is implemented the exception has been sufficiently declared, and if C3 is implemented the exception has been sufficiently handled. C2 is not necessary in either case.

☒ **B, D, E, F,** and **G** are incorrect based on the above. (Objective 2.4)

9. Given:

```
class Swill {
  public static void main(String[] args) {
    String s = "-";
    switch(TimeZone.CST) {
      case EST: s += "e";
      case CST: s += "c";
      case MST: s += "m";
      default:  s += "X";
      case PST: s += "p";
    }
    System.out.println(s);
  }
}
enum TimeZone {EST, CST, MST, PST }
```

What is the result?

A. -c

B. -X

C. -cm

D. -cmp

E. -cmXp

F. Compilation fails.

G. An exception is thrown at runtime.

Answer:

☑ **E** is correct. It's legal to use enums in a `switch`, and normal `switch` fall-through logic applies; i.e., once a match is made the `switch` has been entered, and all remaining blocks will run if no `break` statement is encountered. Note: `default` doesn't have to be last.

☒ **A, B, C, D,** and **F** are incorrect based on the above. (Objective 2.1)

10. Given:

```
class Circus {
  public static void main(String[] args) {
    int x = 9;
    int y = 6;
    for(int z = 0; z < 6; z++, y--) {
      if(x > 2)   x--;
      label:
        if(x > 5) {
          System.out.print(x + " ");
          --x;
          continue label;
        }
      x--;
    }
  }
}
```

What is the result?

A. 8

B. 8 7

C. 8 7 6

D. Compilation fails.

E. An exception is thrown at runtime.

Answer:

☑ **D** is correct. A labeled `continue` works *only* with loops. In this case, although the label is legal, `label` is not a label on a loop statement, it's a label on an `if` statement.

☒ **A, B, C,** and **E** are incorrect based on the above. (Objective 2.2)

11. Which are true? (Choose all that apply.)

A. It is appropriate to use assertions to validate arguments to methods marked `public`.

B. It is appropriate to catch and handle assertion errors.

C. It is NOT appropriate to use assertions to validate command-line arguments.

D. It is appropriate to use assertions to generate alerts when you reach code that should not be reachable.

E. It is NOT appropriate for assertions to change a program's state.

Answer:

☑ **C, D,** and **E** are correct statements.

☒ **A** is incorrect. It *is* acceptable to use assertions to test the arguments of `private` methods.
B is incorrect. While assertion errors can be caught, Sun discourages you from doing so.
(Objective 2.3)

12. Given:

```
1. class Loopy {
2.   public static void main(String[] args) {
3.     int[] x = {7,6,5,4,3,2,1};
4.     // insert code here
5.       System.out.print(y + " ");
6.     }
7. } }
```

Which, inserted independently at line 4, compiles? (Choose all that apply.)

A. `for(int y : x) {`

B. `for(x : int y) {`

C. `int y = 0; for(y : x) {`

D. `for(int y=0, z=0; z<x.length; z++) { y = x[z];`

E. `for(int y=0, int z=0; z<x.length; z++) { y = x[z];`

F. `int y = 0; for(int z=0; z<x.length; z++) { y = x[z];`

Answer:

☑ **A, D,** and **F** are correct. **A** is an example of the enhanced `for` loop. **D** and **F** are examples of the basic `for` loop.

☒ **B** is incorrect because its operands are swapped. **C** is incorrect because the enhanced `for` must declare its first operand. **E** is incorrect syntax to declare two variables in a `for` statement. (Objective 2.2)

13. Given:

```
1. class Ring {
2.   final static int x2 = 7;
3.   final static Integer x4 = 8;
4.   public static void main(String[] args) {
5.     Integer x1 = 5;
6.     String s = "a";
```

```
 7.      if(x1 < 9) s += "b";
 8.      switch(x1) {
 9.        case 5:  s += "c";
10.        case x2: s += "d";
11.        case x4: s += "e";
12.      }
13.      System.out.println(s);
14.    }
15. }
```

What is the result?

A. abc

B. abcde

C. Compilation fails due only to an error on line 7.

D. Compilation fails due only to an error on line 8.

E. Compilation fails due only to an error on line 10.

F. Compilation fails due only to an error on line 11.

G. Compilation fails due to errors on multiple lines.

Answer:

☑ **F** is correct. A `switch` statement requires its `case` expressions to be constants, and wrapper variables (even `final static` ones) aren't considered constants. The rest of the code is correct.

☒ **A, B, C, D, E,** and **G** are incorrect based on the above. (Objective 2.1)

14. Given:

```
class Emu {
  static String s = "-";
  public static void main(String[] args) {
    try {
      throw new Exception();
    } catch (Exception e) {
        try {
          try { throw new Exception();
          } catch (Exception ex) { s += "ic "; }
          throw new Exception(); }
        catch (Exception x) { s += "mc "; }
        finally { s += "mf "; }
    } finally { s += "of "; }
    System.out.println(s);
  } }
```

What is the result?

A. `-ic of`

B. `-mf of`

C. `-mc mf`

D. `-ic mf of`

E. `-ic mc mf of`

F. `-ic mc of mf`

G. Compilation fails.

Answer:

☑ **E** is correct. There is no problem nesting `try / catch` blocks. As is normal, when an exception is thrown, the code in the `catch` block runs, then the code in the `finally` block runs.

☒ **A, B, C, D,** and **F** are incorrect based on the above. (Objective 2.5)

15. Given:

```
class Mineral { }
class Gem extends Mineral { }
class Miner {
  static int x = 7;
  static String s = null;
  public static void getWeight(Mineral m) {
    int y = 0 / x;
    System.out.print(s + " ");
  }
  public static void main(String[] args) {
    Mineral[] ma = {new Mineral(), new Gem()};
    for(Object o : ma)
      getWeight((Mineral) o);
  }
}
```

And the command-line invocation:

```
java Miner.java
```

What is the result?

A. `null`

B. `null null`

C. A `ClassCastException` is thrown.

D. A `NullPointerException` is thrown.

E. A `NoClassDefFoundError` is thrown.

F. An `ArithmeticException` is thrown.

G. An `IllegalArgumentException` is thrown.

H. An `ArrayIndexOutOfBoundsException` is thrown.

Answer:

☑ **E** is correct. The invocation should be `java Miner`, in which case `null null` would be produced.

☒ **A, B, C, D, F, G,** and **H** are incorrect based on the above. (Objective 2.6)

---

16. Which are most typically thrown by an API developer or an application developer as opposed to being thrown by the JVM? (Choose all that apply.)

A. `ClassCastException`

B. `IllegalStateException`

C. `NumberFormatException`

D. `IllegalArgumentException`

E. `ExceptionInInitializerError`

Answer:

☑ **B, C,** and **D** are correct. **B** is typically used to report an environment problem such as trying to access a resource that's closed. **C** is often thrown in API methods that attempt to convert poorly formed String arguments to numeric values. **D** is often thrown in API methods that receive poorly formed arguments.

☒ **A** and **E** are thrown by the JVM. (Objective 2.6)

6

Strings, I/O, Formatting, and Parsing

- Using String, StringBuilder, and StringBuffer
- File I/O using the java.io package
- Serialization using the java.io package
- Working with Dates, Numbers, and Currencies

- Using Regular Expressions
- ✓ Two-Minute Drill
- Q&A Self Test

T his chapter focuses on the various API-related topics that were added to the exam for Java 5. J2SE comes with an enormous API, and a lot of your work as a Java programmer will revolve around using this API. The exam team chose to focus on APIs for I/O, formatting, and parsing. Each of these topics could fill an entire book. Fortunately, you won't have to become a total I/O or regex guru to do well on the exam. The intention of the exam team was to include just the basic aspects of these technologies, and in this chapter we cover *more* than you'll need to get through the String, I/O, formatting, and parsing objectives on the exam.

CERTIFICATION OBJECTIVE

String, StringBuilder, and StringBuffer (Exam Objective 3.1)

3.1   Discuss the differences between the String, StringBuilder, and StringBuffer classes.

Everything you needed to know about Strings in the SCJP 1.4 exam, you'll need to know for the SCJP 5 exam…plus, Sun added the *StringBuilder* class to the API, to provide faster, non-synchronized StringBuffer capability. The StringBuilder class has exactly the same methods as the old StringBuffer class, but StringBuilder is faster because its methods aren't synchronized. Both classes give you String-like objects that handle some of the String class's shortcomings (like immutability).

The String Class

This section covers the String class, and the key concept to understand is that once a String object is created, it can never be changed—so what is happening when a String object seems to be changing? Let's find out.

Strings Are Immutable Objects

We'll start with a little background information about strings. You may not need this for the test, but a little context will help. Handling "strings" of characters is a fundamental aspect of most programming languages. In Java, each character in a string is a 16-bit Unicode character. Because Unicode characters are 16 bits (not the skimpy 7 or 8 bits that ASCII provides), a rich, international set of characters is easily represented in Unicode.

In Java, strings are objects. Just like other objects, you can create an instance of a String with the new keyword, as follows:

```
String s = new String();
```

This line of code creates a new object of class String, and assigns it to the reference variable s. So far, String objects seem just like other objects. Now, let's give the String a value:

```
s = "abcdef";
```

As you might expect, the String class has about a zillion constructors, so you can use a more efficient shortcut:

```
String s = new String("abcdef");
```

And just because you'll use strings all the time, you can even say this:

```
String s = "abcdef";
```

There are some subtle differences between these options that we'll discuss later, but what they have in common is that they all create a new String object, with a value of "abcdef", and assign it to a reference variable s. Now let's say that you want a second reference to the String object referred to by s:

```
String s2 = s;    //  refer s2 to the same String as s
```

So far so good. String objects seem to be behaving just like other objects, so what's all the fuss about?...Immutability! (What the heck is immutability?) Once you have assigned a String a value, that value can never change— it's immutable, frozen solid, won't budge, fini, done. (We'll talk about why later, don't let us forget.) The good news is that while the String object is immutable, its reference variable is not, so to continue with our previous example:

```
s = s.concat(" more stuff");  // the concat() method 'appends'
                              // a literal to the end
```

Now wait just a minute, didn't we just say that Strings were immutable? So what's all this "appending to the end of the string" talk? Excellent question: let's look at what really happened…

The VM took the value of String s (which was `"abcdef"`), and tacked `" more stuff"` onto the end, giving us the value `"abcdef more stuff"`. Since Strings are immutable, the VM couldn't stuff this new value into the old String referenced by s, so it created a new String object, gave it the value `"abcdef more stuff"`, and made s refer to it. At this point in our example, we have two String objects: the first one we created, with the value `"abcdef"`, and the second one with the value `"abcdef more stuff"`. Technically there are now three String objects, because the literal argument to concat, `" more stuff"`, is itself a new String object. But we have references only to `"abcdef"` (referenced by s2) and `"abcdef more stuff"` (referenced by s).

What if we didn't have the foresight or luck to create a second reference variable for the `"abcdef"` String before we called s = s.concat(`" more stuff"`);? In that case, the original, unchanged String containing `"abcdef"` would still exist in memory, but it would be considered "lost." No code in our program has any way to reference it—it is lost to us. Note, however, that the original `"abcdef"` String didn't change (it can't, remember, it's immutable); only the reference variable s was changed, so that it would refer to a different String. Figure 6-1 shows what happens on the heap when you reassign a reference variable. Note that the dashed line indicates a deleted reference.

To review our first example:

```
String s = "abcdef";      // create a new String object, with
                          // value "abcdef", refer s to it
String s2 = s;            // create a 2nd reference variable
                          // referring to the same String

// create a new String object, with value "abcdef more stuff",
// refer s to it. (Change s's reference from the old String
// to the new String.) ( Remember s2 is still referring to
// the original "abcdef" String.)

s = s.concat(" more stuff");
```

FIGURE 6-1   String objects and their reference variables

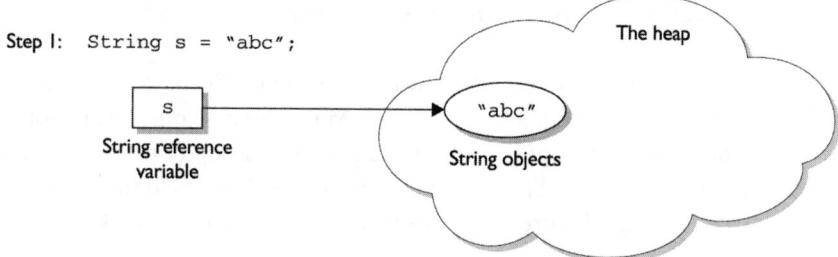

Step 1:   String s = "abc";

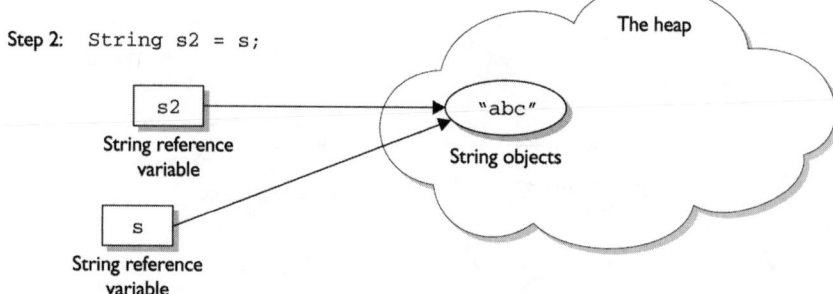

Step 2:   String s2 = s;

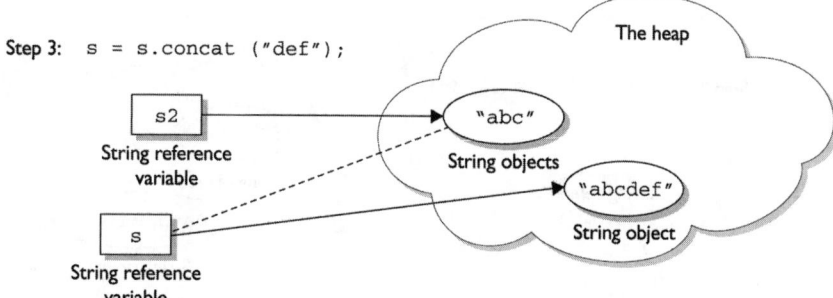

Step 3:   s = s.concat ("def");

Let's look at another example:

```
String x = "Java";
x.concat(" Rules!");
System.out.println("x = " + x);  // the output is "x = Java"
```

The first line is straightforward: create a new String object, give it the value
"Java", and refer x to it. Next the VM creates a second String object with the value
"Java Rules!" but nothing refers to it. The second String object is instantly lost;
you can't get to it. The reference variable x still refers to the original String with the
value "Java". Figure 6-2 shows creating a String without assigning a reference to it.

FIGURE 6-2 A String object is abandoned upon creation

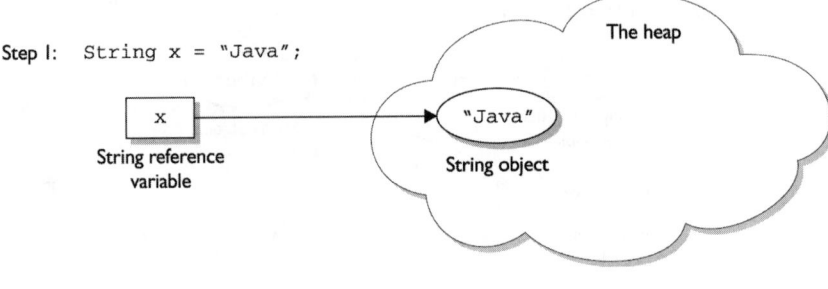

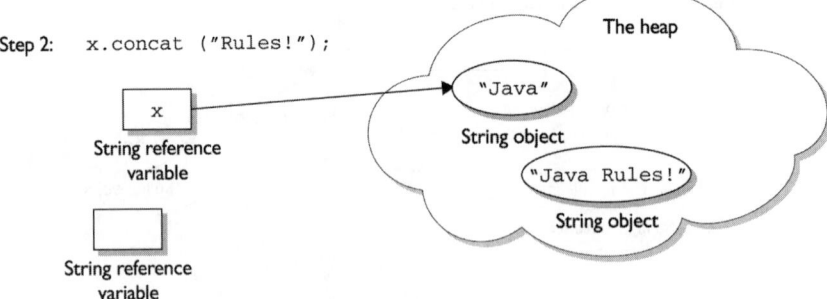

Let's expand this current example. We started with

```
String x = "Java";
x.concat(" Rules!");
System.out.println("x = " + x);   // the output is: x = Java
```

Now let's add

```
x.toUpperCase();
System.out.println("x = " + x);   // the output is still:
                                  // x = Java
```

(We actually did just create a new String object with the value "JAVA", but it was lost, and x still refers to the original, unchanged String "Java".) How about adding

```
x.replace('a', 'X');
System.out.println("x = " + x);   // the output is still:
                                  // x = Java
```

Can you determine what happened? The VM created yet another new String object, with the value "JXvX", (replacing the a's with X's), but once again this new String was lost, leaving x to refer to the original unchanged and unchangeable String object, with the value "Java". In all of these cases we called various String methods to create a new String by altering an existing String, but we never assigned the newly created String to a reference variable.

But we can put a small spin on the previous example:

```
String x = "Java";
x = x.concat(" Rules!");           // Now we're assigning the
                                   // new String to x
System.out.println("x = " + x);    // the output will be:
                                   // x = Java Rules!
```

This time, when the VM runs the second line, a new String object is created with the value of "Java Rules!", and x is set to reference it. But wait, there's more— now the original String object, "Java", has been lost, and no one is referring to it. So in both examples we created two String objects and only one reference variable, so one of the two String objects was left out in the cold. See Figure 6-3 for a graphic depiction of this sad story. The dashed line indicates a deleted reference.

FIGURE 6-3	An old String object being abandoned

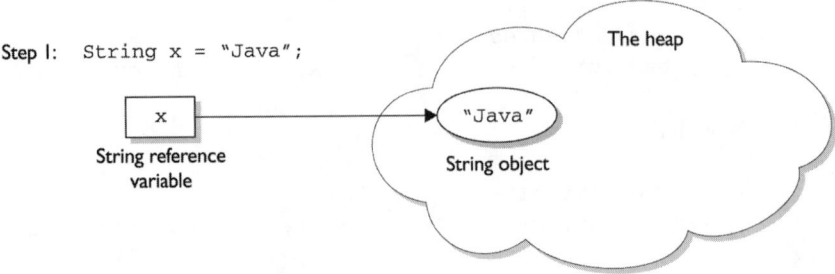

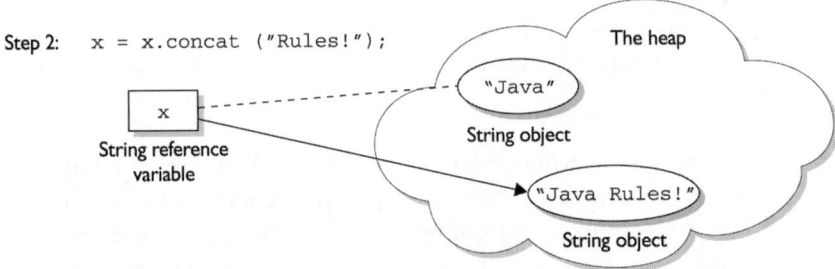

Notice in step 2 that there is no valid reference to the "Java" String; that object has been "abandoned," and a new object created.

Let's take this example a little further:

```
String x = "Java";
x = x.concat(" Rules!");
System.out.println("x = " + x);    // the output is:
                                   // x = Java Rules!

x.toLowerCase();                   // no assignment, create a
                                   // new, abandoned String

System.out.println("x = " + x);    // no assignment, the output
                                   // is still: x = Java Rules!
```

```
x = x.toLowerCase();              // create a new String,
                                  // assigned to x
System.out.println("x = " + x);   // the assignment causes the
                                  // output: x = java rules!
```

The preceding discussion contains the keys to understanding Java String immutability. If you really, really get the examples and diagrams, backwards and forwards, you should get 80 percent of the String questions on the exam correct.

We will cover more details about Strings next, but make no mistake—in terms of bang for your buck, what we've already covered is by far the most important part of understanding how String objects work in Java.

We'll finish this section by presenting an example of the kind of devilish String question you might expect to see on the exam. Take the time to work it out on paper (as a hint, try to keep track of how many objects and reference variables there are, and which ones refer to which).

```
String s1 = "spring ";
String s2 = s1 + "summer ";
s1.concat("fall ");
s2.concat(s1);
s1 += "winter ";
System.out.println(s1 + " " + s2);
```

What is the output? For extra credit, how many String objects and how many reference variables were created prior to the `println` statement?

Answer: The result of this code fragment is "spring winter spring summer". There are two reference variables, `s1` and `s2`. There were a total of eight String objects created as follows: "spring", "summer " (lost), "spring summer", "fall " (lost), "spring fall" (lost), "spring summer spring" (lost), "winter" (lost), "spring winter" (at this point "spring" is lost). Only two of the eight String objects are not lost in this process.

Important Facts About Strings and Memory

In this section we'll discuss how Java handles String objects in memory, and some of the reasons behind these behaviors.

One of the key goals of any good programming language is to make efficient use of memory. As applications grow, it's very common for String literals to occupy large amounts of a program's memory, and there is often a lot of redundancy within the universe of String literals for a program. To make Java more memory efficient, the JVM sets aside a special area of memory called the "String constant pool." When the compiler encounters a String literal, it checks the pool to see if an identical String already exists. If a match is found, the reference to the new literal is directed to the existing String, and no new String literal object is created. (The existing String simply has an additional reference.) Now we can start to see why making String objects immutable is such a good idea. If several reference variables refer to the same String without even knowing it, it would be very bad if any of them could change the String's value.

You might say, "Well that's all well and good, but what if someone overrides the String class functionality; couldn't that cause problems in the pool?" That's one of the main reasons that the String class is marked `final`. Nobody can override the behaviors of any of the String methods, so you can rest assured that the String objects you are counting on to be immutable will, in fact, be immutable.

Creating New Strings

Earlier we promised to talk more about the subtle differences between the various methods of creating a String. Let's look at a couple of examples of how a String might be created, and let's further assume that no other String objects exist in the pool:

```
String s = "abc";    //  creates one String object and one
                     //  reference variable
```

In this simple case, "abc" will go in the pool and s will refer to it.

```
String s = new String("abc");  // creates two objects,
                               // and one reference variable
```

In this case, because we used the new keyword, Java will create a new String object in normal (non-pool) memory, and s will refer to it. In addition, the literal "abc" will be placed in the pool.

Important Methods in the String Class

The following methods are some of the more commonly used methods in the String class, and also the ones that you're most likely to encounter on the exam.

- **charAt()**   Returns the character located at the specified index
- **concat()**   Appends one String to the end of another ("+" also works)
- **equalsIgnoreCase()**   Determines the equality of two Strings, ignoring case
- **length()**   Returns the number of characters in a String
- **replace()**   Replaces occurrences of a character with a new character
- **substring()**   Returns a part of a String
- **toLowerCase()**   Returns a String with uppercase characters converted
- **toString()**   Returns the value of a String
- **toUpperCase()**   Returns a String with lowercase characters converted
- **trim()**   Removes whitespace from the ends of a String

Let's look at these methods in more detail.

public char charAt(int index)   This method returns the character located at the String's specified index. Remember, String indexes are zero-based—for example,

```
String x = "airplane";
System.out.println( x.charAt(2) );        //  output is 'r'
```

public String concat(String s)   This method returns a String with the value of the String passed in to the method appended to the end of the String used to invoke the method—for example,

```
String x = "taxi";
System.out.println( x.concat(" cab") ); // output is "taxi cab"
```

The overloaded + and += operators perform functions similar to the `concat()` method—for example,

```
String x = "library";
System.out.println( x + " card");     // output is "library card"

String x = "Atlantic";
x += " ocean"
System.out.println( x );              // output is "Atlantic ocean"
```

In the preceding "Atlantic ocean" example, notice that the value of x really did change! Remember that the += operator is an assignment operator, so line 2 is really creating a new String, "Atlantic ocean", and assigning it to the x variable. After line 2 executes, the original String x was referring to, "Atlantic", is abandoned.

public boolean equalsIgnoreCase(String s) This method returns a boolean value (true or false) depending on whether the value of the String in the argument is the same as the value of the String used to invoke the method. This method will return true even when characters in the String objects being compared have differing cases—for example,

```
String x = "Exit";
System.out.println( x.equalsIgnoreCase("EXIT"));    // is "true"
System.out.println( x.equalsIgnoreCase("tixe"));    // is "false"
```

public int length() This method returns the length of the String used to invoke the method—for example,

```
String x = "01234567";
System.out.println( x.length() );     // returns "8"
```

public String replace(char old, char new) This method returns a String whose value is that of the String used to invoke the method, updated so that any occurrence of the char in the first argument is replaced by the char in the second argument—for example,

```
String x = "oxoxoxox";
System.out.println( x.replace('x', 'X') );     // output is
                                               // "oXoXoXoX"
```

public String substring(int begin)
public String substring(int begin, int end) The substring() method is used to return a part (or substring) of the String used to invoke the method. The first argument represents the starting location (zero-based) of the substring. If the call has only one argument, the substring returned will include the characters to the end of the original String. If the call has two arguments, the substring returned will end with the character located in the nth position of the original String where n is the

exam
ⓦatch

Arrays have an attribute (not a method), called length. *You may encounter questions in the exam that attempt to use the length() method on an array, or that attempt to use the length attribute on a String. Both cause compiler errors—for example,*

```
String x = "test";
System.out.println( x.length );      // compiler error
```

or

```
String[] x = new String[3];
System.out.println( x.length() );    // compiler error
```

second argument. Unfortunately, the ending argument is not zero-based, so if the second argument is 7, the last character in the returned String will be in the original String's 7 position, which is index 6 (ouch). Let's look at some examples:

```
String x = "0123456789";             // as if by magic, the value
                                     // of each char
                                     // is the same as its index!
System.out.println( x.substring(5) );       // output is  "56789"
System.out.println( x.substring(5, 8));     // output is "567"
```

The first example should be easy: start at index 5 and return the rest of the String. The second example should be read as follows: start at index 5 and return the characters up to and including the 8th position (index 7).

public String toLowerCase()   This method returns a String whose value is the String used to invoke the method, but with any uppercase characters converted to lowercase—for example,

```
String x = "A New Moon";
System.out.println( x.toLowerCase() );      // output is
                                            // "a new moon"
```

public String toString() This method returns the value of the String used to invoke the method. What? Why would you need such a seemingly "do nothing" method? All objects in Java must have a toString() method, which typically returns a String that in some meaningful way describes the object in question. In the case of a String object, what more meaningful way than the String's value? For the sake of consistency, here's an example:

```
String x = "big surprise";
System.out.println( x.toString() );     // output -
                                        // reader's exercise
```

public String toUpperCase() This method returns a String whose value is the String used to invoke the method, but with any lowercase characters converted to uppercase—for example,

```
String x = "A New Moon";
System.out.println( x.toUpperCase() );  // output is
                                        // "A NEW MOON"
```

public String trim() This method returns a String whose value is the String used to invoke the method, but with any leading or trailing blank spaces removed—for example,

```
String x = "      hi        ";
System.out.println( x + "x" );          // result is
                                        // "      hi        x"

System.out.println( x.trim() + "x");    // result is "hix"
```

The StringBuffer and StringBuilder Classes

The java.lang.StringBuffer and java.lang.StringBuilder classes should be used when you have to make a lot of modifications to strings of characters. As we discussed in the previous section, String objects are immutable, so if you choose to do a lot of manipulations with String objects, you will end up with a lot of abandoned String objects in the String pool. (Even in these days of gigabytes of RAM, it's not a good idea to waste precious memory on discarded String pool objects.) On the other hand, objects of type StringBuffer and StringBuilder can be modified over and over again without leaving behind a great effluence of discarded String objects.

on the **!** **Ö**ob

A common use for StringBuffers and StringBuilders is file I/O when large, ever-changing streams of input are being handled by the program. In these cases, large blocks of characters are handled as units, and StringBuffer objects are the ideal way to handle a block of data, pass it on, and then reuse the same memory to handle the next block of data.

StringBuffer vs. StringBuilder

The StringBuilder class was added in Java 5. It has exactly the same API as the StringBuffer class, except StringBuilder is not thread safe. In other words, its methods are not synchronized. (More about thread safety in Chapter 9.) Sun recommends that you use StringBuilder instead of StringBuffer whenever possible because StringBuilder will run faster (and perhaps jump higher). So apart from synchronization, anything we say about StringBuilder's methods holds true for StringBuffer's methods, and vice versa. The exam might use these classes in the creation of thread-safe applications, and we'll discuss how *that* works in Chapter 9.

Using StringBuilder and StringBuffer

In the previous section, we saw how the exam might test your understanding of String immutability with code fragments like this:

```
String x = "abc";
x.concat("def");
System.out.println("x = " + x);      // output is "x = abc"
```

Because no new assignment was made, the new String object created with the concat() method was abandoned instantly. We also saw examples like this:

```
String x = "abc";
x = x.concat("def");
System.out.println("x = " + x);      // output is "x = abcdef"
```

We got a nice new String out of the deal, but the downside is that the old String "abc" has been lost in the String pool, thus wasting memory. If we were using a StringBuffer instead of a String, the code would look like this:

```
StringBuffer sb = new StringBuffer("abc");
sb.append("def");
System.out.println("sb = " + sb);      // output is "sb = abcdef"
```

All of the StringBuffer methods we will discuss operate on the value of the StringBuffer object invoking the method. So a call to `sb.append("def");` is actually appending "def" to itself (StringBuffer `sb`). In fact, these method calls can be chained to each other—for example,

```
StringBuilder sb = new StringBuilder("abc");
sb.append("def").reverse().insert(3, "---");
System.out.println( sb );              // output is  "fed---cba"
```

Notice that in each of the previous two examples, there was a single call to new, concordantly in each example we weren't creating any extra objects. Each example needed only a single StringXxx object to execute.

Important Methods in the StringBuffer and StringBuilder Classes

The following method returns a StringXxx object with the argument's value appended to the value of the object that invoked the method.

public synchronized StringBuffer append(String s)   As we've seen earlier, this method will update the value of the object that invoked the method, whether or not the return is assigned to a variable. This method will take many different arguments, including boolean, char, double, float, int, long, and others, but the most likely use on the exam will be a String argument—for example,

```
StringBuffer sb = new StringBuffer("set ");
sb.append("point");
System.out.println(sb);        // output is "set point"
StringBuffer sb2 = new StringBuffer("pi = ");
sb2.append(3.14159f);
System.out.println(sb2);       // output is  "pi = 3.14159"
```

public StringBuilder delete(int start, int end)   This method returns a StringBuilder object and updates the value of the StringBuilder object that invoked the method call. In both cases, a substring is removed from the original object. The starting index of the substring to be removed is defined by the first argument (which is zero-based), and the ending index of the substring to be removed is defined by the second argument (but it is one-based)! Study the following example carefully:

```
StringBuilder sb = new StringBuilder("0123456789");
System.out.println(sb.delete(4,6));       // output is "01236789"
```

The exam will probably test your knowledge of the difference between String and StringBuffer objects. Because StringBuffer objects are changeable, the following code fragment will behave differently than a similar code fragment that uses String objects:

```
StringBuffer sb = new StringBuffer("abc");
sb.append("def");
System.out.println( sb );
```

In this case, the output will be: "abcdef"

public StringBuilder insert(int offset, String s)
This method returns a StringBuilder object and updates the value of the StringBuilder object that invoked the method call. In both cases, the String passed in to the second argument is inserted into the original StringBuilder starting at the offset location represented by the first argument (the offset is zero-based). Again, other types of data can be passed in through the second argument (`boolean`, `char`, `double`, `float`, `int`, `long`, and so on), but the String argument is the one you're most likely to see:

```
StringBuilder sb = new StringBuilder("01234567");
sb.insert(4, "---");
System.out.println( sb );          //   output is  "0123---4567"
```

public synchronized StringBuffer reverse()
This method returns a StringBuffer object and updates the value of the StringBuffer object that invoked the method call. In both cases, the characters in the StringBuffer are reversed, the first character becoming the last, the second becoming the second to the last, and so on:

```
StringBuffer s = new StringBuffer("A man a plan a canal Panama");
sb.reverse();
System.out.println(sb); // output: "amanaP lanac a nalp a nam A"
```

public String toString()
This method returns the value of the StringBuffer object that invoked the method call as a String:

```
StringBuffer sb = new StringBuffer("test string");
System.out.println( sb.toString() );  // output is "test string"
```

That's it for StringBuffers and StringBuilders. If you take only one thing away from this section, it's that unlike Strings, StringBuffer objects and StringBuilder objects can be changed.

exam
w a t c h

Many of the exam questions covering this chapter's topics use a tricky (and not very readable) bit of Java syntax known as "chained methods." A statement with chained methods has this general form:

```
result = method1().method2().method3();
```

In theory, any number of methods can be chained in this fashion, although typically you won't see more than three. Here's how to decipher these "handy Java shortcuts" when you encounter them:

1. Determine what the leftmost method call will return (let's call it x).
2. Use x as the object invoking the second (from the left) method. If there are only two chained methods, the result of the second method call is the expression's result.
3. If there is a third method, the result of the second method call is used to invoke the third method, whose result is the expression's result—for example,

```
String x = "abc";
String y = x.concat("def").toUpperCase().replace('C','x');
//chained methods
System.out.println("y = " + y); // result is "y = ABxDEF"
```

Let's look at what happened. The literal def *was concatenated to* abc, *creating a temporary, intermediate String (soon to be lost), with the value* abcdef. *The* toUpperCase() *method created a new (soon to be lost) temporary String with the value* ABCDEF. *The* replace() *method created a final String with the value* ABxDEF, *and referred* y *to it.*

CERTIFICATION OBJECTIVE

File Navigation and I/O (Exam Objective 3.2)

3.2   Given a scenario involving navigating file systems, reading from files, or writing to files, develop the correct solution using the following classes (sometimes in combination), from java.io: BufferedReader, BufferedWriter, File, FileReader, FileWriter, and PrintWriter.

I/O has had a strange history with the SCJP certification. It was included in all the versions of the exam up to and including 1.2, then removed from the 1.4 exam, and then re-introduced for Java 5.

I/O is a huge topic in general, and the Java APIs that deal with I/O in one fashion or another are correspondingly huge. A general discussion of I/O could include topics such as file I/O, console I/O, thread I/O, high-performance I/O, byte-oriented I/O, character-oriented I/O, I/O filtering and wrapping, serialization, and more. Luckily for us, the I/O topics included in the Java 5 exam are fairly well restricted to file I/O for characters, and serialization.

Here's a summary of the I/O classes you'll need to understand for the exam:

- **File**   The API says that the class File is "An abstract representation of file and directory pathnames." The File class isn't used to actually read or write data; it's used to work at a higher level, making new empty files, searching for files, deleting files, making directories, and working with paths.

- **FileReader**   This class is used to read character files. Its `read()` methods are fairly low-level, allowing you to read single characters, the whole stream of characters, or a fixed number of characters. FileReaders are usually *wrapped* by higher-level objects such as BufferedReaders, which improve performance and provide more convenient ways to work with the data.

- **BufferedReader**   This class is used to make lower-level Reader classes like FileReader more efficient and easier to use. Compared to FileReaders, BufferedReaders read relatively large chunks of data from a file at once, and keep this data in a buffer. When you ask for the next character or line of data, it is retrieved from the buffer, which minimizes the number of times that time-intensive, file read operations are performed. In addition,

BufferedReader provides more convenient methods such as `readLine()`, that allow you to get the next line of characters from a file.

- **FileWriter** This class is used to write to character files. Its `write()` methods allow you to write character(s) or Strings to a file. FileWriters are usually *wrapped* by higher-level Writer objects such as BufferedWriters or PrintWriters, which provide better performance and higher-level, more flexible methods to write data.

- **BufferedWriter** This class is used to make lower-level classes like FileWriters more efficient and easier to use. Compared to FileWriters, BufferedWriters write relatively large chunks of data to a file at once, minimizing the number of times that slow, file writing operations are performed. In addition, the BufferedWriter class provides a `newLine()` method that makes it easy to create platform-specific line separators automatically.

- **PrintWriter** This class has been enhanced significantly in Java 5. Because of newly created methods and constructors (like building a PrintWriter with a File or a String), you might find that you can use PrintWriter in places where you previously needed a Writer to be wrapped with a FileWriter and/or a BufferedWriter. New methods like `format()`, `printf()`, and `append()` make PrintWriters very flexible and powerful.

---

exam

Watch

Stream classes are used to read and write bytes, and Readers and Writers are used to read and write characters. Since all of the file I/O on the exam is related to characters, if you see API class names containing the word "Stream", for instance DataOutputStream, then the question is probably about serialization, or something unrelated to the actual I/O objective.

Creating Files Using Class File

Objects of type File are used to represent the actual files (but not the data in the files) or directories that exist on a computer's physical disk. Just to make sure we're clear, when we talk about an object of type File, we'll say File, with a capital F. When we're talking about what exists on a hard drive, we'll call it a file with a lowercase f (unless it's a variable name in some code). Let's start with a few basic examples of creating files, writing to them, and reading from them. First, let's create a new file and write a few lines of data to it:

```java
import java.io.*;                     // The Java 5 exam focuses on
                                      // classes from java.io
class Writer1 {
  public static void main(String [] args) {
    File file = new File("fileWrite1.txt");    // There's no
                                               // file yet!
  }
}
```

If you compile and run this program, when you look at the contents of your current directory, you'll discover absolutely no indication of a file called `fileWrite1.txt`. When you make a new instance of the class File, *you're not yet making an actual file, you're just creating a filename.* Once you have a File *object*, there are several ways to make an actual file. Let's see what we can do with the File object we just made:

```java
import java.io.*;

class Writer1 {
 public static void main(String [] args) {
   try {                             // warning: exceptions possible
     boolean newFile = false;
     File file = new File            // it's only an object
                 ("fileWrite1.txt");
     System.out.println(file.exists());  // look for a real file
     newFile = file.createNewFile();     // maybe create a file!
     System.out.println(newFile);        // already there?
     System.out.println(file.exists());  // look again
   } catch(IOException e) { }
 }
}
```

This produces the output

```
false
true
true
```

And also produces an empty file in your current directory. If you run the code a *second* time you get the output

```
true
false
true
```

Let's examine these sets of output:

- **First execution** The first call to `exists()` returned `false`, which we expected...remember `new File()` doesn't create a file on the disk! The `createNewFile()` method created an actual file, and returned `true`, indicating that a new file was created, and that one didn't already exist. Finally, we called `exists()` again, and this time it returned `true`, indicating that the file existed on the disk.

- **Second execution** The first call to `exists()` returns `true` because we built the file during the first run. Then the call to `createNewFile()` returns `false` since the method didn't create a file this time through. Of course, the last call to `exists()` returns `true`.

A couple of other new things happened in this code. First, notice that we had to put our file creation code in a try/catch. This is true for almost all of the file I/O code you'll ever write. I/O is one of those inherently risky things. We're keeping it simple for now, and ignoring the exceptions, but we still need to follow the handle-or-declare rule since most I/O methods declare checked exceptions. We'll talk more about I/O exceptions later. We used a couple of File's methods in this code:

- `boolean exists()` This method returns `true` if it can find the actual file.
- `boolean createNewFile()` This method creates a new file if it doesn't already exist.

Remember, the exam creators are trying to jam as much code as they can into a small space, so in the previous example, instead of these three lines code,

```
boolean newFile = false;
...
newFile = file.createNewFile();
System.out.println(newFile);
```

You might see something like the following single line of code, which is a bit harder to read, but accomplishes the same thing:

```
System.out.println(file.createNewFile());
```

Using FileWriter and FileReader

In practice, you probably won't use the FileWriter and FileReader classes without wrapping them (more about "wrapping" very soon). That said, let's go ahead and do a little "naked" file I/O:

```
import java.io.*;

class Writer2 {
  public static void main(String [] args) {
    char[] in = new char[50];          // to store input
    int size = 0;
    try {
      File file = new File(            // just an object
                "fileWrite2.txt");
      FileWriter fw =
                new FileWriter(file);  // create an actual file
                                       // & a FileWriter obj
      fw.write("howdy\nfolks\n");      // write characters to
                                       // the file
      fw.flush();                      // flush before closing
      fw.close();                      // close file when done
```

```
    FileReader fr =
            new FileReader(file);   // create a FileReader
                                    // object
    size = fr.read(in);            // read the whole file!
    System.out.print(size + " ");  // how many bytes read
    for(char c : in)               // print the array
      System.out.print(c);
    fr.close();                    // again, always close
  } catch(IOException e) { }
  }
}
```

which produces the output:

```
12 howdy
folks
```

Here's what just happened:

1. `FileWriter fw = new FileWriter(file)` did three things:

    a. It created a FileWriter reference variable, `fw`.

    b. It created a FileWriter object, and assigned it to `fw`.

    c. It created an actual empty file out on the disk (and you can prove it).

2. We wrote 12 characters to the file with the `write()` method, and we did a `flush()` and a `close()`.

3. We made a new FileReader object, which also opened the file on disk for reading.

4. The `read()` method read the whole file, a character at a time, and put it into the `char[]` in.

5. We printed out the number of characters we read `size`, and we looped through the `in` array printing out each character we read, then we closed the file.

Before we go any further let's talk about `flush()` and `close()`. When you write data out to a stream, some amount of buffering will occur, and you never know for sure exactly when the last of the data will actually be sent. You might perform many write operations on a stream before closing it, and invoking the `flush()` method guarantees that the last of the data you thought you had already written actually gets out to the file. Whenever you're done using a file, either reading it or writing to it, you should invoke the `close()` method. When you are doing file I/O you're using expensive and limited operating system resources, and so when you're done, invoking `close()` will free up those resources.

Now, back to our last example. This program certainly works, but it's painful in a couple of different ways:

1. When we were writing data to the file, we manually inserted line separators (in this case \n), into our data.

2. When we were reading data back in, we put it into a character array. It being an array and all, we had to declare its size beforehand, so we'd have been in trouble if we hadn't made it big enough! We could have read the data in one character at a time, looking for the end of file after each `read()`, but that's pretty painful too.

Because of these limitations, we'll typically want to use higher-level I/O classes like BufferedWriter or BufferedReader in combination with FileWriter or FileReader.

Combining I/O classes

Java's entire I/O system was designed around the idea of using several classes in combination. Combining I/O classes is sometimes called *wrapping* and sometimes called *chaining*. The java.io package contains about 50 classes, 10 interfaces, and 15 exceptions. Each class in the package has a very specific purpose (creating high cohesion), and the classes are designed to be combined with each other in countless ways, to handle a wide variety of situations.

When it's time to do some I/O in real life, you'll undoubtedly find yourself pouring over the java.io API, trying to figure out which classes you'll need, and how to hook them together. For the exam, you'll need to do the same thing, but we've artificially reduced the API. In terms of studying for exam Objective 3.2, we can imagine that the entire java.io package consisted of the classes listed in exam Objective 3.2, and summarized in Table 6-1, our mini I/O API.

TABLE 6-1   java.io Mini API

java.io Class	Extends From	Key Constructor(s) Arguments	Key Methods
File	Object	File, String String String, String	createNewFile() delete() exists() isDirectory() isFile() list() mkdir() renameTo()
FileWriter	Writer	File String	close() flush() write()
BufferedWriter	Writer	Writer	close() flush() newLine() write()
PrintWriter	Writer	File (as of Java 5) String (as of Java 5) OutputStream Writer	close() flush() format()*, printf()* print(), println() write()
FileReader	Reader	File String	read()
BufferedReader	Reader	Reader	read() readLine()
			*Discussed later

Now let's say that we want to find a less painful way to write data to a file and read the file's contents back into memory. Starting with the task of writing data to a file, here's a process for determining what classes we'll need, and how we'll hook them together:

1. We know that ultimately we want to hook to a File object. So whatever other class or classes we use, one of them must have a constructor that takes an object of type File.

2. Find a method that sounds like the most powerful, easiest way to accomplish
    the task. When we look at Table 6-1 we can see that BufferedWriter has
    a `newLine()` method. That sounds a little better than having to manually
    embed a separator after each line, but if we look further we see that
    PrintWriter has a method called `println()`. That sounds like the easiest
    approach of all, so we'll go with it.

3. When we look at PrintWriter's constructors, we see that we can build a
    PrintWriter object if we have an object of type file, so all we need to do to
    create a PrintWriter object is the following:

```
File file = new File("fileWrite2.txt");   // create a File
PrintWriter pw = new PrintWriter(file);   // pass file to
                                          // the PrintWriter
                                          // constructor
```

Okay, time for a pop quiz. Prior to Java 5, PrintWriter did not have constructors
that took either a String or a File. If you were writing some I/O code in Java 1.4,
how would you get a PrintWriter to write data to a File? Hint: You can figure this out
by studying the mini I/O API, Table 6-1.

Here's one way to go about solving this puzzle: First, we know that we'll create
a File object on one end of the chain, and that we want a PrintWriter object on
the other end. We can see in Table 6-1 that a PrintWriter can also be built using
a Writer object. Although Writer isn't a *class* we see in the table, we can see that
several other classes extend Writer, which for our purposes is just as good; any class
that extends Writer is a candidate. Looking further, we can see that FileWriter has
the two attributes we're looking for:

1. It can be constructed using a File.
2. It extends Writer.

Given all of this information, we can put together the following code (remember,
this is a Java 1.4 example):

```
File file = new File("fileWrite2.txt");   // create a File object
FileWriter fw = new FileWriter(file);     // create a FileWriter
                                          // that will send its
                                          // output to a File
```

```
PrintWriter pw = new PrintWriter(fw);     // create a PrintWriter
                                          // that will send its
                                          // output to a Writer

pw.println("howdy");                      // write the data
pw.println("folks");
```

At this point it should be fairly easy to put together the code to more easily read data from the file back into memory. Again, looking through the table, we see a method called `readLine()` that sounds like a much better way to read data. Going through a similar process we get the following code:

```
File file =
      new File("fileWrite2.txt");   // create a File object AND
                                    // open "fileWrite2.txt"
FileReader fr =
        new FileReader(file);       // create a FileReader to get
                                    // data from 'file'
BufferedReader br =
        new BufferedReader(fr);     // create a BufferReader to
                                    // get its data from a Reader
String data = br.readLine();        // read some data
```

exam
watch

You're almost certain to encounter exam questions that test your knowledge of how I/O classes can be chained. If you're not totally clear on this last section, we recommend that you use Table 6-1 as a reference, and write code to experiment with which chaining combinations are legal and which are illegal.

Working with Files and Directories

Earlier we touched on the fact that the File class is used to create files and directories. In addition, File's methods can be used to delete files, rename files, determine whether files exist, create temporary files, change a file's attributes, and differentiate between files and directories. A point that is often confusing is that an object of type File is used to represent *either* a *file* or a *directory*. We'll talk about both cases next.

We saw earlier that the statement

```
File file = new File("foo");
```

always creates a File object, and then does one of two things:

1. If "foo" does NOT exist, no actual file is created.

2. If "foo" *does* exist, the new File object refers to the existing file.

Notice that `File file = new File("foo");` NEVER creates an actual file. There are two ways to create a file:

1. Invoke the `createNewFile()` method on a File object. For example:

```
File file = new File("foo");    // no file yet
file.createNewFile();           // make a file, "foo" which
                                // is assigned to 'file'
```

2. Create a Reader or a Writer or a Stream. Specifically, create a FileReader, a FileWriter, a PrintWriter, a FileInputStream, or a FileOutputStream. Whenever you create an instance of one of these classes, you automatically create a file, unless one already exists, for instance

```
File file = new File("foo"); // no file yet
PrintWriter pw =
    new PrintWriter(file);  // make a PrintWriter object AND
                            // make a file, "foo" to which
                            // 'file' is assigned, AND assign
                            // 'pw' to the PrintWriter
```

Creating a directory is similar to creating a file. Again, we'll use the convention of referring to an object of type File that represents an actual directory, as a Directory File object, capital D, (even though it's of type File.) We'll call an actual directory on a computer a directory, small d. Phew! As with creating a file, creating a directory is a two-step process; first we create a Directory (File) object, then we create an actual directory using the following `mkdir()` method:

```
File myDir = new File("mydir");      // create an object
myDir.mkdir();                       // create an actual directory
```

Once you've got a directory, you put files into it, and work with those files:

```
File myFile = new File(myDir, "myFile.txt");
myFile.createNewFile();
```

This code is making a new file in a subdirectory. Since you provide the subdirectory to the constructor, from then on you just refer to the file by its reference variable. In this case, here's a way that you could write some data to the file `myFile`:

```
PrintWriter pw = new PrintWriter(myFile);
pw.println("new stuff");
pw.flush();
pw.close();
```

Be careful when you're creating new directories! As we've seen, constructing a Reader or Writer will automatically create a file for you if one doesn't exist, but that's not true for a directory:

```
File myDir = new File("mydir");
// myDir.mkdir();                         // call to mkdir() omitted!
File myFile = new File(
             myDir, "myFile.txt");
myFile.createNewFile();                   // exception if no mkdir!
```

This will generate an exception something like

```
java.io.IOException: No such file or directory
```

You can refer a `File` object to an existing file or directory. For example, assume that we already have a subdirectory called `existingDir` in which resides an existing file `existingDirFile.txt`, which contains several lines of text. When you run the following code,

```
File existingDir = new File("existingDir");      // assign a dir
System.out.println(existingDir.isDirectory());
```

```
File existingDirFile = new File(
        existingDir, "existingDirFile.txt");  // assign a file
System.out.println (existingDirFile.isFile());

FileReader fr = new FileReader(existingDirFile);
BufferedReader br = new BufferedReader(fr);     // make a Reader

String s;
while( (s = br.readLine()) != null)              // read data
  System.out.println(s);

br.close();
```

the following output will be generated:

```
true
true
existing sub-dir data
line 2 of text
line 3 of text
```

Take special note of the what the readLine() method returns. When there is no more data to read, readLine() returns a null—this is our signal to stop reading the file. Also, notice that we didn't invoke a flush() method. When reading a file, no flushing is required, so you won't even find a flush() method in a Reader kind of class.

In addition to creating files, the File class also let's you do things like renaming and deleting files. The following code demonstrates a few of the most common ins and outs of deleting files and directories (via delete()), and renaming files and directories (via renameTo()):

```
File delDir = new File("deldir");       // make a directory
delDir.mkdir();

File delFile1 = new File(
        delDir, "delFile1.txt");        // add file to directory
delFile1.createNewFile();

File delFile2 = new File(
        delDir, "delFile2.txt");        // add file to directory
delFile2.createNewFile();
```

```
delFile1.delete();                      // delete a file
System.out.println("delDir is "
                  + delDir.delete());   // attempt to delete
                                        // the directory
File newName = new File(
        delDir, "newName.txt");         // a new object
delFile2.renameTo(newName);             // rename file

File newDir = new File("newDir");       // rename directory
delDir.renameTo(newDir);
```

This outputs

```
delDir is false
```

and leaves us with a directory called `newDir` that contains a file called
`newName.txt`. Here are some rules that we can deduce from this result:

- **delete()** You can't delete a directory if it's not empty, which is why the
  invocation `delDir.delete()` failed.
- **renameTo()** You must give the existing File object a valid new File object
  with the new name that you want. (If `newName` had been `null` we would
  have gotten a NullPointerException.)
- **renameTo()** It's okay to rename a directory, even if it isn't empty.

There's a lot more to learn about using the java.io package, but as far as the
exam goes we only have one more thing to discuss, and that is how to search for a
file. Assuming that we have a directory named `searchThis` that we want to search
through, the following code uses the `File.list()` method to create a String array
of files and directories, which we then use the enhanced `for` loop to iterate through
and print:

```
String[] files = new String[100];
File search = new File("searchThis");
files = search.list();                  // create the list

for(String fn : files)                  // iterate through it
  System.out.println("found " + fn);
```

On our system, we got the following output:

```
found dir1
found dir2
found dir3
found file1.txt
found file2.txt
```

Your results will almost certainly vary :)

In this section we've scratched the surface of what's available in the java.io package. Entire books have been written about this package, so we're obviously covering only a very small (but frequently used) portion of the API. On the other hand, if you understand everything we've covered in this section, you will be in great shape to handle any java.io questions you encounter on the exam (except for serialization, which is covered in the next section).

CERTIFICATION OBJECTIVE

Serialization (Exam Objective 3.3)

3.3   Develop code that serializes and/or de-serializes objects using the following APIs from java.io: DataInputStream, DataOutputStream, FileInputStream, FileOutputStream, ObjectInputStream, ObjectOutputStream, and Serializable.

Imagine you want to save the state of one or more objects. If Java didn't have serialization (as the earliest version did not), you'd have to use one of the I/O classes to write out the state of the instance variables of all the objects you want to save. The worst part would be trying to reconstruct new objects that were virtually identical to the objects you were trying to save. You'd need your own protocol for the way in which you wrote and restored the state of each object, or you could end up setting variables with the wrong values. For example, imagine you stored an object that has instance variables for height and weight. At the time you save the state of the object, you could write out the height and weight as two ints in a file, but the order in which you write them is crucial. It would be all too easy to re-create the object but mix up the height and weight values—using the saved height as the value for the new object's weight and vice versa.

Serialization lets you simply say "save this object and all of its instance variables." Actually its a little more interesting than that, because you can add, "... unless I've explicitly marked a variable as `transient`, which means, don't include the transient variable's value as part of the object's serialized state."

Working with ObjectOutputStream and ObjectInputStream

The magic of basic serialization happens with just two methods: one to serialize objects and write them to a stream, and a second to read the stream and deserialize objects.

```
ObjectOutputStream.writeObject()    // serialize and write

ObjectInputStream.readObject()      // read and deserialize
```

The java.io.ObjectOutputStream and java.io.ObjectInputStream classes are considered to be *higher*-level classes in the java.io package, and as we learned earlier, that means that you'll wrap them around *lower*-level classes, such as java.io.FileOutputStream and java.io.FileInputStream. Here's a small program that creates a (Cat) object, serializes it, and then deserializes it:

```java
import java.io.*;

class Cat implements Serializable { }    // 1

public class SerializeCat {
  public static void main(String[] args) {
    Cat c = new Cat();   // 2
    try {
      FileOutputStream fs = new FileOutputStream("testSer.ser");
      ObjectOutputStream os = new ObjectOutputStream(fs);
      os.writeObject(c);    // 3
      os.close();
    } catch (Exception e) { e.printStackTrace(); }

    try {
      FileInputStream fis = new FileInputStream("testSer.ser");
      ObjectInputStream ois = new ObjectInputStream(fis);
      c = (Cat) ois.readObject();   // 4
      ois.close();
    } catch (Exception e) { e.printStackTrace(); }
  }
}
```

Let's take a look at the key points in this example:

1. We declare that the Cat class implements the Serializable interface. Serializable is a *marker* interface; it has no methods to implement. (In the next several sections, we'll cover various rules about when you need to declare classes Serializable.)

2. We make a new Cat object, which as we know is serializable.

3. We serialize the Cat object c by invoking the `writeObject()` method. It took a fair amount of preparation before we could actually serialize our Cat. First, we had to put all of our I/O-related code in a try/catch block. Next we had to create a FileOutputStream to write the object to. Then we wrapped the FileOutputStream in an ObjectOutputStream, which is the class that has the magic serialization method that we need. Remember that the invocation of `writeObject()` performs two tasks: it serializes the object, and then it writes the serialized object to a file.

4. We de-serialize the Cat object by invoking the `readObject()` method. The `readObject()` method returns an Object, so we have to cast the deserialized object back to a Cat. Again, we had to go through the typical I/O hoops to set this up.

This is a bare-bones example of serialization in action. Over the next set of pages we'll look at some of the more complex issues that are associated with serialization.

Object Graphs

What does it really mean to save an object? If the instance variables are all primitive types, it's pretty straightforward. But what if the instance variables are themselves references to *objects*? What gets saved? Clearly in Java it wouldn't make any sense to save the actual value of a reference variable, because the value of a Java reference has meaning only within the context of a single instance of a JVM. In other words, if you tried to restore the object in another instance of the JVM, even running on the same computer on which the object was originally serialized, the reference would be useless.

But what about the object that the reference refers to? Look at this class:

```
class Dog {
   private Collar theCollar;
   private int dogSize;
   public Dog(Collar collar, int size) {
     theCollar = collar;
     dogSize = size;
```

```
   }
   public Collar getCollar() { return theCollar; }
}
class Collar {
   private int collarSize;
   public Collar(int size) { collarSize = size; }
   public int getCollarSize() { return collarSize; }
}
```

Now make a dog... First, you make a Collar for the Dog:

```
Collar c = new Collar(3);
```

Then make a new Dog, passing it the Collar:

```
Dog d = new Dog(c, 8);
```

Now what happens if you save the Dog? If the goal is to save and then restore a Dog, and the restored Dog is an exact duplicate of the Dog that was saved, then the Dog needs a Collar that is an exact duplicate of the Dog's Collar at the time the Dog was saved. That means both the Dog and the Collar should be saved.

And what if the Collar itself had references to other objects—like perhaps a Color object? This gets quite complicated very quickly. If it were up to the programmer to know the internal structure of each object the Dog referred to, so that the programmer could be sure to save all the state of all those objects...whew. That would be a nightmare with even the simplest of objects.

Fortunately, the Java serialization mechanism takes care of all of this. When you serialize an object, Java serialization takes care of saving that object's entire "object graph." That means a deep copy of everything the saved object needs to be restored. For example, if you serialize a Dog object, the Collar will be serialized automatically. And if the Collar class contained a reference to another object, THAT object would also be serialized, and so on. And the only object you have to worry about saving and restoring is the Dog. The other objects required to fully reconstruct that Dog are saved (and restored) automatically through serialization.

Remember, you do have to make a conscious choice to create objects that are serializable, by implementing the Serializable interface. If we want to save Dog objects, for example, we'll have to modify the Dog class as follows:

```
class Dog implements Serializable {
   // the rest of the code as before
```

```
    // Serializable has no methods to implement
}
```

And now we can save the Dog with the following code:

```
import java.io.*;
public class SerializeDog {
  public static void main(String[] args) {
    Collar c = new Collar(3);
    Dog d = new Dog(c, 8);
    try {
      FileOutputStream fs = new FileOutputStream("testSer.ser");
      ObjectOutputStream os = new ObjectOutputStream(fs);
      os.writeObject(d);
      os.close();
    } catch (Exception e) { e.printStackTrace(); }
  }
}
```

But when we run this code we get a runtime exception something like this

```
java.io.NotSerializableException: Collar
```

What did we forget? The Collar class must ALSO be Serializable. If we modify the Collar class and make it serializable, then there's no problem:

```
class Collar implements Serializable {
    // same
}
```

Here's the complete listing:

```
import java.io.*;
public class SerializeDog {
  public static void main(String[] args) {
    Collar c = new Collar(3);
    Dog d = new Dog(c, 5);
    System.out.println("before: collar size is "
                        + d.getCollar().getCollarSize());
    try {
      FileOutputStream fs = new FileOutputStream("testSer.ser");
```

```
          ObjectOutputStream os = new ObjectOutputStream(fs);
          os.writeObject(d);
          os.close();
        } catch (Exception e) { e.printStackTrace(); }
        try {
          FileInputStream fis = new FileInputStream("testSer.ser");
          ObjectInputStream ois = new ObjectInputStream(fis);
          d = (Dog) ois.readObject();
          ois.close();
        } catch (Exception e) { e.printStackTrace(); }

        System.out.println("after:  collar size is "
                         + d.getCollar().getCollarSize());
    }
  }
  class Dog implements Serializable {
    private Collar theCollar;
    private int dogSize;
    public Dog(Collar collar, int size) {
      theCollar = collar;
      dogSize = size;
    }
    public Collar getCollar() { return theCollar; }
  }
  class Collar implements Serializable {
    private int collarSize;
    public Collar(int size) { collarSize = size; }
    public int getCollarSize() { return collarSize; }
  }
```

This produces the output:

```
    before: collar size is 3
    after:  collar size is 3
```

But what would happen if we didn't have access to the Collar class source code? In other words, what if making the Collar class serializable was not an option? Are we stuck with a non-serializable Dog?

Obviously we could subclass the Collar class, mark the subclass as Serializable, and then use the Collar subclass instead of the Collar class. But that's not always an option either for several potential reasons:

1. The Collar class might be final, preventing subclassing.
   OR

2. The Collar class might itself refer to other non-serializable objects, and without knowing the internal structure of Collar, you aren't able to make all these fixes (assuming you even wanted to TRY to go down that road).
   OR

3. Subclassing is not an option for other reasons related to your design.

So...THEN what do you do if you want to save a Dog?

That's where the `transient` modifier comes in. If you mark the Dog's Collar instance variable with `transient`, then serialization will simply skip the Collar during serialization:

```
class Dog implements Serializable {
   private transient Collar theCollar;   // add transient
   // the rest of the class as before
}

class Collar {                  // no longer Serializable
   // same code
}
```

Now we have a Serializable Dog, with a non-serializable Collar, but the Dog has marked the Collar `transient`; the output is

```
before: collar size is 3
Exception in thread "main" java.lang.NullPointerException
```

So NOW what can we do?

Using writeObject and readObject

Consider the problem: we have a Dog object we want to save. The Dog has a Collar, and the Collar has state that should also be saved as part of the Dog's state. But...the Collar is not Serializable, so we must mark it `transient`. That means when the Dog is deserialized, it comes back with a null Collar. What can we do to somehow make sure that when the Dog is deserialized, it gets a new Collar that matches the one the Dog had when the Dog was saved?

Java serialization has a special mechanism just for this—a set of private methods you can implement in your class that, if present, will be invoked automatically during serialization and deserialization. It's almost as if the methods were defined in the Serializable interface, except they aren't. They are part of a special callback contract the serialization system offers you that basically says, "If you (the programmer) have a pair of methods matching this exact signature (you'll see them in a moment), these methods will be called during the serialization/deserialization process.

These methods let you step into the middle of serialization and deserialization. So they're perfect for letting you solve the Dog/Collar problem: when a Dog is being saved, you can step into the middle of serialization and say, "By the way, I'd like to add the state of the Collar's variable (an `int`) to the stream when the Dog is serialized." You've manually added the state of the Collar to the Dog's serialized representation, even though the Collar itself is not saved.

Of course, you'll need to restore the Collar during deserialization by stepping into the middle and saying, "I'll read that extra `int` I saved to the Dog stream, and use it to create a new Collar, and then assign that new Collar to the Dog that's being deserialized." The two special methods you define must have signatures that look EXACTLY like this:

```
private void writeObject(ObjectOutputStream os) {
  // your code for saving the Collar variables
}

private void readObject(ObjectInputStream os) {
   // your code to read the Collar state, create a new Collar,
   // and assign it to the Dog
}
```

Yes, we're going to write methods that have the same name as the ones we've been calling! Where do these methods go? Let's change the Dog class:

```
class Dog implements Serializable {
  transient private Collar theCollar; // we can't serialize this
  private int dogSize;
  public Dog(Collar collar, int size) {
    theCollar = collar;
    dogSize = size;
  }
  public Collar getCollar() { return theCollar; }
```

```
private void writeObject(ObjectOutputStream os) {
  //  throws IOException {                               // 1
  try {
    os.defaultWriteObject();                             // 2
    os.writeInt(theCollar.getCollarSize());             // 3
  } catch (Exception e) { e.printStackTrace(); }
}
private void readObject(ObjectInputStream is) {
  //  throws IOException, ClassNotFoundException {   // 4
  try {
    is.defaultReadObject();                              // 5
    theCollar = new Collar(is.readInt());               // 6
  } catch (Exception e) { e.printStackTrace(); }
  }
}
```

Let's take a look at the preceding code.

In our scenario we've agreed that, for whatever real-world reason, we can't serialize a Collar object, but we want to serialize a Dog. To do this we're going to implement writeObject() and readObject(). By implementing these two methods you're saying to the compiler: "If anyone invokes writeObject() or readObject() concerning a Dog object, use this code as part of the read and write".

1. Like most I/O-related methods writeObject() can throw exceptions. You can declare them or handle them but we recommend handling them.

2. When you invoke defaultWriteObject() from within writeObject() you're telling the JVM to do the normal serialization process for this object. When implementing writeObject(), you will typically request the normal serialization process, *and* do some custom writing and reading too.

3. In this case we decided to write an extra int (the collar size) to the stream that's creating the serialized Dog. You can write extra stuff before and/or after you invoke defaultWriteObject(). BUT...when you read it back in, you have to read the extra stuff in the same order you wrote it.

4. Again, we chose to handle rather than declare the exceptions.

5. When it's time to deserialize, defaultReadObject() handles the normal deserialization you'd get if you didn't implement a readObject() method.

6. Finally we build a new Collar object for the Dog using the collar size that we manually serialized. (We had to invoke readInt() *after* we invoked defaultReadObject() or the streamed data would be out of sync!)

Remember, the most common reason to implement `writeObject()` and `readObject()` is when you have to save some part of an object's state manually. If you choose, you can write and read ALL of the state yourself, but that's very rare. So, when you want to do only a *part* of the serialization/deserialization yourself, you MUST invoke the `defaultReadObject()` and `defaultWriteObject()` methods to do the rest.

Which brings up another question—why wouldn't *all* Java classes be serializable? Why isn't class Object serializable? There are some things in Java that simply cannot be serialized because they are runtime specific. Things like streams, threads, runtime, etc. and even some GUI classes (which are connected to the underlying OS) cannot be serialized. What is and is not serializable in the Java API is NOT part of the exam, but you'll need to keep them in mind if you're serializing complex objects.

How Inheritance Affects Serialization

Serialization is very cool, but in order to apply it effectively you're going to have to understand how your class's superclasses affect serialization.

If a superclass is Serializable, then according to normal Java interface rules, all subclasses of that class automatically implement Serializable implicitly. In other words, a subclass of a class marked Serializable passes the IS-A test for Serializable, and thus can be saved without having to explicitly mark the subclass as Serializable. You simply cannot tell whether a class is or is not Serializable UNLESS you can see the class inheritance tree to see if any other superclasses implement Serializable. If the class does not explicitly extend any other class, and does not implement Serializable, then you know for CERTAIN that the class is not Serializable, because class Object does NOT implement Serializable.

That brings up another key issue with serialization…what happens if a superclass is not marked Serializable, but the subclass is? Can the subclass still be serialized even if its superclass does not implement Serializable? Imagine this:

```
class Animal { }
class Dog extends Animal implements Serializable {
   // the rest of the Dog code
}
```

Now you have a Serializable Dog class, with a non-Serializable superclass. This works! But there are potentially serious implications. To fully understand those implications, let's step back and look at the difference between an object that comes from deserialization vs. an object created using new. Remember, when an object is constructed using new (as opposed to being deserialized), the following things happen (in this order):

1. All instance variables are assigned default values.
2. The constructor is invoked, which immediately invokes the superclass constructor (or another overloaded constructor, until one of the overloaded constructors invokes the superclass constructor).
3. All superclass constructors complete.
4. Instance variables that are initialized as part of their declaration are assigned their initial value (as opposed to the default values they're given prior to the superclass constructors completing).
5. The constructor completes.

But these things do NOT happen when an object is deserialized. When an instance of a serializable class is deserialized, the constructor does not run, and instance variables are NOT given their initially assigned values! Think about it—if the constructor were invoked, and/or instance variables were assigned the values given in their declarations, the object you're trying to restore would revert back to its original state, rather than coming back reflecting the changes in its state that happened sometime after it was created. For example, imagine you have a class that declares an instance variable and assigns it the int value 3, and includes a method that changes the instance variable value to 10:

```
class Foo implements Serializable {
   int num = 3;
   void changeNum() {  num = 10;   }
}
```

Obviously if you serialize a Foo instance *after* the changeNum() method runs, the value of the num variable should be 10. When the Foo instance is deserialized, you want the num variable to still be 10! You obviously don't want the initialization (in this case, the assignment of the value 3 to the variable num) to happen. Think of constructors and instance variable assignments together as part of one complete object initialization process (and in fact, they DO become one initialization method in the bytecode). The point is, when an object is deserialized we do NOT want any of the normal initialization to happen. We don't want the constructor to run, and we don't want the explicitly declared values to be assigned. We want only the values saved as part of the serialized state of the object to be reassigned.

Of course if you have variables marked transient, they will not be restored to their original state (unless you implement defaultReadObject()), but will instead be given the default value for that data type. In other words, even if you say

```
class Bar implements Serializable {
    transient int x = 42;
}
```

when the Bar instance is deserialized, the variable x will be set to a value of 0. Object references marked transient will always be reset to null, regardless of whether they were initialized at the time of declaration in the class.

So, that's what happens when the object is deserialized, and the class of the serialized object directly extends Object, or has ONLY serializable classes in its inheritance tree. It gets a little trickier when the serializable class has one or more non-serializable superclasses. Getting back to our non-serializable Animal class with a serializable Dog subclass example:

```
class Animal {
    public String name;
}
class Dog extends Animal implements Serializable {
    // the rest of the Dog code
}
```

Because Animal is NOT serializable, any state maintained in the Animal class, even though the state variable is inherited by the Dog, isn't going to be restored with the Dog when it's deserialized! The reason is, the (unserialized) Animal part of the Dog is going to be reinitialized just as it would be if you were making a new Dog (as opposed to deserializing one). That means all the things that happen to an object during construction, will happen—but only to the Animal parts of a Dog. In other words, the instance variables from the Dog's class will be serialized and deserialized correctly, but the inherited variables from the non-serializable Animal superclass will come back with their default/initially assigned values rather than the values they had at the time of serialization.

If you are a serializable class, but your superclass is NOT serializable, then any instance variables you INHERIT from that superclass will be reset to the values they were given during the original construction of the object. This is because the non-serializable class constructor WILL run!

In fact, every constructor ABOVE the first non-serializable class constructor will also run, no matter what, because once the first super constructor is invoked, it of course invokes its super constructor and so on up the inheritance tree.

For the exam, you'll need to be able to recognize which variables will and will not be restored with the appropriate values when an object is deserialized, so be sure to study the following code example and the output:

```java
import java.io.*;
class SuperNotSerial {
  public static void main(String [] args) {

    Dog d = new Dog(35, "Fido");
    System.out.println("before: " + d.name + " "
                        + d.weight);
    try {
      FileOutputStream fs = new FileOutputStream("testSer.ser");
      ObjectOutputStream os = new ObjectOutputStream(fs);
      os.writeObject(d);
      os.close();
    } catch (Exception e) { e.printStackTrace(); }
    try {
      FileInputStream fis = new FileInputStream("testSer.ser");
      ObjectInputStream ois = new ObjectInputStream(fis);
      d = (Dog) ois.readObject();
      ois.close();
    } catch (Exception e) { e.printStackTrace(); }

    System.out.println("after:  " + d.name + " "
                        + d.weight);
  }
}
class Dog extends Animal implements Serializable {
  String name;
```

```
Dog(int w, String n) {
  weight = w;              // inherited
  name = n;                // not inherited
}
}
class Animal {             // not serializable !
  int weight = 42;
}
```

which produces the output:

```
before: Fido 35
after:  Fido 42
```

The key here is that because Animal is not serializable, when the Dog was deserialized, the Animal constructor ran and reset the Dog's inherited weight variable.

If you serialize a collection or an array, every element must be serializable! A single non-serializable element will cause serialization to fail. Note also that while the collection interfaces are not serializable, the concrete collection classes in the Java API are.

Serialization Is Not for Statics

Finally, you might notice that we've talked ONLY about instance variables, not static variables. Should static variables be saved as part of the object's state? Isn't the state of a static variable at the time an object was serialized important? Yes and no. It might be important, but it isn't part of the instance's state at all. Remember, you should think of static variables purely as CLASS variables. They have nothing to do with individual instances. But serialization applies only to OBJECTS. And what happens if you deserialize three different Dog instances, all of which were serialized at different times, and all of which were saved when the value of a static variable in class Dog was different. Which instance would "win"? Which instance's static value would be used to replace the one currently in the one and only Dog class that's currently loaded? See the problem?

Static variables are NEVER saved as part of the object's state…because they do not belong to the object!

ⓦatch

What about DataInputStream and DataOutputStream? They're in the objectives! It turns out that while the exam was being created, it was decided that those two classes wouldn't be on the exam after all, but someone forgot to remove them from the objectives! So you get a break. That's one less thing you'll have to worry about.

on the
Ⓙob

As simple as serialization code is to write, versioning problems can occur in the real world. If you save a Dog object using one version of the class, but attempt to deserialize it using a newer, different version of the class, deserialization might fail. See the Java API for details about versioning issues and solutions.

CERTIFICATION OBJECTIVE

Dates, Numbers, and Currency (Exam Objective 3.4)

3.4   Use standard J2SE APIs in the java.text package to correctly format or parse dates, numbers and currency values for a specific locale; and, given a scenario, determine the appropriate methods to use if you want to use the default locale or a specific locale. Describe the purpose and use of the java.util.Locale class.

The Java API provides an extensive (perhaps a little *too* extensive) set of classes to help you work with dates, numbers, and currency. The exam will test your knowledge of the basic classes and methods you'll use to work with dates and such. When you've finished this section you should have a solid foundation in tasks such as creating new Date and DateFormat objects, converting Strings to Dates and back again, performing Calendaring functions, printing properly formatted currency values, and doing all of this for locations around the globe. In fact, a large part of why this section was added to the exam was to test whether you can do some basic internationalization (often shortened to "i18n").

Working with Dates, Numbers, and Currencies

If you want to work with dates from around the world (and who doesn't?), you'll need to be familiar with at least four classes from the java.text and java.util packages. In fact, we'll admit it right up front, you might encounter questions on the exam that use classes that aren't specifically mentioned in the Sun objective. Here are the four date related classes you'll need to understand:

- **`java.util.Date`** Most of this class's methods have been deprecated, but you can use this class to bridge between the `Calendar` and `DateFormat` class. An instance of `Date` represents a mutable date and time, to a millisecond.

- **`java.util.Calendar`** This class provides a huge variety of methods that help you convert and manipulate dates and times. For instance, if you want to add a month to a given date, or find out what day of the week January 1, 3000 falls on, the methods in the `Calendar` class will save your bacon.

- **`java.text.DateFormat`** This class is used to format dates not only providing various styles such as "01/01/70" or "January 1, 1970," but also to format dates for numerous locales around the world.

- **`java.text.NumberFormat`** This class is used to format numbers and currencies for locales around the world.

- **`java.util.Locale`** This class is used in conjunction with `DateFormat` and `NumberFormat` to format dates, numbers and currency for specific locales. With the help of the `Locale` class you'll be able to convert a date like "10/08/2005" to "Segunda-feira, 8 de Outubro de 2005" in no time. If you want to manipulate dates without producing formatted output, you can use the Locale class directly with the Calendar class.

Orchestrating Date- and Number-Related Classes

When you work with dates and numbers, you'll often use several classes together. It's important to understand how the classes we described above relate to each other, and when to use which classes in combination. For instance, you'll need to know that if you want to do date formatting for a specific locale, you need to create your Locale object before your DateFormat object, because you'll need your Locale object as an argument to your DateFormat factory method. Table 6-2 provides a quick overview of common date- and number-related use cases and solutions using these classes. Table 6-2 will undoubtedly bring up specific questions about individual classes, and we will dive into specifics for each class next. Once you've gone through the class level discussions, you should find that Table 6-2 provides a good summary.

TABLE 6-2	Common Use Cases When Working with Dates and Numbers	

Use Case	Steps
Get the current date and time.	1. Create a Date: `Date d = new Date();` 2. Get its value: `String s = d.toString();`
Get an object that lets you perform date and time calculations in your locale.	1. Create a Calendar: `Calendar c = Calendar.getInstance();` 2. Use `c.add(...)` and `c.roll(...)` to perform date and time manipulations.

Get an object that lets you perform date and time calculations in a different locale.	1. Create a Locale:
	`Locale loc = new Locale(language);` or
	`Locale loc = new Locale(language, country);`
	2. Create a Calendar for that locale:
	`Calendar c = Calendar.getInstance(loc);`
	3. Use `c.add(...)` and `c.roll(...)` to perform date and time manipulations.

Get an object that lets you perform date and time calculations, and then format it for output in different locales with different date styles.	1. Create a Calendar:
	`Calendar c = Calendar.getInstance();`
	2. Create a Locale for each location:
	`Locale loc = new Locale(...);`
	3. Convert your Calendar to a Date:
	`Date d = c.getTime();`
	4. Create a DateFormat for each Locale:
	`DateFormat df = DateFormat.getDateInstance`
	`                    (style, loc);`
	5. Use the format() method to create formatted dates:
	`String s = df.format(d);`

Get an object that lets you format numbers or currencies across many different locales.	1. Create a Locale for each location:
	`Locale loc = new Locale(...);`
	2. Create a NumberFormat:
	`NumberFormat nf = NumberFormat.getInstance(loc);`
	`-or- NumberFormat nf = NumberFormat.`
	`                    getCurrencyInstance(loc);`
	3. Use the format() method to create formatted output:
	`String s = nf.format(someNumber);`

The Date Class

The Date class has a checkered past. Its API design didn't do a good job of handling internationalization and localization situations. In its current state, most of its methods have been deprecated, and for most purposes you'll want to use the Calendar class instead of the Date class. The Date class is on the exam for several reasons: you might find it used in legacy code, it's really easy if all you want is a quick and dirty way to get the current date and time, it's good when you want a universal time that is not affected by time zones, and finally, you'll use it as a temporary bridge to format a Calendar object using the DateFormat class.

As we mentioned briefly above, an instance of the Date class represents a single date and time. Internally, the date and time is stored as a primitive long. Specifically, the long holds the number of milliseconds (you know, 1000 of these per second), between the date being represented and January 1, 1970. Have you ever tried to grasp how big really big numbers are? Let's use the Date class to find out how long it took for a trillion milliseconds to pass, starting at January 1, 1970:

```
import java.util.*;
class TestDates {
  public static void main(String[] args) {
    Date d1 = new Date(1000000000000L);  // a trillion!
    System.out.println("1st date " + d1.toString());
  }
}
```

On our JVM, which has a US locale, the output is

```
1st date Sat Sep 08 19:46:40 MDT 2001
```

Okay, for future reference remember that there are a trillion milliseconds for every 31 and 2/3 years.

Although most of Date's methods have been deprecated, it's still acceptable to use the getTime and setTime methods, although as we'll soon see, it's a bit painful. Let's add an hour to our Date instance, d1, from the previous example:

```
import java.util.*;
class TestDates {
  public static void main(String[] args) {
    Date d1 = new Date(1000000000000L);  // a trillion!
```

```
    System.out.println("1st date " + d1.toString());
    d1.setTime(d1.getTime() + 3600000); // 3600000 millis / hour
    System.out.println("new time " + d1.toString());
  }
}
```

which produces (again, on our JVM):

```
1st date Sat Sep 08 19:46:40 MDT 2001
new time Sat Sep 08 20:46:40 MDT 2001
```

Notice that both `setTime()` and `getTime()` used the handy millisecond scale... if you want to manipulate dates using the Date class, that's your only choice. While that wasn't too painful, imagine how much fun it would be to add, say, a year to a given date.

We'll revisit the Date class later on, but for now the only other thing you need to know is that if you want to create an instance of Date to represent "now," you use Date's no-argument constructor:

```
Date now = new Date();
```

(We're guessing that if you call `now.getTime()`, you'll get a number somewhere between one trillion and two trillion.)

The Calendar Class

We've just seen that manipulating dates using the Date class is tricky. The Calendar class is designed to make date manipulation easy! (Well, easier.) While the Calendar class has about a million fields and methods, once you get the hang of a few of them the rest tend to work in a similar fashion.

When you first try to use the `Calendar` class you might notice that it's an abstract class. You can't say

```
Calendar c = new Calendar();   // illegal, Calendar is abstract
```

In order to create a `Calendar` instance, you have to use one of the overloaded `getInstance()` static factory methods:

```
Calendar cal = Calendar.getInstance();
```

When you get a Calendar reference like `cal`, from above, your Calendar reference variable is actually referring to an instance of a concrete subclass of Calendar. You can't know for sure what subclass you'll get (`java.util.GregorianCalendar` is what you'll almost certainly get), but it won't matter to you. You'll be using Calendar's API. (As Java continues to spread around the world, in order to maintain cohesion, you might find additional, locale-specific subclasses of `Calendar`.)

Okay, so now we've got an instance of Calendar, let's go back to our earlier example, and find out what day of the week our trillionth millisecond falls on, and then let's add a month to that date:

```java
import java.util.*;
class Dates2 {
  public static void main(String[] args) {
    Date d1 = new Date(1000000000000L);
    System.out.println("1st date " + d1.toString());

    Calendar c = Calendar.getInstance();
    c.setTime(d1);                            // #1

    if(c.SUNDAY == c.getFirstDayOfWeek())    // #2
      System.out.println("Sunday is the first day of the week");
    System.out.println("trillionth milli day of week is "
                       + c.get(c.DAY_OF_WEEK));    // #3

    c.add(Calendar.MONTH, 1);                 // #4
    Date d2 = c.getTime();                    // #5
    System.out.println("new date " + d2.toString() );
  }
}
```

This produces something like

```
1st date Sat Sep 08 19:46:40 MDT 2001
Sunday is the first day of the week
trillionth milli day of week is 7
new date Mon Oct 08 20:46:40 MDT 2001
```

Let's take a look at this program, focusing on the five highlighted lines:

1. We assign the Date d1 to the Calendar instance c.

2. We use Calendar's SUNDAY field to determine whether, for our JVM, SUNDAY is considered to be the first day of the week. (In some locales, MONDAY is the first day of the week.) The Calendar class provides similar fields for days of the week, months, the day of the month, the day of the year, and so on.

3. We use the DAY_OF_WEEK field to find out the day of the week that the trillionth millisecond falls on.

4. So far we've used setter and getter methods that should be intuitive to figure out. Now we're going to use Calendar's add() method. This very powerful method let's you add or subtract units of time appropriate for whichever Calendar field you specify. For instance:

```
c.add(Calendar.HOUR, -4);        // subtract 4 hours from c's value
c.add(Calendar.YEAR, 2);          // add 2 years to c's value
c.add(Calendar.DAY_OF_WEEK, -2);  // subtract two days from
                                  // c's value
```

5. Convert c's value back to an instance of Date.

The other Calendar method you should know for the exam is the roll() method. The roll() method acts like the add() method, except that when a part of a Date gets incremented or decremented, larger parts of the Date will not get incremented or decremented. Hmmm…for instance:

```
// assume c is October 8, 2001
c.roll(Calendar.MONTH, 9);        // notice the year in the output
Date d4 = c.getTime();
System.out.println("new date " + d4.toString() );
```

The output would be something like this

```
new date Fri Jul 08 19:46:40 MDT 2001
```

Notice that the year did not change, even though we added 9 months to an October date. In a similar fashion, invoking roll() with HOUR won't change the date, the month or the year.

For the exam, you won't have to memorize the Calendar class's fields. If you need them to help answer a question, they will be provided as part of the question.

The DateFormat Class

Having learned how to create dates and manipulate them, let's find out how to format them. So that we're all on the same page, here's an example of how a date can be formatted in different ways:

```
import java.text.*;
import java.util.*;
class Dates3 {
  public static void main(String[] args) {
    Date d1 = new Date(1000000000000L);

    DateFormat[] dfa = new DateFormat[6];
    dfa[0] = DateFormat.getInstance();
    dfa[1] = DateFormat.getDateInstance();
    dfa[2] = DateFormat.getDateInstance(DateFormat.SHORT);
    dfa[3] = DateFormat.getDateInstance(DateFormat.MEDIUM);
    dfa[4] = DateFormat.getDateInstance(DateFormat.LONG);
    dfa[5] = DateFormat.getDateInstance(DateFormat.FULL);

    for(DateFormat df : dfa)
      System.out.println(df.format(d1));
  }
}
```

which on our JVM produces

```
9/8/01 7:46 PM
Sep 8, 2001
9/8/01
Sep 8, 2001
September 8, 2001
Saturday, September 8, 2001
```

Examining this code we see a couple of things right away. First off, it looks like DateFormat is another abstract class, so we can't use new to create instances of DateFormat. In this case we used two factory methods, getInstance() and getDateInstance(). Notice that getDateInstance() is overloaded; when we discuss locales, we'll look at the other version of getDateInstance() that you'll need to understand for the exam.

Next, we used static fields from the DateFormat class to customize our various instances of DateFormat. Each of these static fields represents a formatting *style*. In this case it looks like the no-arg version of getDateInstance() gives us the same style as the MEDIUM version of the method, but that's not a hard and fast rule. (More on this when we discuss locales.) Finally, we used the format() method to create Strings representing the properly formatted versions of the Date we're working with.

The last method you should be familiar with is the parse() method. The parse() method takes a String formatted in the style of the DateFormat instance being used, and converts the String into a Date object. As you might imagine, this is a risky operation because the parse() method could easily receive a badly formatted String. Because of this, parse() can throw a ParseException. The following code creates a Date instance, uses DateFormat.format() to convert it into a String, and then uses DateFormat.parse() to change it back into a Date:

```
Date d1 = new Date(1000000000000L);
System.out.println("d1 = " + d1.toString());

DateFormat df = DateFormat.getDateInstance(
                                DateFormat.SHORT);
String s = df.format(d1);
System.out.println(s);

try {
  Date d2 = df.parse(s);
  System.out.println("parsed = " + d2.toString());
} catch (ParseException pe) {
  System.out.println("parse exc"); }
```

which on our JVM produces

```
d1 = Sat Sep 08 19:46:40 MDT 2001
9/8/01
parsed = Sat Sep 08 00:00:00 MDT 2001
```

Notice that because we were using a SHORT style, we lost some precision when we converted the Date to a String. This loss of precision showed up when we converted back to a Date object, and it went from being 7:46 to midnight.

on the job

The API for DateFormat.parse() explains that by default, the parse() *method is lenient when parsing dates. Our experience is that* parse() *isn't very lenient about the formatting of Strings it will successfully parse into dates; take care when you use this method!*

The Locale Class

Earlier we said that a big part of why this objective exists is to test your ability to do some basic internationalization tasks. Your wait is over; the `Locale` class is your ticket to worldwide domination. Both the DateFormat class and the NumberFormat class (which we'll cover next) can use an instance of Locale to customize formatted output to be specific to a locale. You might ask how Java defines a locale? The API says a locale is "a specific geographical, political, or cultural region." The two Locale constructors you'll need to understand for the exam are

```
Locale(String language)
Locale(String language, String country)
```

The language argument represents an ISO 639 Language Code, so for instance if you want to format your dates or numbers in Walloon (the language sometimes used in southern Belgium), you'd use `"wa"` as your language string. There are over 500 ISO Language codes, including one for Klingon (`"tlh"`), although unfortunately Java doesn't yet support the Klingon locale. We thought about telling you that you'd have to memorize all these codes for the exam...but we didn't want to cause any heart attacks. So rest assured, you won't have to memorize any ISO Language codes or ISO Country codes (of which there are about 240) for the exam.

Let's get back to how you might use these codes. If you want to represent basic Italian in your application, all you need is the language code. If, on the other hand, you want to represent the Italian used in Switzerland, you'd want to indicate that the country is Switzerland (yes, the country code for Switzerland is `"CH"`), but that the language is Italian:

```
Locale locPT = new Locale("it");        // Italian
Locale locBR = new Locale("it", "CH");  // Switzerland
```

Using these two locales on a date could give us output like this:

```
sabato 1 ottobre 2005
sabato, 1. ottobre 2005
```

Now let's put this all together in some code that creates a Calendar object, sets its date, then converts it to a Date. After that we'll take that Date object and print it out using locales from around the world:

```
Calendar c = Calendar.getInstance();
c.set(2010, 11, 14);                    // December 14, 2010
                                        // (month is 0-based
Date d2 = c.getTime();

Locale locIT = new Locale("it", "IT");  // Italy
Locale locPT = new Locale("pt");        // Portugal
Locale locBR = new Locale("pt", "BR");  // Brazil
Locale locIN = new Locale("hi", "IN");  // India
Locale locJA = new Locale("ja");        // Japan

DateFormat dfUS = DateFormat.getInstance();
System.out.println("US        " + dfUS.format(d2));

DateFormat dfUSfull = DateFormat.getDateInstance(
                                    DateFormat.FULL);
System.out.println("US full  " + dfUSfull.format(d2));

DateFormat dfIT = DateFormat.getDateInstance(
                                    DateFormat.FULL, locIT);
System.out.println("Italy    " + dfIT.format(d2));

DateFormat dfPT = DateFormat.getDateInstance(
                                    DateFormat.FULL, locPT);
System.out.println("Portugal " + dfPT.format(d2));

DateFormat dfBR = DateFormat.getDateInstance(
                                    DateFormat.FULL, locBR);
System.out.println("Brazil   " + dfBR.format(d2));

DateFormat dfIN = DateFormat.getDateInstance(
                                    DateFormat.FULL, locIN);
System.out.println("India    " + dfIN.format(d2));

DateFormat dfJA = DateFormat.getDateInstance(
                                    DateFormat.FULL, locJA);
System.out.println("Japan    " + dfJA.format(d2));
```

This, on our JVM, produces

```
US       12/14/10 3:32 PM
US full  Sunday, December 14, 2010
Italy    domenica 14 dicembre 2010
```

```
Portugal Domingo, 14 de Dezembro de 2010
Brazil   Domingo, 14 de Dezembro de 2010
India    ??????, ?? ??????, ????
Japan    2010?12?14?
```

Oops! Our machine isn't configured to support locales for India or Japan, but you can see how a single Date object can be formatted to work for many locales.

There are a couple more methods in Locale (`getDisplayCountry()` and `getDisplayLanguage()`) that you'll have to know for the exam. These methods let you create Strings that represent a given locale's country and language in terms of both the default locale and any other locale:

```
Calendar c = Calendar.getInstance();
c.set(2010, 11, 14);
Date d2 = c.getTime();

Locale locBR = new Locale("pt", "BR");  // Brazil
Locale locDK = new Locale("da", "DK");  // Denmark
Locale locIT = new Locale("it", "IT");  // Italy

System.out.println("def " + locBR.getDisplayCountry());
System.out.println("loc " + locBR.getDisplayCountry(locBR));

System.out.println("def " + locDK.getDisplayLanguage());
System.out.println("loc " + locDK.getDisplayLanguage(locDK));
System.out.println("D>I " + locDK.getDisplayLanguage(locIT));
```

This, on our JVM, produces

```
def Brazil
loc Brasil
def Danish
loc dansk
D>I danese
```

Given that our JVM's locale (the default for us) is US, the default for the country Brazil is "Brazil", and the default for the Danish language is "Danish". In Brazil, the country is called "Brasil", and in Denmark the language is called "dansk". Finally, just for fun, we discovered that in Italy, the Danish language is called "danese".

The NumberFormat Class

We'll wrap up this objective by discussing the NumberFormat class. Like the DateFormat class, NumberFormat is abstract, so you'll typically use some version of either getInstance() or getCurrencyInstance() to create a NumberFormat object. Not surprisingly, you use this class to format numbers or currency values:

```
float f1 = 123.4567f;
Locale locFR = new Locale("fr");          // France
NumberFormat[] nfa = new NumberFormat[4];

nfa[0] = NumberFormat.getInstance();
nfa[1] = NumberFormat.getInstance(locFR);
nfa[2] = NumberFormat.getCurrencyInstance();
nfa[3] = NumberFormat.getCurrencyInstance(locFR);

for(NumberFormat nf : nfa)
  System.out.println(nf.format(f1));
```

This, on our JVM, produces

```
123.457
123,457
$123.46
123,46 ?
```

Don't be worried if, like us, you're not set up to display the symbols for francs, pounds, rupees, yen, baht, or drachmas. You won't be expected to know the symbols used for currency: if you need one, it will be specified in the question. You might encounter methods other than the format method on the exam. Here's a little code that uses getMaximumFractionDigits(), setMaximumFractionDigits(), parse(), and setParseIntegerOnly():

```
float f1 = 123.45678f;
NumberFormat nf = NumberFormat.getInstance();
System.out.print(nf.getMaximumFractionDigits() + " ");
System.out.print(nf.format(f1) + "  ");

nf.setMaximumFractionDigits(5);
System.out.println(nf.format(f1) + "  ");

try {
  System.out.println(nf.parse("1234.567"));
  nf.setParseIntegerOnly(true);
  System.out.println(nf.parse("1234.567"));
} catch (ParseException pe) {
  System.out.println("parse exc");
}
```

This, on our JVM, produces

```
3   123.457   123.45678
1234.567
1234
```

Notice that in this case, the initial number of fractional digits for the default NumberFormat is three: and that the format() method rounds f1's value, it doesn't truncate it. After changing nf's fractional digits, the entire value of f1 is displayed. Next, notice that the parse() method must run in a try/catch block and that the setParseIntegerOnly() method takes a boolean and in this case, causes subsequent calls to parse() to return only the integer part of Strings formatted as floating-point numbers.

As we've seen, several of the classes covered in this objective are abstract. In addition, for all of these classes, key functionality for every instance is established at the time of creation. Table 6-3 summarizes the constructors or methods used to create instances of all the classes we've discussed in this section.

TABLE 6-3	Instance Creation for Key java.text and java.util Classes
Class	**Key Instance Creation Options**
`util.Date`	`new Date();` `new Date(long millisecondsSince010170);`
`util.Calendar`	`Calendar.getInstance();` `Calendar.getInstance(Locale);`

`util.Locale`	`Locale.getDefault();`
	`new Locale(String language);`
	`new Locale(String language, String country);`

`text.DateFormat`	`DateFormat.getInstance();`
	`DateFormat.getDateInstance();`
	`DateFormat.getDateInstance(style);`
	`DateFormat.getDateInstance(style, Locale);`

`text.NumberFormat`	`NumberFormat.getInstance()`
	`NumberFormat.getInstance(Locale)`
	`NumberFormat.getNumberInstance()`
	`NumberFormat.getNumberInstance(Locale)`
	`NumberFormat.getCurrencyInstance()`
	`NumberFormat.getCurrencyInstance(Locale)`

CERTIFICATION OBJECTIVE

Parsing, Tokenizing, and Formatting (Exam Objective 3.5)

3.5   Write code that uses standard J2SE APIs in the java.util and java.util.regex packages to format or parse strings or streams. For strings, write code that uses the Pattern and Matcher classes and the String.split method. Recognize and use regular expression patterns for matching (limited to: .(dot), *(star), +(plus), ?, \d, \s, \w, [ ], ( )). The use of *, + , and ? will be limited to greedy quantifiers, and the parenthesis operator will only be used as a grouping mechanism, not for capturing content during matching. For streams, write code using the Formatter and Scanner classes and the PrintWriter.format/printf methods. Recognize and use formatting parameters (limited to: %b, %c, %d, %f, %s) in format Strings.

We're going to start with yet another disclaimer: This small section isn't going to morph you from regex newbie to regex guru. In this section we'll cover three basic ideas:

- **Finding stuff** You've got big heaps of text to look through. Maybe you're doing some screen scraping, maybe you're reading from a file. In any case, you need easy ways to find textual needles in textual haystacks. We'll use the java.regex.Pattern, java.regex.Matcher, and java.util.Scanner classes to help us find stuff.

- **Tokenizing stuff** You've got a delimited file that you want to get useful data out of. You want to transform a piece of a text file that looks like: "1500.00,343.77,123.4" into some individual float variables. We'll show you the basics of using the `String.split()` method and the java.util.Scanner class, to tokenize your data.

- **Formatting stuff** You've got a report to create and you need to take a float variable with a value of 32500.000f and transform it into a String with a value of "$32,500.00". We'll introduce you to the java.util.Formatter class and to the `printf()` and `format()` methods.

A Search Tutorial

Whether you're looking for stuff or tokenizing stuff, a lot of the concepts are the same, so let's start with some basics. No matter what language you're using, sooner or later you'll probably be faced with the need to search through large amounts of textual data, looking for some specific stuff.

Regular expressions (regex for short) are a kind of language within a language, designed to help programmers with these searching tasks. Every language that provides regex capabilities uses one or more regex *engines*. regex engines search through textual data using instructions that are coded into *expressions*. A regex expression is like a very short program or script. When you invoke a regex engine, you'll pass it the chunk of textual data you want it to process (in Java this is usually a String or a stream), and you pass it the expression you want it to use to search through the data.

It's fair to think of regex as a language, and we will refer to it that way throughout this section. The regex language is used to create expressions, and as we work through this section, whenever we talk about expressions or expression syntax, we're talking about syntax for the regex "language." Oh, one more disclaimer...we know that you regex mavens out there can come up with better expressions than what we're about to present. Keep in mind that for the most part we're creating these expressions using only a portion of the total regex instruction set, thanks.

Simple Searches

For our first example, we'd like to search through the following *source* String

```
abaaaba
```

for all occurrences (or *matches*) of the *expression*

```
ab
```

In all of these discussions we'll assume that our data sources use zero-based indexes, so if we apply an index to our source string we get

```
source: abaaaba
index:  0123456
```

We can see that we have two occurrences of the expression ab: one starting at position 0 and the second starting at position 4. If we sent the previous source data and expression to a regex engine, it would reply by telling us that it found matches at positions 0 and 4:

```
import java.util.regex.*;
class RegexSmall {
  public static void main(String [] args) {
    Pattern p = Pattern.compile("ab");      // the expression
    Matcher m = p.matcher("abaaaba");       // the source
    boolean b = false;
    while(b = m.find()) {
      System.out.print(m.start() + " ");
    }
  }
}
```

This produces

```
0 4
```

We're not going to explain this code right now. In a few pages we're going to show you a lot more regex code, but first we want to go over some more regex syntax. Once you understand a little more regex, the code samples will make a lot more sense. Here's a more complicated example of a source and an expression:

```
source: abababa
index:  0123456
expression: aba
```

How many occurrences do we get in this case? Well, there is clearly an occurrence starting at position 0, and another starting at position 4. But how about starting at position 2? In general in the world of regex, the `aba` string that starts at position 2 will not be considered a valid occurrence. The first general regex search rule is

In general, a regex search runs from left to right, and once a source's character has been used in a match, it cannot be reused.

So in our previous example, the first match used positions 0, 1, and 2 to match the expression. (Another common term for this is that the first three characters of the source were *consumed*.) Because the character in position 2 was consumed in the first match, it couldn't be used again. So the engine moved on, and didn't find another occurrence of `aba` until it reached position 4. This is the typical way that a regex matching engine works. However, in a few pages, we'll look at an exception to the first rule we stated above.

So we've matched a couple of exact strings, but what would we do if we wanted to find something a little more dynamic? For instance, what if we wanted to find all of the occurrences of hex numbers or phone numbers or ZIP codes?

Searches Using Metacharacters

As luck would have it, regex has a powerful mechanism for dealing with the cases we described above. At the heart of this mechanism is the idea of a *metacharacter*. As an easy example, let's say that we want to search through some source data looking for all occurrences of numeric digits. In regex, the following expression is used to look for numeric digits:

```
\d
```

If we change the previous program to apply the expression \d to the following source string

```
source: a12c3e456f
index:  0123456789
```

regex will tell us that it found digits at positions 1, 2, 4, 6, 7, and 8. (If you want to try this at home, you'll need to "escape" the `compile` method's "\d" argument by making it "\\d", more on this a little later.)

Regex provides a rich set of metacharacters that you can find described in the API documentation for java.util.regex.Pattern. We won't discuss them all here, but we will describe the ones you'll need for the exam:

\d   A digit
\s   A whitespace character
\w   A word character (letters, digits, or "_" (underscore))

So for example, given

```
source: "a 1 56 _Z"
index:   012345678
pattern: \w
```

regex will return positions 0, 2, 4, 5, 7, and 8. The only characters in this source that don't match the definition of a word character are the whitespaces. (Note: In this example we enclosed the source data in quotes to clearly indicate that there was no whitespace at either end.)

You can also specify sets of characters to search for using square brackets and ranges of characters to search for using square brackets and a dash:

[abc]   Searches only for a's, b's or c's
[a-f]   Searches only for a, b, c, d, e, or f characters

In addition, you can search across several ranges at once. The following expression is looking for occurrences of the letters a - f or A - F, it's NOT looking for an fA combination:

[a-fA-F]   Searches for the first six letters of the alphabet, both cases.

So for instance,

```
source: "cafeBABE"
index:   01234567
pattern: [a-cA-C]
```

returns positions 0, 1, 4, 5, 6.

on the job

In addition to the capabilities described for the exam, you can also apply the following attributes to sets and ranges within square brackets: "^" to negate the characters specified, nested brackets to create a union of sets, and "&&" to specify the intersection of sets. While these constructs are not on the exam, they are quite useful, and good examples can be found in the API for the java.util.regex.Pattern class.

Searches Using Quantifiers

Let's say that we want to create a regex pattern to search for hexadecimal literals. As a first step, let's solve the problem for one-digit hexadecimal numbers:

```
0[xX][0-9a-fA-F]
```

The preceding expression could be stated: "Find a set of characters in which the first character is a "0", the second character is either an "x" or an "X", and the third character is either a digit from "0" to "9", a letter from "a" to "f" or an uppercase letter from "A" to "F" ". Using the preceding expression, and the following data,

```
source: "12 0x 0x12 0Xf 0xg"
index:   012345678901234567
```

regex would return 6 and 11. (Note: 0x and 0xg are not valid hex numbers.)

As a second step, let's think about an easier problem. What if we just wanted regex to find occurrences of integers? Integers can be one or more digits long, so it would be great if we could say "one or more" in an expression. There is a set of regex constructs called quantifiers that let us specify concepts such as "one or more." In fact, the quantifier that represents "one or more" is the "+" character. We'll see the others shortly.

The other issue this raises is that when we're searching for something whose length is variable, getting only a starting position as a return value has limited value. So, in addition to returning starting positions, another bit of information that a regex engine can return is the entire match or *group* that it finds. We're going to change the way we talk about what regex returns by specifying each return on its own line, remembering that now for each return we're going to get back the starting position AND then the group:

```
source: "1 a12 234b"
pattern: \d+
```

You can read this expression as saying: "Find one or more digits in a row." This expression produces the regex output

```
0 1
3 12
6 234
```

You can read this as "At position 0 there's an integer with a value of 1, then at position 3 there's an integer with a value of 12, then at position 6 there's an integer with a value of 234." Returning now to our hexadecimal problem, the last thing we need to know is how to specify the use of a quantifier for only part of an expression. In this case we must have exactly one occurrence of 0x or 0X but we can have from one to many occurrences of the hex "digits" that follow. The following expression adds parentheses to limit the "+" quantifier to only the hex digits:

```
0[xX]([0-9a-fA-F])+
```

The parentheses and "+" augment the previous find-the-hex expression by saying in effect: "Once we've found our 0x or 0X, you can find from one to many occurrences of hex digits." Notice that we put the "+" quantifier at the end of the expression. It's useful to think of quantifiers as always quantifying the part of the expression that precedes them.

The other two quantifiers we're going to look at are

* Zero or more occurrences
? Zero or one occurrence

Let's say you have a text file containing a comma-delimited list of all the file names in a directory that contains several very important projects. (BTW, this isn't how we'd arrange our directories :) You want to create a list of all the files whose names start with `proj1`. You might discover .txt files, .java files, .pdf files, who knows? What kind of regex expression could we create to find these various `proj1` files? First let's take a look at what a part of this text might look like:

```
..."proj3.txt,proj1sched.pdf,proj1,proj2,proj1.java"...
```

To solve this problem we're going to use the regex ^ (carat) operator, which we mentioned earlier. The regex ^ operator isn't on the exam, but it will help us create a fairly clean solution to our problem. The ^ is the negation symbol in regex. For instance, if you want to find anything but a's, b's, or c's in a file you could say

```
[^abc]
```

So, armed with the ^ operator and the * (zero or more) quantifier we can create the following:

```
proj1([^,])*
```

If we apply this expression to just the portion of the text file we listed above, regex returns

```
10 proj1sched.pdf
25 proj1
37 proj1.java
```

The key part of this expression is the "give me zero or more characters that aren't a comma."

The last quantifier example we'll look at is the ? (zero or one) quantifier. Let's say that our job this time is to search a text file and find anything that might be a local, 7-digit phone number. We're going to say, arbitrarily, that if we find either seven digits in a row, or three digits followed by a dash or a space followed by 4 digits, that we have a candidate. Here are examples of "valid" phone numbers:

```
1234567
123 4567
123-4567
```

The key to creating this expression is to see that we need "zero or one instance of either a space or a dash" in the middle of our digits:

```
\d\d\d([-\s])?\d\d\d\d
```

The Predefined Dot

In addition to the \s, \d, and \w metacharacters that we discussed, you also have to understand the "." (dot) metacharacter. When you see this character in a regex expression, it means "any character can serve here." For instance, the following source and pattern

```
source: "ac abc a c"
pattern: a.c
```

will produce the output

```
3 abc
7 a c
```

The "." was able to match both the "b" and the " " in the source data.

Greedy Quantifiers

When you use the *, +, and ? quantifiers, you can fine tune them a bit to produce behavior that's known as "greedy," "reluctant," or "possessive." Although you need to understand only the greedy quantifier for the exam, we're also going to discuss the reluctant quantifier to serve as a basis for comparison. First the syntax:

```
? is greedy, ?? is reluctant, for zero or once
* is greedy, *? is reluctant, for zero or more
+ is greedy, +? is reluctant, for one or more
```

What happens when we have the following source and pattern?

```
source:  yyxxxyxx
pattern:  .*xx
```

First off, we're doing something a bit different here by looking for characters that prefix the static (xx) portion of the expression. We think we're saying something like: "Find sets of characters that ends with xx". Before we tell what happens, we at least want you to consider that there are two plausible results...can you find them? Remember we said earlier that in general, regex engines worked from left to right, and consumed characters as they went. So, working from left to right, we might predict that the engine would search the first 4 characters (0-3), find xx starting in position 2, and have its first match. Then it would proceed and find the second xx starting in position 6. This would lead us to a result like this:

```
0  yyxx
4  xyxx
```

A plausible second argument is that since we asked for a set of characters that ends with xx we might get a result like this:

```
0  yyxxxyxx
```

The way to think about this is to consider the name *greedy*. In order for the second answer to be correct, the regex engine would have to look (greedily) at the *entire* source data before it could determine that there was an xx at the end. So in fact, the second result is the correct result because in the original example we used the greedy quantifier *. The result that finds two different sets can be generated by using the reluctant quantifier *?. Let's review:

```
source:  yyxxxyxx
pattern:  .*xx
```

is using the greedy quantifier * and produces

```
0  yyxxxyxx
```

If we change the pattern to

```
source:  yyxxxyxx
pattern:  .*?xx
```

we're now using the reluctant qualifier *?, and we get the following:

```
0  yyxx
4  xyxx
```

The greedy quantifier does in fact read the entire source data, and then it works backwards (from the right) until it finds the rightmost match. At that point, it includes everything from earlier in the source data up to and including the data that is part of the rightmost match.

on the
ʝob

There are a lot more aspects to regex quantifiers than we've discussed here, but we've covered more than enough for the exam. Sun has several tutorials that will help you learn more about quantfiers, and turn you into the go-to person at your job.

When Metacharacters and Strings Collide

So far we've been talking about regex from a theoretical perspective. Before we can put regex to work we have to discuss one more gotcha. When it's time to implement regex in our code, it will be quite common that our source data and/or our expressions will be stored in Strings. The problem is that metacharacters and Strings don't mix too well. For instance. let's say we just want to do a simple regex pattern that looks for digits. We might try something like

```
String pattern = "\d";    // compiler error!
```

This line of code won't compile! The compiler sees the \ and thinks, "Ok, here comes an escape sequence, maybe it'll be a new line!" But no, next comes the d and the compiler says "I've never heard of the \d escape sequence." The way to satisfy the compiler is to add another backslash in front of the \d

```
String pattern = "\\d";    // a compilable metacharacter
```

The first backslash tells the compiler that whatever comes next should be taken literally, not as an escape sequence. How about the dot (.) metacharacter? If we want a dot in our expression to be used as a metacharacter, then no problem, but what if we're reading some source data that happens to use dots as delimiters? Here's another way to look at our options:

```
String p = ".";   // regex sees this as the "." metacharacter
String p = "\.";  // the compiler sees this as an illegal
                  // Java escape sequence
```

```
String p = "\\."; // the compiler is happy, and regex sees a
                  // dot, not a metacharacter
```

A similar problem can occur when you hand metacharacters to a Java program via command-line arguments. If we want to pass the \d metacharacter into our Java program, our JVM does the right thing if we say

```
% java DoRegex "\d"
```

But your JVM might not. If you have problems running the following examples, you might try adding a backslash (i.e. \\d) to your command-line metacharacters. Don't worry, you won't see any command-line metacharacters on the exam!

The Java language defines several escape sequences, including

> \n *= linefeed (which you might see on the exam)*
> \b *= backspace*
> \t *= tab*

And others, which you can find in the Java Language Specification. Other than perhaps seeing a \n *inside a String, you won't have to worry about Java's escape sequences on the exam.*

At this point we've learned enough of the regex language to start using it in our Java programs. We'll start by looking at using regex expressions to find stuff, and then we'll move to the closely related topic of tokenizing stuff.

Locating Data via Pattern Matching

Once you know a little regex, using the java.util.regex.Pattern (Pattern) and java.util.regex.Matcher (Matcher) classes is pretty straightforward. The Pattern class is used to hold a representation of a regex expression, so that it can be used and reused by instances of the Matcher class. The Matcher class is used to invoke the regex engine with the intention of performing match operations. The following program shows Pattern and Matcher in action, and it's not a bad way for you to do your own regex experiments:

```
import java.util.regex.*;
class Regex {
  public static void main(String [] args) {
    Pattern p = Pattern.compile(args[0]);
    Matcher m = p.matcher(args[1]);
    boolean b = false;
    System.out.println("Pattern is " + m.pattern());
    while(b = m.find()) {
      System.out.println(m.start() + " " + m.group());
    }
  }
}
```

This program uses the first command-line argument (args[0]) to represent the regex expression you want to use, and it uses the second argument (args[1]) to represent the source data you want to search. Here's a test run:

```
% java Regex "\d\w" "ab4 56_7ab"
```

Produces the output

```
Pattern is \d\w
4 56
7 7a
```

(Remember, if you want this expression to be represented in a String, you'd use \\d\\w). Because you'll often have special characters or whitespace as part of your arguments, you'll probably want to get in the habit of always enclosing your argument in quotes. Let's take a look at this code in more detail. First off, notice that we aren't using new to create a Pattern; if you check the API, you'll find no constructors are listed. You'll use the overloaded, static compile() method (that takes String expression) to create an instance of Pattern. For the exam, all you'll need to know to create a Matcher, is to use the Pattern.matcher() method (that takes String sourceData).

The important method in this program is the find() method. This is the method that actually cranks up the regex engine and does some searching. The find() method returns true if it gets a match, and remembers the start position of the match. If find() returns true, you can call the start() method to get the starting position of the match, and you can call the group() method to get the string that represents the actual bit of source data that was matched.

on the !Job

A common reason to use regex is to perform search and replace operations. Although replace operations are not on the exam you should know that the Matcher class provides several methods that perform search and replace operations. See the `appendReplacement()`*,* `appendTail()`*, and* `replaceAll()` *methods in the Matcher API for more details.*

The Matcher class allows you to look at subsets of your source data by using a concept called *regions*. In real life, regions can greatly improve performance, but you won't need to know anything about them for the exam.

Searching Using the Scanner Class   Although the java.util.Scanner class is primarily intended for tokenizing data (which we'll cover next), it can also be used to find stuff, just like the Pattern and Matcher classes. While Scanner doesn't provide location information or search and replace functionality, you can use it to apply regex expressions to source data to tell you how many instances of an expression exist in a given piece of source data. The following program uses the first command-line argument as a regex expression, then asks for input using `System.in`. It outputs a message every time a match is found:

```
import java.util.*;
class ScanIn {
  public static void main(String[] args) {
    System.out.print("input: ");
    System.out.flush();
    try {
      Scanner s = new Scanner(System.in);
      String token;
      do {
        token = s.findInLine(args[0]);
        System.out.println("found " + token);
      } while (token != null);
    } catch (Exception e) { System.out.println("scan exc"); }
  }
}
```

The invocation and input

```
java ScanIn "\d\d"
input: 1b2c335f456
```

produce the following:

```
found 33
found 45
found null
```

Tokenizing

Tokenizing is the process of taking big pieces of source data, breaking them into little pieces, and storing the little pieces in variables. Probably the most common tokenizing situation is reading a delimited file in order to get the contents of the file moved into useful places like objects, arrays or collections. We'll look at two classes in the API that provide tokenizing capabilities: String (using the `split()` method) and Scanner, which has many methods that are useful for tokenizing.

Tokens and Delimiters

When we talk about tokenizing, we're talking about data that starts out composed of two things: tokens and delimiters. Tokens are the actual pieces of data, and delimiters are the expressions that *separate* the tokens from each other. When most people think of delimiters, they think of single characters, like commas or backslashes or maybe a single whitespace. These are indeed very common delimiters, but strictly speaking, delimiters can be much more dynamic. In fact, as we hinted at a few sentences ago, delimiters can be anything that qualifies as a regex expression. Let's take a single piece of source data and tokenize it using a couple of different delimiters:

```
source: "ab,cd5b,6x,z4"
```

If we say that our delimiter is a comma, then our four tokens would be

```
ab
cd5b
6x
z4
```

If we use the same source, but declare our delimiter to be \d, we get three tokens:

```
ab,cd
b,
x,z
```

In general, when we tokenize source data, the delimiters themselves are discarded, and all that we are left with are the tokens. So in the second example, we defined digits to be delimiters, so the 5, 6, and 4 do not appear in the final tokens.

Tokenizing with String.split()

The String class's split() method takes a regex expression as its argument, and returns a String array populated with the tokens produced by the split (or tokenizing) process. This is a handy way to tokenize relatively small pieces of data. The following program uses args[0] to hold a source string, and args[1] to hold the regex pattern to use as a delimiter:

```
import java.util.*;
class SplitTest {
  public static void main(String[] args) {
    String[] tokens = args[0].split(args[1]);
    System.out.println("count " + tokens.length);
    for(String s : tokens)
      System.out.println(">" + s + "<");
  }
}
```

Everything happens all at once when the split() method is invoked. The source string is split into pieces, and the pieces are all loaded into the tokens String array. All the code after that is just there to verify what the split operation generated. The following invocation

```
% java SplitTest "ab5 ccc 45 @" "\d"
```

produces

```
count 4
>ab<
> ccc <
><
> @<
```

(Note: Remember that to represent "\" in a string you may need to use the escape sequence "\\". Because of this, and depending on your OS, your second argument might have to be "\\d" or even "\\\\d".)

We put the tokens inside "> <" characters to show whitespace. Notice that every digit was used as a delimiter, and that contiguous digits created an empty token.

One drawback to using the `String.split()` method is that often you'll want to look at tokens as they are produced, and possibly quit a tokenization operation early when you've created the tokens you need. For instance, you might be searching a large file for a phone number. If the phone number occurs early in the file, you'd like to quit the tokenization process as soon as you've got your number. The Scanner class provides a rich API for doing just such on-the-fly tokenization operations.

exam

ⓦatch

Because `System.out.println()` **is so heavily used on the exam, you might see examples of escape sequences tucked in with questions on most any topic, including regex. Remember that if you need to create a String that contains a double quote " or a backslash \ you need to add an escape character first:**

```
System.out.println("\" \\");
```

This prints

```
" \
```

So, what if you need to search for periods (.) in your source data? If you just put a period in the regex expression, you get the "any character" behavior. So, what if you try `\.` **? Now the Java compiler thinks you're trying to create an escape sequence that doesn't exist. The correct syntax is**

```
String s = "ab.cde.fg";
String[] tokens = s.split("\\.");
```

Tokenizing with Scanner

The java.util.Scanner class is the Cadillac of tokenizing. When you need to do some serious tokenizing, look no further than Scanner—this beauty has it all. In addition to the basic tokenizing capabilities provided by `String.split()`, the Scanner class offers the following features:

■ Scanners can be constructed using files, streams, or Strings as a source.

- Tokenizing is performed within a loop so that you can exit the process at any point.
- Tokens can be converted to their appropriate primitive types automatically.

Let's look at a program that demonstrates several of Scanner's methods and capabilities. Scanner's default delimiter is whitespace, which this program uses. The program makes two Scanner objects: `s1` is iterated over with the more generic `next()` method, which returns every token as a String, while `s2` is analyzed with several of the specialized `nextXxx()` methods (where `Xxx` is a primitive type):

```
import java.util.Scanner;
class ScanNext {
  public static void main(String [] args) {
    boolean b2, b;
    int i;
    String s, hits = " ";
    Scanner s1 = new Scanner(args[0]);
    Scanner s2 = new Scanner(args[0]);
    while(b = s1.hasNext()) {
      s = s1.next();  hits += "s";
    }
    while(b = s2.hasNext()) {
      if (s2.hasNextInt()) {
        i = s2.nextInt();  hits += "i";
      } else if (s2.hasNextBoolean()) {
        b2 = s2.nextBoolean();  hits += "b";
      } else {
        s2.next();  hits += "s2";
      }
    }
    System.out.println("hits " + hits);
  }
}
```

If this program is invoked with

```
% java ScanNext "1 true 34 hi"
```

it produces

```
hits  ssssibis2
```

Of course we're not doing anything with the tokens once we've got them, but you can see that s2's tokens are converted to their respective primitives. A key point here is that the methods named `hasNextXxx()` test the value of the next token but do not actually get the token, nor do they move to the next token in the source data. The `nextXxx()` methods all perform two functions: they get the next token, and then they move to the next token.

The Scanner class has `nextXxx()` (for instance `nextLong()`) and `hasNextXxx()` (for instance `hasNextDouble()`) methods for every primitive type except `char`. In addition, the Scanner class has a `useDelimiter()` method that allows you to set the delimiter to be any valid regex expression.

Formatting with printf() and format()

What fun would accounts receivable reports be if the decimal points didn't line up? Where would you be if you couldn't put negative numbers inside of parentheses? Burning questions like these caused the exam creation team to include formatting as a part of the Java 5 exam. The `format()` and `printf()` methods were added to java.io.PrintStream in Java 5. These two methods behave exactly the same way, so anything we say about one of these methods applies to both of them. (The rumor is that Sun added `printf()` just to make old C programmers happy.)

Behind the scenes, the `format()` method uses the `java.util.Formatter` class to do the heavy formatting work. You can use the `Formatter` class directly if you choose, but for the exam all you have to know is the basic syntax of the arguments you pass to the `format()` method. The documentation for these formatting arguments can be found in the Formatter API. We're going to take the "nickel tour" of the formatting String syntax, which will be more than enough to allow you do to a lot of basic formatting work, AND ace all the formatting questions on the exam.

Let's start by paraphrasing the API documentation for format strings (for more complete, way-past-what-you-need-for-the-exam coverage, check out the java.util.Formatter API):

```
printf("format string", argument(s));
```

The format string can contain both normal string literal information that isn't associated with any arguments, and argument-specific formatting data. The clue to determining whether you're looking at formatting data, is that formatting data will always start with a percent sign (`%`). Let's look at an example, and don't panic, we'll cover everything that comes after the `%` next:

```
System.out.printf("%2$d  +  %1$d", 123, 456);
```

This produces

```
456 + 123
```

Let's look at what just happened. Inside the double quotes there is a format string, then a +, and then a second format string. Notice that we mixed literals in with the format strings. Now let's dive in a little deeper and look at the construction of format strings:

```
%[arg_index$][flags][width][.precision]conversion char
```

The values within [ ] are optional. In other words, the only required elements of a format string are the % and a conversion character. In the example above the only optional values we used were for argument indexing. The 2$ represents the second argument, and the 1$ represents the first argument. (Notice that there's no problem switching the order of arguments.) The d after the arguments is a conversion character (more or less the type of the argument). Here's a rundown of the format string elements you'll need to know for the exam:

arg_index An integer followed directly by a $, this indicates which argument should be printed in this position.

flags While many flags are available, for the exam you'll need to know:

- ■ "-" Left justify this argument
- ■ "+" Include a sign (+ or -) with this argument
- ■ "0" Pad this argument with zeroes
- ■ "," Use locale-specific grouping separators (i.e., the comma in 123,456)
- ■ "(" Enclose negative numbers in parentheses

width This value indicates the minimum number of characters to print. (If you want nice even columns, you'll use this value extensively.)

precision For the exam you'll only need this when formatting a floating-point number, and in the case of floating point numbers, precision indicates the number of digits to print after the decimal point.

conversion The type of argument you'll be formatting. You'll need to know:

- b   boolean
- c   char
- d   integer
- f   floating point
- s   string

Let's see some of these formatting strings in action:

```
int i1 = -123;
int i2 = 12345;
System.out.printf(">%1$(7d< \n", i1);
System.out.printf(">%0,7d< \n", i2);
System.out.format(">%+-7d< \n", i2);
System.out.printf(">%2$b + %1$5d< \n", i1, false);
```

This produces:

```
>  (123)<
>012,345<
>+12345 <
>false +  -123<
```

(We added the > and < literals to help show how minimum widths, and zero padding and alignments work.) Finally, it's important to remember that if you have a mismatch between the type specified in your conversion character and your argument, you'll get a runtime exception:

```
System.out.format("%d", 12.3);
```

This produces something like

```
Exception in thread "main" java.util.IllegalFormatConversionEx-
ception: d != java.lang.Double
```

CERTIFICATION SUMMARY

Strings   The most important thing to remember about Strings is that String objects are immutable, but references to Strings are not! You can make a new String by using an existing String as a starting point, but if you don't assign a reference variable to the new String it will be lost to your program—you will have no way to access your new String. Review the important methods in the String class.

The StringBuilder class was added in Java 5. It has exactly the same methods as the old StringBuffer class, except StringBuilder's methods aren't thread-safe. Because StringBuilder's methods are not thread safe, they tend to run faster than StringBuffer methods, so choose StringBuilder whenever threading is not an issue. Both StringBuffer and StringBuilder objects can have their value changed over and over without having to create new objects. If you're doing a lot of string manipulation, these objects will be more efficient than immutable String objects, which are, more or less, "use once, remain in memory forever." Remember, these methods ALWAYS change the invoking object's value, even with no explicit assignment.

File I/O   Remember that objects of type File can represent either files or directories, but that until you call `createNewFile()` or `mkDir()` you haven't actually created anything on your hard drive. Classes in the java.io package are designed to be chained together. It will be rare that you'll use a FileReader or a FileWriter without "wrapping" them with a BufferedReader or BufferedWriter object, which gives you access to more powerful, higher-level methods. As of Java 5, the PrintWriter class has been enhanced with advanced `append()`, `format()`, and `printf()` methods, and when you couple that with new constructors that allow you to create PrintWriters directly from a String name or a File object, you may use BufferWriters a lot less.

Serialization   Serialization lets you save, ship, and restore everything you need to know about a *live* object. And when your object points to other objects, they get saved too. The java.io.ObjectOutputStream and java.io.ObjectInputStream classes are used to serialize and deserialize objects. Typically you wrap them around instances of FileOutputStream and FileInputStream, respectively.

The key method you invoke to serialize an object is `writeObject()`, and to deserialize an object invoke `readMethod()`. In order to serialize an object, it must implement the Serializable interface. Mark instance variables `transient` if you don't want their state to be part of the serialization process. You can augment the serialization process for your class by implementing `writeObject()` and `readObject()`. If you do that, an embedded call to `defaultReadObject()` and `defaultWriteObject()` will handle the normal serialization tasks, and you can augment those invocations with manual *reading from* and *writing to* the stream.

If a superclass implements Serializable then all of its subclasses do too. If a superclass doesn't implement Serializable, then when a subclass object is deserialized the unserializable superclass's constructor runs—be careful! Finally, remember that serialization is about instances, so static variables aren't serialized.

Dates, Numbers, and Currency

Remember that the Sun objective is a bit misleading, and that you'll have to understand the basics of five related classes: java.util.Date, java.util.Calendar, java.util.Locale, java.text.DateFormat, and java.text.NumberFormat. A Date is the number of milliseconds since Jan. 1, 1970, stored in a `long`. Most of Date's methods have been deprecated, so use the Calendar class for your date-manipulation tasks. Remember that in order to create instances of Calendar, DateFormat, and NumberFormat, you have to use static factory methods like `getInstance()`. The Locale class is used with DateFormat and NumberFormat to generate a variety of output styles that are language and/or country specific.

Parsing, Tokenizing, and Formatting

To find specific pieces of data in large data sources, Java provides several mechanisms that use the concepts of regular expressions (regex). regex expressions can be used with the java.util.regex package's Pattern and Matcher classes, as well as with java.util.Scanner and with the `String.split()` method. When creating regex patterns, you can use literal characters for matching or you can use metacharacters, that allow you to match on concepts like "find digits" or "find whitespace." regex provides *quantifiers* that allow you to say things like "find one or more of these things in a row." You won't have to understand the Matcher methods that facilitate replacing strings in data.

Tokenizing is splitting delimited data into pieces. Delimiters are usually as simple as a comma, but they can be as complex as any other regex pattern. The java.util.Scanner class provides full tokenizing capabilities using regex, and allows you to tokenize in a loop so that you can stop the tokenizing process at any point. `String.split()` allows full regex patterns for tokenizing, but tokenizing is done in one step, hence large data sources can take a long time to process.

Formatting data for output can be handled by using the Formatter class, or more commonly by using the new PrintStream methods `format()` and `printf()`. Remember `format()` and `printf()` behave identically. To use these methods, you create a format string that is associated with every piece of data you want to format. You need to understand the subset of format string conventions we covered in the chapter, and you need to remember that if your format string specifies a conversion character that doesn't match your data type, an exception will be thrown.

✔ TWO-MINUTE DRILL

Here are some of the key points from the certification objectives in this chapter.

Using String, StringBuffer, and StringBuilder (Objective 3.1)

❑ String objects are immutable, and String reference variables are not.

❑ If you create a new String without assigning it, it will be lost to your program.

❑ If you redirect a String reference to a new String, the old String can be lost.

❑ String methods use zero-based indexes, except for the second argument of `substring()`.

❑ The String class is `final`—its methods can't be overridden.

❑ When the JVM finds a String literal, it is added to the String literal pool.

❑ Strings have a method: `length()`; arrays have an attribute named `length`.

❑ The StringBuffer's API is the same as the new StringBuilder's API, except that StringBuilder's methods are not synchronized for thread safety.

❑ StringBuilder methods should run faster than StringBuffer methods.

❑ All of the following bullets apply to both StringBuffer and StringBuilder:

  ❑ They are mutable—they can change without creating a new object.

  ❑ StringBuffer methods act on the invoking object, and objects can change without an explicit assignment in the statement.

  ❑ StringBuffer `equals()` is not overridden; it doesn't compare values.

❑ Remember that chained methods are evaluated from left to right.

❑ String methods to remember: `charAt()`, `concat()`, `equalsIgnoreCase()`, `length()`, `replace()`, `substring()`, `toLowerCase()`, `toString()`, `toUpperCase()`, and `trim()`.

❑ Stringbuffer methods to remember: `append()`, `delete()`, `insert()`, `reverse()`, and `toString()`.

File I/O (Objective 3.2)

❑ The classes you need to understand in java.io are File, FileReader, BufferedReader, FileWriter, BufferedWriter, and PrintWriter.

❑ A new File object doesn't mean there's a new file on your hard drive.

❑ File objects can represent either a file or a directory.

❑ The File class lets you manage (add, rename, and delete) files and directories.

❑ The methods `createNewFile()` and `mkDir()` add entries to your file system.

❑ FileWriter and FileReader are low-level I/O classes. You can use them to write and read files, but they should usually be wrapped.

❑ Classes in java.io are designed to be "chained" or "wrapped." (This is a common use of the decorator design pattern.)

❑ It's very common to "wrap" a BufferedReader around a FileReader, to get access to higher-level (more convenient) methods.

❑ It's very common to "wrap" a BufferedWriter around a FileWriter, to get access to higher-level (more convenient) methods.

❑ PrintWriters can be used to wrap other Writers, but as of Java 5 they can be built directly from Files or Strings.

❑ Java 5 PrintWriters have new `append()`, `format()`, and `printf()` methods.

Serialization (Objective 3.3)

❑ The classes you need to understand are all in the java.io package; they include: ObjectOutputStream and ObjectInputStream primarily, and FileOutputStream and FileInputStream because you will use them to create the low-level streams that the ObjectXxxStream classes will use.

❑ A class must implement the Serializable interface before its objects can be serialized.

❑ The `ObjectOutputStream.writeObject()` method serializes objects, and the `ObjectInputStream.readObject()` method deserializes objects.

❑ If you mark an instance variable `transient`, it will not be serialized even thought the rest of the object's state will be.

❑ You can supplement a class's automatic serialization process by implementing the `writeObject()` and `readObject()` methods. If you do this, embedding calls to `defaultWriteObject()` and `defaultReadObject()`, respectively, will handle the part of serialization that happens normally.

❑ If a superclass implements Serializable, then its subclasses do automatically.

❑ If a superclass doesn't implement Serializable, then when a subclass object is deserialized, the superclass constructor will run.

❑ DataInputStream and DataOutputStream aren't actually on the exam, in spite of what the Sun objectives say.

Dates, Numbers, and Currency (Objective 3.4)

❑ The classes you need to understand are java.util.Date, java.util.Calendar, java.text.DateFormat, java.text.NumberFormat, and java.util.Locale.

❑ Most of the Date class's methods have been deprecated.

❑ A Date is stored as a `long`, the number of milliseconds since January 1, 1970.

❑ Date objects are go-betweens the Calendar and Locale classes.

❑ The Calendar provides a powerful set of methods to manipulate dates, performing tasks such as getting days of the week, or adding some number of months or years (or other increments) to a date.

❑ Create Calendar instances using static factory methods (`getInstance()`).

❑ The Calendar methods you should understand are `add()`, which allows you to add or subtract various pieces (minutes, days, years, and so on) of dates, and `roll()`, which works like `add()` but doesn't increment a date's bigger pieces. (For example: adding 10 months to an October date changes the month to August, but doesn't increment the Calendar's year value.)

❑ DateFormat instances are created using static factory methods (`getInstance()` and `getDateInstance()`).

❑ There are several format "styles" available in the DateFormat class.

❑ DateFormat styles can be applied against various Locales to create a wide array of outputs for any given date.

❑ The `DateFormat.format()` method is used to create Strings containing properly formatted dates.

❑ The Locale class is used in conjunction with DateFormat and NumberFormat.

❑ Both DateFormat and NumberFormat objects can be constructed with a specific, immutable Locale.

❑ For the exam you should understand creating Locales using language, or a combination of language and country.

Parsing, Tokenizing, and Formatting (Objective 3.5)

❑ regex is short for regular expressions, which are the patterns used to search for data within large data sources.

❑ regex is a sub-language that exists in Java and other languages (such as Perl).

❑ regex lets you to create search patterns using literal characters or metacharacters. Metacharacters allow you to search for slightly more abstract data like "digits" or "whitespace".

❑ Study the \d, \s, \w, and . metacharacters

❑ regex provides for *quantifiers* which allow you to specify concepts like: "look for one or more digits in a row."

❑ Study the ?, *, and + greedy quantifiers.

❑ Remember that metacharacters and Strings don't mix well unless you remember to "escape" them properly. For instance `String s = "\\d";`

❑ The Pattern and Matcher classes have Java's most powerful regex capabilities.

❑ You should understand the Pattern `compile()` method and the Matcher `matcher()`, `pattern()`, `find()`, `start()`, and `group()` methods.

❑ You WON'T need to understand Matcher's replacement-oriented methods.

❑ You can use java.util.Scanner to do simple regex searches, but it is primarily intended for tokenizing.

❑ Tokenizing is the process of splitting delimited data into small pieces.

❑ In tokenizing, the data you want is called tokens, and the strings that separate the tokens are called delimiters.

❑ Tokenizing can be done with the Scanner class, or with `String.split()`.

❑ Delimiters are single characters like commas, or complex regex expressions.

❑ The Scanner class allows you to tokenize data from within a loop, which allows you to stop whenever you want to.

❑ The Scanner class allows you to tokenize Strings or streams or files.

❑ The `String.split()` method tokenizes the entire source data all at once, so large amounts of data can be quite slow to process.

❑ New to Java 5 are two methods used to format data for output. These methods are `format()` and `printf()`. These methods are found in the PrintStream class, an instance of which is the out in `System.out`.

❑ The `format()` and `printf()` methods have identical functionality.

❑ Formatting data with `printf()` (or `format()`) is accomplished using *formatting strings* that are associated with primitive or string arguments.

❑ The `format()` method allows you to mix literals in with your format strings.

❑ The format string values you should know are

    ❑ Flags: -, +, 0, "," , and (

    ❑ Conversions: b, c, d, f, and s

❑ If your conversion character doesn't match your argument type, an exception will be thrown.

SELF TEST

I. Given:

```
import java.util.regex.*;
class Regex2 {
  public static void main(String[] args) {
    Pattern p = Pattern.compile(args[0]);
    Matcher m = p.matcher(args[1]);
    boolean b = false;
    while(b = m.find()) {
      System.out.print(m.start() + m.group());
    }
  }
}
```

And the command line:

```
java Regex2 "\d*" ab34ef
```

What is the result?

A. 234

B. 334

C. 2334

D. 0123456

E. 01234456

F. 12334567

G. Compilation fails.

2. Given:

```
import java.io.*;
class Player {
  Player() { System.out.print("p"); }
}
class CardPlayer extends Player implements Serializable {
  CardPlayer() { System.out.print("c"); }
  public static void main(String[] args) {
    CardPlayer c1 = new CardPlayer();
```

```
       try {
          FileOutputStream fos = new FileOutputStream("play.txt");
          ObjectOutputStream os = new ObjectOutputStream(fos);
          os.writeObject(c1);
          os.close();
          FileInputStream fis = new FileInputStream("play.txt");
          ObjectInputStream is = new ObjectInputStream(fis);
          CardPlayer c2 = (CardPlayer) is.readObject();
          is.close();
       } catch (Exception x ) { }
    }
  }
```

What is the result?

A. pc

B. pcc

C. pcp

D. pcpc

E. Compilation fails.

F. An exception is thrown at runtime.

3. Given that bw is a reference to a valid BufferedWriter

And the snippet:

```
15.   BufferedWriter b1 = new BufferedWriter(new File("f"));
16.   BufferedWriter b2 = new BufferedWriter(new FileWriter("f1"));
17.   BufferedWriter b3 = new BufferedWriter(new PrintWriter("f2"));
18.   BufferedWriter b4 = new BufferedWriter(new BufferedWriter(bw));
```

What is the result?

A. Compilation succeeds.

B. Compilation fails due only to an error on line 15.

C. Compilation fails due only to an error on line 16.

D. Compilation fails due only to an error on line 17.

E. Compilation fails due only to an error on line 18.

F. Compilation fails due to errors on multiple lines.

4. Given:

```
class TKO {
  public static void main(String[] args) {
    String s = "-";
    Integer x = 343;
    long L343 = 343L;
    if(x.equals(L343))  s += ".e1 ";
    if(x.equals(343))   s += ".e2 ";
    Short s1 = (short)((new Short((short)343)) / (new Short((short)49)));
    if(s1 == 7)           s += "=s ";
    if(s1 < new Integer(7+1))  s += "fly ";
    System.out.println(s);
  }
}
```

Which of the following will be included in the output String s? (Choose all that apply.)

A. `.e1`

B. `.e2`

C. `=s`

D. `fly`

E. None of the above.

F. Compilation fails.

G. An exception is thrown at runtime.

5. Given:

```
1. import java.text.*;
2. class DateOne {
3.   public static void main(String[] args) {
4.     Date d = new Date(1123631685981L);
5.     DateFormat df = new DateFormat();
6.     System.out.println(df.format(d));
7.   }
8. }
```

And given that 1123631685981L is the number of milliseconds between Jan. 1, 1970, and sometime on Aug. 9, 2005, what is the result? (Note: the time of day in option **A** may vary.)

A. 8/9/05 5:54 PM

B. 1123631685981L

C. An exception is thrown at runtime.

D. Compilation fails due to a single error in the code.

E. Compilation fails due to multiple errors in the code.

6. Given:

```
import java.io.*;

class Keyboard { }
public class Computer implements Serializable {
  private Keyboard k = new Keyboard();
  public static void main(String[] args) {
    Computer c = new Computer();
    c.storeIt(c);
  }
  void storeIt(Computer c) {
    try {
      ObjectOutputStream os = new ObjectOutputStream(
        new FileOutputStream("myFile"));
      os.writeObject(c);
      os.close();
      System.out.println("done");
    } catch (Exception x) {System.out.println("exc"); }
  }
}
```

What is the result? (Choose all that apply.)

A. exc

B. done

C. Compilation fails.

D. Exactly one object is serialized.

E. Exactly two objects are serialized.

7. Using the fewest **fragments** possible (and filling the fewest slots possible), complete the **code** below so that the class builds a directory named "dir3" and creates a file named "file3" inside "dir3". Note you can use each fragment either zero or one times.

Code:

```
import java.io._____

class Maker {
  public static void main(String[] args) {

    _____  _____  _____

    _____  _____  _____

    _____  _____  _____

    _____  _____  _____

    _____  _____  _____

    _____  _____  _____

    _____  _____  _____

  }
}
```

Fragments:

```
File;         FileDescriptor;        FileWriter;       Directory;
try {         .createNewDir();       File dir          File
{ }           (Exception x)          ("dir3");         file
file          .createNewFile();      = new File        = new File
dir           (dir, "file3");        (dir, file);      .createFile();
} catch       ("dir3", "file3");     .mkdir();         File file
```

8. Which are true? (Choose all that apply.)

A. The DateFormat.getDate() is used to convert a String to a Date instance.

B. Both `DateFormat` and `NumberFormat` objects can be constructed to be Locale specific.

C. Both Currency and `NumberFormat` objects must be constructed using static methods.

D. If a `NumberFormat` instance's Locale is to be different than the current Locale, it must be specified at creation time.

E. A single instance of `NumberFormat` can be used to create Number objects from Strings and to create formatted numbers from numbers.

9. Which will compile and run without exception? (Choose all that apply.)

A. `System.out.format("%b", 123);`

B. `System.out.format("%c", "x");`

C. `System.out.printf("%d", 123);`

D. `System.out.printf("%f", 123);`

E. `System.out.printf("%d", 123.45);`

F. `System.out.printf("%f", 123.45);`

G. `System.out.format("%s", new Long("123"));`

10. Which about the three java.lang classes String, StringBuilder, and StringBuffer are true? (Choose all that apply.)

A. All three classes have a `length()` method.

B. Objects of type StringBuffer are thread-safe.

C. All three classes have overloaded `append()` methods.

D. The "+" is an overloaded operator for all three classes.

E. According to the API, StringBuffer will be faster than StringBuilder under most implementations.

F. The value of an instance of any of these three types can be modified through various methods in the API.

11. Given that 1119280000000L is roughly the number of milliseconds from Jan. 1, 1970, to June 20, 2005, and that you want to print that date in German, using the LONG style such that "June" will be displayed as "Juni", complete the code using the fragments below. Note: you can use each fragment either zero or one times, and you might not need to fill all of the slots.

Code:

```
import java._____

import java._____

class DateTwo {
  public static void main(String[] args) {
    Date d = new Date(1119280000000L);

    DateFormat df = _____

                    _____ , _____ );

    System.out.println(_____
  }
}
```

Fragments:

io.*;	new DateFormat(	Locale.LONG
nio.*;	DateFormat.getInstance(	Locale.GERMANY
util.*;	DateFormat.getDateInstance(	DateFormat.LONG
text.*;	util.regex;	DateFormat.GERMANY
date.*;	df.format(d));	d.format(df));

12. Given:

```
import java.io.*;
class Directories {
  static String [] dirs = {"dir1", "dir2"};
  public static void main(String [] args) {
    for (String d : dirs) {

      // insert code 1 here

      File file = new File(path, args[0]);

      // insert code 2 here

    }
  }
}
```

and that the invocation

```
java Directories file2.txt
```

is issued from a directory that has two subdirectories, "dir1" and "dir1", and that "dir1" has a file "file1.txt" and "dir2" has a file "file2.txt", and the output is "false true"; which set(s) of code fragments must be inserted? (Choose all that apply.)

A.
```
String path = d;
System.out.print(file.exists() + " ");
```

B.
```
String path = d;
System.out.print(file.isFile() + " ");
```

C.
```
String path = File.separator + d;
System.out.print(file.exists() + " ");
```

D.
```
String path = File.separator + d;
System.out.print(file.isFile() + " ");
```

13. Given:

```
class Polish {
   public static void main(String[] args) {
      int x = 4;
      StringBuffer sb = new StringBuffer("..fedcba");
      sb.delete(3,6);
      sb.insert(3, "az");
      if(sb.length() > 6)   x = sb.indexOf("b");
      sb.delete((x-3), (x-2));
      System.out.println(sb);
   } }
```

What is the result?

A. `.faza`

B. `.fzba`

C. `..azba`

D. `.fazba`

E. `..fezba`

F. Compilation fails.

G. An exception is thrown at runtime.

14.   Given:

```
1. import java.util.*;
2. class Brain {
3.   public static void main(String[] args) {

4.     // insert code block here

5.   }
6. }
```

Which, inserted independently at line 4, compile and produce the output "123 82"?
(Choose all that apply.)

A.
```
Scanner sc = new Scanner("123 A 3b c,45, x5x,76 82 L");
    while(sc.hasNextInt())  System.out.print(sc.nextInt() + " ");
```

B.
```
Scanner sc = new Scanner("123 A 3b c,45, x5x,76 82 L").
                         useDelimiter(" ");
    while(sc.hasNextInt())  System.out.print(sc.nextInt() + " ");
```

C.
```
Scanner sc = new Scanner("123 A 3b c,45, x5x,76 82 L");
    while(sc.hasNext()) {
       if(sc.hasNextInt()) System.out.print(sc.nextInt() + " ");
       else sc.next(); }
```

D.
```
Scanner sc = new Scanner("123 A 3b c,45, x5x,76 82 L").
                   useDelimiter(" ");
    while(sc.hasNext()) {
       if(sc.hasNextInt()) System.out.print(sc.nextInt() + " ");
       else sc.next(); }
```

E.
```
Scanner sc = new Scanner("123 A 3b c,45, x5x,76 82 L");
    do {
       if(sc.hasNextInt()) System.out.print(sc.nextInt() + " ");
       } while ( sc.hasNext() );
```

F.
```
Scanner sc = new Scanner("123 A 3b c,45, x5x,76 82 L").
                   useDelimiter(" ");
    do {
       if(sc.hasNextInt()) System.out.print(sc.nextInt() + " ");
       } while ( sc.hasNext() );
```

15. Given:

```
import java.io.*;

public class TestSer {
  public static void main(String[] args) {
    SpecialSerial s = new SpecialSerial();
    try {
      ObjectOutputStream os = new ObjectOutputStream(
        new FileOutputStream("myFile"));
      os.writeObject(s);  os.close();
      System.out.print(++s.z + " ");

      ObjectInputStream is = new ObjectInputStream(
        new FileInputStream("myFile"));
      SpecialSerial s2 = (SpecialSerial)is.readObject();
      is.close();
      System.out.println(s2.y + " " + s2.z);
    } catch (Exception x) {System.out.println("exc"); }
  }
}
class SpecialSerial implements Serializable {
  transient int y = 7;
  static int z = 9;
}
```

Which are true? (Choose all that apply.)

A. Compilation fails.

B. The output is 10 0 9

C. The output is 10 0 10

D. The output is 10 7 9

E. The output is 10 7 10

F. In order to alter the standard deserialization process you would override the readObject() method in SpecialSerial.

G. In order to alter the standard deserialization process you would override the defaultReadObject() method in SpecialSerial.

SELF TEST ANSWERS

1. Given:

```
import java.util.regex.*;
class Regex2 {
  public static void main(String[] args) {
    Pattern p = Pattern.compile(args[0]);
    Matcher m = p.matcher(args[1]);
    boolean b = false;
    while(b = m.find()) {
      System.out.print(m.start() + m.group());
    }
  }
}
```

And the command line:

```
java Regex2 "\d*" ab34ef
```

What is the result?

A. `234`

B. `334`

C. `2334`

D. `0123456`

E. `01234456`

F. `12334567`

G. Compilation fails.

Answer:

☑ **E** is correct. The `\d` is looking for digits. The `*` is a quantifier that looks for `0` to many occurrences of the pattern that precedes it. Because we specified `*`, the `group()` method returns empty Strings until consecutive digits are found, so the only time `group()` returns a value is when it returns 34 when the matcher finds digits starting in position 2. The `start()` method returns the starting position of the previous match because, again, we said find `0` to many occurrences.

☒ **A, B, C, D, E, F,** and **G** are incorrect based on the above. (Objective 3.5)

2. Given:

```java
import java.io.*;
class Player {
  Player() { System.out.print("p"); }
}
class CardPlayer extends Player implements Serializable {
  CardPlayer() { System.out.print("c"); }
  public static void main(String[] args) {
    CardPlayer c1 = new CardPlayer();
    try {
      FileOutputStream fos = new FileOutputStream("play.txt");
      ObjectOutputStream os = new ObjectOutputStream(fos);
      os.writeObject(c1);
      os.close();
      FileInputStream fis = new FileInputStream("play.txt");
      ObjectInputStream is = new ObjectInputStream(fis);
      CardPlayer c2 = (CardPlayer) is.readObject();
      is.close();
    } catch (Exception x ) { }
  }
}
```

What is the result?

A. pc

B. pcc

C. pcp

D. pcpc

E. Compilation fails.

F. An exception is thrown at runtime.

Answer:

☑ **C** is correct. It's okay for a class to implement Serializable even if its superclass doesn't. However, when you deserialize such an object, the non-serializable superclass must run its constructor. Remember, constructors don't run on deserialized classes that implement Serializable.

☒ **A, B, D, E,** and **F** are incorrect based on the above. (Objective 3.3)

3.   Given:

bw is a reference to a valid `BufferedWriter`

And the snippet:

```
15.  BufferedWriter b1 = new BufferedWriter(new File("f"));
16.  BufferedWriter b2 = new BufferedWriter(new FileWriter("f1"));
17.  BufferedWriter b3 = new BufferedWriter(new PrintWriter("f2"));
18.  BufferedWriter b4 = new BufferedWriter(new BufferedWriter(bw));
```

What is the result?

A.   Compilation succeeds.

B.   Compilation fails due only to an error on line 15.

C.   Compilation fails due only to an error on line 16.

D.   Compilation fails due only to an error on line 17.

E.   Compilation fails due only to an error on line 18.

F.   Compilation fails due to errors on multiple lines.

Answer:

☑   **B** is correct. `BufferedWriters` can be constructed only by wrapping a Writer. Lines 16, 17, and 18 are correct because `BufferedWriter`, `FileWriter`, and `PrintWriter` all extend Writer. (Note: `BufferedWriter` is a decorator class. Decorator classes are used extensively in the java.io package to allow you to extend the functionality of other classes.)

☒   **A, C, D, E,** and **F** are incorrect based on the above. (Objective 3.2)

4.   Given:

```
class TKO {
  public static void main(String[] args) {
    String s = "-";
    Integer x = 343;
    long L343 = 343L;
    if(x.equals(L343))  s += ".e1 ";
    if(x.equals(343))   s += ".e2 ";
    Short s1 = (short)((new Short((short)343)) / (new Short((short)49)));
    if(s1 == 7)         s += "=s ";
    if(s1 < new Integer(7+1))  s += "fly ";
    System.out.println(s);
  } }
```

Which of the following will be included in the output String s? (Choose all that apply.)

A. `.el`

B. `.e2`

C. `=s`

D. `fly`

E. None of the above.

F. Compilation fails.

G. An exception is thrown at runtime.

Answer:

☑ **B, C,** and **D** are correct. Remember, that the `equals()` method for the integer wrappers will only return `true` if the two primitive types and the two values are equal. With **C**, it's okay to unbox and use `==`. For **D**, it's okay to create a wrapper object with an expression, and unbox it for comparison with a primitive.

☒ **A, E, F,** and **G** are incorrect based on the above. (Remember that **A** is using the `equals()` method to try to compare two different types.) (Objective 3.1)

5. Given:

```
1. import java.text.*;
2. class DateOne {
3.    public static void main(String[] args) {
4.       Date d = new Date(1123631685981L);
5.       DateFormat df = new DateFormat();
6.       System.out.println(df.format(d));
7.    }
8. }
```

And given that 1123631685981L is the number of milliseconds between Jan. 1, 1970, and sometime on Aug. 9, 2005, what is the result? (Note: the time of day in option **A** may vary.)

A. 8/9/05 5:54 PM

B. `1123631685981L`

C. An exception is thrown at runtime.

D. Compilation fails due to a single error in the code.

E. Compilation fails due to multiple errors in the code.

Answer:

☑ **E** is correct. The Date class is located in the `java.util` package so it needs an `import`, and `DateFormat` objects must be created using a static method such as `DateFormat.getInstance()` or `DateFormat.getDateInstance()`.

☒ **A, B, C,** and **D** are incorrect based on the above. (Objective 3.4)

6. Given:

```
import java.io.*;

class Keyboard { }
public class Computer implements Serializable {
  private Keyboard k = new Keyboard();
  public static void main(String[] args) {
    Computer c = new Computer();
    c.storeIt(c);
  }
  void storeIt(Computer c) {
    try {
      ObjectOutputStream os = new ObjectOutputStream(
        new FileOutputStream("myFile"));
      os.writeObject(c);
      os.close();
      System.out.println("done");
    } catch (Exception x) {System.out.println("exc"); }
  }
}
```

What is the result? (Choose all that apply.)

A. exc

B. done

C. Compilation fails.

D. Exactly one object is serialized.

E. Exactly two objects are serialized.

Answer:

☑ **A** is correct. An instance of type Computer Has-a Keyboard. Because Keyboard doesn't implement Serializable, any attempt to serialize an instance of Computer will cause an exception to be thrown.

☒ **B, C, D,** and **E** are incorrect based on the above. If Keyboard did implement Serializable then two objects would have been serialized. (Objective 3.3)

7. Using the fewest fragments possible (and filling the fewest slots possible), complete the code below so that the class builds a directory named "dir3" and creates a file named "file3" inside "dir3". Note you can use each fragment either zero or one times.

Code:

```
import java.io._____

class Maker {
  public static void main(String[] args) {

      _____  _____  _____

      _____  _____  _____

      _____  _____  _____

      _____  _____  _____

      _____  _____  _____

      _____  _____  _____

      _____  _____  _____

} }
```

Fragments:

```
File;         FileDescriptor;     FileWriter;     Directory;
try {         .createNewDir();    File dir        File
{ }           (Exception x)       ("dir3");       file
file          .createNewFile();   = new File      = new File
dir           (dir, "file3");     (dir, file);    .createFile();
} catch       ("dir3", "file3");  .mkdir();       File file
```

Answer:

```
import java.io.File;
class Maker {
  public static void main(String[] args) {
    try {
      File dir = new File("dir3");
      dir.mkdir();
      File file = new File(dir, "file3");
      file.createNewFile();
    } catch (Exception x) { }
} }
```

Notes: The new File statements don't make actual files or directories, just objects. You need the mkdir() and createNewFile() methods to actually create the directory and the file. (Objective 3.2)

8. Which are true? (Choose all that apply.)

A. The `DateFormat.getDate()` is used to convert a String to a Date instance.

B. Both `DateFormat` and `NumberFormat` objects can be constructed to be Locale specific.

C. Both Currency and `NumberFormat` objects must be constructed using static methods.

D. If a `NumberFormat` instance's Locale is to be different than the current Locale, it must be specified at creation time.

E. A single instance of `NumberFormat` can be used to create Number objects from Strings and to create formatted numbers from numbers.

Answer:

☑ **B, C, D,** and **E** are correct.

☒ **A** is incorrect, `DateFormat.parse()` is used to convert a String to a Date. (Objective 3.4)

9. Which will compile and run without exception? (Choose all that apply.)

A. `System.out.format("%b", 123);`

B. `System.out.format("%c", "x");`

C. `System.out.printf("%d", 123);`

D. `System.out.printf("%f", 123);`

E. `System.out.printf("%d", 123.45);`

F. `System.out.printf("%f", 123.45);`

G. `System.out.format("%s", new Long("123"));`

Answer:

☑ **A, C, F,** and **G** are correct. The `%b` (boolean) conversion character returns `true` for any non-`null` or non-boolean argument.

☒ **B** is incorrect, the `%c` (character) conversion character expects a character, not a String. **D** is incorrect, the `%f` (floating-point) conversion character won't automatically promote an integer type. **E** is incorrect, the `%d` (integral) conversion character won't take a floating-point number. (Note: The `format()` and `printf()` methods behave identically.) (Objective 3.5)

10. Which about the three java.lang classes String, StringBuilder, and StringBuffer are true? (Choose all that apply.)

A. All three classes have a `length()` method.

B. Objects of type StringBuffer are thread-safe.

C. All three classes have overloaded `append()` methods.

D. The "+" is an overloaded operator for all three classes.

E. According to the API, StringBuffer will be faster than StringBuilder under most implementations.

F. The value of an instance of any of these three types can be modified through various methods in the API.

Answer:

☑ **A** and **B** are correct.

☒ **C** is incorrect because String does not have an "append" method. **D** is incorrect because only String objects can be operated on using the overloaded "+" operator. **E** is backwards; `StringBuilder` is typically faster because it's not thread-safe. **F** is incorrect because String objects are immutable. A String reference can be altered to refer to a different String object, but the objects themselves are immutable. (Objective 3.1)

11. Given that 1119280000000L is roughly the number of milliseconds from Jan. 1, 1970, to June 20, 2005, and that you want to print that date in German, using the LONG style such that "June" will be displayed as "Juni", complete the code using the fragments below. Note: you can use each fragment either zero or one times, and you might not need to fill all of the slots.

Code:

```
import java._____

import java._____

class DateTwo {
  public static void main(String[] args) {
    Date d = new Date(1119280000000L);

    DateFormat df = _____

                    _____ , _____ );

    System.out.println(_____
  }
}
```

Fragments:

```
io.*;        new DateFormat(              Locale.LONG
nio.*;       DateFormat.getInstance(      Locale.GERMANY
util.*;      DateFormat.getDateInstance(  DateFormat.LONG
text.*;      util.regex;                  DateFormat.GERMANY
date.*;      df.format(d));               d.format(df));
```

Answer:

```
import java.util.*;
import java.text.*;
class DateTwo {
  public static void main(String[] args) {
    Date d = new Date(1119280000000L);
  DateFormat df = DateFormat.getDateInstance(
                  DateFormat.LONG, Locale.GERMANY);
    System.out.println(df.format(d));
  }
}
```

Notes: Remember that you must build DateFormat objects using static methods. Also remember that you must specify a Locale for a DateFormat object at the time of instantiation. The getInstance() method does not take a Locale. (Objective 3.4)

12. Given:

```
import java.io.*;

class Directories {
  static String [] dirs = {"dir1", "dir2"};
  public static void main(String [] args) {
    for (String d : dirs) {

      // insert code 1 here

      File file = new File(path, args[0]);

      // insert code 2 here

    }
  }
}
```

and that the invocation

```
java Directories file2.txt
```

is issued from a directory that has two subdirectories, "dir1" and "dir1", and that "dir1" has a file "file1.txt" and "dir2" has a file "file2.txt", and the output is "false true", which set(s) of code fragments must be inserted? (Choose all that apply.)

A. `String path = d;`

   `System.out.print(file.exists() + " ");`

B. `String path = d;`

   `System.out.print(file.isFile() + " ");`

C. `String path = File.separator + d;`

   `System.out.print(file.exists() + " ");`

D. `String path = File.separator + d;`

   `System.out.print(file.isFile() + " ");`

Answer:

☑ **A and B are correct.** Because you are invoking the program from the directory whose direct subdirectories are to be searched, you don't start your path with a `File.separator` character. The `exists()` method tests for either files or directories; the `isFile()` method tests only for files. Since we're looking for a file, both methods work.

☒ **C and D** are incorrect based on the above. (Objective 3.2)

13. Given:

```
class Polish {
  public static void main(String[] args) {
    int x = 4;
    StringBuffer sb = new StringBuffer("..fedcba");
    sb.delete(3,6);
    sb.insert(3, "az");
```

```
              if(sb.length() > 6)  x = sb.indexOf("b");
              sb.delete((x-3), (x-2));
              System.out.println(sb);
          }
      }
```

What is the result?

A. `.faza`

B. `.fzba`

C. `..azba`

D. `.fazba`

E. `..fezba`

F. Compilation fails.

G. An exception is thrown at runtime.

Answer:

☑ **C** is correct. Remember that `StringBuffer` methods use zero-based indexes, and that ending indexes are typically exclusive.

☒ **A, B, D, E, F,** and **G** are incorrect based on the above. (Objective 3.1)

---

14. Given:

```
1. import java.util.*;
2. class Brain {
3.   public static void main(String[] args) {

4.     // insert code block here

5.   }
6. }
```

Which, inserted independently at line 4, compile and produce the output "123 82"? (Choose all that apply.)

A.   `Scanner sc = new Scanner("123 A 3b c,45, x5x,76 82 L");`
     `while(sc.hasNextInt())  System.out.print(sc.nextInt() + " ");`

B.
```
Scanner sc = new Scanner("123 A 3b c,45, x5x,76 82 L").
                              useDelimiter(" ");
     while(sc.hasNextInt())  System.out.print(sc.nextInt() + " ");
```

C.
```
Scanner sc = new Scanner("123 A 3b c,45, x5x,76 82 L");
     while(sc.hasNext()) {
       if(sc.hasNextInt()) System.out.print(sc.nextInt() + " ");
       else sc.next(); }
```

D.
```
Scanner sc = new Scanner("123 A 3b c,45, x5x,76 82 L").
                       useDelimiter(" ");
     while(sc.hasNext()) {
       if(sc.hasNextInt()) System.out.print(sc.nextInt() + " ");
       else sc.next(); }
```

E.
```
Scanner sc = new Scanner("123 A 3b c,45, x5x,76 82 L");
     do {
       if(sc.hasNextInt()) System.out.print(sc.nextInt() + " ");
       } while ( sc.hasNext() );
```

F.
```
Scanner sc = new Scanner("123 A 3b c,45, x5x,76 82 L").
                              useDelimiter(" ");
     do {
       if(sc.hasNextInt()) System.out.print(sc.nextInt() + " ");
       } while ( sc.hasNext() );
```

Answer:

☑ **C** and **D** are correct. Whitespace is the default delimiter, and the while loop advances through the String using `nextInt()` or `next()`.

☒ **A** and **B** are incorrect because the while loop won't progress past the first non-`int`. **E** and **F** are incorrect. The do loop will loop endlessly once the first non-`int` is found because `hasNext()` does not advance through data. (Objective 3.5)

15. Given:

```
import java.io.*;

public class TestSer {
  public static void main(String[] args) {
    SpecialSerial s = new SpecialSerial();
    try {
      ObjectOutputStream os = new ObjectOutputStream(
        new FileOutputStream("myFile"));
      os.writeObject(s);  os.close();
```

```
        System.out.print(++s.z + " ");

        ObjectInputStream is = new ObjectInputStream(
          new FileInputStream("myFile"));
        SpecialSerial s2 = (SpecialSerial)is.readObject();
        is.close();
        System.out.println(s2.y + " " + s2.z);
      } catch (Exception x) {System.out.println("exc"); }
    }
  }
  class SpecialSerial implements Serializable {
    transient int y = 7;
    static int z = 9;
  }
```

Which are true? (Choose all that apply.)

A. Compilation fails.

B. The output is 10 0 9

C. The output is 10 0 10

D. The output is 10 7 9

E. The output is 10 7 10

F. In order to alter the standard deserialization process you would override the readObject() method in SpecialSerial.

G. In order to alter the standard deserialization process you would override the defaultReadObject() method in SpecialSerial.

Answer:

☑ **C** and **F** are correct. **C** is correct because static and transient variables are not serialized when an object is serialized. **F** is a valid statement.

☒ **A, B, D,** and **E** are incorrect based on the above. **G** is incorrect because you don't override the defaultReadObject() method, you call it from within the overridden readObject() method, along with any custom read operations your class needs. (Objective 3.3)

7

Generics and Collections

G enerics are possibly the most talked about feature of Java 5. Some people love 'em, some people hate 'em, but they're here to stay. At their simplest, they can help make code easier to write, and more robust. At their most complex, they can be very, very hard to create, and maintain. Luckily, the exam creators stuck to the simple end of generics, covering the most common and useful features, and leaving out most of the especially tricky bits. Coverage of collections in this exam has expanded in two ways from the previous exam: the use of generics in collections, and the ability to sort and search through collections.

CERTIFICATION OBJECTIVE

Overriding hashCode() and equals() (Objective 6.2)

6.2   Distinguish between correct and incorrect overrides of corresponding hashCode and equals methods, and explain the difference between == and the equals method.

You're an object. Get used to it. You have state, you have behavior, you have a job. (Or at least your chances of getting one will go up after passing the exam.) If you exclude primitives, everything in Java is an object. Not just an *object*, but an Object with a capital O. Every exception, every event, every array extends from java.lang.Object. For the exam, you don't need to know every method in Object, but you will need to know about the methods listed in Table 7-1.

Chapter 9 covers wait(), notify(), and notifyAll(). The finalize() method was covered in Chapter 3. So in this section we'll look at just the hashCode() and equals() methods. Oh, that leaves out toString(), doesn't it. Okay, we'll cover that right now because it takes two seconds.

The toString() Method   Override toString() when you want a mere mortal to be able to read something meaningful about the objects of your class. Code can call toString() on your object when it wants to read useful details about your object. When you pass an object reference to the System.out.println() method, for example, the object's toString() method is called, and the return of toString() is shown in the following example:

TABLE 7-1	Methods of Class Object Covered on the Exam

Method	Description
`boolean equals (Object obj)`	Decides whether two objects are meaningfully equivalent.
`void finalize()`	Called by garbage collector when the garbage collector sees that the object cannot be referenced.
`int hashCode()`	Returns a hashcode `int` value for an object, so that the object can be used in Collection classes that use hashing, including Hashtable, HashMap, and HashSet.
`final void notify()`	Wakes up a thread that is waiting for this object's lock.
`final void notifyAll()`	Wakes up *all* threads that are waiting for this object's lock.
`final void wait()`	Causes the current thread to wait until another thread calls `notify()` or `notifyAll()` on this subject.
`String toString()`	Returns a "text representation" of the object.

```
public class HardToRead {
   public static void main (String [] args) {
     HardToRead h = new HardToRead();
     System.out.println(h);
   }
}
```

Running the HardToRead class gives us the lovely and meaningful,

```
% java HardToRead
HardToRead@a47e0
```

The preceding output is what you get when you don't override the `toString()` method of class Object. It gives you the class name (at least that's meaningful) followed by the @ symbol, followed by the unsigned hexadecimal representation of the object's hashcode.

Trying to read this output might motivate you to override the `toString()` method in your classes, for example,

```
public class BobTest {
   public static void main (String[] args) {
     Bob f = new Bob("GoBobGo", 19);
```

```
        System.out.println(f);
    }
}
class Bob {
    int shoeSize;
    String nickName;
    Bob(String nickName, int shoeSize) {
        this.shoeSize = shoeSize;
        this.nickName = nickName;
    }
    public String toString() {
        return ("I am a Bob, but you can call me " + nickName +
                ". My shoe size is " + shoeSize);
    }
}
```

This ought to be a bit more readable:

```
% java BobTest
I am a Bob, but you can call me GoBobGo. My shoe size is 19
```

Some people affectionately refer to `toString()` as the "spill-your-guts method," because the most common implementations of `toString()` simply spit out the object's state (in other words, the current values of the important instance variables). That's it for `toString()`. Now we'll tackle `equals()` and `hashCode()`.

Overriding equals()

You learned about the `equals()` method in earlier chapters, where we looked at the wrapper classes. We discussed how comparing two object references using the `==` operator evaluates to `true` only when both references refer to the same object (because `==` simply looks at the bits in the variable, and they're either identical or they're not). You saw that the String class and the wrapper classes have overridden the `equals()` method (inherited from class Object), so that you could compare two different objects (of the same type) to see if their contents are meaningfully equivalent. If two different Integer instances both hold the `int` value 5, as far as you're concerned they are equal. The fact that the value 5 lives in two separate objects doesn't matter.

When you really need to know if two references are identical, use `==`. But when you need to know if the objects themselves (not the references) are equal, use the `equals()` method. For each class you write, you must decide if it makes sense to consider two different instances equal. For some classes, you might decide that two objects can never be equal. For example, imagine a class Car that has instance variables for things like make, model, year, configuration—you certainly don't want your car suddenly to be treated as the very same car as someone with a car that has identical attributes. Your car is your car and you don't want your neighbor Billy driving off in it just because, "hey, it's really the same car; the equals() method said so." So no two cars should ever be considered exactly equal. If two references refer to one car, then you know that both are talking about one car, not two cars that have the same attributes. So in the case of a Car you might not ever need, or want, to override the equals() method. Of course, you know that isn't the end of the story.

What It Means If You Don't Override equals()

There's a potential limitation lurking here: if you don't override a class's equals() method, you won't be able to use those objects as a key in a hashtable and you probably won't get accurate Sets, such that there are no conceptual duplicates.

The equals() method in class Object uses only the == operator for comparisons, so unless you override equals(), two objects are considered equal only if the two references refer to the same object.

Let's look at what it means to not be able to use an object as a hashtable key. Imagine you have a car, a very specific car (say, John's red Subaru Outback as opposed to Mary's purple Mini) that you want to put in a HashMap (a type of hashtable we'll look at later in this chapter), so that you can search on a particular car and retrieve the corresponding Person object that represents the owner. So you add the car instance as the key to the HashMap (along with a corresponding Person object as the value). But now what happens when you want to do a search? You want to say to the HashMap collection, "Here's the car, now give me the Person object that goes with this car." But now you're in trouble unless you still have a reference to the exact object you used as the key when you added it to the Collection. *In other words, you can't make an identical Car object and use it for the search.*

The bottom line is this: if you want objects of your class to be used as keys for a hashtable (or as elements in any data structure that uses equivalency for searching for—and/or retrieving—an object), then you must override equals() so that two different instances can be considered the same. So how would we fix the car? You might override the equals() method so that it compares the unique VIN (Vehicle Identification Number) as the basis of comparison. That way, you can use one instance when you add it to a Collection, and essentially re-create an identical instance when you want to do a search based on that object as the key. Of course, overriding the equals() method for Car also allows the potential that more than one object representing a single unique car can exist, which might not be safe in your design. Fortunately, the String and wrapper classes work well as keys in hashtables—they override the `equals()` method. So rather than using the actual car instance as the key into the car/owner pair, you could simply use a String that represents the unique identifier for the car. That way, you'll never have more than one instance representing a specific car, but you can still use the car—or rather, one of the car's attributes—as the search key.

Implementing an equals() Method

Let's say you decide to override `equals()` in your class. It might look like this:

```
public class EqualsTest {
  public static void main (String [] args) {
    Moof one = new Moof(8);
    Moof two = new Moof(8);
    if (one.equals(two)) {
      System.out.println("one and two are equal");
    }
  }
}
class Moof {
  private int moofValue;
  Moof(int val) {
    moofValue = val;
  }
  public int getMoofValue() {
    return moofValue;
  }
  public boolean equals(Object o) {
    if ((o instanceof Moof) && (((Moof)o).getMoofValue()
        == this.moofValue)) {
      return true;
    } else {
      return false;
    }
  }
}
```

Let's look at this code in detail. In the `main()` method of EqualsTest, we create two Moof instances, passing the same value 8 to the Moof constructor. Now look at the Moof class and let's see what it does with that constructor argument—it assigns the value to the `moofValue` instance variable. Now imagine that you've decided two Moof objects are the same if their `moofValue` is identical. So you override the equals() method and compare the two moofValues. It is that simple. But let's break down what's happening in the equals() method:

```
1. public boolean equals(Object o) {
2.   if ((o instanceof Moof) && (((Moof)o).getMoofValue()
          == this.moofValue)) {
3.      return true;
4.    } else {
5.      return false;
6.    }
7.  }
```

First of all, you must observe all the rules of overriding, and in line 1 we are indeed declaring a valid override of the equals() method we inherited from Object.

Line 2 is where all the action is. Logically, we have to do two things in order to make a valid equality comparison.

First, be sure that the object being tested is of the correct type! It comes in polymorphically as type Object, so you need to do an instanceof test on it. Having two objects of different class types be considered equal is usually not a good idea, but that's a design issue we won't go into here. Besides, you'd still have to do the instanceof test just to be sure that you could cast the object argument to the correct type so that you can access its methods or variables in order to actually do the comparison. Remember, if the object doesn't pass the instanceof test, then you'll get a runtime ClassCastException. For example:

```
public boolean equals(Object o) {
    if (((Moof)o).getMoofValue() == this.moofValue){
      // the preceding line compiles, but it's BAD!
      return true;
    } else {
      return false;
    }
}
```

The (Moof)o cast will fail if o doesn't refer to something that IS-A Moof.

Second, compare the attributes we care about (in this case, just moofValue). Only the developer can decide what makes two instances equal. (For best performance, you're going to want to check the fewest number of attributes.)

In case you were a little surprised by the whole ((Moof)o).getMoofValue() syntax, we're simply casting the object reference, o, just-in-time as we try to call a method that's in the Moof class but not in Object. Remember, without the cast, you can't compile because the compiler would see the object referenced by o as simply, well, an Object. And since the Object class doesn't have a `moofvalue()` method, the compiler would squawk (technical term). But then as we said earlier, even with the cast, the code fails at runtime if the object referenced by o isn't something that's castable to a Moof. So don't ever forget to use the `instanceof` test first. Here's another reason to appreciate the short circuit && operator—if the `instanceof` test fails, we'll never get to the code that does the cast, so we're always safe at runtime with the following:

```
if ((o instanceof Moof) && (((Moof)o).getMoofValue()
        == this.moofValue)) {
    return true;
} else {
    return false;
}
```

So that takes care of `equals()`...

Whoa...not so fast. If you look at the Object class in the Java API spec, you'll find what we call a contract specified in the `equals()` method. A Java contract is a set of rules that should be followed, or rather must be followed if you want to provide a "correct" implementation as others will expect it to be. Or to put it another way, if you don't follow the contract, your code may still compile and run, but your code (or someone else's) may break at runtime in some unexpected way.

exam

watch

Remember that the `equals()`, `hashCode()`, *and* `toString()` *methods are all* `public`. *The following would not be a valid override of the* `equals()` *method, although it might appear to be if you don't look closely enough during the exam:*

```
class Foo { boolean equals(Object o) { } }
```

And watch out for the argument types as well. The following method is an overload, but not an override of the `equals()` *method:*

```
class Boo { public boolean equals(Boo b) { } }
```

exam
ⓦatch

Be sure you're very comfortable with the rules of overriding so that you can identify whether a method from Object is being overridden, overloaded, or illegally redeclared in a class. The `equals()` *method in class Boo changes the argument from Object to Boo, so it becomes an overloaded method and won't be called unless it's from your own code that knows about this new, different method that happens to also be named* `equals()`.

The equals() Contract

Pulled straight from the Java docs, the `equals()` contract says

- It is **reflexive**. For any reference value x, `x.equals(x)` should return `true`.
- It is **symmetric**. For any reference values x and y, `x.equals(y)` should return `true` if and only if `y.equals(x)` returns `true`.
- It is **transitive**. For any reference values x, y, and z, if `x.equals(y)` returns `true` and `y.equals(z)` returns `true`, then `x.equals(z)` must return `true`.
- It is **consistent**. For any reference values x and y, multiple invocations of `x.equals(y)` consistently return `true` or consistently return `false`, provided no information used in equals comparisons on the object is modified.
- For any non-`null` reference value x, `x.equals(null)` should return `false`.

And you're so not off the hook yet. We haven't looked at the `hashCode()` method, but `equals()` and `hashCode()` are bound together by a joint contract that specifies if two objects are considered equal using the `equals()` method, then they must have identical hashcode values. So to be truly safe, your rule of thumb should be, if you override `equals()`, override `hashCode()` as well. So let's switch over to `hashCode()` and see how that method ties in to `equals()`.

Overriding hashCode()

Hashcodes are typically used to increase the performance of large collections of data. The hashcode value of an object is used by some collection classes (we'll look at the collections later in this chapter). Although you can think of it as kind of an object ID number, it isn't necessarily unique. Collections such as HashMap and HashSet use the hashcode value of an object to determine how the object should be *stored* in the collection, and the hashcode is used again to help *locate* the object in the collection. For the exam you do not need to understand the deep details of how the collection classes that use hashing are implemented, but you do need to know which collections use them (but, um, they all have "hash" in the name so you should be good there). You must also be able to recognize an appropriate or correct implementation of `hashCode()`. This does not mean legal and does not even mean efficient. It's perfectly legal to have a terribly inefficient hashcode method in your class, as long as it doesn't violate the contract specified in the Object class documentation (we'll look at that contract in a moment). So for the exam, if you're asked to pick out an appropriate or correct use of hashcode, don't mistake appropriate for legal or efficient.

Understanding Hashcodes

In order to understand what's appropriate and correct, we have to look at how some of the collections use hashcodes.

Imagine a set of buckets lined up on the floor. Someone hands you a piece of paper with a name on it. You take the name and calculate an integer code from it by using A is 1, B is 2, and so on, and adding the numeric values of all the letters in the name together. A given name will always result in the same code; see Figure 7-1.

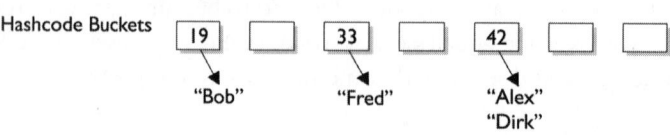

FIGURE 7-1

A simplified hashcode example

Key	Hashcode Algorithm	Hashcode
Alex	A(1) + L(12) + E(5) + X(24)	= 42
Bob	B(2) + O(15) + B(2)	= 19
Dirk	D(4) + I(9) + R(18) + K(11)	= 42
Fred	F(6) + R(18) + E(5) + (D)	= 33

HashMap Collection

Hashcode Buckets: | 19 | [ ] | 33 | [ ] | 42 | [ ] | [ ]

"Bob"   "Fred"   "Alex"
                      "Dirk"

We don't introduce anything random, we simply have an algorithm that will always run the same way given a specific input, so the output will always be identical for any two identical inputs. So far so good? Now the way you use that code (and we'll call it a hashcode now) is to determine which bucket to place the piece of paper into (imagine that each bucket represents a different code number you might get). Now imagine that someone comes up and shows you a name and says, "Please retrieve the piece of paper that matches this name." So you look at the name they show you, and run the same hashcode-generating algorithm. The hashcode tells you in which bucket you should look to find the name.

You might have noticed a little flaw in our system, though. Two different names might result in the same value. For example, the names Amy and May have the same letters, so the hashcode will be identical for both names. That's acceptable, but it does mean that when someone asks you (the bucket-clerk) for the Amy piece of paper, you'll still have to search through the target bucket reading each name until we find Amy rather than May. The hashcode tells you only which bucket to go into, but not how to locate the name once we're in that bucket.

w a t c h

In real-life hashing, it's not uncommon to have more than one entry in a bucket. Hashing retrieval is a two-step process.

1. Find the right bucket (using `hashCode()` *)*

2. Search the bucket for the right element (using `equals()` *).*

So for efficiency, your goal is to have the papers distributed as evenly as possible across all buckets. Ideally, you might have just one name per bucket so that when someone asked for a paper you could simply calculate the hashcode and just grab the one paper from the correct bucket (without having to go flipping through different papers in that bucket until you locate the exact one you're looking for). The least efficient (but still functional) hashcode generator would return the same hashcode (say, 42) regardless of the name, so that all the papers landed in the same bucket while the others stood empty. The bucket-clerk would have to keep going to that one bucket and flipping painfully through each one of the names in the bucket until the right one was found. And if that's how it works, they might as well not use the hashcodes at all but just go to the one big bucket and start from one end and look through each paper until they find the one they want.

This distributed-across-the-buckets example is similar to the way hashcodes are used in collections. When you put an object in a collection that uses hashcodes, the collection uses the hashcode of the object to decide in which bucket/slot the object should land. Then when you want to fetch that object (or, for a hashtable, retrieve the associated value for that object), you have to give the collection a reference to an object that the collection compares to the objects it holds in the collection. As long as the object (stored in the collection, like a paper in the bucket) you're trying to search for has the same hashcode as the object you're using for the search (the name you show to the person working the buckets), then the object will be found. But…and this is a Big One, imagine what would happen if, going back to our name example, you showed the bucket-worker a name and they calculated the code based on only half the letters in the name instead of all of them. They'd never find the name in the bucket because they wouldn't be looking in the correct bucket!

Now can you see why if two objects are considered equal, their hashcodes must also be equal? Otherwise, you'd never be able to find the object since the default hashcode method in class Object virtually always comes up with a unique number for each object, even if the equals() method is overridden in such a way that two or more objects are considered equal. It doesn't matter how equal the objects are if their hashcodes don't reflect that. So one more time: If two objects are equal, their hashcodes must be equal as well.

Implementing hashCode()

What the heck does a real hashcode algorithm look like? People get their PhDs on hashing algorithms, so from a computer science viewpoint, it's beyond the scope of the exam. The part we care about here is the issue of whether you follow the contract. And to follow the contract, think about what you do in the equals() method. You compare attributes. Because that comparison almost always involves instance variable values (remember when we looked at two Moof objects and considered them equal if their int moofValues were the same?). Your hashCode() implementation should use the same instance variables. Here's an example:

```
class HasHash {
  public int x;
  HasHash(int xVal) { x = xVal; }

  public boolean equals(Object o) {
    HasHash h = (HasHash) o; // Don't try at home without
                             // instanceof test
    if (h.x == this.x) {
      return true;
    } else {
      return false;
    }
```

```
   }
   public int hashCode() { return (x * 17); }
}
```

This `equals()` method says two objects are equal if they have the same x value, so objects with the same x value will have to return identical hashcodes.

e x a m

w a t c h

A `hashCode()` *that returns the same value for all instances whether they're equal or not is still a legal—even appropriate—*`hashCode()` *method! For example,*

```
   public int hashCode() { return 1492; }
```

This does not violate the contract. Two objects with an x *value of* 8 *will have the same hashcode. But then again, so will two unequal objects, one with an* x *value of* 12 *and the other a value of* -920. *This* `hashCode()` *method is horribly inefficient, remember, because it makes all objects land in the same bucket, but even so, the object can still be found as the collection cranks through the one and only bucket—using* `equals()`*—trying desperately to finally, painstakingly, locate the correct object. In other words, the hashcode was really no help at all in speeding up the search, even though improving search speed is hashcode's intended purpose! Nonetheless, this one-hash-fits-all method would be considered appropriate and even correct because it doesn't violate the contract. Once more, correct does not necessarily mean good.*

Typically, you'll see `hashCode()` methods that do some combination of ^-ing (XOR-ing) a class's instance variables (in other words, twiddling their bits), along with perhaps multiplying them by a prime number. In any case, while the goal is to get a wide and random distribution of objects across buckets, the contract (and whether or not an object can be found) requires only that two equal objects have equal hashcodes. The exam does not expect you to rate the efficiency of a `hashCode()` method, but you must be able to recognize which ones will and will not work (work meaning "will cause the object to be found in the collection").

Now that we know that two equal objects must have identical hashcodes, is the reverse true? Do two objects with identical hashcodes have to be considered equal? Think about it—you might have lots of objects land in the same bucket because their hashcodes are identical, but unless they also pass the `equals()` test, they won't come up as a match in a search through the collection. This is exactly what you'd get with our very inefficient everybody-gets-the-same-hashcode method. It's legal and correct, just slooooow.

So in order for an object to be located, the search object and the object in the collection must have both identical hashcode values and return `true` for the `equals()` method. So there's just no way out of overriding both methods to be absolutely certain that your objects can be used in Collections that use hashing.

The hashCode() Contract

Now coming to you straight from the fabulous Java API documentation for class Object, may we present (drum roll) the `hashCode()` contract:

- Whenever it is invoked on the same object more than once during an execution of a Java application, the `hashCode()` method must consistently return the same integer, provided no information used in `equals()` comparisons on the object is modified. This integer need not remain consistent from one execution of an application to another execution of the same application.

- If two objects are equal according to the `equals(Object)` method, then calling the `hashCode()` method on each of the two objects must produce the same integer result.

- It is NOT required that if two objects are unequal according to the `equals(java.lang.Object)` method, then calling the `hashCode()` method on each of the two objects must produce distinct integer results. However, the programmer should be aware that producing distinct integer results for unequal objects may improve the performance of hashtables.

And what this means to you is…

Condition	Required	Not Required (But Allowed)
`x.equals(y) == true`	`x.hashCode() == y.hashCode()`	
`x.hashCode() == y.hashCode()`		`x.equals(y) == true`
`x.equals(y) == false`		`No hashCode() requirements`
`x.hashCode() != y.hashCode()`	`x.equals(y) == false`	

So let's look at what else might cause a `hashCode()` method to fail. What happens if you include a transient variable in your `hashCode()` method? While that's legal (compiler won't complain), under some circumstances an object you put in a collection won't be found. As you know, serialization saves an object so that it can be reanimated later by deserializing it back to full objectness. But danger Will Robinson—remember that transient variables are not saved when an object is serialized. A bad scenario might look like this:

```
class SaveMe implements Serializable{
  transient int x;
  int y;
   SaveMe(int xVal, int yVal) {
      x = xVal;
      y = yVal;
   }
  public int hashCode() {
     return (x ^ y);        // Legal, but not correct to
                            // use a transient variable
  }
  public boolean equals(Object o) {
     SaveMe test = (SaveMe)o;
     if (test.y == y && test.x == x) { // Legal, not correct
       return true;
     } else {
       return false;
     }
  }
}
```

Here's what could happen using code like the preceding example:

1. Give an object some state (assign values to its instance variables).
2. Put the object in a HashMap, using the object as a key.
3. Save the object to a file using serialization without altering any of its state.
4. Retrieve the object from the file through deserialization.
5. Use the deserialized (brought back to life on the heap) object to get the object out of the HashMap.

Oops. The object in the collection and the supposedly same object brought back to life are no longer identical. The object's transient variable will come back with a default value rather than the value the variable had at the time it was saved (or put into the HashMap). So using the preceding SaveMe code, if the value of x is 9 when the instance is put in the HashMap, then since x is used in the calculation of the hashcode, when the value of x changes, the hashcode changes too. And when that same instance of SaveMe is brought back from deserialization, x == 0, regardless of the value of x at the time the object was serialized. So the new hashcode calculation will give a different hashcode, and the equals() method fails as well since x is used to determine object equality.

Bottom line: transient variables can really mess with your equals() and hashCode() implementations. Keep variables non-transient or, if they must be marked transient, don't use then to determine hashcodes or equality.

CERTIFICATION OBJECTIVE

Collections (Exam Objective 6.1)

6.1   Given a design scenario, determine which collection classes and/or interfaces should be used to properly implement that design, including the use of the Comparable interface.

Can you imagine trying to write object-oriented applications without using data structures like hashtables or linked lists? What would you do when you needed to maintain a sorted list of, say, all the members in your Simpsons fan club? Obviously you can do it yourself; Amazon.com must have thousands of algorithm books you can buy. But with the kind of schedules programmers are under today, it's almost too painful to consider.

The Collections Framework in Java, which took shape with the release of JDK 1.2 and was expanded in 1.4 and again in Java 5, gives you lists, sets, maps, and queues to satisfy most of your coding needs. They've been tried, tested, and tweaked. Pick the best one for your job and you'll get—at the least—reasonable performance. And when you need something a little more custom, the Collections Framework in the java.util package is loaded with interfaces and utilities.

So What Do You Do with a Collection?

There are a few basic operations you'll normally use with collections:

- Add objects to the collection.
- Remove objects from the collection.

- Find out if an object (or group of objects) is in the collection.
- Retrieve an object from the collection (without removing it).
- Iterate through the collection, looking at each element (object) one after another.

Key Interfaces and Classes of the Collections Framework

For the exam you'll need to know which collection to choose based on a stated requirement. The collections API begins with a group of interfaces, but also gives you a truckload of concrete classes. The core interfaces you need to know for the exam (and life in general) are the following seven:

Collection	Set	SortedSet
List	Map	SortedMap
Queue		

The core concrete implementation classes you need to know for the exam are the following 13 (there are others, but the exam doesn't specifically cover them):

Maps	Sets	Lists	Queues	Utilities
HashMap	HashSet	ArrayList	PriorityQueue	Collections
Hashtable	LinkedHashSet	Vector		Arrays
TreeMap	TreeSet	LinkedList		
LinkedHashMap				

Not all collections in the Collections Framework actually implement the Collection interface. In other words, not all collections pass the IS-A test for Collection. Specifically, none of the Map-related classes and interfaces extend from Collection. So while SortedMap, Hashtable, HashMap, TreeMap, and LinkedHashMap are all thought of as collections, none are actually extended from Collection-with-a-capital-C (see Figure 7-2). To make things a little more confusing, there are really three overloaded uses of the word "collection":

- collection (lowercase *c*), which represents any of the data structures in which objects are stored and iterated over.

- Collection (capital C), which is actually the java.util.Collection interface from which Set, List, and Queue extend. (That's right, extend, not implement. There are no direct implementations of Collection.)

- Collections (capital C and ends with *s*) is the java.util.Collections class that holds a pile of `static` utility methods for use with collections.

FIGURE 7-2   The interface and class hierarchy for collections

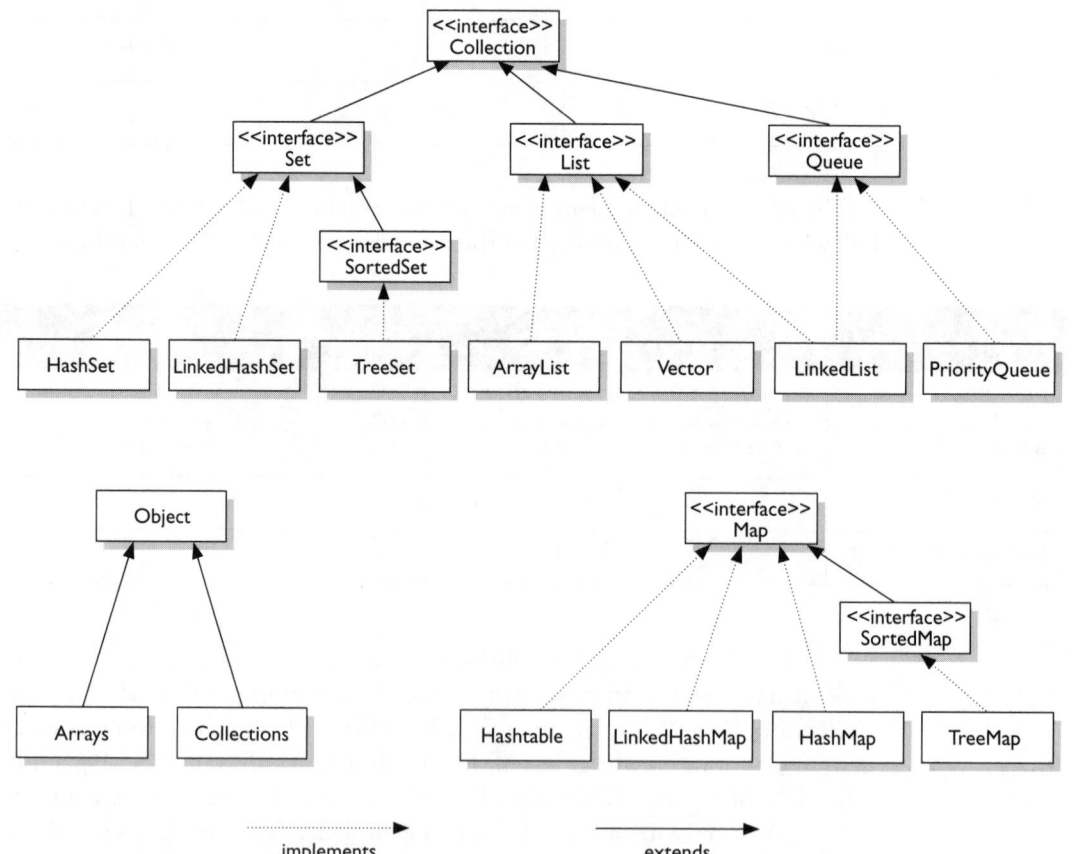

e x a m

🕝 a t c h
You can so easily mistake "Collections" for "Collection"—be careful. Keep in mind that Collections is a class, with static utility methods, while Collection is an interface with declarations of the methods common to most collections including `add()`, `remove()`, `contains()`, `size()`, *and* `iterator()`.

Collections come in four basic flavors:

- **Lists** *Lists* of things (classes that implement List).
- **Sets** *Unique* things (classes that implement Set).
- **Maps** Things with a *unique* ID (classes that implement Map).
- **Queues** Things arranged by the order in which they are to be processed.

Figure 7-3 illustrates the structure of a List, a Set, and a Map.

FIGURE 7-3

The structure of a List, a Set, and a Map

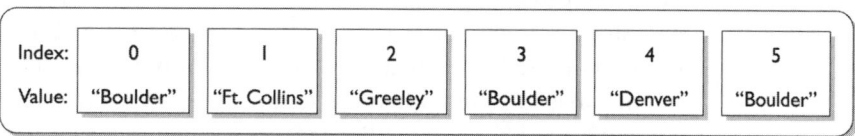

List: The salesman's itinerary (Duplicates allowed)

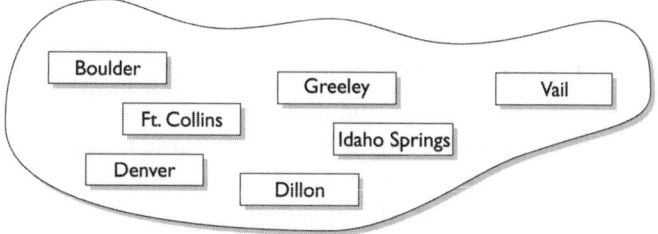

Set: The salesman's territory (No duplicates allowed)

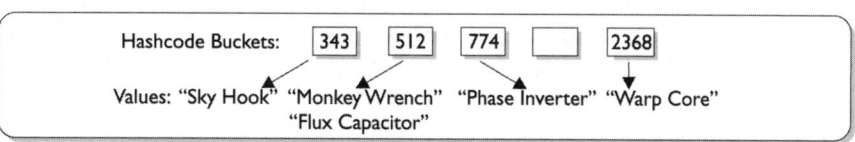

HashMap: the salesman's products (Keys generated from product IDs)

But there are sub-flavors within those four flavors of collections:

Sorted	Unsorted	Ordered	Unordered

An implementation class can be unsorted and unordered, ordered but unsorted, or both ordered and sorted. But an implementation can never be sorted but unordered, because sorting is a specific type of ordering, as you'll see in a moment. For example, a HashSet is an unordered, unsorted set, while a LinkedHashSet is an ordered (but not sorted) set that maintains the order in which objects were inserted.

Maybe we should be explicit about the difference between sorted and ordered, but first we have to discuss the idea of iteration. When you think of iteration, you may think of iterating over an array using, say, a `for` loop to access each element in the array in order ([0], [1], [2], and so on). Iterating through a collection usually means walking through the elements one after another starting from the first element. Sometimes, though, even the concept of *first* is a little strange—in a Hashtable there really isn't a notion of first, second, third, and so on. In a Hashtable, the elements are placed in a (seemingly) chaotic order based on the hashcode of the key. But something has to go first when you iterate; thus, when you iterate over a Hashtable, there will indeed be an order. But as far as you can tell, it's completely arbitrary and can change in apparently random ways as the collection changes.

Ordered   When a collection is ordered, it means you can iterate through the collection in a specific (not-random) order. A Hashtable collection is not ordered. Although the Hashtable itself has internal logic to determine the order (based on hashcodes and the implementation of the collection itself), you won't find any order when you iterate through the Hashtable. An ArrayList, however, keeps the order established by the elements' index position (just like an array). LinkedHashSet keeps the order established by insertion, so the last element inserted is the last element in the LinkedHashSet (as opposed to an ArrayList, where you can insert an element at a specific index position). Finally, there are some collections that keep an order referred to as the natural order of the elements, and those collections are then not just ordered, but also sorted. Let's look at how natural order works for sorted collections.

Sorted   A *sorted* collection means that the order in the collection is determined according to some rule or rules, known as the sort order. A sort order has nothing to do with when an object was added to the collection, or when was the last time it was accessed, or what "position" it was added at. Sorting is done based on properties of the objects themselves. You put objects into the collection, and the collection will figure out what order to put them in, based on the sort order. A collection that keeps an order (such as any List, which uses insertion order) is not really considered *sorted* unless it sorts using some king of sort order. Most commonly, the sort order used is something called the *natural* order. What does that mean?

You know how to sort alphabetically—A comes before B, F comes before G, and so on. For a collection of String objects, then, the natural order is alphabetical. For Integer objects, the natural order is by numeric value—1 before 2, and so on. And for Foo objects, the natural order is...um...we don't know. There is no natural order for Foo unless or until the Foo developer provides one, through an interface (*Comparable*)that defines how instances of a class can be compared to one another (does instance a come before b, or does instance b before a?). If the developer decides that Foo objects should be compared using the value of some instance variable (let's say there's one called `bar`), then a sorted collection will order the Foo objects according to the rules in the Foo class for how to use the bar instance variable to determine the order. Of course, the Foo class might also inherit a natural order from a superclass rather than define its own order, in some cases.

Aside from natural order as specified by the Comparable interface, it's also possible to define other, different sort orders using another interface: *Comparator*. We will discuss how to use both Comparable and Comparator to define sort orders later in this chapter. But for now, just keep in mind that sort order (including natural order) is not the same as ordering by insertion, access, or index.

Now that we know about ordering and sorting, we'll look at each of the four interfaces, and we'll dive into the concrete implementations of those interfaces.

List Interface

A List cares about the index. The one thing that List has that non-lists don't have is a set of methods related to the index. Those key methods include things like `get(int index)`, `indexOf(Object o)`, `add(int index, Object obj)`, and so on. All three List implementations are ordered by index position—a position that you determine either by setting an object at a specific index or by adding it without specifying position, in which case the object is added to the end. The three List implementations are described in the following sections.

ArrayList   Think of this as a growable array. It gives you fast iteration and fast random access. To state the obvious: it is an ordered collection (by index), but not sorted. You might want to know that as of version 1.4, ArrayList now implements the new RandomAccess interface—a marker interface (meaning it has no methods) that says, "this list supports fast (generally constant time) random access." Choose this over a LinkedList when you need fast iteration but aren't as likely to be doing a lot of insertion and deletion.

Vector   Vector is a holdover from the earliest days of Java; Vector and Hashtable were the two original collections, the rest were added with Java 2 versions 1.2 and 1.4. A Vector is basically the same as an ArrayList, but Vector methods are syn-chronized for thread safety. You'll normally want to use ArrayList instead of Vector because the synchronized methods add a performance hit you might not need. And if you do need thread safety, there are utility methods in class Collections that can help. Vector is the only class other than ArrayList to implement RandomAccess.

LinkedList   A LinkedList is ordered by index position, like ArrayList, except that the elements are doubly-linked to one another. This linkage gives you new methods (beyond what you get from the List interface) for adding and removing from the beginning or end, which makes it an easy choice for implementing a stack or queue. Keep in mind that a LinkedList may iterate more slowly than an ArrayList, but it's a good choice when you need fast insertion and deletion. As of Java 5, the LinkedList class has been enhanced to implement the java.util.Queue interface. As such, it now supports the common queue methods: `peek()`, `poll()`, and `offer()`.

Set Interface

A Set cares about uniqueness—it doesn't allow duplicates. Your good friend the `equals()` method determines whether two objects are identical (in which case only one can be in the set). The three Set implementations are described in the following sections.

HashSet   A HashSet is an unsorted, unordered Set. It uses the hashcode of the object being inserted, so the more efficient your `hashCode()` implementation the better access performance you'll get. Use this class when you want a collection with no duplicates and you don't care about order when you iterate through it.

LinkedHashSet   A LinkedHashSet is an ordered version of HashSet that maintains a doubly-linked List across all elements. Use this class instead of HashSet when you care about the iteration order. When you iterate through a HashSet the order is unpredictable, while a LinkedHashSet lets you iterate through the elements in the order in which they were inserted.

e x a m

ⓦ a t c h

When using HashSet or LinkedHashSet, the objects you add to them must override `hashCode()`*. If they don't override* `hashCode()`*, the default* `Object.` `hashCode()` *method will allow multiple objects that you might consider "meaningfully equal" to be added to your "no duplicates allowed" set.*

TreeSet   The TreeSet is one of two sorted collections (the other being TreeMap). It uses a Red-Black tree structure (but you knew that), and guarantees that the elements will be in ascending order, according to natural order. Optionally, you can construct a TreeSet with a constructor that lets you give the collection your own rules for what the order should be (rather than relying on the ordering defined by the elements' class) by using a Comparable or Comparator.

Map Interface

A Map cares about unique identifiers. You map a unique key (the ID) to a specific value, where both the key and the value are, of course, objects. You're probably quite familiar with Maps since many languages support data structures that use a key/value or name/value pair. The Map implementations let you do things like search for a value based on the key, ask for a collection of just the values, or ask for a collection of just the keys. Like Sets, Maps rely on the `equals()` method to determine whether two keys are the same or different.

HashMap   The HashMap gives you an unsorted, unordered Map. When you need a Map and you don't care about the order (when you iterate through it), then HashMap is the way to go; the other maps add a little more overhead. Where the keys land in the Map is based on the key's hashcode, so, like HashSet, the more efficient your `hashCode()` implementation, the better access performance you'll get. HashMap allows one `null` key and multiple `null` values in a collection.

Hashtable   Like Vector, Hashtable has existed from prehistoric Java times. For fun, don't forget to note the naming inconsistency: HashMap vs. Hashtable. Where's the capitalization of *t*? Oh well, you won't be expected to spell it. Anyway, just as Vector is a synchronized counterpart to the sleeker, more modern ArrayList, Hashtable is the synchronized counterpart to HashMap. Remember that you don't synchronize a class, so when we say that Vector and Hashtable are synchronized, we just mean that the key methods of the class are synchronized. Another difference, though, is that while HashMap lets you have `null` values as well as one `null` key, a Hashtable doesn't let you have anything that's `null`.

LinkedHashMap   Like its Set counterpart, LinkedHashSet, the LinkedHashMap collection maintains insertion order (or, optionally, access order). Although it will be somewhat slower than HashMap for adding and removing elements, you can expect faster iteration with a LinkedHashMap.

TreeMap   You can probably guess by now that a TreeMap is a sorted Map. And you already know that by default, this means "sorted by the natural order of the elements." Like TreeSet, TreeMap lets you define a custom sort order (via a Comparable or Comparator) when you construct a TreeMap, that specifies how the elements should be compared to one another when they're being ordered.

Queue Interface

A Queue is designed to hold a list of "to-dos," or things to be processed in some way. Although other orders are possible, queues are typically thought of as FIFO (first-in, first-out). Queues support all of the standard Collection methods and they also add methods to add and subtract elements and review queue elements.

PriorityQueue   This class is new with Java 5. Since the LinkedList class has been enhanced to implement the Queue interface, basic queues can be handled with a LinkedList. The purpose of a PriorityQueue is to create a "priority-in, priority out" queue as opposed to a typical FIFO queue. A PriorityQueue's elements are ordered either by natural ordering (in which case the elements that are sorted first will be accessed first) or according to a Comparator. In either case, the elements' ordering represents their relative priority.

exam
ⓦatch
You can easily eliminate some answers right away if you recognize that, for example, a Map can't be the class to choose when you need a name/value pair collection, since Map is an interface and not a concrete implementation class. The wording on the exam is explicit when it matters, so if you're asked to choose an interface, choose an interface rather than a class that implements that interface. The reverse is also true—if you're asked to choose a class, don't choose an interface type.

Table 7-2 summarizes the 11 of the 13 concrete collection-oriented classes you'll need to understand for the exam. (Arrays and Collections are coming right up!)

TABLE 7-2   Collection Interface Concrete Implementation Classes

Class	Map	Set	List	Ordered	Sorted
HashMap	x			No	No
HashTable	x			No	No
TreeMap	x			Sorted	By *natural order* or custom comparison rules
LinkedHashMap	x			By insertion order or last access order	No
HashSet		x		No	No
TreeSet		x		Sorted	By *natural order* or custom comparison rules
LinkedHashSet		x		By insertion order	No
ArrayList			x	By index	No
Vector			x	By index	No
LinkedList			x	By index	No
PriorityQueue				Sorted	By to-do order

e x a m

w a t c h

Be sure you know how to interpret Table 7-2 in a practical way. For the exam, you might be expected to choose a collection based on a particular requirement, where that need is expressed as a scenario. For example, which collection would you use if you needed to maintain and search on a list of parts, identified by their unique alphanumeric serial number where the part would be of type Part? Would you change your answer at all if we modified the requirement such that you also need to be able to print out the parts in order, by their serial number? For the first question, you can see that since you have a Part class, but need to search for the objects based on a serial number, you need a Map. The key will be the serial number as a String, and the value will be the Part instance. The default choice should be HashMap, the quickest Map for access. But now when we amend the requirement to include getting the parts in order of their serial number, then we need a TreeMap—which maintains the natural order of the keys. Since the key is a String, the natural order for a String will be a standard alphabetical sort. If the requirement had been to keep track of which part was last accessed, then we'd probably need a LinkedHashMap. But since a LinkedHashMap loses the natural order (replacing it with last- accessed order), if we need to list the parts by serial number, we'll have to explicitly sort the collection, using a utility method.

CERTIFICATION OBJECTIVE

Using the Collections Framework (Objective 6.5)

6.5   Use capabilities in the java.util package to write code to manipulate a list by sorting, performing a binary search, or converting the list to an array. Use capabilities in the java.util package to write code to manipulate an array by sorting, performing a binary search, or converting the array to a list. Use the java.util.Comparator and java.lang.Comparable interfaces to affect the sorting of lists and arrays. Furthermore, recognize the effect of the "natural ordering" of primitive wrapper classes and java.lang. String on sorting.

We've taken a high-level, theoretical look at the key interfaces and classes in the Collections Framework, now let's see how they work in practice.

ArrayList Basics

The `java.util.ArrayList` class is one of the most commonly used of all the classes in the Collections Framework. It's like an array on vitamins. Some of the advantages `ArrayList` has over arrays are

- It can grow dynamically.
- It provides more powerful insertion and search mechanisms than arrays.

Let's take a look at using an `ArrayList` that contains Strings. A key design goal of the Collections Framework was to provide rich functionality at the level of the main interfaces: List, Set, and Map. In practice, you'll typically want to instantiate an `ArrayList` polymorphically like this:

```
List myList = new ArrayList();
```

As of Java 5 you'll want to say

```
List<String> myList = new ArrayList<String>();
```

This kind of declaration follows the object oriented programming principle of "coding to an interface", and it makes use of generics. We'll say lots more about generics later in this chapter, but for now just know that, as of Java 5, the <String> syntax is the way that you declare a collection's type. (Prior to Java 5 there was no way to specify the type of a collection, and when we cover generics, we'll talk about the implications of mixing Java 5 (typed) and pre-Java 5 (untyped) collections.)

In many ways, `ArrayList<String>` is similar to a `String[]` in that it declares a container that can hold only Strings, but it's more powerful than a `String[]`. Let's look at some of the capabilities that an `ArrayList` has:

```
import java.util.*;
public class TestArrayList {
  public static void main(String[] args) {
    List<String> test = new ArrayList<String>();
    String s = "hi";
    test.add("string");
    test.add(s);
    test.add(s+s);
    System.out.println(test.size());
    System.out.println(test.contains(42));
```

```
        System.out.println(test.contains("hihi"));
        test.remove("hi");
        System.out.println(test.size());
    } }
```

which produces:

```
3
false
true
2
```

There's lots going on in this small program. Notice that when we declared the `ArrayList` we didn't give it a size. Then we were able to ask the `ArrayList` for its size, we were able to ask it whether it contained specific objects, we removed an object right out from the middle of it, and then we re-checked its size.

Autoboxing with Collections

In general, collections can hold Objects but not primitives. Prior to Java 5, a very common use for the wrapper classes was to provide a way to get a primitive into a collection. Prior to Java 5, you had to wrap a primitive by hand before you could put it into a collection. With Java 5, primitives still have to be wrapped, but autoboxing takes care of it for you.

```
List myInts = new ArrayList();   // pre Java 5 declaration
myInts.add(new Integer(42));     // had to wrap an int
```

As of Java 5 we can say

```
myInts.add(42);                          // autoboxing handles it!
```

In this last example, we are still adding an `Integer` object to `myInts` (not an `int` primitive); it's just that autoboxing handles the wrapping for us.

Sorting Collections and Arrays

Sorting and searching topics have been added to the exam for Java 5. Both collections and arrays can be sorted and searched using methods in the API.

Sorting Collections

Let's start with something simple like sorting an ArrayList of Strings alphabetically. What could be easier? Okay, we'll wait while you go find ArrayList's sort() method...got it? Of course, ArrayList doesn't give you any way to sort its contents, but the java.util.Collections class does:

```java
import java.util.*;
class TestSort1 {
  public static void main(String[] args) {
    ArrayList<String> stuff = new ArrayList<String>(); // #1
    stuff.add("Denver");
    stuff.add("Boulder");
    stuff.add("Vail");
    stuff.add("Aspen");
    stuff.add("Telluride");
    System.out.println("unsorted " + stuff);
    Collections.sort(stuff);                            // #2
    System.out.println("sorted    " + stuff);
  }
}
```

This produces something like this:

```
unsorted [Denver, Boulder, Vail, Aspen, Telluride]
sorted    [Aspen, Boulder, Denver, Telluride, Vail]
```

Line 1 is declaring an ArrayList of Strings, and line 2 is sorting the ArrayList alphabetically. We'll talk more about the Collections class, along with the Arrays class in a later section, for now let's keep sorting stuff.

Let's imagine we're building the ultimate home-automation application. Today we're focused on the home entertainment center, and more specifically the DVD control center. We've already got the file I/O software in place to read and write data between the dvdInfo.txt file and instances of class DVDInfo. Here are the key aspects of the class:

```java
class DVDInfo {
  String title;
  String genre;
  String leadActor;
  DVDInfo(String t, String g, String a) {
```

```
    title = t;  genre = g;  leadActor = a;
  }
  public String toString() {
    return title + " " + genre + " " + leadActor + "\n";
  }
  // getters and setter go here
}
```

Here's the DVD data that's in the `dvdinfo.txt` file:

```
Donnie Darko/sci-fi/Gyllenhall, Jake
Raiders of the Lost Ark/action/Ford, Harrison
2001/sci-fi/??
Caddy Shack/comedy/Murray, Bill
Star Wars/sci-fi/Ford, Harrison
Lost in Translation/comedy/Murray, Bill
Patriot Games/action/Ford, Harrison
```

In our home-automation application, we want to create an instance of `DVDInfo` for each line of data we read in from the `dvdinfo.txt` file. For each instance, we will parse the line of data (remember `String.split()`?) and populate `DVDInfo`'s three instance variables. Finally, we want to put all of the `DVDInfo` instances into an ArrayList. Imagine that the `populateList()` method (below) does all of this. Here is a small piece of code from our application:

```
ArrayList<DVDInfo> dvdList = new ArrayList<DVDInfo>();
populateList();   // adds the file data to the ArrayList
System.out.println(dvdList);
```

You might get output like this:

```
[Donnie Darko sci-fi Gyllenhall, Jake
, Raiders of the Lost Ark action Ford, Harrison
, 2001 sci-fi ??
, Caddy Shack comedy Murray, Bill
, Star Wars sci-fi Ford, Harrison
, Lost in Translation comedy Murray, Bill
, Patriot Games action Ford, Harrison
]
```

(Note: We overrode `DVDInfo`'s `toString()` method, so when we invoked `println()` on the ArrayList it invoked `toString()` for each instance.)

Now that we've got a populated ArrayList, let's sort it:

```
Collections.sort(dvdlist);
```

Oops!, you get something like this:

```
TestDVD.java:13: cannot find symbol
symbol   : method sort(java.util.ArrayList<DVDInfo>)
location: class java.util.Collections
    Collections.sort(dvdlist);
```

What's going on here? We know that the Collections class has a `sort()` method, yet this error implies that Collections does NOT have a `sort()` method that can take a `dvdlist`. That means there must be something wrong with the argument we're passing (`dvdinfo`).

If you've already figured out the problem, our guess is that you did it without the help of the obscure error message shown above…How the heck do you sort instances of `DVDInfo`? Why were we able to sort instances of String? When you look up `Collections.sort()` in the API your first reaction might be to panic. Hang tight, once again the generics section will help you read that weird looking method signature. If you read the description of the one-arg `sort()` method, you'll see that the `sort()` method takes a List argument, and that the objects in the List must implement an interface called Comparable. It turns out that String implements Comparable, and that's why we were able to sort a list of Strings using the `Collections.sort()` method.

The Comparable Interface

The `Comparable` interface is used by the `Collections.sort()` method and the `java.utils.Arrays.sort()` method to sort Lists and arrays of objects, respectively. To implement `Comparable`, a class must implement a single method, `compareTo()`. Here's an invocation of `compareTo()`:

```
int x = thisObject.compareTo(anotherObject);
```

The `compareTo()` method returns an int with the following characteristics:

- negative   If `thisObject` < `anotherObject`
- zero   If `thisObject` == `anotherObject`
- positive   If `thisObject` > `anotherObject`

The sort() method uses compareTo() to determine how the List or object array should be sorted. Since you get to implement compareTo() for your own classes, you can use whatever weird criteria you prefer, to sort instances of your classes. Returning to our earlier example for class DVDInfo, we can take the easy way out and use the String class's implementation of compareTo():

```
class DVDInfo implements Comparable<DVDInfo> {    // #1
  // existing code
  public int compareTo(DVDInfo d) {
    return title.compareTo(d.getTitle());         // #2
} }
```

In line 1 we declare that class DVDInfo implements Comparable in such a way that DVDInfo objects can be compared to other DVDInfo objects. In line 2 we implement compareTo() by comparing the two DVDInfo object's titles. Since we know that the titles are Strings, and that String implements Comparable, this is an easy way to sort our DVDInfo objects, by title. Before generics came along in Java 5, you would have had to implement Comparable something like this:

```
class DVDInfo implements Comparable {
  // existing code
  public int compareTo(Object o) {    // takes an Object rather
                                      // than a specific type
    DVDInfo d = (DVDInfo)o;
    return title.compareTo(d.getTitle());
} }
```

This is still legal, but you can see that it's both painful and risky, because you have to do a cast, and you need to verify that the cast will not fail before you try it.

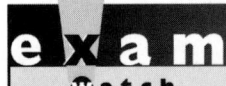

It's important to remember that when you override equals() **you MUST take an argument of type** *Object,* **but that when you override** compareTo() **you should take an argument of the type you're sorting.**

Putting it all together, our DVDInfo class should now look like this:

```
class DVDInfo implements Comparable<DVDInfo> {
  String title;
  String genre;
  String leadActor;
  DVDInfo(String t, String g, String a) {
    title = t;  genre = g;  leadActor = a;
  }
  public String toString() {
    return title + " " + genre + " " + leadActor + "\n";
  }
  public int compareTo(DVDInfo d) {
    return title.compareTo(d.getTitle());
  }
  public String getTitle() {
    return title;
  }
  // other getters and setters
}
```

Now, when we invoke `Collections.sort(dvdlist);` we get

```
[2001 sci-fi ??
, Caddy Shack comedy Murray, Bill
, Donnie Darko sci-fi Gyllenhall, Jake
, Lost in Translation comedy Murray, Bill
, Patriot Games action Ford, Harrison
, Raiders of the Lost Ark action Ford, Harrison
, Star Wars sci-fi Ford, Harrison
]
```

Hooray! Our ArrayList has been sorted by title. Of course, if we want our home automation system to really rock, we'll probably want to sort DVD collections in lots of different ways. Since we sorted our ArrayList by implementing the compareTo() method, we seem to be stuck. We can only implement compareTo() once in a class, so how do we go about sorting our classes in an order different than what we specify in our compareTo() method? Good question. As luck would have it, the answer is coming up next.

Sorting with Comparator

While you were looking up the `Collections.sort()` method you might have noticed that there is an overloaded version of `sort()` that takes a List, AND something called a *Comparator*. The Comparator interface gives you the capability to sort a given collection any number of different ways. The other handy thing about the Comparator interface is that you can use it to sort instances of any class—even classes you can't modify—unlike the Comparable interface, which forces you to change the class whose instances you want to sort. The Comparator interface is also very easy to implement, having only one method, `compare()`. Here's a small class that can be used to sort a List of DVDInfo instances, by `genre`.

```
import java.util.*;
class GenreSort implements Comparator<DVDInfo> {
  public int compare(DVDInfo one, DVDInfo two) {
    return one.getGenre().compareTo(two.getGenre());
  }
}
```

The `Comparator.compare()` method returns an `int` whose meaning is the same as the `Comparable.compareTo()` method's return value. In this case we're taking advantage of that by asking `compareTo()` to do the actual comparison work for us. Here's a test program that lets us test both our Comparable code and our new Comparator code:

```
import java.util.*;
import java.io.*;              // populateList() needs this
public class TestDVD {
  ArrayList<DVDInfo> dvdlist = new ArrayList<DVDInfo>();
  public static void main(String[] args) {
    new TestDVD().go();
  }
  public void go() {
    populateList();
    System.out.println(dvdlist);     // output as read from file
    Collections.sort(dvdlist);
    System.out.println(dvdlist);     // output sorted by title

    GenreSort gs = new GenreSort();
    Collections.sort(dvdlist, gs);
    System.out.println(dvdlist);     // output sorted by genre
  }
```

```
   public void populateList() {
       // read the file, create DVDInfo instances, and
       // populate the ArrayList dvdlist with these instances
   }
}
```

You've already seen the first two output lists, here's the third:

```
[Patriot Games action Ford, Harrison
, Raiders of the Lost Ark action Ford, Harrison
, Caddy Shack comedy Murray, Bill
, Lost in Translation comedy Murray, Bill
, 2001 sci-fi ??
, Donnie Darko sci-fi Gyllenhall, Jake
, Star Wars sci-fi Ford, Harrison
]
```

Because the Comparable and Comparator interfaces are so similar, expect the exam to try to confuse you. For instance you might be asked to implement the compareTo() method in the Comparator interface. Study Table 7-3 to burn in the differences between these two interfaces.

TABLE 7-3   Comparing Comparable to Comparator

java.lang.**Comparable**	java.util.**Comparator**
int objOne.compareTo(objTwo)	int compare(objOne, objTwo)

Returns
   negative   if objOne < objTwo
   zero   if objOne == objTwo
   positive   if objOne > objTwo
	Same as Comparable

You must modify the class whose instances you want to sort.	You build a class separate from the class whose instances you want to sort.
Only **one** sort sequence can be created	**Many** sort sequences can be created
Implemented frequently in the API by: String, Wrapper classes, Date, Calendar...	Meant to be implemented to sort instances of third-party classes.

Sorting with the Arrays Class

We've been using the java.util.Collections class to sort collections; now let's look at using the java.util.Arrays class to sort arrays. The good news is that sorting arrays of objects is just like sorting collections of objects. The `Arrays.sort()` method is overridden in the same way the `Collections.sort()` method is.

- `Arrays.sort(arrayToSort)`
- `Arrays.sort(arrayToSort, Comparator)`

In addition, the `Arrays.sort()` method is overloaded about a million times to provide a couple of sort methods for every type of primitive. The `Arrays.sort()` methods that sort primitives always sort based on natural order. Don't be fooled by an exam question that tries to sort a primitive array using a Comparator.

Finally, remember that the `sort()` methods for both the Collections class and the Arrays class are `static` methods, and that they alter the objects they are sorting, instead of returning a different sorted object.

Searching Arrays and Collections

The Collections class and the Arrays class both provide methods that allow you to search for a specific element. When searching through collections or arrays, the following rules apply:

- Searches are performed using the `binarySearch()` method.
- Successful searches return the `int` index of the element being searched.
- Unsuccessful searches return an `int` index that represents the *insertion point*. The insertion point is the place in the collection/array where the element would be inserted to keep the collection/array properly sorted. Because posi-

tive return values and 0 indicate successful searches, the `binarySearch()` method uses negative numbers to indicate insertion points. Since 0 is a valid result for a successful search, the first available insertion point is -1. Therefore, the actual insertion point is represented as (-(insertion point) -1). For instance, if the insertion point of a search is at element 2, the actual insertion point returned will be -3.

■ The collection/array being searched must be sorted before you can search it.

■ If you attempt to search an array or collection that has not already been sorted, the results of the search will not be predictable.

■ If the collection/array you want to search was sorted in natural order, it *must* be searched in natural order. (This is accomplished by NOT sending a Comparator as an argument to the `binarySearch()` method.)

■ If the collection/array you want to search was sorted using a Comparator, it *must* be searched using the same Comparator, which is passed as the second argument to the `binarySearch()` method. Remember that Comparators cannot be used when searching arrays of primitives.

Let's take a look at a code sample that exercises the `binarySearch()` method:

```java
import java.util.*;
class SearchObjArray {
  public static void main(String [] args) {
    String [] sa = {"one", "two", "three", "four"};

    Arrays.sort(sa);                                        // #1
    for(String s : sa)
      System.out.print(s + " ");
    System.out.println("\none = "
                       + Arrays.binarySearch(sa,"one"));   // #2

    System.out.println("now reverse sort");
    ReSortComparator rs = new ReSortComparator();          // #3
    Arrays.sort(sa,rs);
    for(String s : sa)
      System.out.print(s + " ");
    System.out.println("\none = "
                       + Arrays.binarySearch(sa,"one"));   // #4
    System.out.println("one = "
                     + Arrays.binarySearch(sa,"one",rs));  // #5
  }
```

```
static class ReSortComparator
                 implements Comparator<String> {          // #6
   public int compare(String a, String b) {
     return b.compareTo(a);                              // #7
   }
  }
}
```

which produces something like this:

```
four one three two
one = 1
now reverse sort
two three one four
one = -1
one = 2
```

Here's what happened:

Line 1 Sort the sa array, alphabetically (the natural order).

Line 2 Search for the location of element "one", which is 1.

Line 3 Make a Comparator instance. On the next line we re-sort the array using the Comparator.

Line 4 Attempt to search the array. We didn't pass the binarySearch() method the Comparator we used to sort the array, so we got an incorrect (undefined) answer.

Line 5 Search again, passing the Comparator to binarySearch(). This time we get the correct answer, 2

Line 6 We define the Comparator; it's okay for this to be an inner class.

Line 7 By switching the use of the arguments in the invocation of compareTo(), we get an inverted sort.

When solving searching and sorting questions, two big gotchas are:

1. Searching an array or collection that hasn't been sorted.

2. Using a Comparator in either the sort or the search, but not both.

Converting Arrays to Lists to Arrays

There are a couple of methods that allow you to convert arrays to Lists, and Lists to arrays. The List and Set classes have `toArray()` methods, and the Arrays class has a method called `asList()`.

The `Arrays.asList()` method copies an array into a List. The API says, "Returns a fixed-size list backed by the specified array. (Changes to the returned list 'write through' to the array.)" When you use the `asList()` method, the array and the List become joined at the hip. When you update one of them, the other gets updated automatically. Let's take a look:

```
String[] sa = {"one", "two", "three", "four"};
List sList = Arrays.asList(sa);                 // make a List
System.out.println("size  " + sList.size());
System.out.println("idx2  " + sList.get(2));

sList.set(3,"six");                             // change List
sa[1] = "five";                                 // change array
for(String s : sa)
  System.out.print(s + " ");
System.out.println("\nsl[1] " + sList.get(1));
```

This produces

```
size 4
idx2 three
one five three six
sl[1] five
```

Notice that when we print the final state of the array and the List, they have both been updated with each other's changes. Wouldn't something like this behavior make a great exam question?

Now let's take a look at the `toArray()` method. There's nothing too fancy going on with the `toArray()` method; it comes in two flavors: one that returns a new Object array, and one that uses the array you send it as the destination array:

```
List<Integer> iL = new ArrayList<Integer>();
for(int x=0; x<3; x++)
  iL.add(x);
Object[] oa = iL.toArray();          // create an Object array
Integer[] ia2 = new Integer[3];
ia2 = iL.toArray(ia2);               // create an Integer array
```

Using Lists

Remember that Lists are usually used to keep things in some kind of order. You can use a LinkedList to create a first-in, first-out queue. You can use an ArrayList to keep track of what locations were visited, and in what order. Notice that in both of these examples it's perfectly reasonable to assume that duplicates might occur. In addition, Lists allow you to manually override the ordering of elements by adding or removing elements via the element's index. Before Java 5, and the enhanced for loop, the most common way to examine a List "element by element" was by the use of an Iterator. You'll still find Iterators in use in the Java code you encounter, and you might just find an Iterator or two on the exam. An Iterator is an object that's associated with a specific collection. It let's you loop through the collection step by step. The two Iterator methods you need to understand for the exam are

- **boolean hasNext()** Returns true if there is at least one more element in the collection being traversed. Invoking hasNext() does NOT move you to the next element of the collection.

- **object next()** This method returns the next object in the collection, AND moves you forward to the element after the element just returned.

Let's look at a little code that uses a List and an Iterator:

```
import java.util.*;
class Dog {
  public String name;
  Dog(String n) { name = n; }
}
class ItTest {
  public static void main(String[] args) {
    List<Dog> d = new ArrayList<Dog>();
    Dog dog = new Dog("aiko");
    d.add(dog);
    d.add(new Dog("clover"));
    d.add(new Dog("magnolia"));
    Iterator<Dog> i3 = d.iterator();    // make an iterator
    while (i3.hasNext()) {
      Dog d2 = i3.next();               // cast not required
      System.out.println(d2.name);
    }
    System.out.println("size " + d.size());
    System.out.println("get1 " + d.get(1).name);
    System.out.println("aiko " + d.indexOf(dog));
```

```
    d.remove(2);
    Object[] oa = d.toArray();
    for(Object o : oa) {
      Dog d2 = (Dog)o;
      System.out.println("oa " + d2.name);
    }
  }
}
```

This produces

```
aiko
clover
magnolia
size 3
get1 clover
aiko 0
oa aiko
oa clover
```

First off, we used generics syntax to create the Iterator (an Iterator of type Dog). Because of this, when we used the `next()` method, we didn't have to cast the Object returned by `next()` to a Dog. We could have declared the Iterator like this:

```
Iterator i3 = d.iterator();  // make an iterator
```

But then we would have had to cast the returned value:

```
Dog d2 = (Dog)i3.next();
```

The rest of the code demonstrates using the `size()`, `get()`, `indexOf()`, and toArray() methods. There shouldn't be any surprises with these methods. In a few pages Table 7-5 will list all of the List, Set, and Map methods you should be familiar with for the exam. As a last warning, remember that List is an interface!

Using Sets

Remember that Sets are used when you don't want any duplicates in your collection. If you attempt to add an element to a set that already exists in the set, the duplicate element will not be added, and the `add()` method will return `false`. Remember, HashSets tend to be very fast because, as we discussed earlier, they use hashcodes.

You can also create a TreeSet, which is a Set whose elements are sorted. You must use caution when using a TreeSet (we're about to explain why):

```
import java.util.*;
class SetTest {
  public static void main(String[] args) {
    boolean[] ba = new boolean[5];
    // insert code here

    ba[0] = s.add("a");
    ba[1] = s.add(new Integer(42));
    ba[2] = s.add("b");
    ba[3] = s.add("a");
    ba[4] = s.add(new Object());
    for(int x=0; x<ba.length; x++)
      System.out.print(ba[x] + " ");
    System.out.println("\n");
    for(Object o : s)
      System.out.print(o + " ");
  }
}
```

If you insert the following line of code you'll get output something like this:

```
Set s = new HashSet();        // insert this code

true true true false true
a java.lang.Object@e09713 42 b
```

It's important to know that the order of objects printed in the second for loop is not predictable: HashSets and LinkedHashSets do not guarantee any ordering. Also, notice that the fourth invocation of add() failed, because it attempted to insert a duplicate entry (a String with the value a) into the Set.

If you insert this line of code you'll get something like this:

```
Set s = new TreeSet();        // insert this code

Exception in thread "main" java.lang.ClassCastException: java.
lang.String
        at java.lang.Integer.compareTo(Integer.java:35)
        at java.util.TreeMap.compare(TreeMap.java:1093)
```

```
at java.util.TreeMap.put(TreeMap.java:465)
at java.util.TreeSet.add(TreeSet.java:210)
```

The issue is that whenever you want a collection to be sorted, its elements must be mutually comparable. Remember that unless otherwise specified, objects of different types are not mutually comparable.

Using Maps

Remember that when you use a class that implements Map, any classes that you use as a part of the keys for that map must override the hashCode() and equals() methods. (Well, you only have to override them if you're interested in retrieving stuff from your Map. Seriously, it's legal to use a class that doesn't override equals() and hashCode() as a key in a Map; your code will compile and run, you just won't find your stuff.) Here's some code demonstrating the use of a HashMap:

```java
import java.util.*;
class Dog {
  public Dog(String n) { name = n; }
  public String name;
  public boolean equals(Object o) {
    if((o instanceof Dog) &&
        (((Dog)o).name == name)) {
      return true;
    } else {
      return false;
    }
  }
  public int hashCode() {return name.length(); }
}
class Cat { }

enum Pets {DOG, CAT, HORSE }

class MapTest {
  public static void main(String[] args) {
    Map<Object, Object> m = new HashMap<Object, Object>();

    m.put("k1", new Dog("aiko"));    // add some key/value pairs
    m.put("k2", Pets.DOG);
    m.put(Pets.CAT, "CAT key");
    Dog d1 = new Dog("clover");      // let's keep this reference
```

```
    m.put(d1, "Dog key");
    m.put(new Cat(), "Cat key");

    System.out.println(m.get("k1"));              // #1
    String k2 = "k2";
    System.out.println(m.get(k2));                // #2
    Pets p = Pets.CAT;
    System.out.println(m.get(p));                 // #3
    System.out.println(m.get(d1));                // #4
    System.out.println(m.get(new Cat()));         // #5
    System.out.println(m.size());                 // #6
  }
}
```

which produces something like this:

```
Dog@1c
DOG
CAT key
Dog key
null
5
```

Let's review the output. The first value retrieved is a Dog object (your value will vary). The second value retrieved is an enum value (DOG). The third value retrieved is a String; note that the key was an enum value. Pop quiz: What's the implication of the fact that we were able to successfully use an enum as a key?

The implication of this is that enums override equals() and hashCode(). And, if you look at the java.lang.Enum class in the API, you will see that, in fact, these methods have been overridden.

The fourth output is a String. The important point about this output is that the key used to retrieve the String was made of a Dog object. The fifth output is null. The important point here is that the get() method failed to find the Cat object that was inserted earlier. (The last line of output confirms that indeed, 5 key/value pairs exist in the Map.) Why didn't we find the Cat key String? Why did it work to use an instance of Dog as a key, when using an instance of Cat as a key failed?

It's easy to see that Dog overrode equals() and hashCode() while Cat didn't.

Let's take a quick look at hashcodes. We used an incredibly simplistic hashcode formula in the Dog class—the hashcode of a Dog object is the length of the instance's name. So in this example the hashcode = 4. Let's compare the following two hashCode() methods:

```
public int hashCode() {return name.length(); }    // #1
public int hashCode() {return 4; }                 // #2
```

Time for another pop quiz: Are the preceding two hashcodes legal? Will they successfully retrieve objects from a Map? Which will be faster?

The answer to the first two questions is Yes and Yes. Neither of these hashcodes will be very efficient (in fact they would both be incredibly inefficient), but they are both legal, and they will both work. The answer to the last question is that the first hashcode will be a little bit faster than the second hashcode. In general, the more *unique* hashcodes a formula creates, the faster the retrieval will be. The first hashcode formula will generate a different code for each name length (for instance the name Robert will generate one hashcode and the name Benchley will generate a different hashcode). The second hashcode formula will always produce the same result, 4, so it will be slower than the first.

Our last Map topic is what happens when an object used as a key has its values changed? If we add two lines of code to the end of the earlier MapTest.main(),

```
d1.name = "magnolia"
System.out.println(m.get(d1));
```

we get something like this:

```
Dog@4
DOG
CAT key
Dog key
null
5
null
```

The Dog that was previously found now cannot be found. Because the Dog.name variable is used to create the hashcode, changing the name changed the value of the hashcode. As a final quiz for hashcodes, determine the output for the following lines of code if they're added to the end of MapTest.main():

```
d1.name = "magnolia";
System.out.println(m.get(d1));                       // #1
d1.name = "clover";
System.out.println(m.get(new Dog("clover")));        // #2
d1.name = "arthur";
System.out.println(m.get(new Dog("clover")));        // #3
```

Remember that the hashcode is equal to the length of the name variable. When you study a problem like this, it can be useful to think of the two stages of retrieval:

1. Use the hashcode() method to find the correct bucket
2. Use the equals() method to find the object in the bucket

In the first call to get(), the hashcode is 8 (magnolia) and it should be 6 (clover), so the retrieval fails at step 1 and we get null. In the second call to get(), the hashcodes are both 6, so step 1 succeeds. Once in the correct bucket (the "length of name = 6" bucket), the equals() method is invoked, and since Dog's equals() method compares names, equals() succeeds, and the output is Dog key. In the third invocation of get(), the hashcode test succeeds, but the equals() test fails because arthur is NOT equal to clover.

In a few pages Table 7-5 will summarize the Map methods you should be familiar with for the exam.

Using the PriorityQueue Class

The last collection class you'll need to understand for the exam is the PriorityQueue. Unlike basic queue structures that are first-in, first-out by default, a PriorityQueue orders its elements using a user-defined priority. The priority can be as simple as natural ordering (in which, for instance, an entry of 1 would be a higher priority than an entry of 2). In addition, a PriorityQueue can be ordered using a Comparator, which lets you define any ordering you want. Queues have a few methods not found in other collection interfaces: peek(), poll(), and offer().

```java
import java.util.*;
class PQ {
  static class PQsort
          implements Comparator<Integer> {   // inverse sort
    public int compare(Integer one, Integer two) {
      return two - one;                       // unboxing
    }
  }
  public static void main(String[] args) {
    int[] ia = {1,5,3,7,6,9,8 };             // unordered data
    PriorityQueue<Integer> pq1 =
      new PriorityQueue<Integer>();           // use natural order

    for(int x : ia)                           // load queue
      pq1.offer(x);
    for(int x : ia)                           // review queue
```

```
        System.out.print(pq1.poll() + " ");
      System.out.println("");

      PQsort pqs = new PQsort();              // get a Comparator
      PriorityQueue<Integer> pq2 =
        new PriorityQueue<Integer>(10,pqs);   // use Comparator

      for(int x : ia)                         // load queue
        pq2.offer(x);
      System.out.println("size " + pq2.size());
      System.out.println("peek " + pq2.peek());
      System.out.println("size " + pq2.size());
      System.out.println("poll " + pq2.poll());
      System.out.println("size " + pq2.size());
      for(int x : ia)                         // review queue
        System.out.print(pq2.poll() + " ");
  }
}
```

This code produces something like this:

```
1 3 5 6 7 8 9

size 7
peek 9
size 7
poll 9
size 6
8 7 6 5 3 1 null
```

Let's look at this in detail. The first for loop iterates through the ia array, and uses the offer() method to add elements to the PriorityQueue named pq1. The second for loop iterates through pq1 using the poll() method, which returns the highest priority entry in pq1 AND removes the entry from the queue. Notice that the elements are returned in priority order (in this case, natural order). Next, we create a Comparator—in this case, a Comparator that orders elements in the opposite of natural order. We use this Comparator to build a second PriorityQueue, pq2, and we load it with the same array we used earlier. Finally, we check the size of pq2 before and after calls to peek() and poll(). This confirms that peek() returns the highest priority element in the queue without removing it, and poll() returns the highest priority element, AND removes it from the queue. Finally, we review the remaining elements in the queue.

Method Overview for Arrays and Collections

For these two classes, we've already covered the trickier methods you might encounter on the exam. Table 7-4 lists a summary of the methods you should be aware of. (Note: The `T[]` syntax will be explained later in this chapter; for now, think of it as meaning "any array that's NOT an array of primitives.")

Key Methods in java.util.Arrays	Descriptions
`static List asList(T[])`	Convert an array to a List, (and bind them).
`static int binarySearch(Object[], key)` `static int binarySearch(primitive[], key)`	Search a sorted array for a given value, return an index or insertion point.
`static int binarySearch(T[], key, Comparator)`	Search a Comparator-sorted array for a value.
`static boolean equals(Object[], Object[])` `static boolean equals(primitive[], primitive[])`	Compare two arrays to determine if their contents are equal.
`public static void sort(Object[ ] )` `public static void sort(primitive[ ] )`	Sort the elements of an array by natural order.
`public static void sort(T[], Comparator)`	Sort the elements of an array using a Comparator.
`public static String toString(Object[])` `public static String toString(primitive[])`	Create a String containing the contents of an array.
Key Methods in java.util.Collections	**Descriptions**
`static int binarySearch(List, key)` `static int binarySearch(List, key, Comparator)`	Search a "sorted" List for a given value, return an index or insertion point.
`static void reverse(List)`	Reverse the order of elements in a List.
`static Comparator reverseOrder()` `static Comparator reverseOrder(Comparator)`	Return a Comparator that sorts the reverse of the collection's current sort sequence.
`static void sort(List)` `static void sort(List, Comparator)`	Sort a List either by natural order or by a Comparator.

Method Overview for List, Set, Map, and Queue

For these four interfaces, we've already covered the trickier methods you might encounter on the exam. Table 7-5 lists a summary of the List, Set, and Map methods you should be aware of.

TABLE 7-5	Key Methods in List, Set, and Map

Key Interface Methods	List	Set	Map	Descriptions
boolean **add**(element) boolean **add**(index, element)	X X	X		Add an element. For Lists, optionally add the element at an index point.
boolean **contains**(object) boolean **containsKey**(object key) boolean **containsValue**(object value)	X	X	 X X	Search a collection for an object (or, optionally for Maps a key), return the result as a `boolean`.
object **get**(index) object **get**(key)	X		 X	Get an object from a collection, via an index or a key.
int **indexOf**(object)	X			Get the location of an object in a List.
Iterator **iterator**()	X	X		Get an Iterator for a List or a Set.
Set **keySet**()			X	Return a Set containing a Map's keys.
put(key, value)			X	Add a key/value pair to a Map.
remove(index) **remove**(object) **remove**(key)	X X	 X	 X	Remove an element via an index, or via the element's value, or via a key.
int size()	X	X	X	Return the number of elements in a collection.
Object[] **toArray**() T[] **toArray**(T[])	X	X		Return an array containing the elements of the collection.

For the exam, the PriorityQueue methods that are important to understand are `offer()` (which is similar to `add()`), `peek()` (which retrieves the element at the head of the queue, but doesn't delete it), and `poll()` (which retrieves the head element and removes it from the queue).

exam

ⓦatch

It's important to know some of the details of natural ordering. The following code will help you understand the relative positions of uppercase characters, lowercase characters, and spaces in a natural ordering:

```
String[] sa = {">ff<", "> f<", ">f <", ">FF<" }; // ordered?
PriorityQueue<String> pq3 = new PriorityQueue<String>();
for(String s : sa)
  pq3.offer(s);
for(String s : sa)
  System.out.print(pq3.poll() + " ");
```

This produces:

```
> f< >FF< >f < >ff<
```

If you remember that spaces sort before characters and that uppercase letters sort before lowercase characters, you should be good to go for the exam.

CERTIFICATION OBJECTIVE

Generic Types (Objectives 6.3 and 6.4)

6.3   *Write code that uses the generic versions of the Collections API, in particular the Set, List, and Map interfaces and implementation classes. Recognize the limitations of the non-generic Collections API and how to refactor code to use the generic versions.*

6.4   *Develop code that makes proper use of type parameters in class/interface declarations, instance variables, method arguments, and return types; and write generic methods or methods that make use of wildcard types and understand the similarities and differences between these two approaches.*

Arrays in Java have always been type safe—an array declared as type String (`string []`) can't accept Integers (or `ints`), Dogs, or anything other than Strings. But remember that before Java 5 there was no syntax for declaring a type safe collection. To make an ArrayList of Strings, you said,

```
ArrayList myList = new ArrayList();
```

or, the polymorphic equivalent:

```
List myList = new ArrayList();
```

There was no syntax that let you specify that `myList` will take Strings and only Strings. And with no way to specify a type for the ArrayList, the compiler couldn't enforce that you put only things of the specified type into the list. As of Java 5, we can use generics, and while they aren't only for making type safe collections, that's just about all most developers use generics for. So, while generics aren't just for collections, think of collections as the overwhelming reason and motivation for adding generics to the language.

And it was not an easy decision, nor has it been an entirely welcome addition. Because along with all the nice happy type safety, generics come with a lot of baggage—most of which you'll never see or care about, but there are some gotchas that come up surprisingly quickly. We'll cover the ones most likely to show up in your own code, and those are also the issues that you'll need to know for the exam.

The biggest challenge for Sun in adding generics to the language (and the main reason it took them so long) was how to deal with legacy code built without generics. Sun's Java engineers obviously didn't want to break everyone's existing Java code, so they had to find a way for Java classes with both type safe (generic) and non-type safe (non-generic/pre-Java 5) collections to still work together. Their solution isn't the friendliest, but it does let you use older non-generic code, as well as use generic code that plays with non-generic code. But notice we said "plays," and not "plays WELL."

While you can integrate Java 5 generic code with legacy non-generic code, the consequences can be disastrous, and unfortunately, most of the disasters happen at runtime, not compile time. Fortunately, though, most compilers will generate warnings to tell you when you're using unsafe (meaning non-generic) collections.

The Java 5 exam covers both pre-Java 5 (non-generic) and Java 5 style collections, and you'll see questions that expect you to understand the tricky problems that can come from mixing non-generic and generic code together. And like some of the other topics in this book, you could fill an entire book if you really wanted to cover every detail about generics, but the exam (and this book) covers more than most developers will ever need to use.

The Legacy Way to Do Collections

Here's a review of a pre-Java 5 ArrayList intended to hold Strings. (We say "intended" because that's about all you had—good intentions—to make sure that the ArrayList would hold only Strings).

```
List myList = new ArrayList();   // can't declare a type

myList.add("Fred");              // OK, it will hold Strings

myList.add(new Dog());           // and it will hold Dogs too

myList.add(new Integer(42));     // and Integers...
```

A non-generic collection can hold any kind of object! A non-generic collection is quite happy to hold anything that is NOT a primitive.

This meant it was entirely up to the programmer to be...careful. Having no way to guarantee collection type wasn't very programmer-friendly for such a strongly typed language. We're so used to the compiler stopping us from, say, assigning an `int` to a `boolean` reference or a String to a Dog reference, but with collections, it was, "Come on in! The door is always open! All objects are welcome here any time!"

And since a collection could hold anything, the methods that get objects out of the collection could have only one kind of return type—java.lang.Object. That meant that getting a String back out of our only-Strings-intended list required a cast:

```
String s = (String) myList.get(0);
```

And since you couldn't guarantee that what was coming out really was a String (since you were allowed to put anything in the list), the cast could fail at runtime.

So, generics takes care of both ends (the putting in and getting out) by enforcing the type of your collections. Let's update the String list:

```
List<String> myList = new ArrayList<String>();
myList.add("Fred");             // OK, it will hold Strings
myList.add(new Dog());          // compiler error!!
```

Perfect. That's exactly what we want. By using generics syntax—which means putting the type in angle brackets <String>, we're telling the compiler that this collection can hold only String objects. The type in angle brackets is referred to as either the "parameterized type," "type parameter," or of course just old-fashioned "type." In this chapter, we'll refer to it both new ways.

So, now that what you put IN is guaranteed, you can also guarantee what comes OUT, and that means you can get rid of the cast when you get something from the collection. Instead of

```
String s = (String)myList.get(0);  // pre-generics, when a
                                   // String wasn't guaranteed
```

we can now just say

```
String s = myList.get(0);
```

The compiler already knows that myList contains only things that can be assigned to a String reference, so now there's no need for a cast. So far, it seems pretty simple. And with the new for loop, you can of course iterate over the guaranteed-to-be-String list:

```
for (String s : myList) {
    int x = s.length();
    // no need for a cast before calling a String method! The
    // compiler already knew "s" was a String coming from MyList
}
```

And of course you can declare a type parameter for a method argument, which then makes the argument a type safe reference:

```
void takeListOfStrings(List<String> strings) {
    strings.add("foo");  // no problem adding a String
}
```

The method above would NOT compile if we changed it to

```
void takeListOfStrings(List<String> strings) {
    strings.add(new Integer(42)); // NO!! strings is type safe
}
```

Return types can obviously be declared type safe as well:

```
public Set<Dog> getDogList() {
    Set<Dog> dogs = new HashSet<Dog>();
    // more code to insert dogs
    return dogs;
}
```

The compiler will stop you from returning anything not compatible with a Set<Dog> (although what is and is not compatible is going to get very interesting in a minute). And since the compiler guarantees that only a type safe Dog Set is returned, those calling the method won't need a cast to take Dogs from the Set:

```
Dog d = getDogList().get(0);  // we KNOW a Dog is coming out
```

With pre-Java 5, non-generic code, the getDogList() method would be

```
public Set getDogList() {
    Set dogs = new HashSet();
     // code to add only Dogs... fingers crossed...
    return dogs; // a Set of ANYTHING will work here
}
```

and the caller would need a cast:

```
Dog d = (Dog) getDogList().get(0);
```

(The cast in this example applies to what comes from the Set's get() method; we aren't casting what is returned from the getDogList() method, which is a Set.)

But what about the benefit of a completely heterogeneous collection? In other words, what if you liked the fact that before generics you could make an ArrayList that could hold any kind of object?

```
List myList = new ArrayList();  // old-style, non-generic
```

is almost identical to

```
List<Object> myList = new
                ArrayList<Object>(); // holds ANY object type
```

Declaring a List with a type parameter of <Object> makes a collection that works in almost the same way as the original pre-Java 5, non-generic collection—you can put ANY Object type into the collection. You'll see a little later that non-generic collections and collections of type <Object> aren't entirely the same, but most of the time the differences do not matter.

Oh, if only this were the end of the story...but there are still a few tricky issues with methods arguments, polymorphism, and integrating generic and non-generic code, so we're just getting warmed up here.

Generics and Legacy Code

The easiest generics thing you'll need to know for the exam is how to update non-generic code to make it generic. You just add a type in angle brackets (<>) immediately following the collection type in BOTH the variable declaration and the constructor call, including any place you declare a variable (so that means arguments and return types too). A pre-Java 5 List meant to hold only Integers:

```
List myList = new ArrayList();
```

becomes

```
List<Integer> myList = new ArrayList<Integer>();
```

and a list meant to hold only Strings goes from

```
public List changeStrings(ArrayList s) { }
```

to this:

```
public List<String> changeStrings(ArrayList<String> s) { }
```

Easy. And if there's code that used the earlier non-generic version and performed a cast to get things out, that won't break anyone's code:

```
Integer i = (Integer) list.get(0); // cast no longer needed,
                                    // but it won't hurt
```

Mixing Generic and Non-generic Collections

Now here's where it starts to get interesting...imagine we have an ArrayList, of type Integer, and we're passing it into a method from a class whose source code we don't have access to. Will this work?

```java
// a Java 5 class using a generic collection
import java.util.*;
public class TestLegacy {
    public static void main(String[] args) {
        List<Integer> myList = new ArrayList<Integer>();
                                   // type safe collection
        myList.add(4);
        myList.add(6);
        Adder adder = new Adder();
        int total = adder.addAll(myList);
                          // pass it to an untyped argument
        System.out.println(total);
    }
}
```

The older, non-generics class we want to use:

```java
import java.util.*;
class Adder {
    int addAll(List list) {
        // method with a non-generic List argument,
        // but assumes (with no guarantee) that it will be Integers
        Iterator it = list.iterator();
        int total = 0;
        while (it.hasNext()) {
            int i = ((Integer)it.next()).intValue();
            total += i;
        }
        return total;
    }
}
```

Yes, this works just fine. You can mix correct generic code with older non-generic code, and everyone is happy.

In the previous example, the `addAll()` legacy method assumed (trusted? hoped?) that the list passed in was indeed restricted to Integers, even though when the code was written, there was no guarantee. It was up to the programmers to be careful.

Since the addAll() method wasn't doing anything except getting the Integer (using a cast) from the list and accessing its value, there were no problems. In that example, there was no risk to the caller's code, but the legacy method might have blown up if the list passed in contained anything but Integers (which would cause a ClassCastException).

But now imagine that you call a legacy method that doesn't just *read* a value but *adds* something to the ArrayList? Will this work?

```java
import java.util.*;
public class TestBadLegacy {
    public static void main(String[] args) {
        List<Integer> myList = new ArrayList<Integer>();
        myList.add(4);
        myList.add(6);
        Inserter in  = new Inserter();
        in.insert(myList);  // pass List<Integer> to legacy code
    }
}
class Inserter {
    // method with a non-generic List argument
    void insert(List list) {
        list.add(new Integer(42)); // adds to the incoming list
    }
}
```

Sure, this code works. It compiles, and it runs. The insert() method puts an Integer into the list that was originally typed as <Integer>, so no problem.

But...what if we modify the insert() method like this:

```java
void insert(List list) {
    list.add(new String("42"));  // put a String in the list
                                 // passed in
}
```

Will that work? Yes, sadly, it does! It both compiles and runs. No runtime exception. Yet, someone just stuffed a String into a *supposedly* type safe ArrayList of type <Integer>. How can that be?

Remember, the older legacy code was allowed to put anything at all (except primitives) into a collection. And in order to support legacy code, Java 5 allows your newer type safe code to make use of older code (the last thing Sun wanted to do was ask several million Java developers to modify all their existing code).

So, the Java 5 compiler is *forced* into letting you compile your new type safe code even though your code invokes a method of an older class that takes a non-type safe argument and does who knows what with it.

However, just because the Java 5 compiler allows this code to compile doesn't mean it has to be HAPPY about it. In fact the compiler will warn you that you're taking a big, big risk sending your nice protected ArrayList<Integer> into a dangerous method that can have its way with your list and put in Floats, Strings, or even Dogs.

When you called the addAll() method in the earlier example, it didn't insert anything to the list (it simply added up the values within the collection), so there was no risk to the caller that his list would be modified in some horrible way. It compiled and ran just fine. But in the second version, with the legacy insert() method that adds a String, the compiler generated a warning:

```
javac TestBadLegacy.java
Note: TestBadLegacy.java uses unchecked or unsafe operations.
Note: Recompile with -Xlint:unchecked for details.
```

Remember that *compiler warnings are NOT considered a compiler failure*. The compiler generated a perfectly valid class file from the compilation, but it was kind enough to tell you by saying, in so many words, "I seriously hope you know what you are doing because this old code has NO respect (or even knowledge) of your <Integer> typing, and can do whatever the heck it wants to your precious ArrayList<Integer>."

exam
watch

Be sure you know the difference between "compilation fails" and "compiles without error" and "compiles without warnings" and "compiles with warnings." In most questions on the exam, you care only about compiles vs. compilation fails—compiler warnings don't matter for most of the exam. But when you are using generics, and mixing both typed and untyped code, warnings matter.

Back to our example with the legacy code that does an insert, keep in mind that for BOTH versions of the insert() method (one that adds an Integer and one that adds a String) the compiler issues warnings. The compiler does NOT know whether the `insert()` method is adding the right thing (Integer) or wrong thing (String). The reason the compiler produces a warning is because the method is ADDING something to the collection! In other words, the compiler knows there's a chance the method might add the wrong thing to a collection the caller thinks is type safe.

So far, we've looked at how the compiler will generate warnings if it sees that there's a chance your type safe collection could be harmed by older, non-type-safe code. But one of the questions developers often ask is, "Okay, sure, it compiles, but why does it RUN? Why does the code that inserts the wrong thing into my list work at runtime?" In other words, why does the JVM let old code stuff a String into your ArrayList<Integer>, without any problems at all? No exceptions, nothing. Just a quiet, behind-the-scenes, total violation of your type safety that you might not discover until the worst possible moment.

There's one Big Truth you need to know to understand why it runs without problems—the JVM has no idea that your ArrayList was supposed to hold only Integers. The typing information does not exist at runtime! All your generic code is strictly for the compiler. Through a process called "type erasure," the compiler does all of its verifications on your generic code and then strips the type information out of the class bytecode. At runtime, ALL collection code—both legacy and new Java 5 code you write using generics—looks exactly like the pre-generic version of collections. None of your typing information exists at runtime. In other words, even though you WROTE

```
List<Integer> myList = new ArrayList<Integer>();
```

By the time the compiler is done with it, the JVM sees what it always saw before Java 5 and generics:

```
List myList = new ArrayList();
```

The compiler even inserts the casts for you—the casts you had to do to get things out of a pre-Java 5 collection.

Think of generics as strictly a compile-time protection. The compiler uses generic type information (the <type> in the angle brackets) to make sure that your code doesn't put the wrong things into a collection, and that you do not assign what you get from a collection to the wrong reference type. But NONE of this protection exists at runtime.

This is a little different from arrays, which give you BOTH compile-time protection and runtime protection. Why did they do generics this way? Why is there no type information at runtime? To support legacy code. At runtime, collections are collections just like the old days. What you gain from using generics is compile-time protection that guarantees that you won't put the wrong thing into a typed collection, and it also eliminates the need for a cast when you get something out, since the compiler already knows that only an Integer is coming out of an Integer list.

The fact is, you don't NEED runtime protection...until you start mixing up generic and non-generic code, as we did in the previous example. Then you can have disasters at runtime. The only advice we have is to pay very close attention to those compiler warnings:

```
javac TestBadLegacy.java
Note: TestBadLegacy.java uses unchecked or unsafe operations.
Note: Recompile with -Xlint:unchecked for details.
```

This compiler warning isn't very descriptive, but the second note suggests that you recompile with -Xlint:unchecked. If you do, you'll get something like this:

```
javac -Xlint:unchecked TestBadLegacy.java
TestBadLegacy.java:17: warning: [unchecked] unchecked call to
add(E) as a member of the raw type java.util.List
        list.add(new String("42"));
            ^
1 warning
```

When you compile with the -Xlint:unchecked flag, the compiler shows you exactly which method(s) might be doing something dangerous. In this example, since the list argument was not declared with a type, the compiler treats it as legacy code and assumes no risk for what the method puts into the "raw" list.

On the exam, you must be able to recognize when you are compiling code that will produce warnings but still compile. And any code that compiles (even with warnings) will run! No type violations will be caught at runtime by the JVM, *until* those type violations mess with your code in some other way. In other words, the act of adding a String to an <Integer> list won't fail at runtime *until* you try to treat that String-you-think-is-an-Integer as an Integer.

For example, imagine you want your code to pull something out of your *supposedly* type safe ArrayList<Integer> that older code put a String into. It compiles (with warnings). It runs...or at least the code that actually adds the String to the list runs. But when you take the String-that-wasn't-supposed-to-be-there out of the list, and try to assign it to an Integer reference or invoke an Integer method, you're dead.

Keep in mind, then, that the problem of putting the wrong thing into a typed (generic) collection does not show up at the time you actually do the add() to the collection. It only shows up later, when you try to use something in the list and it doesn't match what you were expecting. In the old (pre-Java 5) days, you always assumed that you might get the wrong thing out of a collection (since they were all non-type safe), so you took appropriate defensive steps in your code. The problem with mixing generic with non-generic code is that you won't be expecting those problems if you have been lulled into a false sense of security by having written type safe code. Just remember that the moment you turn that type safe collection over to older, non-type safe code, your protection vanishes.

Again, pay very close attention to compiler warnings, and be prepared to see issues like this come up on the exam.

exam

Watch

When using legacy (non-type safe) collections—watch out for unboxing problems! If you declare a non-generic collection, the `get()` *method ALWAYS returns a reference of type java.lang.Object. Remember that unboxing can't convert a plain old Object to a primitive, even if that Object reference points to an Integer (or some other primitive) on the heap. Unboxing converts only from a wrapper class reference (like an Integer or a Long) to a primitive.*

Unboxing gotcha, continued:

```
List test = new ArrayList();
test.add(43);
int x = (Integer)test.get(0);      // you must cast !!

List<Integer> test2 = new ArrayList<Integer>();
test2.add(343);
int x2 = test2.get(0);             // cast not necessary
```

*Watch out for missing casts associated with pre-Java 5,
non-generic collections.*

Polymorphism and Generics

Generic collections give you the same benefits of type safety that you've always had with arrays, but there are some crucial differences that can bite you if you aren't prepared. Most of these have to do with polymorphism.

You've already seen that polymorphism applies to the "base" type of the collection:

```
List<Integer> myList = new ArrayList<Integer>();
```

In other words, we were able to assign an ArrayList to a List reference, because List is a supertype of ArrayList. Nothing special there—this polymorphic assignment works the way it always works in Java, regardless of the generic typing.

But what about this?

```
class Parent { }
class Child extends Parent { }
List<Parent> myList = new ArrayList<Child>();
```

Think about it for a minute.
Keep thinking...

No, it doesn't work. There's a very simple rule here—the type of the variable declaration must match the type you pass to the actual object type. If you declare List<Foo> foo then whatever you assign to the foo reference MUST be of the generic type <Foo>. Not a subtype of <Foo>. Not a supertype of <Foo>. Just <Foo>.

These are wrong:

```
List<Object> myList = new ArrayList<JButton>();  // NO!
List<Number> numbers = new ArrayList<Integer>(); // NO!
// remember that Integer is a subtype of Number
```

But these are fine:

```
List<JButton> myList = new ArrayList<JButton>(); // yes
List<Object> myList = new ArrayList<Object>();   // yes
List<Integer> myList = new ArrayList<Integer>(); // yes
```

So far so good. Just keep the generic type of the reference and the generic type of the object to which it refers identical. In other words, polymorphism applies here to only the "base" type. And by "base," we mean the type of the collection class itself—the class that can be customized with a type. In this code,

```
List<JButton> myList = new ArrayList<JButton>();
```

List and ArrayList are the *base* type and JButton is the *generic* type. So an ArrayList can be assigned to a List, but a collection of <JButton> cannot be assigned to a reference of <Object>, even though JButton is a subtype of Object.

The part that feels wrong for most developers is that this is NOT how it works with arrays, where you *are* allowed to do this,

```
import java.util.*;
class Parent { }
class Child extends Parent { }
public class TestPoly {
    public static void main(String[] args) {
        Parent[] myArray = new Child[3];  // yes
    }
}
```

which means you're also allowed to do this

```
Object[] myArray = new JButton[3];   // yes
```

but not this:

```
List<Object> list = new ArrayList<JButton>();   // NO!
```

Why are the rules for typing of arrays different from the rules for generic typing? We'll get to that in a minute. For now, just burn it into your brain that polymorphism does not work the same way for generics as it does with arrays.

Generic Methods

If you weren't already familiar with generics, you might be feeling very uncomfortable with the implications of the previous no-polymorphic-assignment-for-generic-types thing. And why shouldn't you be uncomfortable? One of the biggest benefits of polymorphism is that you can declare, say, a method argument of a particular type and at runtime be able to have that argument refer to any subtype—including those you'd never known about at the time you wrote the method with the supertype argument.

For example, imagine a classic (simplified) polymorphism example of a veterinarian (AnimalDoctor) class with a method checkup(). And right now, you have three Animal subtypes—Dog, Cat, and Bird—each implementing the abstract checkup() method from Animal:

```
abstract class Animal {
    public abstract void checkup();
}
class Dog extends Animal {
    public void checkup() {    // implement Dog-specific code
        System.out.println("Dog checkup");
    }
}
class Cat extends Animal {
    public void checkup() {    // implement Cat-specific code
        System.out.println("Cat checkup");
    }
}
class Bird extends Animal {
    public void checkup() {    // implement Bird-specific code
        System.out.println("Bird checkup");
    }  }
```

Forgetting collections/arrays for a moment, just imagine what the AnimalDoctor class needs to look like in order to have code that takes any kind of Animal and invokes the Animal checkup() method. Trying to overload the AnimalDoctor class with checkup() methods for every possible kind of animal is ridiculous, and obviously not extensible. You'd have to change the AnimalDoctor class every time someone added a new subtype of Animal.

So in the AnimalDoctor class, you'd probably have a polymorphic method:

```
public void checkAnimal(Animal a) {
    a.checkup(); // does not matter which animal subtype each
                 // Animal's overridden checkup() method runs
}
```

And of course we do want the AnimalDoctor to also have code that can take arrays of Dogs, Cats, or Birds, for when the vet comes to the dog, cat, or bird kennel. Again, we don't want overloaded methods with arrays for each potential Animal subtype, so we use polymorphism in the AnimalDoctor class:

```
public void checkAnimals(Animal[] animals) {
    for(Animal a : animals) {
      a.checkup();
    }
  }
```

Here is the entire example, complete with a test of the array polymorphism that takes any type of animal array (Dog[], Cat[], Bird[]).

```
import java.util.*;
abstract class Animal {
    public abstract void checkup();
}
class Dog extends Animal {
    public void checkup() {   // implement Dog-specific code
      System.out.println("Dog checkup");
    }
}
class Cat extends Animal {
    public void checkup() {   // implement Cat-specific code
      System.out.println("Cat checkup");
    }
}
```

```
class Bird extends Animal {
   public void checkup() {      // implement Bird-specific code
      System.out.println("Bird checkup");
   }
}
public class AnimalDoctor  {
   // method takes an array of any animal subtype
   public void checkAnimals(Animal[] animals) {
     for(Animal a : animals) {
       a.checkup();
     }
   }
   public static void main(String[] args) {
      // test it
      Dog[] dogs = {new Dog(), new Dog()};
      Cat[] cats = {new Cat(), new Cat(), new Cat()};
      Bird[] birds = {new Bird()};

      AnimalDoctor doc = new AnimalDoctor();
      doc.checkAnimals(dogs);  // pass the Dog[]
      doc.checkAnimals(cats);  // pass the Cat[]
      doc.checkAnimals(birds); // pass the Bird[]
   }
}
```

This works fine, of course (we know, we know, this is old news). But here's why we brought this up as refresher—this approach does NOT work the same way with type safe collections!

In other words, a method that takes, say, an ArrayList<Animal> will NOT be able to accept a collection of any Animal subtype! That means ArrayList<Dog> cannot be passed into a method with an argument of ArrayList<Animal>, even though we already know that this works just fine with plain old arrays.

Obviously this difference between arrays and ArrayList is consistent with the polymorphism assignment rules we already looked at—the fact that you cannot assign an object of type ArrayList<JButton> to a List<Object>. But this is where you really start to feel the pain of the distinction between typed arrays and typed collections.

We know it won't work correctly, but let's try changing the AnimalDoctor code to use generics instead of arrays:

```
public class AnimalDoctorGeneric  {
```

```
     // change the argument from Animal[] to ArrayList<Animal>
     public void checkAnimals(ArrayList<Animal> animals) {
       for(Animal a : animals) {
         a.checkup();
       }
     }
     public static void main(String[] args) {
         // make ArrayLists instead of arrays for Dog, Cat, Bird
         List<Dog> dogs = new ArrayList<Dog>();
         dogs.add(new Dog());
         dogs.add(new Dog());
         List<Cat> cats = new ArrayList<Cat>();
         cats.add(new Cat());
         cats.add(new Cat());
         List<Bird> birds = new ArrayList<Bird>();
         birds.add(new Bird());
         // this code is the same as the Array version
         AnimalDoctorGeneric doc = new AnimalDoctorGeneric();
         // this worked when we used arrays instead of ArrayLists
         doc.checkAnimals(dogs);   // send a List<Dog>
         doc.checkAnimals(cats);   // send a List<Cat>
         doc.checkAnimals(birds);  // send a List<Bird>
     }
}
```

So what does happen?

```
javac AnimalDoctorGeneric.java
AnimalDoctorGeneric.java:51: checkAnimals(java.util.
ArrayList<Animal>) in AnimalDoctorGeneric cannot be applied to
(java.util.List<Dog>)
      doc.checkAnimals(dogs);
         ^

AnimalDoctorGeneric.java:52: checkAnimals(java.util.
ArrayList<Animal>) in AnimalDoctorGeneric cannot be applied to
(java.util.List<Cat>)
      doc.checkAnimals(cats);
         ^

AnimalDoctorGeneric.java:53: checkAnimals(java.util.
ArrayList<Animal>) in AnimalDoctorGeneric cannot be applied to
(java.util.List<Bird>)
      doc.checkAnimals(birds);
         ^

3 errors
```

The compiler stops us with errors, not warnings. You simply CANNOT assign the individual ArrayLists of Animal subtypes (<Dog>, <Cat>, or <Bird>) to an ArrayList of the supertype <Animal>, which is the declared type of the argument.

This is one of the biggest gotchas for Java programmers who are so familiar with using polymorphism with arrays, where the same scenario (`Animal[]` can refer to `Dog[]`, `Cat[]`, or `Bird[]`) works as you would expect. So we have two real issues:

1. Why doesn't this work?
2. How do you get around it?

You'd hate us and all of the Sun engineers if we told you that there wasn't a way around it—that you had to accept it and write horribly inflexible code that tried to anticipate and code overloaded methods for each specific <type>. Fortunately, there is a way around it.

But first, why can't you do it if it works for arrays? Why can't you pass an ArrayList<Dog> into a method with an argument of ArrayList<Animal>?

We'll get there, but first let's step way back for a minute and consider this perfectly legal scenario:

```
Animal[] animals = new Animal[3];
animals[0] = new Cat();
animals[1] = new Dog();
```

Part of the benefit of declaring an array using a more abstract supertype is that the array itself can hold objects of multiple subtypes of the supertype, and then you can manipulate the array assuming everything in it can respond to the Animal interface (in other words, everything in the array can respond to method calls defined in the Animal class). So here, we're using polymorphism not for the object that the array reference points to, but rather what the array can actually HOLD—in this case, any subtype of Animal. You can do the same thing with generics:

```
List<Animal> animals = new ArrayList<Animal>();
animals.add(new Cat());  // OK
animals.add(new Dog());  // OK
```

So this part works with both arrays and generic collections—we can add an instance of a subtype into an array or collection declared with a supertype. You can add Dogs and Cats to an Animal array (`Animal[]`) or an Animal collection (ArrayList<Animal>).

And with arrays, this applies to what happens within a method:

```
public void addAnimal(Animal[] animals) {
      animals[0] = new Dog();  // no problem, any Animal works
                               // in Animal[]
}
```

So if this is true, and if you can put Dogs into an ArrayList<Animal>, then why can't you use that same kind of method scenario? Why can't you do this?

```
public void addAnimal(ArrayList<Animal> animals) {
      animals.add(new Dog()); // sometimes allowed...
}
```

Actually, you CAN do this under certain conditions. The code above WILL compile just fine IF what you pass into the method is also an ArrayList<Animal>. This is the part where it differs from arrays, because in the array version, you COULD pass a `Dog[]` into the method that takes an `Animal[]`.

The ONLY thing you can pass to a method argument of ArrayList<Animal> is an ArrayList<Animal>! (Assuming you aren't trying to pass a subtype of ArrayList, since remember—the "base" type can be polymorphic.)

The question is still out there—why is this bad? And why is it bad for ArrayList but not arrays? Why can't you pass an ArrayList<Dog> to an argument of ArrayList<Animal>? Actually, the problem IS just as dangerous whether you're using arrays or a generic collection. It's just that the compiler and JVM behave differently for arrays vs. generic collections.

The reason it is dangerous to pass a collection (array or ArrayList) of a subtype into a method that takes a collection of a supertype, is because you might add something. And that means you might add the WRONG thing! This is probably really obvious, but just in case (and to reinforce), let's walk through some scenarios. The first one is simple:

```
public void foo() {
  Dog[] dogs = {new Dog(), new Dog()};
  addAnimal(dogs);  // no problem, send the Dog[] to the method
}
public void addAnimal(Animal[] animals) {
  animals[0] = new Dog();  // ok, any Animal subtype works
}
```

This is no problem. We passed a `Dog[]` into the method, and added a Dog to the array (which was allowed since the method parameter was type `Animal[]`, which can hold any Animal subtype). But what if we changed the calling code to

```
public void foo() {
  Cat[] cats = {new Cat(), new Cat()};
  addAnimal(cats);  // no problem, send the Cat[] to the method
}
```

and the original method stays the same:

```
public void addAnimal(Animal[] animals) {
  animals[0] = new Dog();  // Eeek! We just put a Dog
                           // in a Cat array!
}
```

The compiler thinks it is perfectly fine to add a Dog to an `Animal[]` array, since a Dog can be assigned to an Animal reference. The problem is, if you passed in an array of an Animal subtype (Cat, Dog, or Bird), the compiler does not know. The compiler does not realize that out on the heap somewhere is an array of type `Cat[]`, not `Animal[]`, and you're about to try to add a Dog to it. To the compiler, you have passed in an array of type Animal, so it has no way to recognize the problem.

THIS is the scenario we're trying to prevent, regardless of whether it's an array or an ArrayList. The difference is, the compiler lets you get away with it for arrays, but not for generic collections.

The reason the compiler won't let you pass an ArrayList<Dog> into a method that takes an ArrayList<Animal>, is because within the method, that parameter is of type ArrayList<Animal>, and that means you could put *any* kind of Animal into it. There would be no way for the compiler to stop you from putting a Dog into a List that was originally declared as <Cat>, but is now referenced from the <Animal> parameter.

We still have two questions…how do you get around it and why the heck does the compiler allow you to take that risk for arrays but not for ArrayList (or any other generic collection)?

The reason you can get away with compiling this for arrays is because there is a runtime exception (ArrayStoreException) that will prevent you from putting the wrong type of object into an array. If you send a `Dog` array into the method that takes an `Animal` array, and you add only Dogs (including Dog subtypes, of course) into the array now referenced by `Animal`, no problem. But if you DO try to add a Cat to the object that is actually a `Dog` array, you'll get the exception.

But there IS no equivalent exception for generics, because of type erasure! In other words, at runtime the JVM KNOWS the type of arrays, but does NOT know the type of a collection. All the generic type information is removed during compilation, so by the time it gets to the JVM, there is simply no way to recognize the disaster of putting a Cat into an ArrayList<Dog> and vice versa (and it becomes exactly like the problems you have when you use legacy, non-type safe code).

So this actually IS legal code:

```
public void addAnimal(List<Animal> animals) {
    animals.add(new Dog());   // this is always legal,
                              // since Dog can
                              // be assigned to an Animal
                              // reference
  }
   public static void main(String[] args) {
      List<Animal> animals = new ArrayList<Animal>();
      animals.add(new Dog());
      animals.add(new Dog());
      AnimalDoctorGeneric doc = new AnimalDoctorGeneric();
      doc.addAnimal(animals); // OK, since animals matches
                              // the method arg
   }
```

As long as the only thing you pass to the addAnimals(List<Animal>) is an ArrayList<Animal>, the compiler is pleased—knowing that any Animal subtype you add will be valid (you can always add a Dog to an Animal collection, yada, yada, yada). But if you try to invoke addAnimal() with an argument of any OTHER ArrayList type, the compiler will stop you, since at runtime the JVM would have no way to stop you from adding a Dog to what was created as a Cat collection.

For example, this code that changes the generic type to <Dog>, but without changing the addAnimal() method, will NOT compile:

```
public void addAnimal(List<Animal> animals) {
  animals.add(new Dog());   // still OK as always
}
public static void main(String[] args) {
  List<Dog> animals = new ArrayList<Dog>();
  animals.add(new Dog());
  animals.add(new Dog());
  AnimalDoctorGeneric doc = new AnimalDoctorGeneric();
  doc.addAnimal(animals); // THIS is where it breaks!
}
```

The compiler says something like:

```
javac AnimalDoctorGeneric.java
AnimalDoctorGeneric.java:49: addAnimal(java.util.List<Animal>)
in AnimalDoctorGeneric cannot be applied to (java.util.
List<Dog>)
        doc.addAnimal(animals);
            ^
1 error
```

Notice that this message is virtually the same one you'd get trying to invoke any method with the wrong argument. It's saying that you simply cannot invoke `addAnimal(List<Animal>)` using something whose reference was declared as List<Dog>. (It's the reference type, not the actual object type that matters—but remember—the generic type of an object is ALWAYS the same as the generic type declared on the reference. List<Dog> can refer ONLY to collections that are subtypes of List, but which were instantiated as generic type <Dog>.)

Once again, remember that once inside the `addAnimals()` method, all that matters is the type of the parameter—in this case, List<Animal>. (We changed it from ArrayList to List to keep our "base" type polymorphism cleaner.)

Back to the key question—how do we get around this? If the problem is related only to the danger of adding the wrong thing to the collection, what about the `checkup()` method that used the collection passed in as read-only? In other words, what about methods that invoke Animal methods on each thing in the collection, which will work regardless of which kind of ArrayList subtype is passed in?

And that's a clue! It's the `add()` method that is the problem, so what we need is a way to tell the compiler, "Hey, I'm using the collection passed in just to invoke methods on the elements—and I promise not to ADD anything into the collection." And there IS a mechanism to tell the compiler that you can take any generic subtype of the declared argument type because you won't be putting anything in the collection. And that mechanism is the wildcard <?>.

The method signature would change from

```
public void addAnimal(List<Animal> animals)
```

to

```
public void addAnimal(List<? extends Animal> animals)
```

By saying `<? extends Animal>`, we're saying, "I can be assigned a collection that is a subtype of List and typed for <Animal> or anything that *extends* Animal. And oh yes, I SWEAR that I will not ADD anything into the collection." (There's a little more to the story, but we'll get there.)

So of course the `addAnimal()` method above won't actually compile even with the wildcard notation, because that method DOES add something.

```
public void addAnimal(List<? extends Animal> animals) {
    animals.add(new Dog());   // NO! Can't add if we
                              // use <? extends Animal>
}
```

You'll get a very strange error that might look something like this:

```
javac AnimalDoctorGeneric.java
AnimalDoctorGeneric.java:38: cannot find symbol
symbol  : method add(Dog)
location: interface java.util.List<capture of ? extends Animal>
    animals.add(new Dog());
                ^
1 error
```

which basically says, "you can't add a Dog here." If we change the method so that it doesn't add anything, it works.

But wait—there's more. (And by the way, everything we've covered in this generics section is likely to be tested for on the exam, with the exception of "type erasure," for which you aren't required to know any details.)

First, the `<? extends Animal>` means that you can take any subtype of Animal; however, that subtype can be EITHER a subclass of a class (abstract or concrete) OR a type that implements the interface after the word `extends`. In other words, the keyword `extends` in the context of a wildcard represents BOTH subclasses and interface implementations. There is no `<? implements Serializable>` syntax. If you want to declare a method that takes anything that is of a type that implements Serializable, you'd still use `extends` like this:

```
void foo(List<? extends Serializable> list) // odd, but correct
                                            // to use "extends"
```

This looks strange since you would never say this in a class declaration because Serializable is an interface, not a class. But that's the syntax, so burn it in!

One more time—there is only ONE wildcard keyword that represents *both* interface implementations and subclasses. And that keyword is `extends`. But when you see it, think "Is-a", as in something that passes the `instanceof` test.

However, there is another scenario where you can use a wildcard AND still add to the collection, but in a safe way—the keyword `super`.

Imagine, for example, that you declared the method this way:

```
public void addAnimal(List<? super Dog> animals) {
  animals.add(new Dog());  // adding is sometimes OK with super
}
public static void main(String[] args) {
  List<Animal> animals = new ArrayList<Animal>();
  animals.add(new Dog());
  animals.add(new Dog());
  AnimalDoctorGeneric doc = new AnimalDoctorGeneric();
  doc.addAnimal(animals); // passing an Animal List
}
```

Now what you've said in this line

```
public void addAnimal(List<? super Dog> animals)
```

is essentially, "Hey compiler, please accept any List with a generic type that is of type Dog, or a supertype of Dog. Nothing lower in the inheritance tree can come in, but anything higher than Dog is OK."

You probably already recognize why this works. If you pass in a list of type Animal, then it's perfectly fine to add a Dog to it. If you pass in a list of type Dog, it's perfectly fine to add a Dog to it. And if you pass in a list of type Object, it's STILL fine to add a Dog to it. When you use the `<? super ...>` syntax, you are telling the compiler that you can accept the type on the right-hand side of `super` or any of its supertypes, since—and this is the key part that makes it work—a collection declared as any supertype of Dog will be able to accept a Dog as an element. List<Object> can take a Dog. List<Animal> can take a Dog. And List<Dog> can take a Dog. So passing any of those in will work. So the `super` keyword in wildcard notation lets you have a restricted, but still possible way to add to a collection.

So, the wildcard gives you polymorphic assignments, but with certain restrictions that you don't have for arrays. Quick question: are these two identical?

```
public void foo(List<?> list) { }
public void foo(List<Object> list) { }
```

If there IS a difference (and we're not yet saying there is), what is it?

There IS a huge difference. List<?>, which is the wildcard <?> without the keywords extends or super, simply means "any type." So that means any type of List can be assigned to the argument. That could be a List of <Dog>, <Integer>, <JButton>, <Socket>, whatever. And using the wildcard alone, without the keyword super (followed by a type), means that you cannot ADD anything to the list referred to as List<?>.

List<Object> is completely different from List<?>. List<Object> means that the method can take ONLY a List<Object>. Not a List<Dog>, or a List<Cat>. It does, however, mean that you can add to the list, since the compiler has already made certain that you're passing only a valid List<Object> into the method.

Based on the previous explanations, figure out if the following will work:

```java
import java.util.*;
public class TestWildcards {
  public static void main(String[] args) {
    List<Integer> myList = new ArrayList<Integer>();
    Bar bar = new Bar();
    bar.doInsert(myList);
  }
}
class Bar {
  void doInsert(List<?> list) {
    list.add(new Dog());
  }
}
```

If not, where is the problem?

The problem is in the list.add() method within doInsert(). The <?> wildcard allows a list of ANY type to be passed to the method, but the add() method is not valid, for the reasons we explored earlier (that you could put the wrong kind of thing into the collection). So this time, the TestWildcards class is fine, but the Bar class won't compile because it does an add() in a method that uses a wildcard (without super). What if we change the doInsert() method to this:

```java
public class TestWildcards {
  public static void main(String[] args) {
    List<Integer> myList = new ArrayList<Integer>();
    Bar bar = new Bar();
    bar.doInsert(myList);
  }
}
```

```
class Bar {
  void doInsert(List<Object> list) {
    list.add(new Dog());
  }
}
```

Now will it work? If not, why not?

This time, class Bar, with the doInsert() method, compiles just fine. The problem is that the TestWildcards code is trying to pass a List<Integer> into a method that can take ONLY a List<Object>. And *nothing* else can be substituted for <Object>.

By the way, List<? extends Object> and List<?> are absolutely identical! They both say, "I can refer to any type of object." But as you can see, neither of them are the same as List<Object>. One way to remember this is that if you see the wildcard notation (a question mark ?), this means "many possibilities". If you do NOT see the question mark, then it means the <type> in the brackets, and absolutely NOTHING ELSE. List<Dog> means List<Dog> and not List<Beagle>, List<Poodle>, or any other subtype of Dog. But List<? extends Dog> could mean List<Beagle>, List<Poodle>, and so on. Of course List<?> could be... anything at all.

Keep in mind that the wildcards can be used only for reference declarations (including arguments, variables, return types, and so on). They can't be used as the type parameter when you create a new typed collection. Think about that—while a reference can be abstract and polymorphic, the actual object created must be of a specific type. You have to lock down the type when you make the object using new.

As a little review before we move on with generics, look at the following statements and figure out which will compile:

```
1) List<?> list = new ArrayList<Dog>();
2) List<? extends Animal> aList = new ArrayList<Dog>();
3) List<?> foo = new ArrayList<? extends Animal>();
4) List<? extends Dog> cList = new ArrayList<Integer>();
5) List<? super Dog> bList = new ArrayList<Animal>();
6) List<? super Animal> dList = new ArrayList<Dog>();
```

The correct answers (the statements that compile) are 1, 2, and 5. The three that won't compile are

■ Statement: List<?> foo = new ArrayList<? extends Animal>();
   Problem: you cannot use wildcard notation in the object creation. So the new ArrayList<? extends Animal>() will not compile.

- Statement: `List<? extends Dog> cList =`
  `new ArrayList<Integer>();`

  Problem: You cannot assign an Integer list to a reference that takes only a Dog (including any subtypes of Dog, of course).

- Statement: `List<? super Animal> dList = new ArrayList<Dog>();`

  Problem: You cannot assign a Dog to <? super Animal>. The Dog is too "low" in the class hierarchy. Only <Animal> or <Object> would have been legal.

Generic Declarations

Until now, we've talked about how to create type safe collections, and how to declare reference variables including arguments and return types using generic syntax. But here are a few questions: How do we even know that we're allowed/supposed to specify a type for these collection classes? And does generic typing work with any other classes in the API? And finally, can we declare our own classes as generic types? In other words, can we make a class that requires that someone pass a type in when they declare it and instantiate it?

First, the one you obviously know the answer to—the API tells you when a parameterized type is expected. For example, this is the API declaration for the java.util.List interface:

```
public interface List<E>
```

The <E> is a placeholder for the type you pass in. The List interface is behaving as a generic "template" (sort of like C++ templates), and when you write your code, you change it from a generic List to a List<Dog> or List<Integer>, and so on.

The E, by the way, is only a convention. Any valid Java identifier would work here, but E stands for "Element," and it's used when the template is a collection. The other main convention is T (stands for "type"), used for, well, things that are NOT collections.

Now that you've seen the interface declaration for List, what do you think the add() method looks like?

```
boolean add(E o)
```

In other words, whatever E is when you declare the List, *that's what you can add to it.* So imagine this code:

```
List<Animal> list = new ArrayList<Animal>();
```

The E in the List API suddenly has its waveform collapsed, and goes from the abstract <your type goes here>, to a List of Animals. And if it's a List of Animals, then the add() method of List must obviously behave like this:

```
boolean add(Animal a)
```

When you look at an API for a generics class or interface, pick a type parameter (Dog, JButton, even Object) and do a mental find and replace on each instance of E (or whatever identifier is used as the placeholder for the type parameter).

Making Your Own Generic Class

Let's try making our own generic class, to get a feel for how it works, and then we'll look at a few remaining generics syntax details. Imagine someone created a class Rental, that manages a pool of rentable items.

```java
public class Rental {
    private List rentalPool;
    private int maxNum;
    public Rental(int maxNum, List rentalPool) {
        this.maxNum = maxNum;
        this.rentalPool = rentalPool;
    }
    public Object getRental() {
        // blocks until there's something available
        return rentalPool.get(0);
    }
    public void returnRental(Object o) {
        rentalPool.add(o);
    }
}
```

Now imagine you wanted to make a subclass of Rental that was just for renting cars. You might start with something like this:

```java
import java.util.*;
public class CarRental extends Rental {
    public CarRental(int maxNum, List<Car> rentalPool) {
        super(maxNum, rentalPool);
    }
    public Car getRental() {
        return (Car) super.getRental();
    }
```

```
public void returnRental(Car c) {
   super.returnRental(c);
}
public void returnRental(Object o) {
  if (o instanceof Car) {
    super.returnRental(o);
  } else {
    System.out.println("Cannot add a non-Car");
    // probably throw an exception
} } }
```

But then the more you look at it, the more you realize:

1. You are doing your own type checking in the `returnRental()` method.
   You can't change the argument type of `returnRental()` to take a Car,
   since it's an override (not an overload) of the method from class Rental.
   (Overloading would take away your polymorphic flexibility with Rental).
2. You really don't want to make separate subclasses for every possible kind of
   rentable thing (cars, computers, bowling shoes, children, and so on).

But given your natural brilliance (heightened by this contrived scenario), you
quickly realize that you can make the Rental class a generic type—a template for any
kind of Rentable thing—and you're good to go.
   (We did say contrived…since in reality, you might very well want to have
different behaviors for different kinds of rentable things, but even that could be
solved cleanly through some kind of behavior composition as opposed to inheritance
(using the Strategy design pattern, for example). And no, design patterns aren't on
the exam, but we still think you should read our design patterns book. Think of the
kittens.) So here's your new and improved generic Rental class:

```
import java.util.*;
public class RentalGeneric<T> {   // "T" is for the type
                                  // parameter
   private List<T> rentalPool;    // Use the class type for the
                                  // List type
   private int maxNum;
   public RentalGeneric(
     int maxNum, List<T> rentalPool) { // constructor takes a
                                       // List of the class type
     this.maxNum = maxNum;
     this.rentalPool = rentalPool;
   }
```

```
    public T getRental() {                        // we rent out a T
      // blocks until there's something available
      return rentalPool.get(0);
    }
    public void returnRental(T returnedThing) { // and the renter
                                                // returns a T
      rentalPool.add(returnedThing);
    }
  }
```

Let's put it to the test:

```
class TestRental {
  public static void main (String[] args) {
    //make some Cars for the pool
    Car c1 = new Car();
    Car c2 = new Car();
    List<Car> carList = new ArrayList<Car>();
    carList.add(c1);
    carList.add(c2);
    RentalGeneric<Car> carRental = new
                       RentalGeneric<Car>(2, carList);
    // now get a car out, and it won't need a cast
    Car carToRent = carRental.getRental();
    carRental.returnRental(carToRent);
    // can we stick something else in the original carList?
    carList.add(new Cat("Fluffy"));
  }
}
```

We get one error:

```
kathy% javac1.5 RentalGeneric.java
RentalGeneric.java:38: cannot find symbol
symbol  : method add(Cat)
location: interface java.util.List<Car>
    carList.add(new Cat("Fluffy"));
                ^

1 error
```

Now we have a Rental class that can be *typed* to whatever the programmer chooses, and the compiler will enforce it. In other words, it works just as the

Collections classes do. Let's look at more examples of generic syntax you might find in the API or source code. Here's another simple class that uses the parameterized type of the class in several ways:

```
public class TestGenerics<T> {   // as the class type
   T anInstance;                  // as an instance variable type
   T [] anArrayOfTs;              // as an array type

   TestGenerics(T anInstance) {      // as an argument type
      this.anInstance = anInstance;
   }
   T getT() {                        // as a return type
      return anInstance;
   }
}
```

Obviously this is a ridiculous use of generics, and in fact you'll see generics only rarely outside of collections. But, you do need to understand the different kinds of generic syntax you might encounter, so we'll continue with these examples until we've covered them all.

You can use more than one parameterized type in a single class definition:

```
public class UseTwo<T, X> {
   T one;
   X two;
   UseTwo(T one, X two) {
      this.one = one;
      this.two = two;
   }
   T getT() { return one; }
   X getX() { return two; }

// test it by creating it with <String, Integer>

   public static void main (String[] args) {
      UseTwo<String, Integer> twos =
                  new UseTwo<String, Integer>("foo", 42);

      String theT = twos.getT(); // returns a String
      int theX = twos.getX();    // returns Integer, unboxes to int
   }
}
```

And you can use a form of wildcard notation in a class definition, to specify a range (called "bounds") for the type that can be used for the type parameter:

```
public class AnimalHolder<T extends Animal> { // use "T" instead
                                              // of "?"
  T animal;
  public static void main(String[] args) {
    AnimalHolder<Dog> dogHolder = new AnimalHolder<Dog>(); // OK
    AnimalHolder<Integer> x = new AnimalHolder<Integer>(); // NO!
  }
}
```

Creating Generic Methods

Until now, every example we've seen uses the class parameter type—the type declared with the class name. For example, in the UseTwo<T,X> declaration, we used the T and X placeholders throughout the code. But it's possible to define a parameterized type at a more granular level—a method.

Imagine you want to create a method that takes an instance of any type, instantiates an ArrayList of that type, and adds the instance to the ArrayList. The class itself doesn't need to be generic; basically we just want a utility method that we can pass a type to and that can use that type to construct a type safe collection. Using a generic method, we can declare the method without a specific type and then get the type information based on the type of the object passed to the method. For example:

```
import java.util.*;
public class CreateAnArrayList {
  public <T> void makeArrayList(T t) { // take an object of an
                                       // unknown type and use a
                                       // "T" to represent the type
    List<T> list = new ArrayList<T>(); // now we can create the
                                       // list using "T"
    list.add(t);
  }
}
```

In the preceding code, if you invoke the makeArrayList() method with a Dog instance, the method will behave as though it looked like this all along:

```
public void makeArrayList(Dog t) {
  List<Dog> list = new ArrayList<Dog>();
  list.add(t);
}
```

And of course if you invoke the method with an Integer, then the T is replaced by Integer (not in the bytecode, remember—we're describing how it appears to behave, not how it actually gets it done).

The strangest thing about generic methods is that you must declare the type variable BEFORE the return type of the method:

```
public <T> void makeArrayList(T t)
```

The <T> before `void` simply defines what T is before you use it as a type in the argument. You MUST declare the type like that unless the type is specified for the class. In CreateAnArrayList, the class is not generic, so there's no type parameter placeholder we can use.

You're also free to put boundaries on the type you declare, for example if you want to restrict the `makeArrayList()` method to only Number or its subtypes (Integer, Float, and so on) you would say

```
public <T extends Number> void makeArrayList(T t)
```

exam

watch

It's tempting to forget that the method argument is NOT where you declare the type parameter variable T. In order to use a type variable like T, you must have declared it either as the class parameter type or in the method, before the return type. The following might look right,

```
public void makeList(T t) { }
```

But the only way for this to be legal is if there is actually a class named T, in which case the argument is like any other type declaration for a variable. And what about constructor arguments? They, too, can be declared with a generic type, but then it looks even stranger since constructors have no return type at all:

```
public class Radio {
    public <T> Radio(T t) { }  // legal constructor
}
```

e**x**a m

If you REALLY want to get ridiculous (or fired), you can declare a class with a name that is the same as the type parameter placeholder:

```
class X { public <X> X(X x) { } }
```

Yes, this works. The X that is the constructor name has no relationship to the <X> type declaration, which has no relationship to the constructor argument identifier, which is also, of course, X. The compiler is able to parse this and treat each of the different uses of X independently. So there is no naming conflict between class names, type parameter placeholders, and variable identifiers.

e**x**a m

One of the most common mistakes programmers make when creating generic classes or methods is to use a <?> in the wildcard syntax rather than a type variable <T>, <E>, and so on. This code might look right, but isn't:

```
public class NumberHolder<? extends Number> { }
```

While the question mark works when declaring a reference for a variable, it does NOT work for generic class and method declarations. This code is not legal:

```
public class NumberHolder<?> { ? aNum; }     // NO!
```

But if you replace the <?> with a legal identifier, you're good:

```
public class NumberHolder<T> { T aNum; }     // Yes
```

98% of what you're likely to do with generics is simply declare and use type safe collections, including using (and passing) them as arguments. But now you know much more (but by no means everything) about the way generics works.

If this was clear and easy for you, that's excellent. If it was…painful…just know that adding generics to the Java language very nearly caused a revolt among some of the most experienced Java developers. Most of the outspoken critics are simply unhappy with the complexity, or aren't convinced that gaining type safe collections is worth the ten million little rules you have to learn now. It's true that with Java 5, learning Java just got harder. But trust us…we've never seen it take more than two days to "get" generics. That's 48 consecutive hours.

CERTIFICATION SUMMARY

We began with a quick review of the `toString()` method. The `toString()` method is automatically called when you ask `System.out.println()` to print an object—you override it to return a String of meaningful data about your objects.

Next we reviewed the purpose of `==` (to see if two reference variables refer to the same object) and the `equals()` method (to see if two objects are meaningfully equivalent). You learned the downside of not overriding `equals()`—you may not be able to find the object in a collection. We discussed a little bit about how to write a good `equals()` method—don't forget to use `instanceof` and refer to the object's significant attributes. We reviewed the contracts for overriding `equals()` and `hashCode()`. We learned about the theory behind hashcodes, the difference between legal, appropriate, and efficient hashcoding. We also saw that even though wildly inefficient, it's legal for a `hashCode()` method to always return the same value.

Next we turned to collections, where we learned about Lists, Sets, and Maps, and the difference between ordered and sorted collections. We learned the key attributes of the common collection classes, and when to use which.

We covered the ins and outs of the Collections and Arrays classes: how to sort, and how to search. We learned about converting arrays to Lists and back again.

Finally we tackled generics. Generics let you enforce compile-time type-safety on collections or other classes. Generics help assure you that when you get an item from a collection it will be of the type you expect, with no casting required. You can mix legacy code with generics code, but this can cause exceptions. The rules for polymorphism change when you use generics, although by using wildcards you can still create polymorphic collections. Some generics declarations allow reading of a collection, but allow no updating of the collection.

All in all, one fascinating chapter.

✓ TWO-MINUTE DRILL

Here are some of the key points from this chapter.

Overriding hashCode() and equals() (Objective 6.2)

❑ `equals()`, `hashCode()`, and `toString()` are public.

❑ Override `toString()` so that `System.out.println()` or other methods can see something useful, like your object's state.

❑ Use `==` to determine if two reference variables refer to the same object.

❑ Use `equals()` to determine if two objects are meaningfully equivalent.

❑ If you don't override `equals()`, your objects won't be useful hashing keys.

❑ If you don't override `equals()`, different objects can't be considered equal.

❑ Strings and wrappers override `equals()` and make good hashing keys.

❑ When overriding `equals()`, use the `instanceof` operator to be sure you're evaluating an appropriate class.

❑ When overriding `equals()`, compare the objects' significant attributes.

❑ Highlights of the `equals()` contract:

 ❑ Reflexive: `x.equals(x)` is true.

 ❑ Symmetric: If `x.equals(y)` is true, then `y.equals(x)` must be true.

 ❑ Transitive: If `x.equals(y)` is true, and `y.equals(z)` is true, then `z.equals(x)` is true.

 ❑ Consistent: Multiple calls to `x.equals(y)` will return the same result.

 ❑ Null: If `x` is not `null`, then `x.equals(null)` is false.

❑ If `x.equals(y)` is true, then `x.hashCode() == y.hashCode()` is true.

❑ If you override `equals()`, override `hashCode()`.

❑ HashMap, HashSet, Hashtable, LinkedHashMap, & LinkedHashSet use hashing.

❑ An appropriate `hashCode()` override sticks to the `hashCode()` contract.

❑ An efficient `hashCode()` override distributes keys evenly across its buckets.

❑ An overridden `equals()` must be at least as precise as its `hashCode()` mate.

❑ To reiterate: if two objects are equal, their hashcodes must be equal.

❑ It's legal for a `hashCode()` method to return the same value for all instances (although in practice it's very inefficient).

❑ Highlights of the `hashCode()` contract:

   ❑ Consistent: multiple calls to `x.hashCode()` return the same integer.

   ❑ If `x.equals(y)` is `true`, `x.hashCode() == y.hashCode()` is `true`.

   ❑ If `x.equals(y)` is `false`, then `x.hashCode() == y.hashCode()` can be either `true` or `false`, but `false` will tend to create better efficiency.

❑ `transient` variables aren't appropriate for `equals()` and `hashCode()`.

Collections (Objective 6.1)

❑ Common collection activities include adding objects, removing objects, verifying object inclusion, retrieving objects, and iterating.

❑ Three meanings for "collection":

   ❑ **collection**   Represents the data structure in which objects are stored

   ❑ **Collection**   java.util interface from which Set and List extend

   ❑ **Collections**   A class that holds static collection utility methods

❑ Four basic flavors of collections include Lists, Sets, Maps, Queues:

   ❑ **Lists of things**   Ordered, duplicates allowed, with an index.

   ❑ **Sets of things**   May or may not be ordered and/or sorted; duplicates not allowed.

   ❑ **Maps of things with keys**   May or may not be ordered and/or sorted; duplicate keys are not allowed.

   ❑ **Queues of things to process**   Ordered by FIFO or by priority.

❑ Four basic sub-flavors of collections Sorted, Unsorted, Ordered, Unordered.

   ❑ **Ordered**   Iterating through a collection in a specific, non-random order.

   ❑ **Sorted**   Iterating through a collection in a sorted order.

❑ Sorting can be alphabetic, numeric, or programmer-defined.

Key Attributes of Common Collection Classes (Objective 6.1)

❑ ArrayList: Fast iteration and fast random access.

❑ Vector: It's like a slower ArrayList, but it has synchronized methods.

❑ LinkedList: Good for adding elements to the ends, i.e., stacks and queues.

❑ HashSet: Fast access, assures no duplicates, provides no ordering.

❑ LinkedHashSet: No duplicates; iterates by insertion order.

❑ TreeSet: No duplicates; iterates in sorted order.

- ❏ HashMap: Fastest updates (key/value pairs); allows one `null` key, many `null` values.
- ❏ Hashtable: Like a slower HashMap (as with Vector, due to its synchronized methods). No `null` values or `null` keys allowed.
- ❏ LinkedHashMap: Faster iterations; iterates by insertion order or last accessed; allows one `null` key, many `null` values.
- ❏ TreeMap: A sorted map.
- ❏ PriorityQueue: A to-do list ordered by the elements' priority.

Using Collection Classes (Objective 6.3)

- ❏ Collections hold only Objects, but primitives can be autoboxed.
- ❏ Iterate with the enhanced `for`, or with an Iterator via `hasNext()` & `next()`.
- ❏ `hasNext()` determines if more elements exist; the Iterator does NOT move.
- ❏ `next()` returns the next element AND moves the Iterator forward.
- ❏ To work correctly, a Map's keys must override `equals()` and `hashCode()`.
- ❏ Queues use `offer()` to add an element, `poll()` to remove the head of the queue, and `peek()` to look at the head of a queue.

Sorting and Searching Arrays and Lists (Objective 6.5)

- ❏ Sorting can be in natural order, or via a Comparable or many Comparators.
- ❏ Implement Comparable using `compareTo()`; provides only one sort order.
- ❏ Create many Comparators to sort a class many ways; implement `compare()`.
- ❏ To be sorted and searched, a List's elements must be *comparable*.
- ❏ To be searched, an array or List must first be sorted.

Utility Classes: Collections and Arrays (Objective 6.5)

- ❏ Both of these java.util classes provide
  - ❏ A `sort()` method. Sort using a Comparator or sort using natural order.
  - ❏ A `binarySearch()` method. Search a pre-sorted array or List.
- ❏ `Arrays.asList()` creates a List from an array and links them together.
- ❏ `Collections.reverse()` reverses the order of elements in a List.
- ❏ `Collections.reverseOrder()` returns a Comparator that sorts in reverse.
- ❏ Lists and Sets have a `toArray()` method to create arrays.

Generics (Objective 6.4)

❏ Generics let you enforce compile-time type safety on Collections (or other classes and methods declared using generic type parameters).

❏ An ArrayList<Animal> can accept references of type Dog, Cat, or any other subtype of Animal (subclass, or if Animal is an interface, implementation).

❏ When using generic collections, a cast is not needed to get (declared type) elements out of the collection. With non-generic collections, a cast is required:

```
List<String> gList = new ArrayList<String>();
List list = new ArrayList();
// more code
String s = gList.get(0);            // no cast needed
String s = (String)list.get(0);     // cast required
```

❏ You can pass a generic collection into a method that takes a non-generic collection, but the results may be disastrous. The compiler can't stop the method from inserting the wrong type into the previously type safe collection.

❏ If the compiler can recognize that non-type-safe code is potentially endangering something you originally declared as type-safe, you will get a compiler warning. For instance, if you pass a List<String> into a method declared as

```
void foo(List aList) { aList.add(anInteger); }
```

the compiler will issue a warning because the add() method is potentially an "unsafe operation."

❏ Remember that "compiles without error" is not the same as "compiles without warnings." On the exam, a compilation *warning* is not considered a compilation *error* or *failure*.

❏ Generic type information does not exist at runtime—it is for compile-time safety only. Mixing generics with legacy code can create compiled code that may throw an exception at runtime.

❏ Polymorphic assignments applies only to the base type, not the generic type parameter. You can say

```
List<Animal> aList = new ArrayList<Animal>();    // yes
```

You can't say

```
List<Animal> aList = new ArrayList<Dog>();        // no
```

❑ The polymorphic assignment rule applies everywhere an assignment can be made. The following are NOT allowed:

```
void foo(List<Animal> aList) { }  // cannot take a List<Dog>
List<Animal> bar() { }            // cannot return a List<Dog>
```

❑ Wildcard syntax allows a generic method, accept subtypes (or supertypes) of the declared type of the method argument:

```
void addD(List<Dog> d) {}  // can take only <Dog>
void addD(List<? extends Dog>) {} // take a <Dog> or <Beagle>
```

❑ The wildcard keyword `extends` is used to mean either "extends" or "implements." So in `<? extends Dog>`, Dog can be a class or an interface.

❑ When using a wildcard, `List<? extends Dog>`, the collection can be accessed but not modified.

❑ When using a wildcard, `List<?>`, any generic type can be assigned to the reference, but for access only, no modifications.

❑ `List<Object>` refers only to a `List<Object>`, while `List<?>` or `List<? extends Object>` can hold any type of object, but for access only.

❑ Declaration conventions for generics use T for type and E for element:

```
public interface List<E>  // API declaration for List
boolean add(E o)          // List.add() declaration
```

❑ The generics type identifier can be used in class, method, and variable declarations:

```
class Foo<t> { }       // a class
T anInstance;          // an instance variable
Foo(T aRef) {}         // a constructor argument
void bar(T aRef) {}    // a method argument
T baz() {}             // a return type
```

The compiler will substitute the actual type.

❑ You can use more than one parameterized type in a declaration:

```
public class UseTwo<T, X> { }
```

❑ You can declare a generic method using a type not defined in the class:

```
public <T> void makeList(T t) { }
```

is NOT using T as the return type. This method has a `void` return type, but to use T within the method's argument you must declare the `<T>`, which happens before the return type.

SELF TEST

I. Given:

```
import java.util.*;
class Test {
  public static void main(String[] args) {
    // insert code here
    x.add("one");
    x.add("two");
    x.add("TWO");
    System.out.println(x.poll());
  }
}
```

Which, inserted at // insert code here, will compile? (Choose all that apply.)

A. List<String> x = new LinkedList<String>();

B. TreeSet<String> x = new TreeSet<String>();

C. HashSet<String> x = new HashSet<String>();

D. Queue<String> x = new PriorityQueue<String>();

E. ArrayList<String> x = new ArrayList<String>();

F. LinkedList<String> x = new LinkedList<String>();

2. Given:

```
public static void main(String[] args) {

  // INSERT DECLARATION HERE
  for (int i = 0; i <= 10; i++) {
    List<Integer> row = new ArrayList<Integer>();
    for (int j = 0; j <= 10; j++)
      row.add(i * j);
    table.add(row);
  }
  for (List<Integer> row : table)
    System.out.println(row);
  }
```

Which statements could be inserted at `// INSERT DECLARATION HERE` to allow this code to compile and run? (Choose all that apply.)

A. `List<List<Integer>> table = new List<List<Integer>>();`

B. `List<List<Integer>> table = new ArrayList<List<Integer>>();`

C. `List<List<Integer>> table = new ArrayList<ArrayList<Integer>>();`

D. `List<List, Integer> table = new List<List, Integer>();`

E. `List<List, Integer> table = new ArrayList<List, Integer>();`

F. `List<List, Integer> table = new ArrayList<ArrayList, Integer>();`

G. None of the above.

3. Which statements are true about comparing two instances of the same class, given that the `equals()` and `hashCode()` methods have been properly overridden? (Choose all that apply.)

A. If the `equals()` method returns true, the `hashCode()` comparison `==` might return false.

B. If the `equals()` method returns false, the `hashCode()` comparison `==` might return true.

C. If the `hashCode()` comparison `==` returns true, the `equals()` method must return true.

D. If the `hashCode()` comparison `==` returns true, the `equals()` method might return true.

E. If the `hashCode()` comparison `!=` returns true, the `equals()` method might return true.

4. Given:

```
import java.util.*;
class Flubber {
  public static void main(String[] args) {
    List<String> x = new ArrayList<String>();
    x.add(" x");   x.add("xx");   x.add("Xx");

    // insert code here
    for(String s: x)   System.out.println(s);
} }
```

And the output:

```
xx
Xx
 x
```

Which code, inserted at `// insert code here`, will produce the preceding output? (Choose all that apply.)

A. `Collections.sort(x);`

B. `Comparable c = Collections.reverse();`
`Collections.sort(x,c);`

C. `Comparator c = Collections.reverse();`
`Collections.sort(x,c);`

D. `Comparable c = Collections.reverseOrder();`
`Collections.sort(x,c);`

E. `Comparator c = Collections.reverseOrder();`
`Collections.sort(x,c);`

5. Given:

```
10.     public static void main(String[] args) {
11.         Queue<String> q = new LinkedList<String>();
12.         q.add("Veronica");
13.         q.add("Wallace");
14.         q.add("Duncan");
15.         showAll(q);
16.     }
17.
18.     public static void showAll(Queue q) {
19.         q.add(new Integer(42));
20.         while (!q.isEmpty())
21.             System.out.print(q.remove() + " ");
22.     }
```

What is the result?

A. `Veronica Wallace Duncan`

B. `Veronica Wallace Duncan 42`

C. `Duncan Wallace Veronica`

D. `42 Duncan Wallace Veronica`

E. Compilation fails.

F. An exception occurs at runtime.

6. Given:

```
public static void before() {
  Set set = new TreeSet();
  set.add("2");
  set.add(3);
  set.add("1");
  Iterator it = set.iterator();
    while (it.hasNext())
  System.out.print(it.next() + " ");
}
```

Which of the following statements are true?

A. The before() method will print 1 2

B. The before() method will print 1 2 3

C. The before() method will print three numbers, but the order cannot be determined.

D. The before() method will not compile.

E. The before() method will throw an exception at runtime.

7. Given:

```
import java.util.*;
class MapEQ {
  public static void main(String[] args) {
    Map<ToDos, String> m = new HashMap<ToDos, String>();
    ToDos t1 = new ToDos("Monday");
    ToDos t2 = new ToDos("Monday");
    ToDos t3 = new ToDos("Tuesday");
    m.put(t1, "doLaundry");
    m.put(t2, "payBills");
    m.put(t3, "cleanAttic");
    System.out.println(m.size());
  }
}
class ToDos{
  String day;
  ToDos(String d) { day = d; }
  public boolean equals(Object o) {
    return ((ToDos)o).day == this.day;
  }
  // public int hashCode() { return 9; }
}
```

Which is correct? (Choose all that apply.)

A. As the code stands it will not compile.

B. As the code stands the output will be 2.

C. As the code stands the output will be 3.

D. If the `hashCode()` method is uncommented the output will be 2.

E. If the `hashCode()` method is uncommented the output will be 3.

F. If the `hashCode()` method is uncommented the code will not compile.

8. Given:

```
12. public class AccountManager {
13.       private Map accountTotals = new HashMap();
14.       private int retirementFund;
15.
16.       public int getBalance(String accountName) {
17.           Integer total = (Integer) accountTotals.get(accountName);
18.           if (total == null)
19.               total = Integer.valueOf(0);
20.           return total.intValue();
21.       }
23.       public void setBalance(String accountName, int amount) {
24.           accountTotals.put(accountName, Integer.valueOf(amount));
25.       }
26. }
```

This class is to be updated to make use of appropriate generic types, with no changes in behavior (for better or worse). Which of these steps could be performed? (Choose three.)

A. Replace line 13 with
   `private Map<String, int> accountTotals = new HashMap<String, int>();`

B. Replace line 13 with
   `private Map<String, Integer> accountTotals = new HashMap<String, Integer>();`

C. Replace line 13 with
   `private Map<String<Integer>> accountTotals = new HashMap<String<Integer>>();`

D. Replace lines 17–20 with
   ```
   int total = accountTotals.get(accountName);
   if (total == null)
       total = 0;
   return total;
   ```

E. Replace lines 17–20 with

```
Integer total = accountTotals.get(accountName);
if (total == null)
    total = 0;
return total;
```

F. Replace lines 17–20 with

```
return accountTotals.get(accountName);
```

G. Replace line 24 with

```
accountTotals.put(accountName, amount);
```

H. Replace line 24 with

```
accountTotals.put(accountName, amount.intValue());
```

9. Given a properly prepared String array containing five elements, which range of results could a proper invocation of `Arrays.binarySearch()` produce?

A. 0 through 4

B. 0 through 5

C. -1 through 4

D. -1 through 5

E. -5 through 4

F. -5 through 5

G. -6 through 4

H. -6 through 5

10. Given:

```
interface Hungry<E> { void munch(E x); }
interface Carnivore<E extends Animal> extends Hungry<E> {}
interface Herbivore<E extends Plant> extends Hungry<E> {}
abstract class Plant {}
class Grass extends Plant {}
abstract class Animal {}
class Sheep extends Animal implements Herbivore<Sheep> {
  public void munch(Sheep x) {}
}
class Wolf extends Animal implements Carnivore<Sheep> {
  public void munch(Sheep x) {}
}
```

Which of the following changes (taken separately) would allow this code to compile? (Choose all that apply.)

A. Change the Carnivore interface to
```
interface Carnivore<E extends Plant> extends Hungry<E> {}
```

B. Change the Herbivore interface to
```
interface Herbivore<E extends Animal> extends Hungry<E> {}
```

C. Change the Sheep class to
```
class Sheep extends Animal implements Herbivore<Plant> {
    public void munch(Grass x) {}
}
```

D. Change the Sheep class to
```
class Sheep extends Plant implements Carnivore<Wolf> {
    public void munch(Wolf x) {}
}
```

E. Change the Wolf class to
```
class Wolf extends Animal implements Herbivore<Grass> {
    public void munch(Grass x) {}
}
```

F. No changes are necessary.

11. Which collection class(es) allows you to grow or shrink its size and provides indexed access to its elements, but whose methods are not synchronized? (Choose all that apply.)

A. `java.util.HashSet`

B. `java.util.LinkedHashSet`

C. `java.util.List`

D. `java.util.ArrayList`

E. `java.util.Vector`

F. `java.util.PriorityQueue`

12. Given:
```
import java.util.*;
public class Group extends HashSet<Person> {
    public static void main(String[] args) {
        Group g = new Group();
        g.add(new Person("Hans"));
        g.add(new Person("Lotte"));
```

```
            g.add(new Person("Jane"));
            g.add(new Person("Hans"));
            g.add(new Person("Jane"));
            System.out.println("Total: " + g.size());
        }
        public boolean add(Object o) {
            System.out.println("Adding: " + o);
            return super.add(o);
        }
    }
    class Person {
        private final String name;
        public Person(String name) { this.name = name; }
        public String toString() { return name; }
    }
```

Which of the following occur at least once when the code is compiled and run? (Choose all that apply.)

A. `Adding Hans`

B. `Adding Lotte`

C. `Adding Jane`

D. `Total: 3`

E. `Total: 5`

F. The code does not compile.

G. An exception is thrown at runtime.

13. Given:

```
    import java.util.*;
    class AlgaeDiesel {
      public static void main(String[] args) {
        String[] sa = {"foo", "bar", "baz" };
        // insert method invocations here
      }
    }
```

What `java.util.Arrays` and/or `java.util.Collections` methods could you use to convert sa to a List and then search the List to find the index of the element whose value is `"foo"`? (Choose from one to three methods.)

A. `sort()`

B. `asList()`

C. `toList()`

D. `search()`

E. `sortList()`

F. `contains()`

G. `binarySearch()`

14. Given that String implements java.lang.CharSequence, and:

```
import java.util.*;
public class LongWordFinder {
    public static void main(String[] args) {
        String[] array = { "123", "12345678", "1", "12", "1234567890"};
        List<String> list = Arrays.asList(array);
        Collection<String> resultList = getLongWords(list);
    }
    // INSERT DECLARATION HERE
    {
        Collection<E> longWords = new ArrayList<E>();
        for (E word : coll)
            if (word.length() > 6)  longWords.add(word);
        return longWords;
    }
}
```

Which declarations could be inserted at `// INSERT DECLARATION HERE` so that the program will compile and run? (Choose all that apply.)

A. `public static <E extends CharSequence> Collection<? extends CharSequence>`
   `    getLongWords(Collection<E> coll)`

B. `public static <E extends CharSequence> List<E>`
   `        getLongWords(Collection<E> coll)`

C. `public static Collection<E extends CharSequence>`
   `        getLongWords(Collection<E> coll)`

D. `public static List<CharSequence>`
   `        getLongWords(Collection<CharSequence> coll)`

E. `public static List<? extends CharSequence>`
   `        getLongWords(Collection<? extends CharSequence> coll)`

F. ```
static public <E extends CharSequence> Collection<E>
        getLongWords(Collection<E> coll)
```

G. ```
static public <E super CharSequence> Collection<E>
        getLongWords(Collection<E> coll)
```

15. Given:

```
12.     TreeSet map = new TreeSet();
13.     map.add("one");
14.     map.add("two");
15.     map.add("three");
16.     map.add("four");
17.     map.add("one");
18.     Iterator it = map.iterator();
19.     while (it.hasNext() ) {
20.         System.out.print( it.next() + " " );
21.     }
```

What is the result?

A. Compilation fails.

B. `one two three four`

C. `four three two one`

D. `four one three two`

E. `one two three four one`

F. `one four three two one`

G. An exception is thrown at runtime.

H. The print order is not guaranteed.

16. Given a method declared as:

```
public static <E extends Number> List<? super E> process(List<E> nums)
```

A programmer wants to use this method like this:

```
// INSERT DECLARATIONS HERE

output = process(input);
```

Which pairs of declarations could be placed at // INSERT DECLARATIONS HERE to allow the code to compile? (Choose all that apply.)

A. `ArrayList<Integer> input = null;`
`ArrayList<Integer> output = null;`

B. `ArrayList<Integer> input = null;`
`List<Integer> output = null;`

C. `ArrayList<Integer> input = null;`
`List<Number> output = null;`

D. `List<Number> input = null;`
`ArrayList<Integer> output = null;`

E. `List<Number> input = null;`
`List<Number> output = null;`

F. `List<Integer> input = null;`
`List<Integer> output = null;`

G. None of the above.

SELF TEST ANSWERS

1. Given:

```
import java.util.*;
class Test {
  public static void main(String[] args) {
    // insert code here
    x.add("one");
    x.add("two");
    x.add("TWO");
    System.out.println(x.poll());
  }
}
```

Which, inserted at `// insert code here`, will compile? (Choose all that apply.)

A. `List<String> x = new LinkedList<String>();`

B. `TreeSet<String> x = new TreeSet<String>();`

C. `HashSet<String> x = new HashSet<String>();`

D. `Queue<String> x = new PriorityQueue<String>();`

E. `ArrayList<String> x = new ArrayList<String>();`

F. `LinkedList<String> x = new LinkedList<String>();`

Answer:

☑ **D** and **F** are correct. The `poll()` method is associated with Queues. The LinkedList class implements the Queue interface.

☒ **A** is incorrect because the List interface does not implement Queue, and the polymorphic instantiation would restrict x to invoking only those methods declared in the List interface. **B, C,** and **E** are incorrect, based on the above. (Objective 6.3)

2. Given:

```
public static void main(String[] args) {
  // INSERT DECLARATION HERE
  for (int i = 0; i <= 10; i++) {
    List<Integer> row = new ArrayList<Integer>();
    for (int j = 0; j <= 10; j++)
      row.add(i * j);
    table.add(row);
  }
  for (List<Integer> row : table)
    System.out.println(row);
}
```

Which statements could be inserted at `// INSERT DECLARATION HERE` to allow this code to compile and run? (Choose all that apply.)

A. `List<List<Integer>> table = new List<List<Integer>>();`

B. `List<List<Integer>> table = new ArrayList<List<Integer>>();`

C. `List<List<Integer>> table = new ArrayList<ArrayList<Integer>>();`

D. `List<List, Integer> table = new List<List, Integer>();`

E. `List<List, Integer> table = new ArrayList<List, Integer>();`

F. `List<List, Integer> table = new ArrayList<ArrayList, Integer>();`

G. None of the above.

Answer:

☑ **B** is correct.

☒ **A** is incorrect because List is an interface, so you can't say `new List()` regardless of any generic types. **D, E,** and **F** are incorrect because List only takes one type parameter (a Map would take two, not a List). **C** is tempting, but incorrect. The type argument `<List<Integer>>` must be the same for both sides of the assignment, even though the constructor `new ArrayList()` on the right side is a subtype of the declared type List on the left. (Objective 6.4)

3. Which statements are true about comparing two instances of the same class, given that the `equals()` and `hashCode()` methods have been properly overridden? (Choose all that apply.)

A. If the `equals()` method returns true, the `hashCode()` comparison `==` might return false.

B. If the `equals()` method returns false, the `hashCode()` comparison `==` might return true.

C. If the `hashCode()` comparison `==` returns true, the `equals()` method must return true.

D. If the `hashCode()` comparison `==` returns true, the `equals()` method might return true.

E. If the `hashCode()` comparison `!=` returns true, the `equals()` method might return true.

Answer:

☑ **B** and **D**. **B** is true because often two dissimilar objects can return the same hashcode value. **D** is true because if the `hashCode()` comparison returns `==`, the two objects might or might not be equal.

☒ **A, C,** and **E** are incorrect. **C** is incorrect because the `hashCode()` method is very flexible in its return values, and often two dissimilar objects can return the same hash code value. **A** and **E** are a negation of the `hashCode()` and `equals()` contract. (Objective 6.2)

4. Given:

```
import java.util.*;
class Flubber {
  public static void main(String[] args) {
    List<String> x = new ArrayList<String>();
    x.add(" x");  x.add("xx"); x.add("Xx");

    // insert code here
    for(String s: x)  System.out.println(s);
  }
}
```

And the output:

```
xx
Xx
 x
```

Which code, inserted at `// insert code here`, will produce the preceding output? (Choose all that apply.)

A. `Collections.sort(x);`

B. `Comparable c = Collections.reverse();`
   `Collections.sort(x,c);`

C. `Comparator c = Collections.reverse();`
   `Collections.sort(x,c);`

D. `Comparable c = Collections.reverseOrder();`
   `Collections.sort(x,c);`

E. `Comparator c = Collections.reverseOrder();`
   `Collections.sort(x,c);`

Answer:

☑ **E** is correct. Natural ordering would produce output in reverse sequence to that listed. The `Collections.reverseOrder()` method takes a Comparator not a Comparable to re-sort a Collection.

☒ **A, B, C,** and **D** are incorrect based on the above. (Objective 6.5)

5. Given:

```
10.    public static void main(String[] args) {
11.        Queue<String> q = new LinkedList<String>();
12.        q.add("Veronica");
13.        q.add("Wallace");
14.        q.add("Duncan");
15.        showAll(q);
16.    }
```

```
17.
18.    public static void showAll(Queue q) {
19.        q.add(new Integer(42));
20.        while (!q.isEmpty())
21.            System.out.print(q.remove() + " ");
22.    }
```

What is the result?

A. `Veronica Wallace Duncan`

B. `Veronica Wallace Duncan 42`

C. `Duncan Wallace Veronica`

D. `42 Duncan Wallace Veronica`

E. Compilation fails.

F. An exception occurs at runtime.

Answer:

☑ **B** is correct. There is a compiler warning at line 19 because of an unchecked assignment, but other than that everything compiles and runs fine. Although q was originally declared as Queue<String>, in showAll() it's passed as an untyped Queue—nothing in the compiler or JVM prevents us from adding an Integer after that. The add() method puts things at the end of the queue, while remove() takes them from the beginning, so everything prints in the order they were put in.

☒ **A, C, D, E,** and **F** are incorrect based on the above. (Objective 6.3)

6. Given:

```
public static void before() {
    Set set = new TreeSet();
    set.add("2");
    set.add(3);
    set.add("1");
    Iterator it = set.iterator();
      while (it.hasNext())
    System.out.print(it.next() + " ");
}
```

Which of the following statements are true?

A. The `before()` method will print 1 2

B. The `before()` method will print 1 2 3

C. The `before()` method will print three numbers, but the order cannot be determined.

D. The `before()` method will not compile.

E. The `before()` method will throw an exception at runtime.

Answer:

☑ **E** is correct. You can't put both Strings and `int`s into the same TreeSet. Without generics, the compiler has no way of knowing what type is appropriate for this TreeSet, so it allows everything to compile. At runtime, the TreeSet will try to sort the elements as they're added, and when it tries to compare an Integer with a String it will throw a ClassCastException. Note that although the `before()` method does not use generics, it does use autoboxing. Watch out for code that uses some new features and some old features mixed together.

☒ **A, B, C,** and **D** are incorrect based on the above. (Objective 6.5)

7. Given:

```java
import java.util.*;
class MapEQ {
  public static void main(String[] args) {
    Map<ToDos, String> m = new HashMap<ToDos, String>();
    ToDos t1 = new ToDos("Monday");
    ToDos t2 = new ToDos("Monday");
    ToDos t3 = new ToDos("Tuesday");
    m.put(t1, "doLaundry");
    m.put(t2, "payBills");
    m.put(t3, "cleanAttic");
    System.out.println(m.size());
} }
class ToDos{
  String day;
  ToDos(String d) { day = d; }
  public boolean equals(Object o) {
    return ((ToDos)o).day == this.day;
  }
  // public int hashCode() { return 9; }
}
```

Which is correct? (Choose all that apply.)

A. As the code stands it will not compile.

B. As the code stands the output will be 2.

C. As the code stands the output will be 3.

D. If the `hashCode()` method is uncommented the output will be 2.

E. If the `hashCode()` method is uncommented the output will be 3.

F. If the `hashCode()` method is uncommented the code will not compile.

Answer:

☑ **C** and **D** are correct. If `hashCode()` is not overridden then every entry will go into its own bucket, and the overridden `equals()` method will have no effect on determining equivalency. If `hashCode()` is overridden, then the overridden `equals()` method will view `t1` and `t2` as duplicates.

☒ **A, B, E,** and **F** are incorrect based on the above. (Objective 6.2)

8. Given:

```
12. public class AccountManager {
13.     private Map accountTotals = new HashMap();
14.     private int retirementFund;
15.
16.     public int getBalance(String accountName) {
17.         Integer total = (Integer) accountTotals.get(accountName);
18.         if (total == null)
19.             total = Integer.valueOf(0);
20.         return total.intValue();
21.     }
23.     public void setBalance(String accountName, int amount) {
24.         accountTotals.put(accountName, Integer.valueOf(amount));
25.  } }
```

This class is to be updated to make use of appropriate generic types, with no changes in behavior (for better or worse). Which of these steps could be performed? (Choose three.)

A. Replace line 13 with
```
private Map<String, int> accountTotals = new HashMap<String, int>();
```

B. Replace line 13 with
```
private Map<String, Integer> accountTotals = new HashMap<String, Integer>();
```

C. Replace line 13 with
```
private Map<String<Integer>> accountTotals = new HashMap<String<Integer>>();
```

D. Replace lines 17–20 with
```
int total = accountTotals.get(accountName);
if (total == null)  total = 0;
return total;
```

E. Replace lines 17–20 with
```
Integer total = accountTotals.get(accountName);
if (total == null)  total = 0;
return total;
```

F. Replace lines 17–20 with
```
return accountTotals.get(accountName);
```

G. Replace line 24 with
```
accountTotals.put(accountName, amount);
```

H. Replace line 24 with

```
accountTotals.put(accountName, amount.intValue());
```

Answer:

☑ **B, E,** and **G** are correct.

☒ **A** is wrong because you can't use a primitive type as a type parameter. **C** is wrong because a Map takes two type parameters separated by a comma. **D** is wrong because an int can't autobox to a null, and **F** is wrong because a `null` can't unbox to 0. **H** is wrong because you can't autobox a primitive just by trying to invoke a method with it. (Objective 6.4)

9. Given a properly prepared String array containing five elements, which range of results could a proper invocation of `Arrays.binarySearch()` produce?

A. 0 through 4

B. 0 through 5

C. -1 through 4

D. -1 through 5

E. -5 through 4

F. -5 through 5

G. -6 through 4

H. -6 through 5

Answer:

☑ **G** is correct. If a match is found, `binarySearch()` will return the index of the element that was matched. If no match is found, `binarySearch()` will return a negative number that, if inverted and then decremented, gives you the insertion point (array index) at which the value searched on should be inserted into the array to maintain a proper sort.

☒ **A, B, C, D, E, F,** and **H** are incorrect based on the above. (Objective 6.5)

10. Given:

```
interface Hungry<E> { void munch(E x); }
interface Carnivore<E extends Animal> extends Hungry<E> {}
interface Herbivore<E extends Plant> extends Hungry<E> {}
abstract class Plant {}
class Grass extends Plant {}
abstract class Animal {}
class Sheep extends Animal implements Herbivore<Sheep> {
  public void munch(Sheep x) {}
}
class Wolf extends Animal implements Carnivore<Sheep> {
  public void munch(Sheep x) {}
}
```

Which of the following changes (taken separately) would allow this code to compile? (Choose all that apply.)

A. Change the Carnivore interface to

```
interface Carnivore<E extends Plant> extends Hungry<E> {}
```

B. Change the Herbivore interface to

```
interface Herbivore<E extends Animal> extends Hungry<E> {}
```

C. Change the Sheep class to

```
class Sheep extends Animal implements Herbivore<Plant> {
    public void munch(Grass x) {}
}
```

D. Change the Sheep class to

```
class Sheep extends Plant implements Carnivore<Wolf> {
    public void munch(Wolf x) {}
}
```

E. Change the Wolf class to

```
class Wolf extends Animal implements Herbivore<Grass> {
    public void munch(Grass x) {}
}
```

F. No changes are necessary.

Answer:

☑ **B** is correct. The problem with the original code is that Sheep tries to implement `Herbivore<Sheep>` and Herbivore declares that its type parameter `E` can be any type that extends Plant. Since a Sheep is not a Plant, `Herbivore<Sheep>` makes no sense—the type Sheep is outside the allowed range of Herbivore's parameter `E`. Only solutions that either alter the definition of a Sheep or alter the definition of Herbivore will be able to fix this. So **A, E,** and **F** are eliminated. **B** works, changing the definition of an Herbivore to allow it to eat Sheep solves the problem. **C** doesn't work because an `Herbivore<Plant>` must have a `munch(Plant)` method, not `munch(Grass)`. And **D** doesn't work, because in **D** we made Sheep extend Plant, now the Wolf class breaks because its `munch(Sheep)` method no longer fulfills the contract of Carnivore. (Objective 6.4)

11. Which collection class(es) allows you to grow or shrink its size and provides indexed access to its elements, but whose methods are not synchronized? (Choose all that apply.)

A. `java.util.HashSet`

B. `java.util.LinkedHashSet`

C. `java.util.List`

D. `java.util.ArrayList`

E. `java.util.Vector`

F. `java.util.PriorityQueue`

Answer:

☑ **D** is correct. All of the collection classes allow you to grow or shrink the size of your collection. `ArrayList` provides an index to its elements. The newer collection classes tend not to have synchronized methods. Vector is an older implementation of `ArrayList` functionality and has synchronized methods; it is slower than `ArrayList`.

☒ **A, B, C, E,** and **F** are incorrect based on the logic described above; Notes: **C,** List is an interface, and **F,** `PriorityQueue` does not offer access by index. (Objective 6.1)

12. Given:

```
import java.util.*;
public class Group extends HashSet<Person> {
    public static void main(String[] args) {
        Group g = new Group();
        g.add(new Person("Hans"));
        g.add(new Person("Lotte"));
        g.add(new Person("Jane"));
        g.add(new Person("Hans"));
        g.add(new Person("Jane"));
        System.out.println("Total: " + g.size());
    }
    public boolean add(Object o) {
        System.out.println("Adding: " + o);
        return super.add(o);
    }
}
class Person {
    private final String name;
    public Person(String name) { this.name = name; }
    public String toString() { return name; }
}
```

Which of the following occur at least once when the code is compiled and run? (Choose all that apply.)

A. Adding `Hans`

B. Adding `Lotte`

C. Adding `Jane`

D. Total: 3

E. Total: 5

F. The code does not compile.

G. An exception is thrown at runtime.

Answer:

☑ **F** is correct. The problem here is in Group's `add()` method—it should have been `add(Person)`, since the class extends `HashSet<Person>`. So this doesn't compile. Pop Quiz: What would happen if you fixed this code, changing `add(Object)` to `add(Person)`? Try running the code to see if the results match what you thought.

☒ **A, B, C, D, E,** and **G** are incorrect based on the above. (Objective 6.4)

13. Given:

```
import java.util.*;
class AlgaeDiesel {
  public static void main(String[] args) {
    String[] sa = {"foo", "bar", "baz" };
    // insert method invocations here
  }
}
```

What `java.util.Arrays` and/or `java.util.Collections` methods could you use to convert sa to a List and then search the List to find the index of the element whose value is `"foo"`? (Choose from one to three methods.)

A. `sort()`

B. `asList()`

C. `toList()`

D. `search()`

E. `sortList()`

F. `contains()`

G. `binarySearch()`

Answer:

☑ **A, B,** and **G** are required. The as `List()` method converts an array to a List. You can find the index of an element in a List with the `binarySearch()` method, but before you do that you must sort the list using `sort()`.

☒ **F** is incorrect because `contains()` returns a boolean, not an index. **C, D,** and **E** are incorrect, because these methods are not defined in the List interface. (Objective 6.5)

14. Given that String implements java.lang.CharSequence, and:

```
import java.util.*;
public class LongWordFinder {
    public static void main(String[] args) {
        String[] array = { "123", "12345678", "1", "12", "1234567890"};
        List<String> list = Arrays.asList(array);
        Collection<String> resultList = getLongWords(list);
    }
    // INSERT DECLARATION HERE
    {
        Collection<E> longWords = new ArrayList<E>();
        for (E word : coll)
            if (word.length() > 6)  longWords.add(word);
        return longWords;
    }   }
```

Which declarations could be inserted at `// INSERT DECLARATION HERE` so that the program will compile and run? (Choose all that apply.)

A. `public static <E extends CharSequence> Collection<? extends CharSequence>`
        `getLongWords(Collection<E> coll)`

B. `public static <E extends CharSequence> List<E>`
        `getLongWords(Collection<E> coll)`

C. `public static Collection<E extends CharSequence> getLongWords(Collection<E> coll)`

D. `public static List<CharSequence>`
        `getLongWords(Collection<CharSequence> coll)`

E. `public static List<? extends CharSequence>`
        `getLongWords(Collection<? extends CharSequence> coll)`

F. `static public <E extends CharSequence> Collection<E>`
        `getLongWords(Collection<E> coll)`

G. `static public <E super CharSequence> Collection<E>`
        `getLongWords(Collection<E> coll)`

Answer:

☑ **F** is correct.

☒ **A** is close, but it's wrong because the return value is too vague. The last line of the method expects the return value to be `Collection<String>`, not `Collection<? extends CharSequence>`. **B** is wrong because `longWords` has been declared as a `Collection<E>`, and that can't be implicitly converted to a `List<E>` to match the declared return value. (Even though we know that `longWords` is really an `ArrayList<E>`, the compiler only knows what it's been declared as.) **C, D,** and **E** are wrong because they do not declare a type variable `E` (there's no `<>` before the return value) so the `getLongWords()` method body will not compile. **G** is wrong because `E super CharSequence` makes no sense—super could be used in conjunction with a wildcard but not a type variable like `E`. (Objective 6.3)

15. Given:

```
12.     TreeSet map = new TreeSet();
13.     map.add("one");
14.     map.add("two");
15.     map.add("three");
16.     map.add("four");
17.     map.add("one");
18.     Iterator it = map.iterator();
19.     while (it.hasNext() ) {
20.         System.out.print( it.next() + " " );
21.     }
```

What is the result?

A. Compilation fails.

B. `one two three four`

C. `four three two one`

D. `four one three two`

E. `one two three four one`

F. `one four three two one`

G. An exception is thrown at runtime.

H. The print order is not guaranteed.

Answer:

☑ **D** is correct. TreeSet assures no duplicate entries; also, when it is accessed it will return elements in natural order, which for Strings means alphabetical.

☒ **A, B, C, E, F, G,** and **H** are incorrect based on the logic described above. Note, even though as of Java 5 you don't have to use an Iterator, you still can. (Objective 6.5)

16. Given a method declared as:

```
public static <E extends Number> List<? super E> process(List<E> nums)
```

A programmer wants to use this method like this:

```
// INSERT DECLARATIONS HERE
output = process(input);
```

Which pairs of declarations could be placed at `// INSERT DECLARATIONS HERE` to allow the code to compile? (Choose all that apply.)

A. `ArrayList<Integer> input = null;`
`ArrayList<Integer> output = null;`

B. `ArrayList<Integer> input = null;`
`List<Integer> output = null;`

C. `ArrayList<Integer> input = null;`
`List<Number> output = null;`

D. `List<Number> input = null;`
`ArrayList<Integer> output = null;`

E. `List<Number> input = null;`
`List<Number> output = null;`

F. `List<Integer> input = null;`
`List<Integer> output = null;`

G. None of the above.

Answer:

☑ **B, E,** and **F** are correct.

☒ The return type of process is definitely declared as a `List`, not an `ArrayList`, so **A** and **D** are wrong. **C** is wrong because the return type evaluates to `List<Integer>`, and that can't be assigned to a variable of type `List<Number>`. Of course all these would probably cause a `NullPointerException` since the variables are still null—but the question only asked us to get the code to compile. (Objective 6.4)

8
Inner Classes

- Inner Classes
- Method-Local Inner Classes
- Anonymous Inner Classes

- Static Nested Classes
- ✓ Two-Minute Drill

Q&A Self Test

I nner classes (including static nested classes) appear throughout the exam. Although there are no official exam objectives specifically about inner classes, Objective 1.1 includes inner (a.k.a. nested) classes. More important, the code used to represent questions on virtually *any* topic on the exam can involve inner classes. Unless you deeply understand the rules and syntax for inner classes, you're likely to miss questions you'd otherwise be able to answer. *As if the exam weren't already tough enough.*

This chapter looks at the ins and outs (inners and outers?) of inner classes, and exposes you to the kinds of (often strange-looking) syntax examples you'll see scattered throughout the entire exam. So you've really got two goals for this chapter—to learn what you'll need to answer questions testing your inner class knowledge, and to learn how to read and understand inner class code so that you can correctly process questions testing your knowledge of *other* topics.

So what's all the hoopla about inner classes? Before we get into it, we have to warn you (if you don't already know) that inner classes have inspired passionate love 'em or hate 'em debates since first introduced in version 1.1 of the language. For once, we're going to try to keep our opinions to ourselves here and just present the facts as you'll need to know them for the exam. It's up to you to decide how—and to what extent—you should use inner classes in your own development. We mean it. We believe they have some powerful, efficient uses in very specific situations, including code that's easier to read and maintain, but they can also be abused and lead to code that's as clear as a cornfield maze, and to the syndrome known as "reuseless": *code that's useless over and over again.*

Inner classes let you define one class within another. They provide a type of scoping for your classes since you can make one class *a member of another class.* Just as classes have member *variables* and *methods*, a class can also have member *classes.* They come in several flavors, depending on how and where you define the inner class, including a special kind of inner class known as a "top-level nested class" (an inner class marked `static`), which technically isn't really an inner class. Because a static nested class is still a class defined within the scope of another class, we're still going to cover them in this chapter on inner classes.

Unlike the other chapters in this book, the certification objectives for inner classes don't have official exam objective numbers since they're part of other objectives covered elsewhere. So for this chapter, the Certification Objective headings in the following list represent the four inner class *topics* discussed in this chapter, rather than four official exam *objectives*:

- Inner classes
- Method-local inner classes
- Anonymous inner classes
- Static nested classes

Inner Classes

You're an OO programmer, so you know that for reuse and flexibility/extensibility you need to keep your classes specialized. In other words, a class should have code *only* for the things an object of that particular type needs to do; any *other* behavior should be part of another class better suited for *that* job. Sometimes, though, you find yourself designing a class where you discover you need behavior that belongs in a separate, specialized class, but also needs to be intimately tied to the class you're designing.

Event handlers are perhaps the best example of this (and are, in fact, one of the main reasons inner classes were added to the language in the first place). If you have a GUI class that performs some job like, say, a chat client, you might want the chat-client–specific methods (accept input, read new messages from server, send user input back to server, and so on) to be in the class. But how do those methods get invoked in the first place? A user clicks a button. Or types some text in the input field. Or a separate thread doing the I/O work of getting messages from the server has messages that need to be displayed in the GUI. So you have chat-client–specific methods, but you also need methods for handling the "events" (button presses, keyboard typing, I/O available, and so on) that drive the calls on those chat-client methods. The ideal scenario—from an OO perspective—is to keep the chat-client–specific methods in the ChatClient class, and put the event-handling *code* in a separate event-handling *class*.

Nothing unusual about that so far; after all, that's how you're *supposed* to design OO classes. As *specialists*. But here's the problem with the chat-client scenario: the event-handling code is intimately tied to the chat-client–specific code! Think about it: when the user presses a Send button (indicating that they want their typed-in message to be sent to the chat server), the chat-client code that sends the message needs to read from a *particular* text field. In other words, if the user clicks Button A, the program is supposed to extract the text from the TextField B, *of a particular*

ChatClient instance. Not from some *other* text field from some *other* object, but specifically the text field that a specific instance of the ChatClient class has a reference to. So the event-handling code needs access to the members of the ChatClient object, to be useful as a "helper" to a particular ChatClient instance.

And what if the ChatClient class needs to inherit from one class, but the event handling code is better off inheriting from some *other* class? You can't make a class extend more than one class, so putting all the code (the chat-client– specific code and the event-handling code) in one class won't work in that case. So what you'd really like to have is the benefit of putting your event code in a separate class (better OO, encapsulation, and the ability to extend a class other than the class the ChatClient extends) but still allow the event-handling code to have easy access to the members of the ChatClient (so the event-handling code can, for example, update the ChatClient's private instance variables). You *could* manage it by making the members of the ChatClient accessible to the event-handling class by, for example, marking them `public`. But that's not a good solution either.

You already know where this is going—one of the key benefits of an inner class is the "special relationship" an *inner class instance* shares with *an instance of the outer class*. That "special relationship" gives code in the inner class access to members of the enclosing (outer) class, *as if the inner class were part of the outer class*. In fact, that's exactly what it means: the inner class *is* a part of the outer class. Not just a "part" but a full-fledged, card-carrying *member* of the outer class. Yes, an inner class instance has access to all members of the outer class, *even those marked private*. (Relax, that's the whole point, remember? We want this separate inner class instance to have an intimate relationship with the outer class instance, but we still want to keep everyone *else* out. And besides, if you wrote the outer class, then you also wrote the inner class! So you're not violating encapsulation; you *designed* it this way.)

Coding a "Regular" Inner Class

We use the term *regular* here to represent inner classes that are not:

- Static
- Method-local
- Anonymous

For the rest of this section, though, we'll just use the term "inner class" and drop the "regular". (When we switch to one of the other three types in the preceding list, you'll know it.) You define an inner class within the curly braces of the outer class:

```
class MyOuter {
   class MyInner { }
}
```

Piece of cake. And if you compile it,

```
%javac MyOuter.java
```

you'll end up with *two* class files:

MyOuter.class
MyOuter$MyInner.class

The inner class is still, in the end, a separate class, so a separate class file is generated for it. But the inner class file isn't accessible to you in the usual way. You can't say

```
%java MyOuter$MyInner
```

in hopes of running the main() method of the inner class, because a *regular* inner class can't have static declarations of any kind. *The only way you can access the inner class is through a live instance of the outer class!* In other words, only at runtime when there's already an instance of the outer class to tie the inner class instance to. You'll see all this in a moment. First, let's beef up the classes a little:

```
class MyOuter {
   private int x = 7;

   // inner class definition
   class MyInner {
     public void seeOuter() {
        System.out.println("Outer x is " + x);
     }
   } // close inner class definition

} // close outer class
```

The preceding code is perfectly legal. Notice that the inner class is indeed accessing a private member of the outer class. That's fine, because the inner class is also a member of the outer class. So just as any member of the outer class (say, an instance method) can access any other member of the outer class, private or not, the inner class—also a member—can do the same.

OK, so now that we know how to write the code giving an inner class access to members of the outer class, how do you actually use it?

Instantiating an Inner Class

To create an instance of an inner class, *you must have an instance of the outer class* to tie to the inner class. There are no exceptions to this rule: an inner class instance can never stand alone without a direct relationship to an instance of the outer class.

Instantiating an Inner Class from Within the Outer Class   Most often, it is the outer class that creates instances of the inner class, since it is usually the outer class wanting to use the inner instance as a helper for its own personal use. We'll modify the MyOuter class to create an instance of MyInner:

```
class MyOuter {
   private int x = 7;
   public void makeInner() {
      MyInner in = new MyInner();  // make an inner instance
      in.seeOuter();
   }

   class MyInner {
      public void seeOuter() {
         System.out.println("Outer x is " + x);
      }
   }
}
```

You can see in the preceding code that the MyOuter code treats MyInner just as though MyInner were any other accessible class—it instantiates it using the class name (`new MyInner()`), and then invokes a method on the reference variable (`in.seeOuter()`). But the only reason this syntax works is because the outer class instance method code is doing the instantiating. In other words, *there's already an instance of the outer class—the instance running the* `makeInner()` *method.* So how do you instantiate a MyInner object from somewhere outside the MyOuter class? Is it even possible? (Well, since we're going to all the trouble of making a whole new subhead for it, as you'll see next, there's no big mystery here.)

Creating an Inner Class Object from Outside the Outer Class
Instance Code   Whew. Long subhead there, but it does explain what we're trying to do. If we want to create an instance of the inner class, we must have an instance of the outer class. You already know that, but think about the

implications...it means that, without a reference to an instance of the outer class, you can't instantiate the inner class from a `static` method of the outer class (because, don't forget, in `static` code *there is no* `this` *reference*), or from any other code in any other class. Inner class instances are always handed an implicit reference to the outer class. The compiler takes care of it, so you'll never see anything but the end result—the ability of the inner class to access members of the outer class. The code to make an instance from anywhere outside non-`static` code of the outer class is simple, but you must memorize this for the exam!

```
public static void main(String[] args) {
   MyOuter mo = new MyOuter();      // gotta get an instance!
   MyOuter.MyInner inner = mo.new MyInner();
   inner.seeOuter();
}
```

The preceding code is the same regardless of whether the `main()` method is within the MyOuter class or some *other* class (assuming the other class has access to MyOuter, and sinceMyOuter has default access, that means the code must be in a class within the same package asMyOuter).

If you're into one-liners, you can do it like this:

```
public static void main(String[] args) {
   MyOuter.MyInner inner = new MyOuter().new MyInner();
   inner.seeOuter();
}
```

You can think of this as though you're invoking a method on the outer instance, but the method happens to be a special inner class instantiation method, and it's invoked using the keyword `new`. Instantiating an inner class is the *only* scenario in which you'll invoke `new` *on* an instance as opposed to invoking `new` to *construct* an instance.

Here's a quick summary of the differences between inner class instantiation code that's *within* the outer class (but not `static`), and inner class instantiation code that's *outside* the outer class:

■ From *inside* the outer class instance code, use the inner class name in the normal way:

```
MyInner mi = new MyInner();
```

■ From *outside* the outer class instance code (including static method code within the outer class), the inner class name must now include the outer class's name:

```
MyOuter.MyInner
```

To instantiate it, you must use a reference to the outer class:

```
new MyOuter().new MyInner(); or outerObjRef.new MyInner();
```

if you already have an instance of the outer class.

Referencing the Inner or Outer Instance from Within the Inner Class

How does an object refer to itself normally? By using the `this` reference. Here is a quick review of `this`:

■ The keyword `this` can be used only from within instance code. In other words, not within `static` code.

■ The `this` reference is a reference to the currently executing object. In other words, the object whose reference was used to invoke the currently running method.

■ The `this` reference is the way an object can pass a reference to itself to some other code, as a method argument:

```
public void myMethod() {
  MyClass mc = new MyClass();
  mc.doStuff(this);  // pass a ref to object running myMethod
}
```

Within an inner class code, the `this` reference refers to the instance of the inner class, as you'd probably expect, since `this` always refers to the currently executing object. But what if the inner class code wants an explicit reference to the outer class instance that the inner instance is tied to? In other words, *how do you reference the "outer `this`"*? Although normally the inner class code doesn't need a reference to the outer class, since it already has an implicit one it's using to access the members of the outer class, it would need a reference to the outer class if it needed to pass that reference to some other code as follows:

```
class MyInner {
   public void seeOuter() {
      System.out.println("Outer x is " + x);
      System.out.println("Inner class ref is " + this);
      System.out.println("Outer class ref is " + MyOuter.this);
   }
}
```

If we run the complete code as follows:

```
class MyOuter {
   private int x = 7;
   public void makeInner() {
      MyInner in = new MyInner();
      in.seeOuter();
   }
   class MyInner {
      public void seeOuter() {
         System.out.println("Outer x is " + x);
         System.out.println("Inner class ref is " + this);
         System.out.println("Outer class ref is " + MyOuter.this);
      }
   }
   public static void main (String[] args) {
      MyOuter.MyInner inner = new MyOuter().new MyInner();
      inner.seeOuter();
   }
}
```

the output is something like this:

```
Outer x is 7
Inner class ref is MyOuter$MyInner@113708
Outer class ref is MyOuter@33f1d7
```

So the rules for an inner class referencing itself or the outer instance are as follows:

- To reference the inner class instance itself, from *within* the inner class code, use this.
- To reference the "*outer* this" (the outer class instance) from within the inner class code, use NameOfOuterClass.this (example, MyOuter.this).

Member Modifiers Applied to Inner Classes A regular inner class is a member of the outer class just as instance variables and methods are, so the following modifiers can be applied to an inner class:

- `final`
- `abstract`
- `public`
- `private`
- `protected`
- `static`—*but* `static` *turns it into a* `static` *nested class not an inner class.*
- `strictfp`

Method-Local Inner Classes

A regular inner class is scoped inside another class's curly braces, but outside any method code (in other words, at the same level that an instance variable is declared). But you can also define an inner class within a method:

```
class MyOuter2 {
    private String x = "Outer2";

    void doStuff() {
        class MyInner {
            public void seeOuter() {
                System.out.println("Outer x is " + x);
            } // close inner class method
        } // close inner class definition
    } // close outer class method doStuff()

} // close outer class
```

The preceding code declares a class, `MyOuter2`, with one method, `doStuff()`. But *inside* `doStuff()`, another class, `MyInner`, is declared, and it has a method of its own, `seeOuter()`. The code above is completely useless, however, because *it never instantiates the inner class!* Just because you *declared* the class doesn't mean you created an *instance* of it. So if you want to actually *use* the inner class (say, to invoke its methods), then you must make an instance of it somewhere *within the method but below the inner class definition*. The following legal code shows how to instantiate and use a method-local inner class:

```
class MyOuter2 {
    private String x = "Outer2";
    void doStuff() {
      class MyInner {
        public void seeOuter() {
          System.out.println("Outer x is " + x);
        } // close inner class method
      } // close inner class definition

      MyInner mi = new MyInner();  // This line must come
                                   // after the class
      mi.seeOuter();
    } // close outer class method doStuff()
} // close outer class
```

What a Method-Local Inner Object Can and Can't Do

A method-local inner class can be instantiated only within the method where the inner class is defined. In other words, no other code running in any other method—inside or outside the outer class—can ever instantiate the method-local inner class. Like regular inner class objects, the method-local inner class object shares a special relationship with the enclosing (outer) class object, and can access its `private` (or any other) members. However, *the inner class object cannot use the local variables of the method the inner class is in.* Why not?

Think about it. The local variables of the method live on the stack, and exist only for the lifetime of the method. You already know that the scope of a local variable is limited to the method the variable is declared in. When the method ends, the stack frame is blown away and the variable is history. But even after the method completes, the inner class object created within it might still be alive on the heap if, for example, a reference to it was passed into some other code and then stored in an instance variable. Because the local variables aren't guaranteed to be alive as long as the method-local inner class object, the inner class object can't use them. *Unless the local variables are marked* `final`! The following code attempts to access a local variable from within a method-local inner class.

```
class MyOuter2 {
   private String x = "Outer2";
   void doStuff() {
      String z = "local variable";
      class MyInner {
         public void seeOuter() {
            System.out.println("Outer x is " + x);
            System.out.println("Local variable z is " + z);  // Won't Compile!
         } // close inner class method
      }    // close inner class definition
   }       // close outer class method doStuff()
}          // close outer class
```

Compiling the preceding code *really* upsets the compiler:

```
MyOuter2.java:8: local variable z is accessed from within inner class;
needs to be declared final
            System.out.println("Local variable z is " + z);
                                                          ^
```

Marking the local variable z as `final` fixes the problem:

```
final String z = "local variable";  // Now inner object can use it
```

And just a reminder about modifiers within a method: the same rules apply to method-local inner classes as to local variable declarations. You can't, for example, mark a method-local inner class `public`, `private`, `protected`, `static`, `transient`, and the like. The only modifiers you *can* apply to a method-local inner class are `abstract` and `final`, but as always, never both at the same time.

Anonymous Inner Classes

So far we've looked at defining a class within an enclosing class (a regular inner class) and within a method (a method-local inner class). Finally, we're going to look at the most unusual syntax you might ever see in Java; inner classes declared without any class name at all (hence the word *anonymous*). And if that's not weird enough, you can define these classes not just within a method, but even within an *argument* to a method. We'll look first at the *plain-old* (as if there is such a thing as a plain-old anonymous inner class) version (actually, even the plain-old version comes in two flavors), and then at the argument-declared anonymous inner class.

Perhaps your most important job here is to *learn to not be thrown when you see the syntax*. The exam is littered with anonymous inner class code: you might see it on questions about threads, wrappers, overriding, garbage collection, and... well, you get the idea.

Plain-Old Anonymous Inner Classes, Flavor One

Check out the following legal-but-strange-the-first-time-you-see-it code:

```
class Popcorn {
  public void pop() {
    System.out.println("popcorn");
  }
}
class Food {
  Popcorn p = new Popcorn() {
    public void pop() {
      System.out.println("anonymous popcorn");
    }
  };
}
```

Let's look at what's in the preceding code:

■ We define two classes, Popcorn and Food.

■ Popcorn has one method, pop().

■ Food has one instance variable, declared as type Popcorn. That's it for Food. Food has *no* methods.

And here's the big thing to get:

The Popcorn reference variable refers *not* to an instance of Popcorn, but to *an instance of an anonymous (unnamed) subclass of Popcorn.*

Let's look at just the anonymous class code:

```
2. Popcorn p = new Popcorn() {
3.    public void pop() {
4.       System.out.println("anonymous popcorn");
5.    }
6. };
```

Line 2   Line 2 starts out as an instance variable declaration of type `Popcorn`. But instead of looking like this:

```
Popcorn p = new Popcorn(); // notice the semicolon at the end
```

there's a curly brace at the end of line 2, where a semicolon would normally be.

```
Popcorn p = new Popcorn() { // a curly brace, not a semicolon
```

You can read line 2 as saying,

Declare a reference variable, p, of type `Popcorn`. Then declare a new class that has no name, but that is a *subclass* of `Popcorn`. And here's the curly brace that opens the class definition…

Line 3   Line 3, then, is actually the first statement within the new class definition. And what is it doing? Overriding the `pop()` method of the superclass `Popcorn`. This is the whole point of making an anonymous inner class—to *override one or more methods of the superclass!* (Or to implement methods of an interface, but we'll save that for a little later.)

Line 4   Line 4 is the first (and in this case *only*) statement within the overriding `pop()` method. Nothing special there.

Line 5   Line 5 is the closing curly brace of the `pop()` method. Nothing special.

Line 6   Here's where you have to pay attention: line 6 includes a *curly brace closing off the anonymous class definition* (it's the companion brace to the one on line 2), but there's more! Line 6 also has *the semicolon that ends the statement started on line 2*—the statement where it all began—the statement declaring and initializing the `Popcorn` reference variable. And what you're left with is a `Popcorn` reference to a brand-new *instance* of a brand-new, just-in-time, anonymous (no name) *subclass* of Popcorn.

---

e x a m
w a t c h

The closing semicolon is hard to spot. Watch for code like this:

```
2. Popcorn p = new Popcorn() {
3.    public void pop() {
4.        System.out.println("anonymous popcorn");
5.    }
6. }                        //  Missing the semicolon needed to end
                            //  the statement started on 2!
7. Foo f = new Foo();
```

You'll need to be especially careful about the syntax when inner classes are involved, because the code on line 6 looks perfectly natural. We're not used to seeing semicolons following curly braces (the only other time it happens is with shortcut array initializations).

Polymorphism is in play when anonymous inner classes are involved. Remember that, as in the preceding Popcorn example, we're using a superclass reference variable type to refer to a subclass object. What are the implications? You can only call methods on an anonymous inner class reference that are defined in the reference variable type! This is no different from any other polymorphic references, for example,

```
class Horse extends Animal{
   void buck() { }
}
class Animal {
   void eat() { }
}
```

```
class Test {
   public static void main (String[] args) {
      Animal h = new Horse();
      h.eat();  // Legal, class Animal has an eat() method
      h.buck();  // Not legal! Class Animal doesn't have buck()
   }
}
```

So on the exam, you must be able to spot an anonymous inner class that—rather than overriding a method of the superclass—defines its own new method. The method definition isn't the problem, though; the real issue is how do you invoke that new method? The reference variable type (the superclass) won't know anything about that new method (defined in the anonymous subclass), so the compiler will complain if you try to invoke any method on an anonymous inner class reference that is not in the superclass class definition.

Check out the following, illegal code:

```
class Popcorn {
   public void pop() {
      System.out.println("popcorn");
   }
}

class Food {
   Popcorn p = new Popcorn() {
      public void sizzle() {
         System.out.println("anonymous sizzling popcorn");
      }
      public void pop() {
         System.out.println("anonymous popcorn");
      }
   };

   public void popIt() {
      p.pop();     // OK, Popcorn has a pop() method
      p.sizzle();  // Not Legal! Popcorn does not have sizzle()
   }
}
```

Compiling the preceding code gives us something like,

```
Anon.java:19: cannot resolve symbol
symbol  : method sizzle  ()
```

```
location: class Popcorn
       p.sizzle();
       ^
```

which is the compiler's way of saying, "I can't find method `sizzle()` in class `Popcorn`," followed by, "Get a clue."

Plain-Old Anonymous Inner Classes, Flavor Two

The only difference between flavor one and flavor two is that flavor one creates an anonymous *subclass* of the specified *class* type, whereas flavor two creates an anonymous *implementer* of the specified *interface* type. In the previous examples, we defined a new anonymous subclass of type `Popcorn` as follows:

```
Popcorn p = new Popcorn() {
```

But if `Popcorn` were an *interface* type instead of a *class* type, then the new anonymous class would be an *implementer* of the *interface* rather than a *subclass* of the *class*. Look at the following example:

```
interface Cookable {
   public void cook();
}
class Food {
   Cookable c = new Cookable() {
     public void cook() {
        System.out.println("anonymous cookable implementer");
     }
   };
}
```

The preceding code, like the Popcorn example, still creates an instance of an anonymous inner class, but this time the new just-in-time class is an implementer of the `Cookable` interface. And note that this is the only time you will ever see the syntax

```
new Cookable()
```

where `Cookable` is an *interface* rather than a non-`abstract` class type. Because think about it, *you can't instantiate an interface*, yet that's what the code *looks* like it's doing. But of course it's not instantiating a Cookable object, it's creating an instance of a new, anonymous, implementer of Cookable. You can read this line:

```
Cookable c = new Cookable() {
```

as, "Declare a reference variable of type `Cookable` that, obviously, will refer to an object from a class that implements the `Cookable` interface. But, oh yes, we don't yet *have* a class that implements `Cookable`, so we're going to make one right here, right now. We don't need a name for the class, but it will be a class that implements `Cookable`, and this curly brace starts the definition of the new implementing class."

One more thing to keep in mind about anonymous interface implementers—*they can implement only one interface*. There simply isn't any mechanism to say that your anonymous inner class is going to implement multiple interfaces. In fact, an anonymous inner class can't even extend a class and implement an interface at the same time. The inner class has to choose either to be a subclass of a named class— and not directly implement any interfaces at all—*or* to implement a single interface. By directly, we mean actually using the keyword `implements` as part of the class declaration. If the anonymous inner class is a subclass of a class type, it automatically becomes an implementer of any interfaces implemented by the superclass.

exam
ⓦatch

Don't be fooled by any attempts to instantiate an interface except in the case of an anonymous inner class. The following is not legal,

```
Runnable r = new Runnable(); // can't instantiate interface
```

whereas the following *is* legal, because it's instantiating an implementer of the `Runnable` interface (an anonymous implementation class):

```
Runnable r = new Runnable() {  // curly brace, not semicolon
  public void run() { }
};
```

Argument-Defined Anonymous Inner Classes

If you understood what we've covered so far in this chapter, then this last part will be simple. If you *are* still a little fuzzy on anonymous classes, however, then you should reread the previous sections. If they're not completely clear, we'd like to take full responsibility for the confusion. But we'll be happy to share.

Okay, if you've made it to this sentence, then we're all going to assume you understood the preceding section, and now we're just going to add one new twist. Imagine the following scenario. You're typing along, creating the Perfect Class, when you write code calling a method on a `Bar` object, and that method takes an object of type `Foo` (an interface).

```
class MyWonderfulClass {
   void go() {
      Bar b = new Bar();
      b.doStuff(ackWeDoNotHaveAFoo!); // Don't try to compile this at home
   }
}
interface Foo {
   void foof();
}
class Bar {
   void doStuff(Foo f) { }
}
```

No *problemo*, except that you don't *have* an object from a class that implements Foo, and you can't instantiate one, either, because *you don't even have a class that implements Foo*, let alone an instance of one. So you first need a class that implements Foo, and then you need an instance of that class to pass to the Bar class's `doStuff()` method. Savvy Java programmer that you are, you simply define an anonymous inner class, *right inside the argument*. That's right, just where you least expect to find a class. And here's what it looks like:

```
 1. class MyWonderfulClass {
 2.    void go() {
 3.       Bar b = new Bar();
 4.       b.doStuff(new Foo() {
 5.         public void foof() {
 6.            System.out.println("foofy");
 7.         } // end foof method
 8.       }); // end inner class def, arg, and b.doStuff stmt.
 9.    } // end go()
10. } // end class
11.
12. interface Foo {
13.    void foof();
14. }
15. class Bar {
16.    void doStuff(Foo f) { }
17. }
```

All the action starts on line 4. We're calling doStuff() on a Bar object, but the method takes an instance that IS-A Foo, where Foo is an interface. So we must make both an *implementation* class and an *instance* of that class, all right here in the argument to doStuff(). So that's what we do. We write

```
new Foo() {
```

to start the new class definition for the anonymous class that implements the Foo interface. Foo has a single method to implement, foof(), so on lines 5, 6, and 7 we implement the foof() method. Then on line 8—whoa!—more strange syntax appears. The first curly brace closes off the new anonymous class definition. But don't forget that this all happened as part of a method argument, so the close parenthesis,), finishes off the method invocation, and then we must still end the statement that began on line 4, so we end with a semicolon. Study this syntax! You will see anonymous inner classes on the exam, and you'll have to be very, very picky about the way they're closed. If they're *argument local*, they end like this:

```
});
```

but if they're just plain-old anonymous classes, then they end like this:

```
};
```

Regardless, the syntax is not what you use in virtually any other part of Java, so be careful. Any question from any part of the exam might involve anonymous inner classes as part of the code.

CERTIFICATION OBJECTIVE

Static Nested Classes

We saved the easiest for last, as a kind of treat :)

You'll sometimes hear static nested classes referred to as *static inner classes*, but they really aren't inner classes at all, by the standard definition of an inner class. While an inner class (regardless of the flavor) enjoys that *special relationship* with the outer class (or rather the *instances* of the two classes share a relationship), a static nested class does not. It is simply a non-inner (also called "top-level") class scoped within another. So with static classes it's really more about name-space resolution than about an implicit relationship between the two classes.

A static nested class is simply *a class that's a static member of the enclosing class*:

```
class BigOuter {
   static class Nested { }
}
```

The class itself isn't really "static"; there's no such thing as a static class. The static modifier in this case says that the nested class is *a static member of the outer class*. That means it can be accessed, as with other static members, *without having an instance of the outer class*.

Instantiating and Using Static Nested Classes

You use standard syntax to access a static nested class from its enclosing class. The syntax for instantiating a static nested class from a non-enclosing class is a little different from a normal inner class, and looks like this:

```
class BigOuter {
  static class Nest {void go() { System.out.println("hi"); } }
}
class Broom {
  static class B2 {void goB2() { System.out.println("hi 2"); } }
  public static void main(String[] args) {
    BigOuter.Nest n = new BigOuter.Nest();   // both class names
    n.go();
    B2 b2 = new B2();      // access the enclosed class
    b2.goB2();
  }
}
```

Which produces:

```
hi
hi 2
```

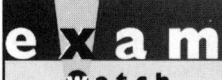

Just as a static method does not have access to the instance variables and non-static methods of the class, a static nested class does not have access to the instance variables and non-static methods of the outer class. Look for static nested classes with code that behaves like a nonstatic (regular inner) class.

CERTIFICATION SUMMARY

Inner classes will show up throughout the exam, in any topic, and these are some of the exam's hardest questions. You should be comfortable with the sometimes bizarre syntax, and know how to spot legal and illegal inner class definitions.

We looked first at "regular" inner classes, where one class is a member of another. You learned that coding an inner class means putting the class definition of the inner class inside the curly braces of the enclosing (outer) class, but outside of any method or other code block. You learned that an inner class *instance* shares a special relationship with a specific *instance* of the outer class, and that this special relationship lets the inner class access all members of the outer class, including those marked `private`. You learned that to instantiate an inner class, you *must* have a reference to an instance of the outer class.

Next we looked at method-local inner classes—classes defined *inside* a method. The code for a method-local inner class looks virtually the same as the code for any other class definition, except that you can't apply an access modifier the way you can with a regular inner class. You learned why method-local inner classes cannot use non-`final` local variables declared within the method—the inner class instance may outlive the stack frame, so the local variable might vanish while the inner class object is still alive. You saw that to *use* the inner class you need to instantiate it, and that the instantiation must come *after* the class declaration in the method.

We also explored the strangest inner class type of all—the *anonymous* inner class. You learned that they come in two forms, normal and argument-local. Normal, ho-hum, anonymous inner classes are created as part of a variable assignment, while argument-local inner classes are actually declared, defined, and automatically instantiated *all within the argument to a method!* We covered the way anonymous inner classes can be either a subclass of the named class type, or an *implementer* of the named interface. Finally, we looked at how polymorphism applies to anonymous inner classes: you can invoke on the new instance only those methods defined in the named class or interface type. In other words, even if the anonymous inner class defines its own new method, no code from anywhere outside the inner class will be able to invoke that method.

As if we weren't already having enough fun for one day, we pushed on to static nested classes, which really aren't inner classes at all. Known as static nested classes, a nested class marked with the `static` modifier is quite similar to any other non-inner class, except that to access it, code must have access to both the nested and enclosing class. We saw that because the class is `static`, no instance of the enclosing class is needed, and thus the static nested class *does not share a special relationship with any instance of the enclosing class.* Remember, static inner classes can't access instance methods or variables.

TWO-MINUTE DRILL

Here are some of the key points from this chapter.

Inner Classes

❑ A "regular" inner class is declared *inside* the curly braces of another class, but *outside* any method or other code block.

❑ An inner class is a full-fledged member of the enclosing (outer) class, so it can be marked with an access modifier as well as the `abstract` or `final` modifiers. (Never both `abstract` and `final` together— remember that `abstract` *must* be subclassed, whereas `final` *cannot* be subclassed).

❑ An inner class instance shares a special relationship with an instance of the enclosing class. This relationship gives the inner class access to *all* of the outer class's members, including those marked `private`.

❑ To instantiate an inner class, you must have a reference to an instance of the outer class.

❑ From code within the enclosing class, you can instantiate the inner class using only the name of the inner class, as follows:

```
MyInner mi = new MyInner();
```

❑ From code outside the enclosing class's instance methods, you can instantiate the inner class only by using both the inner and outer class names, and a reference to the outer class as follows:

```
MyOuter mo = new MyOuter();
MyOuter.MyInner inner = mo.new MyInner();
```

❑ From code within the inner class, the keyword `this` holds a reference to the inner class instance. To reference the *outer* `this` (in other words, the instance of the outer class that this inner instance is tied to) precede the keyword `this` with the outer class name as follows: `MyOuter.this;`

Method-Local Inner Classes

❑ A method-local inner class is defined within a method of the enclosing class.

❑ For the inner class to be used, you must instantiate it, and that instantiation must happen within the same method, but *after* the class definition code.

❑ A method-local inner class cannot use variables declared within the method (including parameters) unless those variables are marked `final`.

❏ The only modifiers you can apply to a method-local inner class are `abstract` and `final`. (Never both at the same time, though.)

Anonymous Inner Classes

❏ Anonymous inner classes have no name, and their type must be either a subclass of the named type or an implementer of the named interface.

❏ An anonymous inner class is always created as part of a statement; don't forget to close the statement after the class definition with a curly brace. This is a rare case in Java, a curly brace followed by a semicolon.

❏ Because of polymorphism, the only methods you can call on an anonymous inner class reference are those defined in the reference variable class (or interface), even though the anonymous class is really a subclass or implementer of the reference variable type.

❏ An anonymous inner class can extend one subclass *or* implement one interface. Unlike non-anonymous classes (inner or otherwise), an anonymous inner class cannot do both. In other words, it cannot both extend a class *and* implement an interface, nor can it implement more than one interface.

❏ An argument-local inner class is declared, defined, and automatically instantiated as part of a method invocation. The key to remember is that the class is being defined within a method argument, so the syntax will end the class definition with a curly brace, followed by a closing parenthesis to end the method call, followed by a semicolon to end the statement: `});`

Static Nested Classes

❏ Static nested classes are inner classes marked with the `static` modifier.

❏ A static nested class is *not* an inner class, it's a top-level nested class.

❏ Because the nested class is static, it does not share any special relationship with an instance of the outer class. In fact, you don't need an instance of the outer class to instantiate a static nested class.

❏ Instantiating a static nested class requires using both the outer and nested class names as follows:

```
BigOuter.Nested n = new BigOuter.Nested();
```

❏ A static nested class cannot access non-static members of the outer class, since it does not have an implicit reference to any outer instance (in other words, the nested class instance does not get an *outer* `this` reference).

SELF TEST

The following questions will help you measure your understanding of the dynamic and life-altering material presented in this chapter. Read all of the choices carefully. Take your time. Breathe.

1. Given:

```
public class MyOuter {
    public static class MyInner {  public static void foo() { } }
}
```

Which, if placed in a class *other* than MyOuter or MyInner, instantiates an instance of the nested class?

A. `MyOuter.MyInner m = new MyOuter.MyInner();`

B. `MyOuter.MyInner mi = new MyInner();`

C. `MyOuter m = new MyOuter();`
   `MyOuter.MyInner mi = m.new MyOuter.MyInner();`

D. `MyInner mi = new MyOuter.MyInner();`

2. Which are true about a static nested class? (Choose all that apply.)

A. You must have a reference to an instance of the enclosing class in order to instantiate it.

B. It does not have access to non-`static` members of the enclosing class.

C. Its variables and methods must be `static`.

D. If the outer class is named `MyOuter`, and the nested class is named `MyInner`, it can be instantiated using `new MyOuter.MyInner();`.

E. It must extend the enclosing class.

3. Given:

```
public interface Runnable { void run(); }
```

Which construct an anonymous inner class instance? (Choose all that apply.)

A. `Runnable r = new Runnable() { };`

B. `Runnable r = new Runnable(public void run() { });`

C. `Runnable r = new Runnable { public void run(){}};`

D. `Runnable r = new Runnable() {public void run{}};`

E. `System.out.println(new Runnable()  {public void run() { }});`

F. `System.out.println(new Runnable(public void run() {}));`

4. Given:

```
class Boo {
    Boo(String s) { }
    Boo() { }
}
class Bar extends Boo {
    Bar() { }
    Bar(String s) {super(s);}
    void zoo() {
    // insert code here
    }
}
```

Which create an anonymous inner class from within class Bar? (Choose all that apply.)

A. `Boo f = new Boo(24) { };`

B. `Boo f = new Bar() { };`

C. `Boo f = new Boo() {String s; };`

D. `Bar f = new Boo(String s) { };`

E. `Boo f = new Boo.Bar(String s) { };`

5. Given:

```
1. class Foo {
2.    class Bar{ }
3. }
4. class Test {
5.    public static void main(String[] args) {
6.        Foo f = new Foo();
7.        // Insert code here
8.    }
9. }
```

Which, inserted at line 7, creates an instance of Bar? (Choose all that apply.)

A. `Foo.Bar b = new Foo.Bar();`

B. `Foo.Bar b = f.new Bar();`

C. `Bar b = new f.Bar();`

D. `Bar b = f.new Bar();`

E. `Foo.Bar b = new f.Bar();`

6. Which are true about a method-local inner class? (Choose all that apply.)

A. It must be marked `final`.

B. It can be marked `abstract`.

C. It can be marked `public`.

D. It can be marked `static`.

E. It can access private members of the enclosing class.

7. Which are true about an anonymous inner class? (Choose all that apply.)

A. It can extend exactly one class and implement exactly one interface.

B. It can extend exactly one class and can implement multiple interfaces.

C. It can extend exactly one class or implement exactly one interface.

D. It can implement multiple interfaces regardless of whether it also extends a class.

E. It can implement multiple interfaces if it does not extend a class.

8. Given:

```
public class Foo {
    Foo() {System.out.print("foo");}
    class Bar{
        Bar() {System.out.print("bar");}
        public void go() {System.out.print("hi");}
    }
    public static void main(String[] args) {
        Foo f = new Foo();
        f.makeBar();
    }
    void makeBar() {
        (new Bar() {}).go();
    }
}
```

What is the result?

A. Compilation fails.

B. An error occurs at runtime.

C. `foobarhi`

D. `barhi`

E. `hi`

F. `foohi`

9. Given:

```
1. public class TestObj {
2.    public static void main(String[] args) {
3.       Object o = new Object() {
4.          public boolean equals(Object obj) {
5.             return true;
6.          }
7.       }
8.       System.out.println(o.equals("Fred"));
9.    }
10. }
```

What is the result?

A. An exception occurs at runtime.

B. `true`

C. `Fred`

D. Compilation fails because of an error on line 3.

E. Compilation fails because of an error on line 4.

F. Compilation fails because of an error on line 8.

G. Compilation fails because of an error on a line other than 3, 4, or 8.

10. Given:

```
1. public class HorseTest {
2.    public static void main(String[] args) {
3.       class Horse {
4.          public String name;
5.          public Horse(String s) {
6.             name = s;
7.          }
8.       }
9.       Object obj = new Horse("Zippo");
10.      Horse h = (Horse) obj;
11.      System.out.println(h.name);
12.   }
13. }
```

What is the result?

A. An exception occurs at runtime at line 10.

B. `Zippo`

C. Compilation fails because of an error on line 3.

D. Compilation fails because of an error on line 9.

E. Compilation fails because of an error on line 10.

F. Compilation fails because of an error on line 11.

11. Given:

```
1. public class HorseTest {
2.    public static void main(String[] args) {
3.       class Horse {
4.          public String name;
5.          public Horse(String s) {
6.             name = s;
7.          }
8.       }
9.       Object obj = new Horse("Zippo");
10.      System.out.println(obj.name);
11.    }
12. }
```

What is the result?

A. An exception occurs at runtime at line 10.

B. `Zippo`

C. Compilation fails because of an error on line 3.

D. Compilation fails because of an error on line 9.

E. Compilation fails because of an error on line 10.

12. Given:

```
public abstract class AbstractTest {
    public int getNum() {
        return 45;
    }
    public abstract class Bar {
      public int getNum() {
        return 38;
      }
    }
    public static void main(String[] args) {
        AbstractTest t = new AbstractTest() {
            public int getNum() {
                return 22;
            }
        };
        AbstractTest.Bar f = t.new Bar() {
            public int getNum() {
                return 57;
            }
        };
        System.out.println(f.getNum() + " " + t.getNum());
    }
}
```

What is the result?

A. 57 22

B. 45 38

C. 45 57

D. An exception occurs at runtime.

E. Compilation fails.

SELF TEST ANSWERS

1. Given:

```
public class MyOuter {
    public static class MyInner {  public static void foo() { } }
}
```

Which, if placed in a class *other* than MyOuter or MyInner, instantiates an instance of the nested class?

A. `MyOuter.MyInner m = new MyOuter.MyInner();`

B. `MyOuter.MyInner mi = new MyInner();`

C. `MyOuter m = new MyOuter();`
`MyOuter.MyInner mi = m.new MyOuter.MyInner();`

D. `MyInner mi = new MyOuter.MyInner();`

Answer:

☑ **A** is correct. MyInner is a static nested class, so it must be instantiated using the fully scoped name of MyOuter.MyInner.

☒ **B** is incorrect because it doesn't use the enclosing name in the new. **C** is incorrect because it uses incorrect syntax. When you instantiate a nested class by invoking new on an instance of the enclosing class, you do not use the enclosing name. The difference between **A** and **C** is that **C** is calling new on an instance of the enclosing class rather than just new by itself. **D** is incorrect because it doesn't use the enclosing class name in the variable declaration.

2. Which are true about a static nested class? (Choose all that apply.)

A. You must have a reference to an instance of the enclosing class in order to instantiate it.

B. It does not have access to non-`static` members of the enclosing class.

C. Its variables and methods must be `static`.

D. If the outer class is named `MyOuter`, and the nested class is named `MyInner`, it can be instantiated using `new MyOuter.MyInner();`.

E. It must extend the enclosing class.

Answer:

☑ **B** and **D**. **B** is correct because a static nested class is not tied to an instance of the enclosing class, and thus can't access the non-`static` members of the class (just as a `static` method can't access non-static members of a class). **D** uses the correct syntax for instantiating a static nested class.

> ☒ **A** is incorrect because static nested classes do not need (and can't use) a reference to an instance of the enclosing class. **C** is incorrect because static nested classes can declare and define non-static members. **E** is wrong because…it just is. There's no rule that says an inner or nested class has to extend anything.

3. Given:

```
public interface Runnable { void run(); }
```

Which construct an anonymous inner class instance? (Choose all that apply.)

A. `Runnable r = new Runnable() { };`

B. `Runnable r = new Runnable(public void run() { });`

C. `Runnable r = new Runnable { public void run(){}};`

D. `Runnable r = new Runnable() {public void run{}};`

E. `System.out.println(new Runnable()  {public void run() { }});`

F. `System.out.println(new Runnable(public void run() {}));`

Answer:

> ☑ **E** is correct. It defines an anonymous inner class instance, which also means it creates an instance of that new anonymous class at the same time. The anonymous class is an implementer of the `Runnable` interface, it must override the `run()` method of `Runnable`.
>
> ☒ **A** is incorrect because it doesn't override the `run()` method, so it violates the rules of interface implementation. **B, C,** and **D** use incorrect syntax.

4. Given:

```
class Boo {
    Boo(String s) { }
    Boo() { }
}
class Bar extends Boo {
    Bar() { }
    Bar(String s) {super(s);}
    void zoo() {
    // insert code here
    }
}
```

Which create an anonymous inner class from within class Bar? (Choose all that apply.)

A. `Boo f = new Boo(24) { };`

B. `Boo f = new Bar() { };`

C. `Boo f = new Boo() {String s; };`

D. `Bar f = new Boo(String s) { };`

E. `Boo f = new Boo.Bar(String s) { };`

Answer:

☑ **B** and **C. B** is correct because anonymous inner classes are no different from any other class when it comes to polymorphism. That means you are always allowed to declare a reference variable of the superclass type and have that reference variable refer to an instance of a subclass type, which in this case is an anonymous subclass of Bar. Since Bar is a subclass of Boo, it all works. **C** uses correct syntax for creating an instance of Boo.

☒ **A** is incorrect because it passes an `int` to the Boo constructor, and there is no matching constructor in the Boo class. **D** is incorrect because it violates the rules of polymorphism; you cannot refer to a superclass type using a reference variable declared as the subclass type. The superclass doesn't have everything the subclass has. **E** uses incorrect syntax.

5. Given:

```
1. class Foo {
2.    class Bar{ }
3. }
4. class Test {
5.    public static void main(String[] args) {
6.        Foo f = new Foo();
7.        // Insert code here
8.    }
9. }
```

Which, inserted at line 7, creates an instance of Bar? (Choose all that apply.)

A. `Foo.Bar b = new Foo.Bar();`

B. `Foo.Bar b = f.new Bar();`

C. `Bar b = new f.Bar();`

D. `Bar b = f.new Bar();`

E. `Foo.Bar b = new f.Bar();`

Answer:

☑ **B** is correct because the syntax is correct—using both names (the enclosing class and the inner class) in the reference declaration, then using a reference to the enclosing class to invoke new on the inner class.

☒ **A, C, D,** and **E** all use incorrect syntax. **A** is incorrect because it doesn't use a reference to the enclosing class, and also because it includes both names in the call to new. **C** is incorrect because it doesn't use the enclosing class name in the reference variable declaration, and because the new syntax is wrong. **D** is incorrect because it doesn't use the enclosing class name in the reference variable declaration. **E** is incorrect because the new syntax is wrong.

6. Which are true about a method-local inner class? (Choose all that apply.)

A. It must be marked `final`.

B. It can be marked `abstract`.

C. It can be marked `public`.

D. It can be marked `static`.

E. It can access private members of the enclosing class.

Answer:

☑ **B** and **E**. **B** is correct because a method-local inner class can be `abstract`, although it means a subclass of the inner class must be created if the `abstract` class is to be used (so an `abstract` method-local inner class is probably not useful). **E** is correct because a method-local inner class works like any other inner class—it has a special relationship to an instance of the enclosing class, thus it can access all members of the enclosing class.

☒ **A** is incorrect because a method-local inner class does not have to be declared `final` (although it is legal to do so). **C** and **D** are incorrect because a method-local inner class cannot be made `public` (remember—local variables can't be `public`) or `static`.

7. Which are true about an anonymous inner class? (Choose all that apply.)

A. It can extend exactly one class and implement exactly one interface.

B. It can extend exactly one class and can implement multiple interfaces.

C. It can extend exactly one class or implement exactly one interface.

D. It can implement multiple interfaces regardless of whether it also extends a class.

E. It can implement multiple interfaces if it does not extend a class.

Answer:

☑ **C** is correct because the syntax of an anonymous inner class allows for only one named type after the `new`, and that type must be either a single interface (in which case the anonymous class implements that one interface) or a single class (in which case the anonymous class extends that one class).

☒ **A, B, D,** and **E** are all incorrect because they don't follow the syntax rules described in the response for answer **C**.

8. Given:

```
public class Foo {
   Foo() {System.out.print("foo");}
   class Bar{
      Bar() {System.out.print("bar");}
      public void go() {System.out.print("hi");}
   }
   public static void main(String[] args) {
```

```
        Foo f = new Foo();
        f.makeBar();
     }
     void makeBar() {
       (new Bar() {}).go();
     }
   }
```

What is the result?

A. Compilation fails.

B. An error occurs at runtime.

C. `foobarhi`

D. barhi

E. `hi`

F. `foohi`

Answer:

☑ **C** is correct because first the Foo instance is created, which means the Foo constructor runs and prints `foo`. Next, the `makeBar()` method is invoked, which creates a `Bar`, which means the Bar constructor runs and prints `bar`, and finally an instance is created (of an anonymous subtype of Bar), from which the `go()` method is invoked. Note that the line `(new Bar() {}).go();` creates a little tiny anonymous inner class, a subtype of Bar.

☒ **A, C, D, E,** and **F** are incorrect based on the program logic described above.

9. Given:

```
1. public class TestObj {
2.    public static void main(String[] args) {
3.       Object o = new Object() {
4.          public boolean equals(Object obj) {
5.             return true;
6.          }
7.       }
8.       System.out.println(o.equals("Fred"));
9.    }
10. }
```

What is the result?

A. An exception occurs at runtime.

B. `true`

C. `fred`

D. Compilation fails because of an error on line 3.

E. Compilation fails because of an error on line 4.

F. Compilation fails because of an error on line 8.

G. Compilation fails because of an error on a line other than 3, 4, or 8.

Answer:

☑ **G.** This code would be legal if line 7 ended with a semicolon. Remember that line 3 is a statement that doesn't end until line 7, and a statement needs a closing semicolon!

☒ **A, B, C, D, E,** and **F** are incorrect based on the program logic described above. If the semicolon were added at line 7, then answer **B** would be correct—the program would print `true`, the return from the `equals()` method overridden by the anonymous subclass of `Object`.

10. Given:

```
1. public class HorseTest {
2.   public static void main(String[] args) {
3.     class Horse {
4.       public String name;
5.       public Horse(String s) {
6.         name = s;
7.       }
8.     }
9.     Object obj = new Horse("Zippo");
10.     Horse h = (Horse) obj;
11.     System.out.println(h.name);
12.   }
13. }
```

What is the result?

A. An exception occurs at runtime at line 10.

B. `Zippo`

C. Compilation fails because of an error on line 3.

D. Compilation fails because of an error on line 9.

E. Compilation fails because of an error on line 10.

F. Compilation fails because of an error on line 11.

Answer:

☑ **B.** The code in the HorseTest class is perfectly legal. Line 9 creates an instance of the method-local inner class Horse, using a reference variable declared as type Object. Line

10 casts the Horse object to a Horse reference variable, which allows line 11 to compile. If line 10 were removed, the HorseTest code would not compile, because class Object does not have a *name* variable.

☒   **A, C, D, E,** and **F** are incorrect based on the program logic described above.

11. Given:

```
1. public class HorseTest {
2.    public static void main(String[] args) {
3.       class Horse {
4.          public String name;
5.          public Horse(String s) {
6.             name = s;
7.          }
8.       }
9.       Object obj = new Horse("Zippo");
10.      System.out.println(obj.name);
11.   }
12. }
```

What is the result?

A.   An exception occurs at runtime at line 10.

B.   `Zippo`

C.   Compilation fails because of an error on line 3.

D.   Compilation fails because of an error on line 9.

E.   Compilation fails because of an error on line 10.

Answer:

☑   **E.** This code is identical to the code in question 10, except the casting statement has been removed. If you use a reference variable of type `Object`, you can access only those members defined in class `Object`.

☒   **A, B, C,** and **D** are incorrect based on the program logic described above.

12. Given:

```
public abstract class AbstractTest {
    public int getNum() {
        return 45;
    }
    public abstract class Bar {
        public int getNum() {
            return 38;
        }
    }
    public static void main(String[] args) {
        AbstractTest t = new AbstractTest() {
            public int getNum() {
                return 22;
            }
        };
        AbstractTest.Bar f = t.new Bar() {
            public int getNum() {
                return 57;
            }
        };
        System.out.println(f.getNum() + " " + t.getNum());
    }  }
```

What is the result?

A. 57 22

B. 45 38

C. 45 57

D. An exception occurs at runtime.

E. Compilation fails.

Answer:

☑ **A.** You can define an inner class as `abstract`, which means you can instantiate only concrete subclasses of the abstract inner class. The object referenced by the variable `t` is an instance of an anonymous subclass of AbstractTest, and the anonymous class overrides the `getNum()` method to return 22. The variable referenced by `f` is an instance of an anonymous subclass of `Bar`, and the anonymous Bar subclass also overrides the `getNum()` method (to return 57). Remember that to create a Bar instance, we need an instance of the enclosing AbstractTest class to tie to the new `Bar` inner class instance. AbstractTest can't be instantiated because it's `abstract`, so we created an anonymous subclass (non-abstract) and then used the instance of that anonymous subclass to tie to the new Bar subclass instance.

☒ **B, C, D, E,** and **F** are incorrect based on the program logic described above.

9

Threads

CERTIFICATION OBJECTIVE

Defining, Instantiating, and Starting Threads (Objective 4.1)

4.1   Write code to define, instantiate, and start new threads using both java.lang.Thread and java.lang.Runnable.

Imagine a stockbroker application with a lot of complex capabilities. One of its functions is "download last stock option prices," another is "check prices for warnings," and a third time-consuming operation is "analyze historical data for company XYZ."

In a single-threaded runtime environment, these actions execute one after another. The next action can happen *only* when the previous one is finished. If a historical analysis takes half an hour, and the user selects to perform a download and check afterward, the warning may come too late to, say, buy or sell stock as a result.

We just imagined the sort of application that cries out for multithreading. Ideally, the download should happen in the background (that is, in another thread). That way, other processes could happen at the same time so that, for example, a warning could be communicated instantly. All the while, the user is interacting with other parts of the application. The analysis, too, could happen in a separate thread, so the user can work in the rest of the application while the results are being calculated.

So what exactly is a thread? In Java, "thread" means two different things:

■ An instance of class java.lang.Thread

■ A thread of execution

An instance of Thread is just...an object. Like any other object in Java, it has variables and methods, and lives and dies on the heap. But a *thread of execution* is an individual process (a "lightweight" process) that has its own call stack. In Java, there is *one thread per call stack*—or, to think of it in reverse, *one call stack per thread*. Even if you don't create any new threads in your program, threads are back there running.

The `main()` method, that starts the whole ball rolling, runs in one thread, called (surprisingly) the *main* thread. If you looked at the main call stack (and you can, any time you get a stack trace from something that happens after main begins, but not within another thread), you'd see that `main()` is the first method on the stack—

the method at the bottom. But as soon as you create a *new* thread, a new stack materializes and methods called from *that* thread run in a call stack that's separate from the `main()` call stack. That second new call stack is said to run concurrently with the main thread, but we'll refine that notion as we go through this chapter.

You might find it confusing that we're talking about code running *concurrently*— as if in *parallel*—given that there's only one CPU on most of the machines running Java. What gives? The JVM, which gets its turn at the CPU by whatever scheduling mechanism the underlying OS uses, operates like a mini-OS and schedules *its* own threads regardless of the underlying operating system. In some JVMs, the Java threads are actually mapped to native OS threads, but we won't discuss that here; native threads are not on the exam. Nor is it required to understand how threads behave in different JVM environments. In fact, the most important concept to understand from this entire chapter is this:

When it comes to threads, very little is guaranteed.

So be very cautious about interpreting the behavior you see on *one* machine as "the way threads work." The exam expects you to know what is and is not guaranteed behavior, so that you can design your program in such a way that it will work regardless of the underlying JVM. *That's part of the whole point of Java.*

on the **Job**

Don't make the mistake of designing your program to be dependent on a particular implementation of the JVM. As you'll learn a little later, different JVMs can run threads in profoundly different ways. For example, one JVM might be sure that all threads get their turn, with a fairly even amount of time allocated for each thread in a nice, happy, round-robin fashion. But in other JVMs, a thread might start running and then just hog the whole show, never stepping out so others can have a turn. If you test your application on the "nice turn-taking" JVM, and you don't know what is and is not guaranteed in Java, then you might be in for a big shock when you run it under a JVM with a different thread scheduling mechanism.

The thread questions are among the most difficult questions on the exam. In fact, for most people they *are* the toughest questions on the exam, and with four objectives for threads you'll be answering a *lot* of thread questions. If you're not already familiar with threads, you'll probably need to spend some time experimenting. Also, one final disclaimer: *This chapter makes almost no attempt to teach you how to design a good, safe, multithreaded application. We only scratch the surface of that huge topic in this chapter!* You're here to learn the basics of threading, and what you need to get through the thread questions on the exam. Before you can write decent multithreaded code, however, you really need to study more on the complexities and subtleties of multithreaded code.

(Note: The topic of daemon threads is NOT on the exam. All of the threads discussed in this chapter are "user" threads. You and the operating system can create a second kind of thread called a daemon thread. The difference between these two types of threads (user and daemon) is that the JVM exits an application only when all user threads are complete—the JVM doesn't care about letting daemon threads complete, so once all user threads are complete, the JVM will shut down, regardless of the state of any daemon threads. Once again, this topic is NOT on the exam.)

Making a Thread

A thread in Java begins as an instance of java.lang.Thread. You'll find methods in the Thread class for managing threads including creating, starting, and pausing them. For the exam, you'll need to know, at a minimum, the following methods:

```
start()
yield()
sleep()
run()
```

The action happens in the run() method. Think of the code you want to execute in a separate thread as *the job to do*. In other words, you have some work that needs to be done, say, downloading stock prices in the background while other things are happening in the program, so what you really want is that *job* to be executed in its own thread. So if the *work* you want done is the *job*, the one *doing* the work (actually executing the job code) is the *thread*. And the *job always starts from a* run() *method* as follows:

```
public void run() {
  // your job code goes here
}
```

You always write the code that needs to be run in a separate thread in a run() method. The run() method will call other methods, of course, but the thread of execution—the new call stack—always begins by invoking run(). So where does the run() method go? In one of the two classes you can use to define your thread job. You can define and instantiate a thread in one of two ways:

■ Extend the java.lang.Thread class.

■ Implement the Runnable interface.

You need to know about both for the exam, although in the real world you're much more likely to implement Runnable than extend Thread. Extending the Thread class is the easiest, but it's usually not a good OO practice. Why? Because subclassing should be reserved for specialized versions of more general superclasses. So the only time it really makes sense (from an OO perspective) to extend Thread is when you have a more specialized version of a Thread class. In other words, because *you have more specialized thread-specific behavior*. Chances are, though, that the thread work you want is really just a job to be done *by* a thread. In that case, you should design a class that implements the Runnable interface, which also leaves your class free to extend from some *other* class.

Defining a Thread

To define a thread, you need a place to put your run() method, and as we just discussed, you can do that by extending the Thread class or by implementing the Runnable interface. We'll look at both in this section.

Extending java.lang.Thread

The simplest way to define code to run in a separate thread is to

■ Extend the java.lang.Thread class.

■ Override the run() method.

It looks like this:

```
class MyThread extends Thread {
   public void run() {
      System.out.println("Important job running in MyThread");
   }
}
```

The limitation with this approach (besides being a poor design choice in most cases) is that if you extend Thread, *you can't extend anything else*. And it's not as if you really need that inherited Thread class behavior, because in order to use a thread you'll need to instantiate one anyway.

Keep in mind that you're free to overload the `run()` method in your Thread subclass:

```
class MyThread extends Thread {
  public void run() {
    System.out.println("Important job running in MyThread");
  }
  public void run(String s) {
    System.out.println("String in run is " + s);
  }
}
```

But know this: *The overloaded* `run(String s)` *method will be ignored by the Thread class unless you call it yourself. The Thread class expects a* `run()` *method with no arguments, and it will execute this method for you in a separate call stack after the thread has been started.* With a `run(String s)` method, the Thread class won't call the method for you, and even if you call the method directly yourself, execution won't happen in a new thread of execution with a separate call stack. It will just happen in the same call stack as the code that you made the call from, just like any other normal method call.

Implementing java.lang.Runnable

Implementing the Runnable interface gives you a way to extend from any class you like, but still define behavior that will be run by a separate thread. It looks like this:

```
class MyRunnable implements Runnable {
  public void run() {
    System.out.println("Important job running in MyRunnable");
  }
}
```

Regardless of which mechanism you choose, you've now got yourself some code that can be run by a thread of execution. So now let's take a look at *instantiating* your thread-capable class, and then we'll figure out how to actually get the thing *running*.

Instantiating a Thread

Remember, every thread of execution begins as an instance of class Thread. Regardless of whether your `run()` method is in a Thread subclass or a Runnable implementation class, you still need a Thread object to do the work.

If you extended the Thread class, instantiation is dead simple (we'll look at some additional overloaded constructors in a moment):

```
MyThread t = new MyThread()
```

If you implement Runnable, instantiation is only slightly less simple. To have code run by a separate thread, *you still need a Thread instance*. But rather than combining both the *thread* and the *job* (the code in the run() method) into one class, you've split it into two classes—the Thread class for the *thread-specific* code and your Runnable implementation class for your *job-that-should-be-run-by-a-thread* code. (Another common way to think about this is that the Thread is the "worker," and the Runnable is the "job" to be done.)

First, you instantiate your Runnable class:

```
MyRunnable r = new MyRunnable();
```

Next, you get yourself an instance of java.lang.Thread (*somebody* has to run your job…), and you *give it your job*!

```
Thread t = new Thread(r);  // Pass your Runnable to the Thread
```

If you create a thread using the no-arg constructor, the thread will call its own run() method when it's time to start working. That's exactly what you want when you extend Thread, but when you use Runnable, you need to tell the new thread to use *your* run() method rather than its own. The Runnable you pass to the Thread constructor is called the *target* or the *target Runnable*.

You can pass a single Runnable instance to multiple Thread objects, so that the same Runnable becomes the target of multiple threads, as follows:

```
public class TestThreads {
   public static void main (String [] args) {
     MyRunnable r = new MyRunnable();
     Thread foo = new Thread(r);
     Thread bar = new Thread(r);
     Thread bat = new Thread(r);
   }
}
```

Giving the same target to multiple threads means that several threads of execution will be running the very same job (and that the same job will be done multiple times).

e x a m

ⓦ **a t c h** *The Thread class itself implements Runnable. (After all, it has a* `run()` *method that we were overriding.) This means that you could pass a Thread to another Thread's constructor:*

```
Thread t = new Thread(new MyThread());
```

This is a bit silly, but it's legal. In this case, you really just need a Runnnable, and creating a whole other Thread is overkill.

Besides the no-arg constructor and the constructor that takes a Runnable (the target, i.e., the instance with the job to do), there are other overloaded constructors in class Thread. The constructors we care about are

- `Thread()`
- `Thread(Runnable target)`
- `Thread(Runnable target, String name)`
- `Thread(String name)`

You need to recognize all of them for the exam! A little later, we'll discuss some of the other constructors in the preceding list.

So now you've made yourself a Thread instance, and it knows which `run()` method to call. *But nothing is happening yet.* At this point, all we've got is a plain old Java object of type Thread. *It is not yet a thread of execution.* To get an actual thread—a new call stack—we still have to *start* the thread.

When a thread has been instantiated but not started (in other words, the `start()` method has not been invoked on the Thread instance), the thread is said to be in the *new* state. At this stage, the thread is not yet considered to be *alive*. Once the `start()` method is called, the thread is considered to be *alive* (even though the `run()` method may not have actually started executing yet). A thread is considered *dead* (no longer *alive*) after the `run()` method completes. The `isAlive()` method is the best way to determine if a thread has been started but has not yet completed its `run()` method. (Note: The `getState()` method is very useful for debugging, but you won't have to know it for the exam.)

Starting a Thread

You've created a Thread object and it knows its target (either the passed-in Runnable or itself if you extended class Thread). Now it's time to get the whole thread thing happening—to launch a new call stack. It's so simple it hardly deserves its own subheading:

```
t.start();
```

Prior to calling `start()` on a Thread instance, the thread (when we use lowercase `t`, we're referring to the *thread of execution* rather than the Thread class) is said to be in the *new* state as we said. The new state means you have a Thread *object* but you don't yet have a *true thread*. So what happens after you call `start()`? The good stuff:

- A new thread of execution starts (with a new call stack).
- The thread moves from the *new* state to the *runnable* state.
- When the thread gets a chance to execute, its target `run()` method will run.

Be *sure* you remember the following: You start a *Thread*, not a *Runnable*. You call `start()` on a Thread instance, not on a Runnable instance. The following example demonstrates what we've covered so far—defining, instantiating, and starting a thread:

```java
class FooRunnable implements Runnable {
    public void run() {
        for(int x =1; x < 6; x++) {
            System.out.println("Runnable running");
        }
    }
}

public class TestThreads {
    public static void main (String [] args) {
        FooRunnable r = new FooRunnable();
        Thread t = new Thread(r);
        t.start();
    }
}
```

Running the preceding code prints out exactly what you'd expect:

```
% java TestThreads
Runnable running
Runnable running
Runnable running
Runnable running
Runnable running
```

(If this isn't what you expected, go back and re-read everything in this objective.)

---

exam

ⓦatch

There's nothing special about the `run()` method as far as Java is concerned. Like `main()`, it just happens to be the name (and signature) of the method that the new thread knows to invoke. So if you see code that calls the `run()` method on a Runnable (or even on a Thread instance), that's perfectly legal. But it doesn't mean the `run()` method will run in a separate thread! Calling a `run()` method directly just means you're invoking a method from whatever thread is currently executing, and the `run()` method goes onto the current call stack rather than at the beginning of a new call stack. The following code does not start a new thread of execution:

```
Runnable r = new Runnable();
r.run();  // Legal, but does not start a separate thread
```

So what happens if we start multiple threads? We'll run a simple example in a moment, but first we need to know how to print out which thread is executing. We can use the `getName()` method of class Thread, and have each Runnable print out the name of the thread executing that Runnable object's `run()` method. The following example instantiates a thread and gives it a name, and then the name is printed out from the `run()` method:

```
class NameRunnable implements Runnable {
   public void run() {
       System.out.println("NameRunnable running");
       System.out.println("Run by "
         + Thread.currentThread().getName());
```

```
      }
   }
public class NameThread {
   public static void main (String [] args) {
     NameRunnable nr = new NameRunnable();
     Thread t = new Thread(nr);
     t.setName("Fred");
     t.start();
   }
}
```

Running this code produces the following, extra special, output:

```
% java NameThread
NameRunnable running
Run by Fred
```

To get the name of a thread you call—who would have guessed—getName() on the Thread instance. But the target Runnable instance doesn't even *have* a reference to the Thread instance, so we first invoked the static Thread.currentThread() method, which returns a reference to the currently executing thread, and then we invoked getName() on that returned reference.

Even if you don't explicitly name a thread, it still has a name. Let's look at the previous code, commenting out the statement that sets the thread's name:

```
public class NameThread {
   public static void main (String [] args) {
     NameRunnable nr = new NameRunnable();
     Thread t = new Thread(nr);
     // t.setName("Fred");
     t.start();
   }
}
```

Running the preceding code now gives us

```
% java NameThread
NameRunnable running
Run by Thread-0
```

And since we're getting the name of the current thread by using the static Thread.currentThread() method, we can even get the name of the thread running our main code,

```
public class NameThreadTwo {
  public static void main (String [] args) {
    System.out.println("thread is "
      + Thread.currentThread().getName());
  }
}
```

which prints out

```
% java NameThreadTwo
thread is main
```

That's right, the main thread already has a name—*main*. (Once again, what are the odds?) Figure 9-1 shows the process of starting a thread.

FIGURE 9-1

Starting a thread

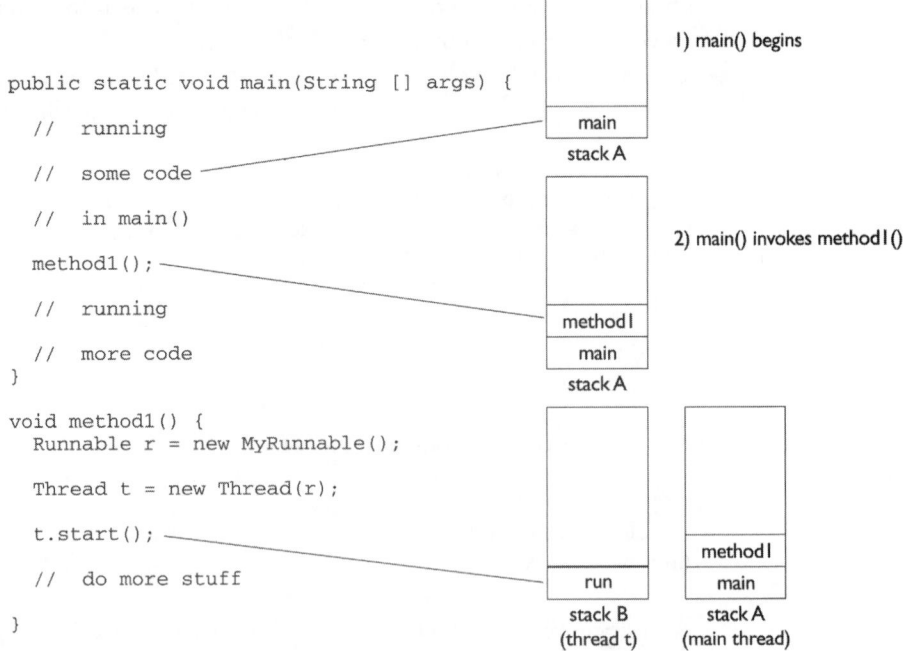

```
public static void main(String [] args) {

  //   running

  //   some code

  //   in main()

  method1();

  //   running

  //   more code
}

void method1() {
  Runnable r = new MyRunnable();

  Thread t = new Thread(r);

  t.start();

  //   do more stuff

}
```

1) main() begins

2) main() invokes method1()

3) method1() starts a new thread

main
stack A

method1
main
stack A

run
stack B
(thread t)

method1
main
stack A
(main thread)

Starting and Running Multiple Threads

Enough playing around here; let's actually get multiple threads going (more than two, that is). We already had two threads, because the main() method starts in a thread of its own, and then t.start() started a *second* thread. Now we'll do more. The following code creates a single Runnable instance and three Thread instances. All three Thread instances get the same Runnable instance, and each thread is given a unique name. Finally, all three threads are started by invoking start() on the Thread instances.

```java
class NameRunnable implements Runnable {
    public void run() {
        for (int x = 1; x <= 3; x++) {
            System.out.println("Run by "
                    + Thread.currentThread().getName()
                    + ", x is " + x);
        }
    }
}
public class ManyNames {
    public static void main(String [] args) {
        // Make one Runnable
        NameRunnable nr = new NameRunnable();
        Thread one = new Thread(nr);
        Thread two = new Thread(nr);
        Thread three = new Thread(nr);

        one.setName("Fred");
        two.setName("Lucy");
        three.setName("Ricky");
        one.start();
        two.start();
        three.start();
    }
}
```

Running this code might produce the following:

```
% java ManyNames
Run by Fred, x is 1
Run by Fred, x is 2
Run by Fred, x is 3
```

```
Run by Lucy, x is 1
Run by Lucy, x is 2
Run by Lucy, x is 3
Run by Ricky, x is 1
Run by Ricky, x is 2
Run by Ricky, x is 3
```

Well, at least that's what it printed when we ran it—this time, on our machine. But the behavior you see above is not guaranteed. This is so crucial that you need to stop right now, take a deep breath, and repeat after me, "The behavior is not guaranteed." You need to know, for your future as a Java programmer as well as for the exam, that there is nothing in the Java specification that says threads will start running in the order in which they were started (in other words, the order in which `start()` was invoked on each thread). And there is no guarantee that once a thread starts executing, it will keep executing until it's done. Or that a loop will complete before another thread begins. No siree Bob. Nothing is guaranteed in the preceding code except this:

Each thread will start, and each thread will run to completion.

Within each thread, things will happen in a predictable order. But the actions of different threads can mix together in unpredictable ways. If you run the program multiple times, or on multiple machines, you may see different output. Even if you don't see different output, you need to realize that the behavior you see is not guaranteed. Sometimes a little change in the way the program is run will cause a difference to emerge. Just for fun we bumped up the loop code so that each `run()` method ran the `for` loop 400 times rather than 3, and eventually we did start to see some wobbling:

```java
public void run() {
    for (int x = 1; x <= 400; x++) {
        System.out.println("Run by "
                + Thread.currentThread().getName()
                + ", x is " + x);
    }
}
```

Running the preceding code, with each thread executing its run loop 400 times, started out fine but then became nonlinear. Here's just a snip from the command-line output of running that code. To make it easier to distinguish each thread, we put Fred's output in italics and Lucy's in bold, and left Ricky's alone:

Run by Fred, x is 345
Run by Lucy, x is 337
Run by Ricky, x is 310
Run by Lucy, x is 338
Run by Ricky, x is 311
Run by Lucy, x is 339
Run by Ricky, x is 312
Run by Lucy, x is 340
Run by Ricky, x is 313
Run by Lucy, x is 341
Run by Ricky, x is 314
Run by Lucy, x is 342
Run by Ricky, x is 315
Run by Fred, x is 346
Run by Lucy, x is 343
Run by Fred, x is 347
Run by Lucy, x is 344

... it continues on ...

Notice that there's not really any clear pattern here. If we look at only the output from Fred, we see the numbers increasing one at a time, as expected:

Run by Fred, x is 345
Run by Fred, x is 346
Run by Fred, x is 347

And similarly if we look only at the output from Lucy, or Ricky. Each one individually is behaving in a nice orderly manner. But together—chaos! In the fragment above we see Fred, then Lucy, then Ricky (in the same order we originally started the threads), but then Lucy butts in when it was Fred's turn. What nerve! And then Ricky and Lucy trade back and forth for a while until finally Fred gets another chance. They jump around like this for a while after this. Eventually (after the part shown above) Fred finishes, then Ricky, and finally Lucy finishes with a long sequence of output. So even though Ricky was started third, he actually completed second. And if we run it again, we'll get a different result. Why? Because it's up to the scheduler, and we don't control the scheduler! Which brings up another key point to remember: Just because a series of threads are started in a particular order doesn't mean they'll run in that order. For any group of started threads, order is not guaranteed by the scheduler. And duration is not guaranteed. You don't know, for example, if one thread will run to completion before the others have a chance to get in or whether they'll all take turns nicely, or whether they'll do a combination of both. There is a way, however, to start a thread but tell it not to run until some other thread has finished. You can do this with the `join()` method, which we'll look at a little later.

A thread is done being a thread when its target `run()` *method completes.*

When a thread completes its `run()` method, the thread ceases to be a thread of execution. The stack for that thread dissolves, and the thread is considered dead. Not dead and gone, however, just dead. It's still a Thread *object*, just not a *thread of execution*. So if you've got a reference to a Thread instance, then even when that Thread instance is no longer a thread of execution, you can still call methods on the Thread instance, just like any other Java object. What you can't do, though, is call `start()` again.

Once a thread has been started, it can never be started again.

If you have a reference to a Thread, and you call `start()`, it's started. If you call `start()` a second time, it will cause an exception (an IllegalThreadStateException, which is a kind of RuntimeException, but you don't need to worry about the exact type). This happens whether or not the `run()` method has completed from the first `start()` call. Only a new thread can be started, and then only once. A runnable thread or a dead thread cannot be restarted.

So far, we've seen three thread states: *new*, *runnable*, and *dead*. We'll look at more thread states before we're done with this chapter.

The Thread Scheduler

The thread scheduler is the part of the JVM (although most JVMs map Java threads directly to native threads on the underlying OS) that decides which thread should run at any given moment, and also takes threads *out* of the run state. Assuming a single processor machine, only one thread can actually *run* at a time. Only one stack can ever be executing at one time. And it's the thread scheduler that decides *which* thread—of all that are eligible—will actually *run*. When we say *eligible*, we really mean *in the runnable state*.

Any thread in the *runnable* state can be chosen by the scheduler to be the one and only running thread. If a thread is not in a runnable state, then it cannot be chosen to be the *currently running* thread. And just so we're clear about how little is guaranteed here:

The order in which runnable threads are chosen to run is not guaranteed.

Although *queue* behavior is typical, it isn't guaranteed. Queue behavior means that when a thread has finished with its "turn," it moves to the end of the line of the runnable pool and waits until it eventually gets to the front of the line, where it can be chosen again. In fact, we call it a runnable *pool*, rather than a runnable *queue*, to help reinforce the fact that threads aren't all lined up in some guaranteed order.

Although we don't *control* the thread scheduler (we can't, for example, tell a specific thread to run), we can sometimes influence it. The following methods give us some tools for *influencing* the scheduler. Just don't ever mistake influence for control.

Methods from the java.lang.Thread Class   Some of the methods that can help us influence thread scheduling are as follows:

```
public static void sleep(long millis) throws InterruptedException
public static void yield()
public final void join() throws InterruptedException
public final void setPriority(int newPriority)
```

Note that both `sleep()` and `join()` have overloaded versions not shown here.

Methods from the java.lang.Object Class   Every class in Java inherits the following three thread-related methods:

```
public final void wait() throws InterruptedException
public final void notify()
public final void notifyAll()
```

The wait() method has three overloaded versions (including the one listed here).

   We'll look at the behavior of each of these methods in this chapter. First, though, we're going to look at the different states a thread can be in.

CERTIFICATION OBJECTIVE

Thread States and Transitions (Objective 4.2)

4.2   Recognize the states in which a thread can exist, and identify ways in which a thread can transition from one state to another.

We've already seen three thread states— *new, runnable,* and *dead*—but wait! There's more! The thread scheduler's job is to move threads in and out of the *running* state. While the thread scheduler can move a thread from the running state back to runnable, other factors can cause a thread to move out of running, but *not* back to runnable. One of these is when the thread's run() method completes, in which case the thread moves from the running state directly to the dead state. Next we'll look at some of the other ways in which a thread can leave the running state, and where the thread goes.

Thread States

A thread can be only in one of five states (see Figure 9-2):

- **New**   This is the state the thread is in after the Thread instance has been created, but the start() method has not been invoked on the thread. It is a live Thread object, but not yet a thread of execution. At this point, the thread is considered *not alive*.

■ **Runnable**   This is the state a thread is in when it's eligible to run, but the scheduler has not selected it to be the running thread. A thread first enters the runnable state when the `start()` method is invoked, but a thread can also return to the runnable state after either running or coming back from a blocked, waiting, or sleeping state. When the thread is in the runnable state, it is considered *alive*.

■ **Running**   This is it. The "big time." Where the action is. This is the state a thread is in when the thread scheduler selects it (from the runnable pool) to be the currently executing process. A thread can transition out of a running state for several reasons, including because "the thread scheduler felt like it." We'll look at those other reasons shortly. Note that in Figure 9-2, there are several ways to get to the runnable state, but only *one* way to get to the running state: the scheduler chooses a thread from the runnable pool.

Transitioning between thread states

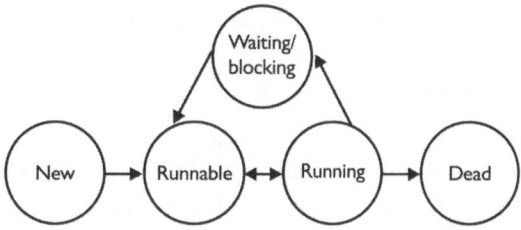

■ **Waiting/blocked/sleeping**   This is the state a thread is in when it's eligible to run. Okay, so this is really three states combined into one, but they all have one thing in common: the thread is still alive, but is currently not eligible to run. In other words, it is not *runnable*, but it might *return* to a runnable state later if a particular event occurs. A thread may be *blocked* waiting for a resource (like I/O or an object's lock), in which case the event that sends it back to runnable is the availability of the resource—for example, if data comes in through the input stream the thread code is reading from, or if the object's lock suddenly becomes available. A thread may be *sleeping* because the thread's run code *tells* it to sleep for some period of time, in which case the event that sends it back to runnable is that it wakes up because its sleep time has expired. Or the thread may be *waiting*, because the thread's run code *causes* it to wait, in which case the event that sends it back to runnable is that another thread sends a notification that it may no longer be necessary for the thread to wait. The important point is that one thread does not *tell* another thread to block. Some methods may *look* like they tell another thread to block, but they don't. If you have a reference t to another thread, you can write something like this:

```
t.sleep();   or      t.yield()
```

But those are actually static methods of the Thread class—*they don't affect the instance* t; instead they are defined to always affect the thread that's currently executing. (This is a good example of why it's a bad idea to use an instance variable to access a static method—it's misleading. There *is* a method, suspend(), in the Thread class, that lets one thread tell another to suspend, but the suspend() method has been deprecated and won't be on the exam (nor will its counterpart resume()). There is also a stop() method, but it too has been deprecated and we won't even go there. Both suspend() and stop() turned out to be very dangerous, so you shouldn't use them and again, because they're deprecated, they won't appear on the exam. Don't study 'em, don't use 'em. Note also that a thread in a blocked state is still considered to be *alive*.

■ **Dead**   A thread is considered dead when its run() method completes. It may still be a viable Thread object, but it is no longer a separate thread of execution. Once a thread is dead, it can never be brought back to life! (The whole "I see dead threads" thing.) If you invoke start() on a dead Thread instance, you'll get a runtime (not compiler) exception. And it probably doesn't take a rocket scientist to tell you that if a thread is dead, it is no longer considered to be *alive*.

Preventing Thread Execution

A thread that's been stopped usually means a thread that's moved to the dead state. But Objective 4.2 is also looking for your ability to recognize when a thread will get kicked out of running but *not* be sent back to either runnable or dead.

For the purpose of the exam, we aren't concerned with a thread blocking on I/O (say, waiting for something to arrive from an input stream from the server). We *are* concerned with the following:

■ Sleeping
■ Waiting
■ Blocked because it needs an object's lock

Sleeping

The `sleep()` method is a `static` method of class Thread. You use it in your code to "slow a thread down" by forcing it to go into a sleep mode before coming back to runnable (where it still has to beg to be the currently running thread). When a thread sleeps, it drifts off somewhere and doesn't return to runnable until it wakes up.

So why would you want a thread to sleep? Well, you might think the thread is moving too quickly through its code. Or you might need to force your threads to take turns, since reasonable turn-taking isn't guaranteed in the Java specification. Or imagine a thread that runs in a loop, downloading the latest stock prices and analyzing them. Downloading prices one after another would be a waste of time, as most would be quite similar—and even more important, it would be an incredible waste of precious bandwidth. The simplest way to solve this is to cause a thread to pause (sleep) for five minutes after each download.

You do this by invoking the static `Thread.sleep()` method, giving it a time in milliseconds as follows:

```
try {
  Thread.sleep(5*60*1000);  // Sleep for 5 minutes
} catch (InterruptedException ex) { }
```

Notice that the `sleep()` method can throw a checked InterruptedException (you'll usually know if that is a possibility, since another thread has to explicitly do the interrupting), so you must acknowledge the exception with a handle or declare. Typically, you wrap calls to `sleep()` in a `try/catch`, as in the preceding code.

Let's modify our Fred, Lucy, Ricky code by using `sleep()` to *try* to force the threads to alternate rather than letting one thread dominate for any period of time. Where do you think the `sleep()` method should go?

```
class NameRunnable implements Runnable {
   public void run() {
      for (int x = 1; x < 4; x++) {
         System.out.println("Run by "
           + Thread.currentThread().getName());
```

```
            try {
              Thread.sleep(1000);
            } catch (InterruptedException ex) { }
        }
      }
}

public class ManyNames {
    public static void main (String [] args) {

        // Make one Runnable
        NameRunnable nr = new NameRunnable();

        Thread one = new Thread(nr);
        one.setName("Fred");
        Thread two = new Thread(nr);
        two.setName("Lucy");
        Thread three = new Thread(nr);
        three.setName("Ricky");

        one.start();
        two.start();
        three.start();
    }
}
```

Running this code shows Fred, Lucy, and Ricky alternating nicely:

```
% java ManyNames
Run by Fred
Run by Lucy
Run by Ricky
Run by Fred
Run by Lucy
Run by Ricky
Run by Fred
Run by Lucy
Run by Ricky
```

Just keep in mind that the behavior in the preceding output is still not guaranteed. You can't be certain how long a thread will actually run *before* it gets put to sleep, so you can't know with certainty that only one of the three threads will be in the runnable state when the running thread goes to sleep. In other words, if there are two threads awake and in the runnable pool, you can't know with certainty that the least recently used thread will be the one selected to run. *Still, using* sleep() *is the best way to help all threads get a chance to run!* Or at least to guarantee that one thread doesn't get in and stay until it's done. When a thread encounters a sleep call, it *must* go to sleep for *at least* the specified number of milliseconds (unless it is interrupted before its wake-up time, in which case it immediately throws the InterruptedException).

e x a m
ⓦatch

Just because a thread's sleep() *expires, and it wakes up, does not mean it will return to running! Remember, when a thread wakes up, it simply goes back to the runnable state. So the time specified in* sleep() *is the minimum duration in which the thread won't run, but it is not the exact duration in which the thread won't run. So you can't, for example, rely on the* sleep() *method to give you a perfectly accurate timer. Although in many applications using* sleep() *as a timer is certainly good enough, you must know that a* sleep() *time is not a guarantee that the thread will start running again as soon as the time expires and the thread wakes.*

Remember that sleep() is a static method, so don't be fooled into thinking that one thread can put another thread to sleep. You can put sleep() code anywhere, since *all* code is being run by *some* thread. When the executing code (meaning the currently running thread's code) hits a sleep() call, it puts the currently running thread to sleep.

EXERCISE 9-1

Creating a Thread and Putting It to Sleep

In this exercise we will create a simple counting thread. It will count to 100, pausing one second between each number. Also, in keeping with the counting theme, it will output a string every ten numbers.

1. Create a class and extend the Thread class. As an option, you can implement the Runnable interface.

2. Override the `run()` method of Thread. This is where the code will go that will output the numbers.

3. Create a `for` loop that will loop 100 times. Use the modulo operation to check whether there are any remainder numbers when divided by 10.

4. Use the `static` method `Thread.sleep()` to pause. The *long* number represents milliseconds.

Thread Priorities and yield( )

To understand `yield()`, you must understand the concept of thread *priorities*. Threads always run with some priority, usually represented as a number between 1 and 10 (although in some cases the range is less than 10). The scheduler in most JVMs uses preemptive, priority-based scheduling (which implies some sort of time slicing). *This does not mean that all JVMs use time slicing.* The JVM specification does not require a VM to implement a time-slicing scheduler, where each thread is allocated a fair amount of time and then sent back to runnable to give another thread a chance. Although many JVMs do use time slicing, some may use a scheduler that lets one thread stay running until the thread completes its `run()` method.

In most JVMs, however, the scheduler does use thread priorities in one important way: If a thread enters the runnable state, and it has a higher priority than any of the threads in the pool and a higher priority than the currently running thread, *the lower-priority running thread usually will be bumped back to runnable and the highest-priority thread will be chosen to run.* In other words, at any given time the currently running thread usually will not have a priority that is lower than any of the threads in the pool. *In most cases, the running thread will be of equal or greater priority than the highest priority threads in the pool.* This is as close to a guarantee about scheduling as you'll get from the JVM specification, so you must never rely on thread priorities to guarantee the correct behavior of your program.

on the job

Don't rely on thread priorities when designing your multithreaded application. Because thread-scheduling priority behavior is not guaranteed, use thread priorities as a way to improve the efficiency of your program, but just be sure your program doesn't depend on that behavior for correctness.

What is also *not* guaranteed is the behavior when threads in the pool are of equal priority, or when the currently running thread has the same priority as threads in the pool. All priorities being equal, a JVM implementation of the scheduler is free to do just about anything it likes. That means a scheduler might do one of the following (among other things):

■ Pick a thread to run, and run it there until it blocks or completes.

■ Time slice the threads in the pool to give everyone an equal opportunity to run.

Setting a Thread's Priority   A thread gets a default priority that is *the priority of the thread of execution that creates it*. For example, in the code

```
public class TestThreads {
  public static void main (String [] args) {
    MyThread t = new MyThread();
  }
}
```

the thread referenced by t will have the same priority as the *main* thread, since the main thread is executing the code that creates the MyThread instance.

You can also set a thread's priority directly by calling the setPriority() method on a Thread instance as follows:

```
FooRunnable r = new FooRunnable();
Thread t = new Thread(r);
t.setPriority(8);
t.start();
```

Priorities are set using a positive integer, usually between 1 and 10, and the JVM will never change a thread's priority. However, the values 1 through 10 are not guaranteed. Some JVM's might not recognize ten distinct values. Such a JVM might merge values from 1 to 10 down to maybe values from 1 to 5, so if you have, say, ten threads each with a different priority, and the current application is running in a JVM that allocates a range of only five priorities, then two or more threads might be mapped to one priority.

Although *the default priority is 5*, the Thread class has the three following constants (static final variables) that define the range of thread priorities:

```
Thread.MIN_PRIORITY   (1)
Thread.NORM_PRIORITY  (5)
Thread.MAX_PRIORITY   (10)
```

The yield( ) Method So what does the static `Thread.yield()` have to do with all this? Not that much, in practice. What `yield()` is *supposed* to do is make the currently running thread head back to runnable to allow other threads of the same priority to get their turn. So the intention is to use `yield()` to promote graceful turn-taking among equal-priority threads. In reality, though, the `yield()` method isn't guaranteed to do what it claims, and even if `yield()` does cause a thread to step out of running and back to runnable, *there's no guarantee the yielding thread won't just be chosen again over all the others!* So while `yield()` might—and often does—make a running thread give up its slot to another runnable thread of the same priority, there's no guarantee.

A `yield()` won't ever cause a thread to go to the waiting/sleeping/ blocking state. At most, a `yield()` will cause a thread to go from running to runnable, but again, it might have no effect at all.

The join( ) Method

The non-static `join()` method of class Thread lets one thread "join onto the end" of another thread. If you have a thread B that can't do its work until another thread A has completed *its* work, then you want thread B to "join" thread A. This means that thread B will not become runnable until A has finished (and entered the dead state).

```
Thread t = new Thread();
t.start();
t.join();
```

The preceding code takes the currently running thread (if this were in the `main()` method, then that would be the main thread) and *joins* it to the end of the thread referenced by `t`. This blocks the current thread from becoming runnable until after the thread referenced by `t` is no longer alive. In other words, the code `t.join()` means "Join me (the current thread) to the end of `t`, so that `t` must finish before I (the current thread) can run again." You can also call one of the overloaded versions of `join()` that takes a timeout duration, so that you're saying, "wait until thread `t` is done, but if it takes longer than 5,000 milliseconds, then stop waiting and become runnable anyway." Figure 9-3 shows the effect of the `join()` method.

FIGURE 9-3   The join() method

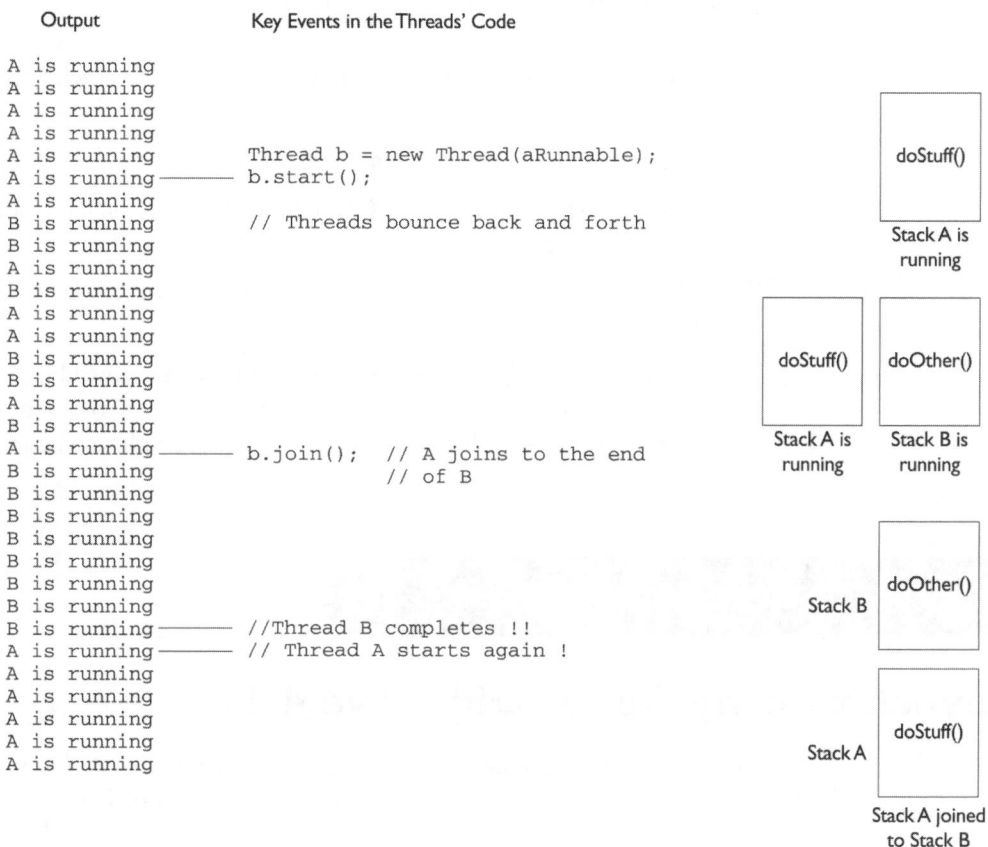

```
Output                     Key Events in the Threads' Code

A is running
A is running
A is running
A is running
A is running            Thread b = new Thread(aRunnable);
A is running ─────────  b.start();
A is running
B is running            // Threads bounce back and forth
B is running
A is running
B is running
A is running
A is running
B is running
B is running
A is running
B is running
A is running ────────── b.join();  // A joins to the end
B is running                        // of B
B is running
B is running
B is running
B is running
B is running
B is running
B is running ─────────  //Thread B completes !!
A is running ─────────  // Thread A starts again !
A is running
A is running
A is running
A is running
A is running
```

So far we've looked at three ways a running thread could leave the running state:

- **A call to sleep()**   Guaranteed to cause the current thread to stop executing for at least the specified sleep duration (although it might be *interrupted* before its specified time).

- **A call to yield()**   Not guaranteed to do much of anything, although typically it will cause the currently running thread to move back to runnable so that a thread of the same priority can have a chance.

- **A call to join()**   Guaranteed to cause the current thread to stop executing until the thread it joins with (in other words, the thread it calls join()

on) completes, or if the thread it's trying to join with is not alive, however, the current thread won't need to back out.

Besides those three, we also have the following scenarios in which a thread might leave the running state:

■ The thread's `run()` method completes. Duh.

■ A call to `wait()` on an object (we don't call `wait()` on a *thread*, as we'll see in a moment).

■ A thread can't acquire the *lock* on the object whose method code it's attempting to run.

■ The thread scheduler can decide to move the current thread from running to runnable in order to give another thread a chance to run. No reason is needed—the thread scheduler can trade threads in and out whenever it likes.

CERTIFICATION OBJECTIVE

Synchronizing Code (Objective 4.3)

4.3   Given a scenario, write code that makes appropriate use of object locking to protect static or instance variables from concurrent access problems.

Can you imagine the havoc that can occur when two different threads have access to a single instance of a class, and both threads invoke methods on that object...and those methods modify the state of the object? In other words, what might happen if *two* different threads call, say, a setter method on a *single* object? A scenario like that might corrupt an object's state (by changing its instance variable values in an inconsistent way), and if that object's state is data shared by other parts of the program, well, it's too scary to even visualize.

But just because we enjoy horror, let's look at an example of what might happen. The following code demonstrates what happens when two different threads are accessing the same account data. Imagine that two people each have a checkbook for a single checking account (or two people each have ATM cards, but both cards are linked to only one account).

In this example, we have a class called Account that represents a bank account. To keep the code short, this account starts with a balance of 50, and can be used only for withdrawals. The withdrawal will be accepted even if there isn't enough money in the account to cover it. The account simply reduces the balance by the amount you want to withdraw:

```
class Account {
   private int balance = 50;
   public int getBalance() {
      return balance;
   }
   public void withdraw(int amount) {
      balance = balance - amount;
   }
}
```

Now here's where it starts to get fun. Imagine a couple, Fred and Lucy, who both have access to the account and want to make withdrawals. But they don't want the account to ever be overdrawn, so just before one of them makes a withdrawal, he or she will first check the balance to be certain there's enough to cover the withdrawal. Also, withdrawals are always limited to an amount of 10, so there must be at least 10 in the account balance in order to make a withdrawal. Sounds reasonable. But that's a two-step process:

1. Check the balance.

2. If there's enough in the account (in this example, at least 10), make the withdrawal.

What happens if something separates step 1 from step 2? For example, imagine what would happen if Lucy checks the balance and sees that there's just exactly enough in the account, 10. *But before she makes the withdrawal, Fred checks the balance and also sees that there's enough for his withdrawal.* Since Lucy has verified the balance, but not yet made her withdrawal, Fred is seeing "bad data." He is seeing the account balance *before* Lucy actually debits the account, but at this point that debit is certain to occur. Now both Lucy and Fred believe there's enough to make their withdrawals. So now imagine that Lucy makes *her* withdrawal, and now there isn't enough in the account for Fred's withdrawal, but he thinks there is since when he checked, there was enough! Yikes. In a minute we'll see the actual banking code, with Fred and Lucy, represented by two threads, each acting on the same Runnable, and that Runnable holds a reference to the one and only account instance—so, two threads, one account.

The logic in our code example is as follows:

1. The Runnable object holds a reference to a single account.

2. Two threads are started, representing Lucy and Fred, and each thread is given a reference to the same Runnable (which holds a reference to the actual account)

3. The initial balance on the account is 50, and each withdrawal is exactly 10.

4. In the `run()` method, we loop 5 times, and in each loop we

   - Make a withdrawal (if there's enough in the account).

   - Print a statement *if the account is overdrawn* (which it should never be, since we check the balance *before* making a withdrawal).

5. The `makeWithdrawal()` method in the test class (representing the behavior of Fred or Lucy) will do the following:

   - Check the balance to see if there's enough for the withdrawal.

   - If there is enough, print out the name of the one making the withdrawal.

   - Go to sleep for 500 milliseconds—just long enough to give the other partner a chance to get in before you actually *make* the withdrawal.

   - Upon waking up, complete the withdrawal and print that fact.

   - If there wasn't enough in the first place, print a statement showing who you are and the fact that there wasn't enough.

So what we're really trying to discover is if the following is possible: for one partner to check the account and see that there's enough, but before making the actual withdrawal, the other partner checks the account and *also* sees that there's enough. When the account balance gets to 10, if both partners check it before making the withdrawal, both will think it's OK to withdraw, and the account will overdraw by 10!

Here's the code:

```
public class AccountDanger implements Runnable {
    private Account acct = new Account();
    public static void main (String [] args) {
        AccountDanger r = new AccountDanger();
        Thread one = new Thread(r);
        Thread two = new Thread(r);
        one.setName("Fred");
        two.setName("Lucy");
```

```
      one.start();
      two.start();
    }
  public void run() {
   for (int x = 0; x < 5; x++) {
      makeWithdrawal(10);
      if (acct.getBalance() < 0) {
        System.out.println("account is overdrawn!");
      }
    }
  }
}
  private void makeWithdrawal(int amt) {
      if (acct.getBalance() >= amt) {
        System.out.println(Thread.currentThread().getName()
                    + " is going to withdraw");
        try {
          Thread.sleep(500);
        } catch(InterruptedException ex) { }
        acct.withdraw(amt);
        System.out.println(Thread.currentThread().getName()
                    + " completes the withdrawal");
      } else {
        System.out.println("Not enough in account for "
                    + Thread.currentThread().getName()
                    + " to withdraw " + acct.getBalance());
      }
    }
  }
}
```

So what happened? Is it possible that, say, Lucy checked the balance, fell asleep, Fred checked the balance, Lucy woke up and completed *her* withdrawal, then Fred completes *his* withdrawal, and in the end they overdraw the account? Look at the (numbered) output:

```
% java AccountDanger
 1. Fred is going to withdraw
 2. Lucy is going to withdraw
 3. Fred completes the withdrawal
 4. Fred is going to withdraw
 5. Lucy completes the withdrawal
 6. Lucy is going to withdraw
 7. Fred completes the withdrawal
 8. Fred is going to withdraw
 9. Lucy completes the withdrawal
```

```
10. Lucy is going to withdraw
11. Fred completes the withdrawal
12. Not enough in account for Fred to withdraw 0
13. Not enough in account for Fred to withdraw 0
14. Lucy completes the withdrawal
15. account is overdrawn!
16. Not enough in account for Lucy to withdraw -10
17. account is overdrawn!
18. Not enough in account for Lucy to withdraw -10
19. account is overdrawn!
```

Although each time you run this code the output might be a little different, let's walk through this particular example using the numbered lines of output. For the first four attempts, everything is fine. Fred checks the balance on line 1, and finds it's OK. At line 2, Lucy checks the balance and finds it OK. At line 3, Fred makes his withdrawal. At this point, the balance Lucy checked for (and believes is still accurate) has actually changed since she last checked. And now Fred checks the balance *again*, before Lucy even completes her first withdrawal. By this point, even Fred is seeing a potentially inaccurate balance, because we know Lucy is going to complete her withdrawal. It is possible, of course, that Fred will complete his before Lucy does, but that's not what happens here.

On line 5, Lucy completes her withdrawal and then before Fred completes his, Lucy does another check on the account on line 6. And so it continues until we get to line 8, where Fred checks the balance and sees that it's 20. On line 9, Lucy completes a withdrawal (that she had checked for earlier), and this takes the balance to 10. On line 10, Lucy checks again, sees that the balance is 10, so she knows she can do a withdrawal. *But she didn't know that Fred, too, has already checked the balance on line 8 so he thinks it's safe to do the withdrawal!* On line 11, Fred completes the withdrawal he approved on line 8. This takes the balance to zero. But Lucy still has a pending withdrawal that she got approval for on line 10! You know what's coming.

On lines 12 and 13, Fred checks the balance and finds that there's not enough in the account. But on line 14, Lucy completes her withdrawal and BOOM! The account is now overdrawn by 10—*something we thought we were preventing by doing a balance check prior to a withdrawal.*

Figure 9-4 shows the timeline of what can happen when two threads concurrently access the same object.

FIGURE 9-4

Problems with
concurrent access

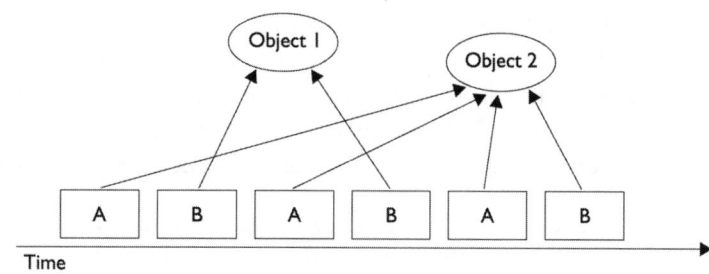

Time

Thread A will access Object 2 only

Thread B will access Object 1, and then Object 2

This problem is known as a "race condition," where multiple threads can access the same resource (typically an object's instance variables), and can produce corrupted data if one thread "races in" too quickly before an operation that should be "atomic" has completed.

Preventing the Account Overdraw   So what can be done? The solution is actually quite simple. We must guarantee that the two steps of the withdrawal— *checking* the balance and *making* the withdrawal—are never split apart. We need them to always be performed as one operation, even when the thread falls asleep in between step 1 and step 2! We call this an "atomic operation" (although the physics is a little outdated, in this case "atomic" means "indivisible") because the operation, regardless of the number of actual statements (or underlying byte code instructions), is completed *before* any other thread code that acts on the same data.

You can't guarantee that a single thread will stay running throughout the entire atomic operation. But you *can* guarantee that even if the thread running the atomic operation moves in and out of the running state, *no other running thread will be able to act on the same data.* In other words, If Lucy falls asleep after checking the balance, we can stop Fred from checking the balance until *after* Lucy wakes up and completes her withdrawal.

So how do you protect the data? You must do two things:

- Mark the variables `private`.
- Synchronize the code that modifies the variables.

Remember, you protect the variables in the normal way—using an access control modifier. It's the method code that you must protect, so that only one thread at a time can be executing that code. You do this with the synchronized keyword.

We can solve all of Fred and Lucy's problems by adding one word to the code. We mark the makeWithdrawal() method synchronized as follows:

```
private synchronized void makeWithdrawal(int amt) {
  if (acct.getBalance() >= amt) {
    System.out.println(Thread.currentThread().getName() +
                         " is going to withdraw");
    try {
      Thread.sleep(500);
    } catch(InterruptedException ex) { }
    acct.withdraw(amt);
    System.out.println(Thread.currentThread().getName() +
                         " completes the withdrawal");
  } else {
    System.out.println("Not enough in account for "
                     + Thread.currentThread().getName()
                     + " to withdraw " + acct.getBalance());
  }
}
```

Now we've guaranteed that once a thread (Lucy or Fred) starts the withdrawal process (by invoking makeWithdrawal()), the other thread cannot enter that method until the first one completes the process by exiting the method. The new output shows the benefit of synchronizing the makeWithdrawal() method:

```
% java AccountDanger
Fred is going to withdraw
Fred completes the withdrawal
Lucy is going to withdraw
Lucy completes the withdrawal
Fred is going to withdraw
Fred completes the withdrawal
Lucy is going to withdraw
Lucy completes the withdrawal
Fred is going to withdraw
Fred completes the withdrawal
Not enough in account for Lucy to withdraw 0
Not enough in account for Fred to withdraw 0
Not enough in account for Lucy to withdraw 0
Not enough in account for Fred to withdraw 0
Not enough in account for Lucy to withdraw 0
```

Notice that now both threads, Lucy and Fred, always check the account balance *and* complete the withdrawal before the other thread can check the balance.

Synchronization and Locks

How does synchronization work? With locks. Every object in Java has a built-in lock that only comes into play when the object has synchronized method code. When we enter a synchronized non-static method, we automatically acquire the lock associated with the current instance of the class whose code we're executing (the this instance). Acquiring a lock for an object is also known as getting the lock, or locking the object, locking *on* the object, or synchronizing on the object. We may also use the term *monitor* to refer to the object whose lock we're acquiring. Technically the lock and the monitor are two different things, but most people talk about the two interchangeably, and we will too.

Since there is only one lock per object, if one thread has picked up the lock, no other thread can pick up the lock until the first thread releases (or returns) the lock. This means no other thread can enter the synchronized code (which means it can't enter any synchronized method of that object) until the lock has been released. Typically, releasing a lock means the thread holding the lock (in other words, the thread currently in the synchronized method) exits the synchronized method. At that point, the lock is free until some other thread enters a synchronized method on that object. Remember the following key points about locking and synchronization:

- Only methods (or blocks) can be synchronized, not variables or classes.
- Each object has just one lock.
- Not all methods in a class need to be synchronized. A class can have both synchronized and non-synchronized methods.
- If two threads are about to execute a synchronized method in a class, and both threads are using the same instance of the class to invoke the method, only one thread at a time will be able to execute the method. The other thread will need to wait until the first one finishes its method call. In other words, once a thread acquires the lock on an object, no other thread can enter any of the synchronized methods in that class (for that object).

- If a class has both `synchronized` and non-`synchronized` methods, multiple threads can still access the class's non-`synchronized` methods! If you have methods that don't access the data you're trying to protect, then you don't need to synchronize them. Synchronization can cause a hit in some cases (or even deadlock if used incorrectly), so you should be careful not to overuse it.

- If a thread goes to sleep, it holds any locks it has—it doesn't release them.

- A thread can acquire more than one lock. For example, a thread can enter a `synchronized` method, thus acquiring a lock, and then immediately invoke a `synchronized` method on a different object, thus acquiring that lock as well. As the stack unwinds, locks are released again. Also, if a thread acquires a lock and then attempts to call a `synchronized` method on that same object, no problem. The JVM knows that this thread already has the lock for this object, so the thread is free to call other `synchronized` methods on the same object, using the lock the thread already has.

- You can synchronize a block of code rather than a method.

Because synchronization does hurt concurrency, you don't want to synchronize any more code than is necessary to protect your data. So if the scope of a method is more than needed, you can reduce the scope of the synchronized part to something less than a full method—to just a block. We call this, strangely, a *synchronized block*, and it looks like this:

```
class SyncTest {
  public void doStuff() {
    System.out.println("not synchronized");
    synchronized(this) {
      System.out.println("synchronized");
    }
  }
}
```

When a thread is executing code from within a `synchronized` block, including any method code invoked from that `synchronized` block, the code is said to be executing in a synchronized context. The real question is, synchronized on what? Or, synchronized on which object's lock?

When you synchronize a method, the object used to invoke the method is the object whose lock must be acquired. But when you synchronize a block of code, you specify which object's lock you want to use as the lock, so you could, for example, use some third-party object as the lock for this piece of code. That gives you the ability to have more than one lock for code synchronization within a single object.

Or you can synchronize on the current instance (this) as in the code above. Since that's the same instance that synchronized methods lock on, it means that you could always replace a synchronized method with a non-synchronized method containing a synchronized block. In other words, this:

```java
public synchronized void doStuff() {
    System.out.println("synchronized");
}
```

is equivalent to this:

```java
public void doStuff() {
    synchronized(this) {
        System.out.println("synchronized");
    }
}
```

These methods both have the exact same effect, in practical terms. The compiled bytecodes may not be exactly the same for the two methods, but they *could* be—and any differences are not really important. The first form is shorter and more familiar to most people, but the second can be more flexible.

So What About Static Methods? Can They Be Synchronized?

static methods can be synchronized. There is only one copy of the static data you're trying to protect, so you only need one lock per class to synchronize static methods—a lock for the whole class. There is such a lock; every class loaded in Java has a corresponding instance of java.lang.Class representing that class. It's that java.lang.Class instance whose lock is used to protect the static methods of the class (if they're synchronized). There's nothing special you have to do to synchronize a static method:

```java
public static synchronized int getCount() {
    return count;
}
```

Again, this could be replaced with code that uses a `synchronized` block. If the method is defined in a class called MyClass, the equivalent code is as follows:

```
public static int getCount() {
    synchronized(MyClass.class) {
        return count;
    }
}
```

Wait—what's that `MyClass.class` thing? That's called a *class literal*. It's a special feature in the Java language that tells the compiler (who tells the JVM): go and find me the instance of Class that represents the class called MyClass. You can also do this with the following code:

```
public static void classMethod() {
    Class cl = Class.forName("MyClass");
    synchronized (cl) {
        // do stuff
    }
}
```

However that's longer, ickier, and most important, *not on the SCJP exam*. But it's quick and easy to use a class literal—just write the name of the class, and add `.class` at the end. No quotation marks needed. Now you've got an expression for the Class object you need to synchronize on.

EXERCISE 9-2

Synchronizing a Block of Code

In this exercise we will attempt to synchronize a block of code. Within that block of code we will get the lock on an object, so that other threads cannot modify it while the block of code is executing. We will be creating three threads that will all attempt to manipulate the same object. Each thread will output a single letter 100 times, and then increment that letter by one. The object we will be using is StringBuffer.

We could synchronize on a String object, but strings cannot be modified once they are created, so we would not be able to increment the letter without generating a new String object. The final output should have 100 As, 100 Bs, and 100 Cs all in unbroken lines.

1. Create a class and extend the Thread class.

2. Override the `run()` method of Thread. This is where the `synchronized` block of code will go.

3. For our three thread objects to share the same object, we will need to create a constructor that accepts a StringBuffer object in the argument.

4. The `synchronized` block of code will obtain a lock on the StringBuffer object from step 3.

5. Within the block, output the StringBuffer 100 times and then increment the letter in the StringBuffer. You can check Chapter 5 for StringBuffer methods that will help with this.

6. Finally, in the `main()` method, create a single StringBuffer object using the letter A, then create three instances of our class and start all three of them.

What Happens If a thread Can't Get the Lock?

If a thread tries to enter a `synchronized` method and the lock is already taken, the thread is said to be blocked on the object's lock. Essentially, the thread goes into a kind of pool for that particular object and has to sit there until the lock is released and the thread can again become runnable/running. Just because a lock is released doesn't mean any particular thread will get it. There might be three threads waiting for a single lock, for example, and there's no guarantee that the thread that has waited the longest will get the lock first.

When thinking about blocking, it's important to pay attention to which objects are being used for locking.

- Threads calling non-`static` `synchronized` methods in the same class will only block each other if they're invoked using the same instance. That's because they each lock on `this` instance, and if they're called using two different instances, they get two locks, which do not interfere with each other.

- Threads calling `static` `synchronized` methods in the same class will always block each other—they all lock on the same Class instance.

- A `static` `synchronized` method and a non-`static` `synchronized` method will not block each other, ever. The `static` method locks on a Class instance while the non-`static` method locks on the `this` instance—these actions do not interfere with each other at all.

■ For `synchronized` blocks, you have to look at exactly what object has been used for locking. (What's inside the parentheses after the word `synchronized`?) Threads that synchronize on the same object will block each other. Threads that synchronize on different objects will not.

Table 9-1 lists the thread-related methods and whether the thread gives up its lock as a result of the call.

| TABLE 9-1 | Methods and Lock Status | |

Give Up Locks	Keep Locks	Class Defining the Method
`wait ()`	`notify()` (Although the thread will probably exit the synchronized code shortly after this call, and thus give up its locks.)	`java.lang.Object`
	`join()`	`java.lang.Thread`
	`sleep()`	`java.lang.Thread`
	`yield()`	`java.lang.Thread`

So When Do I Need To Synchronize?

Synchronization can get pretty complicated, and you may be wondering why you would want to do this at all if you can help it. But remember the earlier "race conditions" example with Lucy and Fred making withdrawals from their account. When we use threads, we usually need to use some synchronization somewhere to make sure our methods don't interrupt each other at the wrong time and mess up our data. Generally, any time more than one thread is accessing mutable (changeable) data, you synchronize to protect that data, to make sure two threads aren't changing it at the same time (or that one isn't changing it at the same time the other is reading it, which is also confusing). You don't need to worry about local variables— each thread gets its own copy of a local variable. Two threads executing the same method at the same time will use different copies of the local variables, and they won't bother each other. However, you do need to worry about `static` and non-`static` fields, if they contain data that can be changed.

For changeable data in a non-`static` field, you usually use a non-`static` method to access it. By synchronizing that method, you will ensure that any threads trying to run that method *using the same instance* will be prevented from simultaneous access. But a thread working with a *different* instance will not be affected, because it's acquiring a lock on the other instance. That's what we want—threads working with the same data need to go one at a time, but threads working with different data can just ignore each other and run whenever they want to; it doesn't matter.

For changeable data in a `static` field, you usually use a static method to access it. And again, by synchronizing the method you ensure that any two threads trying to access the data will be prevented from simultaneous access, because both threads will have to acquire locks on the Class object for the class the `static` method's defined in. Again, that's what we want.

However—what if you have a non-`static` method that accesses a `static` field? Or a `static` method that accesses a non-`static` field (using an instance)? In these cases things start to get messy quickly, and there's a very good chance that things will not work the way you want. If you've got a `static` method accessing a non-`static` field, and you synchronize the method, you acquire a lock on the Class object. But what if there's another method that also accesses the non-`static` field, this time using a non-`static` method? It probably synchronizes on the current instance (`this`) instead. Remember that a `static synchronized` method and a non-`static synchronized` method will not block each other—they can run at the same time. Similarly, if you access a `static` field using a non-`static` method, two threads might invoke that method using two different `this` instances. Which means they won't block each other, because they use different locks. Which means two threads are simultaneously accessing the same `static` field—exactly the sort of thing we're trying to prevent.

It gets very confusing trying to imagine all the weird things that can happen here. To keep things simple: in order to make a class thread-safe, methods that access changeable fields need to be `synchronized`.

Access to static fields should be done from `static synchronized` *methods. Access to non-`static` fields should be done from non-`static` synchronized methods.* For example:

```
public class Thing {
    private static int staticField;
    private int nonstaticField;
    public static synchronized int getStaticField() {
        return staticField;
    }
    public static synchronized void setStaticField(
                                        int staticField) {
```

```
        Thing.staticField = staticField;
    }
    public synchronized int getNonstaticField() {
        return nonstaticField;
    }
    public synchronized void setNonstaticField(
                                    int nonstaticField) {
        this.nonstaticField = nonstaticField;
    }
}
```

What if you need to access both static and non-static fields in a method? Well, there are ways to do that, but it's beyond what you need for the exam. You will live a longer, happier life if you JUST DON'T DO IT. Really. Would we lie?

Thread-Safe Classes

When a class has been carefully synchronized to protect its data (using the rules just given, or using more complicated alternatives), we say the class is "thread-safe." Many classes in the Java APIs already use synchronization internally in order to make the class "thread-safe." For example, StringBuffer and StringBuilder are nearly identical classes, except that all the methods in StringBuffer are synchronized when necessary, while those in StringBuilder are not. Generally, this makes StringBuffer safe to use in a multithreaded environment, while StringBuilder is not. (In return, StringBuilder is a little bit faster because it doesn't bother synchronizing.) However, even when a class is "thread-safe," it is often dangerous to rely on these classes to provide the thread protection you need. (C'mon, the repeated quotes used around "thread-safe" had to be a clue, right?) You still need to think carefully about how you use these classes, As an example, consider the following class.

```
import java.util.*;
public class NameList {
    private List names = Collections.synchronizedList(
                                    new LinkedList());
    public void add(String name) {
        names.add(name);
    }
    public String removeFirst() {
        if (names.size() > 0)
            return (String) names.remove(0);
        else
            return null;
```

```
        }
    }
```

The method `Collections.synchronizedList()` returns a List whose methods are all `synchronized` and "thread-safe" according to the documentation (like a Vector—but since this is the 21st century, we're not going to use a Vector here). The question is, can the NameList class be used safely from multiple threads? It's tempting to think that yes, since the data in names is in a synchronized collection, the NameList class is "safe" too. However that's not the case—the `removeFirst()` may sometimes throw a NoSuchElementException. What's the problem? Doesn't it correctly check the `size()` of names before removing anything, to make sure there's something there? How could this code fail? Let's try to use NameList like this:

```
public static void main(String[] args) {
    final NameList nl = new NameList();
    nl.add("Ozymandias");
    class NameDropper extends Thread {
        public void run() {
            String name = nl.removeFirst();
            System.out.println(name);
        }
    }
    Thread t1 = new NameDropper();
    Thread t2 = new NameDropper();
    t1.start();
    t2.start();
}
```

What might happen here is that one of the threads will remove the one name and print it, then the other will try to remove a name and get `null`. If we think just about the calls to `names.size()` and `names.get(0)`, they occur in this order:

Thread `t1` executes `names.size()`, which returns 1.
Thread `t1` executes `names.remove(0)`, which returns `Ozymandias`.
Thread `t2` executes `names.size()`, which returns 0.
Thread `t2` does not call `remove(0)`.

The output here is

```
Ozymandias
null
```

However, if we run the program again something different might happen:

Thread `t1` executes `names.size()`, which returns 1.
Thread `t2` executes `names.size()`, which returns 1.
Thread `t1` executes `names.remove(0)`, which returns `Ozymandias`.
Thread `t2` executes `names.remove(0)`, which throws an exception because the list is now empty.

The thing to realize here is that in a "thread-safe" class like the one returned by `synchronizedList()`, each *individual* method is synchronized. So `names.size()` is synchronized, and `names.remove(0)` is synchronized. But nothing prevents another thread from doing something else to the list *in between* those two calls. And that's where problems can happen.

There's a solution here: don't rely on `Collections.synchronizedList()`. Instead, synchronize the code yourself:

```java
import java.util.*;
public class NameList {
    private List names = new LinkedList();
    public synchronized void add(String name) {
        names.add(name);
    }
    public synchronized String removeFirst() {
        if (names.size() > 0)
            return (String) names.remove(0);
        else
            return null;
    }
}
```

Now the entire `removeFirst()` method is `synchronized`, and once one thread starts it and calls `names.size()`, there's no way the other thread can cut in and steal the last name. The other thread will just have to wait until the first thread completes the `removeFirst()` method.

The moral here is that just because a class is described as "thread-safe" doesn't mean it is *always* thread-safe. If individual methods are synchronized, that may not be enough—you may be better off putting in synchronization at a higher level (i.e., put it in the block or method that *calls* the other methods). Once you do that, the original synchronization (in this case, the synchronization inside the object returned by `Collections.synchronizedList()`) may well become redundant.

Thread Deadlock

Perhaps the scariest thing that can happen to a Java program is deadlock. Deadlock occurs when two threads are blocked, with each waiting for the other's lock. Neither can run until the other gives up its lock, so they'll sit there forever.

This can happen, for example, when thread A hits synchronized code, acquires a lock B, and then enters another method (still within the synchronized code it has the lock on) that's also synchronized. But thread A can't get the lock to enter this synchronized code—block C—because another thread D has the lock already. So thread A goes off to the waiting-for-the-C-lock pool, hoping that thread D will hurry up and release the lock (by completing the synchronized method). But thread A will wait a very long time indeed, because while thread D picked up lock C, it then entered a method synchronized on lock B. Obviously, thread D can't get the lock B because thread A has it. And thread A won't release it until thread D releases lock C. But thread D won't release lock C until after it can get lock B and continue. And there they sit. The following example demonstrates deadlock:

```
1. public class DeadlockRisk {
2.    private static class Resource {
3.      public int value;
4.    }
5.    private Resource resourceA = new Resource();
6.    private Resource resourceB = new Resource();
7.    public int read() {
8.      synchronized(resourceA) { // May deadlock here
9.        synchronized(resourceB) {
10.          return resourceB.value + resourceA.value;
11.        }
12.      }
13.    }
14.
15.    public void write(int a, int b) {
16.      synchronized(resourceB) { // May deadlock here
17.        synchronized(resourceA) {
18.          resourceA.value = a;
19.          resourceB.value = b;
20.        }
21.      }
22.    }
23. }
```

Assume that read() is started by one thread and write() is started by another. If there are two different threads that may read and write independently, there is a risk of deadlock at line 8 or 16. The reader thread will have resourceA, the writer thread will have resourceB, and both will get stuck waiting for the other.

Code like this almost never results in deadlock because the CPU has to switch from the reader thread to the writer thread at a particular point in the code, and the chances of deadlock occurring are very small. The application may work fine 99.9 percent of the time.

The preceding simple example is easy to fix; just swap the order of locking for either the reader or the writer at lines 16 and 17 (or lines 8 and 9). More complex deadlock situations can take a long time to figure out.

Regardless of how little chance there is for your code to deadlock, the bottom line is, if you deadlock, you're dead. There are design approaches that can help avoid deadlock, including strategies for always acquiring locks in a predetermined order.

But that's for you to study and is beyond the scope of this book. We're just trying to get you through the exam. If you learn everything in this chapter, though, you'll still know more about threads than most experienced Java programmers.

CERTIFICATION OBJECTIVE

Thread Interaction (Objective 4.4)

4.4   Given a scenario, write code that makes appropriate use of wait, notify. or notifyAll.

The last thing we need to look at is how threads can interact with one another to communicate about—among other things—their locking status. The Object class has three methods, wait(), notify(), and notifyAll() that help threads communicate about the status of an event that the threads care about. For example, if one thread is a mail-delivery thread and one thread is a mail-processor thread, the mail-processor thread has to keep checking to see if there's any mail to process. Using the wait and notify mechanism, the mail-processor thread could check for mail, and if it doesn't find any it can say, "Hey, I'm not going to waste my time checking for mail every two seconds. I'm going to go hang out, and when the mail deliverer puts something in the mailbox, have him notify me so I can go back to runnable and do some work." In other words, using wait() and notify() lets one thread put itself into a "waiting room" until some *other* thread notifies it that there's a reason to come back out.

One key point to remember (and keep in mind for the exam) about wait/notify is this:

wait (), notify (), and notifyAll () must be called from within a synchronized context! A thread can't invoke a wait or notify method on an object unless it owns that object's lock.

Here we'll present an example of two threads that depend on each other to proceed with their execution, and we'll show how to use wait() and notify() to make them interact safely and at the proper moment.

Think of a computer-controlled machine that cuts pieces of fabric into different shapes and an application that allows users to specify the shape to cut. The current version of the application has one thread, which loops, first asking the user for instructions, and then directs the hardware to cut the requested shape:

```
public void run(){
    while(true){
        // Get shape from user
        // Calculate machine steps from shape
        // Send steps to hardware
    }
}
```

This design is not optimal because the user can't do anything while the machine is busy and while there are other shapes to define. We need to improve the situation.

A simple solution is to separate the processes into two different threads, one of them interacting with the user and another managing the hardware. The user thread sends the instructions to the hardware thread and then goes back to interacting with the user immediately. The hardware thread receives the instructions from the user thread and starts directing the machine immediately. Both threads use a common object to communicate, which holds the current design being processed.

The following pseudocode shows this design:

```
public void userLoop(){
    while(true){
        // Get shape from user
        // Calculate machine steps from shape
        // Modify common object with new machine steps
```

```
        }
    }

    public void hardwareLoop(){
        while(true){
            // Get steps from common object
            // Send steps to hardware
        }
    }
}
```

The problem now is to get the hardware thread to process the machine steps as soon as they are available. Also, the user thread should not modify them until they have all been sent to the hardware. The solution is to use wait() and notify(), and also to synchronize some of the code.

The methods wait() and notify(), remember, are instance methods of Object. In the same way that every object has a lock, every object can have a list of threads that are waiting for a signal (a notification) from the object. A thread gets on this waiting list by executing the wait() method of the target object. From that moment, it doesn't execute any further instructions until the notify() method of the target object is called. If many threads are waiting on the same object, only one will be chosen (in no guaranteed order) to proceed with its execution. If there are no threads waiting, then no particular action is taken. Let's take a look at some real code that shows one object waiting for another object to notify it (take note, it is somewhat complex):

```
1.   class ThreadA {
2.       public static void main(String [] args) {
3.           ThreadB b = new ThreadB();
4.           b.start();
5.
6.           synchronized(b) {
7.               try {
8.                   System.out.println("Waiting for b to complete...");
9.                   b.wait();
10.              } catch (InterruptedException e) {}
11.              System.out.println("Total is: " + b.total);
12.          }
13.      }
14.  }
15.
16.  class ThreadB extends Thread {
17.      int total;
```

```
18.
19.     public void run() {
20.         synchronized(this) {
21.             for(int i=0;i<100;i++) {
22.                 total += i;
23.             }
24.             notify();
25.         }
26.     }
27. }
```

This program contains two objects with threads: ThreadA contains the main thread and ThreadB has a thread that calculates the sum of all numbers from 0 through 99. As soon as line 4 calls the `start()` method, ThreadA will continue with the next line of code in its own class, which means it could get to line 11 before ThreadB has finished the calculation. To prevent this, we use the `wait()` method in line 9.

Notice in line 6 the code synchronizes itself with the object b—this is because in order to call `wait()` on the object, ThreadA must own a lock on b. For a thread to call `wait()` or `notify()`, the thread has to be the owner of the lock for that object. When the thread waits, it temporarily releases the lock for other threads to use, but it will need it again to continue execution. It's common to find code like this:

```
synchronized(anotherObject) { // this has the lock on anotherObject
    try {
        anotherObject.wait();
        // the thread releases the lock and waits
        // To continue, the thread needs the lock,
        // so it may be blocked until it gets it.
    } catch(InterruptedException e){}
}
```

The preceding code waits until `notify()` is called on `anotherObject`.

```
synchronized(this) { notify(); }
```

This code notifies a single thread currently waiting on the `this` object. The lock can be acquired much earlier in the code, such as in the calling method. Note that if the thread calling `wait()` does not own the lock, it will throw an `IllegalMonitorStateException`. This exception is not a checked exception, so you don't have to *catch* it explicitly. You should always be clear whether a thread has the lock of an object in any given block of code.

Notice in lines 7–10 there is a `try`/`catch` block around the `wait()` method. A waiting thread can be interrupted in the same way as a sleeping thread, so you have to take care of the exception:

```
try {
    wait();
} catch(InterruptedException e) {
    // Do something about it
}
```

In the fabric example, the way to use these methods is to have the hardware thread wait on the shape to be available and the user thread to notify after it has written the steps. The machine steps may comprise global steps, such as moving the required fabric to the cutting area, and a number of substeps, such as the direction and length of a cut. As an example they could be

```
int fabricRoll;
int cuttingSpeed;
Point startingPoint;
float[] directions;
float[] lengths;
etc..
```

It is important that the user thread does not modify the machine steps while the hardware thread is using them, so this reading and writing should be synchronized. The resulting code would look like this:

```
class Operator extends Thread {
    public void run() {
        while(true) {
            // Get shape from user
            synchronized(this) {
                // Calculate new machine steps from shape
                notify();
            }
        }
    }
}
class Machine extends Thread {
    Operator operator; // assume this gets initialized
```

```java
public void run(){
    while(true){
        synchronized(operator){
            try {
                operator.wait();
            } catch(InterruptedException ie) {}
            // Send machine steps to hardware
        }
    }
}
```

The machine thread, once started, will immediately go into the waiting state and will wait patiently until the operator sends the first notification. At that point it is the operator thread that owns the lock for the object, so the hardware thread gets stuck for a while. It's only after the operator thread abandons the `synchronized` block that the hardware thread can really start processing the machine steps.

While one shape is being processed by the hardware, the user may interact with the system and specify another shape to be cut. When the user is finished with the shape and it is time to cut it, the operator thread attempts to enter the `synchronized` block, maybe blocking until the machine thread has finished with the previous machine steps. When the machine thread has finished, it repeats the loop, going again to the waiting state (and therefore releasing the lock). Only then can the operator thread enter the `synchronized` block and overwrite the machine steps with the new ones.

Having two threads is definitely an improvement over having one, although in this implementation there is still a possibility of making the user wait. A further improvement would be to have many shapes in a queue, thereby reducing the possibility of requiring the user to wait for the hardware.

There is also a second form of `wait()` that accepts a number of milliseconds as a maximum time to wait. If the thread is not interrupted, it will continue normally whenever it is notified or the specified timeout has elapsed. This normal continuation consists of getting out of the waiting state, but to continue execution it will have to get the lock for the object:

```java
synchronized(a){ // The thread gets the lock on 'a'
  a.wait(2000); // Thread releases the lock and waits for notify
  // only for a maximum of two seconds, then goes back to Runnable
  // The thread reacquires the lock
  // More instructions here
}
```

e x a m
w a t c h

When the `wait()` *method is invoked on an object, the thread executing that code gives up its lock on the object immediately. However, when* `notify()` *is called, that doesn't mean the thread gives up its lock at that moment. If the thread is still completing synchronized code, the lock is not released until the thread moves out of synchronized code. So just because* `notify()` *is called doesn't mean the lock becomes available at that moment.*

Using notifyAll( ) When Many Threads May Be Waiting

In most scenarios, it's preferable to notify *all* of the threads that are waiting on a particular object. If so, you can use `notifyAll()` on the object to let all the threads rush out of the waiting area and back to runnable. This is especially important if you have several threads waiting on one object, but for different reasons, and you want to be sure that the *right* thread (along with all of the others) gets notified.

```
notifyAll(); // Will notify all waiting threads
```

All of the threads will be notified and start competing to get the lock. As the lock is used and released by each thread, all of them will get into action without a need for further notification.

As we said earlier, an object can have many threads waiting on it, and using `notify()` will affect only one of them. Which one, exactly, is not specified and depends on the JVM implementation, so you should never rely on a particular thread being notified in preference to another.

In cases in which there might be a lot more waiting, the best way to do this is by using `notifyAll()`. Let's take a look at this in some code. In this example, there is one class that performs a calculation and many readers that are waiting to receive the completed calculation. At any given moment many readers may be waiting.

```
1.   class Reader extends Thread {
2.      Calculator c;
3.
4.      public Reader(Calculator calc) {
5.         c = calc;
```

```
6.      }
7.
8.      public void run() {
9.          synchronized(c) {
10.             try {
11.                 System.out.println("Waiting for calculation...");
12.                 c.wait();
13.             } catch (InterruptedException e) {}
14.             System.out.println("Total is: " + c.total);
15.         }
16.     }
17.
18.     public static void main(String [] args) {
19.         Calculator calculator = new Calculator();
20.         new Reader(calculator).start();
21.         new Reader(calculator).start();
22.         new Reader(calculator).start();
23.         calculator.start();
24.     }
25. }
26.
27. class Calculator extends Thread {
28.     int total;
29.
30.     public void run() {
31.         synchronized(this) {
32.             for(int i=0;i<100;i++) {
33.                 total += i;
34.             }
35.             notifyAll();
36.         }
37.     }
38. }
```

The program starts three threads that are all waiting to receive the finished calculation (lines 18–24), and then starts the calculator with its calculation. Note that if the run() method at line 30 used notify() instead of notifyAll(), only one reader would be notified instead of all the readers.

Using wait( ) in a Loop

Actually both of the previous examples (Machine/Operator and Reader/Calculator) had a common problem. In each one, there was at least one thread calling wait(), and another thread calling notify() or notifyAll(). This works well enough as long as the waiting threads have actually started waiting before the other thread executes the `notify()` or `notifyAll()`. But what happens if, for example, the Calculator runs first and calls `notify()` before the Readers have started waiting? This could happen, since we can't guarantee what order the different parts of the thread will execute in. Unfortunately, when the Readers run, they just start waiting right away. They don't do anything to see if the event they're waiting for has already happened. So if the Calculator has already called `notifyAll()`, it's not going to call `notifyAll()` again—and the waiting Readers will keep waiting forever. This is probably *not* what the programmer wanted to happen. Almost always, when you want to wait for something, you also need to be able to check if it has already happened. Generally the best way to solve this is to put in some sort of loop that checks on some sort of conditional expressions, and only waits if the thing you're waiting for has not yet happened. Here's a modified, safer version of the earlier fabric-cutting machine example:

```
class Operator extends Thread {
  Machine machine; // assume this gets initialized
  public void run() {
    while (true) {
      Shape shape = getShapeFromUser();
      MachineInstructions job =
                       calculateNewInstructionsFor(shape);
      machine.addJob(job);
    }
  }
}
```

The operator will still keep on looping forever, getting more shapes from users, calculating new instructions for those shapes, and sending them to the machine. But now the logic for `notify()` has been moved into the `addJob()` method in the Machine class:

```
class Machine extends Thread {
  List<MachineInstructions> jobs =
                       new ArrayList<MachineInstructions>();

  public void addJob(MachineInstructions job) {
    synchronized (jobs) {
      jobs.add(job);
      jobs.notify();
```

```
      }
    }
    public void run() {
      while (true) {
        synchronized (jobs) {
          // wait until at least one job is available
          while (jobs.isEmpty()) {
            try {
              jobs.wait();
            } catch (InterruptedException ie) { }
          }
          // If we get here, we know that jobs is not empty
          MachineInstructions instructions = jobs.remove(0);
          // Send machine steps to hardware
        }
      }
    }
}
```

A machine keeps a list of the jobs it's scheduled to do. Whenever an operator adds a new job to the list, it calls the addJob() method and adds the new job to the list. Meanwhile the run() method just keeps looping, looking for any jobs on the list. If there are no jobs, it will start waiting. If it's notified, it will stop waiting and then recheck the loop condition: is the list still empty? In practice this double-check is probably not necessary, as the only time a notify() is ever sent is when a new job has been added to the list. However, it's a good idea to require the thread to recheck the isEmpty() condition whenever it's been woken up, because it's possible that a thread has accidentally sent an extra notify() that was not intended. There's also a possible situation called *spontaneous wakeup* that may exist in some situations—a thread may wake up even though no code has called notify() or notifyAll(). (At least, no code you know about has called these methods. Sometimes the JVM may call notify() for reasons of its own, or code in some other class calls it for reasons you just don't know.) What this means is, when your thread wakes up from a wait(), you don't know for sure why it was awakened. By putting the wait() method in a while loop and re-checking the condition that represents what we were waiting for, we ensure that *whatever* the reason we woke up, we will re-enter the wait() if (and only if) the thing we were waiting for has not happened yet. In the Machine class, the thing we were waiting for is for the jobs list to not be empty. If it's empty, we wait, and if it's not, we don't.

Note also that both the `run()` method and the `addJob()` method synchronize on the same object—the jobs list. This is for two reasons. One is because we're calling `wait()` and `notify()` on this instance, so we need to synchronize in order to avoid an IllegalThreadState exception. The other reason is, the data in the jobs list is changeable data stored in a field that is accessed by two different threads. We need to synchronize in order to access that changeable data safely. Fortunately, the same `synchronized` blocks that allow us to `wait()` and `notify()` also provide the required thread safety for our other access to changeable data. In fact this is a main reason why synchronization is required to use `wait()` and `notify()` in the first place—you almost always need to share some mutable data between threads at the same time, and that means you need synchronization. Notice that the `synchronized` block in `addJob()` is big enough to also include the call to `jobs.add(job)`—which modifies shared data. And the `synchronized` block in `run()` is large enough to include the whole `while` loop—which includes the call to `jobs.isEmpty()`, which accesses shared data.

The moral here is that when you use `wait()` and `notify()` or `notifyAll()`, you should almost always also have a `while` loop around the `wait()` that checks a condition and forces continued waiting until the condition is met. And you should also make use of the required synchronization for the `wait()` and `notify()` calls, to also protect whatever other data you're sharing between threads. If you see code which fails to do this, there's usually something wrong with the code—even if you have a hard time seeing what exactly the problem is.

TABLE 9-2	Key Thread Methods	
Class Object	**Class Thread**	**Interface Runnable**
wait ()	start()	run()
notify()	*yield()*	
notifyAll()	*sleep()*	
	join()	

CERTIFICATION SUMMARY

This chapter covered the required thread knowledge you'll need to apply on the certification exam. Threads can be created by either extending the Thread class or implementing the Runnable interface. The only method that must be overridden in the Runnable interface is the run() method, but the thread doesn't become a *thread of execution* until somebody calls the Thread object's start() method. We also looked at how the sleep() method can be used to pause a thread, and we saw that when an object goes to sleep, it holds onto any locks it acquired prior to sleeping.

We looked at five thread states: new, runnable, running, blocked/waiting/sleeping, and dead. You learned that when a thread is dead, it can never be restarted even if it's still a valid object on the heap. We saw that there is only one way a thread can transition to running, and that's from runnable. However, once running, a thread can become dead, go to sleep, wait for another thread to finish, block on an object's lock, wait for a notification, or return to runnable.

You saw how two threads acting on the same data can cause serious problems (remember Lucy and Fred's bank account?). We saw that, to let one thread execute a method, but prevent other threads from running the same object's method, we use the synchronized keyword. To coordinate activity between different threads, use the wait(), notify(), and notifyAll() methods.

✓ TWO-MINUTE DRILL

Here are some of the key points from each certification objective in this chapter. Photocopy it and sleep with it under your pillow for complete absorption.

Defining, Instantiating, and Starting Threads (Objective 4.1)

❑ Threads can be created by extending Thread and overriding the `public void run()` method.

❑ Thread objects can also be created by calling the Thread constructor that takes a Runnable argument. The Runnable object is said to be the *target* of the thread.

❑ You can call `start()` on a Thread object only once. If `start()` is called more than once on a Thread object, it will throw a RuntimeException.

❑ It is legal to create many Thread objects using the same Runnable object as the target.

❑ When a Thread object is created, it does not become a *thread of execution* until its `start()` method is invoked. When a Thread object exists but hasn't been started, it is in the *new* state and is not considered *alive*.

Transitioning Between Thread States (Objective 4.2)

❑ Once a new thread is started, it will always enter the runnable state.

❑ The thread scheduler can move a thread back and forth between the runnable state and the running state.

❑ For a typical single-processor machine, only one thread can be running at a time, although many threads may be in the runnable state.

❑ There is no guarantee that the order in which threads were started determines the order in which they'll run.

❑ There's no guarantee that threads will take turns in any fair way. It's up to the thread scheduler, as determined by the particular virtual machine implementation. If you want a guarantee that your threads will take turns regardless of the underlying JVM, you can use the `sleep()` method. This prevents one thread from hogging the running process while another thread starves. (In most cases, though, `yield()` works well enough to encourage your threads to play together nicely.)

❑ A running thread may enter a blocked/waiting state by a `wait()`, `sleep()`, or `join()` call.

- ❑ A running thread may enter a blocked/waiting state because it can't acquire the lock for a synchronized block of code.
- ❑ When the sleep or wait is over, or an object's lock becomes available, the thread can only reenter the runnable state. It will *go* directly from waiting to running (well, for all practical purposes anyway).
- ❑ A dead thread cannot be started again.

Sleep, Yield, and Join (Objective 4.2)

- ❑ Sleeping is used to delay execution for a period of time, and no locks are released when a thread goes to sleep.
- ❑ A sleeping thread is guaranteed to sleep for at least the time specified in the argument to the `sleep()` method (unless it's interrupted), but there is no guarantee as to when the newly awakened thread will actually return to running.
- ❑ The `sleep()` method is a `static` method that sleeps the currently executing thread's state. One thread *cannot* tell another thread to sleep.
- ❑ The `setPriority()` method is used on Thread objects to give threads a priority of between 1 (low) and 10 (high), although priorities are not guaranteed, and not all JVMs recognize 10 distinct priority levels—some levels may be treated as effectively equal.
- ❑ If not explicitly set, a thread's priority will have the same priority as the priority of the thread that created it.
- ❑ The `yield()` method *may* cause a running thread to back out if there are runnable threads of the same priority. There is no guarantee that this will happen, and there is no guarantee that when the thread backs out there will be a *different* thread selected to run. A thread might yield and then immediately reenter the running state.
- ❑ The closest thing to a guarantee is that at any given time, when a thread is running it will usually not have a lower priority than any thread in the runnable state. If a low-priority thread is running when a high-priority thread enters runnable, the JVM will usually preempt the running low-priority thread and put the high-priority thread in.
- ❑ When one thread calls the `join()` method of another thread, the currently running thread will wait until the thread it joins with has completed. Think of the `join()` method as saying, "Hey thread, I want to join on to the end of you. Let me know when you're done, so I can enter the runnable state."

Concurrent Access Problems and Synchronized Threads (Obj. 4.3)

❑ `synchronized` methods prevent more than one thread from accessing an object's critical method code simultaneously.

❑ You can use the `synchronized` keyword as a method modifier, or to start a synchronized block of code.

❑ To synchronize a block of code (in other words, a scope smaller than the whole method), you must specify an argument that is the object whose lock you want to synchronize on.

❑ While only one thread can be accessing synchronized code of a particular instance, multiple threads can still access the same object's *un*synchronized code.

❑ When a thread goes to sleep, its locks will be unavailable to other threads.

❑ `static` methods can be `synchronized`, using the lock from the java.lang.Class instance representing that class.

Communicating with Objects by Waiting and Notifying (Obj. 4.4)

❑ The `wait()` method lets a thread say, "there's nothing for me to do now, so put me in your waiting pool and notify me when something happens that I care about." Basically, a `wait()` call means "wait me in your pool," or "add me to your waiting list."

❑ The `notify()` method is used to send a signal to one and only one of the threads that are waiting in that same object's waiting pool.

❑ The `notify()` method can NOT specify which waiting thread to notify.

❑ The method `notifyAll()` works in the same way as `notify()`, only it sends the signal to *all* of the threads waiting on the object.

❑ All three methods—`wait()`, `notify()`, and `notifyAll()`—must be called from within a `synchronized` context! A thread invokes `wait()` or `notify()` on a particular object, and the thread must currently hold the lock on that object.

Deadlocked Threads (Objective 4.4)

❑ Deadlocking is when thread execution grinds to a halt because the code is waiting for locks to be removed from objects.

❑ Deadlocking can occur when a locked object attempts to access another locked object that is trying to access the first locked object. In other words, both threads are waiting for each other's locks to be released; therefore, the locks will *never* be released!

❑ Deadlocking is bad. Don't do it.

SELF TEST

The following questions will help you measure your understanding of the material presented in this chapter. If you have a rough time with some of these at first, don't beat yourself up. Some of these questions are long and intricate, expect long and intricate questions on the real exam too!

1. Given:

```java
public class Messager  implements Runnable {
    public static void main(String[] args) {
        new Thread(new Messager("Wallace")).start();
        new Thread(new Messager("Gromit")).start();
    }
    private String name;
    public Messager(String name) { this.name = name; }
    public void run() {
        message(1);
        message(2);
    }
    private synchronized void message(int n) {
        System.out.print(name + "-" + n + " ");
    }
}
```

Which of the following is a possible result? (Choose all that apply.)

A. `Wallace-1 Wallace-2 Gromit-1`

B. `Wallace-1 Gromit-2 Wallace-2 Gromit-1`

C. `Wallace-1 Gromit-1 Gromit-2 Wallace-2`

D. `Gromit-1 Gromit-2`

E. `Gromit-2 Wallace-1 Gromit-1 Wallace-2`

F. The code does not compile.

G. An error occurs at run time.

2. Given:

```java
public class Letters extends Thread {
    private String name;
    public Letters(String name) {
        this.name = name;
    }
```

```
        public void write() {
            System.out.print(name);
            System.out.print(name);
        }
        public static void main(String[] args) {
            new Letters("X").start();
            new Letters("Y").start();
        }
    }
```

We want to guarantee that the output can be either XXYY or YYXX, but never XYXY or any other combination. Which of the following method definitions could be added to the Letters class to make this guarantee? (Choose all that apply.)

A. `public void run() { write(); }`

B. `public synchronized void run() { write(); }`

C. `public static synchronized void run() { write(); }`

D. `public void run() { synchronized(this) { write(); } }`

E. `public void run() { synchronized(Letters.class) { write(); } }`

F. `public void run() { synchronized(System.out) { write(); } }`

G. `public void run() { synchronized(System.out.class) { write(); } }`

3. The following block of code creates a Thread using a Runnable target:

```
    Runnable target = new MyRunnable();
    Thread myThread = new Thread(target);
```

Which of the following classes can be used to create the target, so that the preceding code compiles correctly?

A. `public class MyRunnable extends Runnable{public void run(){}}`

B. `public class MyRunnable extends Object{public void run(){}}`

C. `public class MyRunnable implements Runnable{public void run(){}}`

D. `public class MyRunnable implements Runnable{void run(){}}`

E. `public class MyRunnable implements Runnable{public void start(){}}`

4. Given:

```
2.   class MyThread extends Thread {
3.     public static void main(String [] args) {
4.       MyThread t = new MyThread();
5.       t.start();
6.       System.out.print("one. ");
7.       t.start();
8.       System.out.print("two. ");
9.     }
10.    public void run() {
11.      System.out.print("Thread ");
12.    }
13.  }
```

What is the result of this code?

A. Compilation fails.

B. An exception occurs at runtime.

C. `Thread one. Thread two.`

D. The output cannot be determined.

5. Given:

```
3.   class MyThread extends Thread {
4.     public static void main(String [] args) {
5.       MyThread t = new MyThread();
6.       Thread x = new Thread(t);
7.       x.start();
8.     }
9.     public void run() {
10.      for(int i=0;i<3;++i) {
11.        System.out.print(i + "..");
12.      }
13.    }
14.  }
```

What is the result of this code?

A. Compilation fails.

B. 1..2..3..

C. 0..1..2..3..

D. 0..1..2..

E. An exception occurs at runtime.

6. Given the following

```
3.  class Test {
4.      public static void main(String [] args) {
5.          printAll(args);
6.      }
7.      public static void printAll(String[] lines) {
8.          for(int i=0;i<lines.length;i++){
9.              System.out.println(lines[i]);
10.             Thread.currentThread().sleep(1000);
11.         }
12.     }
13. }
```

The `static` method `Thread.currentThread()` returns a reference to the currently executing Thread object. What is the result of this code?

A. Each String in the array `lines` will output, with a 1-second pause between lines.

B. Each String in the array `lines` will output, with no pause in between because this method is not executed in a Thread.

C. Each String in the array `lines` will output, and there is no guarantee there will be a pause because `currentThread()` may not retrieve this thread.

D. This code will not compile.

E. Each String in the `lines` array will print, with at least a one-second pause between lines.

7. Assume you have a class that holds two `private` variables: a and b. Which of the following pairs can prevent concurrent access problems in that class? (Choose all that apply.)

A. ```
    public int read(){return a+b;}
    public void set(int a, int b){this.a=a;this.b=b;}
    ```

B.  ```
    public synchronized int read(){return a+b;}
    public synchronized void set(int a, int b){this.a=a;this.b=b;}
    ```

C. ```
    public int read(){synchronized(a){return a+b;}}
    public void set(int a, int b){synchronized(a){this.a=a;this.b=b;}}
    ```

D.  ```
    public int read(){synchronized(a){return a+b;}}
    public void set(int a, int b){synchronized(b){this.a=a;this.b=b;}}
    ```

E. ```
    public synchronized(this) int read(){return a+b;}
    public synchronized(this) void set(int a, int b){this.a=a;this.b=b;}
    ```

F.  ```
    public int read(){synchronized(this){return a+b;}}
    public void set(int a, int b){synchronized(this){this.a=a;this.b=b;}}
    ```

8. Which are methods of the Object class? (Choose all that apply.)

A. `notify();`

B. `notifyAll();`

C. `isInterrupted();`

D. `synchronized();`

E. `interrupt();`

F. `wait(long msecs);`

G. `sleep(long msecs);`

H. `yield();`

9. Given the following

```
1.   public class WaitTest {
2.      public static void main(String [] args) {
3.         System.out.print("1 ");
4.         synchronized(args){
5.            System.out.print("2 ");
6.            try {
7.               args.wait();
8.            }
9.            catch(InterruptedException e){}
10.         }
11.         System.out.print("3 ");
12.      }
13.   }
```

What is the result of trying to compile and run this program?

A. It fails to compile because the `IllegalMonitorStateException` of `wait()` is not dealt with in line 7.

B. `1 2 3`

C. `1 3`

D. `1 2`

E. At runtime, it throws an `IllegalMonitorStateException` when trying to wait.

F. It will fail to compile because it has to be synchronized on the `this` object.

10. Assume the following method is properly synchronized and called from a thread A on an object B:

```
wait(2000);
```

After calling this method, when will the thread A become a candidate to get another turn at the CPU?

A. After object B is notified, or after two seconds.

B. After the lock on B is released, or after two seconds.

C. Two seconds after object B is notified.

D. Two seconds after lock B is released.

11. Which are true? (Choose all that apply.)

A. The `notifyAll()` method must be called from a synchronized context.

B. To call `wait()`, an object must own the lock on the thread.

C. The `notify()` method is defined in class `java.lang.Thread`.

D. When a thread is waiting as a result of `wait()`, it release its lock.

E. The `notify()` method causes a thread to immediately release its lock.

F. The difference between `notify()` and `notifyAll()` is that `notifyAll()` notifies all waiting threads, regardless of the object they're waiting on.

12. Given the scenario: This class is intended to allow users to write a series of messages, so that each message is identified with a timestamp and the name of the thread that wrote the message:

```java
public class Logger {
    private StringBuilder contents = new StringBuilder();
    public void log(String message) {
        contents.append(System.currentTimeMillis());
        contents.append(": ");
        contents.append(Thread.currentThread().getName());
        contents.append(message);
        contents.append("\n");
    }
    public String getContents() { return contents.toString(); }
}
```

How can we ensure that instances of this class can be safely used by multiple threads?

A. This class is already thread-safe.

B. Replacing `StringBuilder` with `StringBuffer` will make this class thread-safe.

C. Synchronize the `log()` method only.

D. Synchronize the `getContents()` method only.

E. Synchronize both `log()` and `getContents()`.

F. This class cannot be made thread-safe.

13. Given:

```
public static synchronized void main(String[] args) throws
  InterruptedException {
    Thread t = new Thread();
    t.start();
    System.out.print("X");
    t.wait(10000);
    System.out.print("Y");
}
```

What is the result of this code?

A. It prints X and exits.

B. It prints X and never exits.

C. It prints XY and exits almost immeditately.

D. It prints XY with a 10-second delay between X and Y.

E. It prints XY with a 10000-second delay between X and Y.

F. The code does not compile.

G. An exception is thrown at runtime.

14. Given the following,

```
class MyThread extends Thread {
  MyThread() {
    System.out.print(" MyThread");
  }
  public void run() {
```

```
        System.out.print(" bar");
      }
    public void run(String s) {
        System.out.print(" baz");
    }
  }
}
public class TestThreads {
  public static void main (String [] args) {
    Thread t = new MyThread() {
      public void run() {
        System.out.print(" foo");
      }
    };
    t.start();
} }
```

What is the result?

A. foo

B. MyThread foo

C. MyThread bar

D. foo bar

E. foo bar baz

F. bar foo

G. Compilation fails.

H. An exception is thrown at runtime.

15. Given

```
public class ThreadDemo {
    synchronized void a() { actBusy(); }
    static synchronized void b() { actBusy(); }
    static void actBusy() {
        try {
            Thread.sleep(1000);
        } catch (InterruptedException e) {}
    }
    public static void main(String[] args) {
        final ThreadDemo x = new ThreadDemo();
```

```
        final ThreadDemo y = new ThreadDemo();
        Runnable runnable = new Runnable() {
            public void run() {
                int option = (int) (Math.random() * 4);
                switch (option) {
                    case 0: x.a(); break;
                    case 1: x.b(); break;
                    case 2: y.a(); break;
                    case 3: y.b(); break;
                }
            }
        };
        Thread thread1 = new Thread(runnable);
        Thread thread2 = new Thread(runnable);
        thread1.start();
        thread2.start();
    }
}
```

Which of the following pairs of method invocations could NEVER be executing at the same time? (Choose all that apply.)

A. `x.a()` in `thread1`, and `x.a()` in `thread2`

B. `x.a()` in `thread1`, and `x.b()` in `thread2`

C. `x.a()` in `thread1`, and `y.a()` in `thread2`

D. `x.a()` in `thread1`, and `y.b()` in `thread2`

E. `x.b()` in `thread1`, and `x.a()` in `thread2`

F. `x.b()` in `thread1`, and `x.b()` in `thread2`

G. `x.b()` in `thread1`, and `y.a()` in `thread2`

H. `x.b()` in `thread1`, and `y.b()` in `thread2`

16. Given the following,

```
1. public class Test {
2.  public static void main (String [] args) {
3.    final Foo f = new Foo();
4.    Thread t = new Thread(new Runnable() {
5.        public void run() {
6.        f.doStuff();
```

```
7.           }
8.    });
9.    Thread g = new Thread() {
10.     public void run() {
11.             f.doStuff();
12.         }
13.      };
14.      t.start();
15.      g.start();
16.  }
17. }
1. class Foo {
2.    int x = 5;
3.   public void doStuff() {
4.       if (x < 10) {
5.           // nothing to do
6.           try {
7.              wait();
8.           } catch(InterruptedException ex) { }
9.         } else {
10.          System.out.println("x is " + x++);
11.          if (x >= 10) {
12.              notify();
13.          }
14.      }
15.   }
16. }
```

What is the result?

A. The code will not compile because of an error on line 12 of class Foo.

B. The code will not compile because of an error on line 7 of class Foo.

C. The code will not compile because of an error on line 4 of class Test.

D. The code will not compile because of some other error in class Test.

E. An exception occurs at runtime.

F. x is 5
   x is 6

17. Given:

```
public class TwoThreads {
    static Thread laurel, hardy;
    public static void main(String[] args) {
        laurel = new Thread() {
            public void run() {
                System.out.println("A");
                try {
                    hardy.sleep(1000);
                } catch (Exception e) {
                    System.out.println("B");
                }
                System.out.println("C");
            }
        };
        hardy = new Thread() {
            public void run() {
                System.out.println("D");
                try {
                    laurel.wait();
                } catch (Exception e) {
                    System.out.println("E");
                }
                System.out.println("F");
            }
        };
        laurel.start();
        hardy.start();
    }
}
```

Which letters will eventually appear somewhere in the output? (Choose all that apply.)

A. A

B. B

C. C

D. D

E. E

F. F

G. The answer cannot be reliably determined.

H. The code does not compile.

SELF TEST ANSWERS

Note: Some code has been re-formatted to fit your screen.

1. Given:

```
public class Messager implements Runnable {
    public static void main(String[] args) {
        new Thread(new Messager("Wallace")).start();
        new Thread(new Messager("Gromit")).start();
    }
    private String name;
    public Messager(String name) { this.name = name; }
    public void run() {
        message(1);  message(2);
    }
    private synchronized void message(int n) {
        System.out.print(name + "-" + n + " ");
    }
}
```

Which of the following is a possible result? (Choose all that apply.)

A. `Wallace-1 Wallace-2 Gromit-1`

B. `Wallace-1 Gromit-2 Wallace-2 Gromit-1`

C. `Wallace-1 Gromit-1 Gromit-2 Wallace-2`

D. `Gromit-1 Gromit-2`

E. `Gromit-2 Wallace-1 Gromit-1 Wallace-2`

F. The code does not compile.

G. An error occurs at run time.

Answer:

☑ **C** is correct. Both threads will print two messages each. `Wallace-1` must be before `Wallace-2`, and `Gromit-1` must be before `Gromit-2`. Other than that, the Wallace and Gromit messages can be intermingled in any order.

☒ **A, B, D, E, F,** and **G** are incorrect based on the above. (Objective 4.1)

2. Given:

```
public class Letters extends Thread {
    private String name;
    public Letters(String name) { this.name = name; }
    public void write() {
        System.out.print(name);
        System.out.print(name);
```

```
        }
        public static void main(String[] args) {
            new Letters("X").start();
            new Letters("Y").start();
    }   }
```

We want to guarantee that the output can be either XXYY or YYXX, but never XYXY or any other combination. Which of the following method definitions could be added to the Letters class to make this guarantee? (Choose all that apply.)

A. `public void run() { write(); }`

B. `public synchronized void run() { write(); }`

C. `public static synchronized void run() { write(); }`

D. `public void run() { synchronized(this) { write(); } }`

E. `public void run() { synchronized(Letters.class) { write(); } }`

F. `public void run() { synchronized(System.out) { write(); } }`

G. `public void run() { synchronized(System.out.class) { write(); } }`

Answer:

☑ **E** and **F** are correct. **E** and **F** both cause both threads to lock on the same object, which will prevent the threads from running simultaneously, and guarantee XXYY or YYXX. It's a bit unusual to lock on an object like `System.out`, but it's perfectly legal, and both threads are locking on the same object.

☒ **A** can't guarantee anything since it has no synchronization. **B** and **D** both synchronize on an instance of the Letters class—but since there are two different instances in the `main()` method, the two threads do not block each other and may run simultaneously, resulting in output like XYXY. **C** won't compile because it tries to override `run()` with a `static` method, and also calls a non-`static` method from a `static` method. **G** won't compile because `System.out.class` is nonsense. A class literal must start with a class name. `System.out` is a field not a class, so `System.out.class` is not a valid class literal. (Objective 4.3)

3. The following block of code creates a Thread using a Runnable target:

```
Runnable target = new MyRunnable();
Thread myThread = new Thread(target);
```

Which of the following classes can be used to create the target, so that the preceding code compiles correctly?

A. `public class MyRunnable extends Runnable{public void run(){}}`

B. `public class MyRunnable extends Object{public void run(){}}`

C. `public class MyRunnable implements Runnable{public void run(){}}`

D. `public class MyRunnable implements Runnable{void run(){}}`

E. `public class MyRunnable implements Runnable{public void start(){}}`

Answer:

☑ **C** is correct. The class implements the Runnable interface with a legal `run()` method.

☒ **A** is incorrect because interfaces are implemented, not extended. **B** is incorrect because even though the class has a valid `public void run()` method, it does not implement the Runnable interface. **D** is incorrect because the `run()` method must be `public`. **E** is incorrect because the method to implement is `run()`, not `start()`. (Objective 4.1)

4. Given the following,

```
2.    class MyThread extends Thread {
3.        public static void main(String [] args) {
4.            MyThread t = new MyThread();
5.            t.start();
6.            System.out.print("one. ");
7.            t.start();
8.            System.out.print("two. ");
9.        }
10.       public void run() {
11.           System.out.print("Thread ");
12.   }   }
```

What is the result of this code?

A. Compilation fails.

B. An exception occurs at runtime.

C. `Thread one. Thread two.`

D. The output cannot be determined.

Answer:

☑ **B** is correct. When the `start()` method is attempted a second time on a single Thread object, the method will throw an `IllegalThreadStateException`. (Although this behavior is specified in the API, some JVMs don't consistently throw an exception in this case). Even if the thread has finished running, it is still illegal to call `start()` again.

☒ **A** is incorrect because compilation will succeed. For the most part, the Java compiler only checks for illegal syntax, rather than class-specific logic. **C** and **D** are incorrect because of the logic explained above. (Objective 4.1)

5.   Given the following

```
3.   class MyThread extends Thread {
4.      public static void main(String [] args) {
5.          MyThread t = new MyThread();
6.          Thread x = new Thread(t);
7.          x.start();
8.      }
9.      public void run() {
10.         for(int i=0;i<3;++i) {
11.             System.out.print(i + "..");
12.   } } }
```

What is the result of this code?

A. Compilation fails.

B. 1..2..3..

C. 0..1..2..3..

D. 0..1..2..

E. An exception occurs at runtime.

Answer:

☑ **D** is correct. The thread `MyThread` will start and loop three times (from 0 to 2).

☒ **A** is incorrect because the Thread class implements the Runnable interface; therefore, in line 5, Thread can take an object of type Thread as an argument in the constructor (this is NOT recommended). **B** and **C** are incorrect because the variable `i` in the `for` loop starts with a value of 0 and ends with a value of 2. **E** is incorrect based on the above. (Obj. 4.1)

6.   Given the following

```
3.   class Test {
4.      public static void main(String [] args) {
5.          printAll(args);
6.      }
7.      public static void printAll(String[] lines) {
8.          for(int i=0;i<lines.length;i++){
9.              System.out.println(lines[i]);
10.             Thread.currentThread().sleep(1000);
11.   } } }
```

The `static` method `Thread.currentThread()` returns a reference to the currently executing Thread object. What is the result of this code?

A. Each String in the array `lines` will print, with exactly a 1-second pause between lines.

B. Each String in the array `lines` will print, with no pause in between because this method is not executed in a Thread.

C. Each String in the array `lines` will print, and there is no guarantee there will be a pause because `currentThread()` may not retrieve this thread.

D. This code will not compile.

E. Each String in the `lines` array will print, with at least a one-second pause between lines.

Answer:

☑ **D** is correct. The `sleep()` method must be enclosed in a `try/catch` block, or the method `printAll()` must declare it throws the `InterruptedException`.

☒ **E** is incorrect, but it would be correct if the `InterruptedException` was dealt with (**A** is too precise). **B** is incorrect (even if the `InterruptedException` was dealt with) because all Java code, including the `main()` method, runs in threads. **C** is incorrect. The `sleep()` method is `static`, it always affects the currently executing thread. (Objective 4.2)

7. Assume you have a class that holds two `private` variables: a and b. Which of the following pairs can prevent concurrent access problems in that class? (Choose all that apply.)

A. ```
public int read(){return a+b;}
public void set(int a, int b){this.a=a;this.b=b;}
```

B. ```
public synchronized int read(){return a+b;}
public synchronized void set(int a, int b){this.a=a;this.b=b;}
```

C. ```
public int read(){synchronized(a){return a+b;}}
public void set(int a, int b){synchronized(a){this.a=a;this.b=b;}}
```

D. ```
public int read(){synchronized(a){return a+b;}}
public void set(int a, int b){synchronized(b){this.a=a;this.b=b;}}
```

E. ```
public synchronized(this) int read(){return a+b;}
public synchronized(this) void set(int a, int b){this.a=a;this.b=b;}
```

F. ```
public int read(){synchronized(this){return a+b;}}
public void set(int a, int b){synchronized(this){this.a=a;this.b=b;}}
```

Answer:

☑ **B** and **F** are correct. By marking the methods as `synchronized`, the threads will get the lock of the `this` object before proceeding. Only one thread will be setting or reading at any given moment, thereby assuring that `read()` always returns the addition of a valid pair.

☒ **A** is incorrect because it is not synchronized; therefore, there is no guarantee that the values added by the `read()` method belong to the same pair. **C** and **D** are incorrect; only objects can be used to synchronize on. **E** fails— it is not possible to select other objects (even `this`) to synchronize on when declaring a method as `synchronized`. (Obj. 4.3)

8. Which are methods of the Object class? (Choose all that apply.)

A. `notify();`

B. `notifyAll();`

C. `isInterrupted();`

D. `synchronized();`

E. `interrupt();`

F. `wait(long msecs);`

G. `sleep(long msecs);`

H. `yield();`

Answer:

☑ **A, B,** and **F** are correct. They are all related to the list of threads waiting on the specified object.

☒ **C, E, G,** and **H** are incorrect answers. The methods `isInterrupted()` and `interrupt()` are instance methods of Thread. The methods `sleep()` and `yield()` are static methods of Thread. **D** is incorrect because `synchronized` is a keyword and the `synchronized()` construct is part of the Java language. (Objective 4.2)

9. Given the following

```
1.   public class WaitTest {
2.      public static void main(String [] args) {
3.          System.out.print("1 ");
4.          synchronized(args){
5.              System.out.print("2 ");
6.              try {
7.                  args.wait();
8.              }
9.              catch(InterruptedException e){}
10.         }
11.         System.out.print("3 ");
12.   }  }
```

What is the result of trying to compile and run this program?

A. It fails to compile because the `IllegalMonitorStateException` of `wait()` is not dealt with in line 7.

B. `1 2 3`

C. `1 3`

D. `1 2`

E. At runtime, it throws an `IllegalMonitorStateException` when trying to wait.

F. It will fail to compile because it has to be synchronized on the `this` object.

Answer:

- ☑ **D** is correct. 1 and 2 will be printed, but there will be no return from the `wait` call because no other thread will notify the main thread, so 3 will never be printed. It's frozen at line 7.

- ☒ **A** is incorrect; `IllegalMonitorStateException` is an unchecked exception. **B and C** are incorrect; 3 will never be printed, since this program will wait forever. **E** is incorrect because `IllegalMonitorStateException` will never be thrown because the `wait()` is done on `args` within a block of code synchronized on `args`. **F** is incorrect because any object can be used to synchronize on and `this` and `static` don't mix. (Objective 4.4)

10. Assume the following method is properly synchronized and called from a thread A on an object B:

```
wait(2000);
```

After calling this method, when will the thread A become a candidate to get another turn at the CPU?

- **A.** After object B is notified, or after two seconds.
- **B.** After the lock on B is released, or after two seconds.
- **C.** Two seconds after object B is notified.
- **D.** Two seconds after lock B is released.

Answer:

- ☑ **A** is correct. Either of the two events will make the thread a candidate for running again.

- ☒ **B** is incorrect because a waiting thread will not return to runnable when the lock is released, unless a notification occurs. **C** is incorrect because the thread will become a candidate immediately after notification. **D** is also incorrect because a thread will not come out of a waiting pool just because a lock has been released. (Objective 4.4)

11. Which are true? (Choose all that apply.)

- **A.** The `notifyAll()` method must be called from a synchronized context.
- **B.** To call `wait()`, an object must own the lock on the thread.
- **C.** The `notify()` method is defined in class `java.lang.Thread`.
- **D.** When a thread is waiting as a result of `wait()`, it release its lock.
- **E.** The `notify()` method causes a thread to immediately release its lock.
- **F.** The difference between `notify()` and `notifyAll()` is that `notifyAll()` notifies all waiting threads, regardless of the object they're waiting on.

Answer:

☑ **A** is correct because `notifyAll()` (and `wait()` and `notify()`) must be called from within a synchronized context. **D** is a correct statement.

☒ **B** is incorrect because to call `wait()`, the thread must own the lock on the object that `wait()` is being invoked on, not the other way around. **C** is wrong because `notify()` is defined in `java.lang.Object`. **E** is wrong because `notify()` will not cause a thread to release its locks. The thread can only release its locks by exiting the synchronized code. **F** is wrong because `notifyAll()` notifies all the threads waiting on a particular locked object, not all threads waiting on *any* object. (Objective 4.4)

12. Given the scenario: This class is intended to allow users to write a series of messages, so that each message is identified with a timestamp and the name of the thread that wrote the message:

```
public class Logger {
    private StringBuilder contents = new StringBuilder();
    public void log(String message) {
        contents.append(System.currentTimeMillis());
        contents.append(": ");
        contents.append(Thread.currentThread().getName());
        contents.append(message);
        contents.append("\n");
    }
    public String getContents() { return contents.toString(); }
}
```

How can we ensure that instances of this class can be safely used by multiple threads?

A. This class is already thread-safe.

B. Replacing `StringBuilder` with `StringBuffer` will make this class thread-safe.

C. Synchronize the `log()` method only.

D. Synchronize the `getContents()` method only.

E. Synchronize both `log()` and `getContents()`.

F. This class cannot be made thread-safe.

Answer:

☑ **E** is correct. Synchronizing the `public` methods is sufficient to make this safe, so **F** is false. This class is not thread-safe unless some sort of synchronization protects the changing data.

☒ **B** is not correct because although a `StringBuffer` is synchonized internally, we call `append()` multiple times, and nothing would prevent two simultaneous `log()` calls from mixing up their messages. **C** and **D** are not correct because if one method remains unsynchronized, it can run while the other is executing, which could result in reading the contents while one of the messages is incomplete, or worse. (You don't want to call `getString()` on the `StringBuffer` as it's resizing its internal character array.) (Objective 4.3)

13. Given:

```
public static synchronized void main(String[] args) throws
  InterruptedException {
    Thread t = new Thread();
    t.start();
    System.out.print("X");
    t.wait(10000);
    System.out.print("Y");
}
```

What is the result of this code?

A. It prints X and exits.

B. It prints X and never exits.

C. It prints XY and exits almost immeditately.

D. It prints XY with a 10-second delay between X and Y.

E. It prints XY with a 10000-second delay between X and Y.

F. The code does not compile.

G. An exception is thrown at runtime.

Answer:

☑ **G** is correct. The code does not acquire a lock on t before calling t.wait(), so it throws an IllegalThreadStateException. The method is synchronized, but it's not synchronized on t so the exception will be thrown. If the wait were placed inside a synchronized(t) block, then the answer would have been **D**.

☒ **A, B, C, D, E,** and **F** are incorrect based the logic described above. (Objective 4.2)

14. Given the following:

```
class MyThread extends Thread {
   MyThread() {
     System.out.print(" MyThread");
   }
   public void run() { System.out.print(" bar"); }
   public void run(String s) { System.out.print(" baz"); }
}
public class TestThreads {
  public static void main (String [] args) {
    Thread t = new MyThread() {
      public void run() { System.out.print(" foo"); }
    };
    t.start();
  } }
```

What is the result?

A. foo

B. MyThread foo

C. MyThread bar

D. foo bar

E. foo bar baz

F. bar foo

G. Compilation fails.

H. An exception is thrown at runtime.

Answer:

☑ **B** is correct. The first line of main we're constructing an instance of an anonymous inner class extending from MyThread. So the MyThread constructor runs and prints MyThread. Next, main() invokes start() on the new thread instance, which causes the overridden run() method (the run() method in the anonymous inner class) to be invoked.

☒ **A, C, D, E, F, G** and **H** are incorrect based on the logic described above. (Objective 4.1)

15. Given

```java
public class ThreadDemo {
    synchronized void a() { actBusy(); }
    static synchronized void b() { actBusy(); }
    static void actBusy() {
        try { Thread.sleep(1000); }
        catch (InterruptedException e) {}
    }
    public static void main(String[] args) {
        final ThreadDemo x = new ThreadDemo();
        final ThreadDemo y = new ThreadDemo();
        Runnable runnable = new Runnable() {
            public void run() {
                int option = (int) (Math.random() * 4);
                switch (option) {
                    case 0: x.a(); break;
                    case 1: x.b(); break;
                    case 2: y.a(); break;
                    case 3: y.b(); break;
                } }
        };
        Thread thread1 = new Thread(runnable);
        Thread thread2 = new Thread(runnable);
        thread1.start();
        thread2.start();
    } }
```

Which of the following pairs of method invocations could NEVER be executing at the same time? (Choose all that apply.)

A. `x.a()` in `thread1`, and `x.a()` in `thread2`

B. `x.a()` in `thread1`, and `x.b()` in `thread2`

C. `x.a()` in `thread1`, and `y.a()` in `thread2`

D. `x.a()` in `thread1`, and `y.b()` in `thread2`

E. `x.b()` in `thread1`, and `x.a()` in `thread2`

F. `x.b()` in `thread1`, and `x.b()` in `thread2`

G. `x.b()` in `thread1`, and `y.a()` in `thread2`

H. `x.b()` in `thread1`, and `y.b()` in `thread2`

Answer:

☑ **A, F,** and **H. A** is a right answer because when `synchronized` instance methods are called on the same *instance*, they block each other. **F** and **H** can't happen because `synchronized` `static` methods in the same class block each other, regardless of which instance was used to call the methods. (An instance is not required to call `static` methods; only the class.)

☒ **C** could happen because `synchronized` instance methods called on different instances do not block each other. **B, D, E,** and **G** could all happen because instance methods and `static` methods lock on different objects, and do not block each other. (Objective 4.3)

16. Given the following,

```
1.  public class Test {
2.  public static void main (String [] args) {
3.     final Foo f = new Foo();
4.     Thread t = new Thread(new Runnable() {
5.          public void run() {
6.           f.doStuff();
7.          }
8.     });
9.     Thread g = new Thread() {
10.    public void run() {
11.         f.doStuff();
12.     }
13.     };
14.     t.start();
15.     g.start();
16.  }
```

```
17. }
 1. class Foo {
 2.    int x = 5;
 3.    public void doStuff() {
 4.       if (x < 10) {
 5.          // nothing to do
 6.          try {
 7.             wait();
 8.          } catch(InterruptedException ex) { }
 9.       } else {
10.          System.out.println("x is " + x++);
11.          if (x >= 10) {
12.             notify();
13.          }
14.       }
15.    }
16. }
```

What is the result?

A. The code will not compile because of an error on line 12 of class Foo.

B. The code will not compile because of an error on line 7 of class Foo.

C. The code will not compile because of an error on line 4 of class Test.

D. The code will not compile because of some other error in class Test.

E. An exception occurs at runtime.

F. x is 5
    x is 6

Answer:

☑ **E** is correct because the thread does not own the lock of the object it invokes wait() on. If the method were synchronized, the code would run without exception.

☒ **A, B, C,** and **D** are incorrect because the code compiles without errors. **F** is incorrect because the exception is thrown before there is any output. (Objective 4.4)

17. Given:

```java
public class TwoThreads {
    static Thread laurel, hardy;
    public static void main(String[] args) {
        laurel = new Thread() {
            public void run() {
                System.out.println("A");
                try {
                    hardy.sleep(1000);
                } catch (Exception e) {
                    System.out.println("B");
                }
                System.out.println("C");
            }
        };
        hardy = new Thread() {
            public void run() {
                System.out.println("D");
                try {
                    laurel.wait();
                } catch (Exception e) {
                    System.out.println("E");
                }
                System.out.println("F");
            }
        };
        laurel.start();
        hardy.start();
    }
}
```

Which letters will eventually appear somewhere in the output? (Choose all that apply.)

A. A

B. B

C. C

D. D

E. E

F. F

G. The answer cannot be reliably determined.

H. The code does not compile.

Answer:

☑ **A, C, D, E,** and **F** are correct. This may look like `laurel` and `hardy` are battling to cause the other to `sleep()` or `wait()`—but that's not the case. Since `sleep()` is a `static` method, it affects the current thread, which is `laurel` (even though the method is invoked using a reference to `hardy`). That's misleading but perfectly legal, and the Thread `laurel` is able to sleep with no exception, printing A and C (after a 1-second delay). Meanwhile `hardy` tries to call `laurel.wait()`—but hardy has not `synchronized` on `laurel`, so calling `laurel.wait()` immediately causes an `IllegalThreadStateException`, and so `hardy` prints D, E, and F. Although the *order* of the output is somewhat indeterminate (we have no way of knowing whether A is printed before D, for example) it is guaranteed that A, C, D, E, and F will all be printed in some order, eventually—so **G** is incorrect.

☒ **B, G,** and **H** are incorrect based on the above. (Objective 4.4)

EXERCISE ANSWERS

Exercise 9-1: Creating a Thread and Putting It to Sleep

The final code should look something like this:

```
class TheCount extends Thread {
   public void run() {
      for(int i = 1;i<=100;++i) {
         System.out.print(i + "  ");
         if(i % 10 == 0)  System.out.println("Hahaha");
         try { Thread.sleep(1000); }
         catch(InterruptedException e) {}
      }
   }
   public static void main(String [] args) {
      new TheCount().start();
   }
}
```

Exercise 9-2: Synchronizing a Block of Code

Your code might look something like this when completed:

```
class InSync extends Thread {
  StringBuffer letter;
  public InSync(StringBuffer letter) { this.letter = letter; }
  public void run() {
    synchronized(letter) {        // #1
      for(int i = 1;i<=100;++i) System.out.print(letter);
      System.out.println();
      char temp = letter.charAt(0);
      ++temp;            // Increment the letter in StringBuffer:
      letter.setCharAt(0, temp);
    }      // #2
  }
  public static void main(String [] args) {
    StringBuffer sb = new StringBuffer("A");
    new InSync(sb).start();  new InSync(sb).start();
    new InSync(sb).start();
  }
}
```

Just for fun, try removing lines 1 and 2 then run the program again. It will be unsynchronized—watch what happens.

10

Development

Y ou want to keep your classes organized. You need to have powerful ways for your classes to find each other. You want to make sure that when you're looking for a particular class you get the one you want, and not another class that happens to have the same name. In this chapter we'll explore some of the advanced capabilities of the java and javac commands. We'll revisit the use of packages in Java, and how to search for classes that live in packages.

CERTIFICATION OBJECTIVES

Using the javac and java Commands (Exam Objectives 7.1, 7.2, and 7.5)

7.1   *Given a code example and a scenario, write code that uses the appropriate access modifiers, package declarations, and import statements to interact with (through access or inheritance) the code in the example.*

7.2   *Given an example of a class and a command-line, determine the expected runtime behavior.*

7.5   *Given the fully-qualified name of a class that is deployed inside and/or outside a JAR file, construct the appropriate directory structure for that class. Given a code example and a classpath, determine whether the classpath will allow the code to compile successfully.*

So far in this book, we've probably talked about invoking the java and java commands about 1000 times; now we're going to take a closer look.

Compiling with javac

The javac command is used to invoke Java's compiler. In Chapter 5 we talked about the assertion mechanism and when you might use the -source option when compiling a file. There are many other options you can specify when running javac, options to generate debugging information or compiler warnings for example. For the exam, you'll need to understand the -classpath and -d options, which we'll cover in the next few pages. Here's the structural overview for javac:

```
javac [options] [source files]
```

There are additional command-line options called @argfiles, but you won't need to study them for the exam. Both the [options] and the [source files] are optional parts of the command, and both allow multiple entries. The following are both legal javac commands:

```
javac -help
javac -classpath com:. -g Foo.java Bar.java
```

The first invocation doesn't compile any files, but prints a summary of valid options. The second invocation passes the compiler two options (-classpath, which itself has an argument of com:. and -g), and passes the compiler two .java files to compile (Foo.java and Bar.java). Whenever you specify multiple options and/or files they should be separated by spaces.

Compiling with -d

By default, the compiler puts a .class file in the same directory as the .java source file. This is fine for very small projects, but once you're working on a project of any size at all, you'll want to keep your .java files separated from your .class files. (This helps with version control, testing, deployment...) The -d option lets you tell the compiler in which directory to put the .class file(s) it generates (d is for destination). Let's say you have the following directory structure:

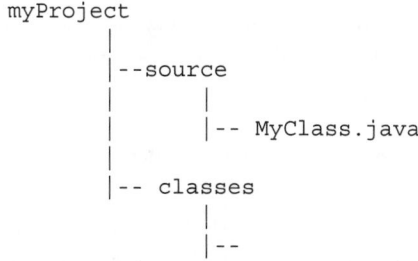

```
myProject
     |
     |--source
     |     |
     |     |-- MyClass.java
     |
     |-- classes
            |
            |--
```

The following command, issued from the myProject directory, will compile MyClass.java and put the resulting MyClass.class file into the classes directory. (Note: This assumes that MyClass does not have a package statement; we'll talk about packages in a minute.)

```
cd myProject
javac -d classes source/MyClass.java
```

This command also demonstrates selecting a `.java` file from a subdirectory of the directory from which the command was invoked. Now let's take a quick look at how packages work in relationship to the `-d` option.

Suppose we have the following `.java` file in the following directory structure:

```
package com.wickedlysmart;
public class MyClass { }
```

```
myProject
      |
      |--source
      |      |
      |      |--com
      |             |
      |             |--wickedlysmart
      |                          |
      |                          |--MyClass.java
      |
      |--classes
      |      |
      |      |--com
      |             |
      |             |--wickedlysmart
      |                          |
      |                          |-- (MyClass.class goes here)
```

If you were in the `source` directory, you would compile `MyClass.java` and put the resulting `MyClass.class` file into the `classes/com/wickedlysmart` directory by invoking the following command:

```
javac -d ../classes com/wickedlysmart/MyClass.java
```

This command could be read: "To set the destination directory, `cd` back to the `myProject` directory then `cd` into the `classes` directory, which will be your destination. Then compile the file named `MyClass.java`. Finally, put the resulting `MyClass.class` file into the directory structure that matches its package, in this case, `classes/com/wickedlysmart`." Because `MyClass.java` is in a package, the compiler knew to put the resulting `.class` file into the `classes/com/wickedlysmart` directory.

Somewhat amazingly, the `javac` command can sometimes help you out by building directories it needs! Suppose we have the following:

```
package com.wickedlysmart;
public class MyClass { }
```

```
myProject
     |
     |--source
     |      |
     |      |--com
     |             |
     |             |--wickedlysmart
     |                       |
     |                       |--MyClass.java
     |
     |--classes
     |      |
```

And the following command (the same as last time):

```
javac -d ../classes com/wickedlysmart/MyClass.java
```

In this case, the compiler will build two directories called `com` and `com/wickedlysmart` in order to put the resulting `MyClass.class` file into the correct package directory (`com/wickedlysmart/`) which it builds within the existing `.../classes` directory.

The last thing about `-d` that you'll need to know for the exam is that if the destination directory you specify doesn't exist, you'll get a compiler error. If, in the previous example, the `classes` directory did NOT exist, the compiler would say something like:

```
java:5: error while writing MyClass: classes/MyClass.class (No
such file or directory)
```

Launching Applications with java

The `java` command is used to invoke the Java virtual machine. In Chapter 5 we talked about the assertion mechanism and when you might use flags such as `-ea` or `-da` when launching an application. There are many other options you can specify when running the `java` command, but for the exam, you'll need to understand the `-classpath` (and its twin `-cp`) and `-D` options, which we'll cover in the next few pages. In addition, it's important to understand the structure of this command. Here's the overview:

```
java [options] class [args]
```

The `[options]` and `[args]` parts of the `java` command are optional, and they can both have multiple values. You must specify exactly one class file to execute, and the `java` command assumes you're talking about a `.class` file, so you don't specify the `.class` extension on the command line. Here's an example:

```
java -DmyProp=myValue MyClass x 1
```

Sparing the details for later, this command can be read as "Create a *system property* called `myProp` and set its value to `myValue`. Then launch the file named `MyClass.class` and send it two String *arguments* whose values are x and 1."

Let's look at system properties and command-line arguments more closely.

Using System Properties

Java 5 has a class called `java.util.Properties` that can be used to access a system's persistent information such as the current versions of the operating system, the Java compiler, and the Java virtual machine. In addition to providing such default information, you can also add and retrieve your own properties. Take a look at the following:

```java
import java.util.*;
public class TestProps {
  public static void main(String[] args) {
    Properties p = System.getProperties();
    p.setProperty("myProp", "myValue");
    p.list(System.out);
  }
}
```

If this file is compiled and invoked as follows:

```
java -DcmdProp=cmdVal TestProps
```

You'll get something like this:

```
...
os.name=Mac OS X
myProp=myValue
...
java.specification.vendor=Sun Microsystems Inc.
user.language=en
java.version=1.5.0_02
...
cmdProp=cmdVal
...
```

where the . . . represent lots of other name=value pairs. (The *name* and *value* are sometimes called the *key* and the *property*.) Two name=value properties were added to the system's properties: myProp=myValue was added via the setProperty method, and cmdProp=cmdVal was added via the -D option at the command line. When using the -D option, if your value contains white space the entire value should be placed in quotes like this:

```
java -DcmdProp="cmdVal take 2" TestProps
```

Just in case you missed it, when you use -D, the name=value pair must follow *immediately*, no spaces allowed.

The getProperty() method is used to retrieve a single property. It can be invoked with a single argument (a String that represents the name (or key)), or it can be invoked with two arguments, (a String that represents the name (or key), and a default String value to be used as the property if the property does not already exist). In both cases, getProperty() returns the property as a String.

Handling Command-Line Arguments

Let's return to an example of launching an application and passing in arguments from the command line. If we have the following code:

```
public class CmdArgs {
  public static void main(String[] args) {
    int x = 0;
    for(String s : args)
      System.out.println(x++ + " element = " + s);
  }
}
```

compiled and then invoked as follows

```
java CmdArgs x 1
```

the output will be

```
0 element = x
1 element = 1
```

Like all arrays, `args` index is zero based. Arguments on the command line directly follow the class name. The first argument is assigned to `args[0]`, the second argument is assigned to `args[1]`, and so on.

Finally, there is some flexibility in the declaration of the `main()` method that is used to start a Java application. The order of `main()`'s modifiers can be altered a little, the String array doesn't have to be named `args`, and as of Java 5 it can be declared using var-args syntax. The following are all legal declarations for `main()`:

```
static public void main(String[] args)
public static void main(String... x)
static public void main(String bang_a_gong[])
```

Searching for Other Classes

In most cases, when we use the `java` and `javac` commands, we want these commands to search for other classes that will be necessary to complete the operation. The most obvious case is when classes we create use classes that Sun provides with J2SE (now sometimes called Java SE), for instance when we use classes in `java.lang` or `java.util`. The next common case is when we want to compile a file or run a class that uses other classes that have been created outside of what Sun provides, for instance our own previously created classes. Remember that for any given class, the `java` virtual machine will need to find exactly the same supporting classes that the `javac` compiler needed to find at compilation time. In other words, if `javac` needed access to `java.util.HashMap` then the `java` command will need to find `java.util.HashMap` as well.

Both `java` and `javac` use the same basic search algorithm:

1. They both have the same list of places (directories) they search, to look for classes.

2. They both search through this list of directories in the same order.

3. As soon as they find the class they're looking for, they stop searching for that class. In the case that their search lists contain two or more files with the same name, the first file found will be the file that is used.

4. The first place they look is in the directories that contain the classes that come standard with J2SE.

5. The second place they look is in the directories defined by classpaths.

6. Classpaths should be thought of as "class search paths." They are lists of directories in which classes might be found.

7. There are two places where classpaths can be declared:

    A classpath can be declared as an operating system environment variable. The classpath declared here is used by default, whenever `java` or `javac` are invoked.

    A classpath can be declared as a command-line option for either `java` or `javac`. *Classpaths declared as command-line options override the classpath declared as an environment variable, but they persist only for the length of the invocation.*

Declaring and Using Classpaths

Classpaths consist of a variable number of directory locations, separated by delimiters. For Unix-based operating systems, forward slashes are used to construct directory locations, and the separator is the colon (:). For example:

```
-classpath /com/foo/acct:/com/foo
```

specifies two directories in which classes can be found: `/com/foo/acct` and `/com/foo`. In both cases, these directories are absolutely tied to the root of the file system, which is specified by the leading forward slash. It's important to remember that when you specify a subdirectory, you're NOT specifying the directories above it. For instance, in the preceding example the directory `/com` will NOT be searched.

e x a m

ⓦ a t c h
Most of the path-related questions on the exam will use Unix conventions. If you are a Windows user, your directories will be declared using backslashes (\) and the separator character you use will be a semicolon (;). But again, you will NOT need any shell-specific knowledge for the exam.

A very common situation occurs in which java or javac complains that it can't find a class file, and yet you can see that the file is IN the current directory! When searching for class files, the java and javac commands don't search the current directory by default. You must *tell* them to search there. The way to tell java or javac to search in the current directory is to add a dot (.) to the classpath:

```
-classpath /com/foo/acct:/com/foo:.
```

This classpath is identical to the previous one EXCEPT that the dot (.) at the end of the declaration instructs java or javac to *also* search for class files in the current directory. (Remember, we're talking about class files—when you're telling javac which .java file to compile, javac looks in the current directory by default.)

It's also important to remember that classpaths are searched from left to right. Therefore in a situation where classes with duplicate names are located in several different directories in the following classpaths, different results will occur:

```
-classpath /com:/foo:.
```

is not the same as

```
-classpath .:/foo:/com
```

Finally, the java command allows you to abbreviate -classpath with -cp. The Java documentation is inconsistent about whether the javac command allows the -cp abbreviation. On most machines it does, but there are no guarantees.

Packages and Searching

When you start to put classes into packages, and then start to use classpaths to find these classes, things can get tricky. The exam creators knew this, and they tried to create an especially devilish set of package/classpath questions with which to confound you. Let's start off by reviewing packages. In the following code:

```
package com.foo;
public class MyClass { public void hi() { } }
```

we're saying that MyClass is a member of the com.foo package. This means that the fully qualified name of the class is now com.foo.MyClass. Once a class is in a package, the package part of its fully qualified name is *atomic*—it can never be divided. You can't split it up on the command line, and you can't split it up in an import statement.

Now let's see how we can use com.foo.MyClass in another class:

```
package com.foo;
public class MyClass { public void hi() { } }
```

And in another file:

```
import com.foo.MyClass;    // either import will work
import com.foo.*;

public class Another {
  void go() {
    MyClass m1 = new MyClass();                        // alias name
    com.foo.MyClass m2 = new com.foo.MyClass();  // full name
    m1.hi();
    m2.hi();
  }
}
```

It's easy to get confused when you use import statements. The preceding code is perfectly legal. The import statement is like an alias for the class's fully qualified name. You define the fully qualified name for the class with an import statement (or with a wildcard in an import statement of the package). Once you've defined the fully qualified name, you can use the "alias" in your code—but the alias is referring back to the fully qualified name.

Now that we've reviewed packages, let's take a look at how they work in conjunction with classpaths and command lines. First we'll start off with the idea that when you're searching for a class using its fully qualified name, that fully qualified name relates closely to a specific directory structure. For instance, relative to your current directory, the class whose source code is

```
package com.foo;
public class MyClass { public void hi() { } }
```

would *have* to be located here:

```
com/foo/MyClass.class
```

In order to find a class in a package, you have to have a directory in your classpath that has the package's leftmost entry (the package's "root") as a subdirectory.

This is an important concept, so let's look at another example:

```
import com.wickedlysmart.Utils;
class TestClass {
  void doStuff() {
    Utils u = new Utils();                      // simple name
    u.doX("arg1", "arg2");
    com.wickedlysmart.Date d =
                new com.wickedlysmart.Date();   // full name
    d.getMonth("Oct");
  }
}
```

In this case we're using two classes from the package com.wickedlysmart. For the sake of discussion we imported the fully qualified name for the Utils class, and we didn't for the Date class. The *only* difference is that because we listed Utils in an import statement, we didn't have to type its fully qualified name inside the class. In both cases the package is com.wickedlysmart. When it's time to compile or run TestClass, the classpath will have to include a directory with the following attributes:

- A subdirectory named com (we'll call this the "package root" directory)
- A subdirectory in com named wickedlysmart
- Two files in wickedlysmart named Utils.class and Date.class

Finally, the directory that has all of these attributes has to be accessible (via a classpath) in one of two ways:

1. The path to the directory must be absolute, in other words, from the root (the file system root, not the package root).

or

2. The path to the directory has to be correct relative to the current directory.

Relative and Absolute Paths

A classpath is a collection of one or more paths. Each path in a classpath is either an absolute path or a relative path. An absolute path in Unix begins with a forward slash (/) (on Windows it would be something like c:\). The leading slash indicates that this path is starting from the root directory of the system. Because it's starting from the root, it doesn't *matter* what the current directory is—*a directory's absolute path is always the same*. A *relative* path is one that does NOT start with a slash. Here's an example of a full directory structure, and a classpath:

```
/ (root)
    |
    |--dirA
        |
        |-- dirB
             |
             |--dirC

-cp dirB:dirB/dirC
```

In this example, `dirB` and `dirB/dirC` are relative paths (they don't start with a slash /). Both of these relative paths are meaningful *only* when the current directory is `dirA`. Pop Quiz! If the current directory is `dirA`, and you're searching for class files, and you use the classpath described above, which directories will be searched?

```
dirA?  dirB?  dirC?
```

Too easy? How about the same question if the current directory is the root (/)? When the current directory is `dirA`, then `dirB` and `dirC` will be searched, but not dirA (remember, we didn't specify the current directory by adding a dot (.) to the classpath). When the current directory is root, since dirB is not a direct subdirectory of root, no directories will be searched. Okay, how about if the current directory is dirB? Again, no directories will be searched! This is because dirB doesn't have a subdirectory named dirB. In other words, Java will look in dirB for a directory named dirB (which it won't find), without realizing that it's already in dirB.

Let's use the same directory structure and a different classpath:

```
/ (root)
    |
    |--dirA
        |
        |-- dirB
            |
            |--dirC


-cp /dirB:/dirA/dirB/dirC
```

In this case, what directories will be searched if the current directory is dirA? How about if the current directory is root? How about if the current directory is dirB? In this case, both paths in the classpath are absolute. It doesn't matter what the current directory is; since absolute paths are specified the search results will always be the same. Specifically, only dirC will be searched, regardless of the current directory. The first path (/dirB) is invalid since dirB is not a direct subdirectory of root, so dirB will never be searched. And, one more time, for emphasis, since dot (.) is not in the classpath, the current directory will only be searched if it happens to be described elsewhere in the classpath (in this case, dirC).

CERTIFICATION OBJECTIVE

JAR Files (Objective 7.5)

7.5   Given the fully-qualified name of a class that is deployed inside and/or outside a JAR file, construct the appropriate directory structure for that class. Given a code example and a classpath, determine whether the classpath will allow the code to compile successfully.

JAR Files and Searching

Once you've built and tested your application, you might want to bundle it up so that it's easy to distribute and easy for other people to install. One mechanism that Java provides for these purposes is a JAR file. JAR stands for Java Archive. JAR files are used to compress data (similar to ZIP files) and to archive data.

Let's say you've got an application that uses many different classes that are located in several different packages. Here's a partial directory tree:

```
test
    |
    |--UseStuff.java
    |--ws
        |
        |--(create MyJar.jar here)
        |--myApp
            |
            |--utils
            |    |
            |    |--Dates.class         (package myApp.utils;)
            |    |--Conversions.class       "           "
            |
            |--engine
                |
                |--rete.class           (package myApp.engine;)
                |--minmax.class             "           "
```

You can create a single JAR file that contains all of the class files in myApp, and also maintains myApp's directory structure. Once this JAR file is created, it can be moved from place to place, and from machine to machine, and all of the classes in the JAR file can be accessed via classpaths and used by java and javac. All of this can happen without ever unJARing the JAR file. Although you won't need to know how to make JAR files for the exam, let's make the current directory ws, and then make a JAR file called MyJar.jar:

```
cd ws
jar -cf MyJar.jar myApp
```

The jar command will create a JAR file called MyJar.jar and it will contain the myApp directory and myApp's entire subdirectory tree and files. You can look at the contents of the JAR file with the next command (this isn't on the exam either):

```
jar -tf MyJar.jar
```

which will list the JAR's contents something like this:

```
META-INF/
META-INF/MANIFEST.MF
myApp/
myApp/.DS_Store
myApp/utils/
myApp/utils/Dates.class
myApp/utils/Conversions.class
myApp/engine/
myApp/engine/rete.class
myApp/engine/minmax.class
```

Okay, now back to exam stuff. Finding a JAR file using a classpath is similar to finding a package file in a classpath. The difference is that when you specify a path for a JAR file, *you must include the name of the JAR file at the end of the path.* Let's say you want to compile `UseStuff.java` in the `test` directory, and `UseStuff.java` needs access to a class contained in `myApp.jar`. To compile `UseStuff.java` you would say

```
cd test
javac -classpath ws/myApp.jar UseStuff.java
```

Compare the use of the JAR file to using a class in a package. If `UseStuff.java` needed to use classes in the `myApp.utils` package, and the class was not in a JAR, you would say

```
cd test
javac -classpath ws UseStuff.java
```

Remember when using a classpath, the last directory in the path must be the super-directory of the *root* directory for the package. (In the preceding example, `myApp` is the root directory of the package `myApp.utils`.) Notice that `myApp` can be the root directory for more than one package (`myApp.utils` and `myApp.engine`), and the `java` and `javac` commands can find what they need across multiple *peer* packages like this. In other words, if `ws` is on the classpath and `ws` is the super-directory of `myApp`, then classes in both the `myApp.utils` and `myApp.engine` packages will be found.

Using .../jre/lib/ext with JAR files

When you install Java, you end up with a huge directory tree of Java-related stuff, including the JAR files that contain the classes that come standard with J2SE. As we discussed earlier, `java` and `javac` have a list of places that they access when searching for class files. Buried deep inside of your Java directory tree is a subdirectory tree named `jre/lib/ext`. If you put JAR files into the `ext` subdirectory, `java` and `javac` can find them, and use the class files they contain. You don't have to mention these subdirectories in a classpath statement—searching this directory is a function that's built right into Java. Sun recommends, however, that you use this feature only for your own internal testing and development, and not for software that you intend to distribute.

Using Static Imports (Exam Objective 7.1)

7.1   Given a code example and a scenario, write code that uses the appropriate access modifiers, package declarations, and import statements to interact with (through access or inheritance) the code in the example.

Note: In Chapter 1 we covered most of what's defined in this objective, but we saved static imports for this chapter.

Static Imports

We've been using `import` statements throughout the book. Ultimately, the only value `import` statements have is that they save typing and they can make your code easier to read. In Java 5, the `import` statement was enhanced to provide even greater keystroke-reduction capabilities...although some would argue that this comes at the expense of readability. This new feature is known as *static imports*. Static imports can be used when you want to use a class's `static` members. (You can use this feature on classes in the API and on your own classes.) Here's a "before and after" example:

Before static imports:

```
public class TestStatic {
  public static void main(String[] args) {
    System.out.println(Integer.MAX_VALUE);
    System.out.println(Integer.toHexString(42));
  }
}
```

After static imports:

```
import static java.lang.System.out;             // 1
import static java.lang.Integer.*;              // 2
public class TestStaticImport {
  public static void main(String[] args)  {
    out.println(MAX_VALUE);                     // 3
    out.println(toHexString(42));               // 4
  }
}
```

Both classes produce the same output:

```
2147483647
2a
```

Let's look at what's happening in the code that's using the static import feature:

1. Even though the feature is commonly called "static import" the syntax MUST be `import static` followed by the fully qualified name of the `static` member you want to import, or a wildcard. In this case we're doing a static import on the `System` class's out object.

2. In this case we might want to use several of the `static` members of the `java.lang.Integer` class. This static import statement uses the wildcard to say, "I want to do static imports of ALL the `static` members in this class."

3. Now we're finally seeing the *benefit* of the static import feature! We didn't have to type the `System` in `System.out.println`! Wow! Second, we didn't have to type the `Integer` in `Integer.MAX_VALUE`. So in this line of code we were able to use a shortcut for a `static` method AND a constant.

4. Finally, we do one more shortcut, this time for a method in the `Integer` class.

We've been a little sarcastic about this feature, but we're not the only ones. We're not convinced that saving a few keystrokes is worth possibly making the code a little harder to read, but enough developers requested it that it was added to the language.
    Here are a couple of rules for using static imports:

- You must say `import static`; you can't say `static import`.

- Watch out for ambiguously named `static` members. For instance, if you do a static import for both the `Integer` class and the `Long` class, referring to `MAX_VALUE` will cause a compiler error, since both `Integer` and `Long` have a `MAX_VALUE` constant, and Java won't know which `MAX_VALUE` you're referring to.

- You can do a static import on `static` object references, constants (remember they're `static` and `final`), and `static` methods.

CERTIFICATION SUMMARY

We started by exploring the `javac` command more deeply. The `-d` option allows you to put class files generated by compilation into whatever directory you want to. The `-d` option lets you specify the destination of newly created class files.

Next we talked about some of the options available through the `java` application launcher. We discussed the ordering of the arguments `java` can take, including `[options] class [args]`. We learned how to query and update system properties in code and at the command line using the `-D` option.

The next topic was handling command-line arguments. The key concepts are that these arguments are put into a String array, and that the first argument goes into array element 0, the second argument into array element 1, and so on.

We turned to the important topic of how `java` and `javac` search for other class files when they need them, and how they use the same algorithm to find these classes. There are search locations predefined by Sun, and additional search locations, called *classpaths* that are user defined. The syntax for Unix classpaths is different than the syntax for Windows classpaths, and the exam will tend to use Unix syntax.

The topic of packages came next. Remember that once you put a class into a package, its name is atomic—in other words, it can't be split up. There is a tight relationship between a class's fully qualified package name and the directory structure in which the class resides.

JAR files were discussed next. JAR files are used to compress and archive data. They can be used to archive entire directory tree structures into a single JAR file. JAR files can be searched by `java` and `javac`.

We finished the chapter by discussing a new Java 5 feature, static imports. This is a convenience-only feature that reduces keying long names for `static` members in the classes you use in your programs.

✓ TWO-MINUTE DRILL

Here are the key points from this chapter.

Using javac and java (Objective 7.2)

❑ Use `-d` to change the destination of a class file when it's first generated by the `javac` command.

❑ The `-d` option can build package-dependent destination classes on-the-fly if the *root* package directory already exists.

❑ Use the `-D` option in conjunction with the `java` command when you want to set a system property.

❑ System properties consist of name=value pairs that must be appended directly behind the `-D`, for example, `java -Dmyproperty=myvalue`.

❑ Command-line arguments are always treated as Strings.

❑ The `java` command-line argument 1 is put into array element 0, argument 2 is put into element 1, and so on.

Searching with java and javac (Objective 7.5)

❑ Both `java` and `javac` use the same algorithms to search for classes.

❑ Searching begins in the locations that contain the classes that come standard with J2SE.

❑ Users can define secondary search locations using classpaths.

❑ Default classpaths can be defined by using OS environment variables.

❑ A classpath can be declared at the command line, and it overrides the default classpath.

❑ A single classpath can define many different search locations.

❑ In Unix classpaths, forward slashes (`/`) are used to separate the directories that make up a path. In Windows, backslashes (`\`) are used.

❑ In Unix, colons (:) are used to separate the paths within a classpath. In Windows, semicolons (;) are used.

❑ In a classpath, to specify the current directory as a search location, use a dot (.)

❑ In a classpath, once a class is found, searching stops, so the order of locations to search is important.

Packages and Searching (Objective 7.5)

❑ When a class is put into a package, its fully qualified name must be used.

❑ An `import` statement provides an alias to a class's fully qualified name.

❑ In order for a class to be located, its fully qualified name must have a tight relationship with the directory structure in which it resides.

❑ A classpath can contain both relative and absolute paths.

❑ An absolute path starts with a / or a \.

❑ Only the final directory in a given path will be searched.

JAR Files (Objective 7.5)

❑ An entire directory tree structure can be archived in a single JAR file.

❑ JAR files can be searched by `java` and `javac`.

❑ When you include a JAR file in a classpath, you must include not only the directory in which the JAR file is located, but the name of the JAR file too.

❑ For testing purposes, you can put JAR files into `.../jre/lib/ext`, which is somewhere inside the Java directory tree on your machine.

Static Imports (Objective 7.1)

❑ You must start a static import statement like this: `import static`

❑ You can use static imports to create shortcuts for `static` members (static variables, constants, and methods) of any class.

SELF TEST

1. Given these classes in different files:

```
package xcom;
public class Useful {
    int increment(int x) { return ++x; }
}
```

```
import xcom.*;                              // line 1
class Needy3 {
    public static void main(String[] args) {
        xcom.Useful u = new xcom.Useful();      // line 2
        System.out.println(u.increment(5));
    }
}
```

Which statements are true? (Choose all that apply.)

A. The output is 0.

B. The output is 5.

C. The output is 6.

D. Compilation fails.

E. The code compiles if line 1 is removed.

F. The code compiles if line 2 is changed to read

```
Useful u = new Useful();
```

2. Given the following directory structure:

```
org
  | -- Robot.class
  |
  | -- ex
        |-- Pet.class
        |
        |-- why
              |-- Dog.class
```

And the following source file:

```
class MyClass {
   Robot r;
   Pet p;
   Dog d;
}
```

Which statement(s) *must* be added for the source file to compile? (Choose all that apply.)

A. `package org;`

B. `import org.*;`

C. `package org.*;`

D. `package org.ex;`

E. `import org.ex.*;`

F. `package org.ex.why;`

G. `package org.ex.why.Dog;`

3. Given:

```
1. // insert code here
2. class StatTest {
3.    public static void main(String[] args) {
4.       System.out.println(Integer.MAX_VALUE);
5.    }
6. }
```

Which, inserted independently at line 1, compiles? (Choose all that apply.)

A. `import static java.lang;`

B. `import static java.lang.Integer;`

C. `import static java.lang.Integer.*;`

D. `import static java.lang.Integer.*_VALUE;`

E. `import static java.lang.Integer.MAX_VALUE;`

F. None of the above statements are valid import syntax.

4. Given:

```
import static java.lang.System.*;
class _ {
  static public void main(String... __A_V_) {
    String $ = "";
    for(int x=0; ++x < __A_V_.length; )
      $ += __A_V_[x];
    out.println($);
  }
}
```

And the command line:

```
java _ - A .
```

What is the result?

A. -A

B. A.

C. -A.

D. -A.

E. _-A.

F. Compilation fails.

G. An exception is thrown at runtime.

5. Given the default classpath:

```
/foo
```

And this directory structure:

```
foo
 |
  test
```

```
    |
    xcom
       |--A.class
       |--B.java
```

And these two files:

```
package xcom;
public class A { }

package xcom;
public class B extends A { }
```

Which allows B.java to compile? (Choose all that apply.)

A. Set the current directory to xcom then invoke
    `javac B.java`

B. Set the current directory to xcom then invoke
    `javac -classpath . B.java`

C. Set the current directory to test then invoke
    `javac -classpath . xcom/B.java`

D. Set the current directory to test then invoke
    `javac -classpath xcom B.java`

E. Set the current directory to test then invoke
    `javac -classpath xcom:. B.java`

6. Given two files:

```
package xcom;
public class Stuff {
  public static final int MY_CONSTANT = 5;
  public static int doStuff(int x) { return (x++)*x; }
}

import xcom.Stuff.*;
import java.lang.System.out;
class User {
  public static void main(String[] args) {
    new User().go();
```

```
        }
        void go() { out.println(doStuff(MY_CONSTANT)); }
    }
```

What is the result?

A. 25

B. 30

C. 36

D. Compilation fails.

E. An exception is thrown at runtime.

7. Given two files:

```
a=b.java
c_d.class
```

Are in the current directory, which command-line invocation(s) could complete without error? (Choose all that apply.)

A. `java -Da=b c_d`

B. `java -D a=b c_d`

C. `javac -Da=b c_d`

D. `javac -D a=b c_d`

8. Given three files:

```
package xcom;
public class A {
   // insert code here
}

package xcom;
public class B extends A {public void doB() { System.out.println("B.doB"); } }
```

```
import xcom.B;
class TestXcom {
  public static void main(String[] args) {
    B b = new B();  b.doB();  b.go();
  }
}
```

Which, inserted at `// insert code here` will allow all three files to compile? (Choose all that apply.)

A. `void go() { System.out.println("a.go"); }`

B. `public void go() { System.out.println("a.go"); }`

C. `private void go() { System.out.println("a.go"); }`

D. `protected void go() { System.out.println("a.go"); }`

E. None of these options will allow the code to compile.

9. Given:

```
class TestProps {
  public static void main(String[] args) {
    String s = System.getProperty("aaa","bbb");
  }
}
```

And the command-line invocation:

```
java -Daaa=ccc TestProps
```

What is always true? (Choose all that apply.)

A. The value of property aaa is aaa.

B. The value of property aaa is bbb.

C. The value of property aaa is ccc.

D. The value of property bbb is aaa.

E. The value of property bbb is ccc.

F. The invocation will not complete without error.

10. If three versions of `MyClass.java` exist on a file system:

> Version 1 is in `/foo/bar`
> Version 2 is in `/foo/bar/baz`
> Version 3 is in `/foo/bar/baz/bing`

And the system's classpath includes:

> `/foo/bar/baz`

And this command line is invoked from `/foo`

> `javac -classpath /foo/bar/baz/bing:/foo/bar MyClass.java`

Which version will be used by `javac`?

- **A.** `/foo/MyClass.java`
- **B.** `/foo/bar/MyClass.java`
- **C.** `/foo/bar/baz/MyClass.java`
- **D.** `/foo/bar/baz/bing/MyClass.java`
- **E.** The result is not predictable.

11. Which are true? (Choose all that apply.)

- **A.** The `java` command can access classes from more than one package, from a single JAR file.
- **B.** JAR files can be used with the `java` command but not with the `javac` command.
- **C.** In order for JAR files to be used by `java`, they MUST be placed in the /jre/lib/ext subdirectory within the J2SE directory tree.
- **D.** In order to specify the use of a JAR file on the command line, the JAR file's path and filename MUST be included.
- **E.** When a part of a directory tree that includes subdirectories with files is put into a JAR file, all of the files are saved in the JAR file, but the subdirectory structure is lost.

12.   Given two files:

```
package pkg;
public class Kit {
   public String glueIt(String a, String b) { return a+b; }
}
```

```
import pkg.*;
class UseKit {
   public static void main(String[] args) {
      String s = new Kit().glueIt(args[1], args[2]);
      System.out.println(s);
   }
}
```

And the following sub-directory structure:

```
test
    |--UseKit.class
    |
    com
       |--KitJar.jar
```

If the current directory is test, and the file pkg/Kit.class is in KitJar.jar, which command line will produce the output bc ? (Choose all that apply.)

A.   java UseKit b c
B.   java UseKit a b c
C.   java -classpath com UseKit b c
D.   java -classpath com:. UseKit b c
E.   java -classpath com/KitJar.jar UseKit b c
F.   java -classpath com/KitJar.jar UseKit a b c
G.   java -classpath com/KitJar.jar:. UseKit b c
H.   java -classpath com/KitJar.jar:. UseKit a b c

SELF TEST ANSWERS

1. Given these classes in different files:

```
package xcom;
public class Useful {
  int increment(int x) { return ++x; }
}
```

```
import xcom.*;                                // line 1
class Needy3 {
  public static void main(String[] args) {
    xcom.Useful u = new xcom.Useful();       // line 2
    System.out.println(u.increment(5));
  }
}
```

Which statements are true? (Choose all that apply.)

A. The output is 0.

B. The output is 5.

C. The output is 6.

D. Compilation fails.

E. The code compiles if line 1 is removed.

F. The code compiles if line 2 is changed to read

```
Useful u = new Useful();
```

Answer:

☑ **D** is correct. The `increment()` method must be marked `public` to be accessed outside of the package. If `increment()` was `public`, **C, E,** and **F** would be correct.

☒ **A** and **B** are incorrect output, even if `increment()` is `public`. (Objective 7.1)

2. Given the following directory structure:

```
org
  | -- Robot.class
```

```
|
| -- ex
      |-- Pet.class
      |
      |-- why
             |-- Dog.class
```

And the following source file:

```
class MyClass {
  Robot r;
  Pet p;
  Dog d;
}
```

Which statement(s) *must* be added for the source file to compile? (Choose all that apply.)

A. `package org;`

B. `import org.*;`

C. `package org.*;`

D. `package org.ex;`

E. `import org.ex.*;`

F. `package org.ex.why;`

G. `package org.ex.why.Dog;`

Answer:

☑ **B, E,** and **F** are required. The only way to access class Dog is via **F**, which is a package statement. Since you can have only one package statement in a source file, you have to get access to class Robot and class Pet using `import` statements. Option **B** accesses Robot, and option **E** accesses Pet.

☒ **A, C, D,** and **G** are incorrect based on the above. Also, **C** and **G** are incorrect syntax. (Objective 7.1)

3. Given:

```
1. // insert code here
2. class StatTest {
3.   public static void main(String[] args) {
4.     System.out.println(Integer.MAX_VALUE);
5.   }
6. }
```

Which, inserted independently at line 1, compiles? (Choose all that apply.)

A. `import static java.lang;`

B. `import static java.lang.Integer;`

C. `import static java.lang.Integer.*;`

D. `import static java.lang.Integer.*_VALUE;`

E. `import static java.lang.Integer.MAX_VALUE;`

F. None of the above statements are valid import syntax.

Answer:

☑ **C** and **E** are correct syntax for static imports. Line 4 isn't making use of `static imports`, so the code will also compile with none of the imports.

☒ **A, B, D,** and **F** are incorrect based on the above. (Objective 7.1)

4. Given:

```
import static java.lang.System.*;
class _ {
  static public void main(String... __A_V_) {
    String $ = "";
    for(int x=0; ++x < __A_V_.length; )
      $ += __A_V_[x];
    out.println($);
  }
}
```

And the command line:

```
java _ - A .
```

What is the result?

A. `-A`

B. `A.`

C. `-A.`

D. `-A.`

E. `_-A.`

F. Compilation fails.

G. An exception is thrown at runtime.

Answer:

☑ **B** is correct. This question is using valid (but inappropriate and weird) identifiers, static imports, var-args in `main()`, and pre-incrementing logic.

☒ **A, C, D, E, F,** and **G** are incorrect based on the above. (Objective 7.2)

5. Given the default classpath:

```
/foo
```

And this directory structure:

```
foo
 |
  test
    |
    xcom
        |--A.class
        |--B.java
```

And these two files:

```
package xcom;
public class A { }

package xcom;
public class B extends A { }
```

Which allows `B.java` to compile? (Choose all that apply.)

A. Set the current directory to `xcom` then invoke
```
javac B.java
```

B. Set the current directory to `xcom` then invoke
```
javac -classpath . B.java
```

C. Set the current directory to `test` then invoke
```
javac -classpath . xcom/B.java
```

D. Set the current directory to `test` then invoke
```
javac -classpath xcom B.java
```

E. Set the current directory to `test` then invoke
```
javac -classpath xcom:. B.java
```

Answer:

☑ **C** is correct. In order for `B.java` to compile, the compiler first needs to be able to find `B.java`. Once it's found `B.java` it needs to find `A.class`. Because `A.class` is in the `xcom` package the compiler won't find `A.class` if it's invoked from the `xcom` directory. Remember that the `-classpath` isn't looking for `B.java`, it's looking for whatever classes `B.java` needs (in this case `A.class`).

☒ **A, B,** and **D** are incorrect based on the above. **E** is incorrect because the compiler can't find `B.java`. (Objective 7.2)

6. Given two files:

```
package xcom;
public class Stuff {
  public static final int MY_CONSTANT = 5;
  public static int doStuff(int x) { return (x++)*x; }
}

import xcom.Stuff.*;
import java.lang.System.out;
class User {
  public static void main(String[] args) {
    new User().go();
  }
  void go() { out.println(doStuff(MY_CONSTANT)); }
}
```

What is the result?

A. 25

B. 30

C. 36

D. Compilation fails.

E. An exception is thrown at runtime.

Answer:

☑ **D** is correct. To import static members, an `import` statement must begin: `import static`.

☒ **A, B, C,** and **E** are incorrect based on the above. (Objective 7.1)

---

7. Given two files:

```
a=b.java
c_d.class
```

Are in the current directory, which command-line invocation(s) could complete without error? (Choose all that apply.)

A. `java -Da=b c_d`

B. `java -D a=b c_d`

C. `javac -Da=b c_d`

D. `javac -D a=b c_d`

Answer:

☑ **A** is correct. The `-D` flag is NOT a compiler flag, and the name=value pair that is associated with the `-D` must follow the `-D` with no spaces.

☒ **B, C,** and **D** are incorrect based on the above. (Objective 7.2)

---

8. Given three files:

```
package xcom;
public class A {
  // insert code here
}
```

```
package xcom;
public class B extends A {public void doB() { System.out.println("B.doB"); } }

import xcom.B;
class TestXcom {
  public static void main(String[] args) {
    B b = new B();  b.doB();  b.go();
  }
}
```

Which, inserted at// insert code here will allow all three files to compile? (Choose all that apply.)

A. `void go() { System.out.println("a.go"); }`

B. `public void go() { System.out.println("a.go"); }`

C. `private void go() { System.out.println("a.go"); }`

D. `protected void go() { System.out.println("a.go"); }`

E.   None of these options will allow the code to compile.

> Answer:
>
> ☑ **B** is correct. The `public` access modifier is the only one that allows code from outside a package to access methods in a package—regardless of inheritance.
>
> ☒ **A, B, D,** and **E** are incorrect based on the above. (Objective 7.1)

9.   Given:

```
class TestProps {
  public static void main(String[] args) {
    String s = System.getProperty("aaa","bbb");
  }
}
```

And the command-line invocation:

```
java -Daaa=ccc TestProps
```

What is always true? (Choose all that apply.)

A. The value of property aaa is aaa.

B. The value of property aaa is bbb.

C. The value of property aaa is ccc.

D. The value of property bbb is aaa.

E. The value of property bbb is ccc.

F. The invocation will not complete without error.

Answer:

☑ **C** is correct. The value of aaa is set at the command line. If aaa had no value when getProperty was invoked, then aaa would have been set to bbb.

☒ **A, B, D, E,** and **F** are incorrect based on the above. (Objective 7.2)

10. If three versions of MyClass.java exist on a file system:

> Version 1 is in /foo/bar
> Version 2 is in /foo/bar/baz
> Version 3 is in /foo/bar/baz/bing

And the system's classpath includes:

> /foo/bar/baz

And this command line is invoked from /foo

```
javac -classpath /foo/bar/baz/bing:/foo/bar MyClass.java
```

Which version will be used by javac?

A. /foo/MyClass.java

B. /foo/bar/MyClass.java

C. /foo/bar/baz/MyClass.java

D. /foo/bar/baz/bing/MyClass.java

E. The result is not predictable.

Answer:

☒ **D** is correct. A -classpath included with a `javac` invocation overrides a system classpath. When `javac` is using any classpath, it reads the classpath from left to right, and uses the first match it finds.

☒ **A, B, C,** and **E** are incorrect based on the above. (Objective 7.5)

11. Which are true? (Choose all that apply.)

A. The `java` command can access classes from more than one package, from a single JAR file.

B. JAR files can be used with the `java` command but not with the `javac` command.

C. In order for JAR files to be used by `java`, they MUST be placed in the /jre/lib/ext subdirectory within the J2SE directory tree.

D. In order to specify the use of a JAR file on the command line, the JAR file's path and filename MUST be included.

E. When a part of a directory tree that includes subdirectories with files is put into a JAR file, all of the files are saved in the JAR file, but the subdirectory structure is lost.

Answer:

☑ **A** and **D** are correct.

☒ **B** is incorrect because `javac` can also use JAR files. **C** is incorrect because JARs can be located in ../jre/lib/ext, but they can also be accessed if they live in other locations. **E** is incorrect, JAR files maintain directory structures. (Objective 7.5)

12. Given two files:

```
package pkg;
public class Kit {
  public String glueIt(String a, String b) { return a+b; }
}
import pkg.*;
class UseKit {
  public static void main(String[] args) {
    String s = new Kit().glueIt(args[1], args[2]);
    System.out.println(s);
  }
}
```

And the following sub-directory structure:

```
test
  |--UseKit.class
  |
  com
    |--KitJar.jar
```

If the current directory is `test`, and the file `pkg/Kit.class` is in `KitJar.jar`, which command line will produce the output `bc`? (Choose all that apply.)

A. `java UseKit b c`

B. `java UseKit a b c`

C. `java -classpath com UseKit b c`

D. `java -classpath com:. UseKit b c`

E. `java -classpath com/KitJar.jar UseKit b c`

F. `java -classpath com/KitJar.jar UseKit a b c`

G. `java -classpath com/KitJar.jar:. UseKit b c`

H. `java -classpath com/KitJar.jar:. UseKit a b c`

Answer:

☑ **H** is correct.

☒ **A, C, E,** and **G** are incorrect if for no other reason than `args[]` is 0-based. **B, D,** and **F** are incorrect because java needs a classpath that specifies two directories, one for the class file (the . directory), and one for the JAR file (the `com` directory). Remember, to find a JAR file, the classpath must include the name of the JAR file, not just its directory. (Objective 7.5)

A

About the CD

The CD-ROM included with this book comes complete with MasterExam and the electronic version of the book. The software is easy to install on any Windows 98/ NT/2000/XP computer and must be installed to access the MasterExam features. You may, however, browse the electronic book directly from the CD without installation. To register for a second bonus MasterExam, simply click the Bonus Material link on the Main Page and follow the directions to the free online registration.

System Requirements

Software requires Windows 98 or higher and Internet Explorer 5.0 or above and 20 MB of hard disk space for full installation. The Electronic book requires Adobe Acrobat Reader.

Installing and Running MasterExam

If your computer CD-ROM drive is configured to auto run, the CD will automatically start up upon inserting the disk. From the opening screen you may install MasterExam by pressing the MasterExam buttons. This will begin the installation process and create a program group named "LearnKey." To run MasterExam, choose Start | Programs | LearnKey. If the auto run feature did not launch your CD, browse to the CD and click RunInstall.

MasterExam

MasterExam provides you with a simulation of the actual exam. The number of questions, types of questions, and the time allowed are intended to be an accurate representation of the exam environment. You have the option to take an open-book exam, including hints, references, and answers; a closed-book exam; or the timed MasterExam simulation.

When you launch MasterExam, a digital clock display will appear in the upper-left corner of your screen. The clock will continue to count down to zero unless you choose to end the exam before the time expires. To register for a second bonus MasterExam, simply click the Bonus Material link on the Main Page and follow the directions to the free online registration.

Electronic Book

The entire contents of the Study Guide are provided in PDF format. Adobe's Acrobat Reader has been included on the CD.

Help

A help file is provided through the Help button on the main page in the lower-left corner. Individual help features are also available through MasterExam and LearnKey's Online Training.

Removing Installation(s)

MasterExam is installed on your hard drive. For best results for removal of programs use the Start | Programs | LearnKey | Uninstall options to remove MasterExam.

If you want to remove the Real Player, use the Add/Remove Programs icon from your Control Panel. You may also remove the LearnKey training program from this location.

Technical Support

For questions regarding the technical content of the electronic book, or MasterExam, please visit www.osborne.com or e-mail customer.service@mcgraw-hill.com. For customers outside the 50 United States, e-mail international_cs@mcgraw-hill.com.

LearnKey Technical Support

For technical problems with the software (installation, operation, removing installations), and for questions regarding any LearnKey Online Training content, please visit www.learnkey.com or e-mail techsupport@learnkey.com.

M

N

Q

R

S

T

U

V

W

X

Y